UNIX® Programmer's Reference

John Valley

QUe™

CORPORATION

LEADING COMPUTER KNOWLEDGE

UNIX® Programmer's Reference

D EDICATION ▼

I dedicate this book to my wife Terri,
as an apology for the many hours I spent with my
terminal, instead of her, while writing this book, and
in appreciation for her tolerance, understanding, and
support during those seemingly endless months.

Publishing Director

Richard K. Swadley

Product Manager

Joseph B. Wikert

Acquisitions/Development

Linda Sanning

Technical Editor

Peter Holsberg

Editors

Lynn Brown, Brown Editorial Service
Susan Christophersen
Andy Saff

Editorial Assistant

Pam Bowley

Illustrations

Susan Moore

Cover Design

Dan Armstrong

Index

Brown Editorial Service

Book Design and Production

Martin Coleman
Joelynn Gifford
Sandy Grieshop
Bob LaRoche
Michele Laseau
Sarah Leatherman
Howard Peirce
Joyce Petersen
Cindy Phipps
Joe Ramon
Dennis Sheehan
Lisa Wilson

*Composed in Garamond and OCRB
by Que Corporation.*

ABOUT THE AUTHOR ▼

John Valley

J ohn Valley began his career in 1972 as a night shift operator of an IBM mainframe computer. Over the next eight years he progressed from applications programmer to systems programmer and analyst, worked briefly as a DOS/VSE consultant in Detroit, then moved to Richmond, Virginia, in 1980 to join an operating system development team with the Nixdorf Computer Corporation.

For the next six years he supervised the development and maintenance of operating systems for a line of mainframe computers. In 1986 he taught himself UNIX and the C programming language in order to develop support software for an international project to build a new version of a Nixdorf operating system.

He currently works with Capricorn Systems Associates, a software engineering firm in Richmond, Virginia, where for the last four years he has led a research and development effort designing an experimental CASE system for the UNIX System V environment.

John Valley lives in Richmond with his wife Terri and his golden retriever Brandon. He likes to compose classical chamber music in his spare time, and he and his wife enjoy traveling to foreign countries.

CONTENT OVERVIEW ▼

TABLE OF CONTENTS ▼

3   UNIX in Action 45

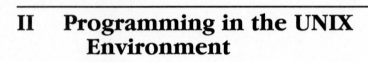

II Programming in the UNIX Environment

IV   **Operating System Services** ▼

13   **Kernel Internals** 307

14   **Signals and IPC** 343

V Reference

C Library Functions 473

The UNIX Shell 635

Appendixes

A Regular Expressions

B Error Codes

C Important Header Files

ACKNOWLEDGMENTS

The reader often believes that a book is primarily the work of its author. It would be a grievous error if I were to allow that belief to go unchallenged.

This book would not exist without the generous support and assistance of the people at Que, and especially Linda Sanning. Her efforts, often protracted well into the evening hours, deserve far more acknowledgement than these few words can convey.

David Rodman gave birth to the original idea for this book, and wrote much of the first five chapters before other more pressing concerns forced him to abandon work on the book.

Sydney Weinstein contributed Chapter 12, "Programming Serial Devices." His mastery of the technicalities of that subject far exceeds my own.

Pete Holsberg deserves many thanks and a share of the credit for his masterful summary of System V Release 4 changes in Chapter 16, and for his role as a technical editor.

Don Gloistein has helped in many capacities with this book, including as a technical editor; unfortunately, more urgent business prevented him from authoring a chapter for the book, a fact which I learned with genuine disappointment.

Among the many others who have helped in one way or another, special thanks must go to Frank Reynolds, Rich Wells, and Jack Ehrhardt, all co-workers of mine, whose review and critiques of many of the chapters improved them more than anyone else will ever know.

TRADEMARK ACKNOWLEDGMENTS

Que Corporation has made every attempt to supply trademark information about company names, products, and services mentioned in this book. Trademarks indicated below were derived from various sources. Que Corporation cannot attest to the accuracy of this information.

AT&T, UNIX, UNIX System V, and XENIX are registered trademark of AT&T.

CP/M is a registered trademark of Digital Research Inc.

IBM is a registered trademark of International Business Machines Corporation.

Microsoft and MS-DOS are registered trademarks of Microsoft Corporation.

Motorola is a registered trademark of Motorola, Inc.

NFS is a trademark of Sun Microsystems, Inc.

X Window System is a trademark of the Massachusetts Institute of Technology.

Zenith is a registered trademark of Zenith Electronics Corp.

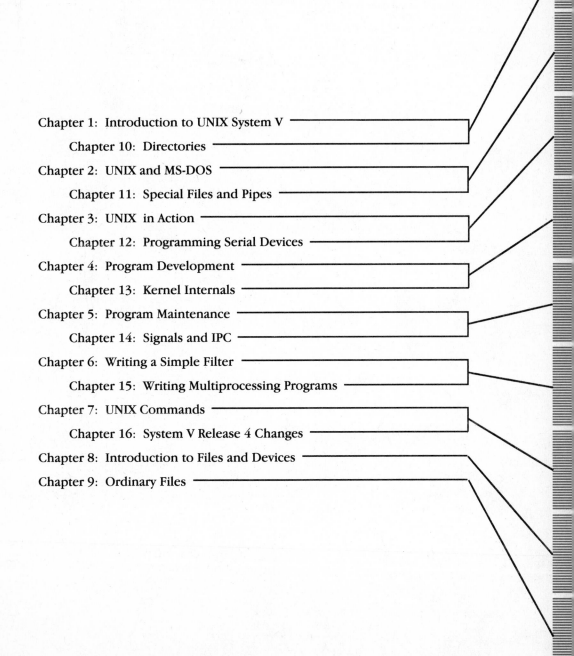

Introduction

A colleague of mine once asked me how I learned UNIX programming. He asked this with some frustration after I answered a question he had just spent nearly an hour researching in the UNIX manuals. The sad fact is that UNIX, unlike most other operating systems, cannot really be learned from the manuals. Experienced UNIX programmers have had to glean information from many sources including magazine articles, lectures, classes, seminars, and word of mouth. *UNIX Programmer's Reference* is an attempt to bring together in published form much of the knowledge that has been pieced together by just such means, and to present it to you in an easily digested, logically ordered presentation. If you already know the C programming language and want to learn how to write programs for UNIX System V, this book is for you.

This is not an introductory text, however. You should already know how to log in, how to use a text editor, how to manage files and directories with the `cp`, `mv`, `ls`, `rm`, `mkdir`, `rmdir`, and `cat` commands, and how to compile and link edit a C program. You should also be familiar with the stream I/O functions (`fopen`, `fclose`, `printf`, `getchar`, `putchar`, and so on).

If you are not familiar with any of these topics, you might pick up a copy of *The C Programming Language* by Kernighan and Ritchie (Prentice-Hall, 1988), and an introduction to UNIX such as *The Waite Group's UNIX System V Primer* by Waite, Prata, and Martin (SAMS, 1990).

What You Will Learn

If you already have a basic acquaintance with UNIX, the following chapters will extend your knowledge with an understanding of the file system and its mechanisms, give you insight into the operation and usage of system calls, and teach you how to use pipes, signals, raw I/O, interprocess communication, daemons, and other advanced UNIX techniques.

The topics covered are intended to give you the foundation you need to tackle more advanced subjects such as writing device drivers, programming with X Windows, and developing network applications with TCP/IP. The knowledge you gain here will enable you to write your own shell, build a data base system, or design efficient business software.

In other words, you will become a UNIX master.

Organization of the Book

UNIX Programmer's Reference is organized into five parts.

Part I, "Introduction to the UNIX System," sketches the early history of UNIX and introduces the principal components of the operating system. These chapters are intended to be light reading for you, but they build an overview of UNIX in your mind that is essential; without a clear picture of the facilities available to you, you can't hope to make full and efficient use of UNIX.

Part II, "Programming in the UNIX Environment," presents some of the utilities available to assist you with the programming process itself. These utilities enable you to make the best use of your time and to improve the quality of your products. UNIX includes many such tools; unfortunately, there isn't room in one book to cover them all in depth.

Part III, "UNIX Files and Devices," teaches you how the UNIX file system works and how to use it. The details of its implementation are not discussed, because the design of UNIX allows for differences among hardware. If you expect to learn the structure and format of device tables, disk volumes, and files, you will be disappointed. However, UNIX System V comes complete with a guarantee that the file system will behave in certain ways, as seen by the C programmer, and these chapters acquaint you with the terms of the contract.

Part IV, "Operating System Services," deals with the UNIX kernel, the system start-up procedure, process management, memory management, signals and interprocess communication, in fact all of the facilities provided by the UNIX kernel with the exception of the file system. Because of this variety of material, you may feel drowned in a sea of unrelated topics. You should skim these chapters on a first reading, and study them more closely only when you have an actual need to use a particular facility. You do not need to learn UNIX all at once, and most programs do not use all of the features of the operating system.

Part V, "Reference," provides complete reference sections for the C library functions and the shell, and also includes a description of the new and changed features of UNIX System V Release 4.

Notation and Conventions

Text is sometimes set in a special type style to clarify its meaning.

`Monospace type` is used for command and function names. This type style is also used for path names, header file names, and code listings.

Variable names in function calls are shown in *italics*; when the variable is later explained in the text, the variable name is *italicized* to tie the explanation back to the command or function call format. Also, technical terms that are special to UNIX are shown in italics when used for the first time. Sometimes, though, italics are used just to *emphasize* a word or phrase.

ANSI C function prototypes are used to describe the format of library function calls. However, there are many versions of UNIX System V that do not provide an ANSI C compiler. If you are using an ANSI C compiler, then the prototypes for functions are already provided for you in the header files, and you do not normally need to type them yourself in your programs. If you are using a K&R compiler, the function prototypes are *not* already provided for you in header files, but you don't use them either, because the older K&R compilers don't support function prototyping. If you try to use code from this book with a K&R C compiler, you will have to convert function prototypes to the older form.

To convert function prototypes to K&R C, just observe these two rules:

1:    K&R function *declarations* do not permit arguments; just drop the argument list from the function declaration. For example, if the sample code shows

```
extern char *strcpy(char *s1, const char *s2);
```

then enter the function declaration as follows:

```
extern char *strcpy();
```

2:    K&R function *definitions* do not allow type qualification of argument names; just move the type specifications of arguments outside the parentheses. For example, if the sample code shows

```
int main(int argc, char *argv[])
```

then enter the function definition as follows:

```
int main(argc, argv)
int argc;
char *argv[];
{
...
}
```

❏ Lastly, K&R C does not recognize a few of the type qualifiers allowed in ANSI C. Ignore any occurrences of the type qualifiers `signed` or `const`.

If you are not already familiar with ANSI standard C, you should get a book that describes its syntax because an ANSI standard C compiler is in your future; beginning with release 3.2.2, all AT&T UNIX System V systems include an ANSI standard compiler. For the time being, the newer compilers also support K&R syntax, so program conversion is not a task that immediately confronts you. Nonetheless, whenever possible you should write all new programs in the new language.

One final word before you begin. Often discussion of a command or library function begins without first presenting the command or function format. The format is omitted, because Part V, "Reference," already contains a complete description of all function formats. When you are unfamiliar with a command or function mentioned in the text, please turn to the reference section and look up its format. The text discussion will be much clearer to you if you do.

Part I

Introduction to the
UNIX System

1

Introduction to UNIX System V

I n 1969, working at Bell Laboratories on an unused DEC PDP-7 computer, Ken Thompson wrote the first implementation of what eventually became the UNIX operating system. The initial motivation for this not insubstantial effort was to provide an environment for a computerized spaceship simulation game that he was working on at the time as part of a research project. Shortly thereafter, Thompson and Dennis Ritchie implemented the first C compiler, using this system as their programming environment. In 1973 Ritchie and Thompson rewrote the operating system in C, breaking with the long-standing tradition that systems software must always be written in assembly language. Thus they gave birth to the system we know today as UNIX.

In 1974, AT&T first began to license the system to universities "for educational purposes," and the number of UNIX installations stood at about 100 systems.

Now, almost 20 years later, there are tens of thousands of UNIX systems installed throughout the world, and most computer manufacturers offer some version of UNIX on their machines. The original implementation was extended and enhanced at the Berkeley campus of the University of California, giving rise to the *BSD* version which now stands at release 4.3. Bell Labs developed a different implementation called Version 7, which somewhat later became the basis for Microsoft's XENIX, and AT&T's own System V. No one really knows how many different versions of UNIX now exist.

What stands out in the history of UNIX is that it was never the protege of the big corporation, designed and built to sell machines. The early history of UNIX contains no marketing plans, no tantalizing press releases, no advertising campaigns, and no shrink-wrapped packages.

UNIX found its way out into the world slowly, hand-copied and hand-carried to first one machine and then another, gradually building a community of users dedicated to enhancing it and encouraging its dissemination.

Given this background, you have to wonder what it is about UNIX that keeps it alive and nurtures its growth without any of the motivations that usually drive the selection of an operating system. What justifies the importance of UNIX today?

The answer is that UNIX is a good environment for developing programs.

Now this is somewhat surprising. We expect a successful product to have a user-friendly interface—UNIX doesn't. We expect glossy documentation with an eighth-grade vocabulary and lots of diagrams—but UNIX documentation is terrible. We expect easy installation, but until recently installing UNIX has been more like solving a jigsaw puzzle.

UNIX defies all these expectations and succeeds anyway, because UNIX was written by programmers for programmers, not for users.

High-quality applications are more likely to emerge from an environment that supports the programmer than from an environment that caters to users. Why? Because users don't write programs, programmers do. How easy it is to forget that fact and to attempt complex development projects on systems designed solely for the user, leaving the programming staff to struggle with inadequate tools and unsupportive environments. Little wonder that software development projects are traditionally late and over-budget.

This chapter tells about the genesis of the UNIX operating system—the environment in which the code evolved, the impetus behind its development, and the rationale of its designers. The chapter discusses the philosophy of UNIX and tries to convey the reasons for its growing popularity. Finally, the chapter examines the major components of UNIX to show how they are related.

The History of UNIX

Although the history of UNIX would make an interesting study in itself, this chapter takes a brief look at its origins here mainly to explain the thinking behind some of its unusual features.

UNIX was more revolutionary in its design than it appears today because many of its ideas have been borrowed and reused by other operating systems. When it was new, UNIX was a surprising beast that looked strange and wonderful (or ugly) to everyone who encountered it. That anyone found this new beast wonderful indicates just how crude and unfriendly most systems in the early 1970s were.

Computers before the Age of Operating Systems

In the very earliest days of computing, computers were very large and expensive and yet, by today's standards, very crude. Programmers were also electronics engineers. When you started up a computer (a very complex process in itself), it was not unusual to have to monitor an oscilloscope to tell when the voltage and current levels in the machine had become sufficiently stable that you could use it.

The machine could execute only one program at a time, and it had to be loaded each time (computers had no permanent memory). Typically the computer contained no operating system whatsoever; and the operating procedures were so complex that a programmer usually ran his or her own jobs. This meant that one programmer was the sole user of the machine at a time. A program was developed at the computer console and debugged at the computer console. Typically the first debugging run that worked was also the final, production run; the programmer took the results and went off to study them while someone else took over the machine.

As computers became more powerful and less difficult to use, people eventually realized that they were wasting much of the capacity of these expensive machines while a single programmer typed away at the console. This led to the development of a new kind of software called a *batch-job monitor*. This kind of program was not intended to produce results at all; instead, it was supposed to administer the computer itself by taking work that had been prepared in advance and running it automatically.

This approach allowed more computer runs per hour, because no manual setup time was needed between jobs. All the setup time was expended "off-line" by the programmer, who punched the source programs and data onto cards, wrapped the deck of cards in a special set of run instructions called JCL (job control language), and then presented this sandwich of cards to a new person on the staff: the computer operator. The computer operator would stack these jobs in the card reader, collect the cards as they came out, remove the output from the printer, and return both cards and printout to the programmer.

Batch job monitors introduced the idea of efficiency to the computer community. Programmers no longer needed to punch their programs into card decks: Keypunch operators did that. Programmers no longer needed to run their programs: Computer operators did that. Apparently programmers did not even need to debug their programs on the machine: If the program failed, the operator returned whatever output there was plus a memory dump to the programmer; presumably the programmer could use the output and dump to find out what had gone wrong with the program.

Invariably the programming staff complained about this state of affairs. They didn't like being pushed out of the computer room. The keypunch operators didn't understand their programs and always made keying errors. Then programmers had to wait while the operators punched up replacement cards, all in the interest of efficiency! And although the memory dumps were better than nothing, a snapshot of memory at the time of program failure was no help when the programmer needed to know how the program had generated the error in the first place.

Programmers still wanted time at the computer console to debug their programs. This became known as "test time," and programmers fought for their slice of the computer's precious time, accepting midnight hours and weekend work as part of their occupation.

Meanwhile, computer manufacturers kept increasing the power of their machines, and the software developers kept looking for better ways to use that power. Operating systems designers recognized it was a huge waste of computer resources to execute only one program at a time when that program only needed two tape drives and some memory; the computer probably had dozens of tape drives and staggering quantities of memory (maybe as much as 48K)! The problem was to find a way to let two or three programs all run at once, each using a temporarily dedicated set of resources so that they didn't interfere with each other.

This technique was called *multiprogramming*. Because allocating and scheduling machine resources was a task very similar to the task already performed by the batch-job monitor, it seemed natural to assign resource scheduling to a more complex version of the monitor. Thus were born the first primitive operating systems.

Streamlining Computer Operations with Operating Systems

The operating system idea caught on rapidly and had an astounding effect on the computer industry. With multiprogramming operating systems, there was no limit to the size and power of the computer that could be efficiently used; if the computer was bigger, you could just run more jobs at once. Although the size of the computer itself was dwindling, the computer room remained large, crammed now with printers and disks and tape drives.

But the programmers had never gotten over their frustration at having to work with the computer at a distance. As a matter of fact, things got worse. The machine was now so large and expensive that dedicating it to a single person, no matter for what purpose, became ludicrous. Test time became scarce. The time needed to develop new application programs ballooned. The skill and ingenuity needed to develop complex applications skyrocketed, and programmers became very expensive.

Thus the software crisis evolved. Managers complain to this day that the cost of software development is unreasonable, the reliability of software deplorable, and the development lead times unbearable. Most puzzling of all, no one seems to know the reason for this state of affairs.

In the mid-1960s, when everyone believed OS/360 (IBM's mainframe operating system) was the height of technical sophistication and the application backlog had grown to intolerable proportions, something quiet was happening on college campuses.

The big universities were laboring with a problem that seemed not to affect the business community: with enrollments in computer science courses soaring, and the cost of computing very high, how could researchers (and even students) be given the hands-on computer time they needed?

With no expectation that their work would ever have practical importance, a few computer scientists began to experiment with a new way of using the machine. If the computer could execute more than one task at a time, they reasoned, why couldn't it be made to look as if it were several computers, each one dedicated to an individual user sitting in front of a terminal? A number of projects were attempted.

One of these resulted in the invention of the BASIC (Beginner's All-purpose Symbolic Instruction Code) language in 1965. The idea here was that a special programming language was needed to support simultaneous on-line programming at a terminal. If everyone programmed in assembly language, even a simple programming error could crash the machine, so data processing managers needed some way to buffer the computer from users' errors. What better way than to use an *interpreter*? Interpreters check every instruction before execution and errors are brought to the attention of the programmer before the system is damaged.

But by far the most ambitious project undertaken was the MULTICS operating system, a joint undertaking of Bell Laboratories, Massachusetts

Institute of Technology, and General Electric Corporation. MULTICS was to be a special operating system designed from the ground up to support time-sharing. It was to provide an environment that was secure and robust, that would give its users unrestricted access to the full power of the machine and any programming language they chose, and that was to provide special tools for communication between its users.

Unfortunately, for reasons beyond the scope of this book, MULTICS didn't succeed. The system worked, and it achieved many of its objectives, but the cost per user was prohibitive. The project suffered from the "too many cooks" phenomenon. The very diversity of talents and ideas that, early on, seemed to presage a wonderful universality in the system instead led to a series of communication breakdowns and lack of coordination that ultimately caused the project's demise. Perhaps with a sardonic sense of having attempted too much with too many, Brian Kernighan (one of the members of the original UNIX development group) first coined the term "UNICS," changing the "MULT" in MULTICS to "UN" (from the Latin *unus* meaning "one"), which was almost immediately revised to "UNIX."

Ken Thompson Creates UNIX

The story of UNIX continued at Bell Laboratories, where one of the MULTICS researchers, Ken Thompson, was working on a computer spaceship simulation game. He had implemented the program on the MULTICS system, but now that MULTICS was no longer available he had to search for an alternate platform for his program.

The focus for this research project was neither frivolous nor unusual. Games provide a perfect context for doing computing research: They have well-defined parameters that are easily programmed, and they often quickly develop a complexity that pushes the implementer toward ever more so-phisticated algorithms. Games also provide a means of keeping the researcher's interest level up while making it easy to gauge the progress of a new system. (For example, in the early days of the LISP language, the game of chess replaced Spacewar as the lunchtime activity at MIT's artificial intelligence laboratory. The question, "How well is it playing this week?" always had a different answer, and both the LISP language and the techniques of knowledge representation and problem solving were advanced by the game.)

But in the 1960s the Bell Laboratories computing research group did not command the budget it has today. Thompson could not just choose a computer and buy it. He found an old unused PDP-7 with the graphics hardware he needed and cobbled together an operating system of his own, basing its design on many elements of the now-defunct MULTICS. He used a cross-assembler on another computer to build the initial system for the PDP-7 machine. Every time he changed his system, he had to punch the object program onto paper tape, carry the tape over to the PDP-7, and reinstall everything. After a few iterations of this procedure, Thompson put together a native assembler for the PDP-7.

Sooner or later though, UNIX would have to justify its existence in practical terms or be scrapped. The Patent department at Bell Labs needed a text-processing application, and a PDP-11/20 was available for the project. Seeing an opportunity, Thompson decided to port the operating system to the new computer.

At about this same time, a number of other groups at Bell Laboratories and elsewhere were working on language development. In their attempts to share algorithms with each other, it soon became clear that English was not precise enough and FORTRAN was not expressive enough to serve as a language for stating their algorithms. Algol 68 was created to fill that void, as was BCPL (Basic Combined Programming Language). These two languages strongly influenced the future development of C.

Thompson was aware of these language developments and was dismayed by the prospect of moving his system to a different computer (because that would entail developing a whole new assembler and then completely rewriting his entire operating system in the new assembler language). So Thompson decided to solve the problem once and for all by making his system more portable.

He created a new programming language, B, using BCPL as a starting point. B was an interpreter, however, and predictably slow in execution. Also, having no `char` type, Thompson's interpreter could not take advantage of the byte-oriented instructions of the PDP machines.

Dennis Ritchie took on the project of developing a code generator for B that would use byte-oriented instructions, and called his new compiler C.

Because Thompson and Ritchie intended to use the new language for rewriting their operating system, they designed their compiler to produce compact, efficient code while supporting portability and low-level control. The advantages of a high-level language over assembler, together with the functional structure of the language, attracted many talented programmers to the UNIX project and furthered the development of the operating system.

In 1973, Thompson and Ritchie rewrote the complete operating system in C, and UNIX became the first operating system to be implemented in a high-level language.

In retrospect, we can easily pick out the crucial choices that have made UNIX the environment of choice for software development.

First was Thompson's decision to base the design of his experimental operating system on MULTICS. This provided the fundamental ideas of an operating system intended expressly to support time-sharing, levels of security to allow individual users to protect their files from each other, and message passing between programs. These and other elements chosen from MULTICS form the basic core of functionality in UNIX.

A second critical decision was to write his system in a high-level language to simplify the chore of porting it from one hardware platform to another. This has made UNIX easy to port to new computers, with the result that it is usually the first if not the only operating system to be supported on new machines. Businesses also like UNIX because it is hardware *neutral*, allowing its users to select whatever vendor's equipment provides the best price and performance.

But the most significant choice of all was not even a conscious choice. Thompson designed his operating system to be used, not by clerks, accountants, or managers, but by the other members of his research team, all of whom by definition were chiefly engaged in programming. He solved the greatest computing problem of his age without even realizing it, finally bringing the programmer back into contact with the machine, giving the programmer the opportunity and the tools to boost programming productivity and effectiveness back up to the level that employers demand, and that the programmer desires.

UNIX can be easily ported to almost any hardware environment, so there's no convincing reason why UNIX can't be used as the development environment for any applications system. And until it or a system like it is used for every development project, programming managers can continue to expect the same old story of cost and schedule overruns that have become so familiar in the past. As recently as 1975 there were good reasons to incur such costs. Those reasons have vanished.

A New File System

UNIX implements a *hierarchical* file system. Files are organized into directories, which may in turn be contained within other directories. At the top of this structure is a single directory, called the *root* directory because all other directories and files branch from it like the limbs and leaves of a tree. This is a very simple but extremely powerful concept.

The hierarchical nature of UNIX resulted directly from Thompson's absorbing interest in file systems. He wanted to implement a file system that permitted a more logical, organized structuring of information than was possible with existing operating systems.

His file system reflects the nature of human problem solving. Just as people break large tasks into smaller, more manageable units, so a hierarchical file system breaks a large collection of files into smaller, more conveniently sized collections. Just as people can recall the same fact using several different trains of thought, so a hierarchical file system can access the same file by many different paths. This capability is central to the UNIX structure. Chapter 10, "Directories," describes the file system in detail.

The UNIX file structure has great utility to a programmer, because it allows the user to organize files by project and to keep shared files in a common directory that is easily accessible to anyone. The structure also lets the user control the context in which programs and users operate. Programs can refer to files that are in "the current directory" instead of naming a specific directory. The user can change the current directory before running a program and by doing so, change the context within which the program runs.

The hierarchical file structure also aids portability. As UNIX has evolved, the system has, by convention, kept standard utilities in one directory, common header files in another, device drivers in another, and so on. With standardized directory names, a developer can write a package consisting of several programs and files, and still set up an installation procedure that stores the programs and files correctly on the user's machine. This is one of many ways in which UNIX supports multiprogrammer, multisite projects.

The rest of the UNIX operating system was designed around the file system, and that has had much to do with the way processes and devices are implemented, as you will see later.

The Philosophy of UNIX

An operating system, like the constitution of a country, defines certain rules of behavior and guarantees access to certain resources. An operating system also makes many implicit (or explicit) statements about the way things are and the way they ought to be. These statements compose a philosophy, and every operating system expresses its philosophy through its design, documentation, and uses. As nations succeed or fail according to how they were conceived, so do operating systems. The longevity of UNIX and its acceptance as a standard are entirely due to the philosophy the system embodies.

The UNIX philosophy partially expresses the motivations of the UNIX designers, because the operating system does indeed provide a unique support system for communal computing and close communication. UNIX provides an unusual degree of support for the individual programmer: all the resources of the operating system are available in ways that other systems lack. For example, useful programs can be promoted to system utility status without any special magic or reprogramming. The *shell*, which is the user interface of the system, is an application program. There is nothing to prevent you from building your own shell. You could use it for your own purposes or make it available to other users. If your new shell becomes sufficiently important to the community of users, it can be promoted to a system utility and be made available to all.

The UNIX philosophy is also partly a product of the environment in which it grew up. Small computers with a 64K limit on address space required small, efficient system utilities, which led to the "building-block" approach that characterizes a well-designed UNIX program. Moving from one computer to another several times in its early years made UNIX somewhat like a mongrel; the system is tough, adaptable, and street smart.

Computer Time Is Cheaper than People Time

UNIX was developed in an environment where computer time was cheaper than people time. The system administration policies of UNIX reflect that evaluation. For example, the system's commands and utilities are designed to require a minimum of human intervention. The UNIX philosophy is that it is better to spend 5 minutes to set up a 3-hour run than to run the job in an hour and a half but have to interact with the system every 15 minutes. As a result, many UNIX utilities are designed to form part of a cooperative, ad hoc sequence of steps called a *pipeline*, which can be set up on a single command line. The syntax for pipelines is intuitive, a fine example of the UNIX style, enabling you to do something very useful with minimum effort and in a perfectly simple and logical way.

The noninteractive nature of most UNIX utilities also makes it easier to create large, complicated programs by combining several small utilities. Most utilities let you specify processing options with command-line arguments, making it relatively easy to invoke the utility to do exactly what you want without bothering the user with a lot of questions. Alternatively, you can use the capabilities of the UNIX shell to build an interactive front end for the UNIX commands; many software products do just that with the standard utilities.

Software for Grownups

UNIX programs are usually silent unless they encounter errors. This avoids cluttering up the user's terminal with status messages and comments that would be ignored anyway. Noisy dialog wastes time and makes it difficult to build pipelines; UNIX utilities are "software for grownups" who don't need a lot of handholding.

Good UNIX programs make maximum use of available resources. From its beginning, the UNIX system pioneered the use of inexpensive computers by more than one user, which won UNIX a fond place in the budgets of colleges and universities all over the world and has much to do with how you came to be reading this book. The resources of the operating system itself are also fully used; UNIX does not force you to "reinvent wheels" that are part of the system. You can call them as subroutines or put them into your own pipelines, whichever is appropriate.

Hierarchical File System and Process Control

The cornerstone of the UNIX philosophy is hierarchy. Both files and processes are managed hierarchically. This enables you to integrate several small, simple units (files, programs, or whatever) into larger units, to combine several of these larger units into still larger units, and so on. The system helps you build up quite complicated structures in a straightforward manner.

Because the shell is hierarchically above the programs it invokes, it has complete control over the input, output, and environment of these programs, whereas the programs themselves have no idea how they were called or what the larger process is within which they execute. Thus, if a program ultimately takes input from a laboratory device and sends output to a logging device, you can fully test the program by feeding input from a file or from your keyboard and sending the program's output to a file, printer, or your screen. No change is required to the program to accomplish this test under UNIX.

The hierarchical file system eases problems caused by having many users on the same system at the same time. Each user can freely create and name files in his or her own directory, without fear of using a name that conflicts with another user's choice. If my personal directory contained a file called *chap02*, it would not be confused with file *chap02* in your personal directory, because the context in which I refer to the name *chap02* is my directory, and the context for your *chap02* is your directory.

This capability of holding a context within which commands are understood is another characteristic of the UNIX system.

Major Components of the UNIX Operating System

As defined by AT&T, the UNIX operating system consists of the base system and a number of extensions. The base system comprises the kernel, the shell, and the base utilities. The extensions include the kernel extension, the graphics extension, and the network services extension (all of which are enhancements to the kernel itself), and a series of application-level extensions: the advanced utilities extension, the administered systems extension, the software development extension, and the terminal interface extension.

Although not explicitly mentioned in the base system definition, the functionality of the shell is included in the base system. Therefore, all command interpreters that claim System V compliance share a certain basic set of functions, described in this section.

The bad news is that all the extensions are optional; in any compliant implementation of System V, only the base system is absolutely required. The good news is that there is a tremendous amount of functionality even in the base system, and that many of the extensions are included as "standard equipment" in many commercially available implementations of System V.

The UNIX Kernel

The kernel is the nucleus of the operating system. The *System V Interface Definition*, issue 3 (a large and very technical document published by AT&T) provides for implementation of the System V kernel in two main parts: the base system (which is required in all implementations of System V) and the kernel extension (which is optional and need not be present in all versions of System V). The kernel defined for the base system provides the minimum set of services needed to operate a UNIX system, whereas the kernel extensions provide advanced features such as Interprocess Communication (*IPC*) and advanced networking capability.

The following overview highlights some of the principal services included in the base system.

Time

The time system call returns the current date and time as the number of seconds elapsed since midnight, January 1, 1970. Various routines are provided in the standard library for converting this number to more meaningful units.

By using the `times` system call, a program can determine the amount of CPU time that it has used. Many I/O functions suspend the calling program until data is available. You can use the `alarm` system call to avoid an undesirably long wait. `Alarm` forces an interruption to occur after a set amount of time elapses. The interruption sends a signal to the calling program and effectively forces program execution to resume.

Memory

Memory can be dynamically allocated with the `malloc` function and released by a call to `free`.

`realloc` (part of the `malloc` family of functions) changes the size of a previously allocated block of memory by extending or contracting the block if possible. The `realloc` function also allocates a new memory area and releases the old if necessary. `realloc` preserves the original contents of the block even if it is moved.

The `mallopt` function provides a mechanism for managing many small memory blocks more efficiently than `malloc`; `mallopt` causes `malloc` to preallocate large blocks of memory and then parcel out small pieces as they are required.

Devices

UNIX represents a physical device as a *special* file. As with any other type of file, a *special* file is represented by a directory entry and has a file name. By allocating a directory entry to represent a device, UNIX enables users to define the name that will represent a device; unlike some other operating systems, there are no reserved names built into the system to stand for devices.

Devices (and therefore *special* files) are categorized into two main types: character and block. A *character device* reads and writes streams of characters. Terminals are considered character devices. A *block device* reads and writes data in fixed-size blocks. A disk drive must be defined to the system as a block device and may also be accessible as a character device.

Because devices are represented by directory entries, you can rename devices like any other file. The standard home for device files is the `/dev` directory.

The traditional path name of the system's master console is `/dev/console`. The kernel and many system utilities write their error output to `/dev/console`. The `/dev/console` file can be linked to a remote terminal, thereby configuring the system for remote operation with a single `ln` command.

The /dev/null file is the standard null device. When opened for output, it acts like a bit bucket: all output written to /dev/null just disappears. When opened for input, the /dev/null file returns the end-of-file (EOF) to all read requests.

The /dev/tty file is another standard file: it is a special file that acts as a pseudonym for your active terminal. The file is used when standard input or standard output may have been redirected and you want to be sure to read the keyboard or write to the screen. The /dev/tty file can also be used as a generic "this terminal" file name, making it easy to refer to the terminal even when you do not know its real path name.

The File System

The base system definition includes the UNIX file system, without which the system could not operate. The file system is a strategy for storing and organizing files on disk; it dictates a hierarchical structure starting with the root directory, which may in turn contain files and other directories.

All directories include at least two entries: . and .. (pronounced "dot" and "dot dot"). The . entry refers to the directory itself, and the .. entry refers to the directory's parent directory. The file system has a single top-level directory (the root directory). The root directory is named / and is distinguished from other directories only in that its parent is itself.

Directory entries are called *links*; they associate a file name with an *inode* number, which is used to locate the data area of the file. No information other than the file name and the inode number is stored in the directory entry. The number of directory entries that can contain the same inode number is not restricted: the same physical file can be listed in more than one directory; it can also be represented by two or more names in the same directory.

Files are uniquely identified by a *path name*, which describes the path from a reference directory to the file in question. If the path name starts with a /, the reference directory is taken to be the root directory. Such a path name is called *absolute*, because it always locates the same unique file. If the path name does *not* start with a leading /, it is called a *relative* path name, and the reference directory is assumed to be the *current* directory. You can change the current directory with the chdir system call, thereby changing the file to which a relative path name resolves.

Slashes separate the names of the directories intervening between the reference directory and the name of the file. For example, the path name /usr/spool/uucp (an absolute path name) refers to the file uucp located in the *spool* directory, which is in turn located in the usr directory, which is to be found as an entry in the / directory. It is impossible to tell whether /usr/spool/ uucp is a file or a directory just by looking at the path name.

Files with more than one link can be referred to by more than one path name. Files are created by the creat system call (or by the open system call, when specified with the appropriate options). Directories are created by the mknod call, which is restricted to authorized processes. (However, the mkdir command creates directories for a user if the user has the necessary permissions.)

UNIX provides no facility for explicitly deleting a file; instead, a file may be *unlinked*, meaning that one of the directory entries naming the file is removed. When the number of links to a file drops to 0, the file's space is freed, effectively deleting the file. The rm utility, UNIX's counterpart to the MS-DOS ERASE command, does not delete a file. Rather, it executes the unlink system call for the file, removing the named directory entry and decrementing the file's link count by one.

File I/O is performed by a set of kernel routines to open, close, read, and write files. At the level of file access implemented by these system calls, a file is an undifferentiated series of bytes without structure; you may read or write as many or as few bytes as you want in one call.

Above this basic I/O level, the base system defines a set of file access routines called the standard I/O (or stdio) package. These routines perform buffering, and implement stream I/O on files and character devices. The stdio package also defines three special stream files that are always open whenever a program is started: *standard input*, *standard output*, and *standard error*. By default, standard input is opened on the user's keyboard, and the standard output and standard error files are opened on the user's screen.

An open file is identified by an integer called a *file descriptor*. Each *process* (a program in execution) has its own table of file descriptors that point to a system-wide table of open files. The first file opened is always assigned file descriptor number 0, the second is assigned number 1, and so on. Before execution of a user program begins, the shell always opens the standard files in the following order:

1. Standard input

2. Standard output

3. Standard error

For this reason the standard input is always file 0, standard output is always file 1, and standard error is always file 2. The standard I/O library defines structures for dealing with files as streams. Three pointers are defined that correspond to the three standard files. The predefined names of these pointers are stdin, stdout, and stderr, respectively. All the stream I/O functions can be called with one of these file pointers as an argument without previously opening the file (because the shell has already opened it).

Programs typically write sign-on messages, warnings, and error messages to the standard error file, and the programs write normal output to the standard output file. This makes it possible to pipe the output of a program to another program without having the output interspersed with warnings or other nondata output.

The shell provides I/O redirection to enable the standard files to refer to a device other than the user's terminal. I/O redirection also allows the output of one program to become the input of another, an arrangement called a *pipe*, without requiring any changes to the programs themselves.

Terminal I/O

The base system provides a generalized terminal interface called *termio*. Terminals can be defined as local or remote, which determines whether modem control signals are ignored by the system or honored.

The system assigns a special meaning to a number of character values when presented to the termio interface. These characters (called *control* characters) are used to manage terminal operations. Some of them can be originated by the terminal to indicate to the program special events such as the press of a function key; others cause a predefined action to occur when they are sent to the terminal. For example, when the ERASE character is received from the terminal, it causes the operating system to delete the previously entered character within a line of input. Although the default character assigned to the ERASE function is #, most users change ERASE to correspond to the backspace key on the terminal keyboard.

The termio interface provides the programmer with control over the I/O bit rate, case conversions, and various other terminal features. Chapter 12, "Programming Serial Devices," describes the termio interface.

Processes

The kernel creates processes and manages their execution. A process is an instance of a program being run and is identified by a process-ID (PID), an integer that the kernel assigns when it creates the process. Two different invocations of the same program will have two different process-IDs. You create a new process by invoking the fork system call.

The `fork` function creates a new process that almost duplicates the calling process; the processes differ in the return value of the `fork` call itself, which for the calling (*parent*) process is the process-ID of the newly created (*child*) process. The `fork` call that creates the child process returns 0, which is how the process can tell that it is the child. Typically, the child process immediately replaces itself by invoking one of the `exec` system calls.

See Chapter 13, "Kernel Internals," for a detailed discussion of process management.

Each process has a root directory and a current working directory. These directories set the context for associating path names with the files to which they refer. By default, the root directory of a process is the root directory of the file system, but the root directory can be changed by the `chroot` system call to any other desired directory in the file system. A relative path name (one that does not begin with /) is resolved by beginning the path name search from the current working directory.

Chapter 8, "Introduction to Files and Devices," covers this facility in detail.

If the effective user-ID of a process is 0, the process is a superuser process. Super-user processes are not restricted by the normal permissions governing directory and file access and process manipulation.

Processes terminate by calling the `exit` system routine, which closes all open files and returns a value (the *exit* code) to the parent process.

Interprocess Communication

The base system supports a simple method of interprocess communication called *signals*. A signal, in this sense, is just a software interrupt. Any process can signal any other process whose PID is known, as long as the signaled process is a member of the same *process group* (has the same parent or is a child of the signaling process). A superuser process, however, can signal any process. Signals are most often used to immediately terminate a program. This use is analogous to the way that the Ctrl-Break software interrupt is used by MS-DOS.

Device drivers use signals to notify a program of events, such as a dropped carrier on a communications line.

Processes can also communicate using pipes. A pipe is created by the kernel in response to a `pipe` system call. The pipe is opened for writing by one process and for reading by another process. Both processes can then perform ordinary file I/O on the pipe. The kernel automatically provides synchronization between the reading and writing processes: A writing process will be forced to wait if the pipe becomes full, and a reading process will wait if the pipe becomes empty.

With named pipes, the processes do not have to be "relatives" to communicate. A named pipe is created by the `mknod` system call. This call creates a directory entry to represent the pipe, and, because a directory entry has a name, any process can then open the pipe for either input or output. Named pipes enable unrelated processes to communicate in a fairly crude but nonetheless useful way.

The Kernel Extension

The kernel extension defines several more sophisticated forms of interprocess communication: semaphores, message queues, and shared-memory segments.

A *semaphore* is a counter typically used to control access to a limited pool of shared resources. In such an application, the semaphore is preset to the number of resource units available. Subsequently, when process requires one or more of the resources managed by the semaphore, the process decrements the semaphore in an attempt to reserve the required number of units. If the numerical value of the semaphore is too small, so a decrement would reduce it to a negative value, the user process is suspended until another process releases enough to permit the decrement to occur. (Although this sounds tricky, it only means that, if a process wants to allocate seven units when the semaphore shows that only four units are available, the process must wait until three units are returned to the resource pool.)

Message queues provide a more verbose method of communication and are typically used in a client-server scenario to exchange a small amount of data between the client and server processes. The client process sends a message to the server, which then replies with a message. The kernel manages messages in queues, a process that makes implementing such features as print spoolers quite straightforward.

Shared-memory segments enable an area of memory to be shared in common among several unrelated processes. In place of pipes, shared memory segments can be used for moving large chunks of data between processes, as in a database server for example.

The Shell

A program can submit a command line for execution by executing the `system` function call. The command line is not executed by the kernel; instead, the `system` function invokes the program `/bin/sh` as a child process, which in turn interprets and executes the command.

Neither the shell program `/bin/sh` nor the library function `system` are part of the System V kernel. Nevertheless they are included in the base system definition and so must be present and must comply with the System V Interface Definition if the operating system is to be considered a true implementation of UNIX System V.

A command line contains a required command name and may be followed by one or more options and arguments. Multiple command lines can be combined into a single command line by separating each command with a semicolon. Commands separated by newlines or semicolons are executed in the order written.

A pipeline can be formed by joining two commands with the vertical bar character (¦). The effect of the vertical bar is to redirect the standard output of the first command so that it is also the standard input of the second command; the data path between the two programs is a pipe. Because a pipeline is itself a command, several pipelines can be joined together. Output is passed left to right starting with the first program in the pipeline until finally read by the last command in the pipeline.

All of the commands in a pipeline are executed simultaneously as child processes of the shell. Because all the commands are simultaneously active, the first line of output generated by the first command in the pipeline can be processed all the way through the pipeline, and output can be produced from the last command of the pipeline, before the first command generates its second line. When the last command in the pipeline terminates, the entire command line terminates.

There are other shell commands to run programs in the background, to conditionally execute commands, and to repetitively execute a group of commands, giving the shell all the capabilities of a full-fledged programming language.

Using the shell's redirection operators, the standard input for a command can be changed to point to any arbitrary file instead of the user's terminal; the standard output and standard error files can be similarly redirected. The redirection operators allow the output of a command to replace an existing file, to be appended to an existing file, or to create a new file. Each command in a compound command line can have its own set of redirection operators specified independently of the other commands on the command line. Further, the redirections that can be performed are not in any way limited by any redirection of the input or output of the shell itself. All of this amounts to incredibly complete control over the input and output of every command contained in a shell program.

"The UNIX Shell" reference section provides a comprehensive guide to programming with the shell.

The Standard Libraries

System V includes an extensive set of subroutine libraries for programmers who use the C and FORTRAN languages. These libraries include functions for the following:

❏ String manipulation

❏ Mathematics

❏ Graphics

❏ Sorting and searching

❏ Regular expression parsing

❏ I/O character typing and translating

❏ Encrypting and decrypting

❏ Time and date reporting

❏ Random number generating

❏ Process creation and control

❏ Database operations

❏ Efficient memory-block manipulation

There are standard library functions that accomplish the following:

❏ Compare strings

❏ Find characters within strings

❏ Concatenate strings

❏ Deliver delimited tokens from strings

❏ Deliver variously defined parts of strings

There are conversion routines to convert character strings to internal numeric values, and the reverse.

The math library includes all the standard trigonometric, exponential, hyperbolic, and transcendental functions.

The graphics library includes line-drawing, curve-fitting, and plotting routines that use a device-independent graphical interface.

Many UNIX commands allow the use of regular expressions for describing search patterns. Unfortunately, in the early days of the system's development there was no regular expression parsing library. As a result, the way in which string patterns are specified tends to differ markedly from command to command.

Summary

This first chapter described the more significant features and capabilities of the UNIX operating system. If you come away with only one impression, it should be that the UNIX environment offers an incredible wealth of tools to the programmer and to the technical user, most of which are not available at all or only at significant expense in other operating system environments.

Although these tools can be used directly, their main purpose is to be incorporated in larger programs—shell programs when possible, compiled programs when necessary. The variety and richness of the UNIX tool set makes almost any programming job easier in the UNIX environment than elsewhere. The implication, of course, is that in other programming environments the programmer must either build these tools (at great time and effort) or settle for a less-than-desirable application design to keep its schedule and cost within bounds.

UNIX can help to alleviate the software production crisis in *your* organization, for *your* projects, because, being a timesharing system, it puts the programmer in direct and comfortable contact with the machine. UNIX is not the only operating environment that does this; there are many others, including the personal computer with MS-DOS, and the giant OS/MVS/TSO and VM/SP time-sharing systems.

The later sections of this chapter showed that when you sit down to a UNIX terminal you have much more than just a time-sharing operating system at your fingertips—you have more than 20 years' worth of highly gifted, extremely skillful programmers' and computer scientists' efforts ready at hand to help you with your project. I don't know of any other operating system environment that provides all these benefits.

Just because you are now embarking on a course of learning to program in the UNIX environment doesn't necessarily imply that you are already enthralled with UNIX, as I am, or that you freely chose this course, as I did. Therefore, I'll offer some advice.

First, don't be put off by the dense, murky documentation, by the queer and often nonintuitive commands or the shell syntax, by the unfamiliar and often inconsistent user interfaces. These are only the surface of UNIX, and if you are patient, you will eventually find that these externals fade into insignificance as you master them.

Second, be patient. UNIX is large. There are hundreds of library functions and hundreds of commands. They will not be learned all at once. It can take years to become proficient with UNIX. The purpose behind the size of UNIX is not so much to challenge you as to serve you, when you are ready, and as you need.

To learn a new tool such as the `vi` text editor or the `awk` programming language, become familiar with just enough to do something useful with it, then set it aside. Use what you know and don't worry about the rest. Later, when you have time, study the tool a little more, add a little to your knowledge, then set the books aside and use what you know, ignoring the rest. Your goal should be to learn enough to be useful but to take specific, intentional measures to avoid frustrating yourself, as can easily happen to anyone new to UNIX. Let me be the first to welcome you to the world of UNIX!

UNIX and MS-DOS

This chapter explores the similarities and differences between UNIX and MS-DOS. If you have a fairly good knowledge of MS-DOS, this chapter will help you bring that knowledge to your work with UNIX.

UNIX and MS-DOS share many common features. This is not surprising, because MS-DOS has been enhanced or rewritten several times by people with a strong UNIX background. Apparently, many MS-DOS users think that MS-DOS influenced the development of UNIX, but the truth is just the opposite.

For programmers making the transition from MS-DOS to UNIX, the presence of similar facilities is not always helpful. Although you certainly can transfer much of your experience from one system to the other, you must be wary: Similarities between MS-DOS and UNIX are often superficial at best. The UNIX version often provides more capabilities and more options, is complicated by multitasking considerations, and is more consistent and more complete than the MS-DOS counterpart.

Facilities Provided by Both UNIX and MS-DOS

This section covers the major facilities that are common to both systems and compares the original UNIX version of a facility with its more simplified MS-DOS version. This chapter won't go into great detail about the UNIX facilities; each of them is addressed more fully in its own chapter.

The Command Interpreter

UNIX and MS-DOS both have command interpreters that are separate programs rather than built-in functions of the system kernel. (In this chapter, I'll use the term *shell* to refer to the command interpreter in either system.)

The purpose of the shell is to provide a buffer between the user and the operating system, to arrange for the loading and running of programs, and to create an interactive environment for using the system. The shell, in a sense, surrounds the operating system and provides access to its services through well-defined interfaces.

The great advantage to separating the shell from the kernel is that this independence enables you to choose the shell you will use. In both the MS-DOS and UNIX environments, there are numerous command interpreters to choose among.

In UNIX, the standard shell is called s h; in MS-DOS, it is called COMMAND.COM. In either system, you can execute a new copy of the shell by typing its name as a command. The new shell is then invoked as if it were a subroutine of the current shell, and the current shell simply waits for the new shell to complete.

In UNIX, however, both the old and the new shell are actually separate and independent processes. As a result, UNIX also provides ways to invoke a new copy of the shell that allows both copies to continue execution in parallel.

This ability to run two or more shells at once is a great advantage, because it enables you to overlap the execution of your applications. Of course, the system must also keep the two shells from fighting over the terminal, but in the UNIX environment this is not difficult to do.

Shell Programming

The MS-DOS shell provides a rudimentary programming capability called the *batch* facility. The term comes from the early batch-processing days of the industry when work was submitted to the system for unattended execution; here, the term refers to the ability to execute a number of commands without having to type in each one by hand.

The batch facility enables you to combine commands that are frequently used together into a new command of your own making. This is a form of programming, and the batch facility is in fact a kind of programming language. The programming power of the UNIX shell far exceeds the capabilities of the MS-DOS batch facility.

A program written for the UNIX shell is called a *shell script*; in MS-DOS, the same thing is called a *batch file*. Some of the commands permitted inside an MS-DOS batch file are not processible when you are typing a command at the keyboard. UNIX, on the other hand, makes no distinction between shell commands in a file and shell commands typed at the keyboard; to the UNIX shell, the keyboard is just another file (the *standard input* file, to be precise). In fact, you can think of your entire session with UNIX, from the time you log in to the time you log out, as one long shell script.

Environment Variables

Like the MS-DOS shell, the UNIX shell provides environment variables. The environment in both systems is a set of strings of the form `NAME=VALUE`. These strings can be used to store parameters and options for programs to use. Using environment variables, you can change the options or functions to be performed by a program without having to key a command-line option every time you invoke the program.

Some environment variables are used by the shell itself, such as PATH. Unfortunately, in MS-DOS, the value of an environment can be referenced only from within a batch file or a program, and not from the command line. If you want to add a directory to your PATH, it would be a great time-saver if you could just type something such as:

```
SET PATH=%PATH%;D:\NEW\DIR
```

but that would not work under MS-DOS.

In UNIX, though, remembering that the shell makes no distinction between commands entered in a file and those entered at the keyboard, we only need to enter the command line:

```
path=$path:/new/dir
```

to add the directory `/new/dir` to the existing search path. Note that the UNIX shell does not use the `set` command for setting environment values.

Program Control Constructs

The MS-DOS batch facility uses program control constructs that are limited to one line. The UNIX originals of these constructs are not so limited, and that makes it possible to write well-structured code in the shell's language.

For instance, if you have a sequence of commands that you want to execute for each file in a given directory, in MS-DOS you would write a batch file containing those commands and use a parameter to stand for the name of the file. The batch file might look like that in the following listing:

```
SORT %1 >\TMP\%1
PRINT \TMP\%1
```

You can then use this batch file to sort and print a set of files by typing the command:

```
FOR %F IN (*.WK) DO SPRT %F
```

In UNIX, the same operation would look like this:

```
for F in *.wk
do
sort $F >/tmp/$F
lp /tmp/$F
done
```

Because UNIX shell commands like `for` do not have to be complete on one line, you don't need to crank out a batch file for every multistep procedure, and the practical result is that you often find yourself writing a loop to handle a one-time task right at the keyboard.

While you are entering a multiline command, the UNIX shell prompts you for additional input that is needed to complete the current statement. The normal prompt is the environment string PS1, and the secondary prompt is the environment string PS2. Typically, PS1 is a dollar sign ($) followed by a space, and PS2 is a greater-than sign (>) followed by a space, but these prompt strings are as easy to change as any other environment variable, for example:

```
PS2="+ "
```

will change the prompt for continuation lines to the plus (+) character.

Standard Input and Output, and Redirection

Both systems maintain tables in private memory to manage open files. Under MS-DOS, the index into this table is called a *file handle*; under UNIX, the index is called a *file descriptor*. Programs that read and write files use the handle, or file descriptor, to tell the operating system which file is to be used. All programs start out with three files already open: the standard input, standard output, and standard error files. These file descriptors are 0, 1, and 2, respectively.

Both MS-DOS and UNIX provide a capability known as *redirection*. The essential idea behind redirection is that a program is isolated from specific knowledge of where its input comes from and where its output goes. The advantage of redirection is that programs become naturally device-independent. A program written to control a digital tape machine can be tested by another program written to simulate the tape machine. Neither program "knows" what type of device is being used; to either program, the file appears to be nothing more than a stream of characters coming in or going out.

Be aware, though, that I/O redirection only works with programs that use stream I/O.

Any program that reads from its standard input and writes to its standard output is called a *filter*. This term alludes to the pipe-fitting analogy used to describe how one program's output becomes connected to another's input.

MS-DOS provides a pipe facility, but because MS-DOS is not a multitasking system and cannot execute two programs at once, it has to store the entire output of the first program in a temporary file, which is then read by the second program. UNIX, on the other hand, executes both programs at once and can therefore actually pass output data as it is generated directly to the second program without having to use an intermediate file. Chapter 14, "Signals and IPC," covers pipes in detail.

The syntax for performing simple redirection is the same for both systems: < for input redirection and > for output redirection. UNIX provides additional redirection facilities, which "UNIX Commands" covers in detail.

Pipelines

A facility that is little used in MS-DOS because of the overhead involved, the pipeline feature really become powerful in UNIX. A pipeline is a series of commands arranged so that the output of each command becomes the input of the next. Although other, earlier operating systems (notably MULTICS) provided a roughly comparable capability, UNIX was the first system to offer this capability so that it was simple to use and required no special application programming. The pipeline feature characterizes the UNIX philosophy: Build small tools, build them well, and put them together into larger tools.

The MS-DOS implementation of pipelines is straightforward but inefficient. As data is written to the pipe, it is stored in a temporary file; when a command later reads from the pipe, the data is actually retrieved from the temporary file and passed to the program. This is inefficient because two disk accesses are required for every block of data—one to write the block and another to read it back in. No other implementation is practical under MS-DOS, because MS-DOS is not a multitasking system. The two programs sharing the pipe cannot both be in execution at once.

The UNIX implementation of pipelines creates actual coroutines; that is, all programs in the pipeline are executed simultaneously as multiple tasks owned by the shell. Data is passed from one program to the next through a pipe, which is a buffer in kernel-owned memory that emulates a pair of files. A pipe looks like a file open for output to the left-hand program in a pipeline, but the same pipe looks like a file open for input to the right-hand program. Because the data is passed in a memory buffer and because all the programs are active tasks at the same time, there is a significant gain in overall efficiency. More important than the performance gain, though, is the ability to combine several programs into one large processing unit. This is a capability worth having even if, instead of actually gaining efficiency, you had to give up some efficiency to get it.

Both UNIX and MS-DOS use the same syntax for pipelines, the split vertical bar. When using MS-DOS, the command to print a sorted directory listing would be:

```
DIR ¦ SORT > PRN
```

whereas the corresponding UNIX command would be

```
ls ¦ sort >/dev/lp
```

Although the command names differ (and the sort operation is really superfluous for the UNIX version), the commands nonetheless have the same syntactical structure.

In both systems it is actually the shell that performs the I/O redirection. The programs themselves simply read from standard input and write to standard output. Chapter 13, "Kernel Internals," covers the exact details of creating a new process under UNIX.

Bootstrap Activities

When you first boot up MS-DOS, it takes configuration parameters from a file called CONFIG.SYS and then executes the commands in a file called AUTOEXEC.BAT. When UNIX first boots up, it takes configuration parameters from a file called /etc/inittab and then executes the commands in a file called /etc/rc. As usual, the parallel is inexact, but the purpose underlying CONFIG.SYS (/etc/inittab) and AUTOEXEC.BAT (/etc/rc) is the same: to get the system running with a minimum of user interaction.

CONFIG.SYS, the MS-DOS configuration file, is primarily used for loading device drivers and setting parameters such as the number of files and buffers allowed. In UNIX, these same functions are performed through a much more tedious process that involves rebuilding the operating system kernel itself; fortunately, the kernel only needs to be rebuilt when the hardware configuration changes, and not on every boot. Chapter 13, "Kernel Internals," discusses system configuration issues.

The UNIX file /etc/inittab determines which programs will run during the various stages of a UNIX system life cycle, from single-user mode to multiuser mode to rebooting. The primary functions of /etc/inittab are to define which ports have terminals connected to them and what the initial setup is for each terminal; see Chapter 3, "UNIX in Action," for more information.

The MS-DOS file AUTOEXEC.BAT is a batch file that is automatically executed when MS-DOS is started and that is normally used to initialize the user's runtime environment. The UNIX file /etc/rc is a shell script and performs a very similar function for the system as a whole. Because UNIX is a multiuser system, it must provide not only for automatic system initialization, but also for initializing each user's environment when a new user logs in; this latter task is performed by the /etc/profile shell script, which can be tailored to local requirements by the system administrator. Optionally, each user can also have a customized initialization script, called .profile, which is executed by the login process. Chapter 3, "UNIX in Action," details the complete sequence.

File System Structure

UNIX and MS-DOS both have hierarchical file systems. One important difference between the two systems is the relative simplicity of the UNIX directory, containing as it does only the file name and a pointer to the file's data. One consequence of the UNIX implementation is the ease by which aliases for file names can be established; file name aliases are not supported by MS-DOS at all, with the result that in some situations you may be forced to keep a second or third copy of a file, whereas in the same situation UNIX would keep only pointers to the file.

MS-DOS manages a PC and is therefore limited to two (or at least a few) disk drives. MS-DOS 4.0 supports partitions up to 512K. UNIX supports the largest mainframes manufactured and can allow the attachment of literally hundreds of disk drives. In mainframe environments, the capacity of a disk drive can easily exceed 600MB. The UNIX file system is therefore necessarily more flexible and more capacious than that of MS-DOS.

A more subtle difference between the two systems is the fact that, in MS-DOS, path names can refer only to directories and disk files, whereas in UNIX a path name can refer to a disk file, a directory, a device, or a pipe. This means no special provisions are made in user programming for device prefixes ("A:" does not occur in UNIX), and as a result, a device or a pipe can be named wherever a disk file can be named.

MS-DOS, on the other hand, retains the idea of separate disks—actual or logical—a concept that it inherited from its ancestor operating system, CP/M. Whereas UNIX allows only one root directory in the entire system, MS-DOS has a root directory for each disk drive. Therefore, to fully specify a file's path name to MS-DOS, you must also include the drive prefix.

For single-user systems, drive prefixes may be acceptable because (presumably) you know where you have put your files. But on a large system with many users and a system operator, it can be difficult for a user to know from day to day on which disk a particular file happens to be.

UNIX handles this situation by an operation called `mounting` a volume. Before a disk volume can be mounted, an empty directory must be created somewhere in the file system that is already mounted. (The system's root file system is usually used for this purpose because it is always mounted.) Then when the disk is mounted on the empty directory, the root directory of the disk drive appears to cover up the empty directory. In place of the empty directory, users see the entire hierarchical structure that exists on the newly mounted disk drive.

Suppose the root file system looks like figure 2.1.

***Fig. 2.1.** File systems before mount.*

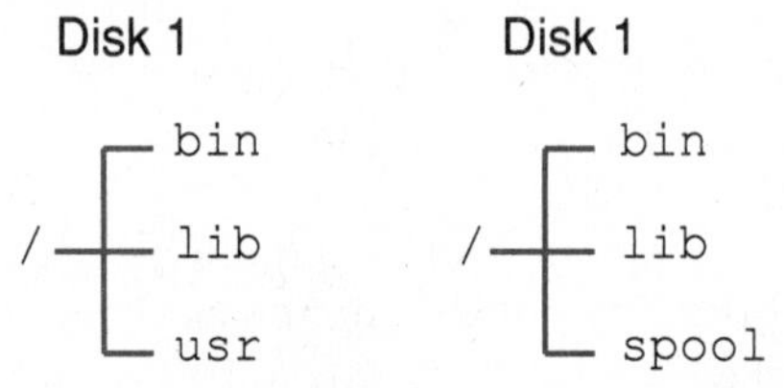

```
       Disk 1                Disk 1

         ┌─ bin                ┌─ bin
  /──────┼─ lib         /──────┼─ lib
         └─ usr                └─ spool
```

If we now mount another disk drive onto the root file system using the *usr* directory as the mount point, the file system will look like figure 2.2.

Because the effect of mounting a disk volume is to extend the current file system, the user needs only to specify the appropriate path name to refer to a file; the system keeps track of which disk contains that file and requires no assistance from the user to find it.

Fig. 2.2. File systems after mount.

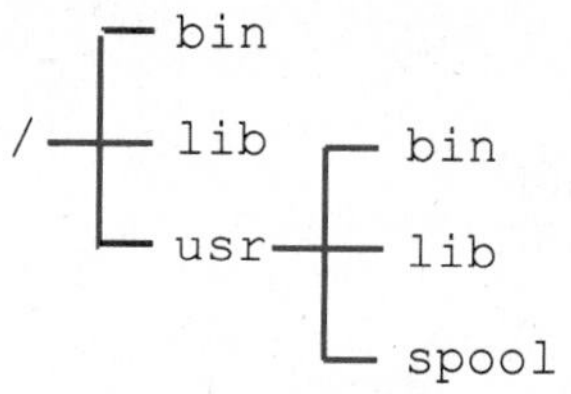

```
              ┌─ bin
              │
     / ─┼─── lib   ┌─ bin
              │     │
              └─ usr┼─ lib
                    │
                    └─ spool
```

Loadable and Linkable Device Drivers

Both UNIX and MS-DOS provide a means of adding support for new devices. Support for a specific kind of device is provided by a module called a *device driver*, which must handle all I/O requests for that device type. Although a device driver behaves like part of the operating system, it is not usually considered as such, because it may be provided by the vendor of the device or by the user.

After a driver is written and installed, both systems access it through the file system.

UNIX defines all device drivers in the directory /dev. A device driver, and its definition in the /dev directory, appears to all application-level programs as if it were an ordinary file; programs can issue open, close, read, and write requests to them. The operating system directs these operations to the appropriate device drivers by using special flags in the device's definition. UNIX refers to one of these device definitions as a *special file*; these files have attribute flags that designate them as such.

MS-DOS uses a similar scheme. Device drivers are given special names like PRN or NUL, and—as with UNIX—they can be opened, closed, read, and written just like ordinary files. Although UNIX block devices follow the same conventions as UNIX character devices, MS-DOS block devices receive disk designations rather than special file names. Therefore, under UNIX, you can read and write a disk directly, as if it were a file. Under MS-DOS, you cannot.

Because UNIX devices are represented by directory entries with special attributes, they can easily be replaced for testing. For example, if you have problems with a printer that is represented by /dev/lp, you may want to put all output destined for that printer into a file instead, to see whether the problem is with the data or the printer. You don't have to change any programs; you only need to replace the file /dev/lp with an ordinary file of the same name. Under MS-DOS, of course, this technique is not available.

File Attributes

MS-DOS files have attributes; so do UNIX files. Under MS-DOS, the attributes of a file may include the following:

READ ONLY: The file can be read but not erased or modified.

ARCHIVE: The file has been changed. This attribute is set when the file is modified and is cleared by some backup programs.

HIDDEN: The file entry is not displayed by the DIR command when this attribute is set.

SYSTEM: Like the Hidden format, but also prevents modification and erasure of the file.

VOLUME ID: The file name of a directory entry having this attribute is taken to be the name of the entire disk volume and does not refer to an actual file.

UNIX file attributes are collectively called the *file mode*. The command (and system call) that changes a file's mode is chmod, which is the origin of the MS-DOS system call of the same name.

The UNIX file mode consists of the permission bits, which are three groups of three bits each, and three additional bits that are covered fully in Chapter 8, "Introduction to Files and Devices." The three groups of permission bits specify whether the system provides read, write, or execute permission to three classes of users: the owner of the file, members of a named group of users, and everybody else. Owners and groups are identifications that are assigned to files, processes, and users in whatever manner desired. Chapter 8 gives all the details on permissions, user-IDs, and group-IDs.

TSRs and Daemons

MS-DOS supports a kind of background process called a *terminate and stay resident (TSR)*. A TSR is not an independent process such as UNIX supports. It is really an interrupt handler that can steal the machine from the active program but that has no independent life of its own. Anyone who has written a TSR is familiar with the difficult, awkward programming that it requires.

UNIX, being a multitasking system, truly supports the simultaneous execution of two or more independent programs. This capability is accessible to the C-language programmer, and also to any user through the facilities of the shell. By simply ending a command with the ampersand (&) symbol, the shell executes the command in the *background*. This means that the command begins to run on its own while the shell comes back immediately with another prompt. You can then execute a second command, and both the new command and the background command execute at the same time.

If you are executing two or more commands at a time using this technique, things can get confusing if both commands try to read from or write to the terminal. Here you can use redirection to provide separate standard input and standard output files for the background command(s) you initiate, while you use the terminal for interactive commands.

If you arrange for the background command to become disassociated with your terminal, the background command becomes a *daemon*. For example, UNIX print spoolers are implemented as daemons; they wake up every so often and send print jobs to the printer and then go back to sleep.

No special programming is required to make a program run as a background task. A daemon, however, must include the necessary programming to detach itself from the terminal. Chapter 15, "Writing Multiprocessing Programs," describes background processes and daemons in detail.

UNIX Facilities Not Provided by MS-DOS

UNIX provides a wealth of resources and support systems that are either completely absent from MS-DOS or available only as third-party, add-on software. This section focuses on the facilities that are not provided in any form under MS-DOS.

Multiuser Operation

UNIX is a multiuser operating system. It supports the distinctions between one user and another. Each user is identified by a name and a number; the system prompts for these identifications when a user logs into the system and remembers them until the user logs out. All processes that the user initiates, and all files that the user creates, are marked with his or her user-ID. UNIX provides a system of file permissions to protect the files created by one user from various levels of access and alteration by other users. UNIX provides each user with a set of directories so that he or she can create and manage files without interfering with other users. UNIX provides each user with a way to initialize his or her environment at login time.

In contrast, MS-DOS is a single-user system. MS-DOS does not require the user's identity and provides no way to identify files or processes as belonging to an individual user. MS-DOS provides no login procedure to confirm a user's authorization to access the system. It is primarily the single-user design of MS-DOS that makes it so much simpler to use and more limited in functionality than UNIX.

UNIX is a multitasking system primarily because any system intended to be used by more than one person at a time must be capable of running more than one program at once. MS-DOS does not support multitasking primarily because that operating system was never intended to support more than one user at a time.

Because UNIX supports multiple users, it must provide some means to administer global system resources in an orderly fashion and a way to limit the administrative capability to a subset of the system's users. UNIX solves this problem with the concept of the *superuser*. The superuser is simply that user whose user-ID is equal to 0. Any programs executed by such a user are allowed to bypass the system's normal security and protection schemes, a necessary capability to enable the superuser (and therefore any programs the superuser runs) to manage all of the system's resources. Chapter 8, "Introduction to Files and Devices," explores some of the ways the superuser concept affects your use of the system.

Multitasking

UNIX is a multitasking system. Any user can run several tasks at once by using the shell's background execution facility. A program can create new tasks, control them, communicate with them, and wait for their completion before continuing.

Multitasking is implemented within the UNIX kernel. All tasks are managed by a simple but very effective task scheduler that constantly adjusts the priority of tasks according to their resource usage, time already spent in execution, and a user-defined priority setting. UNIX provides several forms of communication among processes, as well as capabilities for process creation, control, and destruction.

Chapter 13, "Kernel Internals," covers all the details of task management.

UNIX implements a swapping procedure by which low-priority tasks can be temporarily removed from the machine's memory, then brought back when there is no higher-priority work to do. A area of the disk is reserved for swapping space.

In UNIX, user tasks (*processes*) are maintained in a hierarchy. The *root* of the process hierarchy is task 1, called the `init` process. This process is run automatically as you start up the operating system and is responsible for creating all additional processes. A parent-child relationship exists between a process and any other processes it creates. Pipes can be used by a process to communicate with its parent and child processes, but not with other processes. When a process terminates, its parent is informed. A process inherits environment variables and open files from its parent. As was mentioned earlier in the discussion of daemons, processes can be detached from their parents. In such cases, `init` becomes the parent of the detached process.

UNIX processes can share their code so that, when several users are running the same program at the same time, only one copy of the program is in memory. To be sharable, a program must be appropriately link edited. Even when the program code is shared among several users, a separate data area is allocated for each invocation of the program. A related facility enables you to specify that a heavily used program such as a text editor or compiler be locked in memory even when not being used, to reduce the overhead of repeatedly loading such programs into memory.

Needless to say, because MS-DOS is not a multitasking system, it provides none of the capabilities and features described in this section.

Security

UNIX provides security mechanisms in several areas. File permissions control access to files, directories, and devices. A password scheme prevents unauthorized users from logging in. Encryption is available from within the standard text editors as well as on a file-by-file basis, and a C program can call the encryption subroutine to encrypt arbitrary blocks of data.

MS-DOS offers no file security features, despite the fact that it allows the setting of a read-only attribute of a file. No special permission or privilege is required to set the read-only attribute, and none is required to remove it. Therefore, the only possible use of the MS-DOS file attribute is to help in avoiding accidental erasure of files. This is fundamentally different from the UNIX security mechanism, that actively prevents unauthorized users from modifying or deleting a file and that also prevents those same unauthorized users from removing the protection controls of the file.

The adequacy of UNIX security has been the subject of debate for years. A detailed review of UNIX security holes and how to deal with them is beyond the scope of this book. Suffice it to say that in the inevitable trade-off between ease of use and tightness of security, UNIX designers and administrators traditionally have chosen ease of use. Nonetheless, by fully implementing the facilities that UNIX provides and by adding physical security and good personnel and data management, you can achieve a level of security that should be adequate for anything except government and military work.

Standard Utilities

UNIX comes with a collection of programs, languages, design tools, and subroutine libraries that is impressive as much for its richness and variety as for its sheer size. The following is just a smattering of the features available:

❏ awk is an interpretive programming language for processing ASCII files. awk can be used for complicated string editing and parsing, for reformatting files, or for report writing and data base applications.

❏ bc and dc are programmable scientific calculators.

❏ diff generates a text file describing the differences between two files. The diff family of utilities includes a number of programs besides diff itself, including diff3, sdiff, and diffmk.

❏ grep, fgrep, and egrep provide a pattern-matching facility for searching one or several files.

❏ make, a program for maintaining programs, has been widely imitated for the MS-DOS marketplace. As in so many other areas, UNIX originated the idea and even now, 20 years later, still has the best implementation.

❏ The Source Code Control System (SCCS). If you develop commercial-grade software, you will never want to be without this version and revision control package.

❏ Yet Another Compiler Compiler (YACC). This parser generator has unusual staying power; it has been around since the early 1970s and is still widely used today.

This list of facilities and tools barely begins to scratch the surface of what's available.

Links

UNIX provides a facility called *linking*, whereby a single file is represented by more than one directory entry. Linking performs a number of chores easier than they would be performed using MS-DOS. For example, consider the problem of organizing a set of memoranda. You may want to maintain the memoranda by the author, subject, recipient, and project it references.

In MS-DOS, you can create a set of subdirectories for the most important differentiating characteristic and possibly use a database or other software to organize the files according to other criteria. The difficulty of maintaining such a system soon would lead you to use a specialized software package or to abandon the idea.

Under UNIX, you put the files into subdirectories according to author (for example), then create additional subdirectories for the other criteria, and then link the files into the new directories. In this way, a file appears to be "in" each of the directories that has an entry for it. When the file is changed, it is changed on disk regardless of which directory entry was used to open the file. The other directory entries do not need to be updated, because they contain no information about the file, only a pointer to the information.

Named Pipes

Named pipes, also called FIFOs (first-in, first-out), are an extension of the pipe facility used to achieve communication among tasks that are not necessarily executing at the same time. A named pipe consists of a directory entry that points to a special file-information block in the kernel's memory; the block designates this file as a named pipe. After a named pipe is created, it continues to exist independently of any particular process. Any process with appropriate permissions can read or write the named pipe, without necessarily being synchronized with each other.

One application for named pipes is communication between different processors sharing a disk. Consider a PC that is connected to a UNIX system in such a way that drive D on the PC is the UNIX file system. You can transfer files from the PC to the UNIX system by using the MS-DOS COPY command. This application is a common networking arrangement. Suppose you want to implement a remote execution facility; you want to create a shell script on the PC and have the UNIX system execute it. One way to do this is to set up a named pipe on the UNIX system and execute a copy of the shell with the named pipe as its standard input. You can arrange for the shell to wait indefinitely for a command line to appear in the named pipe. Then, to execute a UNIX command, you copy it to the named pipe, which appears to be an ordinary MS-DOS file on drive D.

Hardware Independence

Unlike MS-DOS, which is supported only for the Intel 8086 family of processions, UNIX is currently available for dozens of different computer architectures, UNIX is portable to processors with widely differing characteristics, mainly because it was written in C rather than in assembly language.

Hardware other than the processor itself is also a factor in the portability of UNIX. Unlike most other operating systems, UNIX makes no assumptions about any of the hardware it runs on. The system console can be any terminal for which a device driver is written. Similarly, the disks are not limited to some arbitrary table of possible characteristics, as the disks are under MS-DOS.

Summary

This chapter mentioned many of the similarities and differences between UNIX and MS-DOS. This is not an exhaustive list. The most important similarities lie in the area of the command language, important because the shell is the primary interface between the user and the system, whether MS-DOS or UNIX.

The most important difference lies in the very multiuser nature of UNIX; this difference colors nearly every other aspect of using the UNIX system. To become comfortable with UNIX, you must not only learn the new command language (ls instead of DIR, rm instead of DEL, cat instead of TYPE, and so on), you must learn the basic concepts of ownership and permissions. Once these are mastered, learning UNIX is nothing more than slowly building familiarity with its utilities and programming functions.

Although learning the shell and the UNIX commands is important, file management concepts (including ownership and permissions) are more difficult to master for new UNIX users. For that reason, much of this book will deal with the features of the UNIX file system.

CHAPTER 3

UNIX in Action

This chapter details the UNIX bootstrap procedure and identifies the processes that are automatically started when UNIX is initialized. Many of these details are not specified in the *System V Interface Definition (SVID)* and can therefore vary from one implementation of System V to another, or are configurable by the local system administrator. This chapter describes the basic requirements of the *SVID*, as well as traditional practice by system administrators.

As a general system user, you need to have some understanding of the system bootstrap procedure in order to discriminate between actions you should provide in your login profile and actions that would be redundant. Knowledge of the process also helps you to recognize those aspects of the system's operation that the local system administrator can adjust for you.

As an applications programmer, you need an even better understanding of the bootstrap procedure so that you can take advantage of bootstrap system start-up options that may be useful to your applications.

If you provide system administration services for one or more machines, you will have to customize the bootstrap procedure to meet the needs of your environment, and to do that job you will have to understand the procedure very well indeed.

The Bootstrap Procedure

Just what functions does the start-up procedure perform? When UNIX is booted, it:

❏ Reads the operating system into memory and enters its initialization routine.

❏ Initializes the disk buffer pool and system memory areas.

❏ Calls the initialization entry point of every device driver.

❏ Calls the fork system routine to start the init process as proc1.

❏ Transfers control to the system's swapper routine, which remains active throughout the remaining life of the system as proc0.

The terms proc0 and proc1 often refer to the swapper and init system processes, because they always receive process-ID numbers 0 and 1, respectively. The output of any ps command will show processes 0 and 1; it is to the swapper and init processes that they refer.

Now let's go back over these steps in greater detail. When you first power on or reset the machine, it automatically jumps to a routine in read-only memory. Exactly what this routine does depends on the particular machine, but its purpose is always the same: to find a working disk drive, read the contents of a software boot program into memory, and transfer control to it. The idea here is that the hardware manufacturer provides just enough functionality in the CPU to allow the operating system implementer to get a "seed" program into memory and running. This program, called the *bootstrap* routine, must usually be small and is often required to fit into one disk block. The operating system programmer must arrange to get the entire system loaded and running, starting only with the bootstrap code—sometimes a formidable task.

This step, although very basic, is crucial. The machine's bootstrap capability must be extremely generic; otherwise, the machine would be limited to supporting only one operating system. It is this first bootstrap program read from the disk that determines whether MS-DOS, UNIX, or some other operating system will be brought into memory.

When the bootstrap routine receives control, the system is not yet in memory. At this point, UNIX bootstrap routines typically prompt the system operator to ask which kernel file should be loaded from the disk. The operator can choose a standard kernel, can choose to load a new version of the kernel to test, or, if there are several kernels available offering different features and options, the operator can choose from among them. To exercise a choice, you must have previously stored different versions of the kernel on the disk, because that is where the bootstrap routine will look.

Regardless of whether the bootstrap routine provides this option or any other option, the routine ultimately reads the contents of an executable kernel program file into memory. Once the kernel is loaded, the real operating system is in memory and the machine can begin to operate as a UNIX system.

The bootstrap routine jumps to the kernel's entry point, where the system's basic initialization code is found, and the second phase of the system start-up procedure begins.

CPU memory is given a quick check to determine how much memory there is. Some available memory is allocated to the system for its own use; the remainder is available for user processes. The initialization routine usually reports these allocations on the console so that the system administrator can monitor the use of memory. Some of the memory reserved for use by the system will be allocated to the disk buffer pool, about which I will say more in later chapters.

The third phase of initialization begins next. The kernel contains routines to initialize itself, but because all knowledge of I/O devices is relegated to device drivers, the kernel cannot initialize I/O devices by itself. Instead, each device driver has the option of declaring an initialization routine that is to be called during start-up; the kernel initialization routine now calls each driver to prepare its devices for normal operation.

The kernel now has only two jobs left to finish its own initialization. In the first of these, the kernel issues a `fork` system call, loading and starting the `init` process. Its second and final job is to branch into the `swapper` routine, from which it will never exit. This ends the kernel's initialization, which now simply waits for active processes to call for service.

Only one useful process is active at this time, though: the `init` process. The system is still not in a usable state, and a great deal of work remains to be done before it becomes usable, so we turn now to the `init` process as the complex job of starting the system enters its next major phase.

The init Process

The purpose of the `init` process is simply to spawn other processes. All processes except process 0 and process 1 are directly or indirectly children of `init`. The `init` process is a good example of the UNIX approach to solving problems. The designers of UNIX realized that a number of processes must be started during system initialization: processes to solicit logins at user terminals, processes to set up the file system for normal use, processes to perform print spooling functions, and so on. They also realized that they could not predict exactly what processes would be required because the requirements are determined by the number and type of terminals installed, the number and type of disk drives, and many other factors that are user configurable.

As a result, the designers decided to create a general-purpose engine for starting up processes and to let the superuser decide what processes are needed. The result of this decision was init.

When started, the init process looks for a file called /etc/inittab. This text file, a script file for init, contains the commands init must issue to configure the system for normal operation. Each line of /etc/inittab describes a shell command containing any options and arguments you may desire—those that as the system administrator you feel need to be executed during system start-up.

This facility enables you to completely control what happens after the bootstrap procedure is completed.

Run Levels

The /etc/inittab file describes one or more states, called *run levels*, that the system may enter. These run levels are not defined in the operating system kernel or referenced by any system calls; they are purely inventions for the benefit of the init process. A given run level is simply a shorthand designation for a configuration of the system.

One of the possible run levels, and the level that init enters if no /etc/inittab file exists, is the so-called singleuser or S run level.

As its name implies, the single-user state is intended to permit only one user (presumably the superuser) to log into the system. The state is typically used to perform maintenance functions such as installing new software packages, changing file system allocations, adding and testing new devices, and other activities that would interfere with (or be disrupted by) the activities of other users.

The init process recognizes seven other run levels in addition to S. These levels are numbered 0–6. No intrinsic meaning is attached to any of the states 0–6; you may use them for any convenient purpose.

For each run level, the /etc/inittab file designates which commands are to be executed when the system enters that particular run level. Commands for controlling the transition from one level to another may also be specified. The superuser can instruct the init process to switch the system from one state to another at any time using the telinit command.

You will want to assign a meaning to at least some of the run levels. In the following descriptions of typical run-level commands, be aware of the distinction between a "command" and a "process." A *command* is a line of text interpreted by the shell and results in the execution of one or more programs. A *process*, on the other hand, refers to a stream of execution without concern for which program may be under execution; two processes may both be executing the same command, perhaps with differing options and arguments, perhaps not.

The following is a typical assignment of run levels:

0: Run level 0 is often used to perform a general shutdown of the system. Users are warned to log out; file systems are unmounted; daemon processes are terminated; system activity is quiesced; and, if possible, the machine is instructed to turn itself off.

1: The commands for this single-user mode usually are designed to switch from multiuser to single-user mode and therefore include commands to kill the standard background processes, unmount file systems, and essentially undo most of what happens when the system enters state 2. State 1 is not the same as state s, which is defined internally and is not dependent on the file /etc/inittab.

2: Run mode 2, the *multiuser* state, is usually designated as the state init is to enter immediately after the system bootstrap procedure is completed. This state mounts the user file systems, starts up the normal daemon processes, and initiates a getty process for each user terminal.

3,4: These states are often used for alternative multiuser environments. For example, on systems that are part of a network, state 3 may be the full-networked state, which would perform all tasks that state 2 does and also initiate the network server and client processes.

5: On systems that have a firmware debugger, this state could be used to perform a complete system shutdown and then transfer control to the debugger.

6: This state usually is defined as a "down-and-up" state; that is, the system is completely shut down, as for state 0, and then restarted as if from a cold, power-off condition. This state is intended for use in testing a new kernel or in performing a periodic system reboot without human intervention.

The /etc/inittab Script

The /etc/inittab file consists of lines delimited by newline characters. Each line can be up to 512 bytes long; there is no limit on the number of lines permitted. Each line contains a number of logical fields separated by colons. The following fields are defined:

ID: A string of up to four characters that uniquely identifies the entry. An optional field, ID is not used by any of the internal processes.

RUN-LEVEL: A string designating the set of run levels for which the command in the next field is to be executed. If null, the value 0123456 is assumed (all run levels).

ENTRY-TYPE: A keyword designating the type of entry for the current line. The entry types are defined below.

COMMAND: Any shell command to be issued by init. A comment, beginning with the # character, can be appended to the command.

The RUN-LEVEL field need not be a single character; for example, 023 is a valid entry and indicates that the command will be executed whenever the system switches from any other state to states 0, 1, or 2. A process that is active in the old run level but not in the new one is terminated before the transition to the new run level. If a transition is in progress from one level to another, a process that is active in both run levels is not disturbed.

Terminating an active process is a two-step operation. First, a warning signal is sent to the process. This signal, SIGTERM, is a request for the receiving process to terminate. Programs can be written to trap this signal and perform shutdown operations or to completely ignore the signal. After a slight pause (typically 15 to 30 seconds), a second signal is sent; this time, the signal is SIGKILL, which cannot be trapped or ignored.

In addition to the defined system states, the *run-level* entry can be a, b, or c. These entries do not correspond to actual run levels; they only cause init to execute the commands associated with the entries. When one of these pseudostates is used, it does not affect the actual run level of the system; therefore, no processes are terminated and no transition is made.

Entry Types

The ENTRY-TYPE defines how init interprets an entry. The boot and bootwait entry types carry a special restriction: they are executed only if their associated run-level is the level first entered when the system is bootstrapped. If the system enters the single-user state when UNIX is first started, the boot and bootwait entries apply to the first state selected when leaving run-mode s. The following are the possible entry types and their meanings:

boot: If the previously described conditions are met, the associated command is executed; the init process does not wait for the command to terminate, and it is not restarted when it does terminate.

bootwait: If the previously described conditions are met, the associated command is executed. The init process waits for the process to terminate before continuing with the other entries in /etc/inittab. The command is not restarted when it terminates.

initdefault: The first entry with this type determines init's initial run level when the system is bootstrapped. The command for this entry is ignored. If more than one run level appears in the run level field for this entry, the last run level is effective and the others are ignored. Because 0123456 is assumed for an empty run level, omitting the run level for an initdefault entry results in a default level of 6. On virtually all UNIX systems, this default level results in one of two disasters: the system continually reboots itself or boots into a completely brain-dead state for which no processes are defined.

off: If the process described by the command entry is active, it is killed according to the previously described sequence; otherwise, this entry is ignored. The off entry type normally is used to disable user terminal processes while keeping their definitions in the /etc/inittab file for later use. When a terminal connection is to be reinstated, you only need change the off to a respawn (see the description of the respawn entry) rather than reenter the line.

once: When init first enters the run level associated with this entry type, the process designated is run. The init process does not wait for it to terminate, and it cannot be restarted when it does terminate.

ondemand: This entry type, which is identical to respawn (see the description of the respawn entry), is given a different keyword because it is intended for use only with the pseudostates a, b, and c, which are indeed "on-demand" actions.

powerfail: The associated command is executed when init is in the state designated by this entry's RUN-LEVEL, and a power failure interrupt (SIGPWR) occurs. The init process does not await the process, and the process is not restarted when it terminates.

powerwait: The associated command is executed under the same conditions as a powerfail entry; the init process waits for the process to terminate before continuing with the other entries in /etc/inittab.

respawn: If this entry's COMMAND field designates a process that already is running, init does nothing and continues to scan /etc/inittab. Otherwise, the command is executed. When the process thus created terminates, init restarts it. This entry type usually is associated with user terminals; see the discussion of the telinit command.

sysinit: This entry type designates a process that is executed before UNIX attempts to communicate with the system console. The command is executed before the initial run level is determined, and init waits for the process to terminate before continuing to scan /etc/inittab. Entries of this type should be limited to the fewest required to set up communication with the system console; on most systems, no such special action is required.

Let's take a look now at a sample /etc/inittab file:

```
fs::bootwait:/etc/bcheckrc </dev/console >/dev/console 2>&1
mt::bootwait:/etc/brc </dev/console >/dev/console 2>&1
ck::bootwait:/etc/bsetdate </dev/console >/dev/console 2>&1
```

These lines describe the basic system start-up procedure. Because the action is bootwait, they are only executed during the boot procedure, when /etc/init is first invoked. System V defines the /etc/bcheckrc shell script to perform the initial file system check of the root file system, /etc/brc to initialize the system mount table (/etc/mnttab), and /etc/bsetdate to allow the operator to set the system date and time before normal system operations begin:

```
is:2:initdefault: # Start local terminals only
```

This line specifies that an initial system boot should enter run level 2 automatically. By custom, run level 2 is the normal multiuser configuration with all user terminals enabled. No command action is performed for the initdefault action.

```
pf::powerfail:/etc/powerfail >/dev/console 2>&1
```

The powerfail action is ignored during normal system start-up, but if a power failure recovery should occur, this line specifies that the shell script /etc/powerfail should be invoked. Execution of this action has no affect on the current run level of the system.

```
s0:0:wait:/etc/rc0 </dev/console >/dev/console 2>&1
s2:2:wait:/etc/rc2 </dev/console >/dev/console 2>&1
s3:3:wait:/etc/rc3 </dev/console >/dev/console 2>&1
r0:0:wait:/etc/uadmin 2 0          # halt and power off if possible
```

These lines complete the system initialization according to the type of run level being entered. You cannot infer the purpose of run levels 0, 2, and 3 from these lines, but examination of the shell scripts named in the command field would disclose that run level 0 is entered when the system is to be shut down; run level 2 is entered to begin local multiuser operation; and run level 3 is the same as run level 2, except that it also starts getty processes on the remote tty lines.

```
co:23:respawn:/etc/getty console console
t1:23:respawn:/etc/getty tty0 9600 vt100
t2:23:respawn:/etc/getty tty1 9600 vt100
t3:23:respawn:/etc/getty tty2 9600 vt100
r1:3:respawn:/etc/getty tty01 2400
r2:3:respawn:/etc/getty tty02 2400
r3:3:respawn:/etc/getty tty03 1200
r4:3:respawn:/etc/getty tty04 1200
```

These script lines cause a getty process to be started for each of the local terminals and remote lines in the system, and therefore finally achieve the long-awaited goal of soliciting user logins and beginning normal system operation. Note that the dial-up lines tty01–tty04 are only activated when the system enters run level 3. In the default run level, only the local terminals are available.

This completes the overview of the special processes 0 and 1 and of the /etc/inittab script that establishes the basic system global processes. At this point, if your interest leans more toward programming UNIX systems than administering them, you may feel that this information is of little use to you. Fear not. When Chapter 15, "Multiprocessing Programs," discusses coprocessing and daemons, you may find that you can add some interesting features to your system by combining a modest amount of programming with the capabilities of init.

On the other hand, if your relationship with UNIX is primarily that of a superuser and system administrator, this discussion covered only the rudiments of configuration management. The story continues with a description of the `getty` program and its associated `/etc/gettydefs` control file, by which you instruct `getty` in the details of how to solicit logins from the various kinds of terminals and lines attached to the system.

The telinit Command

When changes are made to `/etc/inittab`, `init` does not see them immediately. When the system is next rebooted or the run level changes, `init` rereads the file. You can force `init` to read `/etc/inittab` immediately by running the command `telinit` with the argument `q`.

The `telinit` command typically is used to disable a user terminal for a period of time without bringing the whole system down. To disable a user terminal this way, you edit `/etc/inittab` and change `respawn` to `off` in the line that describes the terminal connection. Then you execute the following:

```
telinit q
```

which causes `init` to reread the file, kill the existing process on the line, and leave the terminal disabled. The reverse procedure reawakens the terminal.

The /etc/utmp File

When starting a process that has the `respawn` characteristic, `init` keeps track of when the process starts and stops. For all active processes, this information is recorded in the file `/etc/utmp`. When such a process dies, if the file `/etc/wtmp` exists, `init` writes a record into `/etc/wtmp` showing when the process started and when and why the process terminated. The `who` command reads the `/etc/utmp` file and reports on all current users. (Processes that are invoked with a `respawn` entry are assumed to be running for users at terminals.)

User Processes

After the system completes the bootstrap procedure and enters the multiuser state, a process is initiated for each port that can support a logged-in user. UNIX usually sets up a process for a logged-in user as follows:

1. Run `/etc/getty` to establish the physical connection to the user's terminal; the connection includes the data communications settings and any required character mapping, as

well as the initial settings for erase and kill characters and for command echo.

2. Run /bin/login to validate the user's name and password and to determine the initial directory and shell.

3. Run the shell determined in step 2.

After this sequence is completed successfully, the user is logged in and the shell is ready to interpret commands from the terminal. The following sections detail each of these steps and describe the files that are used in the steps.

The getty Program and the gettydefs File

The program /etc/getty initializes the data link between the user's terminal and the UNIX system. (The program is named for the phrase "get tty," which is a throwback to the days when all UNIX terminals were, in fact, Teletype machines.) The getty program must set the bit rate, parity, stop bits, data bits, handshaking protocol, character mapping, and character processing modes of the data link to those required for the terminal currently using the line. The general form of the getty command is as follows:

```
/etc/getty [-hy] [-t timeout] line [speed [type [ldisc]]]
```

The -h flag prevents getty from disconnecting the line before proceeding. Normally, getty sets the line speed to 0 when the command is first invoked; this setting signals the device driver to disconnect any remote terminal if possible.

The -t flag followed by a value measured in seconds causes getty to exit if no activity occurs on the line after that number of seconds passes.

The line argument is the name of the special file describing the line or terminal getty is to service. The file must be a character-special file (a device driver for a character device).

The optional speed argument does not represent the line speed directly; rather, the argument is used to look up an entry in the file /etc/gettydefs. If this argument is omitted or no /etc/gettydefs file exists, getty uses a default set of parameters that are intended for communicating with a dumb terminal at 300 bps. (The phrase *dumb terminal* does not reflect on anyone's intelligence; it is standard UNIX terminology for an ASCII terminal with no special capabilities.)

The optional type argument designates a terminal type. This argument is used to allow getty to support device-dependent terminal capabilities. If you have a choice on your local UNIX system, you should not use this argument, because it varies in interpretation and is likely to be replaced in future versions of UNIX by a much more generalized technique for supporting device-dependent characteristics.

The optional ldisc argument designates one of several line disciplines to be used. I do not recommend that you use this argument; it is implementation-dependent and could become obsolete in future versions of UNIX.

The getty program begins its tasks by setting the line characteristics according to an entry in the table /etc/gettydefs. As is typical with UNIX, this table is an ASCII file that the system administrator can easily modify by using one of the available editors. Each record in /etc/gettydefs contains the following five fields, which are separated by pound signs (#):

LABEL:
: A string that uniquely identifies a record. This string is matched against the second command-line argument. The value of LABEL is usually the speed argument of the getty command (for example, 1200) or the name of a dedicated device such as console.

INITIAL-SETTINGS:
: A set of keywords chosen from among those supported by the stty command that determines the terminal features to be assumed by getty when attempting to read a login name. You should specify the most general settings possible to maximize the chances of a successful login.

FINAL-SETTINGS:
: A set of keywords chosen from among those supported by the stty command that determines the line characteristics that getty sets just before invoking /bin/login. Typically, these characteristics include delay settings for tabs and form feeds, tab expansion options, and the HUPCL setting, which causes the driver to hang up the line when the shell process terminates.

PROMPT:
: A field containing the exact phrase that is used to solicit a login name from the user. Spaces, tabs, and new lines are not ignored in this field and are part of the prompt if they are present. On some systems, this field is left empty or set to just a single character for dial-up lines to befuddle hackers. The standard C escape sequences are recognized in this and all fields, so the use of special terminal capabilities is possible.

NEXT: A string designating the LABEL field of an alternate entry in the `gettydefs` file to be tried if the current one fails. Failing is defined specifically as the receipt of a null character or a break (a null character plus a framing error). Thus, if garbage is on the screen, the user can press the Break key to cause `getty` to proceed with the next group of settings. With Release 3, autobaud detection was added to this facility. With autobaud detection, the user can continue to press the carriage return key and `getty` will determine the proper baud rate.

A typical entry in the `/etc/gettydefs` file might look like this:

```
console# B9600 HUPCL PARENB CS7 OPOST ONLCR #
B9600 HUPCL SANE IXANY TAB3 NLO CRO BSO VTO FFO CLOCAL ECHOE ECHOK #
Console Login: #console
```

This sample actually appears in the file as one line, even though it is shown as three lines here.

The first entry, `console`, is the symbolic name of this line. The name has no significance except that other lines in the `/etc/gettydefs` file can use it to refer back to this line.

The second entry, `B9600 HUPCL PARENB CS7 OPOST ONLCR`, specifies the terminal settings that `getty` should set as it tries to write the login message to the terminal. Any line parameters that are valid for the `stty` command may be specified in this field of the line. When using this specification, `getty` does the following:

❑ Selects a line speed of 9600 bits per second (`B9600`).

❑ Hangs up the line when the user logs out (`HUPCL`).

❑ Enables parity checking (`PARENB`). Because PARODD is not also specified, the line will default to even parity checking.

❑ Selects seven-bit character size (`CS7`).

❑ Performs post-processing on characters written to the remote terminal (`OPOST`).

❑ On output, converts an NL character to the CR-NL sequence (`ONLCR`).

The third field, `B9600 HUPCL SANE IXANY TAB3 NLO CRO BSO VTO FFO CLOCAL ECHOE ECHOK`, specifies the terminal settings that `getty` should set if the user accepts the login message. The values will be in effect when the login program is called. The specifications cause `getty` to configure the line with the following settings:

❏ Set a line speed of 9600 bits per second (`B9600`).

❏ Hang up the line when the user logs out (`HUPCL`).

❏ Set the line to default values (`SANE`).

❏ Enable START/STOP control, using any keyboard input to resume transmission (`IXANY`).

❏ Expand tabs to spaces on output (`TAB3`).

❏ Disable the use of delay padding (`NL0 CR0 BS0 VT0 FF0`).

❏ Assume a locally connected terminal by suppressing the use of modem control signals (`CLOCAL`).

❏ Echo the backspace operation (`ECHOE`).

❏ Echo an `NL` character when the KILL key is pressed, to confirm that the last input line will be deleted (`ECHOK`).

The fourth field specifies the string that `getty` is to send when requesting the user to log in:

```
Console Login:
```

The actual text of the login message is often chosen to provide the user a hint about what kind of line he is using; in this case, the message implies that the user is at the system console.

The login message should always end with the string `ogin:`, because many communications programs look for this character sequence when attempting to log in to a UNIX system.

The fifth and final field, console, tells getty what to do if the user presses the break key after the login message is sent. The value in this field must be the name of a line in the `/etc/gettydefs` file. `getty` simply fetches the line in `/etc/gettydefs` with that name, reconfigures the terminal according to the specifications in the new line, and tries to send the login message again. In the example, the alternate terminal description is named console, which is the name of the same line. If the user presses the Break key, `getty` simply reinitializes the terminal and tries again with the same control settings.

In theory, a long string of alternate terminal descriptions could be chained together using the fifth entry; `getty` would try each one in turn as the user presses the Break key. Presumably, a readable login message will be displayed for one of the chained entries, at which point `getty` will configure the terminal settings given in the third field and call the login routine. Alternate terminal descriptions enable `getty` to support many different kinds of terminals.

A blank line must follow each record in `/etc/gettydefs`. If you change `/etc/gettydefs`, keep a copy of the original file and run your changed version through `getty` with the `-c` option, as follows:

```
/etc/getty -c /etc/gettydefs
```

This causes `getty` to check the file for valid, consistent, and plausible entries. It also displays all the settings, so you can verify that everything you thought was in the file is actually seen by `getty`.

Dueling gettys

When it begins, `getty` prints the login prompt and then waits for results. If you have two computers connected by a dedicated line and you want them to be capable of bidirectional traffic, you cannot run `getty` on both ends of the line. Each computer sends the prompt, gets back the other's prompt, and responds. The solution is to use the `uugetty` program instead. This program, whose full path name is `/usr/lib/uucp/uugetty`, is a standard part of the UUCP (UNIX-to-UNIX copy) facility. It is the most common way of connecting UNIX machines to transfer files and exchange electronic mail.

The `uugetty` program does the same things that `getty` does, with one difference: `uugetty` waits for input from the line before giving the login prompt. In addition, the `uugetty` protocol is understood by UUCP. If UUCP tries to dial out while `uugetty` is using the line, UUCP disables `uugetty` so that it does not interfere with UUCP activity.

The login Process and the /etc/passwd File

After successfully determining the line characteristics, `getty` passes control to `/bin/login` by giving it the name that was typed in response to the login prompt. The login process looks for this name in another table, called `/etc/passwd`. This table is also an ASCII file that can be modified with a text editor. However, most Release 3 systems and all Release 4 systems come with administration tools that maintain the `/etc/passwd` file. If your system has such tools, use them! They protect you against errors that are easily made and difficult to find. This protection is especially valuable with the `/etc/passwd` file, which is difficult to read because of its format. Furthermore, the tools become even more important when Release 4 implementations (and some Release 3 implementations) separate the contents of `/etc/passwd` into two files for security reasons.

The /etc/passwd file is a plain ASCII text file that consists of records terminated by line feeds. Each record contains the following seven fields:

LOGNAME:

This field contains the login name of the user. The /bin/login program uses this field as the key for finding the record corresponding to the login name given by the user. If multiple entries have the same login name, only the first entry will be found.

PASSWORD:

This field contains the user's password in an encrypted form. If the field is left blank, no password exists. Because all users must be able to read this file (so that other information is accessible), the presence of the password, even encrypted, is a security problem. Recent versions of UNIX address this problem by placing only the letter X in the PASSWORD field and maintaining the user passwords and aging information in a second file, called /etc/shadow, which is not generally accessible.

USERID:

This field contains the user-ID as a number in the range 0 to 65535 corresponding to the LOGNAME field. No other entry in the /etc/passwd file should specify the same user-ID as is given here. The user-ID is the primary means that UNIX uses to refer to users. When a user's login name or other information is required, the user-ID is used as a key to search /etc/passwd sequentially; thus, a user can log in under one name but be referred to by another if two or more entries are in /etc/passwd with the same user-ID. This procedure is not recommended; it is described only because it often happens accidentally, especially when the user-maintenance tools are not used.

GROUPID:

This field contains a number that represents the group to which the user belongs. Groups are identified by name in the /etc/group file. It is common for several users to share the same group-ID. While logged in, a user can switch to another group-ID to change access privileges.

COMMENT:

Many installations use this field to identify a user to other systems and provide contact information (such as office number and phone extension) or other locally defined information.

INITIAL-DIRECTORY: This field contains the full path name of the directory that is to be the current working directory of the user's login shell. For most users, this working directory is the user's own directory. For entries that represent network programs, background processes, or other special entries, the initial directory usually is the one that contains the programs or files that the utility uses.

LOGIN-SHELL: This field designates the program to be executed after the login program validates the user. The default is /bin/sh, which is the Bourne Shell. This field can designate any executable program, so you can set up a tightly defined environment for a user.

Password Security and Aging

You can make a UNIX system very secure, but the more secure you make your system, the less convenient it is to use. However, you can balance security and convenience in several ways. A case in point is the password facility. It is entirely acceptable to set up the /etc/passwd file to omit the password entry for some (or even all) users; in some environments, such as single-user systems, passwords serve no useful purpose. However, most UNIX systems are used by more than one user or by a user who occasionally makes mistakes, and for both of these conditions, having passwords is beneficial.

Most versions of UNIX require passwords to be at least six characters long and to contain at least two nonalphabetic characters. When a password is changed, the new password cannot be a simple variant of the old one. For example, if your password is trev33, you cannot change it to 3trev3 on most systems. Only the first eight characters of the password are significant, so the password 30something is equivalent to the password 30someth. The superuser (a user whose effective user-ID is 0) is not bound by these restrictions and can create arbitrary passwords.

The password aging scheme is intended to increase the security of the system. The scheme provides a means for the system administrator to determine how often users must change their passwords. Passwords can be set to expire in a number of weeks, immediately after first use, or never. Users are prevented from changing their passwords more frequently than a preset limit.

To many administrators, forcing users to change their passwords fairly often would seem, at first thought, to be likely to improve security. The idea behind such a scheme is that if a user's password becomes known to another user by mistake, the hole is eventually plugged when the compromised password is changed. In practice, however, most users do not memorize a large number of passwords, so these users either change their passwords in a simple cycle (such as kitten1, peaches2, kitten2, peaches1, and so on) or make up irrelevant, wonderfully unpredictable passwords and write them down in obvious places in case they forget the password.

UNIX uses login passwords in the following manner.

The login program takes the name passed by /etc/getty and looks for the name sequentially in /etc/passwd. Whether or not the name is found, login then prompts for a password. If the combination of login name and password cannot be found in the /etc/passwd file, login displays the message login incorrect and asks the user to try again. After five incorrect attempts, if the file /usr/adm/loginlog exists, a record of the failed login is entered in the file and the terminal connection is dropped.

If the user enters a valid name and password, login sets the user-ID and group-ID of the current process to the corresponding numbers in the password file, arranges for the designated login directory to be the current directory, and executes the login shell specified in the /etc/passwd entry.

When the login shell is called, argument 0 will contain the name of the shell prefixed by a hyphen character. The shell can therefore easily determine that it is a login shell and take the appropriate action. For the standard System V shell, these actions set each environment variable as follows:

❏ HOME is set to the login directory.

❏ LOGNAME is set to the login name.

❏ MAIL is set to the full path name of the user's private mailbox.

❏ MAILCHECK is set to the number of seconds between tests for incoming mail.

❏ PATH is set to :/bin:/usr/bin.

❏ PS1 is set to $.

❏ PS2 is set to >.

❏ IFS is set to the default set of internal field separators.

❏ SHELL is set to the full path name of the login shell. The shell then executes the /etc/profile and .profile scripts.

Standard Daemons and Start-ups

In addition to running the user processes, UNIX normally has several background processes running. Remember from Chapter 2 that UNIX background processes are called *daemons*. Network servers and some devices require that specific programs be run once after the system is first booted. Making this code part of the device driver itself would use up valuable memory in the kernel, so the same mechanism employed to start the standard daemons is used, when practical, for the start-up code.

The standard daemons are the print spooler, the timed-execution processor (cron), and the error logger. Network support systems usually have daemons also.

Daemons, along with other start-up code, are started by a collection of shell scripts that are normally kept in subdirectories under /etc and executed according to the current run level. For example, the directory /etc/rc2.d usually contains scripts to be executed when init enters run level 2. A simple mechanism executes these run-level-specific programs: a line in /etc/inittab specifies that, when the system first enters run level 2, the shell script /etc/rc2 should be executed and completed before any further processing is done. As an exercise, create this mechanism by constructing the appropriate /etc/inittab entry. You can check your answer in the /etc/inittab file on your own UNIX system—don't cheat!

The shell script /etc/rc2 typically runs the script /etc/TIMEZONE, which sets and exports the TZ variable used to determine the local time. The /etc/rc2 script also typically contains code that searches the directory /etc/rc2.d for executable files and executes them. The order in which these programs are executed can be important; for example, the mountable file systems must be mounted before the files they contain can be used.

The /usr file system holds several important files and programs, many of which even the other start-up programs are likely to use. The cron daemon keeps its tables in the directory /usr/spool/cron/crontabs, so the /usr file system must be mounted before the cron daemon is started. To do this, the script that does the mounting of file systems normally is named MOUNT rather than mount, so that the script alphabetically precedes the other scripts and thus is executed first.

Summary

When UNIX is bootstrapped, the operating system itself is read into memory and executed. After initializing the memory buffers and devices, UNIX starts two processes: the swapper as process 0 and init as process 1. The init process is responsible for starting all the other processes. The init process uses the file /etc/inittab to determine which processes to run and when to run them. The /etc/inittab file is a simple text file that the system administrator can modify. Among the processes started under the direction of this file are all the user-terminal processes. These processes start the init-getty-login shell cycle: init starts getty; getty determines the line characteristics, collects a login name from the user, and passes control to login; login verifies the user name and password, sets the user-ID, group-ID, and login directories, and passes control to the shell. When the shell terminates, control returns to init, which starts the process again because of the respawn entry in /etc/inittab for each user terminal.

When the system enters run level 2, a shell script called /etc/rc2 executes all device drivers, network processors, standard daemons, and required start-up code. When the system enters other run levels, corresponding /etc/rc scripts are executed (etc/rc3 at run level 3, and so on). With this simple mechanism, the system administrator configures the running states of UNIX without programming or even relinking the operating system.

Part II

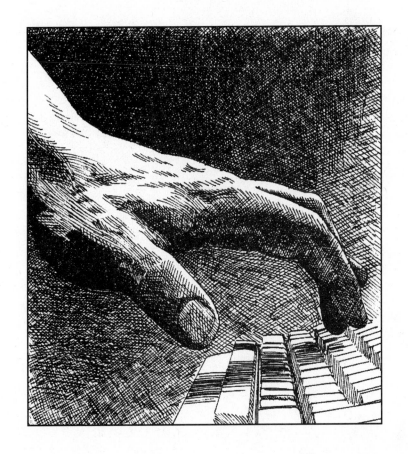

Programming in the
UNIX Environment

4

Program Development

As you would expect of a system developed by programmers for programmers, UNIX provides excellent support for program development. UNIX itself was written in C, using UNIX and the tools it provides for creating, compiling, testing, and maintaining programs.

Programs vary greatly in size and complexity, ranging from small throw-away modules to fully matured operating systems. The amount of time and energy spent designing and documenting the former clearly should not be as great as for the latter. However, the small throw-away program, as a basis for extensions and modifications, often turns out to be useful for purposes far beyond the author's original intent. Reusing another author's code is much easier when it was originally written to be readable, to conform to standards of style and format, to document itself well with comments, and to employ a logical organization.

This chapter develops a simple application to demonstrate the program design principles that work well in the UNIX environment. My intention is to show you how to divide a project into small, well-defined programs, each of which does a single thing well and that fits together naturally into the larger whole.

There are many books available that teach good C programming style, including the use of comments, indenting, modular structure, and the like. This chapter does not rehash these subjects. Rather, this chapter takes you through the process of designing, writing, and maintaining programs for UNIX, using the standard UNIX tools. The focus is on the programming facilities available rather than on the internal organization of the program itself.

The chapter discusses the use of the shell for prototyping. A prototyping tool enables you to quickly develop a model of a new application system, showing the principal user interfaces and processing algorithms of the system for evaluation and study. Often, the shell scripts will be adequate for production usage and can be put into service immediately; other times, you will wish to reimplement the scripts in a compiled language. We'll take a look at some of the factors you should consider when deciding whether to reimplement.

Finally, the chapter will describe the elements of program design that allow a new program to integrate well into the UNIX environment. You'll find that some of the programming techniques you take for granted in a PC or mainframe environment are not appropriate for UNIX, and this section highlights the techniques that you should be using instead.

If you use the UNIX environment as it was intended to be used, you'll find that you will not just be using new commands, editors, debuggers, and other tools to do your work, but that your entire approach to programming will change. You will become more efficient, and your programs more sophisticated.

Prototyping

It is often helpful to build a working model of a new system (called a *prototype*) as early as possible in its design process. Prototyping enables you to experiment with the user interface, trying different approaches until you find one that works well. The best user interface will probably not be the first one that occurs to you. A good prototyping tool will also help you to explore the processing requirements of your application by testing different data formats and structures until you find one that feels right. As with any engineering discipline, prototyping allows the designer to detect flaws and errors early in the design process, before a lot of time and effort have been expended in code production.

The UNIX shell is an excellent prototyping tool because shell scripts can be written, tested, debugged, and modified much more quickly than can compiled programs. The shell also is a powerful programming language itself when combined with the data manipulation utilities that are a standard part of UNIX.

In fact, many shell scripts that start out only as prototypes end up being used in the final application.

The power of the shell language derives not so much from the language as from the power and diversity of the UNIX commands that can be invoked from a shell. "UNIX Commands" presents a basic tool kit of commands that tend to be used over and over in shell scripts; time spent studying that chapter will be rewarded many times over by your increased effectiveness at shell programming and at using UNIX in general.

Just as an extensive library of subroutines make a C program much easier to develop, so the set of UNIX commands and utilities makes prototyping easier. You should skim the entire UNIX manual and familiarize yourself with the types of services available. Don't try to memorize the commands. Instead, try to develop a feel for the kinds of functions that can be performed with available commands. You can always study a particular command as needed, but first you have to know that the command exists.

Shell Scripts

Shell scripts are simple to create and to modify because they are text files. To create a shell script, follow these steps:

1. Use your favorite editor to create the file.

2. Make the file executable by setting on the file's execute permissions.

3. You can then execute the shell script simply by typing its file name as a command.

If you are unfamiliar with this process, perform the following exercise. Create a file called `td` containing the following line:

```
echo It is now ; date
```

Then enter the following command:

```
chmod +x td
```

You now have a new command called `td` that you can execute simply by entering the line:

```
td
```

Note: If your first attempt to execute the `td` command fails, check the value of your PATH shell variable. Whenever you enter a command at the terminal, the shell scans a list of directories looking for a file with the same name as the first word of the command line. You may be surprised to learn that the shell does *not* search your current directory for commands unless the name of your current directory is mentioned in PATH, the shell's list of directories to be searched.

To check the list of directories that will be searched for commands, just enter the `env` command. The shell's current set of environment variables will be displayed at your terminal, and the display will resemble the following:

```
CDPATH=.:...:/u/nsh
HOME=/u/nsh
LOGNAME=nsh
MAIL=/usr/mail/nsh
PATH=.:/u/nsh/bin:/bin:/usr/bin
TERM=ansi
TZ=EST5EDT
```

This sample output shows that the value of the PATH environment variable is as follows:

```
PATH=.:/u/nsh/bin:/bin:/usr/bin
```

The colons (:) separate names of directories in the list. In this case, the directories that the shell will search are ., /u/nsh/bin, /bin, and /usr/bin. The first of these, namely ., represents the current directory no matter which directory is current, so we can see at once that the current directory will be searched by the shell. Furthermore, because the . directory occurs first in the list, we also know that it will be the first directory searched. This is good, because it means that if your new command name happens to be the same as some other command, the shell will execute your program in preference to the other.

If the . directory is *not* listed in your PATH value, you can add it to the shell search path by entering the following statement:

```
PATH=.:$PATH
```

This causes the new value of PATH to be set to the old value prefixed with the current directory. Once you set the PATH variable to include the . directory in your search path, the PATH variable will stay set; you do not need to enter the PATH= statement every time you want to execute the `td` command.

A Prototyping Example Using Shell Scripts

The `td` command gave you practice in creating a shell script, making the script file executable, and then executing the file. But `td` is not a very useful command. For a more practical exercise, suppose that you are a programmer employed by the Tasty Foods Corporation (TFC) and that you've just been given an assignment.

The Tasty Foods Corporation is organized into a number of departments. Each month, TFC produces a month-end closing report for each department and then consolidates these reports into a summary for the monthly board meeting. Every department has an accountant who is responsible for closing the department's books at the end of every month. When all the departments have closed their month-end reports, the company's comptroller produces the consolidated report for the board meeting.

Your job is to set up a computerized procedure whereby the individual department accountants can signal that they have completed their respective month-end closings and that allows the comptroller to determine when all the departments have closed.

Developing the User Interface

Take a minute to design a program or set of programs that could be used by the department accountant to signal completion of month-end closing and by the comptroller to check that all departments have closed. For now, concentrate on the main functions of the program. In the process of designing our sample application, the first issue to address is the appearance of the user interface. To keep the exercise simple, we will assume that the user can be asked to enter a UNIX command, but we still have to decide what information the user will enter. Discussion of the internal details of our program must be deferred until the user interface is designed; otherwise, we risk wasting a lot of time and effort developing a program that can't be used.

Unfortunately, programmers often gloss over the design of the user interface, assuming that the design of the user interface is simple and obvious, or that the design of the user interface will flow naturally from the development of the program's internals.

Suppose you were to design an engine without first considering the kind of vehicle it would power. Would you build a large engine or a small? Would it use a two-cycle or four-cycle combustion? Would it be air-cooled or water-cooled? How many brake-horsepower would it develop? What would be its compression ratio? If you did not have to consider the engine's application, you would probably make these and other choices based on personal perceptions of the characteristics of some ideal engine, or maybe you would model the kind of engine that you prefer. Unfortunately, your favorite engine design might not be suitable for any application.

Just as a design engineer must create an engine to meet the requirements of its application, perhaps expending a great deal of effort to fit it into a small space yet still deliver adequate power, so too the programmer must be prepared to undertake extremely complex or awkward implementations if the user's needs justify the effort. Clearly, then, program design must proceed "outside in," starting from the user's known requirements and working toward a detailed internal program design to meet those requirements.

We start, then, by considering the user's interface to our application. Each department accountant needs a command to execute (we assume for the sake of this exercise that each accountant has a terminal) that will make a note in the system someplace that the month-end closing is complete for that accountant's department. We can choose any name we like for the command; I'll choose the name closed. The closed command will require one argument: the name of the department to be noted as closed.

The comptroller needs a command that will determine whether the consolidation can be performed yet. Let's call this command consok. It will not require any arguments.

For this example, the departments are Inside Sales, Outside Sales, Production, and Service. Before continuing, think about how you would design this application:

❏ How would you represent the data?

❏ What processing algorithms would you use?

❏ What error detection and recovery processes do you need?

I'll return to this example several times throughout the rest of the chapter, adding facilities, exploring different ways of doing things, and generally making the example more realistic.

Developing the Data Structure

You need a small database to keep track of the closed status of each department's books. A handy hierarchical database system is included with UNIX: the file system. Let's use it.

The data structure of our application should begin with a top directory called tfc. All the other files and directories used by the application will be located in the tfc directory.

It will be convenient to use a collection of files to represent the current status of each department. Because the idea of a collection of files suggests a directory, let's create a directory in tfc to hold the department files. Not being particularly creative at naming things, I call the department directory dept to hint at its contents. Because the dept directory is a member of the tfc directory, its full path name will be tfc/dept.

The tfc/dept directory can now contain one file per department, and the contents of each file can indicate the current status of the corresponding department, whether its books are currently *open* or *closed*.

The directory structure for the application looks like that in figure 4.1

***Fig. 4.1.** Structure of database for the TFC application.*

```
tfc/
      dept/
              inside
              outside
              production
              service
```

The following commands will create the database:

```
mkdir tfc tfc/dept
for DEPT in inside outside production service
do
      echo open >tfc/dept/$DEPT
done
```

The for loop creates the department files named inside, outside, production, and service and initializes them to contain the word open, indicating that the books of each department are not yet closed. To indicate that the books have been closed for a particular department, we can write closed in the department file.

We can now write the first version of a shell script to be used by the department's accountant to indicate that he has finished his month-end closing. It will contain the following single instruction:

```
echo closed >tfc/dept/$1
```

where $1 will stand for the department name.

Certainly this first version of the closed command is not a very sophisticated program. In fact, our program already has some bugs:

❑ It always assumes that the tfc directory is located in the user's current working directory.

❑ It doesn't check whether $1 is a valid department name.

We can immediately solve the first of these problems by using a mechanism with which we are already familiar: environment variables. Let's choose a name for a new environment variable and use it in our shell script. The value of the variable will be the path name of the directory containing the t f c directory. If we also arrange for the system administrator to set the proper value of the TFC variable in the system profile script /etc/profile, for example by adding the following line to the script:

```
TFC=/usr/acctg/commercial/tfc
```

the variable will always be available to our programs and the application's users will not have to bother with setting it.

Assuming that the /etc/profile script has been modified, we can now edit the closed file containing our shell script, changing its one line of text to read as follows:

```
echo closed >$TFC/dept/$1
```

Our one-line shell script, as written, would allow the user to enter any department name as the value of the $1 argument. As long as the tfc/dept directory already exists, the echo command will simply create a new file with the department name given and write the word closed in it.

For example, if one of the accountants were to enter this command:

```
closed coffee
```

we would find a new file listed in the tfc/dept directory called coffee. (If you don't believe me, try it yourself. The file coffee is created because the shell redirection operator > first creates the file named to its right if it doesn't already exist and then writes to it.) Unfortunately, there is no department called "coffee" in the organization of the Tasty Foods Corporation.

We would, therefore, like to arrange for the shell script to validate the department name before trying to use it. We could embed a list of the valid department names in the shell script itself, and check that the name given by the user matches one of the names in the internal list, but there is a better way. The application database already contains a list of the valid department names—it's simply the list of files in the tfc/dept directory. The shell script should test for the existence of the given department's file before attempting to write the word closed into it. The existence test in effect allows the system administrator (or anyone with the necessary permissions) to define a new department name simply by creating the appropriate file in the tfc/dept/ directory.

There is a UNIX feature that can test for the existence of a file; the command is called test. The test command evaluates an expression for true or false.

The exit code of the test command indicates the result of the evaluation. (The exit code is similar to the MS-DOS ERRORLEVEL variable.)

To test whether a file exists, use the following command:

```
test -f filename
```

The exit code set by test will be 0 if the test is successful, or nonzero if it fails.

Using the test command, we can extend our closed shell script as follows:

```
if test -f $TFC/dept/$1
then
      echo closed >$TFC/dept/$1
      exit 0
else
      echo \"$1\" is not a valid department
      exit 1
fi
```

The shell provides an alternate form for the test command that makes the if statement read a little more naturally. Using the alternate form, the if statement would read as follows:

```
if [-f $TFC/dept/$1]
```

However, keep in mind that the [ ] expression is really a command invocation. In fact, any command can appear in the body of the if statement; the exit code of the command determines the outcome of the if. Later, we will use other commands with the if statement.

Although we are developing just a tiny sample program, adding at least a rudimentary check on the validity of the arguments is good practice. In particular, the closed command as written completely ignores the possibility that the user invoked the closed command with no department name at all. In such a case, the value of the $1 variable would be the null string, and the echo command would try to write the word closed into the file tfc/dept/, which is a valid path name but unfortunately refers to the directory itself and not to any file within the directory.

Dealing with Errors

So what should the shell script do if no argument is specified, and how can it test for an omitted argument? Although the shell script could be written to just print an error message, it is standard practice when programmers write UNIX commands to briefly explain the correct usage of the program when a user invokes it without arguments or with invalid arguments.

The additional code would look like this:

```
if [$# -lt 1]
then
     echo "usage: $0 <department>"
     exit 1
fi
```

The variable $# is a special, so-called *built-in argument* maintained by the shell. Its value is always the number of $n arguments that were typed on the command line. The added code uses the variable $# in another form of the test command; the form shown will have an exit value of 0 (corresponding to TRUE) only when the value of $# is less than (-lt) 1. The net effect is that the then clause will be executed only when no arguments are specified on the closed command line. The then clause itself consists of two commands: an echo to issue the prescribed usage message, and an exit command to terminate execution of the shell script.

Generating Final Code

After inserting the argument check, the closed shell script looks like the following list:

```
# closed - close a department accounting cycle"
if [ $# -lt 1 ]
then
     echo "usage: $0 <department>"
     exit 1
fi
if [ -f $TFC/dept/$1 ]
then
     echo closed >$TFC/dept/$1
     exit 0
else
     echo \"$1\" is not a valid department
     exit 1
fi
```

Making Program Enhancements

So far we've developed a more or less workable version of the command we intend the departmental accountants to use. We still have no command to be used by the company's comptroller to determine whether to begin the month-end consolidation.

In brief, the processing requirement for the consok command is to check whether every file in the tfc/dept directory contains the word closed. If so, the comptroller can be given an output message that it is okay to proceed with month-end consolidation. But if any departments still have not closed their books, it would probably be more useful to the comptroller to identify the departments for which books are still open, rather than to simply report that consolidation cannot proceed.

The following shell program will do precisely this job.

```
1   # consok - test if all departments are closed
2   cd $TFC/dept
3   if fgrep -l open *
4   then
5       echo "** Above departments not closed"
6       exit 1
7   else
8       echo "** All departments closed."
9   fi
```

I have numbered the lines of the shell script in this listing to make it easier to refer to individual script lines; the line numbers would not be entered when you actually typed in the shell script.

Notice that this shell script contains no $n variables. The consok command requires no arguments because there is no information that the command requires from the comptroller; all the information needed by consok is already present in the tfc database.

Line 1 is a typical comment inserted at the top of the shell script. It tells the reader the name of the shell script (helpful when you're looking at a printout of the script and can't check its file name), and gives a brief description of its purpose. You should always include some descriptive comments at the start of every shell script.

Line 2 switches the current directory to the directory containing the department status files. This will allow the shell script to refer to department files without using their full path name. But the real reason for the cd command has to do with line 3.

Line 3 does the real work of the shell script. In a nutshell, the fgrep command is used to search the entire tfc/dept directory for files containing the word open. Normally, fgrep lists the matching lines it finds on standard output; the -l option causes the command to list only the file names of the files, however, so the net effect of the fgrep command is to list the file name of every file that contains the word open. Because of the application design, the name of a file in the tfc/dept directory is the same as a department name. Therefore, this line lists the names of all the departments that still have not completed their month-end closing.

The reason for line 2 is now evident. If the fgrep command had been written as follows:

```
fgrep -l open $TFC/dept/*
```

the output from `fgrep` would have looked like this:

```
tfc/dept/inside
tfc/dept/outside
** Above departments not closed
```

but because only the department file names themselves appear as arguments on the `fgrep` command, the output will look like this instead:

```
inside
outside
** Above departments not closed
```

In line 3, the `fgrep` command is written as the operand of an `if` statement. The effect of this construction is that the `if` statement tests the exit code from `fgrep`. If `fgrep` finds one or more files matching the search pattern `open`, it sets an exit value of 0; otherwise, its exit value will be 1. The `if` command, in turn, considers an exit value of 0 to indicate successful execution of the command. The upshot is that if the `fgrep` command finds one or more files containing the word `open`, it will execute the `then` clause; otherwise, it will execute the `else` clause.

Lines 4–6 are executed when one or more department files contain the status word `open`. Because consolidation of the month-end reports cannot proceed in this case, line 5 displays a message for the comptroller warning that there are departments still closing their books, and line 6 exits the shell script, setting an exit value of 1. The nonzero exit value is our way of informing any user or other program invoking the `consok` command that `consok` completed *unsuccessfully*.

Lines 7–8 are executed only when `fgrep` considers an error to have occurred; namely, that it searched all the files but found no occurrence of the word `open`. To our command, this is the desired state of affairs, but from the standpoint of the `fgrep` command, which considers its goal to be to find lines matching the pattern, this condition is an error. Thus we handle the case in which no department files remain open in the `else` clause of the `if` statement. The only action in this case is to print a message to the comptroller, saying that all departments show a month-end closing status of `closed`, and therefore the comptroller can proceed with the consolidation procedure.

Line 9 is syntactically required to end the range of the `if` statement; it performs no useful processing.

Admittedly, the sample exercise I've shown in this chapter is contrived and the application system it presents is not very useful. The point of the exercise, however, besides introducing some of the capabilities of the UNIX shell, was to demonstrate the ease by which a new application can be developed using the shell as a programming language.

As the example demonstrates, the shell language itself provides capabilities for managing the flow of control in a program. The actions taken, however, such as displaying a message or checking for the existence of a file, are performed by invoking UNIX commands. As a result, the entire array of UNIX commands is available to be used for processing statements in a shell script.

The shell script implementation fully meets the requirements of the application as initially set forth at the beginning of this chapter. You could implement programs in the C language to execute the processing contained in the closed and consok shell scripts. Each line of the shell script could be used as a model for writing a segment of the C-language programs.

But there would be little advantage to a C implementation of this application. The shell scripts actually perform very little processing, and if you will go to the trouble of entering the scripts on your UNIX system and creating the sample database, you will find from a few trial executions that the shell scripts execute nearly instantaneously. A speedier implementation in a compiled programming language would actually result in no significant savings in the performance of the application but would create a more complex collection of programs to be maintained.

Therefore, for this application, most people would decide that the shell script implementation is satisfactory for real usage. Completion of the prototype achieves completion of the application system.

Maintaining the Program

In this chapter we've developed a new application consisting of a number of shell scripts. The odds are, as time passes and the needs and expectations of the application's users grow, there will be a desire to further modify and extend the shell scripts. In the terminology of the software engineering business, the application is said to enter the "maintenance phase" of its life cycle.

In the next chapter I'll explore some of the UNIX tools that will assist with both the administrative and technical aspects of program maintenance.

UNIX Program Style

UNIX provides a rich set of commands that you can piece together into larger programs by using the facilities of the shell. The building-block approach to application design is typical of the UNIX philosophy, and I urge you to use it in writing your own programs.

What are the characteristics of the TFC example that made them work well together? The programs always write to standard output whenever it makes sense to do so. For instance, fgrep writes the file list to the standard output and does not force the file list to your screen.

UNIX commands use command-line options to modify the way their functions are performed. If fgrep were more "user friendly" by presenting a menu of choices, such as (C)haracters (W)ords, or (L)ines, the command would be completely useless for our purposes in the TFC example.

Because a program never knows when its output may be used as part of another program's command line, UNIX programs usually produce output that is terse and to the point, not cluttered with extraneous sign-on messages and unsolicited information. Programs such as fgrep, which can provide many different forms of output, enable programmers to choose from among the options to design the output needed.

Converting a Shell Script to a C Program

After you finish designing and prototyping an application, you may decide to convert your shell scripts to C programs for a variety of reasons: The application may be too slow, perhaps you want to be able to take advantage of advanced capabilities, or maybe you want to protect your source code before you distribute the program as a commercial product.

Converting a working shell script to a C program is almost a matter of transliteration, done by replacing each shell line with the equivalent C code. The C equivalent of closed is as follows:

```
#include <stdio.h>
#include <sys/types.h>
#include <sys/stat.h>

char *getenv();

main(argc, argv)
int argc;
char *argv[];
```

```
{
        FILE *deptfile;
        char fname[512];
        struct stat s;

        /* Check argument count ... */

        if (argc < 2) {
                fprintf(stderr, "usage: %s <department>\n", *argv);
                exit(1);
        }

        /* Confirm that department file exists */

        sprintf(fname, "%s/dept/%s", getenv("TFC"), argv[1]);
        if (stat(fname, &s) || (s.st_mode & S_IFMT) != S_IFREG) {
          fprintf(stderr, "%s is not a valid department\n",
              argv[1]);
          exit(1);
        }

        /* Echo "closed" to department file */

        if ((deptfile = fopen(argv[1], "r")) == NULL) {
                perror(argv[1]);
                exit(1);
        }
        fprintf(deptfile, "closed\n");
        fclose(deptfile);
        return (0);
}
```

You do not need to be any more careful about possible error conditions with this program than you would need to be with the original shell script. In both cases, a more fully developed application would have to handle errors more carefully.

Summary

In this chapter we looked at some ways in which UNIX assists the development of new programs. Most programs for UNIX systems are developed in either of two languages: the shell language, or C. The UNIX shell, together with the rich command set UNIX provides, is powerful enough to support the implementation of a wide range of useful applications. The C programming language on the other hand gives you direct access to the operating system services.

The shell can be used to develop a protoype version of your application programs. You use the prototype to explore the design of your program's user interface, as well as its primary algorithms. Because a program can be written much more quickly in the shell language than in most other languages, you can easily change a shell program to try out different user interfaces, and to experiment with different ways of implementing the program.

When you have debugged your shell program, and settled on a user interface and main solution strategy, you can either put your shell program into production, or rewrite it in another language (typically C). If the shell version executes with satisfactory speed, and performs all the tasks you want it to, there is little reason to reimplement it in another language. Just store the shell program in a globally accessible directory such as /usr/bin, and you're finished.

If you want to rewrite your shell program, you'll find that it provides a concise statement of the program you want to write; its statements act as a pseudo-code for the C code you need to develop. Because the pseudo-code is precise and unambiguous, unlike most other pseudo-code language, reimplementing the program in C should be straightforward.

The next chapter, "Program Maintenance," discusses some UNIX utilities that help you with the programming process itself. Although the topics are presented in the context of maintaining existing code, many of the tools are also useful when developing the initial version of a program. The make and lint utilities are just as useful for development as for maintenance, for example. Read on, then, to discover other ways in which the UNIX operating system can simplify your programming projects.

5

Program Maintenance

U NIX provides many tools to assist you with maintaining, analyzing, and debugging programs. Of course, if you don't know that the tools exist, don't understand how to use them, or think the tools are unnecessary in your particular situation, you're not likely to benefit much by their existence. My main purpose in this chapter, therefore, is to alert you to the existence of the UNIX tools for program maintenance and to explain why you need them.

The principal UNIX tools for program maintenance include the following:

❏ SCCS and `make`, for program version control

❏ `cb`, `cxref`, `cflow`, and `lint` for analyzing C-language source code

❏ `prof`, for execution profiling

There are other tools that you can bring to bear on your program maintenance and program administration tasks, but those just listed are the major ones and are the subject of this chapter.

The Source Code Control System

The Source Code Control System (SCCS) is a real boon to the programmer who uses it consistently and thoroughly; it is worse than useless to those who use it haphazardly.

How often have you attempted to fix a program bug and simultaneously created another problem? How often have you made several successive tries at fixing a bug, gotten deeper and deeper, and just wished you could go back to the version you started with, bug and all? Did you ever start an ambitious enhancement project for one of your programs, get distracted by other work, and end up with a useless nonworking source code that didn't match your production program? SCCS was designed to eliminate these frustrations.

Properly used, SCCS keeps track of every revision to your source files, enables you to review earlier versions, and even provides ways to discard recent changes to the source code. It does not burden you with a complex backup procedure, nor does it eat up large amounts of disk space storing obsolete versions of your source files.

An Overview of SCCS

SCCS is a file custodian. To use it:

1. Place a source file under SCCS control with the `admin` command.

2. Delete your copy of the plain source file. To make a change to the file, you request a working copy of the file from SCCS with the `get` command. You do not edit the SCCS files directly, but rather a copy of the current version given to you by SCCS.

3. After changing the copy, you store the revision by invoking the SCCS `delta` command, which records your edited copy as a new revision level of the file.

Each revision level of the file is called a *delta*. SCCS can tell you the exact difference between any two deltas and can even generate an editor script that transforms one version into another. SCCS assigns a unique number, called an SCCS ID (SID), to each version of each file. The SID is usually 1.1 for the first version, 1.2 for the next, and so on. You can generate up to a 4-level SID by *branching*. Branching arises in the context of production releases of software products.

When you release a software package, whether to the public, to your boss, or to your user, you freeze that version (say, 1.3) in the SCCS archive. As you continue to develop the program, SCCS stores your changes under a new release number, for example, 2.1. As you develop release 2, you may discover bugs in release 1 that you want to correct without sending out all the changes you're still working on in release 2. This is accomplished by branching. To create a branch:

1. First get a copy of the frozen version (1.3 in this example).

2. When you have completed the changes and give the file back to SCCS, it creates version 1.3.1.1 automatically.

3. You can then continue to develop release 2 while also maintaining release 1. You create a structure that looks something like that in figure 5.1.

Fig. 5.1. *Delta tree with branch.*

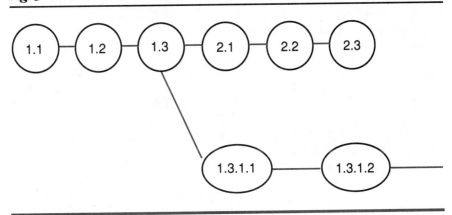

SCCS allows you to branch a file beyond all comprehension. Don't. It's a good idea to keep SCCS archives as simple as possible. You can, for instance, apply changes from an earlier version to a later version, thus combining branches and simplifying the tree. You can also combine several successive deltas into one, which also simplifies the archive.

You can and should embed SCCS keywords in your files. The keywords are expanded automatically when SCCS retrieves a file. These keywords can record the time and date of the last change to a file, the name of the source file, the version number, and a collection of other items. By using keywords to initialize variables, you can embed this information in the object code. The `what` command scans a file for SCCS keywords and reports them.

SCCS also enables you to incorporate descriptive text in an SCCS file. You can arrange for SCCS to treat a file with no keywords as an error, thus ensuring that your files are always marked with the information you want. I strongly recommend that you use this feature.

Features for Tracking Program Modifications

When you create a new delta, SCCS prompts you to enter comments describing the change. You can ask SCCS to print a complete history of changes to the source file, including these delta comments, using the `prs` command. If comments are too informal for describing file changes, SCCS also supports a method for relating source updates to problem report numbers, called Modification Request (or *MR*) numbers. You can configure SCCS to demand a valid Modification Request number for every update stored with the `delta` command. You can supply a program of your own for checking the MR numbers. This facility is valuable for large-scale production projects with many programmers and users generating requests for program changes. If the MR facility is enforced, it is possible to keep a permanent record of the relationship between customer-reported problems and the source code versions that fix them.

If the appropriate option is specified on the `admin` command when you place a file under SCCS control, two or more programmers can be allowed to modify the same file at the same time. You might want to use this capability when project schedules are very tight and two independent features need to be added to the same program; you will have to combine the updates by hand later, but at least the two programmers will be allowed to proceed. In general, however, I don't recommend that you allow *concurrent updates* (the SCCS term) to the same source file.

SCCS provides an optional security facility that is also enabled or disabled by the `admin` command. The facility enables you to specify the login names of those users who will be allowed to update the file; a request by any other user to open an update will be rejected.

Although it is most commonly used for the administration of program source code, SCCS is equally effective in maintaining incremental versions of any other kinds of text files, such as documentation text, or for tracking the successive versions of course materials for a class in UNIX programming.

Using SCCS

To begin to use SCCS to track a file, the first thing you should do is add keywords to the file so that each version is easily identified. For multifile programs, I suggest that you embed the keyword identifiers in the object code for each module. Although this increases the size of the object modules slightly, you can be certain of the exact composition of the final program by using the `what` command.

Use the %W% keyword to identify a module. When a file version is extracted by the get command, every occurrence of the %W% keyword is replaced with the string

```
"@(#)sample.c 2.9
```

The "@(#) mark identifies an SCCS what string and is followed by the name of the module and the SID code of the version.

As you become more familiar with SCCS, you may find a use for some of the other keywords as well. The complete list of SCCS keywords (all of which have the format %<letter>%) is documented with the get command. Let's take the little program I developed in Chapter 4, consol e. The following listing is the final version, with an introductory comment and the SCCS keyword line added to it:

```
# consok - Test whether okay to proceed with month-end consolidation
# %W%

OK_TO_PROCEED=0
for DEPT in $TFC/dept/*
do
      if [ -s $DEPT ]
      then :
      else
            echo $DEPT: not closed
            OK_TO_PROCEED=1
      fi
done
if [ $OK_TO_PROCEED -eq 0 ]
then
      echo All departments closed; okay to proceed with consolidation.
else
      echo Waiting for the above departments to close.
fi
exit $OK_TO_PROCEED
```

As modified, the consok file is ready for turnover to SCCS. The turnover is accomplished with the following command:

```
admin -iconsok.sh -fi s.consok.sh
```

This creates a new file, s.consok.sh, which contains the initial delta. Once you've executed the admin command, remove the original file to avoid confusion:

```
rm consok.sh
```

Now the only copy of the script is in the SCCS file s.consok.sh.

When you retrieve a copy of a file from SCCS, you need to make an important decision: Are you going to change the file and then create a new delta, or do you just want to get the latest version so that you can execute it or print it? If you're only going to process the file, use the get command without options like this:

```
$ get s.consok.sh
1.1
10 lines
$ _
```

The get command creates a read-only copy of the file consok.sh, which you can then print off or execute.

Any keywords in the file are expanded when this kind of a get is done, as the following would demonstrate:

```
$ what consok.sh
consok.sh 1.1
$ _
```

It's easy to understand where the what command gets its information: Take a look at the consok.sh file. The string "a(#)" is recognized by what, which then prints the characters that follow on the same line.

If your reason for executing the get command is to retrieve a copy of the file for editing and you want to store the revised copy back into the SCCS file as a new source version, you must execute get with the -e option (where the *e* stands for *edit*). For example:

```
$ get -e s.consok.sh
1.1 new delta 1.2
10 lines
$ _
```

When you use the -e option of get, SCCS creates a read/write copy of the file, without the keywords expanded. The keywords are not expanded because you're going to put the file back in the archive, and you want to keep the keywords, not their current expansion.

When you "get for edit," the get command also creates a control file that SCCS uses to keep track of the delta process. The control file is used later to determine which is the current version of the SCCS file and who has permission to create a new version.

If you change your mind about editing a file after you've already gotten a read/write version, you can use the unget command to cancel the effects of the get -e command.

Once you've gotten a working copy of a file, you can edit it freely, even completely replace it with another file. When the new version is ready to save, you create a new delta as follows:

```
$ delta s.consok.sh
comments?
```

In response to the prompt, explain why you made this change:

```
Added test for valid department
```

The delta command then responds with the following status report:

```
1.2
3 inserted
2 deleted
8 unchanged
$ _
```

The delta command prompts for comments unless you put them on the command line with the -y option:

```
delta '-yAdded test for valid department' s.consok.sh
```

If you are using the MR facility, delta will also ask for and verify a list of modification request numbers.

After checking that you have permission to update the file, the delta command then performs a comparison between the last archived version and your new version. The changes, in a compact form, are stored as the new entry in the SCCS archive. The comparison between versions is done by a variant of the diff command. Comparison is done on a line-by-line basis; changes are stored as instructions to delete lines, insert new lines, or to change lines by a combination of deletion and insertion. If you change just a single character, the entire line containing it is treated as changed, and SCCS records one deleted line and one inserted line.

The prs command can list the history of an SCCS archive. It's most often used to trace the update activity from one version to the next.

The -d option of the prs command enables you to specify the format of the command's output. The -d option is actually used to specify a string which can contain both literal text and substitution flags. The command can be used just to discover the current revision status of a file, for example:

```
$ prs -d:Dt: s.myprog.c
D 2.3 90/04/05 05:07:09 jjv 4 3
$ _
```

The output from the :Dt: flag gives, left to right, the delta status D, the current SID code (2.3), the date (90/04/05) and time (05:07:09) of the last update to the file, and the login ID of the programmer who made this change (jjv). The numbers 4 and 3 are meaningful only to SCCS but are displayed by the :Dt: flag anyway.

The same information could be presented in a more meaningful fashion with the following command:

```
$ prs "-d:M: SID=:I: created by :P: on :D: :T:" -e s.xcview.c
xcview.c SID=2.3 created by jjv on 90/04/05 05:07:09
xcview.c SID=2.2 created by jjv on 90/04/02 15:25:16
xcview.c SID=2.1 created by jjv on 90/04/01 07:52:05
xcview.c SID=1.1 created by jjv on 90/03/24 23:29:17
$ _
```

Here, I used the -e option of prs to print not just the latest delta, but information for all deltas in the file. Finally, here is the default output of the prs command:

```
/u/jjv/src/xcomm/archive/s.xcview.c:

D 2.3 90/04/05 05:07:09 jjv 4 3 00006/00007/00246
MRs:
COMMENTS:
Added a help facility

D 2.2 90/04/02 15:25:16 jjv 3 2 00099/00067/00154
MRs:
COMMENTS:
Fixed a bug in the UP command

D 2.1 90/04/01 07:52:05 jjv 2 1 00107/00188/00114
MRs:
COMMENTS:
Added thread linkage and navigation

D 1.1 90/03/24 23:29:17 jjv 1 0 00302/00000/00000
MRs:
COMMENTS:
date and time created 90/03/24 23:29:17 by jjv
```

As you can see, SCCS generates a large amount of information about the file and each revision of the file.

SCCS provides a tool to assist the programmer in managing updates to a collection of controlled source files. SCCS prevents damage to and loss of important source files due to incomplete or improper file revisions by allowing undesirable file changes to be discarded and earlier versions of a source file to be retrieved.

To achieve full effectiveness, the SCCS tool must be used to administer source files as early as possible in the code development process. When an important source file has been damaged beyond repair, it is too late to employ SCCS to remedy the loss.

Although SCCS is most often used for medium to large software development projects, it is also useful for small projects and small numbers of source files. All files, regardless of size or complexity, are subject to irreparable damage by improper updating techniques.

SCCS can provide the basis for sophisticated development administration systems. A shortcoming of SCCS is that the user of SCCS must have write access to all SCCS files, thus exposing the master SCCS files to risk of damage or destruction by accidental user error. This shortcoming can be remedied, but only by imposing an additional layer of programming through which all SCCS file administration requests are to be mediated. In general, SCCS is suitable for use in small and medium scale projects, but is not well suited to large or very large scale projects unless augmented with user programming because of its lack of library administration capabilities. SCCS administration considers a source file in isolation and is not useful in resolving issues of source file composition for a multifile program.

The make Facility

Whereas SCCS is a tool for the administration of source files, make assists with the generation and maintenance of executable program libraries. The make command, together with an appropriate list of instructions called a *makefile*, can regenerate object and executable files from the corresponding source or SCCS files in a completely automated manner.

make and SCCS were designed independently, but the System V implementations of these features embody extensions to the original facilties that permit close and meaningful cooperation between the two tools. This chapter concentrates on the basic capabilities of the make command. Once you understand the basic concepts, you should be able to understand and use the standard documentation for the make command well enough to employ all its capabilities.

Basic Concepts

The basic concept underlying the operation of the make command is that of a *dependency* between two files, for example between a source file, prog.c, and the object file generated from it, prog.o. Where such a relationship exists, we say that prog.o is *dependent* on prog.c, because any change to prog.c logically necessitates the reconstruction of `prog.o`, typically by compiling `prog.c`.

`make` recognizes a time relationship that most hold between a file and its dependent: the dependent file (`file.o`) is considered *up to date* when its date and time of last modification as shown by the `ls` command is newer than the file on which it is dependent. When the source file `prog.c` is compiled to generate the object file `prog.o`, the compiled object file `prog.o` is necessarily newer (i.e., created more recently) than the source file `prog.c` because the compiler does not modify the source file but by definition writes a new object file.

When `make` finds that the proper time relationship does *not* hold between a source file and the dependent files generated from it (called the *target* files), `make` attempts to regenerate the target files by executing a user-specified list of commands, on the assumption that the commands will restore the proper older-newer relationship between the source and its dependent files.

The `make` command supports the specification of a hierarchical set of dependency relations such as frequently occur in a programming project. Thus a set of header files may be included by one or several C-language source programs, which in turn must be compiled into a number of object modules, then linked to create executable files.

Consider the following example.

An application consists of five header files—`defs.h`, `io.h`, `accounts.h`, `cust.h`, and `trans.h`—that are copied by inclusion into each of five C-language source files:

`main.c, accts.c, cust.c, trans.c, report.c`

that must be compiled to create the object files `main.o`, `accts.o`, `cust.o`, `trans.o`, and `report.o`. From these five object files, three executable programs can be generated:

```
main.o accts.o report.o -> accts
main.o cust.o report.o -> cust
main.o trans.o report.o -> trans
```

A natural dependency relationship exists between each of the four types of files: headers, C sources, objects, and executables. If a C source file is changed, for example as the result of editing by a programmer, the related `.o` file must be regenerated from the modified source file by the execution of a compilation. Until the compilation is performed, the `.c` file will continue to be newer than the corresponding `.o` file, because the `.c` file was changed but the `.o` file has not been touched since the last compile. After compilation, the `.o` file will be newer than the `.c` file.

The `make` command uses this time relationship and a specification of the dependency relationships between files to determine when a generation procedure (such as compilation) is required. If `make` did not use the time relationship, it would be obligated to rebuild all components of the system if any of them changed. Recompiling all `.c` files, then relinking all `.o` files, in order to derive new versions of the three executables would not be invalid; it would merely be wasteful. As a result, the `make` command, by using the timestamps of the source and target files and an understanding of the dependency relationships between the files, optimizes the regeneration procedure by executing only the build steps that are required.

The Makefile

A verbal description of the dependency relationships between files in a programming project can be confusing to follow even when only a modest number of files are involved, such as in the previous example. When hundreds of files are involved, an English description of the relationships would be completely unusable.

Yet the `make` command requires some definition of the relationships between files. Otherwise, the command will be forced to make assumptions that might not be valid in all the situations where you want to employ `make`. As a result, the `make` command requires you to prepare an auxiliary file—the makefile—that describes the proper dependency relationships between the files of an application.

There are actually two kinds of information that must be encoded in a makefile: dependency relations and generation commands. The dependency relations determine when a file must be regenerated from its supporting source files. The generation commands tell `make` how to build the out-of-date files from the supporting source files. The makefile therefore contains two distinct line formats: one called *rules* (or sometimes *dependency* rules), the other called *commands*.

A rule begins in the first position of the line, and has the following format:

```
name [name ...] : [name ...]
```

The name or names to the left of the colon are the names of target files; that is, files that `make` should build. At least one name must always be specified to the left of the colon, because obviously a dependency relation (which is what the rule line describes) must rebuild at least one file.

The name or names to the right of the colon are the names of the files on which the targets are dependent. In other words, if one or more of the files on the right side of the rule are newer than a name on the left side, then the left-side name is a file that must be rebuilt.

No file names need be specified on the right-hand side of the rule. If the right-hand side is empty, make assumes that the targets on the left-hand side are up to date as long as they exist at all.

The dependency rule may be followed by one or more *command* lines. A command line *must* begin with at least one tab character; otherwise, it will not be recognized as a command line by make and will probably result in a syntax error message. Be careful: Not all text editors that you might use to write a makefile necessarily reproduce tabs that you type at the keyboard into the file you write to disk. Failing to introduce a tab at the beginning of a command line is the primary reason why beginning users have difficulty using the make command.

Other than being required to begin with a tab character, make imposes no restrictions on what you can write in a command line. When make uses command lines to rebuild an out-of-date target file, the lines are passed one by one to the shell for execution. As a command line in a makefile, you can therefore write any command that would be acceptable to the shell. Once again, a word of caution is in order: some shell commands have an effect that endures only as long as the process in which they are executed; such commands will have no effect when issued from a makefile command line. This is because make invokes a new shell in a new process for each command line it executes; when the command finishes, the shell exits, and the effects of any commands such as cd or umask are lost. This restriction can be circumvented by combining shell commands on one line; for example, the following command:

```
cd ../source; cc -c prog.c
```

will have the expected effect.

Using your current level of knowledge about makefiles, you should be able to recognize the following as a description of the dependency relationships and generation commands for our sample application:

```
accts:   main.o accts.o report.o
      cc main.o accts.o report.o -o accts

cust:    main.o cust.o report.o
      cc main.o cust.o report.o -o cust

trans:   main.o trans.o report.o
      cc main.o cust.o report.o -o trans
```

```
main.o:    main.c defs.h io.h accounts.h cust.h trans.h
    cc -c main.c
accts.o:   accts.c defs.h io.h accounts.h cust.h trans.h
    cc -c accts.c
cust.o:    cust.c defs.h io.h accounts.h cust.h trans.h
    cc -c cust.c
trans.o:   trans.c defs.h io.h accounts.h cust.h trans.h
    cc -c trans.c
report.o:  report.c defs.h io.h accounts.h cust.h trans.h
    cc -c report.c
```

Pay attention to the dependency rules for the .o files. You may have expected to find rules in the makefile similar to the following:

```
cust.c: defs.h io.h accounts.h ...
```

Instead, I've listed the header files on the .o dependency rules. This is because, at least for the C programming language, the content of the .c files does *not* depend on the content of the header files. Suppose you change one of the header files. Will you find it necessary to regenerate any of the .c files on account of the header file changes? Of course not. The content of the .c files is determined by you, the programmer, and established by the use of a text editor. Although you may indeed have to adjust one or more of the C source files as a result of a change to a header file, you can hardly expect the make command to invoke the editor for you and automatically insert the requisite text changes. The relationship between header files and C source files is not at all a clear one, and in any case, there is no way to *automatically* alter a source program to allow for changes in a header file.

On the contrary, the only visible effect of a change to a header file is that the object code for one or more of the source files is likely to change.

Our first version of the sample makefile can be significantly shortened by using some of the more advanced capabilities of the make command. However, even as it stands, the makefile represents a substantial potential improvement in our productivity and effectiveness as programmers. I can cite three reasons for this.

First, existence of the written makefile implies that knowledge of the generation procedure for the sample application system will no longer reside only in the heads of programmers. The application's generation procedure has been written down and can be automatically applied whenever the executable programs need to be rebuilt from changed sources. This is a tremendous advantage to the company that considers the application system to be an asset, because the company will still retain full value in the asset even if the programmers who are familiar with the application's generation procedure leave the company.

Second, the programmer time and effort required to rebuild the application after a source change will be considerably reduced. The programmer will not need to type every compile command by hand and will not need to remember the specific compile options required for each module, nor the exact sequence of generation steps required. In most cases, rebuilding the system from source will require only the following single command:

```
make
```

because all other variables in the procedure have been specified in the makefile.

Third, programmer time will not be wasted diagnosing spurious errors caused by improper or incomplete regeneration. The programmer does not even have to remember whether any sources have been changed; execution of the `make` command will result in no action if all dependent files are up-to-date, so any uncertainty at all in the currency of the object files is sufficient justification for invoking the `make` command.

Advanced Features

The `make` command affords many facilities to simplify the task of preparing makefiles. Among these are the use of implicit rules, symbolic variables, special variables, and SCCS support. These advanced facilities do not alter the way make *works*. They are only intended to ease the burden of preparing makefiles for large, complex applications. I would urge you to try your hand at building a few makefiles using the techniques presented in this chapter, and then to get the documentation for the `make` command for your system. Study it at your earliest opportunity and try your hand at writing makefiles that use the advanced features. I believe you will come to think of the `make` command as more important even than the compiler commands and second in importance only to your favorite text editor.

Note also that the `make` command works with more than program files. It is useful in any situation where derived files need to be generated by applying processing programs to base files, and the need to perform a generation step can be judged according to the timestamps of the files involved. You can use the `make` command and suitably prepared makefiles to automate your `lint` procedures, to print changed documentation files, to generate reports from data files, to selectively back up important files, in fact for an infinitely varied array of tasks.

Analyzing Source Code

Now that you have the tools to administer your source code and generate your object and executable code, take a look at other tools that help to improve the quality of your code.

UNIX provides tools to analyze the meaning of your code, to display and even improve the structure of your code, to improve the performance and efficiency of your code, and to verify the correctness of your code. You can even run a program that rewrites your code, using a consistent scheme of indentation that reveals the structure more clearly. I'll treat these tools in alphabetical order in this section.

cb

The `cb` program ("C beautifier") is the program-rewriting feature. It takes a C-language source file as input and produces the same program as output, reformatted to a consistent style of formatting and indentation.

If you have to maintain code written by others, `cb` can make your job a lot easier. The following is an example of a program you might come across when digging through an old source library.

```
#include <stdio.h>

main() { int c;
while ((c = getchar()) != EOF){
if (c=='\n')
{putchar(c);continue;} if (c>127)
{putchar('M');putchar('-');c&=0x7f;} if (
c<32){putchar
('^');putchar(c|0x40);}else if(c==127){putchar('^');putchar('?');}
else putchar (C);}}
```

After executing the command:

```
cb -s vis.c >vis.cb
```

the file `vis.cb` will contain the text in the following listing:

```
#include <stdio.h>

main()
{
    int   c;
    while ((c = getchar()) != EOF) {
        if (c == '\n') {
```

```
            putchar(c);
            continue;
    }
    if (c > 127) {
        putchar('M');
        putchar('-');
        c &= 0x7f;
    }
    if (c < 32) {
        putchar('^');
        putchar(c | 0x40);
    } else if (c == 127) {
        putchar('^');
        putchar('?');
    } else
        putchar(c);
}
}
```

Before reformatting the program, you probably would be unable to guess its purpose; afterward you might recognize it as a program to make control characters and non-ASCII characters in a file visible on the terminal screen.

Although you may not prefer the program style generated by cb, at least in a large project it has the advantage of imposing a consistent style on all the source files. Consistency is often more important than any other virtue when you have to study a large amount of source code.

Do not ignore the cb program merely because you have no need for its reformatting capabilities. It is also a useful diagnostic tool.

Here is a fragment of code as originally written by the programmer:

```
plotpoint(x,y)
{
    for (n = 0; n < 127; n++) {
        if (x < y) /* Check for variables within range */
                printf("(%d,%d) Data out of range", x, y);
                continue;
        plot(x,y);
    }
}
```

and after reformatting by cb:

```
plotpoint(x, y)
{
    for (n = 0; n < 127; n++) {
        if (x < y) /* Check for variables within range */
                printf("(%d,%d) Data out of range", x, y);
        continue;
        plot(x, y);
    }
}
```

Notice that the reformatted version shows the `continue` statement shifted one tab position to the left. The programmer apparently intended both the `printf` and `continue` statements to be executed as part of the `if` statement but forgot to enclose the two statements inside braces. The reformatted version shows exactly how the C compiler will interpret the program. The `plot` function call will never be executed!

cflow

The `cflow` program creates a flow-of-control analysis of the source files you give it. For each function, `cflow` shows the functions it calls as well as the functions that call it. The program supports source files written in the C, `lex`, and YACC languages, and can even identify function calls in assembler (`.s`) and object (`.o`) files.

The program is a bit tricky to use. If the C, `lex`, and YACC source files to be analyzed are normally compiled with the `I` option, indicating that they include header files not located in either the current directory or the standard include directory, you must specify the appropriate `-I` option on the `cflow` command as well.

The `-ix` option causes `cflow` to include global and external symbols in the output listing; normally the output shows only function definitions and calls.

Use the `cflow` program when you are unfamiliar with a system composed of multiple source files and you need to know all the places where a function is called or a global variable is referenced.

cxref

The `cxref` program produces a complete cross-reference of symbol usage in the source files you name. It can be useful when you are attempting to locate references to global symbols in a program consisting of multiple source files.

lint

`lint` is the precursor of all C-language debuggers and error-checkers. Now characterized in the official System V documenation as "a C program checker," its original manual page said "pick bits of fluff from C programs," which I think is more precise. That's what `lint` is all about: It goes through your source code and is extremely picky about what it finds there.

The `lint` program identifies variables that are defined but not used and that are used but not defined. It checks the declaration and usage of external functions against standard lint library files. It complains about variables that are assigned values that are never used. It checks for consistent usage of function parameter lists, both between distinct calls of the function, and between a call of a function and the definition of the function. lint catches a lot of discrepancies that are not errors at all; for example, it lists all the functions whose returned values are always (or sometimes) ignored.

When a program consists of more than one source file, lint can process all the source files together and check for consistent usage of functions and global variables among the files. You can create your own lint libraries to check that functions in your own function libraries are used correctly in C source files.

The output of lint is a sectional listing that shows all the errors and questionable code it has found in the source files.

The following is a sample program I call bad.c, written merely to demonstrate some of lint's checking.

```
 1 #include <stdio.h>
 2
 3 char    buff[180];
 4
 5 main(argc, argv)
 6 {
 7             int exit_value = 4;
 8
 9             while (fgets(buff, sizeof(buff), stdin) != NULL) {
10                     if (strchr(buf, '=') == NULL)
11                             printf("Invalid format: %s\n", buf);
12                     fputs(buf, stdout);
13             }
14             return (0);
15 }
```

The command

    lint bad.c

will generate the following output:

```
bad.c
==============
(10)   buf undefined
(10)   warning: buf may be used before set
(15)   warning: exit_value unused in function main
warning: argument unused in function:
      (15)   argc in main
      (15)   argv in main
```

```
===============
value type used inconsistently
     strchr     llib-lc.c(424) :: bad.c(10)
value type declared inconsistently
     strchr     llib-lc.c(424) :: bad.c(10)
function argument ( number ) used inconsistently
     strchr( arg 1 )     llib-lc.c(424) :: bad.c(10)
     fputs( arg 1 )      llib-lc.c(385) :: bad.c(12)
function returns value which is always ignored
     printf          fputs
```

Let me translate some of the lint listing for you.

When you see the lines:

```
bad.c
===============
```

you know that what follows are errors and inconsistencies that lint found in the one specific file bad.c. On the other hand, the following header:

```
===============
```

without any filename above the bar indicates that what follows are general complaints, or problems lint found involving usage between source files; in other words, the following messages do not pertain to any one particular file.

Output lines of the following format:

```
(10)   buf undefined
```

indicate that lint found an error in line 10 of the file; if you attempt to compile this program, you can expect the compiler to complain about the offending line. On the other hand, a line of the format

```
(10)   warning: buf may be used before set
```

will not result in a compiler diagnostic, but it is doubtful that you really intended to write what lint found on line 10 of the source file.

Lines of the following type:

```
function argument ( number ) used inconsistently
     strchr( arg 1 )      llib-lc.c(424) :: bad.c(10)
```

appear often in lint output. This particular message indicates that the first argument in the function call of strchr in the file llib-lc.c, which appears on line 424 of that file, is not in agreement with the declaration of the first argument in the strchr call on line 10 of the file bad.c. lint of course has no idea which usage is correct, so it draws your attention to the inconsistency and leaves it to you to determine whether both, either, or neither call is in error.

By the way, the message function argument (number) is merely telling you that the format of the following lines consists of function names followed by argument numbers enclosed in parentheses, even though the message sounds more like it's complaining about the number of arguments in a function call.

Actually, there's not that much wrong with bad.c. The following list shows the corrected version, called (of course) good.c:

```c
#include <stdio.h>
#include <string.h>

char    buf[180];

main()
{
        int exit_value = 0;

        while (fgets(buf, sizeof(buf), stdin) != NULL) {
            if (strchr(buf, '=') == NULL) {
                    printf("Invalid format: %s\n", buf);
                    exit_value = 4;
            }
            fputs(buf, stdout);
        }
        return (exit_value);
}
```

produces the following "residual" lint output:

```
==============
function returns value which is always ignored
     printf          fputs
```

I recommend using lint periodically during the program development cycle to help detect violations of the C-language rules that may pass the compiler's minimal checking. The C compiler is intentionally lax about syntax rules to enable the programmer to do anything that is certain to work. Unfortunately, such loose checking also often passes errors that were not intended and that may not show up in casual testing. You're always free to ignore the warnings from lint, so you have nothing to lose and much to gain from frequently using it on your code.

Optimizing Performance

UNIX offers an important and powerful tool for optimizing the performance of your C programs.

Historically, software developers took a sledge-hammer approach to achieving performance goals: They wrote all programs in assembly language. There are many disadvantages to assembly language programming. Programmer productivity is very low in such a detailed language, so the development cost of assembler programs is very high. Even if this cost can be born, however, another disadvantage often cannot: Assembly language programs remain irrevocably tied to one machine architecture. Assembly language programs are not portable.

The technique that has evolved to achieve adequate performance levels in programs written with a high-level language is based on the idea of eliminating performance *bottlenecks*, and the process of eliminating performance bottlenecks is called *tuning*.

A bottleneck is simply any block of code in the program that consumes an inordinately large percentage of the program's total execution time. The process of tuning is iterative. When tuning a program, you find the first bottleneck in the program code, using a method called *execution profiling*, and recode the routine using a more efficient algorithm. If no more efficient way can be found to code the routine using the original high-level language, the routine may be rewritten in assembly language but the use of assembly language is a last resort, because the routine will have to be rewritten every time the program is ported to a different machine architecture.

The process of locating and then removing a bottleneck is repeated, reducing the runtime cost of the worst bottleneck in the program on each iteration, until the desired level of performance is achieved. Usually only two or three iterations are necessary, because by definition each iteration optimizes that one routine in the program that consumes the greatest amount of execution time. Typically only 5 to 10 percent of the program will have been recoded, but the program's total run time will have been reduced by 50 percent or greater. Performance tuning can result in a final program that requires only 10 percent of the execution time that the initial version required.

To identify a bottleneck in a C program, it is first necessary to recompile the program to include *profiling* code. This is easily done: Simply include the -p option on the cc command! You may combine this option any others you want.

You will notice nothing unusual about the program that has been compiled with the -p option, but when the program is executed, a file will mysteriously appear in the current directory named mon.out. The file is actually the output of the profiling code that has been linked with your program. It contains elapsed-time measures and frequency counts for each function in the C program.

To view the execution profile, enter the following command:

```
prof <progname>
```

Typical output from the command looks like this:

%Time	Seconds	Cumsecs	#Calls	msec/call	Name
78.9	8.98	8.98	587	15.30	stat
13.8	1.57	10.55	719	2.18	read
3.8	0.43	10.98	41	10.6	open
1.2	0.13	11.12	587	0.23	ftw
0.9	0.10	11.22	1295	0.077	strcmp
0.7	0.08	11.30			_mcount
0.7	0.08	11.38	41	2.0	close
0.0	0.00	11.38	2	0.	profil
0.0	0.00	11.38	1	0.	creat
0.0	0.00	11.38	3	0.	getenv
0.0	0.00	11.38	1	0.	getuid
0.0	0.00	11.38	587	0.00	display
0.0	0.00	11.38	42	0.0	strcpy
0.0	0.00	11.38	1	0.	main
0.0	0.00	11.38	41	0.0	malloc
0.0	0.00	11.38	41	0.0	free
0.0	0.00	11.38	2	0.	sbrk
0.0	0.00	11.38	41	0.0	strlen
0.0	0.00	11.38	1	0.	write

From left to right, the columns of the listing show the following:

1. Percentage of the total runtime that the function used

2. Actual number of seconds spent in the function

3. Total number of seconds that were spent in this function, and all previously listed functions; i.e., the total cumulative run time including this function

4. Number of times this function was called

5. Number of milliseconds required for one execution of this function

6. Name of this function

This sample prof output shows that the subject program spends nearly 80 percent of its time in one function. The function is identified as stat, the system call for retrieving the description of a file.

If you could redesign the program to avoid the use of the stat system call, you would reduce its overall runtime from 11.38 seconds down to about 2.5 seconds. In other words, the code would run over four and a half times faster!

Suppose, on the other hand, that the s t a t call were indispensable to the application and could not be eliminated. Would rewriting the entire program in assembly language improve performance? Would optimizing the other parts of the program be helpful? Clearly not. Even if all other parts of the program were removed, the program would still require over nine seconds of execution time, which would represent a modest improvement.

Profiling not only shows you the performance problem areas in your program but also shows those areas of the code where any effort expended on optimization would be wasteful. It usually turns out that most parts of a program contribute little or nothing to the total run time.

Summary

This chapter discussed some tools that help with the programming process. Foremost among these tools is the SCCS (Source Code Control System).

SCCS administrates the product of your labors: your program source code. If preservation and protection of your source code is at all important to you, learn to use SCCS whenever you need to make a change to an existing source file. Learning to use SCCS is second in importance only to acquiring the habit of backing up your files.

The second most important tool I presented is the m a k e utility. You use the m a k e utility to generate executable programs from source files. Just as you learn to use SCCS for editing source files, you should get in the habit of using m a k e to compile your programs. Makefiles are easy to write for simple programs. If you get in the habit of writing a makefile even for simple programs, you will find it easier to develop more complex programs, where the use of makefiles is essential from the very beginning of the project.

This chapter mentions several other utilities, including l i n t, c b, c f l o w, and c x r e f, which you can use to develop or document your source code. But UNIX provides many other utilities that you will find useful in special situations. The s d b and a d b debuggers will help you find errors in your executable program, for example. The y a c c and l e x utilities build automatic syntax analyzers and parsers, and enable you to develop sophisticated user interfaces with little programming effort.

UNIX was designed to be used by programmers. It is no exaggeration to say that every command in System V is a programming aid in one situation or another. There is no command that you should spurn or ignore as you learn UNIX and begin to use it in your work. Unlike any other operating system you can buy, UNIX truly was designed from the beginning to be used by programmers, and is still the best programming aid on the market today.

6

Writing a Simple Filter

In this chapter we are introduced to the UNIX principle of standard input/ output files, and we use this feature to write some simple programs. You may want to skip ahead if you are already familiar with the UNIX standard input/output (stdio) package. I will not explore the stdio package in depth because the UNIX bookshelves are already full of texts that do so. The UNIX concept of a *file*, however, is basic to understanding the material in following chapters.

The UNIX File Interface

UNIX strives to present the same programming interface for all files, whether disk, tape, terminal, printer, or pipe. As part of this strategy, detailed information about a file's characteristics is generally hidden from the user program. Whereas many other operating systems represent a file by a table (often called a *file control block*) that must be coded in the application program itself, UNIX represents a file by a small interger called the *file descriptor*. This number becomes associated with the file when it is opened and must be presented to the operating system with every I/O request. It becomes available for reuse when the file is closed.

The term *file descriptor* is a poor choice of words because the number itself describes nothing about the file. When the builders of MS-DOS emulated the design of UNIX in this area, they chose the term *handle* to refer to the same small interger. But UNIX professionals always use the term *file descriptor* to refer to this number, as I shall, and you should, too.

Whichever term is used, the concept is the same: all detailed knowledge of the physical characteristics of a file is hidden from the program, so that all application programs must treat the file interface as a black box. The benefits of this design strategy are twofold: the operating system must handle all device-dependent considerations because it does not allow the program to do so; and we, the UNIX user community, are not bewildered with a maze of utilities and programming interfaces specialized for each type of device or file. The price we pay for this generic style of I/O interface is poorer performance, because some programs treat certain kinds of devices or files inefficiently.

Ken Thompson and Dennis Ritchie, the original designers of UNIX, were fully aware of the tradeoffs involved in their choice of I/O interface, and intentionally broke with the prevalent custom—still followed by the mainframe systems of today—of sacrificing ease of use and ease of programming to machine efficiency. It was their belief that the *people* cost of developing, maintaining, and operating computers is far greater than the hardware cost, and that machines and operating systems which are easiest for application programmers and end users to use will achieve the greatest success. This design principle has largely been vindicated by history as we witness the steady rise in hardware performance levels and an even more rapid decline in hardware prices, while the lead time and cost of software development continually rise.

Nowhere is the application of this design philosophy more evident than in the UNIX file system. All devices and file types respond in essentially the same manner to the open, read, write, and close calls, and all are referenced by the same abstract file descriptor.

A file descriptor is obtained by saving the return value from the open system call. It must be specified in all the basic I/O operations—read, write, and close—to designate the file to be operated on. All files are treated as if they were a simple array of bytes accessed by an index called the *file pointer*.

The read call reads the specified number of bytes into the program's data area, starting at the current position defined by the file pointer associated with the file. Similarly, the write call writes bytes to the file, storing them at the position defined by the current value of the file pointer. In either case, the file pointer is always advanced by the number of bytes transferred.

The file pointer can be incremented or decremented in units as small as one byte, thus allowing the program to reference areas in a file in a device-independent manner. This is one of the characteristics of the UNIX file system design philosophy that simplifies application programming.

The file pointer is always modified by the read and write operations. It also can be modified under program control by the lseek call, which can be used to set the file pointer to any desired value. In theory, this makes random access to files very easy to program. But there is one catch: the file pointer can be adjusted only for some kinds of files. For others, the file pointer value is implicit and cannot be modified by programming.

Consider a printer file, for example. Data written to the file is output in a standard fashion with successive characters forming a line and successive lines appearing on the page. For most kinds of printers, it makes no sense to talk about skipping around printing characters here and there; the data must be presented to the device in the same order that it is to appear on the page. Many devices are limited in the same way, for example, ASCII terminals and communications lines.

The only kind of file for which UNIX guarantees support of file pointer modification under lseek control is the disk file. Other kinds of files (such as diskette and magnetic tape drives) may be capable of lseek control, depending on the specific hardware and software implementation. Still, the lseek call can be invoked for any file; if the operation is not appropriate to the file, it is simply ignored.

This is an irritating flaw in the otherwise smooth edifice of device independence presented by UNIX; programs that are intended to work primarily with disk files and that therefore capitalize on the convenience and efficiency of the lseek system call will probably not work correctly when applied to other types of files. The flaw is inherent in any device-independent file interface because it is caused by fundamental differences in device characteristics. You can easily avoid the problem in practice, simply by being aware that some programs (such as ar) are usable only on disk files, and other programs (such as tar) are efficient only when used with magnetic tape drives, and that an attempt to read from a printer file will fail regardless of the cleverness of our programming technique.

The file pointer is one of the attributes of a file that is hidden from the direct view of the program. It can be examined or modified only by invoking system calls that explicitly or implicitly operate on it. As we examine the UNIX file system in greater detail, we will encounter many other hidden attributes, such as the size of a disk sector or a tape block. Not all file characteristics can be examined or manipulated by application programming.

The Standard I/O Package

The UNIX file interface appears both simple to use and adequate (at least as a basis) for any purpose. The fact is, though, that the UNIX file interface is a bit too simple. It leaves too much work to the application program to be practical for everyday use.

Because the operating system allows user programs to access arbitrary byte ranges of a file, you might suppose that it provides all the necessary buffering needed to make such access efficient. This is not the case. The operating system contains mechanisms to make such access *possible*, but no more. For reasons best left to later chapters, simplistic use of the file interface can result in very poor performance for the typical program.

What is generally considered *improper use* especially includes sequential file access, which accounts for the vast majority of all I/O requests in a typical system. In the standard C library, UNIX includes a set of functions that have been designed to provide optimum performance for sequential file access. These functions are collectively called the *standard I/O* package, and are bread and butter to the UNIX C programmer.

The standard I/O package includes functions analogous to the basic I/O calls, such as fopen, fread, fwrite, and fclose, as well as fseek, which is a direct replacement for the lseek system call. Unlike the basic I/O functions, these calls are library routines, not system calls, so they can be invoked with much less system overhead (see Chapter 13, "Kernel Internals"). Moreover, most requests to fread and fwrite can be satisfied by fast transfers from a memory buffer and often do not require physical device access.

The standard I/O package offers functions to optimize file access in terms of lines and characters. Most basic among these are the getchar and putchar requests, which respectively read one byte from the standard input file, and write one byte to the standard output file.

The usefulness of these two functions can hardly be exaggerated. Other operating systems prefer to handle input/output in large units called *records* or *blocks*. Although such I/O is possible in UNIX, the standard I/O package transforms UNIX into an operating system that prefers data transfer one byte at a time. Because getchar and putchar buffer all data transfers in a large memory area and are implemented as macros, their use is quite efficient.

Due to the simplicity of the UNIX file design, getchar and putchar (as well as the related getc and putc functions) are also powerful. We can use them to write a program that can copy any file, as in the following sample program I call cat:

```
#include <stdio.h>

void main()
{
     int c; /* The current input character */

     while ((c = getchar()) != EOF)
         putchar(C);
}
```

This program can be applied by the following command:

```
cat <file >newfile<M>
```

There are not many operating systems in which such a general-purpose file copying utility would be so easy to implement. The sample `cat` program can indeed be used with any kind of file, without restrictions. It is immaterial whether the file contains non-ASCII characters or nulls, simply because none of these characters is equal in value to `EOF`, and is thus transferred with the same impartiality as any other character values.

Central to the design of this program is the concept of standard files, by which I mean files that are assigned, opened, and ready for use when the program begins execution. This is a feature of both the standard I/O package and the UNIX shells. The standard I/O package supports the use of pre-opened files by defining the `stdin`, `stdout`, and `stderr` symbols to permit easy reference to the standard files, and by providing functions such as `getchar` and `putchar` to access them. The UNIX shells provide a command syntax by which the user can specify the assignment of the standard files.

There are three standard files: standard input, standard output, and standard error. The *standard input file,* represented in a program by the `stdin` predefined symbol, is normally used to read data typed at the terminal by the user. But by the use of shell redirection, the standard input file can be assigned to any disk or device file so that a program reading `stdin` will read from the redirected file or device instead.

The *standard output file,* represented by the `stdout` predefined symbol, is normally assigned to the user's terminal so that program output written to `stdout` will be displayed on the terminal. By the use of shell redirection, program output written to `stdout` can be directed to a disk or device file and saved for later use.

The *standard error file* (`stderr`) is also assigned to the user's terminal by default, and is intended to be used to write error messages so that they can be seen immediately by the user even when standard output is redirected to a file. It can be redirected to a disk or device file just like `stdout`.

Because of these defaults, if you execute the sample program without specifying any redirection, such as by entering the command

```
cat
```

the program would simply echo everything you type at the terminal back to the terminal. This is not useful, so the program would usually be invoked with I/O redirection to change the assignment of one of the standard files. The command

```
cat <text
```

displays the contents of the `text` file on the terminal because standard input (denoted by < in the command) is changed to the `text` file, and the standard output file remains the user's terminal. On the other hand, the command

```
cat >text
```

turns your computer into a typewriter, taking down everything that you type into the file named `text`.

I/O redirection (as the < and > operators are called) is a powerful feature because it allows the user to easily specify the inputs and outputs of a program. But the feature is usable only if you design your program to use the standard files. If a program ignores those files, redirecting them with the shell will be ineffective. Thus, I feel obligated to reiterate the advice given to all beginning UNIX programmers: always use `stdin` to read your input, `stdout` to write your output, and `stderr` to write error messages, unless you have a good reason to do otherwise. If you follow this advice, your program will be usable as a filter.

Using Standard I/O to Write a Filter

Programs that read their primary input from `stdin` and write their output to `stdout` are called *filters* because of the special role they play in constructing a form of shell command called a *pipeline*. Although filters have a simple I/O structure, they can be complex programs; `awk`, `sort`, and `nroff` are examples of sophisticated filters.

Because of their I/O structure, filters change an input data stream into a different form of data. By the use of pipes, several filters can be linked to perform complex data processing, in which each filter in the pipeline performs one step of the processing and passes its results to the next filter. For example, the following shell command (actually several commands linked to form a pipeline) generates a table of the frequency of occurrence of each word in the file named `text`:

```
deroff -w text | sort | uniq -c | sort +0 -1n >table
```

This pipeline performs four transformations on the original text file and uses redirection to store the final output in a file called `table`. (If the `deroff` program were not available to transform the lines of text into a list of words, the same function could be constructed from a pipeline of several `tr` commands.)

Many useful filters are quite simple programs. For example, consider the following listing. It is called `upper` because it converts all lowercase letters in its input to uppercase letters on output.

```
#include <stdio.h>

int main()
{
    int c;  /* The current character */

    while ((c = getchar()) != EOF)
        putchar(toupper(c));

    return (0); /* No error! */
}
```

This is a very simple program, yet it performs a task that can be useful in many different ways. For example, you could use it to eliminate case differences when sorting or searching lines of text.

The usefulness of a filter derives from the fact that it can be used at any stage in a pipeline. For example:

```
cut -d: -f1,3,5 /etc/passwd | tr : '\11' | sort
```

produces the following report on standard output:

```
adm       4    admin
bin       2    admin
jjv       100  John Valley
lp        71   lp
nsh       101  development
nuucp     6    uucp
root      0    admin
sys       3    admin
uucp      5    uucp
```

The pipeline uses three filters to accomplish its task. Although `cut` is a filter, it allows a file name to be specified on the command line, as do many system utilities. This is convenient when a program occupies the first position in a pipeline. If `cut` did not allow explicit naming of the input file on its command line, we would have had to write the command as

```
cut -d: -f1,3,5 </etc/passwd | tr : '\11' | sort
```

or

```
cat /etc/passwd | cut -d: -f1,3,5 | tr : '\11' | sort
```

Both work just as well as the original version of the command, but are more awkward.

Any program that writes its output to `stdout` or can be instructed to write its output to `stdout` can be used as the first command in a pipeline. More programs can be used as the first stage of a pipeline than can be used in the middle or end positions, simply because not all programs can obtain their input from `stdin`. Examples of programs that do not read `stdin` abound, and include basic utilities such as `rm`, `mv`, `cp` and most editors such as `vi`. Some of these programs, such as the `ar` command, can still be useful in the first stage of a pipeline, as in the command

```
ar t /lib/libc.a | sort | pr -t -5
```

This command produces a five-column, sorted listing of all the files in the C standard library.

On the other hand, programs like `cut`, `tr`, and `sort` are pure filters, because they can be used in any stage of a pipeline.

Just because a program is a filter does not mean that it must process its input one character at a time. Following is an example of a program that collects data and generates its output in lines:

```c
#include <stdio.h>
#include <string.h>
#include <ctype.h>

char line [BUFSIZ];
int maxline = 72;

main()
{
    char *lp;          /* Output line pointer */
    char *word;        /* Next input 'word' */
    char *getword();   /* Function to read a 'word' */
    int gap = 0;       /* Num of leading blanks needed */
    int need, space;   /* For computing space */
    int ctr;           /* Utility counter */

    lp = line;
```

```
        space = maxline;

        while ( (word = getword()) != NULL) {
            need = strlen(word);
            if ((need + gap) > space) {
                puts(line);
                lp = line;
                *lp = '\0';
                gap = 0;
                space = maxline;
            }
            for (ctr = 0; ctr < gap; ctr++)
                *lp++ = ' ';
            strcpy(lp, word);
            lp += need;
            space -= (need + gap);
        gap = (word[need-1] == '.') ? 2 : 1; }
        puts(line); /* Write the last line */
        return (0);
}
char *getword()
{
        char word[50];
        int wl = 0;
        int c;

while ((c = getchar()) != EOF && isascii(c) && isspace(c)) ;
/* Skip leading white space */

        while (c != EOF && !(isascii(c) && isspace(c))) {
            if (wl < (sizeof(word) - 1))
                word[wl++] = c;
            c = getchar();
        }
        word[wl] = '\0';

        return (wl == 0 && c == EOF ? NULL : word);
}
```

This filter will accept streams of words separated by white space, and flow the words into 72-character lines. It could be used for many purposes, for example, when called from the v i editor to justify comments in a program. You could add many features to the program by supporting a few options and by establishing a convention for setting paragraph breaks.

The point of this example, however, is that many useful applications can be written in the form of a filter. The only restrictions are that a filter must read its primary input from s t d i n and must write its primary output to s t d o u t. This does not preclude the usefulness of supporting auxiliary or additional files. For example, the `sed`, `awk`, and `fgrep` commands permit an auxiliary file to be specified with the `-f` option, and the `sort` command can process other files along with its standard input.

Using Command Arguments

Many UNIX programs allow the user to specify arguments on the command line, either to provide a list of file names, to specify one or more processing options, or both. You may wonder how the program retrieves arguments specified on the command line. UNIX makes it easy.

Every C program must contain one function called `main` that will receive control when the program begins. As with any other function, the `main` function can have arguments. But unlike other functions, you are not free to choose the arguments to the `main` function; they are defined by the UNIX operating system. The full declaration of the `main` function is

```
int main(int argc, char *argv[], char *envp);
```

You may choose to ignore the *envp* argument, both the *argv* and *envp* arguments, or all three arguments (*argc*, *argv*, and *envp*).

The *argc* argument contains the number of strings separated by white space that were typed on the command line. This count includes the first word of the command line, which for UNIX systems is always the name (or path name) of the program itself; its value is therefore always at least 1.

The *argv* argument is a pointer to an array, each element of which is in turn a pointer to a null-terminated character string. Each string is then one of the command-line arguments. By convention, the array is terminated by a NULL pointer so that the end of the array can be detected easily. These strings are stored in the active address space of the process, as is the array of pointers; the program is free to modify the contents of any argument string, or the array itself. The number of elements in the array pointed to by *argv* (excluding the final NULL entry) is equal to the value of *argc*.

To reference the first command-line argument, use the `argv[1]` expression. To reference the first character of the first argument string, use the `argv[1][0]` expression, where the first subscript selects the second element of the pointer array and the second subscript selects the first character of the string. As previously mentioned, the `argv[0]` string is the name by which the program was invoked. Note that if the program is invoked by a path name, the value of the `argv[0]` string is the path name and not just the simple file name of the program.

The *envp* argument points to a data structure identical to that of *argv*, except that the strings pointed to by the elements of the array are environment strings, not command-line arguments. Although you can alter the pointer array or any of the strings pointed to by elements of the array, the alteration will be propagated to any programs that your program calls because the environment string array is passed to the called program. Individual strings pointed to by elements of the *envp* array will be in the general format name=value, such as

```
HOME=/usr/guest
```

or

```
PATH=:/bin:/usr/bin
```

The getenv and putenv functions can be used to find strings in the array or to modify the value of an environment string.

Note that in all standard UNIX systems, the environ external variable, declared as

```
extern char *environ[];
```

is always defined, and points to the same pointer array as the *envp* argument. Thus, it is rare that programs explicitly declare the *envp* argument.

With this information, we can modify the sample cat program to accept a list of file names on the command line. In the following listing, the contents of all named files will be copied to the standard output file.

```
/* cat version 2--copy files named on the command line */

#include <stdio.h>

int main( int argc, char *argv[])
{
        FILE *input;
        char *filename;
        int rc = 0;
        int ch;

        ++argv;      /* Skip over the program name */

        /* For each file name in the argument list ... */
        while ((filename = *argv++) != NULL) {

            /* Open the input file */
            if ((input = fopen(filename, "r")) == NULL) {
                perror(filename);
                rc = 1; /* Remember that an error occurred */ continue;
            }
```

```
    /* Copy its contents to standard output */
    while ((ch = getc(input)) != EOF)
        putchar(ch);

    /* And close the input file */
    fclose(input);
}

    return (rc); /* Nonzero if any file could not be copied */
}
```

Notice that this listing does not refer to the elements of the argv pointer array by explicit subscripts. Instead, it progressively increments the argv pointer to point to successive elements of the array using the *argv++ expression. This technique destroys the initial value of argv; after the program has scanned the argument list, it can no longer identify its command-line arguments. This is not a problem in this example because after the strings have been processed, they do not need to be referenced again.

This listing uses the fopen and fclose functions, whereas the previous version of cat did not. These functions are simple to use. For additional details about them, you can refer to the "Reference" section. One feature of the program worthy of note is the test for a return value of NULL from the fopen function. All calls to fopen should be similarly checked because there is no assurance that the file you want to open exists. The fopen function returns a NULL value to notify you that an error prevented the opening of the file. You can then test the errno global variable to identify the cause of the failure, or invoke the perror function to write a suitable error message, as was done here.

Although this second version of cat now supports explicit naming of the files to be copied, you can no longer use shell redirection to designate the input file. The new version has lost a useful and desirable feature of the old program. To correct this deficiency, the program must test for and handle the case where no file name arguments are present. This is done easily enough, as the version in the following listing shows:

```
/* cat version 3
   Copy the standard input file or named files */

#include <stdio.h>

int main( int argc, char *argv[])
{
    FILE *input;
    char *filename;
    int rc = 0;
    int ch;
```

```
    ++argv;      /* Skip over the program name */

    if (argc == 1) {
        /* No file names given on the command line */
        while ((ch = getchar()) != EOF)
            putchar(ch);
    }

    /* If no arguments are present, the following loop will
       do nothing; otherwise, it will copy the contents of
       each named file to standard output. */

    while ((filename = *argv++) != NULL) {

        /* Open the input file */
        if ((input = fopen(filename, "r")) == NULL) {
            perror(filename);
            rc = 1; /* Remember that an error occurred */
            continue;
        }

        /* Copy its contents to standard output */
        while ((ch = getc(input)) != EOF)
            putchar(ch);

        /* And close the input file */
        fclose(input);
    }

    return (rc); /* Nonzero if any file could not be copied */
}
```

This last version of `cat` is almost good enough to put into production use, and is close to the `cat` utility included as a standard part of the UNIX operating system. You might find it an interesting exercise to complete the program by adding the remaining features supported by the real version of `cat`.

Other Standard I/O Functions

So far, we have looked closely at the `getchar` and `putchar` functions and glanced at the `fopen` and `fclose` functions. The `stdio` package contains many more functions to ease your programming effort. The "Reference" section contains a detailed explanation of each of them. I will mention the remainder here, so that you will at least have heard of them all.

The `fopen` and `fclose` functions provide fundamental support by allowing you to specify the files you want to process during program execution. Two other functions, `fdopen` and `freopen`, are occasionally useful.

The fdopen function is intended to be used when you already have an open file descriptor, but want to access the file using the standard I/O function set. The fdopen function will create a standard I/O file around the open file descriptor so that you can use the other stdio functions to access it.

With freopen, you can reuse a FILE block (the structure returned by fopen) for a different file. The freopen function is usually used to switch the file to which stdin, stdout, or stderr is assigned, and is the only practical way to change the assignment of one of the standard files from your program.

In addition to getchar, which always reads a character from stdin, you can also avail yourself of the getc and fgetc functions, which read a character from a specified file instead of the standard input. The difference between getc and fgetc is that getc is a macro, and fgetc is a real function. When possible, use getc rather than fgetc because a macro requires no overhead for its invocation.

If you want to read input in units of lines rather than characters, you can use either the gets or fgets function. The gets function reads the next line from standard input; fgets reads the next line from the named file. The gets function is dangerous to use because it does not check that the line will fit in the input area you provide. If an input line is too long, gets will continue to read characters over whatever follows your input area, destroying program instructions and data until either the end of the line is found or your program dies of corruption. You should always use fgets in preference to gets, but fgets has its own set of problems and limitations.

Unlike gets, which requires only one parameter (a pointer to the area of memory where the input line should be stored), fgets requires three: the file to be read, a pointer to the area where the line should be stored, and the size of your input area. If the input line exceeds the size of your area, fgets simply stops reading when you run out of room. The remaining characters in the line are not discarded, however; you receive them on your next call to fgets. Unless you design your program to handle long lines received in segments, your program will erroneously process each segment of a long line as if it were a separate line. The most straightforward solution to this problem is to write a function to read lines. However, fgets is designed to accumulate the characters of the input line in a very efficient manner, and you will lose this performance advantage if you write your own routine.

I think it is better to have a bulletproof program than to have a fast one. Until you are proficient enough to do better, I would recommend a function similar to the following for reading lines:

```
/* getline--a safe function for reading lines */
#include <stdio.h>
static char buffer [BUFSIZ];
char *getline(FILE *file)
{
    int len = 0;
    int ch;

    while ((ch = getc(file)) != EOF && ch != '\n')
    if (len < (BUFSIZ - 1))
            buffer[len++] = ch;
    buffer[len] = '\0'; /* Terminate the new line */
    return ((ch == EOF && len == 0) ? NULL : buffer);
}
```

This routine always returns the next input line to the calling routine. If the next line is longer than BUFSIZ, it simply discards input characters up to the end of the line. This is usually reasonable, because you are obviously not prepared to handle lines longer than BUFSIZ characters anyway. The only safe alternatives are to terminate the program or continue processing with a truncated input line. Either alternative is better than the program dying because the input line was too long.

One other function is provided for input operations: fread. This function reads a specified number of characters from the file into your input area. A newline character is treated just like any other character, so the only time the read can be truncated is when the end of file is reached. The fread function is typically used when a file is organized as a series of structures instead of as a series of lines.

The output functions provided by the standard I/O package include putchar, putc, fputc, puts, fputs, and fwrite. The putchar function is analogous to getchar: it writes one character to the standard output file. The putc function, like getc, is provided as a macro to achieve maximum performance, and writes a specified character to a file. The fputc function performs the same operation as putc; fputc is a real function and therefore incurs a performance penalty in comparison to putc, but it can be used when putc would cause problems.

The puts function writes a string to standard output, and then writes a newline character to the standard output file. The fputs function is similar to puts, but writes the string to any named file. The fputs function does not append a newline, however, so the string presented to fputs must contain the newline character. This difference is tricky because it is easily forgotten; remember that the advantage of being able to write to any file with fputs is offset by the burden of having to append newline characters.

The fwrite function is similar to fread in that it writes a specified number of characters to the file regardless of the occurrence of newlines in the written data. The fread function is used to read a file organized as a series of structures; fwrite is used to create such a file.

The fseek function is available to change the current position in the input or output file. It is not exactly identical to the lseek system call; lseek merely alters the file pointer, whereas the fseek call may have to discard the current data buffer if the new file position lies outside the range of characters currently held in the buffer. In other words, fseek incurs more overhead than lseek. Remember, you *must* use fseek with standard I/O files (those opened with the fopen function) but you *must not* use it with basic files (those opened with the open function). Also, remember that fseek is guaranteed to be effective only with disk files; for other kinds of files it may have no effect on the current file position.

A short form of fseek—rewind—is available when you just want to reposition the file to its beginning. The rewind function is a short form of fseek, requiring no arguments. The ftell function is somewhat the inverse of fseek—instead of altering the file pointer to a specified value, it returns the current value of the file pointer to you.

I cannot leave the discussion of the standard I/O package without mentioning two powerful sets of functions that you will probably use frequently. The scanf family of functions (consisting of scanf, fscanf, and sscanf) can be used to scan input, converting it from its external ASCII representation into its equivalent internal representation. The other set, consisting of printf, fprintf, sprintf, vprintf, vfprintf, and vsprintf, generates ASCII text by substituting the values of variables into a format text.

These functions are too complex to describe here; see the "Reference" section for details. It can take time to learn the set of format codes accepted by the scanf and printf functions, but your study will be rewarded by the impressive power of these functions. The scanf family of functions can be surprisingly tricky and difficult to use. I suggest that you experiment with them; experience is the only effective teacher when it comes to learning scanf.

The remainder of this book contains many examples of using the standard I/O function set. With few exceptions, the examples do not depend on an in-depth understanding of the standard I/O package. Look up the function definitions whenever you do not understand what they are doing. You will find that their operation slowly takes on a natural, intuitive feel that will become as familiar to you as an old sweater.

Summary

In this chapter, we looked at our first programming topic: techniques and considerations for using the standard I/O package.

In the first section, "The UNIX File Interface," you were introduced to the UNIX file system and learned that, just like the MS-DOS file system, the UNIX file system represents disk files as a continuous stream of bytes. Although the stream I/O package represents a file by a FILE structure, the underlying physical file interface represents a file by an integer called a *file descriptor* (the analog of the MS-DOS *handle*).

The UNIX file system implements a procedure called *mounting*, whereby an offline volume is connected to the online file system by mapping the root directory of the new volume onto one of the directories of the online file system. Because UNIX supports the mounting of disk volumes, you do not need to use drive letters as you do with MS-DOS.

After reviewing the standard files standard input, standard output, and standard error, we used the `getchar` and `putchar` functions to write a simple file copying program. This became the basis for a discussion of *filters*, a type of program designed to work with pipes. *Pipes* allow the output of one program to be read directly by another without ever being written to disk. We saw that any program can be used as a filter as long as it reads its primary input from the standard input file, and writes its primary output to the standard output file.

We improved the sample program by adding support for *command-line arguments*. UNIX makes it easy to inspect the operands of a command from an application program, parsing the command line into strings and passing the array of string pointers to your program's main function. We modified the `cat` command to allow the names of the files to be copied to be entered on the command line.

Finally, this chapter reviewed the other important functions in the standard I/O package: `fopen`, `fclose`, `getc`, `putc`, `fgets`, `fputs`, the `printf` family, and the `scanf` family.

The ability to use the standard I/O package effectively is essential to the UNIX programmer, because more than 90 percent of all file access is performed using standard I/O, even in the most sophisticated applications.

Good programming style requires us to write our programs to read input from standard input, and to write output to standard output, whenever possible. Such programs are compatible with the shell's redirection and pipelining capabilities, and achieve the maximum flexibility for the end user.

CHAPTER 7

UNIX Commands

For most of this book we have concentrated on application development using the C programming language, examining many of the system calls and library functions of System V along the way. But C is not the only programming language available to the UNIX programmer, and it is not always the best choice for every job. The shell is the most powerful programming language afforded by the UNIX environment, simply because so much can be accomplished in so few lines of code. You should use the C language only as your programming language of last resort, when there is no other way to do a job or when performance is of paramount importance. When a shell implementation is feasible and provides adequate performance, it is the better choice because your coding and testing time will be minimized.

As noted in the "Prototyping" section in Chapter 4, the shell language provides only a framework for a shell program; most of the processing in a shell script is performed by UNIX commands and programs you write, usually in C. The shell script ties the commands and programs together, deciding when a command will be executed and specifying the options, arguments, and redirections needed to apply the command to the problem at hand.

As a result, successful shell programmers are experienced in the use of UNIX commands for processing information. A chat with them, though, would quickly disclose that even the most experienced UNIX programmers do not claim intimate familiarity with all UNIX commands. They would tell you that there is a relatively small set of generally available UNIX commands that they use over and over in writing shell scripts.

125

Counted among the set of UNIX commands are programs such as `init`, `login`, `getty`, `mount`, `mkfs`, `clri`, and `fsdb` that are intended for very specialized system control functions and rarely appear in user-written shell scripts. Others among the huge UNIX command set, such as `vi`, the visual editor, are usually not appropriate for invocation from a shell script; these commands are more often entered directly by the user.

So it shouldn't be surprising that the commands most useful to the shell programmer provide a general-purpose data manipulation function. High on the list are the commands `sed`, `expr`, `grep` and its variants (`fgrep` and `egrep`), `cut`, `sort`, `echo`, and my personal favorite, `awk`.

The UNIX documentation provides exhaustively detailed explanations of the function and command-line options of each of these commands; I will not repeat the command descriptions here. My purpose is to identify the commands you should keep in your personal "tool box" of shell programming aids and provide examples that show how these commands, when combined with the capabilities of the shell language itself, provide extremely powerful general-purpose data manipulation functions.

Data Manipulation Commands

The following UNIX commands are of special importance to the shell programmer. You should add them to your repertoire of UNIX commands and think of them as your basic toolkit for writing shell scripts.

`awk`   More a language than a command, the `awk` utility provides the capability to process the lines of an ASCII format file field-by-field. The utility can be used to alter the format of a file, to extract selected lines from a file, to tabulate numeric information in a file, or even to prepare a full-scale report from a sorted data file.

`cat`   The `cat` command is most commonly entered at the keyboard to simply list a file. But from a shell script, the `cat` command is more likely to be used to concatenate two or more files into one larger file, which is then piped to another command.

`cut`   The `cut` command copies selected columns or fields of each input line to standard output. The same results can be achieved using `sed` or `awk`, but when `cut` will do the job, its simple command syntax is preferable.

`expr`   The `expr` command is often used to perform simple arithmetic in a Bourne shell script. It can be used also to pick out the portion of a string that matches a specified pattern.

false   The false command returns an exit value of 255, which the shell interprets as a logical false condition.

grep   The grep, fgrep, and egrep commands can be used to select lines from a file according to specified search criteria; lines matching the search pattern are copied to standard output.

join   Often overlooked by shell programmers, the join command provides a way to select lines from a file using another file to specify the lines wanted. The join command can be a bit tricky to use, but it provides a processing function that is almost impossible to implement any other way except by writing your own C program.

sed   The sed command, called the "stream editor," is more restrictive than awk. It provides most of the capabilities of a text editor, and can be used to perform straightforward editing of a file of lines on standard input. The input to sed often comes from a pipe.

sort   Use the sort command to change the ordering of lines in a file, or to eliminate duplicate records from a file.

true   The true command returns an exit value of 0, which the shell interprets as a logical true condition.

xargs   The xargs command is truly a wizard. With it, you can transform the output of another command into a whole series of commands. The xargs command works by taking the words or lines of the standard input file and tacking them onto the end of a model command specified as an argument to xargs; each generated line is then passed to the shell for execution. The shell programmer usually arranges for the input to xargs to come from a pipe.

I will discuss some of these commands at greater length in the remainder of this chapter. The list itself is useful, though. If you take my hint, at your earliest convenience you will sit down with the manual of UNIX commands and study the description of each command in this list. To make sure you understand a command, try it out at the keyboard. For example, you might try the exercise with the true command:

```
$ if true
> then echo "true is true!"
> else echo "true is false?"
> fi
true is true!
$ _
```

If you get any other result, check your typing against the listing.

Regular Expressions

Five of the toolkit commands (`awk`, `egrep`, `expr`, `grep`, and `sed`) are pattern-matching utilities. To use them effectively, you must know how to describe a string pattern. If you are familiar with the shell or with MS-DOS, you already know one way to specify a string pattern.

Wild cards are a familiar way to refer to a group of files that have a similar file name. For example, you can ask for a list of all the C program source files in the current directory using the command

```
ls *.c
```

The MS-DOS user specifies the same operation using identical wild-card notation:

```
DIR *.c
```

Only the command name is different. The asterisk is a wild card that means "any string," and the phrase `*.c` is really a pattern-matching expression. The strings against which the pattern `*.c` are matched are the file names in the current directory.

UNIX commands often use a different language for specifying pattern-matching expressions; this language is called *regular expressions*. A regular expression (abbreviated *RE*) is simply a string made up of *literal* characters (characters that stand for themselves) and *metacharacters* (characters that have a special meaning). Regular expressions are more powerful than the shell wild cards. Any pattern that can be described using shell wild cards can be described by a regular expression, but the opposite is not true; many regular expressions cannot be converted into an equivalent pattern using shell wild-card notation.

To use regular expressions, you must learn the set of metacharacters that make up the alphabet of the language, just as you had to learn the meaning of the shell wild cards. Unfortunately, UNIX commands vary in the extent to which they support regular expression notation; some commands implement only a minimal set of metacharacters and others recognize a richer set. Appendix A shows which regular expressions are supported by each command. The basic set of metacharacters follow:

.   The dot matches any character except the newline character at the end of a line. Use the dot in any context where you would use the shell ? wild card.

*   The asterisk means "zero or more occurrences of the preceding regular expression." Thus, the `.*` regular expression

matches any sequence of characters, and is equivalent to the *
shell wild card. Note that the * regular expression by itself
means nothing, and is an improper expression, because no
literal or metacharacter precedes *.

[...] Characters enclosed in brackets define a character set that will
match one occurrence of any character in the set. A list of
characters can be written out in full. For example, [abc]
means that the expression will match any one of the characters *a*, *b*, or *c*. A set of characters may be designated also by
naming the first and last characters in a range. For example,
[a-f] is equivalent to [abcdef]. A character range can be
described by naming the characters that are *not* in the set, by
following the opening bracket with a caret. For example, the
expression [^cgmCGM] means any character other than *c, g,*
m, C, G, or *M,* and the expression [^a-z] matches any
character except the lowercase letters. Note that more than
one range can be specified in the same character-set expression: [a-zA-Z_] denotes the set of all alphabetic characters
and the underscore. Be careful where you put the hyphen.
The expression [-+*=] identifies the minus, plus, times, and
divide arithmetic operators, but the expression [+-*/] is
interpreted as "the range of characters from + to * inclusive,
and /." By coincidence, the ASCII character set defines *
before +, so the expression [+-*/] actually denotes a
negative range. The interpretation of a negative range depends on the way a command implements regular expressions. Finally, note that you can include the brackets
themselves in a character set by writing them immediately
after the opening bracket (but after the caret, if present).

\ When the backslash is placed before a metacharacter, it causes
the special meaning of the metacharacter to be ignored. For
example, the expression \\ represents the literal \ itself, and
\. means the dot character.

\(RE\) An RE enclosed in escaped parentheses is equivalent to the RE
itself, but most commands interpret this expression as a
request to save the character string that the RE matches in an
internal register. The saved character string may later be
referenced using the special notation \1. If more than one
\(...\) group occurs in an expression, the first is referenced
by \1, the second by \2, and so on.

^   When the caret is outside the `[...]` expression, it represents the start of the current line. A regular expression of the form `^RE` restricts a match on *RE* to occur only at the beginning of the line.

$ When the dollar sign is outside the `[...]` expression, it represents the end of the current line. A regular expression of the form `RE$` restricts a match on *RE* to occur only at the end of the line.

Using regular-expression notation, the `*.c` shell pattern would be written `.*\.c`. Note that `\` is used to quote the second *dot*, which must match a dot in the input string. We will study many more examples of regular expressions as we look at the individual toolkit commands.

awk

`awk` is the name of a UNIX command and the name of a programming language. The peculiar name of this command, often said by quipsters like myself to refer to the *awk*ward language, is actually the combination of the initials of its three authors, Al Aho, Peter Weinberger, and Brian Kernighan. Like the BASIC language, the `awk` language is not compiled; it is interpreted, meaning that a program written in the `awk` language is compiled and executed all at once.

There are two ways to write an `awk` program:

❏ Store the program as a series of statements in a plain ASCII file, and name the file on the `awk` command line.

❏ Code the statements to be executed right on the `awk` command line.

Simple programs are usually written on the command line, and enclosed in quotation marks to avoid conflict with characters that have a special meaning to the shell. More complex programs are stored in a file so that the entire `awk` program doesn't have to be typed every time it is used.

There is no lack of good introductory texts for the `awk` language. You'll find useful descriptions in the UNIX commands manual, as well as in *UNIX System V Programmer's Guide* (Prentice-Hall, 1987) and *The UNIX Programming Environment* by Kernighan and Pike (Prentice-Hall, 1984). Space considerations prohibit me from giving a complete introduction to the language here. After a brief introduction to the basic concepts, we'll look at some examples of its use.

Command Format

The awk command has the following format:

```
awk [ -Fc ] [ -f prog ] [ pattern ] [ filename ...]
```

Although any individual argument can be omitted, in practice at least one argument must be provided on the command line: you can code the -f option and specify for *prog* the name of the file containing awk instructions, or code the *pattern* argument, giving the awk program on the command line itself. Note that awk expects the -f flag and the *prog* file name to be separate arguments. You *must* provide at least one space or tab between -f and the file name of your awk program file.

awk works on fields in the input file. By default, the fields of a line are assumed to be separated by white space (blanks or tab characters). You can use another separator by coding the -F option and specifying the separator character immediately after the F. You would almost always specify the -F: option when processing the /etc/passwd file, for example, because logical fields are separated by : in the /etc/passwd file.

By default, awk reads its input data from the standard input file, but if one or more files are named on the command line, awk will ignore the standard input file and read its input from the named files. When multiple files are named, awk treats the files as if they were concatenated, automatically closing one and opening the next until the end of the last file is reached. The standard input can be named explicitly as an input file by writing - as one of the *filename* arguments.

Introduction to the awk Language

awk is fundamentally a pattern-matching language. Statements in the language take the general form

```
pattern { action }
.
.
.
```

The *pattern* and *action* parts of a statement are optional, but one of the parts must be present. If the *pattern* part is omitted, the *action* part is always executed. Otherwise, the *action* part is executed only when the *pattern* part matches the current line of input. If the *action* part is omitted, the default action is performed, which is to print the current line of input. (Note that, when describing awk actions, *print* actually means to write a line to the standard output file.)

awk executes an automatic processing cycle for each line of input it reads. Your awk program does not need to describe the steps of this cycle, and in fact has very little influence over the cycle. In each cycle, awk does the following:

1. Reads the next input line.

2. Assigns the full text of the line to the $0 symbolic variable.

3. Breaks the line into its individual fields.

4. Assigns the string value of the first field to the $1 symbolic variable, the string value of the second field to the $2 variable, and so on for as many fields as are contained in the line.

5. Attempts to match the pattern part of the first statement in your awk program against the current line.

6. If a match is found, executes the action for the statement.

7. Steps to the next line of your awk program and repeats the matching operation.

8. When the last statement in the awk program has been processed, starts over at the top with the next line of input.

Because awk attempts to execute every statement in the program for each line of input, zero, one, or several statements may be executed for any given input line. This means that the effect of the actions for each statement must be considered in light of the other statements in the program. When planning your awk program, you can choose to perform all the processing for an input line in one statement, or you can distribute the processing for an input line over several statements, using the pattern part of a statement to apply an action only when appropriate.

Patterns

A pattern can be as simple as /RE/, where any regular expression, enclosed between matching delimiters, is matched against each input line. If the pattern is found anywhere in the input line, the action part of the statement is executed; otherwise, awk simply goes on to the next statement in the program. Enter the following command at your UNIX terminal:

```
awk '/[uU]ucp/' /etc/passwd
```

My system generates the following output:

```
uucp:x:5:3:0000-uucp(0000):/usr/lib/uucp:
nuucp:*x:6:3:0000-uucp(0000):/usr/spool/uucppublic:/usr/l
ib/uucp/uucico
Unixric:x:7:3:0000-uucp(0000):/usr/spool/uucppublic:/usr/l
ib/uucp/uucico
```

The `awk` program contained one statement consisting of a pattern (namely, `/[uU]ucp/`) and an omitted action. Because the default action is to print the current line, the `awk` command prints every line in the password file that contains either the word *uucp* or *Uucp* anywhere in the line.

A pattern can also be a logical expression formed using any of the following operators:

```
==

!=

>

<

>=

<=

~

!~

&&

||
```

Except for `~` and `!~`, these have the same interpretation as in the C language. The `~` operator means *contains*, and the `!~` operator means *does not contain*. The program

```
awk -F: '$3 >= 100' /etc/passwd
```

prints all lines from the password file having a user-ID number of at least 100. My system prints:

```
jjv::100:7:John Valley:/u/jjv:
nsh::101:7:nsh development:/u/nsh:
prof::102:1:Business Files:/u/prof:
cmf::104:10:CMF development:/u/cmf:
bbs::105:7:Bulletin Board Services:/u/bbs:
```

Note that in this example we see that `awk` understands numeric fields and relationships as well as strings.

Actions

Actions are actually small programs. An action may consist of any number of instructions separated by newlines or semicolons.

As with any programming language, awk supports the use of variables and literal values. Except for the field values of the current input line, which are represented by the variables $0, $1,...$n, all variable names are required to be a sequence of letters and digits, the first of which must be a letter.

There are two types of literal values: string literals and numeric literals. A *string literal* is an arbitrary sequence of characters enclosed in double quotation marks. The expression *"ABC"* is a valid string literal, *'ABC'* causes a syntax error, and *ABC* is taken as a variable name. A *numeric literal* is any string of digits, possibly containing an embedded decimal point. Note that awk fully supports floating-point arithmetic. Hence, 41.25 is a valid number, and the value of the expression 41.25 / 3.5 is correctly computed to be 11.7857.

An awk instruction may be one of the following types:

```
var = exp
```
The *assignment* statement computes the value of an expression and assigns the result to the variable named to the left of the equal sign. Expressions are written using the C-style operators shown in table 16.1. A variable name is any sequence of letters or digits beginning with a letter; do *not* prefix variable names with the $ symbol.

```
if ( exp ) stmt1 [ else stmt2 ]
```
If the expression *exp* evaluates to a nonzero value, *stmt1* is executed; otherwise *stmt2* is executed.

```
while ( exp ) stmt
```
The *stmt* statement is executed as long as the expression *exp* continues to evaluate to a nonzero value.

```
for ( exp1; exp2; exp3 ) stmt
```
The *exp1* expression is executed at loop initialization time, and the *exp3* expression is executed after each iteration of *stmt*. The loop is executed as long as the result of *exp2* is true (i.e., nonzero).

```
for ( var in arrayname ) stmt
```
Similar to the for statement of the shell, the *var* variable is set to each of the values of the one-dimensional array *arrayname* in turn as *stmt* is executed.

```
break
```
Immediately exits the currently active while or for loop.

```
continue
```
Immediately starts the next iteration of the currently active while or for loop, ignoring all remaining instructions in the loop.

```
print exp [ [ , ] exp ... ]
```
Each of the *exp* values is computed and printed as one line to the standard output file. Values separated by a comma are separated by the OFS (output filed separator) character (usually the space) in the output line; values not separated by the comma are run together in the output line.

```
printf format [ , exp ... ]
```
The values of each *exp* are computed and substituted into the string *format* according to the rules for the `printf` C library function.

```
next
```
Processing of the remainder of the current statement, and all remaining statements in the `awk` program, are immediately bypassed. Processing continues in the normal fashion with the next input line.

```
exit
```
Processing of the input file and the `awk` program are immediately terminated.

Table *7.1. awk Expression Operators*

Operator	Meaning
+	Addition
-	Subtraction
*	Multiply
/	Division
%	Remainder (modulus)
(sp)	Concatenation of string values
++	Increment
—	Decrement
+=	Add to variable
-=	Subtract from variable
*=	Multiply variable by exp
/=	Divide variable by exp

Unlike C, the following relational operators cannot be used in an assignment expression:

```
==
```

```
!=
```

```
<
```

```
>

<=

>=
```

There are a number of built-in variables, the values of which are automatically assigned and maintained by awk itself. These variables follow:

FS
: The field separator character as specified by the -F command-line option. Its default value is the space character.

FILENAME
: The pathname of the current input file, either as supplied to awk in the *filename* arguments of the command line, or - if input is being taken from the standard input file.

NF
: The number of fields in the current input line, that is, the highest value of $n defined for the current line.

NR
: The line number of the current input line.

OFMT
: The format for numbers written with the print instruction, %.6g by default.

OFS
: The output field separator, printed by print for each occurrence of a comma. The default value of OFS is the space character.

ORS
: The output record separator, printed by print at the end of each line written. The default value of ORS is the newline character.

awk also recognizes a number of built-in functions that can be used wherever an expression is permitted, including in the *pattern* part of a statement. These functions follow:

length(exp)
: The length in characters of the string representation of *exp*.

split(s,a[,d])
: The *s* string is split into fields using the first character of the string value of *d*, or the value of FS if the *d* argument is omitted. Each of the fields is stored into successive elements of the array named *a* starting with element 1. The value of the function is the number of fields stored. Thus, split("10/16/91",dt,"/") has a

value of 3, and causes the following
assignments to be made:

```
dt[1] = 10
dt[2] = 16
dt[3] = 91
```

substr(s,m[,n])

The value of the substr function is the
sequence of characters in the string value
of *s* beginning at the *m*th character (relative to 1) and extending for a length of *n*
characters. If the argument *n* is omitted,
the remaining length of the *s* string is
taken. Thus, the value of
substr("abcdef",3) is cdef, but the
value of substr("abcdef",3,2) is cd.

index(s1,s2)

The value of the index function is the
integer offset in the s1 string of the first
occurrence of the s2 string, or 0 if the s2
string does not occur in s1. For example,
substr("abcdef","cd") returns the
value 2.

sprintf(format[,arg...])

The value returned by the sprintf
function is the string resulting from
substitution of the *arg* values into the
format string. The rules for coding the
format string are the same as for the
printf C library function.

getline

The value returned by the getline
function is 0 if end-of-file occurred when
the function tried to read the next input
line, or 1 if the next input line was read
successfully. The NR built-in variable is
changed to reflect the record number of
the line just read, the value of $0 is set to
the value of the line just read, and the
variables $1, $2,... are set to the respective
fields of the line. Note: the getline
function requires no argument list; the
getline() expression generates a syntax
error.

Simple Applications

Because of awk's built-in processing cycle, useful programs are often quite short. The following sample awk program demonstrates the use of awk to reformat a file. It will print the /etc/passwd file in a more readable form, showing only the user name, user-ID, group-ID, and home directory. The output is displayed in a neat columnar format.

```
awk -F: 'BEGIN {OFS="\t"}
{print $1, $3, $4, $6}' /etc/passwd
```

This single command is spread over two lines because the awk program, which is specified here on the command line, contains two statements. The entire program is contained between apostrophes; the shell considers a newline occurring within a quoted string to be part of the string, so awk sees the command-line program as two lines.

The first statement, BEGIN {OFS="\t"}, uses the special pattern BEGIN to tell awk that the action should be processed before reading the first line of input. This is a handy way to perform any initialization that the program may need. In this example, the required initialization is to set the output field separator character used by the print instruction to the tab character. Note that within string literals, awk recognizes backslash sequences such as \n and \t just like the C language.

The second statement, {print $1, $3, $4, $6}, has no pattern, which causes awk to execute the action for every input line. Sample output from the program follows. I think you would agree that it is a lot more readable than the /etc/passwd file itself.

```
root      0     3     /
daemon    1     12    /
bin       2     2     /usr/local
sys       3     3     /usr/adm
adm       4     4     /usr/adm
uucp      5     3     /usr/lib/uucp
nuucp     6     3     /usr/spool/uucppublic
Unixric   7     3     /usr/spool/uucppublic
CMF       10    10    /u/CMF
sync      67    1     /
lp        71    4     /usr/spool/lp
jjv       100   7     /u/jjv
nsh       101   7     /u/nsh
prof      102   1     /u/prof
tlvv      103   7     /u/tlvv
cmf       104   10    /u/cmf
bbs       105   7     /u/bbs
server    107   15    /u/server
```

awk can be used to analyze a file in various ways. In such applications, the output from awk might be information that was not contained in the input file at all. When the following awk program

```
{ if ($3 > maxuid) maxuid = $3; }
END {print "Highest user-ID = " maxuid}
```

is executed with the following command

```
awk -F: -f maxuid /etc/passwd
```

it prints the message

```
Highest user-ID = 107
```

This program uses another special pattern, END, to specify an action that should be performed after the last input line is processed. The action is simple enough: print a string literal followed by the value of a variable.

The value of the maxuid variable is computed by the first statement of the program. Having no pattern, the first statement is executed for every input line. The action is just to test whether the third field of the input line ($3) is larger than the current value of maxuid, and if so, to save the new higher value in maxuid. Note, though, that the program contains no instructions to initialize the value of maxuid to 0. Such instructions are unnecessary because awk automatically considers an undefined variable to be initially the null string, or if used numerically, the value 0.

Let's look at a different kind of problem: file editing. As you will see in the section on sed later in this chapter, there are other tools than awk for editing files. Because of its computational power, though, awk is sometimes the better choice. Consider the problem of resequencing a column of numbers in a file. For our example, we will assume that the set of user-ID numbers in the /etc/passwd file has become haphazard, and we want to assign new numbers. Ignoring other considerations, here is an awk program that will do just that:

```
BEGIN   { FS=":"; OFS=":" }
        { $3 = uid++; print }
```

You might be surprised by the brevity of this program. Its simplicity is the result of capitalizing on a poorly documented feature of awk.

The initialization code, namely {FS=":"; OFS=":"}, sets the input field separator (the FS variable) to the colon so that the -F: flag need not be specified on the awk command itself; this is a convenience for the user and need not be specified in the program. The OFS assignment forces the output field separator (OFS) to be the colon also, and this *is* necessary to write the output file in the proper format.

The second statement is executed for all input lines because it has a null pattern. The action consists of two instructions:

```
$3 = uid++;
```

which assigns the value of the third input field to the current value of a counter. The ++ operator increments the uid variable, but not until after the variable's current value is assigned. I chose this technique based on the assumption that the first line of the /etc/passwd file defines the user root, which absolutely *must* have a user-ID of 0. The second instruction simply prints the input line.

At first sight, it would appear that the assignment to the $3 variable is without effect, because the variable is not subsequently used. Remember, however, that awk immediately splits an input record into fields upon reading it. The implication is that the value of $0 is *defined* to be the collection of all $n variables, and the print instruction simply prints the value of $0 if given no operands. Consequently, the effect of the assignment is to alter the appearance of the original input record, which is then used to full effect by the print instruction.

If you were not aware of the effect of an assignment to a $n variable, you might have been inclined to write the program as follows:

```
BEGIN    { FS=":"; OFS=":" }
         { print $1, $2, uid, $4, $5, $6, $7; uid = uid + 1; }
```

This version is not only more work to write, it is also inferior to the original version. The original version of the program supports an indefinite number of fields on the line, and will even work correctly when a line contains comments; it also uses the more terse ++ operator to good effect.

expr

The expr command finds little practical application at the keyboard; it is used almost exclusively as a tool for extending the capabilities of the shell. Both the C shell and the Korn shell provide some arithmetic capability. The Bourne shell does not, and it is in the Bourne shell that the math functions of expr are most used.

Arithmetic Expressions

Enter the following command (note that the spaces are necessary):

```
expr 2 + 3 \* 5
```

The number 17 is displayed. Now enter the command

```
num1=`expr 2 + 3 \* 5`
```

This time, nothing is displayed. But if you type the following command:

```
$ echo $num1
17
$ _
```

you will see that the value 17 has been assigned to the num1 variable. Now type

```
expr 2 \* 3 + 5
```

and note the result; the screen should display 11. Finally, enter the following command:

```
expr 2 \* \( 3 + 5 \)
```

If you have typed the command correctly, paying special attention to the backslash sequences, you will see the number 16 displayed.

The point of all this is to show that expr is a formula calculator. It follows the standard operator priority rules, performing multiplication and division before addition and subtraction, and treating expressions in parentheses in the normal manner. The output of expr can be assigned to a shell variable using the back-quote operator (`). The expr command can be used to write a small shell program, which you can type at your keyboard, as follows:

```
$ n=5
$ while [ $n -gt 0 ]
> do
> echo $n
> n=`expr $n - 1`
> done
5
4
3
2
1
$ _
```

Unfortunately, this little program doesn't run very quickly. The system has to start a new process to run expr for every iteration of the loop.

You now know two things about expr: it can evaluate arithmetic expressions, and it should be used sparingly because it is slow. After a little experimentation, you would probably discover on your own the set of operators supported by expr. They are listed in table 7.2.

Table 7.2. *Arithmetic Operators Supported by expr*

Operator	Meaning
+	Addition
-	Subtraction
*	Multiplication
/	Integer division
%	Integer remainder (modulus)
( )	Grouping
=	Equality
!=	Inequality
>	Greater than
<	Less than
>=	Greater than or equal to
<=	Less than or equal to

The relational operators display 1 if the relation is true, or 0 if the relation is false. Thus:

```
expr 2 = 3
```

prints 0 (meaning false), and

```
expr 4 != 5
```

prints 1 (meaning true).

There are two rules to remember when using `expr`:

1. Each numeric term and each operator in the expression must be a separate argument. If you try to enclose the expression in quotation marks to save typing, for example by entering

   ```
   expr '2 * ( 3 + 5 )'
   ```

   the output will not be what you expect (try it). Your only choice, then, is between backslashing and quoting each occurrence of a shell metacharacter in the expression.

2. The `expr` command can set a nonzero exit value even when it generates an otherwise valid result. For example, `expr` returns an exit value of 1 when the result of a subtraction is 0, which can cause unexpected side effects in a shell program, especially if you sometimes issue the `set -e` option to catch command processing errors.

String Expressions

The capabilities of `expr` include string operations as well as arithmetic calculations. For users of the C and Korn shells, the string handling capabilities will probably be more important than the arithmetic capabilities.

The most frequently used string operation is the : operator, which compares its two arguments. The first argument must be a literal string. The second argument must be a regular expression. The \(and \) metacharacters can be used to extract a substring from the first argument, as in the example

```
expr filename.ext : '[^.]*\.\(.*\)'
```

This prints the string `ext`.

Regular expressions often look very strange and can be quite difficult to read. Let's take a closer look at the regular expression in the preceding example.

The `[^.]` characters define a single-character expression, which is a character set. This RE will match any single character that is not a period. It is used to start the RE because, to find the file name suffix, we need to skip all characters up to the first period; this expression, however, recognizes only one character.

The next term, `*`, means "zero or more occurrences of the previous," and in this case the `*` applies to the `[^.]` expression. Its effect is to apply the `[^.]` RE until it fails to match an input character. Although `[^.]` by itself recognizes only the *f* in `filename.ext`, the `[^.]*` RE recognizes *filename* and stops at the following period.

The next term, `\.`, is backslashed because we want `expr` to recognize the period in the input string; without the backslash, `expr` would construe the period to mean *any character*, not just the dot.

Up to this point, the `[^.]*\.` RE has recognized the `filename.` string in the input string. The remainder of the string is the file name's suffix, and we want the suffix to be the output from `expr`. Consequently, the remaining expression is of the form `\(...\)` to cause `expr` to *remember* the string it finds in the parentheses.

The last part of the RE, namely `.*` between the backslashed parentheses, is the string that `expr` is to recognize. But the `.` is the operator meaning *any character,* and the `*` character causes any number of periods to be recognized. Consequently, `expr` will recognize any character string from this point.

Let's try this same `\(...\)` expression on some more examples. The command

```
expr aabcdefaa : 'aa\([a-z]*\)aa'
```

prints `bcdef`, and the command

```
expr aaabcaaa : 'aa\([a-z]*\)aa'
```

prints `abca`. In both cases, the `aa\([a-z]*\)aa` regular expression told `expr` to recognize a string starting and ending with `aa`, and to remember (and therefore print) whatever lowercase letters occur between `aa` and `aa`. For the `aaabcaaa` input string, `expr` is not confused by the leading `aaa` because it is looking for two initial and two trailing *a*'s; finding those, it is easy to extract the remaining alphabetic characters between them.

At this point, you are probably starting to catch on. The `expr` command is particularly adept at recognizing a string and returning any subpart of the string. The goal in writing a regular expression is to identify *all* the characters in the string, and to surround the part of the regular expression that recognizes the characters in which we are interested by the symbols `\(\)`.

In the `expr` expression `string : string`, the second string need not contain a `\(\)` operator. If it does not, `expr` prints the number of characters matched by the RE given as the second string. For example:

```
expr filename.ext : '.*'
```

prints `12` because that is the number of characters in the string `filename.ext`, and the `.*` RE recognizes any sequence of characters. The command invocation

```
expr bigboy : big
```

prints `3` because three characters in `bigboy` were matched before the pattern expression `big` was exhausted.

There are many practical applications of the `expr` command. Perhaps the most familiar application is the `basename` command, which extracts the file name part of a path. You might find it interesting to try writing an `expr` command to return the file name portion of a path. This problem has already been solved, though, in the `basename` shell script, which is a part of any UNIX system. (You didn't realize that the `basename` command is a shell script? Many UNIX commands are implemented as shell scripts, following the rule set forth at the beginning of this chapter: *Write in a compiled language only as a matter of last resort.* A shell script is the preferred implementation except when functionality or performance requirements prohibit it.)

On my system, the basename shell script contains the following statements:

```
A=${1-.}
A=`expr //$A : "\(.*\)\/$" \¦ $A`
B=`expr //$A : ´.*/\(.*\)´`
expr $B : "\(.*\)$2$" \¦ $B
```

This script is every bit as difficult to understand as it looks. I leave it to you to figure out what it is really doing.

sed

I think everyone tends to approach sed, the "stream editor," with some reluctance. This is easily understood by scanning the manual page for sed in the commands section of the UNIX manual. The text is terse, sometimes opaque, and often impenetrable. If you scan the manual page, you will undoubtedly see mention of a *pattern space* sprinkled throughout the text, but at no time will you see a definition of this term.

In fact, you would do best to avoid the standard documentation for sed. As long as you have some understanding of regular expressions, the operation of the command is straightforward.

sed is an editor. Unlike most editors, the sed user interface was designed with the expectation that editing commands would not be entered directly from the console. Rather, editing commands for sed must be placed in a text file, or entered on the command line, and are executed automatically while sed is running. In other words, sed is a batch program, whereas most other text editors are interactive.

Because of the poor documentation for sed, as well as the nonintuitive operation of many of its functions, most of the program's capabilities are rarely used. There are four sed functions with which I would like you to be intimately familiar: d, used to delete lines from the input file; p, to print lines from the input file; q, to quit the sed editor before reaching the end of the input file; and s, to substitute one string for another in one, some, or all of the input lines. If you have the time and patience, study some of the other sed functions, but you should feel assured that if you know the four functions I mentioned, you will be able to do as much with sed as most people.

The syntax of the substitute function is

```
s/RE/text/[flags]
```

where *RE* must be a regular expression, *text* is any substitution text to replace the string matching *RE*, and *flags* (an optional operand) modifies the behavior of the substitute function in one of several ways.

For our first sample problem, we will try an exercise in renaming files. Suppose a number of files in your current directory end in *.txt*, and you would like to rename these files so that the suffix of each is changed to *.asc*.

The brute-force method would be to sit down at the keyboard and enter the following series of commands:

```
mv history.txt history.asc
mv geography.txt geography.asc
mv math.txt math.asc
...
```

You would repeat the mv operation until all files have been renamed. Obviously, the brute-force method requires a lot of redundant typing, which is not only error-prone, but worse, wastes a lot of your precious time. (You should think of your time as precious; your employer does!)

One solution you might try for this problem would be

```
$ for FILE in *.txt
> do
> fn=`basename $FILE .txt`
> mv $fn.txt $fn.asc
> done
$ _
```

A more efficient way to do this job, though, is to use the sed command. Look at the following pipeline:

```
ls *.txt | sed 's/\([^.]*\)\.txt/mv \1.txt \1.asc/' | sh -v
```

The thinking behind this pipeline is as follows:

❏ Use the ls command to get a list of all the files ending in *.txt*

❏ Using sed, for each occurrence of *x*.txt substitute the string
   mv *x*.txt *x*.asc

❏ Pipe the resulting tailored mv commands to the shell for execution. The -v option is not required; it merely causes the shell to list each command it executes, which in this case gives a visual display of each mv command as it is executed.

Looking at the sed command, you should find the \([^.]*\) subexpression familiar from the section on expr earlier in this chapter. The [^.]* expression matches all leading characters of the input line that are not periods, and the

\(...\) phrase causes sed to remember the matching text in the pseudo-register \1. The remainder of the RE, namely \.txt, is present to cause sed to replace the entire file name with the text following the second slash.

The mv \1.txt \1.asc replacement string simply uses the \1 register, which was set in the RE, to construct the mv command.

Let's look at a slightly different example. For some reason, you'd like to discover the user name and group-ID of the current user. You could check the value of the LOGNAME environment, but the user can set the value of LOGNAME to any value, so LOGNAME is not reliable. You could look at the output of the command

```
who am i
```

but it shows the name under which the user logged in, which is not necessarily the real user-ID. So for these and other reasons, you decide that the values you need are those shown by the id command, which generates an output line similar to the following:

```
uid=101(jjv) gid=7(user)
```

But this output is not in a usable format. The shell statement you need is

```
set `id | sed something`
```

which would set $1 and $2 to the values jjv and user, respectively. The problem, then, is to convert the string

```
uid=101(jjv) gid=7(user)
```

into the jjv user string.

The sed command you are looking for is this:

```
sed 's/uid=[0-9]*(\([^)]*\))/\1/
s/gid=[0-9]*(\([^)]*\))/\1/'
```

This command spans two lines, so the sed command sees two edit commands. Remember, according to the Bourne shell rules, when a newline occurs within a quoted string, the newline is also considered part of the string.

The sed command line can specify more than one function. This is only reasonable, if we think of sed as a batch-mode file editor. What is unusual about these two consecutive functions is that they both apply to the same input line. There are ways to restrict the scope of edit functions so that some functions apply to one range of lines in the input file, and other functions apply to a different range, but I haven't shown you how to do that yet. Without instructions to the contrary, sed simply applies all edit functions to the current input line, reads the next input line, and repeats all the edit functions on that line as well.

The first of the two substitute functions, namely:

```
s/uid=[0-9]*(\([^)]*\)))/\1/
```

consists of the regular expression `uid=[0-9]*(\([^)]*\))`, and the replacement text `\1`. The pattern itself is in the general form `uid=`*num*`(`*value*`)` where *num* is represented by `[0-9]*` and *value*, which is the user-ID string we are looking for, is represented by the `[^)]*` RE.

As in past examples, the `[...]*` character-set RE was chosen to identify a variable in the input text. The problem in writing any such regular expression is to choose the best way to typify a particular character string. By the time `sed` scans through `uid=[0-9](` it will have already identified the opening parenthesis preceding the user's name, so I can safely say that any character string up to the closing parenthesis is the user's name. The `[^)]*` RE does just that by repeatedly collecting characters from the input until a character that violates the character-set rule I have chosen, namely a `)` character, is found. To make the substitution pattern complete, I need to enclose the part of the character string in which I'm interested in `\(...\)`. Thus, `\([^)]*\)` is the tail of the pattern that begins `uid=[0-9]*(`.

To summarize, the first substitution function replaces the `uid=101(jjv)` string with the `jjv` string, and the second substitution function replaces the `gid=7(user)` string with the `user` string.

As is always the case, `sed` writes the modified text lines to standard output. By enclosing the `sed` command in back quotes like so:

```
`id | sed ...`
```

the output of `sed` becomes text that can be substituted on a shell command line. So by writing

```
set `id | sed ...`
```

in the shell script, the shell replaces the back-quoted pipeline with the output

```
set jjv user
```

and assigns the `jjv` string to the `$1` shell variable, and the `user` string to the `$2` shell variable. Mission accomplished.

Another useful `sed` feature is the capability to delete lines of an input file. Suppose that you are doing program development with the SCCS facility described in Chapter 5, "Program Maintenance." Your working directory will contain several files with names in the general format `s.filename.c`, assuming that you are working with the C language.

To compile a set of files administrated by SCCS, you have to issue the `get` command to retrieve a copy of the current version of each file. When you do

so, you will have two sets of files in the current directory, one named
s.*filename*.c and one named *filename*.c. When the compile job is finished,
it is a good idea to get rid of the temporary copies of the SCCS files. But if you
just issue the command

```
rm *.c
```

you will have a problem when rm tries to delete the write-protected s.*.c files,
which also end with .c.

What to do? Generate a list of all the files ending in .c, then delete lines that
begin with s. from the list. The command line to do this task is

```
rm `ls *.c | sed '/^s\./d'`
```

This sed edit script consists of one function, d. Whereas the substitute
function took a long list of values after the s, there is nothing with which to
modify the d function; to delete is to delete. However, we don't want to delete
every line in the input file (which is the output of the ls command). The /RE/
expression, called an *address*, restricts the range of input lines to which the
function applies—to lines beginning with s. in this example. Notice that the
specified RE, /^s\./, backslashes the period, because the s. pattern would
match lines beginning with s and followed by any character, which is not what
we want.

Several forms of line addressing are supported by sed. The syntax of each
is described in the following:

n	Applies the edit function to line number *n*. For example, 5d deletes line number 5.
n1,n2	Applies the edit function to all lines numbered *n1* through *n2* inclusive. For example, 5,10d deletes lines 5 through 10 of the input file.
n,$	Applies the edit function to all lines starting at line number *n* and continuing through the end of the file. The $ symbol means "end of file," whatever line number that may be.
/RE/	Applies the edit function to all lines where the regular expression, *RE*, matches any part of the line. The /^RE/ notation can be used to restrict *RE* to match only text at the start of the line, and the /RE$/ notation restricts the match of *RE* to occur only at the end of the line.

You should note that the use of addressing is allowed with the s (substitution) function, described in the previous section, as well as the d (delete)
function.

The q function causes sed to abandon reading of the input file and to exit immediately. It would make little sense to code the q function without an address; sed would quit immediately after processing the first line of the input file. Consequently, the quit function is always used in the form *address*q.

Try entering the following command at your terminal:

```
sed 5q /etc/passwd
```

You will immediately see the first five lines of the /etc/passwd file. This experiment demonstrates that the quit function takes effect only *after* sed has processed the addressed line.

Some versions of UNIX include as one of the standard utilities a head command, which prints the front lines of a file. This is in contrast to the tail command, which prints the last lines of a file. If you don't have a head command on your system, you might try to implement the command using the quit function of sed as the working basis.

The sed command implements the p function, used to print selected lines of the input file. Keep in mind, though, that sed prints every line it processes by default, except lines that are deleted. The command

```
sed 5,10p
```

prints every line of the input file once, and lines 5 through 10 twice. To get around this problem, use the -n option of the sed command, as follows:

```
sed -n 5,10p /etc/passwd
```

to print only lines 5 through 10 of the password file.

The print function can be used to implement a shell script that prints selective ranges of a file. When using the print function this way, remember that sed always processes all of the input lines, even if you don't print them. When printing from a large file, you might notice a significant pause after the last line is printed but before the sed command ends; this pause is caused by sed working its way through the thousands of lines remaining in the file that you didn't want to see.

To print only a selected range of lines, and to quit processing at the end of the range, you need to use both the print and the quit functions, as follows:

```
sed -n ´5,10p;10q´ bigfile
```

This version of the command executes a lot faster than the version specifying only the print function.

The command

```
sed -n ´5,$p;10q´ bigfile
```

gives the same result as the preceding example because each s e d function is applied to every line of b i g f i l e. Although the 5,$p function would print from line 5 through the end of b i g f i l e, the 10q function operates independently of the print function, and forces s e d to abandon processing after the tenth line.

Notice that the last example uses a semicolon to separate the functions of the edit script; previously I had mentioned only the use of newlines to separate functions. The semicolon can be a handy way to separate short, simple functions, but breaking a s e d script into multiple lines greatly enhances its readability when the functions are long and complex.

sort

The s o r t command is a basic tool for all users, yet its command syntax is clumsy and difficult to understand. Trying to work with a limited and inadequate understanding of the s o r t command is like trying to work with one hand tied behind your back. In this section, I will explain how to use the s o r t command effectively. The discussion is brief and the material is difficult, so I urge you to complement the explanations given here with careful study of the manual description and ample experimentation.

To aid the discussion, let's assume that you have the following data stored in a file called c o m p u t e r s:

```
Salamander   386SX     22.7     80     1499     Aug 87
Baker        286-20    22.4     40     2199     Aug 88
Baker        286-12    18.5     40     1375     Jul 88
Electra      XT/10     7.9      20     850      Jun 90
Xanthus      386       24.0     100    2250     Mar 89
CompuTech    486/25    41.5     350    7999     Mar 88
```

This sample file contains data you might use when comparison shopping for a personal computer.

Left to right, the columns are

Manufacturer's name (fictitious, of course)

Model name

Machine's performance as a numerical rating

Hard disk size included with the quoted price

Quoted price for the machine

Month of the magazine issue that describes the machine

Year of the magazine issue that describes the machine

Each line of the file contains seven fields (columns). You might want to sort the computers file by price (field 5), by performance rating (field 3), or if you want to go through your stack of magazines and review each machine, by month and date of issue. The sort command can sort the computers file in any of these orders, if you specify the proper options on the command line.

Fortunately, useful work can be accomplished with the sort command even with no options specified on the command line. When no options are specified, sort compares the entire text of each line to determine the proper ordering of the output file. When run against the sample data file, the command

```
sort computers
```

produces the following output:

```
Baker        286-12     18.5     40      1375      Jul 88
Baker        286-20     22.4     40      2199      Aug 88
CompuTech    486/25     41.5     350     7999      Mar 88
Electra      XT/10      7.9      20      850       Jun 90
Salamander   386SX      22.7     80      1499      Aug 87
Xanthus      386        24.0     100     2250      Mar 89
```

If you compare this output with the original file, you will see that not only have the lines been grouped by manufacturer but, where there are two or more lines for the same manufacturer (such as is the case for the Baker company), the model numbers have been ranked. Because the command line contained no options, sort considers each line to be one long field, and continues comparing similar lines until a difference is found between the texts of the two lines.

To put the file into a different order, we have to tell the sort program which fields of each line should be considered to determine the output order. To name a field, the sort program must be given two pieces of information: the relative location in the input line where the field begins, and the location where it ends. That is, the command line must specify a pair of options +*b* and -*e*, where +*b* is the beginning field location and -*e* is the ending field location. You must type the + and – immediately before the field numbers, and the two options must be separated by at least one space or tab on the command line.

The sort command numbers fields starting with 0. For the sample computers file, the first field is field 0, and the last field is field 6.

The following command will sort the lines of the computers file into order according to the price column:

```
sort +4 -5 computer
```

If you can train yourself to think not in terms of the columns of information, but rather in terms of the gaps between the columns, you will find it easier to understand this command line; in these terms, the command line specifies that the file will be sorted according to the data lying to the right of the fourth gap, and to the left of the fifth gap.

The output of the command looks like this:

```
Baker           286-12      18.5        40      1375        Jul  88
Salamander      386SX       22.7        80      1499        Aug  87
Baker           286-20      22.4        40      2199        Aug  88
Electra         XT/10        7.9        20       850        Jun  90
Xanthus         386         24.0       100      2250        Mar  89
CompuTech       486/25      41.5       350      7999        Mar  88
```

Check the fifth column of output. Every line is in the proper order except the line for the Electra computer. Why? The sort program allows only one blank to separate the columns; blanks to the right of the first blank are considered part of the field. That is, the sort program actually views the file as follows:

```
Baker¦          286-12¦     18.5¦       40¦     1375¦       Jul¦88
Salamander¦     386SX¦      22.7¦       80¦     1499¦       Aug¦87
Baker¦          286-20¦     22.4¦       40¦     2199¦       Aug¦88
Electra¦        XT/10¦       7.9¦       20¦      850¦       Jun¦90
Xanthus¦        386¦        24.0¦      100¦     2250¦       Mar¦89
CompuTech¦      486/25¦     41.5¦      350¦     7999¦       Mar¦88
```

I have changed each blank that the sort program considers to be a *field delimiter* with ¦; other blanks are treated as part of the field. If you align the price field as the sort program does when sorting the file, you'll see the following:

```
Baker¦          286-12¦     18.5¦       40¦     1375¦       Jul¦88
  Salamander¦   386SX¦      22.7¦       80¦     1499¦       Aug¦87
  Baker¦          286-20¦   22.4¦       40¦     2199¦       Aug¦88
    Electra¦    XT/10¦       7.9¦       20¦      850¦       Jun¦90
Xanthus¦        386¦        24.0¦      100¦     2250¦       Mar¦89
CompuTech¦      486/25¦     41.5¦      350¦     7999¦       Mar¦88
```

In the ASCII character set, the blank character sorts ahead of any other character, so now it is clear why sort has chosen this particular ordering.

We didn't really want sort to consider blanks as part of the field when sorting the file. To tell sort to ignore leading or trailing blank characters in each field, you must append the b modifier to either the begin or end option, to tell sort to ignore blanks at the beginning or end of the field. For example:

```
sort +4b -5 computers
```

will yield the following sorted output:

```
Baker         286-12      18.5       40       1375        Jul  88
Salamander    386SX       22.7       80       1499        Aug  87
Baker         286-20      22.4       40       2199        Aug  88
Xanthus       386         24.0      100       2250        Mar  89
CompuTech     486/25      41.5      350       7999        Mar  88
Electra       XT/10        7.9       20        850        Jun  90
```

This output is closer to what we expected, but still not quite right. Notice that sort has carefully lined up the first characters of the price field in ascending order; when two adjacent lines start with the same digit, they are then ordered by the second digit, and so on. The reason that the file is still not correctly sorted is because sort has compared the consecutive price fields as if they contained string data, whereas we really wanted sort to order the lines in numeric sequence.

The n modifier character can be appended to a field option to specify that the field should be sorted in numeric order instead of the default alphanumeric order. The command

```
sort +4n -5 computers
```

will finally yield the desired result:

```
Electra       XT/10        7.9       20        850        Jun  90
Baker         286-12      18.5       40       1375        Jul  88
Salamander    386SX       22.7       80       1499        Aug  87
Baker         286-20      22.4       40       2199        Aug  88
Xanthus       386         24.0      100       2250        Mar  89
CompuTech     486/25      41.5      350       7999        Mar  88
```

Notice that I did not provide the b flag on the field option. The b flag is unnecessary when comparing fields numerically. Consequently, options such as +4bn are never necessary and can always be simplified to +4n.

Having successfully sorted the file on an integer numeric field, let's try something else. The command

```
sort +2n -3 computers
```

is our first attempt to sort the file according to performance rating. The output from the command looks like this:

```
Electra       XT/10        7.9       20        850        Jun  90
Baker         286-12      18.5       40       1375        Jul  88
Baker         286-20      22.4       40       2199        Aug  88
Salamander    386SX       22.7       80       1499        Aug  87
Xanthus       386         24.0      100       2250        Mar  89
CompuTech     486/25      41.5      350       7999        Mar  88
```

Notice that the line for the Salamander model 386SX was sorted correctly after the Baker model 286-20 computer. The sort utility supports numbers with decimal points as well as integer numbers. Although our sample file contains no example, `sort` will correctly order signed decimal numbers, ordering numbers with a leading minus sign ahead of numbers without a minus sign.

All the examples we have examined so far sort files in ascending order, where lower valued fields appear first in the output file, followed by higher valued fields. The opposite ordering can be requested by appending the `r` modifier to a field specification. The command

```
sort +3nr -4 computers
```

sorts the file in reverse sequence according to disk size. Here is the result:

```
CompuTech    486/25    41.5    350    7999    Mar 88
Xanthus      386       24.0    100    2250    Mar 89
Salamander   386SX     22.7    80     1499    Aug 87
Baker        286-12    18.5    40     1375    Jul 88
Baker        286-20    22.4    40     2199    Aug 88
Electra      XT/10     7.9     20     850     Jun 90
```

The standard `sort` command can even sort a field containing the month names into proper order. For example, using the `M` flag in the command

```
sort +5bM -6 computers
```

produces the following ordering:

```
CompuTech    486/25    41.5    350    7999    Mar 88
Xanthus      386       24.0    100    2250    Mar 89
Electra      XT/10     7.9     20     850     Jun 90
Baker        286-12    18.5    40     1375    Jul 88
Baker        286-20    22.4    40     2199    Aug 88
Salamander   386SX     22.7    80     1499    Aug 87
```

Frequently, more than one field needs to be considered when sorting the file, as in the preceding example. Rarely would you want to sort on the month field alone; normally, the year number would be considered first, and the month would determine ordering only between records with the same year. A more normal sorting of the file by month within year follows:

```
Salamander   386SX     22.7    80     1499    Aug 87
CompuTech    486/25    41.5    350    7999    Mar 88
Baker        286-12    18.5    40     1375    Jul 88
Baker        286-20    22.4    40     2199    Aug 88
Xanthus      386       24.0    100    2250    Mar 89
Electra      XT/10     7.9     20     850     Jun 90
```

This is obtained by listing multiple sort fields on the command line. The command

```
sort +6n -7 +5Mb -6 computers
```

achieves the desired result. The first pair of arguments (+6n -7) specifies the year number as the major sort field, and the second pair of arguments (+5Mb -6) specifies the month as the minor sort field. The sort command imposes no arbitrary limit on the number of sort fields that can be specified on a single command line.

Notice that different modifier flags can be used on each sort field; you can even sort some fields in ascending order and others in reversed order. The command

```
sort +3nr -4 +4n -5 computers
```

sorts the file in descending order by disk size, and for lines having the same disk size (such as the two 40Mb entries), sorts the lines in ascending order by price. The following output is produced:

```
CompuTech     486/25     41.5      350     7999     Mar 88
Xanthus       386        24.0      100     2250     Mar 89
Salamander    386SX      22.7      80      1499     Aug 87
Baker         286-12     18.5      40      1375     Jul 88
Baker         286-20     22.4      40      2199     Aug 88
Electra       XT/10      7.9       20      850      Jun 90
```

There are many additional features of the sort utility:

❏ The notation +m.n or -m.n can be used to select a portion of a field for determining the sort order

❏ Dictionary ordering of a field can be obtained by using the d flag

❏ The f flag can be used to cause sort to ignore case distinctions in alphanumeric fields

❏ The -u flag can be used at the beginning of the command line to cause sort to discard lines having the same sort key (*u* stands for *unique*)

This list does not exhaust the features of the sort command. The sort command is a powerful full-featured sorting utility that will meet most of your needs.

xargs

The xargs command serves two useful purposes. First, it provides a way to get around the system limit on the number of arguments on a command line. As mentioned in Chapter 13, "Kernel Internals," arguments appearing on the command line have to be saved by the kernel while the command program is being loaded. This is because every process runs in its own private memory, yet the process that reads the command line is not the same process in which the command executes.

The kernel sets aside a buffer of 10K to 20K bytes to preserve the command line while the program is being loaded; it is not overly difficult to exceed that limit. A command such as

```
pr /usr/spool/uucppublic/receive/*/*/*
```

would be used to print all the files that are received by uucp from remote systems and that are waiting to be delivered to users at the local system. If there were 600 such files, and each had a path name length of about 50 bytes (which is not unreasonable because the starting path name is 30 characters long), the total length of the command line would exceed 30K bytes.

The second use of the xargs command is to generate a series of commands from a list of file names or other information. A need for this kind of facility often arises during day-to-day computing, but unless you are familiar with the xargs command, you will waste a lot of time generating commands by hand or with an editor.

The basic method of operation of xargs is to read successive lines from the standard input file, break the lines into words separated by white space, reassemble the words into commands, then pass the generated commands to the shell one by one for execution.

To give a simple example, let's show what xargs does with a list of file names. Enter the command

```
ls | xargs echo cmd
```

You should see one long line displayed, similar in format to the following:

```
cmd clock.c fs.h fs_daemon.c fs_get.c fs_ipc.c fs_main.c fs_put.c fs_share.c
```

Notice how the file names that are output by ls have been collected into a single command line following the arguments that appeared on the xargs command line. The command lines generated by xargs differ from those generated by the shell with wild cards in one important respect: xargs will not build a command line longer than some reasonable upper limit; if the command line would exceed the length limitation, xargs distributes the file name list over two generated command lines.

Although xargs supports a variety of options for controlling command line formatting, which we will examine in a moment, even the basic functionality just shown can be quite useful. For example, it provides a handy way to check for common file names in two directories, using the following command:

```
cd system1; ls | (cd ../system2; xargs ls 2>/dev/null)
```

The list of file names generated by the first `ls` command is converted by `xargs` into a series of explicit `ls` commands, which are then executed in the other directory. Files that cannot be found result in the printing of the error message `filename not found`; the redirection `2>/dev/null` throws away these messages. The only output seen at your terminal is the list of files found by the `xargs`-generated `ls` commands.

Sometimes you don't want a long list of file names appended to the command to be executed. You can use the `-n` option of `xargs` to limit the number of arguments placed on a generated command line. For example, suppose you would like to print the first five lines of every file in your current working directory. The command to do this for one file, as we saw in the section on `sed`, is

```
sed 5q filename
```

But if multiple file names are listed on the command line, `sed` will still print only the first five lines of the first file. To do the job, you must enter the following command:

```
ls ¦ xargs -n1 sed 5q
```

The n1 means one argument per line, and causes `xargs` to generate the following series of commands:

```
sed 5q filename1
sed 5q filename2
sed 5q ...
sed 5q filenameN
```

Notice that so far in this discussion of `xargs`, the commands to be generated consisted of a constant front part, to be followed by one or more names that were simply appended to form the command. Sometimes commands require a different format. For example, we might want to copy an automatically generated list of files to a specified directory. The command to do this task follows:

```
cp filename1 filename2 ... dirname
```

Unfortunately, this doesn't match the `xargs` style of generating commands. The solution is to use the `-i` option of `xargs`.

The following `xargs` command:

```
xargs -iF cp F dirname
```

causes `xargs` to substitute one word from standard input for each occurrence of the letter `F` in the command line. If the input to `xargs` consisted of the lines:

```
main.c
parser.y
scan.l
```

then the commands generated by xargs would be:

```
cp main.c dirname
cp parser.y dirname
cp scan.l dirname
```

This would achieve the desired result.

Fancier command-line manipulation is possible. The following input:

```
history
geography
chemistry
english
```

and the command:

```
xargs -i% mv %.txt %.asc
```

would result in the following series of generated commands:

```
mv history.txt history.asc
mv geography.txt geography.asc
mv chemistry.txt chemistry.asc
mv english.txt english.asc
```

Notice that the character or string following the -i option becomes an argument in the model command text that is replaced by the words input to xargs. Any string may be used as the substitution flag. For example:

```
xargs -iFILE mv FILE.txt FILE.asc
```

produces the same result as the example that used % as the flag value.

The default flag is a pair of braces ({}). The following command takes advantage of that fact:

```
xargs -i mv {}.txt {}.asc
```

Two other useful xargs options are -p and -t. The -p option causes xargs to prompt for permission to execute each generated command before passing the command to the shell. Used with the previous example, you would see the following at your terminal:

```
$ ls | xargs -p -i% mv %.txt %.asc
mv history.txt history.asc ?... y
mv geography.txt geography.asc ?... n
mv chemistry.txt chemistry.asc ?... y
mv english.txt english.asc ?... n
$ _
```

The prompt response was y for the history and chemistry files, and n for the geography and english files. Although it is not obvious from the display, the mv commands were not executed when the response was n.

With the -t (trace) option, xargs prints each generated command, but does not prompt you and executes the command after tracing it.

Applications for the xargs command arise whenever a single command needs to be executed for each of a list of arguments. The xargs command is especially useful when the command arguments already exist as part of a data file. For example, consider the need to examine the login profile of every system user; such a need might arise for the system administrator when making certain kinds of changes to the system. The following command capitalizes on the fact that the /etc/passwd file contains the path name of every user's home directory in the sixth field of each line:

```
cut -d: -f6 /etc/passwd | sed 's|$|/.profile|' | sort -u | xargs more
```

This complex command performs four processing steps:

1. Extract the sixth field of each line in the /etc/passwd file.

2. Append the /.profile string to each line.

3. Sort the resulting path names, discarding duplicates.

4. Finally, display each profile using the more command.

Now, would you have thought of using the xargs command to solve this problem? If not, let me suggest that the reason for your oversight is that you do not yet have the habit of considering xargs in your search for problem solutions. Try to build that habit by pausing to review the commands in your growing UNIX toolkit, including xargs, before choosing a solution strategy. That moment of thought, however brief, will save you much time and effort in the months and years to come.

Summary

The UNIX commands discussed in this chapter are among the more useful for writing shell scripts. The awk, sed, expr, sort, and xargs commands are more difficult to understand, and therefore more difficult to use effectively, than most commands, which is why they are singled out for attention in this chapter.

This should not be taken to imply that other commands are less useful. It would be difficult indeed to write shell scripts without using many other commands including echo, true, false, cat, grep and its related fgrep and egrep, the ubiquitous cut, the exotic join, and the file management utilities ls, cp, mv, rm, mkdir, and rmdir.

The *UNIX System User's Manual*, containing a brief description of every UNIX command, is a treasure trove of tools and utilities that you should keep handy by your desk. Browse its table of contents occasionally. Don't get stuck using the same old utilities day in and day out; add some new ones to your repertoire, to save yourself time and effort. Most important of all, don't write a new program, whether shell script or in C, until you've searched the manual for an existing command to do the job. The chances are good that the service you need is already available.

Part III

UNIX Files
and Devices

8

Introduction to
Files and Devices

In Chapter 6, "Writing a Simple Filter," we looked briefly at the basic concept of a file. We also noted that device considerations intrude on the attempt to provide a common file interface. It should not be surprising to learn that these considerations affect all levels of the file system and give rise to five different kinds of files:

- ❑ ordinary files
- ❑ directories
- ❑ block-special files
- ❑ character-special files
- ❑ pipes

In this chapter, we look at how UNIX implements these file types, and how our use of a file is affected by its type.

Ordinary Files

The first kind of file, which I will call an *ordinary* file, is used for storing data. An ordinary file is always a part of a larger structure called a *filesystem* and can exist only on certain kinds of devices, mainly disk drives. We use ordinary files for both permanent and temporary storage of information. The file can be organized for either sequential or random access, and can be considered to contain an undifferentiated stream of bytes, lines, or fixed-size structures according to our convenience. Ordinary files are the principal focus of Chapter 9, "Ordinary Files."

Directories

A second kind of file, called a *directory*, is used for grouping files together into meaningful categories, in much the same manner as we might collect important papers at home into manilla folders, keeping receipts in one folder, insurance policies in a second, and tax returns in a third. When our records become complex, we might find ourselves storing smaller folders inside larger folders. For example, we might subdivide the tax returns folder into an inner folder for each year, with the inner folders holding such things as copies of W-2 forms, interest statements from the bank, and a copy of the return itself.

Similarly, a UNIX directory can contain multiple occurrences of any file type, including other directories, so that we can keep large quantities of information out of sight when not in use, but quickly locate large collections of files when we need them. The programming and administrative aspects of directories are discussed in Chapter 10, "Directories."

Block-special Files

Both ordinary and directory files reside on disk. Another kind of file is necessary: one that represents the disk itself instead of some partition of it. This is a direct result of two propositions about UNIX that have already been described: first, all input and output under UNIX is performed in terms of files (there is no special form of I/O request for accessing devices); second, a disk contains filesystems subdivided into directories and files. Clearly some method must be available for formatting the disk.

The *block-special* file provides the basic mechanism for this. A block-special file is simply a representation of the entire disk as if it were a single very large ordinary file. Many operations supported on ordinary files are not allowed on block-special files. For example, a block-special file cannot be removed with the rm command, at least not in the same sense as an ordinary file; we can remove the definition, but the space is still there. We cannot add to the end of a block-special file because it is coextensive with the device; to add to the end would imply adding new tracks and cylinders to the disk, something that cannot be accomplished with mere programming. There are many more peculiarities to accessing block-special files; these will be discussed at length in Chapter 11, "Special Files and Pipes."

Character-special Files

Although the three types of files previously mentioned are very important, they overlook an important element of any computer's configuration: byte-oriented I/O devices. Included in this large class of devices are printers, terminals, communication lines, plotters, mice, bar-code readers, and page scanners.

UNIX lumps all these devices into a single large class called *character-special* files. The common characteristics of character-special files follow. One, they require data transfer in units of one byte or a few bytes rather than in blocks or sectors. Second, there is often no way to set or determine device positioning and certainly no common way to do so. Third, these devices are often unidirectional—able to read but not write, or to write but not read.

Little can be said in general terms about this important device class because of the diversity of devices that compose it. Chapter 11, "Special Files and Pipes," provides an introduction to character-special devices, paying special attention to the simpler kinds such as printers and magnetic-tape drives. Chapter 12, "Programming Serial Devices," addresses the more complicated subject of terminals and the interface that allows programming to support the differences between terminals.

Pipes

One other kind of file is supported by UNIX: the *pipe*. This file type was invented by UNIX developers and has proved to be a fertile addition to the theory and practice of operating system design: pipes are now a supported feature of MS-DOS and OS/2 as well, and will probably never disappear from our technical tool kit.

Pipes differ from all other kinds of files in that no peripheral device is involved in their operation. A pipe is a real-time coupling between the output of one program and the input of another, allowing data to be passed immediately from program to program without the need to temporarily store it on an external medium. This capability eliminates two complete passes of the data, one to write the data to disk and the other to read it back into the program that processes it. In addition, this capability implies that the amount of data passed between the two programs is essentially unlimited because it will never reside in its entirety on any external recording device.

Pipes were intended to streamline the traditional data processing paradigm of extract-sort-print that dominated the industry in the 1960s and 1970s. This style of application design required two intermediate files: one to hold the output of the file extract program, and the other to hold the output of the sort program. With pipes, the only data files that occupy any physical space are the original input file and the final output file. Pipes are discussed in detail in Chapter 11, "Special Files and Pipes."

File Permissions

Since UNIX is a time-sharing system, let me take a moment to explain what a time-sharing system is. You are probably familiar with single-user operating systems as exemplified by CP/M, MS-DOS, OS/2, and a host of proprietary monitors implemented on machines such as the 8-bit Atari, Commodore, and Apple. The main purpose of the single-user operating system is to hide the machine interface from the programmer by providing a group of low-level services for I/O, file management, and so on.

A time-sharing operating system is a generalization of the single-user system. Capable of executing several programs at once, the time-sharing system tends to associate every active process with a terminal. Each user at a terminal is given the impression that he or she is working with a single-user operating system, but the machine is rapidly switching from one terminal to the next, slicing its time into equal portions and doling the slices out to individual users.

With a single-user operating system, we need to have little concern with security issues. Only in time-sharing systems, where we give multiple users simultaneous access to the machine, do we need to be concerned with protecting resources from damage by unauthorized users. The mechanisms for this are tightly interwoven with the fundamental design of UNIX. As a result, you will always need to be aware of permissions whenever you are working with UNIX.

Permissions are simply the means by which users are granted access to system resources. You will encounter permissions most often in connection with files.

Associated with every file is a set of nine permission bits. You can see these bits graphically by simply executing the `ls -l` command, which will yield output similar to the following:

```
total 57
-rw-rw-rw-  1 jjv   user 1588    Jul 16 22:21 io
-rwxr-xr-x  1 jjv   user 195     Jul 16 18:07 main
-r--r--r--  1 jjv   user 6321    Jul 16 21:14 part.1
-r--r--r--  1 jjv   user 4635    Jul 17 18:46 part.2
-r--r--r--  1 jjv   user 10284   Jul 16 22:45 part.3
-r--r--r--  1 jjv   user 2875    Jul 16 22:45 part.4
```

The codes at the beginning of each line identify the nine permission bits of each file.

We can take one of these codes, such as `-rwxr-xr-x`, and break it into parts like so:

```
(-) (rwx) (r-x) (r-x)
```

The leading hyphen is not a permission; it merely identifies the file we are looking at as an ordinary file. Sometimes we might see a *d* in this position to signify that the file is a directory.

The next set of marks (*rwx*) indicate whether the owner of the file is allowed to read (*r*), write (*w*), and execute (*x*) the file. If the corresponding permission is not granted, a hyphen is shown instead. The permissions granted to the owner of the file, who is *jjv*, are *read*, *write*, and *execute*.

The second group of permissions (*r-x*) indicate the capabilities of users belonging to a user group. The group name for these files is user, so any user in that group is allowed to read (*r*) or execute (*x*) the file, but not to overwrite it.

The third group of permissions (*r-x*) is the same as the second group. The third set of permissions marks, however, pertains not to the file's group but to the general user, usually called *other*. Users other than the file's owner and group are not allowed to overwrite the file (the *w* flag is missing), but they can read or execute the file.

When a file is created, the user-ID and group-ID of the active user are affixed to the file, and a default set of permission bits is set. You can change any of these parameters—the files's user-ID, its group-ID, or its permission bits—with appropriate system commands.

After a file is created, every attempt to access it is checked against the file's permissions. If the check fails, the access is prohibited. Simple enough, as long as the operation to be performed falls neatly into one of the read, write, or execute categories. But what about other kinds of operations, such as removing a file or changing its permission flags?

This is where the permissions system starts to become nonintuitive. In UNIX, every file has to be defined in some directory—there is no such thing as a file without a folder to keep it in. Well, operations that affect the *existence* of a file, such as creating it or removing it, are alterations of the directory containing the file. Don't you expect the listing of a directory's contents to change when you add or remove a file? Of course you do. But this implies that some program must update the directory, and doing so requires write permission for the directory itself. (As mentioned at the beginning of this chapter, a directory is merely one of the five kinds of files supported by UNIX. Directories therefore have permission bits just like other files.)

The perhaps surprising conclusion is that permission to remove a file is unrelated to the permission bits and ownership of the file; the removal is allowed solely on the basis of your permission to write in the directory containing the file.

What about changes to a file's ownership and permissions bits? These operations do not affect the directory containing the file, nor do they qualify as read, write, or execute operations. UNIX therefore follows a simple and reasonable rule: to alter a file's permissions, owner, or group, you must already be the owner of the file.

That is about all there is to file permissions, except for one small matter. Suppose you make a mistake while typing the `chown` command and accidentally give a file to `bob` instead of `bill`, and `bob` is on vacation this week. Or suppose you mean to type the command `chmod 755 myfile` but type `chown 755 myfile` instead. In either case, the ownership of the file has been accidentally transferred to the wrong user, and the user who received ownership of the file is not available to help you correct the error by changing its ownership back. In the second example, the user who received control of the file (755) doesn't exist (the command is legal nonetheless).

How does UNIX provide for correcting mistakes of this kind? There is one user-ID in the system that is never denied access to any file. This user is unique in having a user-ID value of 0. Traditionally, this user is called `root`, but nothing is special about this user name; the numeric user-ID of 0 is special to the system. This user is often called the *superuser*, because of his or her global powers.

The system cannot know that you were the owner of the file before the disastrous chown just described, so it makes no attempt to allow you to change the ownership back. The error must be corrected by someone who is able to exercise judgement...if the superuser believes your tale of woe, he or she will restore the ownership of your file.

Now for a little trick. If you accidentally change the ownership of a file to the wrong user-ID, you probably do not need the assistance of the superuser to correct the error. As long as the file is listed in a directory you own, or for which you have write permission, you can correct the error with the following sequence of commands:

```
$ chown 775 myfile   # This is an error!
$ cp myfile myfile.x
$ rm myfile
myfile: 644 mode ? y
$ mv myfile.x myfile
```

This sequence of commands works because you still have write permission in the directory containing the file, so you are still allowed to remove the file. Also, presumably, you still have read permission for the file, and can therefore make a copy of it. Given these two capabilities, you can effectively change the ownership of the file to any user you please, as often as you please.

After this description, you probably feel that the UNIX permissions system is more than adequate for any need, maybe even too complicated. Actually, it is not complicated enough. Suppose you want to share write access to a file with one other specific user—we will suppose her user name is kay. How do you go about this?

The current description of your file is as follows:

```
-rw-r--r-- 1 bill      user            1588 Jul 16 22:21 myfile
```

As it stands, only bill (presumably yourself) has access to this file. If you change its permissions to

```
-rw-rw-rw- 1 bill      user            1588 Jul 16 22:21 myfile
```

everyone will be able to modify the file, which is not your intent at all. On the other hand, if you set the permissions to

```
-rw-rw-r-- 1 bill      user            1588 Jul 16 22:21 myfile
```

everyone in the group user will be able to write to the file. This takes in more users than you intended, certainly more than just yourself and kay.

There is only one way to accomplish your objective: ask the superuser to define a new user group (maybe `bk`) that contains only yourself and Kay. You can then change the file permissions to

```
-rw-rw-r--    1 bill      bk           1588 Jul 16 22:21 myfile
```

and everything will work fine. The problem with this approach is that if this kind of file sharing occurs frequently, the system will need a nearly infinite number of group names, one for each possible combination of users!

Several strategies for getting around this problem have been devised. The AIX version of UNIX, for example, allows you to create an *access list* that grants access permissions to a specific list of users. Few people would contend that this is a tidy solution, but it is difficult to imagine a solution that is not based on access lists in some form. We can expect that future versions of UNIX will extend the permissions system, while maintaining full compatibility with the current implementation.

The Standard UNIX Directories

If you have access to a UNIX system, take a moment to browse through its directories. Although you may not immediately notice it, there is a purpose behind the organization. In addition, standards for the directory names and their contents have been in existence since the earliest days of UNIX. These standards are intended to ease the burden of system maintenance and administration, and if you are familiar with the directory scheme, you will be able to locate files more quickly.

Not all versions of UNIX comply rigidly with this scheme, but most come close. AT&T System V, which is the direct descendent of the original implementation of UNIX and has hewed closest to the original philosophy of its inventors, adheres strictly to the directory scheme I describe shortly. Because ports of System V to other machine architectures are based directly on AT&T System V, they also comply closely with this scheme. Other versions have drifted somewhat, causing portability problems.

The UNIX system's directory structure is not itself part of any standard. But systems that deviate markedly from the traditional structure should be viewed with an element of distrust because portability (the porting of software from one machine architecture to another with minimal effort) is threatened by capricious naming conventions.

The remainder of this chapter identifies the most common files and directories in any UNIX system. For some of you, this may make for dry reading.

By all means feel free to skim the rest of this section, but remember where you saw this stuff. If you use UNIX with any frequency, you will eventually commit most of this information to memory.

The root (/) Directory

All UNIX systems must have a root directory. This directory contains all other files and directories. It is called *root* because all other directories branch from it like the branches and leaves of a tree.

Unlike other operating systems such as IBM's MVS or VM/SP, where it can be difficult if not impossible to discover what files are present in the system, the UNIX user has the potential capability of locating any file simply by beginning the search with the root directory.

The /bin Directory

The /bin directory contains executable program files (called *binaries*, hence the directory's name). Other directories contain binaries; what sets this directory apart is that it is the binary directory for the root filesystem. Therefore, this directory contains every program needed to rebuild the system from backups, to install the system from its distribution media, or to perform general system maintenance.

All other filesystems can be, and sometimes need to be, unmounted. It is important that the system administrator maintain in this directory every program needed to get the system started from the initial condition, whatever it may be, including the possibility of having to rebuild the entire system from backups. To this end, keep in mind that, since it is advantageous to create a separate backup for each mountable filesystem, any program needed to rebuild a destroyed filesystem must be available without that filesystem; the normal place to store such programs is this directory.

The /dev Directory

The /dev directory, also located in the root filesystem, is reserved for block-special and character-special files. All block-special and character-special files should be defined in this directory or in a subdirectory of it.

Since the introduction of System V Release 1, the convention is to store all block-special files in the /dev/dsk directory. Other subdirectories are often used to store closely related special files, for example, /dev/mt to contain magnetic tape devices. All special files should be placed in the /dev directory.

If a device-special file is defined in another filesystem, the device will not be available when the filesystem is not mounted.

The /etc Directory

The `/etc` directory must be located in the root filesystem. As its name implies, the `/etc` directory should contain miscellaneous files needed for system operation, administration, and maintenance. Its contents are not limited to binaries, but it does contain many of the program files needed by the superuser for system administration. The reason for hiding such binaries in the `/etc` directory is to avoid cluttering the `/bin` and `/usr/bin` directories with infrequently executed programs. The `/etc` directory contains the most important administrative files in the system:

`/etc/gettydefs`	Terminal support for `getty`
`/etc/group`	List of all valid group names
`/etc/inittab`	System initialization script
`/etc/mnttab`	List of all mounted filesystems
`/etc/motd`	The message of the day
`/etc/passwd`	List of all valid login names
`/etc/utmp`	Log of login processes
`/etc/wtmp`	Log of login processes

The /lib Directory

The `/lib` directory need not be present for all implementations of UNIX. If present, it resides in the root filesystem. Normally, the `/lib` directory contains the C compilation system, including the compiler itself and the function libraries.

The /tmp Directory

The `/tmp` directory is often a mountable filesystem, in which case `/tmp` is simply the mount point. Otherwise, the `/tmp` directory represents the unused space in the root filesystem.

The `/tmp` directory and `/usr/tmp` (described shortly) provide space for temporary files. Because the amount of space in the root filesystem is usually limited, and because any user can not only create but also remove files in the

/tmp directory, you will probably want to avoid placing files in the /tmp directory yourself. Many UNIX commands create temporary files in the /tmp directory as part of their execution. For this reason, the /tmp directory must have read, write, and search permissions for all users.

The /usr Directory

By convention, the /usr directory in the root filesystem is merely a mount point for the usr filesystem. All files that are not required for minimum system operation are placed here. Originally, it was intended that users' home directories would be placed in the /usr directory. But so many system demands are now placed on this filesystem that it has become common practice to locate users' home directories in another filesystem (typically named /u).

The /usr/bin Directory

The /usr/bin directory contains all nonessential executable files that were shipped with the system and are available to the general user. It is considered poor practice to place executable programs in this directory that are not included in the system distribution because the installation of new releases of the system may destroy its contents. Executables of local origin should usually be placed in yet another directory, typically named /usr/local/bin or /usr/lbin. Together the /bin and /usr/bin directories comprise virtually all of the commands and utilities available to the general user that are distributed with the system.

The /usr/lib Directory

The /usr/lib directory is a catchall for files used by system commands and utilities, as well as for a few executable programs not normally used by the general user. The /usr/lib directory was intended to be used by all application packages installed in the system that needed a system global directory. Examples of important files and directories in /usr/lib include the following:

/usr/lib/uucp	Executables and administrative files for uucp
/usr/lib/cron	Administrative files for cron
/usr/lib/help	Data files for the help command
/usr/lib/macros	Macro packages for nroff
/usr/lib/libc.a	Standard function library for C

The /usr/spool Directory

The `/usr/spool` directory contains subdirectories for system packages that need working file space. Examples of its contents include `/usr/spool/lp`, which holds files waiting to be printed, `/usr/spool/uucp`, which is used by UUCP as temporary file space, and `/usr/spool/uucppublic`, which is used by UUCP to contain files waiting to be delivered to their destinations.

The /usr/tmp Directory

The `/usr/tmp` directory represents free space available in the `usr` filesystem for temporary files and work files. Usually, there is more free space in the `/usr/tmp` directory than in `/tmp`. The `P_tmpdir` label defined in `stdio.h` usually names `/usr/tmp` as the preferred directory for temporary files.

However, it is more appropriate for system administrative and maintenance procedures to use the `/tmp` directory for work space, the preferred work area for general users is the `/usr/tmp` directory.

The /usr/include Directory

Although the C programming language is an optional part of UNIX, its presence in the system generally implies that the header files used with the C standard library are stored in the `/usr/include` directory. This is such a common assumption among C programmers that storing standard header files in any other directory can cause excessive difficulty when porting programs developed for other versions of UNIX.

UNIX Devices

In this section, you will learn about device-dependent considerations as they affect applications programming. Before doing so, however, you have to become acquainted with some basic UNIX concepts.

Device Drivers

I use the term *applications program* to refer to any program that executes under the control of the UNIX kernel, as opposed to the kernel itself. The *UNIX kernel* is a single large program that is linked and installed during the system configuration procedure. It is loaded at system startup and manages the computer's resources. In other operating systems, this program is called the *nucleus* or the *supervisor*. The chief purpose of the UNIX kernel is responding to interrupts from external devices and system calls from application programs.

My definition of *application* therefore includes such programs as the Bourne shell, the C shell, the `mv`, `cp`, `rm`, `mkdir`, and `rmdir` file management utilities, `ls`, and `cat`. In UNIX, you are free to rewrite these programs and to implement them in almost any manner. The only part of the system that you ordinarily cannot touch is the UNIX kernel itself.

A class of programs that is linked with the kernel and execute in the machine's privileged state, however, can be written and installed by any authorized user: these are called *device drivers*. These programs are not considered part of UNIX itself; their purpose is to free UNIX from any dependency on device characteristics. The required interface between the kernel and a device driver is well documented and the documentation is widely available. As a result, anyone can write a device driver that will be acceptable to the UNIX kernel, thereby permitting a new kind of peripheral device to be added to the system's configuration. This means that UNIX device support is open-ended; UNIX can support any device for which someone has written a device driver.

This is the main reason why UNIX is often called an *open system*. It is immaterial whether the device is manufactured by the same vendor that provides the computer; you need only a suitable device driver to be able to attach it. The computer, the UNIX operating system, the device driver, and the peripheral device can be made by independent vendors, and integrated with confidence that the resulting system will work properly.

This is a significant departure from the design of most other operating systems, in which support for devices is tightly integrated with the operating system and it is taken for granted that an operating system provided by a hardware manufacturer will support only equipment made by that vendor. The capability of UNIX to attach devices made by different manufacturers is the primary reason why UNIX has been popular with the user community.

This book won't explain the principles of writing device drivers, but it will discuss what can be accomplished with a device driver and how to go about designing it. First, when planning to write a new device driver, remember that you do not have to limit the application program interface to the bare capabilities of the device. As an example, consider a monochrome text display terminal and keyboard. When we write to this device, we embed sequences of special characters in the data stream to do such things as clear the screen, position the cursor, and specify display attributes. As C programmers, we are usually taught to control devices by inserting these control characters in our data stream; we find this more natural than invoking a device control function whenever a control operation is needed.

As a rule, text display terminals do not recognize any control characters for their operation. Typically, the only interface between the computer and the terminal is a display buffer (a two-dimensional array of characters held in main memory that represents the rows and columns of the screen image) and a few hardware registers. To clear the display, the program must store a blank in every position of the display buffer. To position the cursor, an integer representing an offset in the display buffer must be written to a device register. To specify display attributes, additional bits in the appropriate positions of the display buffer must be set or cleared.

But this is not how the terminal appears to the application program! Drivers for video display terminals implement a control-character protocol by mapping fictitious control characters to the kinds of physical actions the terminal requires. For example, the driver might recognize a character with the octal value 037 as the control character for clearing the screen. When the driver finds this character in the data stream presented by the application program, it stores a blank in every position of the display buffer and then discards the 037 character, rather than write the character to the terminal.

This kind of interface mapping is not limited to terminals. Device control requirements for disk drives can be very complex and messy to program. Rather than burden application programs with these requirements, a good driver design will simulate a much simpler protocol for disk operations. Therefore, one of the issues when writing a disk driver is what kind of interface we want to present to the application program.

But a more basic decision is whether the device will be portrayed as a block device or as a character device. As mentioned previously in this chapter, two of the five file types are the block-special file and the character-special file; the remaining three types are ordinary files, directories, and pipes. But ordinary files and directories are subdivisions of disk space, and pipes do not correspond to any physical device. The inescapable conclusion is that UNIX lumps all devices into one of two classes: block devices, which form the underlying physical basis of block-special files, and character devices, which are the physical basis of character-special files.

A device driver is free to present any desired interface to the application program when the device is represented as a character-special file. This is because the UNIX kernel makes no special assumptions about character devices and (with only minor exceptions) does not access them on its own behalf. But block devices must conform to a more rigid specification because the kernel frequently accesses the disk for a variety of purposes.

To the UNIX kernel, a disk is an abstract recording medium. The kernel makes no attempt to optimize its operation to the specific recording formats or capabilities of the disk; to do so would severely limit the range of devices that could be attached as disk drives. Furthermore, the kernel always accesses a disk through the device driver interface to further reduce its dependence on specific device formats. UNIX places only three requirements on the appearance of a disk device: it must be capable of storing and retrieving data in fixed-size units called blocks; it must be capable of accessing blocks in any order; and the time required to access any block should be approximately the same regardless of the block requested.

The kernel also imposes a number of additional responsibilities on drivers for block devices. For example, the kernel assumes that all attached disks can be accessed simultaneously; if this is not the case, the driver must provide any necessary I/O scheduling.

The assumption of block size made by the UNIX kernel is not a limitation on the physical disk drive. Because all accesses to the disk are made through the device driver, the driver is free to map these blocks onto the physical recording medium in any convenient manner. For example, many implementations of UNIX presume a disk block size of 1K (1024) bytes. If the disk has a physical block size of 512 bytes, the driver is free to assign each UNIX disk block to two physical blocks. Similarly, equal access times for all blocks is only an assumption; it is sometimes possible to implement a block device driver for magnetic tape drives. This allows a tape drive to be used as if it were a disk, even though access times to tape blocks are anything but evenly distributed.

Because efficient disk I/O is essential to achieving good overall system performance, all modern implementations of UNIX provide an additional layer of software between the application program and the block device driver to perform *caching*. The following ideas underly this technique: (1) accesses to disk are not, in general, truly random, (2) the same disk blocks tend to be accessed again and again, and (3) a significant amount of time can be saved by keeping in memory a copy of the most recently referenced disk blocks. The set of current disk blocks tends to change over time, so the caching routines implement an algorithm for replacing in-core buffers with new disk blocks as the pattern of references change.

The application program cannot directly perceive the operation of the caching software because its only effect is to reduce the apparent retrieval time for disk data. The device driver, however, is severely constrained by the caching routines because the driver must match the device interface expected by the cache routines. The block device driver, unlike the character device driver, cannot freely choose its interface.

Working with Disks

The most significant difference between writing programs for UNIX and writing for more conventional operating systems lies in the area of disk access. Traditionally, knowledge of the physical characteristics of disk drives is present at all layers of the system, including the application level. An application must be written to support specific brands and models of disk, and must be aware of the device's geometry.

In contrast to the traditional environment, the UNIX programmer has no idea what kind of disk drives the system is using. There are no system calls to return cryptic model numbers, no device characteristics tables to examine, no device commands to be written. Such concepts do not exist outside the UNIX kernel.

There is no practical way to take advantage of device-level knowledge in UNIX even if you have that information. Suppose that you know that a particular disk drive reads and writes data in blocks of 512 bytes. You write your program to always read or write 512 bytes of data at a time. You may discover to your surprise that this has little or no affect on the performance of your program. A little reflection will show why.

The UNIX kernel does not know that the block size for this disk is 512 bytes. If this version of UNIX was designed to use a 1024-byte block size for its disk file systems, it will *always* read and write 1024 bytes at a time, regardless of your program's requests. The result may be that the kernel sometimes re-reads blocks of data from disk. If your program had been written to access disk in blocks of 1024 bytes, the performance would be better even though the physical block size of the disk is 512 bytes.

Programs that contain detailed hardware knowledge need continual modification to support new device types. Worse, a high level of technical competence is needed to understand device-level concepts, learn new technology, and finally modify existing programs to use that technology. Such staff is expensive and difficult to find.

As James Martin explains (on page 5 of *Software Maintenance, the Problem and Its Solutions,* by James Martin and Carma McClure, Prentice-Hall 1983): "Computers have plunged in cost dramatically. It is clear that the spectacular cost reductions will continue.... Programming accounts for an ever increasing proportion of computer costs." His observations underscore the importance of the UNIX philosophy that people costs are higher than machine costs. Device independence simplifies user programming and saves people costs.

Efforts spent improving program performance, on the other hand, will become valueless when you add on that new faster disk drive.

The UNIX approach to disk management is to keep device level details out of your programs and where they belong—in the device driver.

Working with Character Devices

The principal problem we encountered when examining the UNIX treatment of disks was maintaining some level of performance while benefiting from the advantages of device independence. The following chapters will examine ways to use the UNIX I/O facilities efficiently.

The problem we encounter with character devices is almost the opposite. Recall that a character device is any device that cannot be treated as a block device. This device class includes terminals, printers, modems, plotters, bar-code readers, badge readers, and so on through an almost endless list of peripherals.

When we open a file we can test whether it is a block-special file or a character-special file, but we cannot identify the device containing the file with any greater degree of precision than this.

Many kinds of programs do not care what kind of device is involved even to this degree. For example, a sort utility performs a sophisticated operation on a simple data stream. It has little concern for the contents of a record other than its keys, and the values of the record's sort keys are significant only with regard to their collating sequence. As much as possible, the sort utility regards its input and output as simple sequential files to avoid unnecessary complication and maximize its usability.

UNIX supports such generic file handling very well. A program doing simple sequential processing (that is, a program concerned with the logical content of a file instead of its external representation) can successfully ignore all device-dependent considerations. The sort utility can read its input from a disk file, a terminal, or nearly any kind of device because it makes no device-specific demands on the data.

Frequently, however, a program cannot be indifferent to device consider-ations, or we want to capitalize on the features of a device. Programs that are designed to present full-screen displays on video terminals are a good example. We know that not every kind of terminal that can be attached to the computer is capable of full-screen operation. Or suppose we want to write a program to generate fancy text and graphics on a laser printer. Such a program will not work correctly with every kind of printer.

Is there a way to tell that the program has been invoked with the wrong kind of device? If so, it would be possible to issue a helpful error message and end the program gracefully.

Is there a way to tell what kind of device has been provided to the program? If so, the program we can adapt its behavior to the device's capabilities.

In general, the answer to either question is "No." UNIX does not make such information available to the program. I would guess that you are not pleased with that answer. Before I try to convince you that you don't really want any other answer, let me explain how the problem is dealt with traditionally in the UNIX environment.

One way to deal with the question of device capability is to simply assume what the device is. The other way is to provide a command-line option to identify the deivce.

An example of the first method is the `tar` utility, which is intended to be used for writing backup tapes and is therefore specific to magnetic tape drives. Most device drivers for tape drives require that all writes to the device use a fixed block size. Some drivers accept any block size as long as all writes specify the same block size; others insist on one particular block size. The `tar` utility assumes by default that the proper block size is 5120 bytes, and will pad its output to that block size if necessary.

This assumption has a number of consequences. One is that all programmers with sufficient skill to write a device driver know this about the `tar` utility, so you will hardly ever find a magnetic tape device driver that will reject that block size. In other words, it's a chicken-and-egg situation: when `tar` was originally written, a 5120-byte block size generally worked; later, when new device drivers were written for magnetic tape, they were designed to accommodate that block size so that `tar` would continue to work.

On the other hand, should `tar` be invoked for a device that does not accept a write of 5120 bytes, the `tar` utility will fail. The resolution of the problem is simple: use `tar` only with the devices that it supports.

This does not mean that `tar` supports only magnetic tape drives for its output. It can be instructed (by specifying the right option) to write its output to any other file, such as a disk file or a printer. The output is still blocked to a size of 5120 bytes. If your purpose in executing `tar` is to create a short-term backup of a collection of files, where it is convenient to save the backup on disk, this is particularly inefficient and the `tar` format will waste a great deal of disk space. If you don't find that alternative acceptable, you should use `cpio` or `ar` instead.

The modern tar utility supports an option to specify the output block size. However, it still cannot sense whether the specified value is legal, or select an intelligent default for the block device.

Many programs support command-line options or similar means to specify the device type. The vi editor uses the $TERM variable to locate a terminal description in a terminfo database. The technique is completely independent of operating system support, so it is subject to errors such as an incorrect value in $TERM.

If you are accustomed to programs that automatically adjust to their environment, such as can be written for an operating system that makes device description information available to the application, you will consider the UNIX alternatives clumsy and undesirable.

I think UNIX works just fine, however, and here's why. The tar utility and the vi program are completely device independent. If I install a new kind of tape drive that requires tape blocks to be written with a length of 8192 bytes, I can begin to use that tape drive immediately simply by changing my tape backup procedures to specify that block size as an option to tar. Similarly, if I install a new kind of terminal that the UNIX developers never heard of, and that was placed on the market long after vi was written, I can still use vi with that terminal simply by entering the appropriate terminal definition in the terminfo database.

It is precisely because tar does not know anything about specific devices that makes it able to support new devices. It is precisely because vi must be customized by the user that allows the user to customize it. If UNIX provided device-specific information to application programs, one could not expect application developers to ignore the temptation to use it, thereby locking their applications into a rigid device environment. UNIX programs, precisely because they require the environment to be specified by the user rather than the operating system, are adaptable to new environments and permit hardware to be easily changed.

The moral of this story is this: if you want to write a program to use specific device capabilities, go ahead; users will learn not to attempt to use your program with unsuitable devices, and may be able to use your program in the future with devices that didn't exist when you wrote the program. If you want to be able to adapt your program to a range of device features, use program options or environment variables to select the device features applicable in a given program execution.

Summary

We have talked at great length about the device-dependent considerations for disk-type devices and other devices. In neither case, however, did I describe any system facilities to assist with device feature support or performance optimization.

As a result, the interface between your program and the outside world of real devices will seem very fuzzy and undefined. That is the point of this chapter. UNIX simply does not incorporate device-dependent considerations into its design, and therefore has no such information that it can share with your programs. In the remainder of this book, we will concentrate our attention on the only two kinds of devices that UNIX supports: block devices and character devices.

The approach taken by UNIX to the world of devices is radically different from that of most other operating systems. I think the UNIX approach is better, and in support of this, let me give you one final example.

There are a great many similarities between MS-DOS and UNIX, but one area in which they are at variance is terminal support. Anyone who wants to write a program for MS-DOS has a clear idea of the capabilities of the terminal: it is an MDA, a CGA, an EGA, or a VGA, and the specifications for these device interfaces are widely disseminated. A program can test to see which of the various adapters is present, so that the program can adjust its actions to the type of terminal it finds. As a result, many programs executable on any MS-DOS machine use fancy graphics to provide a very attractive user interface.

In the UNIX environment, the situation is far less clear. In general, UNIX permits the attachment of a greater variety of terminals than does the PC. Some of these terminals offer less functionality than the Monochrome Display Adapter; some offer capabilities exceeding even the super-VGA interface. Creeping technology is slowly blurring the certainty that used to prevail in the MS-DOS world. It invaded the world of UNIX long ago simply because there are so many different versions of UNIX and they are used with such an incredible variety of hardware gear.

For UNIX programmers, it is very difficult to design a program that offers advanced user interfaces but also runs in almost any environment. A few tools can assist you. One is curses, which supports most video terminals and provides a good device-independent interface for text displays. But curses offers only the crudest graphic support and is not suitable as a base on which to build a modern graphical user interface. The curses pacakge is attractive to UNIX program designers because it offers device independence—the capability to support your program on many kinds of terminals, most of which you may never even heard of—but aggravating because it doesn't allow designers to achieve the effects they want.

Now, given this description of the two different worlds of MS-DOS and UNIX, in which of the two would you rather write programs? MS-DOS, I suppose. Ah, but you forget or ignore what is happening to that vast library of software for MS-DOS.

As newer and more advanced terminals become available for the PC, commercial software is continuously upgraded to support and take advantage of the new hardware (an effort you pay for when you buy the upgrade packages or the latest version). Thus, you can probably obtain a version of your favorite program that takes advantage of your new 19-inch 1024x768 pixel resolution interlaced-scan super-VGA terminal.

But the large numbers of public domain, shareware, and simply old programs out there are languishing in the cemetery of obsolete device support. Someday, when no one has CGA displays anymore (a day that is not far off) and when no modern terminal includes compatibility for CGA, those programs will all be unusuable. Who will rewrite them?

Why must we make the choice between losing their otherwise good and useful functionality, and spending a great deal of time and effort to upgrade their device support? The answer is simple: these programs were written to work with a specific device of an exact description. Should that device not be available, the entire program is unusable.

I have no idea how old the UNIX utilities are that I use every day, but some of them are really old. They ought to survive until UNIX itself dies of old age.

So, what do you think is the answer to the software crisis of the last ten years? To continue to write throw-away software (at anything but throw-away prices), or to start using the UNIX approach? If you want to learn more about the UNIX approach, the next three chapters will tell you a great deal more about I/O programming.

9

Ordinary Files

I have no wish to belabor the obvious, and any chapter devoted to a discussion of ordinary files runs that risk. Because you are reading a book about programming in the UNIX environment, I assume that you are already familiar with many aspects of managing ordinary files, and have a general understanding of `fopen`, `fclose`, and the various `printf`, `scanf`, `get`, and `put` functions. I also assume that you have a basic understanding of file permissions, ownership, and the use of the `chmod` and `chown` commands.

In this chapter we will build on that knowledge by examining unusual and special uses of file permissions (for example, *set-uid* programs), and the system calls and library functions that provide additional or unusual facilities for managing files.

You may be unfamiliar with (or unaccustomed to using) the basic file I/O functions `open`, `close`, `read`, and `write`. I will discuss the use of these and other basic I/O functions, and get into the ticklish business of when and how to mix basic I/O functions with stream files.

The Filesystem

Before I can talk in detail about files, I have to make a few preliminary remarks about filesystems. First, let's distinguish between the terms *file system* and *filesystem*.

In UNIX, the term *file system* refers to the scheme used for organizing data on disk. Thus, when someone makes a remark about the UNIX file system, they are commenting on the way UNIX organizes data and provides for its storage and retrieval. By way of example, let me make such a remark: the UNIX file system allows the transfer of as little as one byte in an I/O operation.

In contrast, the term *filesystem* refers to a definite, concrete, physical data structure. In your previous experience with UNIX, you have probably learned that the system dynamically manages disk space, automatically determining where to store a file on disk and allocating disk space for the file as needed. It may surprise you to learn that a *filesystem* is the primary unit of disk allocation in UNIX, and that it does not grow or shrink as needed. A filesystem's starting location on a disk volume, and its size expressed as a number of disk blocks, is fixed and constant. All disk space allocation in UNIX is suballocation of the space in a filesystem.

When the administrator installs the UNIX system and configures it according to in-house needs, one of the most important steps is dividing available disk space into fixed-sized areas called filesystems. One such area is used for the files needed to operate the system, and is called the root filesystem. Another such area is usually set aside for temporary files, and is called the /tmp filesystem. If the administrator hasn't made these areas too large and some space is left on the available disk volumes, the system administrator can define other filesystems. For example, /u is often set aside to contain users' home directories and files.

You may think that the fixed permanent allocation of space in filesystems is a disadvantage, but this is not so. The total amount of disk space available is finite, and therefore limited. There is only so much to go around. By setting up filesystems as fixed-sized areas of disk, and then establishing conventions about their usage and contents, the system administrator can achieve some balance between various needs. For example, many important system programs (for example, the C compiler) will not run successfully unless some space is available for temporary files. The system administrator therefore sets aside a reasonable amount of space for this purpose, guaranteeing that some amount of temporary file space is always available regardless of how users may (for good or ill) fill up their own user filesystem.

The filesystem thus enables the system administrator to enforce some constraints on the growth of system and user files, and to ensure that filling one filesystem does not render the system useless or inoperative from lack of disk space.

Filesystems are connected to the system by being *mounted*. The root filesystem is mounted automatically when the system is started; other filesystems are mounted by executing the `mount` command. You can find out what filesystems are mounted by executing the d f command.

An individual filesystem consists of three main areas: the superblock, the inode table, and the data blocks. The superblock is a kind of label used to identify the filesystem and to allow the kernel to find the various areas of the filesystem. Among other things, the superblock identifies

❏ The size of the filesystem, as a number of disk blocks

❏ The location where the disk inode table begins

❏ The number of inodes in the disk inode table

❏ The number of data blocks in the filesystem

❏ Which data block will be used next when one has to be allocated

We will discuss inodes at length in a moment. At this point we need only note that the number of inodes in the disk inode table is a critically important number, because inodes are a type of table of contents for the filesystem. The system administrator decides how many inodes will be in the filesystem; what is left after the superblock and the disk inode blocks are subtracted is available for data blocks.

Data blocks are nondescript; their format is largely determined by what the user decides to put in them. Data blocks that currently contain file data are located by pointers stored in an inode. Data blocks that are currently free and available for allocation are collected into a *free chain*. Of all this structure in the filesystem, the data blocks are the only portion that you can directly read and write.

Inodes and stat

Most files in a filesystem are ordinary files. As users of the system, we find ordinary files more interesting than any other kind. As UNIX programmers, although we sometimes access directories and special files, the largest number of our programs process ordinary files. Because of their great importance, ordinary files are embedded in a complex structure of relationships, the first of which is the relationship of a file to its name.

Unlike some other popular operating systems, UNIX carefully distinguishes the name by which a file is *called* from the file itself. File names are stored in *directories*, and a pointer to the file's description, or *inode*, is listed with each file name. Because UNIX does not treat a file name as if it were the file itself, UNIX allows a file to have many file names (at least 1000 in most versions of the operating system).

Because file names are the principal components of directories, I will have more to say about them in Chapter 10, "Directories." In this chapter, I want to discuss the properties of the file itself.

UNIX collects all the information about a file in one place, the inode. Inodes are not stored with the files themselves, nor are they stored in directories. All of the inodes are collected in a table at the beginning of a filesystem, in the form of an array. This table extends over a contiguous range of disk blocks, with some fixed number of inodes stored in each block (the exact number is a system-dependent parameter).

The role played by the inode is that of a pointer. File names point to inodes, and inodes point to data blocks. The pointer connecting a file name to an inode plays a critical role in the UNIX file system because it defines the data to which a file name refers. In UNIX, this pointer is called a *link*.

A pointer to an inode is an integer number used as an index into the array of inodes on disk; a pointer to a data block is a system-dependent value. An inode pointer may be a byte offset, a block number, or anything that is convenient for the system's implementers. The inode contains thirteen of these pointers, which is enough to locate all of the data blocks in a file.

Ordinarily, an inode cannot be directly accessed by a user program. There are routines in the kernel for fetching inodes from disk and for storing them safely back to disk, but these routines are accessible only to other kernel routines. Two system calls, however, will return to you the most useful parts of an inode: `stat` and `fstat`. Neither one of these accepts an inode number as the designator of the inode to be returned; `stat` requires one of the file names of the file, and `fstat` requires an open file-descriptor number.

The stripped-down inode that is returned by these calls is stored in a buffer of type `struct stat` that you provide. Its format is described in the header file `sys/stat.h`, and in Appendix C, "Important Header Files." You should review these references now.

One of the first things you may notice is that the contents of the `stat` buffer bear a resemblance to the output of the `ls` command. This is no accident, because the `ls` command executes the `stat` system call for each file named on its command line, and prints the contents of the `stat` buffer returned. You can create your own versions of the `ls` command easily, by using `stat` to retrieve the file description and generating the report format that you prefer. The following simple program implements a rudimentary form of `ls` that you might find instructive:

```c
#include <stdio.h>
#include <sys/types.h>
#include <sys/stat.h>
#include <time.h>

char heading[] =
    "  fmode links uid gid   bytes --last modified-- name";
char format[] =
    "%7.5o %5d %3d %3d %7ld %02d/%02d/%02d %02d:%02d:%02d %s\n";

main(int argc, char *argv[])
{
    struct stat buf;
    struct tm *tm;
    char *filename;

    puts(heading);
    while (filename = *++argv) {
        if (stat(filename,&buf) == (-1))
            perror(filename);
        else { /* Print a 'stat' line for this file */
            tm = localtime(&buf.st_mtime);
            printf(format,
                buf.st_mode, buf.st_nlink,
                buf.st_uid, buf.st_gid, buf.st_size,
                tm->tm_year, tm->tm_mon+1, tm->tm_mday,
                tm->tm_hour, tm->tm_min, tm->tm_sec,
                filename
                );
        }
    }
    return 0;
}
```

The output from this program looks like this:

```
 fmode links uid gid    bytes --last modified-- name
100775      1   2   2    68552 85/10/27 02:17:17 /lib/back
100775      1   2   2    35536 85/10/27 02:19:27 /lib/cpp
100775      1   2   2    95280 85/10/27 02:24:37 /lib/front
 40775      2   2   2      144 87/09/14 20:45:02 /lib/large
 40775      4   2   2       64 87/09/14 20:45:18 /lib/libp
100775      1   2   2    78736 85/10/27 03:10:57 /lib/optim
 40775      2   2   2      144 87/09/14 20:46:08 /lib/small
```

This output shows an assortment of regular files (mode 100xxx) and directories (mode 40xxx).

Two of the values in an inode (st_dev and st_rdev) contain major and minor device numbers. These numbers are UNIX identifiers for a device. (For more information, see Chapter 11, "Special Files and Pipes.") These numbers cannot be used to directly address devices, but they have their uses.

The st_dev value defines the relationship between the inode of a file and the device containing the inode. One UNIX rule is that a file's inode must reside in the same filesystem as its data, so the st_dev value also identifies the device where the file's data resides. It can be treated as a *filesystem identifier*, and has been treated as such by several system commands, including pwd and cp.

Consider the problem faced by the cp command: if it is asked to copy a file to itself, opening the output file destroys the contents of the input file. For this reason, the command checks to see whether the input file and the output file are the same. By the normal rules, doing this can be difficult because many different path names can represent the same file, and links can hide the equivalence of two path names. The cp command solves this problem by retrieving the inodes of the source and destination files with stat and comparing their st_dev and st_ino values. If the values are the same, the two files are described by the same inode in the same filesystem, and hence they are the same file.

For accuracy, we should note that st_ino is not present in the real disk inode. It is stored in the stat struct by stat for your information.

The st_rdev value performs a similar service for special files (UNIX terminology for devices). Special files are often named and referenced through links, which could make it difficult to tell whether two special files are the same device. If stat shows that both have the same st_rdev value, the two names refer to the same device.

The st_size value gives the size of the file in bytes. When the file has been written using the lseek and write functions in such a way that it contains "holes," however, the file may be smaller than the value indicated here (in the sense that it occupies less disk space than indicated). The st_size value is the offset in bytes to the end-of-file location for the file.

Links

As mentioned, a link is a pointer from a file name to the inode. The relationship between links and file names is therefore a close one.

There are two principal ways to create a link. One way is to create a new file using the creat or open system call. The system allocates an inode to define the file, and initializes the value of st_size to 0 and st_nlink to 1. Then the system allocates space for the new file name in the directory that will contain the file, and stores the inode number into the directory entry along with the file name. At this point, no data blocks are attached to the file because it contains no data. Nevertheless, the allocation of an inode to the file and the association of a file name with the inode is sufficient to cause the file to exist.

Another way to create a link is to invoke the `link` function. This associates another file name with an existing file. The function requires two arguments, as follows:

```
int link(const char *name1, const char *name2);
```

This call creates a directory entry for *name2* having the same inode number as the directory entry for *name1*. When the new directory entry is created, the system increments the inode count of active links (`st_nlink`) by 1.

The `unlink` command is the opposite of the `link` command. The `unlink` command deletes the directory entry for the specified file name, and reduces the count of active links in the inode by one. When this count reaches 0, the inode for the file is returned to the free inode list for the filesystem, and the data blocks owned by the file are returned to the free data block list. In other words, the file is deleted.

One implication of this unlinking procedure is that there is no delete operation to remove the file and its data in one step. The only way to delete a file is to repeatedly unlink each of the file names by which it is known, thereby destroying every link to the file. The problem with this approach is that it can be difficult to find all the links to a file if they are defined in many different directories.

A careful search of the system calls in System V will fail to discover a rename function to change the names of files. This is because you can use the `link` and `unlink` calls to rename files. A rename operation is nothing more complex than defining the new file name with `link`, and deleting the old file name with `unlink`.

The `unlink` operation can have an undesirable side effect called "breaking links." When two or more links exist for a file, only one copy of the data exists even though the file has two names. If `unlink` is used to delete one of the file names, the file continues to exist under the other file name. If a new file is written with the same file name as was just deleted, the same two file names will exist as before, but now they will point to different data. We say that the first link was broken because it no longer points to the same file data.

This situation arises because text files usually cannot be updated "in place"; the only way to modify such a file is to copy it to a new file name, delete the original, then rename the new file to the old name. If only one link exists for the modified file, no problem occurs. But if two or more links exist, this kind of update results in the retention of the old copy of the file under the other file names.

Programs that update a file in this manner must have a policy about breaking links. If the decision is to warn the user or to refuse to proceed, the program must check the st_nlink value to determine whether multiple links exist. The decision as to whether the links need to be preserved is up to the program (although it may simply ask the user to make the choice).

In general, you need to be concerned about the number of links to a file only if you plan to use the unlink system call to remove it.

The st_nlink value returned by the stat function can be used for another purpose. The cpio and tar utilities use it to avoid copying a file to a backup medium several times (usually once is enough). An st_nlink value greater than one warns these programs that another file name for this file exists, and causes them to check whether the file may already have been processed.

The following sample program is an example of a text update file that breaks links. It takes a simple ASCII text file as its input and changes every lowercase letter in the file to the corresponding uppercase letter. The name of the input file must be given as the program's only command-line argument.

```c
#include <stdio.h>   /* Always needed */
#include <string.h>  /* Needed for strrchr() */
#include <ctype.h>   /* Needed for islower() and _toupper() */
#include <errno.h>   /* Needed for reference to 'errno' */

main(argc, argv)
int argc;
char *argv[];
{

    FILE *in, *out;
    char *tempfile = "__TEMP__";
    char *filename;
    int c;

    /* Switch to the directory containing the file */

    if ((filename = strrchr(argv[1],'/')) == NULL)
        filename = argv[1];
    else  {
        *filename++ = '\0';
        if (chdir(argv[1])) {
            perror(argv[1]);
            exit(1);
            }
    }

    /* Open the input and output files */
```

```
    if ((in = fopen(filename, "r")) == NULL) {
       perror(filename);
       exit(2);
       }

    if ((out = fopen(tempfile, "w")) == NULL) {
       perror(filename);
       exit(3);
       }

    /* Copy the user's file to the temporary file */

    while ((c = getc(in)) != EOF) {
       putc( (islower ? _toupper(c) : c), out);
       if (ferror(in) || ferror(out)) {
           perror("I/O error");
           unlink(tempfile);
           exit(4);
           }
       }
    fclose(out);

    /* Rename temporary file to input filename */

    if (unlink(filename) || link(tempfile,filename)) {
       /* Can't rename the input file */
       perror(filename);
       fprintf(stderr, "Rename failed: output is in '%s'\n",
           tempfile);
       exit(5);
       }

    /* Rename was successful; kill temp filename */
    unlink(tempfile);
    return 0;
}
```

This program attempts to update the input file "in place"; that is, the result file replaces the input file. If more than one link exists for the input file, the link represented by the input file name will be broken. The other file names for the file will continue to refer to the original file, but the input file name will refer to the updated text.

Despite this, the technique is basically a good one because it saves users the trouble of using the mv command later. The program makes every effort to avoid loss of data so that its use is risk-free for the user. Let's take a closer look at its main points.

The program begins by using the chdir function to change the current directory to the directory containing the file to be updated. Because we will be renaming the temporary output file to the original file name, the output file must be in the same filesystem as the input. Remember, a link cannot point outside the filesystem that contains it.

After the program is in the correct directory, it performs its main processing by copying the input file to a temporary file name, making the text changes as it goes. When the copy is finished, the text exists in both its original form and in the modified form. Now comes the tricky business of trying to rename the new file. The first step has to be to unlink the input file so that the original file name is no longer in use. If this step fails, the file still exists under its original name, so the program just exits with an error message.

If the unlink operation succeeds, the program is in a sensitive condition because the original input file is gone and the new version of the file exists under a name that is unfamiliar to the user. If the program exits at this point, the user may believe that the original file was destroyed, not realizing that a usable version exists under the name __TEMP__. It would be a good idea to use the `signal` function to minimize the risk of the program ending at this point. But I omitted the code to do this because we haven't discussed signals yet.

If the link that renames the new temporary file name to the original file name succeeds, it is clear sailing from there on. The only chores left are to destroy the temporary copy of the file, which exists under two file names, and to exit. If the link fails, we have essentially renamed the user's file from its original name to __TEMP__, so we warn the user that this has happened and exit immediately.

I show this example not because I want to encourage risky programming practices, but because it is a good example of using `link` and `unlink` to manage file names, and because most programmers will try this sort of thing at one time or another. This example shows a fairly safe way to perform the renaming operation. I encourage you to enter this program, compile it, and experiment with ways to break it and ways to make it more secure (such as adding signal trapping).

There is one important feature of links this program does not demonstrate well. You may notice that the program does not contain an `fclose` call for the input file. This means that the input file remains open throughout the program's execution. System V ordinarily deletes a file when its link count goes to 0, so you would expect that the `unlink` call would delete the input file, which is clearly its intent. Nonetheless, the system does not immediately delete the file.

As long as any program in the system has the file open for input (and clearly the file remains open in this program), the system will not delete the file; it continues to exist until the program exits, at which time the file is automatically closed. The system deletes a file only when the link count in the inode goes to 0 *and* all programs using the file have closed it.

This fact is sometimes used to good effect when using temporary files. If you open a file and then unlink it immediately, the file continues to exist while your program is running, but vanishes when your program closes the file or exits for any reason. If this sounds like magic, consider that `unlink` removes the directory entry for the file even though the file continues to exist. This implies that any number of programs could open the same file name (although not simultaneously) and read and write it as a temporary file, as long as each program unlinks the file name just after opening it. Each such file would be a different file even though it started out with the same name every time.

Permissions

Associated with any file, even the most humble, are a strange and wonderful set of bits and codes called *permissions*. I am sure you already have some acquaintance with the UNIX concept of file permissions, but don't skip ahead yet. Permissions are not as simple as they seem.

The first myth about UNIX permissions I would like to dispel is the belief that they have something to do with that most mythical of all creatures, the user. This is quite untrue, and you don't deserve to be tricked by such statements. You see, users don't really exist.

I realize that as you sit at your terminal you are quite confident that you both are a user and exist. But inside the UNIX system there are no users, only programs and data and other ordinary objects. You are outside the computer, not inside it, so how can any program (even an operating system as clever as UNIX) deal with something that has no memory address, such as yourself?

Then what are permissions? File permissions are similar to a lock-and-key arrangement. Each file is protected by a set of locks. Every program running in the system carries a set of keys. When one of the keys carried by a program fits one of the locks on a data file, the program can open the file.

This is a nice arrangement, because it is quite simple. Let's see how complicated we can make it. UNIX arranges for every program to have two keys, its owner key and its group key. (For reasons that really do make sense, these keys are known as the *process effective user-ID* and the *process effective group-ID*, respectively.)

Every file has nine categories of permission, two locks, three special attributes, and one type code associated with it. So much for simplicity. Associated with each file is an *owner-ID* (which is a number) and a *group-ID*

(which is another number). The object of the permissions game is for a program to try to get its owner key to fit into the owner lock for a file and, failing that, to get the group key to fit into the group lock for the file. The owner key is never tested in the group lock, nor the group key in the owner lock; a key has to fit into the same sort of lock.

When one of the program's keys matches the corresponding file lock, the program is authorized to use the file in the kinds of ways specified by the permission bits. There are three sets of permission bits. Each set contains a bit to allow reading the file, a bit to allow writing the file, and a bit to allow executing the file. One set is used when the program's owner key matches the file's owner-ID; a second set is used when the program's group key matches the file's group-ID; a third set is used when neither key matches.

Each one of these nine permissions is a solitary bit. A program is either granted the corresponding permission when the bit is 1, and denied permission when the bit is 0. When all these bits are lined up with the owner permissions on the left, the group permissions in the middle, and anyone else's permissions on the right, we get the rwxrwxrwx string.

Because these are bits, we can also write a set of permissions as an octal number (octal because each octal digit corresponds to one of the three sets of permissions). Friendly people like to set directories to the permissions 755 (rwxr-xr-x) and files to the permissions 644 (rw-r--r--). Paranoid people use values like 700 and 600. The gullible (and uucp) use permissions like 777 and 666. (I suggest you work out the meanings of these numbers; you will have to code them as arguments to various system calls, so it's time to wean yourself from the rwx strings.)

It would seem natural to assume that if a program has been granted permission to write to a file, it would also have permission to read the file. Not so. To use a file in a particular way, the program must have the corresponding permission for the file. It's possible to set up file permissions in a manner that makes no sense. For example, you can define the permissions of a file so that any program except the owner can write in the file, while a program having the group key can also read the file, and a program having the owner key cannot use the file at all. (This is the permission 062, or ---rw--w-.)

If I've done a passable job of explaining, you now have a fair grasp of the basics of permissions. But I haven't yet talked about the *set-uid* flag, the *set-gid* flag, and the "sticky" bit. (No one calls this last attribute by its proper name: the *save-text*-image flag.)

You'll remember that I said every file is assigned an owner number and a group number as its lock values. Because executable programs are stored in files, they also have owner and group numbers associated with them. When a program file has the `set-uid` bit set as part of its permissions and someone invokes the program, the system sets the owner key of the invoking process to the owner-ID of the program file.

The effect of this is remarkable. Most of the time, programs that you execute run with a set of owner and group keys that are related in an indirect way to who you are. But when the `set-uid` flag is set, the program you executed suddenly gains the power and authority of whatever owner-ID is attached to the file. If the program file has an owner-ID of *root*, you are wielding the power of the superuser, probably without realizing it. It is equally true that if the program file has an owner-ID of `joe` (and the `set-uid` bit is set) you are suddenly restricted to the capabilities Joe has.

Programs you use all the time use this trick. The `mkdir` and `rmdir` commands are examples. Did you know that only the superuser can create a directory? Imagine if the superuser had to be interrupted every time someone wanted to create a new directory. The problem is solved, and the superuser left safely undisturbed, by letting the `mkdir` program borrow the superuser's privilege level just long enough, and just for the purpose of creating a new directory for you. This is safe to do for two reasons: you can get the program to do only what it was written to do (and `mkdir` only makes directories), and the program was written to check that it is safe to allow you to create that directory.

You can use this feature of the permissions system for your own purposes. Suppose that you write a program to do maintenance chores on a special file or set of files in your `$HOME` directory. You can extend the capability to use the program on those files to other users by setting the `set-uid` flag in the permissions of your program along with the execute permission. If you include checks in the program to ensure that it is being used only for its intended purpose, you can rest assured that letting others borrow your user-ID when using that program will do no harm.

The `set-gid` flag works the same way as the `set-uid` flag, except a program file with this bit set assumes the group-ID of the program file, rather than its owner-ID. The `set-gid` flag is somewhat less useful than the `set-uid` flag because group permissions are falling out of fashion in the UNIX world (for good reasons). Still, the `mail` and `mailx` programs use the `set-gid` flag to good effect by allowing both you and the mail programs to manipulate your mail file in the `/usr/mail` directory while preventing others from bothering your mail. You ought to take a brief look at the permissions on the `/bin/mail` program, the `/usr/mail` directory, and files in that directory; you will see a good example of how to put the `set-gid` flag to work for your own programs.

One note: you can set the `set-uid` and `set-gid` flags (permission bits

04000 and 02000, respectively) on shell script files, but it will do no good. The reason is that the key switching described previously is performed only by the system's program loader when reading a binary file. Shell scripts are read by the shell processor, not by the system program loader, so these two flags never get tested for shell scripts.

The third file attribute flag is called the *save-text-image* flag (known in `sys/stat.h` as `S_ISVTX` and having the octal value 01000), or the "sticky" or "tacky" bit. It is usable only by the superuser. When set for an executable program file, the instruction portion of the program (but not the data area) is preserved in memory after the execution of the program is completed, and is reused whenever the program is reexecuted. The `save-text-image` flag is used to improve overall system performance by reducing the amount of system time spent reading frequently used programs into memory from disk. The flag has no other salutary or detrimental affects on the capabilities of your programs, so it is useful mainly to the superuser.

At the beginning of this section, I promised to explain where the permissions keys associated with programs ordinarily come from, for those programs that do not have the `set-uid` or `set-gid` flag set. When users log in to the system, they must enter a user name and a password to prove that they are who they say they are. The user name is read by the `/bin/login` program, which executes with the privileges of the superuser. The `/bin/login` program searches the `/etc/passwd` file, looking for a match on the user name it has just read from the terminal. When a match is found, and assuming that the password is correct, the third and fourth fields of the `/etc/passwd` line specify a user-ID and a group-ID value.

Before loading and executing the shell program, the `login` program sets the real user-ID and real group-ID values of the process to the values given in the password file using the `setuid` and `setgid` system calls. When the shell is loaded, these keys are retained and become associated with the shell. When the shell subsequently executes user commands, the `fork` and `exec` system calls simply pass the real user-ID and real group-ID of the parent process to the new process.

The key values for every program run by the user are thus inherited from the original shell initiated for the user when the user first logged on to the system. A program with superuser privilege can set any values as the user and group keys of the current process, but other programs are restricted to inheriting these values from their parent process.

In other words, the normal keys of programs executed by the user are simply the two values appearing in the `/etc/passwd` file beside the name with which the user logged onto the system. So the user is nothing more than a name and two numeric values stored in a simple ASCII file.

The permissions system I have just described can be manipulated by your programs.

The stat and fstat system calls can be used to identify (but not modify) the owner-ID, group-ID, and permission bits of an arbitrary file. The getuid, geteuid, getgid, and getegid system calls can be used to discover the keys associated with the current process.

The stat call returns the owner-ID of the file in the st_uid member of the stat structure. If the set-uid and execute flags appear in the permissions bits of st_mode, this will be the user-ID with which the program file will execute. Otherwise, it is the user-ID required for owner access privileges to the file.

The group-ID of the file is returned in the st_gid member of the stat buffer. If the set-gid and execute flags appear in the permissions bits, this will be the group-ID with which the program file will execute. Otherwise, it is the group-ID required for group access privileges to the file.

The permissions of a file, as well as a code indicating the general type of file, appear in the st_mode field of the struct stat returned by stat and fstat. A number of bit fields are packed into the st_mode value. Use the mask values defined in the sys/stat.h header file to select an individual bit field.

To identify the file type, extract the format bits using code along the following lines:

```c
int ftype (const char *path)
{
    struct stat buf;

    if (stat(path, &buf) == 0)
        switch(buf.st_mode & S_IFMT) {
            case S_IFDIR: /* Directory */
                return 'd';
            case S_IFREG: /* Regular file */
                return 'f';
            case S_IFBLK: /* Block-special file */
                return 'b';
            case S_IFCHR: /* Character-special file */
                return 'c';
            case S_IFIFO: /* Named pipe */
                return 'p';
            default: /* Unknown type */
                return '?';
        }
    return EOF; /* Type unknown */
}
```

This is an easy function to write, and is more useful than the `exists()` type of function. You might like to add it to your personal library of functions.

Some system implementations define names in the `sys/stat.h` header file for all the permission bits; some do not. For the best program portability, do not rely on the header file to contain names for all the permission bits. The following code sample tests for various permissions:

```
if (buf.st_mode & S_ISUID)
    /* Has set-uid flag set */ ;
if (buf.st_mode & S_ISGID)
    /* Has set-gid flag set */ ;
if (buf.st_mode & 0444)
    /* Has read permission for owner, group, or other */
    ;
if (buf.st_mode & 0222)
    /* Has write permission for owner, group, or other */
    ;
if (buf.st_mode & 0111)
    /* Has execute permission for owner, group, or other */
    ;
```

You can fill in your own code where the comments appear, or adapt the code to your needs.

You can change the owner-ID and group-ID of a file with the `chown` system call, as follows:

```
chown(path, new_uid, new_gid);
```

Note that the call sets both a new owner-ID and a new group-ID at the same time; you cannot set just one or the other. To execute this call, your process must have an effective user-ID (remember, this is the owner key of your process) equal to the current owner-ID of the file. You can't change the ownership of a file unless you already own the file. (The call is permitted anyway if the effective user-ID of the process is `superuser`.) Furthermore, if successfully executed, the `set-uid` and `set-gid` flags of the file are forced off. This prevents an unscrupulous user from creating a `set-uid` program for a user-ID other than the user's own, which would result in the user gaining permissions to which the user has no rightful claim. It also means that if you set the `set-uid` or `set-gid` flags, and change ownership in the wrong order, you lose the flags you just set.

Some systems disallow, or can be configured by the superuser to disallow, use of the `chown` system call by regular users. Applications that depend on the capability to use `chown` are therefore risking problems when ported to another system implementation (or even another installation). The purpose of such a restriction is to enhance overall system security at the expense of user capabilities, which is sometimes a justifiable sacrifice.

You can change the permissions of a file you own (or a file that you don't own if your program is executing with a `superuser` ID) by executing the call

```
chmod(path, 4755);
```

where 4755 are the new permission bits. (An integer variable could have been used as well.)

Both the `chown` and `chmod` calls alter the inode of the affected file. But because the inode does not reside in a directory, the calls do not require write permission for the directory containing the file. The `creat`, `open`, `link`, and `unlink` calls, however, add or delete an entry to a directory, and require write permission for the directory to contain the file.

Other Services

The inode and the `stat` buffer contain three values we have not yet mentioned: `st_atime`, `st_mtime`, and `st_ctime`. The values are system clock values, of the same type returned by the `time` system call. They record when certain events last occurred for the file.

The `st_atime` member is updated with the current system clock value whenever the file is opened for *read* access. Therefore, it remembers when the file was last used. The value can be used to tell when the file has become obsolete and useless.

The `st_mtime` member is updated with the current system clock value when the file is opened for *write* access. Therefore, it remembers when the file was last created or last changed. The value is used primarily to tell when the file has been modified since the last system backup, so that a new backup will be made. This value is also used by the `make` program to tell when a source file has been changed and its related object files need to be rebuilt.

The `st_ctime` member is updated when the inode for the file is changed but the file itself is not, that is, when the file status changes because of the `chown` or `chmod` system call.

The `st_atime` and `st_mtime` values can be altered by the `utime` system call in one of the following ways. `utime` can be invoked with a call of the type:

```
utime(path, (struct timbuf *)&newtimes)
```

where `newtimes` is defined by

```
struct { time_t atime, mtime; } newtimes;
```

The value of the member `atime` replaces the value of `st_atime` in the file inode, and the value of `mtime` replaces the value of `st_mtime` in the file inode. To successfully execute this call, your program must have an effective user-ID matching the file's owner-ID. This means that only the owner of the file may intentionally set artificial values into the timestamps of the file. This restriction is intended to safeguard your own files and system files from users who may want to make a file look too old to be backed up, or have a file removed automatically by system clean-up utilities.

If your program has write access to a file (or ownership of the file), you can invoke the special form of `utime` as follows:

```
utime(path,NULL)
```

This simply sets the file last-access and last-modification times to the current time. The system is more generous with permission to do this because it is generally harmless.

The `umask` system call is called as follows:

```
int umask(int mask);
```

This call sets the *process file-creation mask* to the value *mask*.

The process file-creation mask modifies the permissions of every file created by the process. The modification consists of setting to 0 every bit in the permissions of the new file where the process file-creation mask contains a 1. If `umask` is used to set a process file-creation mask of 022, a new data file created with permissions 666 is actually written with the permissions 644. A new executable program written by the `cc` command with permissions of 777 is actually written with permissions 755. The effect of `umask` in this case is to deny write permission to group and other users, reserving it solely to the file's owner.

When creating a file, your programs should set all the permission bits to 1, specifying 666 for data files and 777 for executable files and directories. The user's process file-creation mask will restrict the scope of access to a smaller range if the user wants to do so.

You may want to code the `umask` system call directly in some of your programs. This is appropriate when writing a program to be used with the `set-uid` flag, for the purpose of managing files in an application directory rather than in the user's own directories. If you do not use `umask` to set the process file-creation mask, new files will be created with inconsistent permissions, using whatever file-creation mask the user of the moment happens to have set.

Therefore, you should override the user's file-creation mask to a value that makes sense for your application.

The mask call is a little peculiar in that it is also used to determine the current setting of the process file-creation mask, because it returns the previous value of the mask. This means that the only way to fetch the mask value without changing it is to use umask to change the mask to any value, then invoke it again to restore its original value.

ulimit is the last system call that we will examine for managing files. The function's calling format is

```
long ulimit (int func, int newlimit);
```

Although the function will perform several services, the two that are of interest for file management are those performed for *func* values of 1 and 2. A value of 1 for *func* returns the current value of the file-size limit of the current process. (The *newlimit* argument is not used and can be omitted when *func* is 1.)

A value of 2 for *func* sets the process file-size limit to the value of *newlimit*. This call will succeed only if the specified file-size limit is less than the current limit or the current process user is superuser.

The file-size limit is specified in units of filesystem blocks, 512 bytes or 1024 bytes. The file-size limit applies only to writing a file, not to reading it. An attempt to write to the end of a file when its size is already equal to the file-size limit results in an error return with *errno* set to ENOSPC, which means that the filesystem is out of room and there is no space for the additional data. When the error is caused by the file-size limitation, the filesystem is not really out of room.

The default file-size limit is usually comfortably large, but you should be aware of this limitation when developing applications that write very large files. You can use a *func* value of 1 to find out the maximum file size permitted by the current shell, and take steps to avoid running out of space, or at least to issue a suitable error message. Perhaps the worst thing you could do is to ignore error return values from functions such as putc, or to omit bothering with ferror checks. This casual approach to error detection and handling can give the impression that writing a large file ended successfully when in fact an unknown number of bytes at the end of the file were lost.

If your program might write a file larger than a megabyte, be careful to check for write errors that may be caused by the ulimit file-size limitation. And don't forget the possibility that the filesystem could run out of space.

Using Low-level I/O

You are probably familiar with the `fopen`, `fclose`, `getc`, and `putc` stream I/O functions. These and the other stream I/O functions provide an efficient, easy-to-use package that meets most programming needs. When they do not, you will need to resort to the low-level I/O functions.

The "Reference" section in this book, as well as the user manuals accompanying your UNIX system, provide a terse description of the low-level I/O functions. But they do not provide much help when you need to know how to use the functions. This section will try to fill that gap.

You need to use the low-level I/O functions when the characteristics of the stream I/O package that are its principal advantages turn into liabilities. The most significant feature of stream I/O is *buffering*. The idea behind buffering is to access the device for data transfer as rarely as possible by reading or writing as much as possible with every transfer.

The implementation of buffering involves allocating a large area of memory called a *buffer*, and then reading ahead of the device by grabbing as much data as will fit in the buffer. When your program wants to read a few bytes, the data is extracted from the buffer, and an internal pointer is advanced so that your next request will retrieve new characters instead of the ones just returned.

Writing works the same way. Requests to write a single character or a few bytes are satisfied by storing the character or characters into the buffer and advancing a pointer to show where subsequent bytes can be stored. When the buffer is full, data is written to the device by writing the entire buffer in a single I/O.

This generally increases the performance of a program dramatically. There are several reasons why:

❑ Devices are much slower than the computer, so it takes a tremendous amount of time to access a device when compared with the speed at which a typical program is executed.

❑ Most devices can transfer bytes only in groups, called *blocks*. Without buffering, requests to read a few bytes at a time may mean that the operating system has to reread (or rewrite) the same block several times.

❑ It takes considerably more time to call the operating system than it would take to call a function linked with your program. The overhead involved in operating system calls is considerable, and is described in

Chapter 13, "Kernel Internals." Unfortunately, every low-level I/O function is a system call.

All of these reasons conspire to make low-level I/O calls inefficient for most applications. Using the stream I/O calls can easily eliminate 90 percent of the low-level calls that a program would otherwise need to make, and that can mean an improvement in the performance of your program by a factor of 10 to 20 or more.

If stream I/O is so beneficial, you may wonder why anyone would want to bypass it. Here are a few reasons.

Small Files

Suppose your program opens a small administrative file, writes a few bytes to it, then closes the file. To the stream I/O functions, the job is not that simple. First the FILE block must be initialized, then a buffer must be allocated. The I/O functions must update counters and pointers as each byte is written into the buffer. When you close the file, the standard I/O package must check whether any data remains in the buffer, write the data out, deallocate the buffer, then deallocate the FILE block. This effort can be compounded even further by using printf to format the output data.

This overhead can be substantially reduced by using low-level I/O. For a small file, you need to read or write only one block of data, so there is no advantage to using stream I/O.

Here is a piece of code that writes a few scraps of information into an administrative file:

```c
#include <fcntl.h>
struct {
    time_t  last_run;   /* Date of last run */
    char    last_user [9];/* User who last ran the report */
    int lines;      /* Num of lines printed */
    int items;      /* Num of items reported */
} ctl_rec;

int update_ctl (char *filename)
{
    int ctl;    /* File descriptor */

    if ((ctl = open(filename, O_RDWR)) < 0)
        return ERROR;
    write(ctl, &ctl_rec, sizeof(ctl_rec));
    close(ctl);
    return OK;
}
```

It isn't important what the administrative file represents. It is meant to be typical of the small files often used by applications for recording and remembering operational parameters. The point is that small files can be manipulated more efficiently with low-level I/O calls than with stream I/O.

Two points in the preceding listing are worth noting. First, note that the control information is written in a machine-dependent format, that is, as a struct. This format is easier to use than formats requiring printf and scanf to encode and decode. Notice that the information in the control record can be used as soon as it is read when stored in this manner, and no formatting is required when writing the file.

The second point involves testing the write call for errors. In principle, the return value from write should be checked for an error, for example with the following code:

```
if (write(ctl, &ctl_rec, sizeof(ctl_rec)) == ERROR)
    {
    perror("ctl file");
    return ERROR;
    }
```

Would you check printf in a similar situtation?

Probably not. Yet the printf call would not write any data to the output file, due to the effects of buffering. The fclose call, on the other hand, must flush all previously unwritten data remaining in the buffer to the output device. Because of the small size of the file, the fclose call will be the only point where any data is written. But fclose is the call least often checked for errors by most programmers.

Considering how often we get by with such slipshod coding techniques, you might wonder whether the write call needs to be checked for errors. My advice would be to check the write call when doing low-level I/O, and check the fclose call when using stream I/O.

Random I/O

Most file processing is sequential, which means that each byte of the file is read in consecutive order from the first to the last. This kind of file processing is well suited to the stream I/O package because the read-ahead buffering technique it uses always "guesses" correctly that data which has not yet been asked for will be asked for in the future.

I am implying that I/O buffering as performed by the stream I/O package is a kind of forecasting technique. The package assumes that it will be efficient to read a full block into memory even though only a few bytes have been requested, because sequential processing is the most common type of file processing. This is not always the case, however. Files can be processed also in random order.

The fseek function repositions a stream file to any byte within it. If the new position is outside the current contents of the file buffer, the entire contents of the buffer are discarded and the next input request (for example, fread or fgets) reads the block containing the new file position into the buffer. Sequential processing resumes from the new position.

This is reasonably efficient when repositioning is infrequent. But if the file processing technique is primarily random, as is the case with some advanced file management systems, the use of stream I/O calls is wasteful. The overhead in managing the buffer serves no useful purpose, and if the stream buffer is larger than a device block, more data will be read than used.

A form of buffering that is useful for random file processing is called *caching*, but it is not supported by stream I/O. Caching allocates multiple buffers, each the same size as a disk block, and keeps the most frequently referenced blocks in the buffers. Less frequently referenced blocks are discarded and the buffers they occupy are reused to satisfy requests for new blocks. Caching will result in a net performance improvement when disk blocks are repeatedly referenced.

Let's take a look at the basic programming needed to manage a disk cache. We will start with a routine to initialize the cache:

```
#include <stdio.h>
#include <fcntl.h>
#include <errno.h>
#include <unistd.h>
#include <sys/types.h>

#define BUF_NB   512      /* Size of a buffer */
#define BUF_NO   12       /* Number of buffers in cache */

/* FORMAT OF A DISK CACHE BUFFER */

struct cbuf {
   struct cbuf *
      prev,              /* Backward chain of cbufs*/
      next;              /* Forward chain of cbufs*/
   off_t   blkno;         /* Block occupying the buffer*/
   char    block [BUF_NB]; /* Disk block*/
   };
/* DISK CACHE CONTROLS */
struct cbuf
   cache,                 /* Anchor for active buffers*/
   *c_free;               /* Buffers in inactive list*/
```

```
int c_file;                 /* File descriptor for file*/

/* CACHE INITIALIZATION ROUTINE */

void init_cache (void)
{
   int b;
   struct cbuf *buf;     /* Current buffer pointer */

   for (b = 0; b < BUF_NO; b++)
   {
      buf = (struct cbuf *) malloc( sizeof(struct cbuf) );
      buf->next = c_free, c_free = buf;
   }

   cache.next = cache.prev = &cache;
}
```

The initialization routine must be called before any I/O routines to chain the cache buffers into a free list. Also noteworthy is the routine's use of a dummy buffer, called cache, which is used to organize active buffers into a circular list. This technique simplifies the insertion and removal of buffers from the active list, as we shall see in the next example.

The readb function reads a block of data into one of the cache buffers, but first it searches the list of active buffers for the requested block. If the block is already in memory, the routine needs only to return a pointer to the buffer. But the readb routine will do a little more in this case. Because we have just had a cache hit, it is reasonable to guess that this block may be referenced again. To increase the probability that this block, which has now been referenced at least twice, will be in the buffer the next time it is needed, the buffer gets moved higher in the buffer list. Because buffers are reused starting at the end of the active buffer list, this will keep the disk block in memory longer.

```
/* READ A DATA BLOCK */

struct cbuf *
readb (off_t offset)
{
   off_t         b;
   struct cbuf *buf;

   b = offset / BUF_NB;
   for (buf = cache.next; buf != &cache; buf = buf->next)
     if (buf->blkno == b)
     {
        /* Remove buffer from busy list */
        buf->prev->next = buf->next;
        buf->next->prev = buf->prev;
```

```
            /* Add to the head of the list */
            buf->next = cache.next;
            buf->prev = &cache;
            buf->prev->next =
            buf->next->prev = buf;
            return buf;
        }
    /* Not in memory--allocate a buffer for the block */

    if (c_free) {
        buf = c_free, c_free = buf->next;
        /* Add to the tail of the list */
        buf->next = &cache;
        buf->prev = cache.prev;
        buf->prev->next = buf->next->prev = buf;
        }

    /* Use the last buffer in the list in any case */

    buf = cache.prev;
    buf->blkno = b;
    lseek(c_file, b * BUF_NB, SEEK_SET);
    read(c_file, buf->block, BUF_NB);

    return buf;
}
```

If the desired block cannot be found, `readb` allocates a buffer and reads the disk block in. The routine prefers to select a previously unused buffer from the free list created by `init_cache`. But if the free list is empty, the last buffer in the cache is selected.

The write routine is much simpler than this, if we assume that a block can be written only if it has previously been read. In such cases, the block is already present in one of the buffers and the only action needed is to call `write` to write the modified block out to the device. The block can continue to occupy the buffer in case it is referenced again. If the block is not referenced again, the buffer containing it will eventually be reused when the buffer falls to the bottom of the busy list.

The `readb` routine can read blocks that fall at integral multiples of the block size only, but often an application may want to reference only part of a block. To support this, we need a higher-level function that can handle requests for a group of bytes that span two blocks, and assemble the two parts into the caller's record area. The implementation of such a function is straightforward, so I will not show it here.

Before leaving this subject, it is worth noting that the caching scheme described is useful only when the program has a tendency to repeatedly access the same collection of disk blocks over a short period of time. The blocks need not be close together in the file. When file references are more scattered, a larger number of buffers may be needed to achieve a high hit ratio. When the references tend to concentrate in particular parts of the file, a smaller number of buffers will suffice. If you are ambitious, the algorithm I have shown could be improved in the following ways:

❑ Monitor the hit ratio using a moving or weighted average. Increase the number of buffers in the cache when the ratio of hits to accesses falls below a minimum threshold. Release buffers when the hit ratio exceeds an upper satisfactory level (90 percent is usually considered very good).

❑ Include a reference counter in each cache buffer, and instead of reordering buffers, select the buffer with the lowest reference count when a free buffer is needed.

In general, the size of a cache buffer for random I/O should not be much larger than the average size of an application record. Larger sizes tend to waste buffer space because there is no assurance that the application will ever reference the other records in the buffer. Buffer sizes may be smaller than a device block size, but this will result in good performance only when the hit ratio is large. The operating system usually has to read or write an entire block regardless of the size specified on a read or write request. Thus, smaller buffer sizes provide no improvement in I/O speed and may overlook hits that would otherwise occur with a larger buffer size.

Extending fopen( )

The system has no built-in restrictions against using both stream I/O and low-level I/O calls for the same file. Mixing calls can cause problems if it is done haphazardly, primarily because low-level I/O is executed immediately but stream I/O is buffered. Let's look at some cases where mixed calls work well.

Chief among these cases may be the use of the open system call in preference to fopen in some situations. The fopen function supports six kinds (or modes) of file access. Each of these modes corresponds to a *mode* value that can be specified on the open call as well. The modes supported by fopen, and the equivalent open modes, are as follows:

"r"   Open the file for input only. The file must already exist. Equivalent to

```
open(fd,O_RDONLY)
```

"r+" Open the file for input and output (*update*). The file must already exist. Equivalent to

```
open(fd,O_RDWR)
```

"w" Open the file for output only. The file will be created if it does not exist; otherwise, it will be truncated to zero length. Equivalent to

```
open(fd, O_WRONLY | O_CREAT | O_TRUNC, 0666)
```

"w+" Open the file for input or append. The file will be created if it does not exist; otherwise, it will be truncated to zero length. All writes are forced to occur at the end of the file, but reads may occur anywhere within the file. Equivalent to

```
open(fd, O_RDWR | O_APPEND | O_CREAT | O_TRUNC, 0666)
```

"a" Open the file for output append. The file will be created if it does not exist; it is never truncated. All writes are forced to occur at the end of the file. Equivalent to

```
open(fd, O_WRONLY | O_APPEND | O_CREAT, 0666)
```

"a+" Open the file for input or append. The file will be created if it does not exist; it is never truncated. All writes are forced to occur at the end of the file, but reads may occur anywhere within the file. Equivalent to

```
open(fd, O_RDWR | O_APPEND | O_CREAT, 0666)
```

As you might guess, not all possible combinations of the open flags are provided by fopen. For example, suppose an application needs to update a file, but if the file does not exist it should be created. The closest fopen mode is "r+", but this option will not create the file. We can get around this limitation by combining the open and fdopen functions as follows:

```
int fd;
FILE *file;

if ((fd = open(fname, O_RDWR | O_CREAT, 0666)) < 0)
    perror(fname), exit(1);
if ((file = fdopen(fd, "r+")) == NULL)
    perror(fname), exit(1);
```

The fdopen function performs all of the actions normally performed by fopen, except for actually opening the file. The *fd* argument must specify a file descriptor number that is already open. It creates a stream FILE block that can be used just like any other stream. The result of the two calls achieves the desired objective.

Using fileno()

There are a number of system calls for low-level file management that we occasionally would like to use with stream files. Examples are the fstat and fcntl calls. But for a stream file, all we have is a pointer to a FILE structure, not a file descriptor number.

The fileno macro defined in stdio returns the file descriptor number underlying the open stream. The fstat call can then be written as follows:

```
FILE *fp;
struct stat i;

/* Call fstat for the open file *fp */

if (fstat(fileno(fp)))
    perror("fstat"), exit(1);

/* Use the returned stat buf: */

if ((i.st_mode & S_IFMT) != S_IFREG) {
    fprintf(stderr, "Not a regular file\n");
    exit(2);
    }
```

If you are using the exec system call in your program, you sometimes may want to set the close-on-exec flag in the file descriptor. This is easy, as in the following example:

```
FILE *fp;

if ((fp = fopen(fname, "r")) == NULL)
    perror(fname), exit(1);
fcntl(fileno(fp), F_SETFD, 1); /* Close on exec! */
```

You can also modify the access mode of a file with fcntl, for example, to add the O_APPEND flag so that all writes occur at the end of the file. The following example opens a file with the "w+" mode so that the file will be created if it doesn't exist. In addition, "w+" mode allows both read and write operations on the file. The fcntl call is then used to change the mode to "a+" for write-append:

```
FILE *fp;

if ((fp = fopen(fname, "w+")) == NULL)
    perror(fname), exit(1);
fcntl(fileno(fp), F_SETFL, O_APPEND); /* Append mode! */
```

You can use a minimal level of advisory file locking with stream files, although the manual cautions against it. As long as the entire file is locked, either for shared or exclusive access, the buffering used with stream files is irrelevant. The cautions in the manual advise you against trying to lock the portion of a file corresponding to one record; when stream buffering is used, a buffer may contain more than one record at a time.

The following example opens a file for input and sets a shared lock on the entire file:

```
FILE *example (char *filename)
{
    FILE *f;
    struct flock lockw;

    lockw.l_type = F_RDLCK;
    lockw.l_whence = SEEK_SET;
    lockw.l_start = 0L;
    lockw.l_len = 0L;

    if ((f = fopen(filename, "r")) == NULL)
        return NULL; /* Open failed */
    fcntl(fileno, F_SETLKW, &lockw);

    return f;
}
```

This lock remains in effect until the file is closed, and it applies to the entire length of the file. The program calling this function may now perform any desired stream operations on the file; no interference between the file locking mechanism and stream I/O will occur.

Summary

On the surface, the UNIX file system appears very simple. The representation of a file as a continuous unstructured stream of bytes is one reason for its apparent simplicity. Another is the UNIX dictum that every device, whether disk, tape, printer, communications line, or printer, will exhibit the same programming interface as a standard disk file. Add to this the spare elegance of the file descriptor and the basic I/O calls `open`, `close`, `read`, `write`, and `lseek`, and the subject of ordinary files might appear to be one quickly dealt with.

However, the competent UNIX programmer must eventually deal with the complexity underlying the UNIX file system. The standard I/O package is convenient and easy to use, but not appropriate for every situation; knowing when not to use standard I/O is an important part of understanding the standard I/O package. Knowing how to replace it with the basic read and write calls is the other part.

This chapter has explained some of the shortcomings of the standard I/O package, and has shown how to remedy them. Using the basic I/O calls effectively, however, requires an understanding of the basic mechanisms by which UNIX operates; we won't be finished with the intricacies of basic I/O until Chapter 15, "Writing Multiprocessing Programs."

10

Directories

Directories are the essential feature of the UNIX file system. One of the pleasures—and one of the difficulties—of working with UNIX is the flexibility and power of nesting directories within directories.

You have been introduced to methods of using directories as a general user and as a shell programmer. Now we will take a close look at what makes directories work, and see how they affect your C programs.

Directory Permissions

In most respects, a directory is a file like any other file. For example, you can name it as the file to be printed by cat. If you do, you will immediately see that it is not a standard ASCII file. Still, this demonstrates that a directory is a file that can be opened and read by your programs. It is special in that the operating system has some built-in knowledge about the organization and contents of a directory, and restricts some of the ways you can handle it.

The file permissions of a directory are similar to those of regular files, but not identical. File permissions are stored in the inode of the file, in a field called the *file mode*. The high-order portion of the field identifies the type of file, in this case a directory. The low-order twelve bits (octal mask 07777) describe the permission to be granted to the directory's owner, members of its group, and to other users for various kinds of operations.

217

The read permission bits (0444) have the same meaning for directory files as for regular files. If the effective user-ID of the current process is the same as the directory's owner-ID, and the permissions contain the mask 0400, the process can read the directory. If the effective user-ID of the current process is not the same as the directory's owner-ID but is the same as the file's group-ID, and permission 0040 is set, the directory can be read because of group affiliation. If the effective user-ID of the current process is not the same as the directory's owner-ID or the file's group-ID, but permission 0004 is set, the directory can be read by any process.

When no read permission for a directory exists, its contents cannot be listed (`ls` will fail) because the attempt by `ls` to open the directory for read access is rejected. This sometimes has dire consequences for system back-up procedures. These procedures, unless they are run by the superuser, will be unable to access the files in the directory. Thus, the contents of the directory will not be backed up.

The write permissions for a directory are represented by the 0222 bits of the file mode, as usual. You will find that you cannot write to a directory, however, even if you have write permission. The system makes a special exception to its interpretation of file permissions for directories. Write permission to the directory is granted by the system open routines only if the requesting process has an effective user-ID of superuser. This restriction is circumvented by only the `creat`, `open`, and `mkdir` system calls, which must write to the directory to do their job.

Setting the write-permission bits on or off for a directory is still useful, but the effect is to allow (or disallow) creating and removing files in the directory. These are the only valid conditions for writing in the directory because it is really just a list of the files it contains. Therefore, the system allows writes to the directory only to create and remove files, and the calls to perform these operations must originate from other system routines such as `creat` and `mkdir`.

Execute permission is represented by the 0111 bits of the file mode: 0100 indicates execute permission for the directory's owner, 0010 indicates execute permission for the directory's group, and 0001 indicates execute permission by others.

Normally, execute permissions are set only for executable files, because these permissions have no meaning and no effect for other types of files. But for directories, the execute permissions have a special interpretation: if the appropriate permission is set (owner, group, or other), the requesting process is allowed to search the directory; if not set, the process cannot search it. Consequently, for a directory, these bits are known as the search permissions; they are called execute permissions only for regular files.

The search permissions have nothing to do with searching the directory; the only way to search a directory is to read through it looking for specific file names, but searching in this sense requires read permission. Search permission actually grants the right to retrieve the inode of one of the files listed in the directory. To use search permission without read permission, you have to know that a file is present without looking for it.

Although unusual, it is not uncommon to want to examine a particular file in some directory, for example when the file names in the directory are predefined or follow a standard naming convention. We will consider the case in which you want to retrieve the inode of a file known to exist in some directory.

If you cannot retrieve the inode of a file, you cannot open it, you cannot produce an ls listing of its status, you cannot execute it, you cannot cd to it (if it is a directory). You cannot use it in any way. This is true regardless of whether you have the necessary access permissions for the file itself. If the directory containing the file does not grant search permission, you cannot access any file in the directory even if you know it is there, and even if you have the necessary read, write, or execute permission to use it.

It is normal to grant to everyone both read and search permissions for a directory. Sometimes, however, you might want to withhold read permission but still grant search permission.

For example, suppose a directory is used for public storage of mail files intended to be delivered to specific users. It is your job to make sure that security is maintained. If your only concern is to ensure that just the intended user and the mail system can read and write a mail file, it would be sufficient to allow only the mail system to have write access to the directory, and it would do no harm to allow all users to read the directory. (Mail files would have read permission only for the intended recipient and the mail system.)

On the other hand, it may be a matter of security to prevent unauthorized users from even finding out who uses the mail system, and who has messages waiting in the public mail directory. In this case, both read and write permission to the mail directory must be denied to other users. But if search permission is granted, then if you know there is a mail file in that directory for you, and you know the name of the file, you can still read the file. Because the mail directory does not grant read permissions to all users, only you will know that the file is there.

Now that you've gone through this example, the benefit of denying read permission should be apparent. Denying read access to the directory does not prevent users from accessing files in the directory, but it does prevent users from discovering what files are present. And without knowing a file's name, you cannot read it. The following example demonstrates the effect of denying read permission:

```
cd $HOME                    # Switch to your home directory
mkdir hidden                # Create a new directory
echo junk >hidden/1         # Make three junk files
echo junk >hidden/2
echo junk >hidden/3
chmod u-r hidden            # Now you don't have read permission
cat hidden/*                # What do you get?
rm -r hidden                # Can't read directory
chmod u+r hidden            # Okay because I'm the owner
rm -r hidden                # Now it works
```

Consider the reverse situation: read access is granted but search access is denied. In this case, the l s command can be used to list the file names in the directory; this requires only read permission. But any attempt to access one of the files in the directory is denied. Even certain forms of the l s command fail, such as a long listing (option - l), because the inode of a file must be retrieved to print out the file's status.

The other permission bits in the file mode, namely the set-uid, set-group-ID, and "sticky" bits (bits 4000, 2000, and 1000, respectively), have no significance when set for a directory because a directory by definition is not an executable file.

File Names

A directory is just a list of file names. The directory file itself consists of a series of records in a standard format defined by the operating system. This format may vary slightly from one version of UNIX to another, but in any version the significant information in an entry is the name of a member file and a pointer to the inode of the file.

The inode will be discussed in more detail later. The file name consists of from one to fourteen characters. (Future releases of System V are expected to increase the maximum length of a file name considerably.) Only the null character (\0) and the slash (/) cannot appear in a file name; all other characters are allowed, including spaces, control characters, and non-ASCII codes. This flexibility can be an advantage. Some users set the file names of a number of shell scripts to the control sequence sent by their terminals when function keys are pressed, so that pressing the key invokes the corresponding shell script as a command. It can also be a disadvantage. A file name consisting of embedded spaces, characters special to the shell, or control codes can be difficult to delete, or even to list.

Two file names are always present in any directory, and cannot be written (or removed). These are the . and .. file names, called *dot* and *dot-dot*, respectively. These file names are written when the directory is created (by the mkdir system call or the mkdir system command). If these files are not present, or are removed by the superuser (who can do anything), the directory is not usable, and represents a threat to system integrity.

The . file is itself a directory. It is a link to the directory that contains it. As a result, a reference to the . file is always a reference to the current directory. The . file is required by UNIX mainly as a convenience to its users. It is much more convenient to type in the command

```
find . -type f -print
```

than using a full path name such as

```
find /u/jjv/cmf/v4/development/source -type f -print
```

The .. file is also a directory. It is a link to the directory containing the current directory, often called the *parent* directory. Just as with the . file, the .. link is present as an aid to filesystem navigation. For example, you can move from the current directory to a "sibling" directory called executables by simply typing

```
cd ../executables
```

instead of the much more lengthy

```
cd /u/jjv/cmf/v4/development/executables
```

Following the chain of .. links is the only way the pwd command can discover the path name of the current directory! If one of the directories in this chain (../../../ and so on) cannot be read, the pwd command will be unable to print the current directory name.

If you have ever listed a freshly created directory, you may have noticed that there are two links to it. The first of these is the link from the name of the directory itself to the data area of the directory on disk, the second is the link from the . file name (in the directory) to the directory's data area. And the directory is not empty; there is no such thing as a directory of size 0, even though files of length 0 commonly exist. This is because the directory file initially contains two entries (. and ..), and therefore has a size equal to the length in bytes of the two entries.

One other feature of directory names is the class of files often called *hidden* files. These are file names beginning with a dot. The shell profile is a hidden file, with a predefined name of .profile in your home directory. You can create hidden files freely, simply by choosing a file name beginning with the dot character.

There is nothing special about these file names, except that some programs (notably ls) ignore them. The -a option of the ls command simply indicates whether ls will list file names beginning with a dot. From the standpoint of the ls command, these file names are not hidden; the ls command simply ignores them unless the -a option is specified. Similarly, the find command, when invoked with the operands

```
find . -print
```

prints the . file name (along with all the other file names in the current directory) but not the .. file name because the . file is in the current directory (it *is* the current directory), but .. is not.

As an interesting aside into how things work, change to your home directory and issue the following two commands:

```
ls .*
```

and

```
ls -d .*
```

In the first example, you get a lengthy listing of all your dot files, all the files in your home directory, all the directories in the parent of your home directory, and a few other files as well. In the second example, you get a clean listing of all your dot files.

The reason for this difference lies hidden in the meaning of the . and .. files. Without the -d option, ls lists the contents of every directory named on the command line. Because the . and .. files are directories, the ls command lists their contents as well, which means the full contents of your current directory and its parent are listed. In the second case, ls just lists the status of directories as if they were regular files and ignores their contents. You may say that you didn't list the . and .. files on the command line, but you did.

Now enter the following command:

```
echo .*
```

and you will get a listing similar to

```
. .. .news_time .profile
```

This proves that the shell does not hide the . and .. files; they are expanded by file name generation just like any other dot file names.

If you write programs that read directory files, you must make the choice between processing or ignoring dot files, and you must especially be aware of the . and .. files.

Inode Numbers

An inode number is simply an index into a disk file table. This table is kept at the beginning of each filesystem. Each entry in the table is a fixed-sized number of bytes. The number of entries in the table is set by the system programmer when the filesystem is created. Each entry is called an inode; the *i* stands for *information*. Inodes come in two varieties, free and used. The number of inodes in a filesystem is fixed when the filesystem is created, but the number of active files in a filesystem varies over time.

When you create a file of any variety, whether regular, directory, or special, the kernel allocates an inode to contain a description of the file. The inode is filled in with all the information needed to manage and administrate the file, except the file name. The information contained in the inode is already familiar to you; it is just the information displayed by a long ls listing.

Because the number of inodes in a filesystem is limited, the number of files (including directories) that can be stored in the filesystem is also limited. The two limitations on the capacity of a filesystem are the number of disk blocks in it and the number of inodes in it. When all the disk blocks are in use, there is no room for another file. Unfortunately, the file system can have vast amounts of free space, but when all the inodes are in use, you still cannot create another file because it cannot be cataloged. It is the system administrator's job to strike a balance between allocating disk space to inodes and data blocks. All implementations of UNIX are alike in that the parameters of a filesystem (its location on disk, the number of inodes allocated, and the total number of data blocks allocated) are fixed values. Filesystems cannot grow or shrink as files and directories do, because in general a filesystem corresponds to a disk volume, and disk volumes certainly do not grow or shrink.

An important piece of information carried in the inode is the number of outstanding links to the file. (The number of links to an inode is displayed by ls.) A link is a pointer in a directory entry to an inode. It establishes the correspondence between a file name and the block of data bytes in the file.

Any number of directory entries can point to the same inode. It doesn't matter whether some of the entries are in the same directory, or whether some are in one directory and some in another. The only restriction is that all directory entries pointing to an inode must be in the same filesystem.

When two directory entries point to the same inode, two different path names represent the same file. I use *path name* rather than *file name* because the same name in different directories normally represents different files. But when the two files are linked to the same inode, the data in the files is the same. If the file is changed using either one of its names, the change is visible when the file is accessed by the other name as well.

This amounts to what in other operating systems is called an *alias*: two (or more) names for the same file. This can be very handy. Do you tire of typing a long path name over and over during a work session? You might feel tempted to copy the file into your current directory so that you don't have to continually type its full pathname. You promise yourself that you will delete the file, but do you? A better alternative is to link the file into your current directory, thus establishing an alias for the path name of the file. (The closest thing in MS-DOS is the subst command, but it makes a drive name an alias for a path name, and it works only with directories, not files.) When you link the file, the system always reminds you that the file in your current directory is a "copy" of the real file, by showing that there are two links to the file in the output of the ls command. Using links is better than copying for other reasons. You save disk space because the file isn't present on disk twice. In addition, if the file is changed using its original path name, your linked copy is also changed—in other words, the link is a dynamic copy.

Let's dispel one of the common misconceptions about links: the question about which of the two files is linked, and which is the original. If you have ever wondered about this, you have probably also tried in vain to find a command that will show the distinction. There is no difference between the two files other than their name. They both have the same permissions, owner, group-ID, size, date and time created...everything about the files is the same except the file names. And if you understand that a directory entry is nothing more than a file name with an inode number, the mystery of links vanishes. Two links simply means that the same block of data on disk is connected to two different file names.

Now what happens if you delete one of the files? The answer is simple and straightforward. The directory entry that you deleted is removed, and the number of links shown in the inode of the file is decremented by 1. As long as the number of links in the inode is greater than 0, the file data is preserved because one or more file names still refer to the data. When the number of links shown in the file's inode goes to 0, the file is removed. So the removal of the last directory entry referring to a file causes the removal of the file.

Now we can see what would happen if either one of two links to a file is deleted. In either case, one of the path names still refers to the file, so the file continues to exist. Only the link count is decremented.

The Root Directory

The root directory is unique in a number of ways. First, the .. link in the root directory points to the root directory itself, rather than its parent because the root directory has no parent. The root directory is the topmost directory of the system.

Because of this convention, you can write a pathname such as ../../ ../../ with any number of .. references, because sooner or later the root directory is encountered, and all subsequent .. references loop back to the root directory.

Second, the root directory of the system is a filesystem. It may be the only filesystem on your machine, or other filesystems may be mounted on it. To find out how many filesystems are actually on-line, issue the df command; it prints a status report for each mounted filesystem.

Each filesystem is formatted as if it were a directory; it may also contain several subdirectories, just as root does. But the top directory of every filesystem contains a .. file that points to itself. This means that in UNIX, no directory entry ever points outside the filesystem that contains it. This follows from the fact that inode numbers are not unique between filesystems. Each filesystem counts its first usable inode as inode number 2, and the rest of the inodes are numbered from there. Thus, if a directory entry links a file name to inode number 1206, the system cannot be confused about whether this means inode number 1206 in filesystem x, or inode number 1206 in filesystem y, because by convention the directory entry always refers to the same filesystem as that containing the directory entry.

The root directory is automatically mounted by the system boot procedure. By definition, the root directory is the top directory of the volume from which the system was booted.

After the root filesystem is mounted, all the directories in it become accessible. It is also possible to mount other filesystems so that their contents can be accessed.

When a filesystem is mounted, one of the directories of an already mounted filesystem is chosen as a *mount point*. The mount command simply overlays the chosen directory with the root directory of the new filesystem. The original contents of the overlaid directory are no longer accessible, because references to that directory are translated by the kernel into a reference to the mounted filesystem. Thus, while we may smoothly write a pathname like /usr/ include, its access may involve passing from the root directory (/) across a mount point (usr), and possibly across another mount point (include, mounted on usr).

Programming

Programming for directories involves three kinds of activities:

❏ Recognizing a directory from its response to the stat system call

❏ Reading a directory to find out what files are in it

❏ Walking a directory hierarchy, visiting every file in every subdirectory nested inside the starting directory

The first of these is the simplest task, and we will look at it first. Reading directories can be easy or difficult, depending on the degree to which you are concerned with portability issues. We will consider methods for reading directories second. Walking a directory tree, although difficult conceptually, is simple in practice because the C functions library includes a function called ftw that does just this. We will take a look at using ftw at the end of this chapter.

Recognizing a Directory

Identifying a file as a directory starts with having a path name for the directory. You might get this path name from the user, or you might discover it as a file name listed in another directory. In either case, a typical question your programs must address is whether to open the path name as a standard file or as a directory.

To find out, invoke the stat function, or the fstat function if you have already opened a file descriptor for the file. The stat and fstat functions return file status information in a stat buffer. The sys/stat.h header file contains a description of the stat struct, so include this in your program when using stat or fstat.

The stat buffer returned by stat contains the member st_mode, commonly called the file mode. The bits of the file mode corresponding to the value of S_IFMT (also defined in sys/stat.h) contain a code that identifies the file type. The possible codes are shown in table 10.1. The ls command prints this code as one of the characters *b*, *c*, *d*, *p*, or - at the start of a long listing line.

Table 10.1. *File-mode File Types*

Value	File type
S_IFBLK	Block-special file
S_IFCHR	Character-special file
S_IFDIR	Directory file
S_IFIFO	Named pipe
S_IFREG	Regular file

The following example shows how to test the path name for a directory using these codes:

```
#include <sys/types.h>
#include <sys/stat.h>

int
is_directory(const char *filename)
{
    struct stat buf;

    if (stat(filename, &buf)) {
        perror(filename);
        return (0);
        }

    return ((buf.st_mode & S_IFMT) == S_IFDIR);
}
```

Several things are worth noting in this example. First, we remember to test the return value of the stat system call by placing it in an if statement. If we did not to do this, the return statement could end up testing a garbage value in struct stat because the whole struct is automatic (it is allocated at function entry).

Second, although the statement

```
if (stat(filename, &buf) != 0)
```

would be more explicit when checking for an error return, the test for nonzero is redundant because the if statement does this. Therefore, when checking for an error return from a system call, where a successful return is always indicated by a return value of 0, it is necessary only to write the system call inside the if expression and use the then statement to handle the error.

Note that when stat fails, the function performs a perror call before returning because in this case we do not know whether the path name refers to a directory. We have a fifty-fifty chance of guessing wrong when we return 0 to mean that *filename* is not a directory. This means that the calling routine may behave incorrectly when it tries to base further processing on the return value of is_directory. The error message documents a reason why this incorrect behavior might have occurred.

We do all the work of checking for a directory in the return statement. The test consists of two steps. First, the & operation uses the S_IFMT mask defined in sys/stat.h to isolate the file format flag in the st_mode field. We have to do this because the st_mode field also contains other values such as the permission bits; thus, it is important to discard the irrelevant bits of st_mode. Then we test the isolated file format value for being equal to the code for directory. The S_IFDIR label is the value we are looking for in st_mode.

Reading a Directory

There are several methods for reading directories, depending on your needs. If you can count on running your program on a System V Release 3 (or higher release) system, the best method is to use the *dirent* package.

If you must support earlier releases of the system, you can try reading the directory directly, but this is dangerous because different versions of UNIX use different directory formats. Generally, System V implementations are sufficiently similar that you will often succeed with this approach. Try it if you want, but be aware that you may have portability problems.

As a final alternative, you could try invoking the ls command as a child process, and reading its output from a pipe. Although this certainly entails a lot of overhead, it will work on almost any version of UNIX (as long as you avoid option flags on the command, and support multicolumn output as well as a simple list). If you are really interested in this approach, start by reading the manual page for the popen function.

The *dirent* package, available in System V Release 3 and above, is remarkably easy to use. The package provides six functions:

The opendir function opens a directory file for read access. The function returns a pointer to a DIR, analogous to the FILE pointer returned by fopen.

The closedir function closes a directory file. This function requires a pointer to a DIR returned by a previous opendir call.

The readdir function reads the next directory entry from the directory file identified by a DIR pointer. As long as the seekdir and rewinddir functions are not used, readdir simply returns the active entries of the directory file one after another, or EOF when the end of the directory is reached. (Note that a UNIX directory file may contain "holes"—inactive entries—left by previous unlink operations.)

The seekdir function modifies the current location in the directory file pointed to by DIR so that the next readdir call will retrieve the directory entry corresponding to the *loc* argument. The seekdir function requires two arguments: a DIR pointer to identify the directory file, and a long to designate a new directory location for the seek. Usually, the value of *loc* is a byte offset from the beginning of the directory file; its value should correspond to the start of a directory entry. The *loc* value is not defined to be a file offset, however, so all *loc* values passed to seekdir should be values obtained from previous telldir calls, without arithmetic or other alterations having been performed on them.

The telldir function returns the current location in the directory file pointed to by the DIR argument. The value returned can be used in a subsequent seekdir call to restore the directory position to the location in effect when the telldir function was called.

The rewinddir function is a macro that invokes the seekdir function in such a way that the current directory position is reset to the beginning of the directory. The directory entry returned by the next readdir call will be the first active directory entry in the file.

The *dirent* package also provides the dirent.h header file, which defines, among other things, the DIR object used by all the functions and the format of a directory entry as returned by readdir.

The value returned by readdir is a pointer to a directory entry structure. The format of this structure (struct dirent) does not necessarily agree with that of actual directory entries in your version of UNIX. It is a system-independent format that will be the same for all implementations of System V Release 3 and up. Its format therefore supports portable programming.

The dirent structure contains two members of general interest, namely an inode number and a file name. The inode number is generally not of much use. The proper way to retrieve an inode is to use the stat or fstat function, so you will generally ignore the inode number. The inode number is not useless, however. As long as you know that two path names lie in the same filesystem, you can use the inode number to tell whether the two path names refer to the same file. This is the criterion used by the cp command to detect and avoid an attempt to copy a file to itself.

The file name member is a character array of undefined length containing the file name of the file, ending with a null character (\0). The array size is not really undefined for any given implementation of System V, but the maximum length of a file name can vary from one implementation to another. Generally, you should not be concerned with the size of a file name, but if you must know, the dirent.h header file defines the MAXNAMLEN value to correspond to the array size that will be sufficient to contain all the characters of a file name plus a trailing null character. The file name is a simple name containing no slashes; the file referred to is by definition a member of the directory being read. Therefore, the full path name of a file in the directory is simply the path name of the directory, plus a slash, plus the file name. There is no point in storing full path names in directory entries, and in fact this is not done in UNIX.

The following simple program reads a directory using the *dirent* functions, and prints the file names and inode numbers it finds:

```
#include <stdio.h>
#include <sys/types.h>
#include <dirent.h>

main(int argc, char *argv[])
{
    DIR *dir;
    struct dirent *entry;

    if (argc != 2) {
        fprintf( stderr, "Usage: %s dir-path\n", *argv);
        exit(2);
        }

    if ((dir = opendir(argv[1])) == NULL) {
        perror(argv[1]);
        exit(1);
        }

    while ((entry = readdir(dir)) != NULL)
        printf("%7ld  %s\n", (long)entry->d_ino, entry->d_name);

    closedir(dir);
    return 0;
}
```

Taking it from the top, you will notice that three header files are required: stdio.h because we want to use the standard I/O package to do printing, dirent.h because we want to use the *dirent* functions, and sys/types.h because the dirent.h header uses it internally (which is why it is placed before rather than after dirent.h).

The `main` function declaration is written in ANSI C style; you may have to change this to the older K&R style if your system does not include an ANSI compiler. The K&R version of this function is

```
main(argc, argv)
int argc;
char *argv[];
{
...
}
```

The next order of business is declarations, of which we need two. The first defines a variable of type "pointer to `DIR`" that we will use for referring to the directory file. The second is a pointer to a struct of type `dirent`. It will hold the return value from `readdir` so that we can examine the directory entries. These are the only variables we will need.

We expect that the program will get the path name of the directory from the command arguments. But to assume that the argument is present would be poor form, so we check that the number of arguments is as expected. The correct number is two: in UNIX, the first argument is always the name used to invoke the program, and the second is the first command argument. If the expected number of arguments is not present (finding either more or less), we indicate an error by printing a usage message, on the assumption that users would have entered a correct command if they had remembered the command syntax.

The directory file is opened in much the same fashion as a standard stream file. But notice that `opendir` does not require a mode argument as does `fopen`. Because directories can only be read, it would be redundant to require an `"r"` argument. Also, `opendir` returns a pointer to a `DIR` structure, not to a `FILE`. As with `fopen`, a NULL return value indicates that the file could not be opened, and `perror` can be used to explain the problem to the user.

Reading the directory entries is trivial. Our example loops until a NULL pointer is returned, which indicates that the end of the directory file has been reached. The `printf` function is used to print the contents of each entry. The inode is printed as a seven-digit number. I used a field width for printing the inode numbers to force the file names to line up in a printed column, and chose a width of seven digits because on some of the bigger UNIX systems, a filesystem can be large and the inode numbers for really big filesystems can easily be in the six-digit range.

Also important for maintaining program portability is to not make assumptions about the size of a field. In this example, I cast the inode number to `long` so that I could use the `%ld` format for printing, thus handling both large and small values of the inode number. (If you have peeked at the dirent.h on your system and found that d_ino *is* a long, I can assure you that on some system it is defined as a short.) I also arranged to print the file name at the end of the line, thus avoiding any need to know the maximum length of a file name. Portability consists largely of careful attention to such details.

We have seen that reading directories can be easy when Release 3 of System V is available and the *dirent* functions can be used. But what if you have to write a program that must run on Release 2, or even XENIX? As mentioned, there are no guarantees that you can do this. With this caution in mind, we can observe that Release 2 includes a dir.h header file (usually in the /usr/include/sys directory) that gives us at least a chance of doing so.

This header defines at least two members (d_ino and d_name) as components of a struct direct, as well as a symbolic value DIRSIZ representing the maximum length of a file name. This header defines the structure of a real directory entry, so it varies from one implementation of UNIX to another.

In UNIX, directories can be read as if they were files. Thus, we can combine the capability to read files with the information about the structure of a directory entry to make a reasonably portable program. The following sample works on one version of a System V Release 2 system, as well as on a machine with a Berkeley BSD4.2 file system:

```c
#include <stdio.h>
#include <sys/types.h>
#include <sys/stat.h>
#include <sys/dir.h>

main(argc, argv) int argc; char *argv[];
{
    FILE *dir;
    char *filename;
    struct stat buf;
    static struct {
        struct direct entry;
        char nulls[2];
    } io;

    if (argc != 2) {
        fprintf( stderr, "Usage: %s dir-path\n", *argv);
        exit(2);
        }

    filename = argv[1];

    if ((dir = fopen(filename, "r")) == NULL ||
        fstat(fileno(dir), &buf)) {
        perror(filename);
        exit(1);
        }
```

```
    if ((buf.st_mode & S_IFMT) != S_IFDIR) {
        fprintf( stderr, "%s: not a directory\n", filename);
        exit(2);
        }

    while ( fread((char *)&io.entry, sizeof io.entry, 1, dir)) {
        printf("%7ld  %s\n", (long)io.entry.d_ino, io.entry.d_name);
        }

    fclose(dir);
    return 0;
}
```

This program uses f s t a t to test whether the input file is a directory; the previous program did not because the o p e n d i r function performs this service internally for the caller. The example uses one i f statement to test for both an open failure and an f s t a t error because the same action is required in both cases.

The two example process the directory entries is a manner that is not completely dissimilar. The d i r . h version, however, must read each directory entry into a buffer; there is no r e a d d i r routine to return a pointer to it. The entries are read using the f r e a d function, which gives us the advantage of using stream-file I/O buffering. The r e a d low-level function could also have been used but would have incurred greater overhead than f r e a d.

You are probably wondering why the s t r u c t d i r e c t is embedded in another s t r u c t. The reason is that the D I R S I Z value defined in d i r . h specifies the maximum length of a file name *excluding* a trailing null character. To conserve disk space, the real directory entry does not reserve a byte location to hold a trailing null for the file name. As a result, the s t r u c t d i r e c t does not include space for a trailing null either.

Therefore, if we print output directly from the directory entry, maximum length file names could be printed as garbage. To avoid that risk, the example embeds the directory entry I/O buffer in a larger s t r u c t that does have trailing null characters following the directory entry. This allows us to print the file name directly from the I/O buffer without having to move the file name to another larger area to append a null. Note, however, that this technique works only if the file name occurs at the end of the directory entry; there is no guarantee that this is the case for all versions of UNIX.

When I run this example on my home directory, the output looks like this:

```
154    .
  2    ..
209    .profile
117    .news_time
```

```
116   lib
173   bin
 45   .logout
 46   notes
 79   mbox
944   src
  0   test
  0   map
712   .trashcan
  0   terminfo
  0   floppy.count
```

Notice that the file names are not in sorted order. The program prints directory entries in the order in which it finds them. UNIX does not keep directories in sorted sequence, which may be a surprise to you because most utility programs (including ls and even the shell) print file names in alphabetical order.

But what are these lines with 0s for inode numbers? Remember, the readdir function returns only active directory entries; it automatically skips inactive entries. Once again, our portable example reads actual directory entries, so it is responsible for identifying and skipping inactive ones. The lines with 0 inode numbers are for files that have been removed. They no longer physically exist.

The portable example should be modified so that it tests for 0 inode numbers and skips them. I left the test out of the example so that you could see the result of its omission. You might enjoy running this program on some of your directories.

Walking a Directory Tree

Processing directories recursively is a frequent request, and UNIX has long had a function in the standard libraries for doing just that. The ftw function is simple to use, although it requires some C programming techniques you may not have used before.

The ftw function has the following calling syntax:

```
int ftw (const char *pathname, int (*fn)(), int depth);
```

I am sure that the *pathname* argument presents no problem; it is simply a pointer you provide to a null-terminated string containing the path name of the directory to be traversed. The ftw function does not examine any higher-level directories.

After ftw processes each file in the starting directory, it goes to the next file in the directory. If ftw finds a file that is itself a directory, it temporarily suspends reading in the current directory, remembers its position so that it can come back to it later, opens the new directory file it just found, and begins scanning the entries in that directory one by one. If ftw finds a directory in that directory, it does the same, now figuratively keeping two place holders to remember where it was, and begins processing that directory. When ftw comes to the end of a directory, it closes the directory file and returns to the last-remembered place in the most recently opened directory. This process continues, with ftw pushing directories on and popping directories off an internal stack, until ftw works its way through all the subdirectories of the starting directory, and all of their subdirectories, and so on, until it finally comes to the end of the starting directory. Then it quits and returns to its caller.

This brings us to the second argument of ftw, namely *fn*. This must be a pointer to a function you have written and included in your program (*fn* here stands for *function*). As you may recall from your study of the C programming language, the name of a function is defined to be a pointer, just like the name of an array. So it is not difficult to get a pointer to a function, despite the rather intimidating appearance of the argument's declaration. You just write the name of the function as the second argument to ftw.

With each file and directory that ftw finds, it calls your function and passes it a few items of useful information. Specifically, ftw assumes that your function is declared as follows:

```
int fn (const char *path, struct stat *statbuf, int flag);
```

(I will explain these arguments in a moment.) When your function is entered, you may do whatever you like. You should not, however, use the chdir function to change the current directory. The ftw function assumes a constant current working directory. If you change the current directory, ftw will become lost and its file reports will be meaningless.

What you do in the function is up to you. You might want to open the file that ftw has found and process it, or you might like to print its path name. The *path* argument that ftw passes to your routine is a pointer to a null-terminated character string containing the path name of the file it has found. The string begins with a verbatim copy of the path name you provided to ftw as its starting directory. This is followed by the names of the subdirectories ftw has open when it found this file, separated by slashes. Finally, the file name is tacked on the end. In the sample program for ftw, you will see how the path name of the starting directory can be removed from the front of the path name passed to your routine to get only the path name of the file relative to the starting directory.

The second argument passed to your routine by ftw, namely *statbuf*, is a pointer to a stat structure. The ftw function will have already performed a stat system call on the path name pointed to by *path*, filling in the stat structure that it is passing to you. The ftw function has to perform a stat function call to determine whether the file it is looking at is a directory, so it passes a pointer to the returned stat structure to your routine so that you can avoid the overhead of performing two stat calls for every file.

The third argument passed to your routine, namely *flag*, is a code that tells you something about the file that is being passed. These codes are defined in the ftw.h header file that you must include in your program, and are listed in table 10.2.

Table 10.2. *FTW Flags*

Flag value	Meaning
FTW_F	Regular file
FTW_D	Directory
FTW_DNR	Unreadable directory
FTW_NS	No status in statbuf

The first two flags, FTW_F and FTW_D, are for your convenience. You could have figured out whether the file was a directory simply by examining the contents of the stat structure passed by ftw.

The FTW_DNR flag warns you that although ftw has performed a stat function for the file and determined that the file is a directory, it cannot open the directory because you do not have read permission for it. You can ignore this warning; it means that you will receive no file reports for any files in this directory because ftw cannot read it. The call by ftw with the FTW_DNR flag set is the last you will hear of this directory. The ftw function is forced to go to the next file in the currently open directory, ignoring any contents in the unreadable directory.

The FTW_NS flag is perhaps a more severe warning. It tells you that, although ftw has been able to find this file by reading the currently open directory, the stat buffer pointed to by the *statbuf* argument contains only garbage because the stat call for this file failed. When the FTW_NS flag is set, you should not examine the contents of the struct pointed to by the *statbuf* argument; its contents are unrelated to the file for which your *fn* function is being called.

But the implications of the FTW-NS flag are more severe than this. Because ftw cannot retrieve the file status, it cannot determine whether the file is a regular file or a directory. (The inability to retrieve the file status implies that an attempt to open the file will fail, because you do not have search permission for the directory that f t w is currently reading.) Just as with F T W_D N R, if this file is a directory, the directory will be ignored. Unlike F T W_D N R, we do not know whether the file was a directory, so we may or may not be missing some files.

At this point, there is still one argument to the f t w function that we have not discussed. The *depth* argument of f t w has nothing to do with specifying or limiting the nesting depth to which f t w will process directories. The *depth* argument is somewhat misnamed, although this is what it is called in the UNIX manuals.

The *depth* argument specifies how many different file descriptors the f t w function can open for reading directories (it opens none for any other purpose). The problem is that the nesting level of a directory structure is virtually unlimited, whereas the number of file descriptors that a process may have open at one time is definitely limited. The easiest way for f t w to scan a directory is to open a new file descriptor and read it. This is also the most efficient way because the directory that f t w was reading will remain open. The f t w function can resume reading it when finished with the new directory simply by picking up where it left off.

There is a less efficient way to read nested directories, and f t w is prepared to use it if necessary. The method is to save the current position in the open directory on an internal stack managed by f t w, then close the file descriptor and reopen it for the new lower-level directory. When f t w has finished reading the new directory, it has to pop the stack, reopen the directory that it was previously reading, then execute the l s e e k system call to restore its position in the directory.

Because this method is just as effective as opening new file descriptors, f t w can get by with a *depth* value as small as 1. With higher values, f t w can defer opening and closing directories to save file descriptors until it reaches a nesting level in the directory hierarchy that requires it. With values greater than ten, it is unlikely that f t w will ever have to resort to the slower method...how often have you seen a directory tree greater than ten levels deep?

Unfortunately, you may not be able to afford allocating ten or more file descriptors to f t w for its use. The traditional limit of open file descriptors per process is twenty; many installations allow more (it is a configuration parameter), but some do not. It is true that f t w is prepared to automatically switch to reusing file descriptors if an attempt to open one fails, so why do you need to specify a *depth* value? The answer lies in the fact that you may want to open one or more files in your *fn* routine. If f t w has already opened all available file descriptors, you will be able to open none. Furthermore, f t w has no way of knowing how many files you want to open in your *fn* routine, so the *depth* argument is the only way you can reserve some for your own use.

If you want some file descriptors left over for your routine, you have to count the number of file descriptors you will already have open when you call ftw, add one each for the standard input, standard output, and standard error files, then add the number you want to use in your *fn* routine. Subtract the sum of these counts from the total number of file descriptors your system allows open per process. (The number is usually defined in the stdio.h header file as the value _NFILE, though to be safe you should check with your system administrator. The system adiministrator can change the limit without altering the stdio.h file.) The difference is the value you should specify for *depth*.

At this point I can finally present an example of a program that uses the ftw function to perform a useful task:

```
/********************************************************************
NAME
    wro - find files writable by others
SYNOPSIS
    wro [ pathname ]

DESCRIPTION
    This program is an example of the use of the ftw library
    function to visit all the files in all the subdirectories
    of a directory. If an argument is supplied, it is taken
    as the path name of the starting directory to be searched;
    otherwise, we start with the current directory (".").

    Each file found that extends write permission to others
    and is owned by the current process-ID (presumably "me")
    is listed on standard output.

********************************************************************/

#include <stdio.h>          /* Needed for stream I/O */
#include <string.h>         /* String function package */
#include <ftw.h>            /* Needed for use of ftw() */
#include <sys/types.h>      /* Prerequisite for sys/stat.h */
#include <sys/stat.h>       /* Stat structure definitions */

char* start_dir;            /* Path of starting directory */
int me;                     /* Real user-ID of current proc */
int display();              /* Pathname logging function */

main(argc, argv)
int argc;
char *argv[];
{
    /*
```

```
       Check for a path name on the command line.
       If none is supplied, we will use the current directory
       as the default.
       */

       start_dir = ".";

       if (argc > 1)
           start_dir = argv[1];

       /*
       Invoke ftw...it will in turn invoke the display routine
       for each file or directory it finds.
       */

       me = getuid();
       return ftw(start_dir, display, 15);
}

/* ---------------------------------------------------------
   DISPLAY - check for write-by-others permissions
   ----------------------------------------------------- */

int display (pathname, buf, flag)
char *pathname;
struct stat *buf;
int flag;
{
    switch (flag) {

    case FTW_DNR:   /* Unreadable directory */
        fprintf( stderr, "%s: unreadable directory\n",
            pathname);

        /* Fall through to test the directory itself. */
    case FTW_F: /* Normal file */
    case FTW_D: /* Directory */
        if ((buf->st_mode & 022) && buf->st_uid == me)
            puts(pathname); /* This file is in danger! */
        break;

    case FTW_NS:    /* File, no status available */
        fprintf( stderr, "%s: no status, file ignored.\n",
            pathname);
        break;

    }

    return 0; /* Normal return */
}
```

If you have ever used uucp, you know that files received for you are stored in a public directory (/usr/spool/uucppblic) until you retrieve them. These files are always stored with open-door permissions (rw-rw-rw-). I often forget to correct them to the permission setting I prefer, namely (rw-r--r--). The sample program searches the directory named on its command line (and, through ftw, all subordinate directories) for files having write permission for other users. The path name of each file found is written to standard output. You could collect these path names in a file, or pipe the output to the xargs command, to correct the permissions of the errant files.

I am sure you can find ways to improve the program and customize it to your specific needs. I developed it primarily because I found it too awkward to set up the find command to do the job.

Summary

This chapter explains the general structure of a directory. As with most things in UNIX, directories are really very simple objects. A directory is simply a list of filenames together with pointers to the files named. The file system itself is not hierarchical; it is simply a collection of files together with a table of contents, the entries of which are called *inodes*.

The directory enables you to organize these files any way you want, simply by listing the files that you want to be considered included in the directory. Because a directory only contains pointers to files, you can include the same file in multiple directories.

The UNIX term for a directory entry is a *link*, because it links a filename with the file itself. The link system call creates new directory entries; the unlink system call removes them. The creat, open, and mknod system calls create both a file and a link, because a file cannot exist without at least one directory entry to point to it.

Directories are an essential part of the UNIX operating system; you will encounter them constantly. The ability to access directories from within our programs is essential if your programs are to execute efficiently; it is hardly efficient to invoke the ls system command whenever you need to scan a directory.

This chapter presented three ways to process a directory. The ftw library function is the simplest of the three to use, and is available in all implementations of UNIX; its use is preferred when the full extent of its services is required, or when portability of program code is of paramount importance; its major disadvantage is that it incurs a lot of overhead and therefore runs rather slowly.

The *dirent* function package provides the most elegant of the three directory access interfaces. It is designed to be independent of both the hardware and software environment, and therefore provides excellent program portability. Its use is preferred when you need to scan the contents of a directory, but do not necessarily need to examine subdirectories that might be contained in the directory.

Unfortunately, the *dirent* package is only available beginning with release 3 of UNIX System V. If you need to support earlier releases of System V, or to support other versions of UNIX, you may need to read a directory with the normal I/O calls. This chapter presents a sample program that can read a directory using only the fopen and fread calls. Although the program is likely to work in almost any environment, it cannot be guaranteed to work. The sample is given to show you how you might go about reading directories without the *dirent* package; you will have to adapt it to your specific environment.

The remaining chapters do not depend very strongly on the contents of this chapter. Because it deals with directories, though, and directories are central to UNIX, it is essential that you study this chapter carefully. If you have access to a UNIX system, write a sample program for each method of directory access, and get it to work. Many of the programs you write in the future will depend on the knowledge you gain through such exercises.

CHAPTER __ **11**

Special Files and Pipes

I n the previous two chapters we have discussed filesystems, regular files, and directories. In this chapter we will look at the remaining file types.

Special files are of two kinds: block-special files and character-special files. The subject of block-special files will be completed in this chapter. The discussion of character-special files (especially terminals and similar devices) will continue into Chapter 12, "Programming with Serial Devices." Because a detailed explanation of the workings of pipes has not been given elsewhere, both regular and named pipes will be described in this chapter.

Special Files

In addition to ordinary files and directories, which we have already discussed, UNIX supports a class of files called *special files*. These come in three varieties: *character-special*, *block-special*, and *pipes*.

None of these are files in the ordinary sense. Character-special and block-special files are devices. Named pipes are neither files nor devices; we discuss this type of file later.

The original designers of UNIX had to choose some way to represent devices to users and application programs. For various reasons, they chose to depart from the more traditional methods and to represent devices as if they were just more files in the UNIX file system.

243

The major advantage reaped from this choice is that today we can use a device as easily as a disk file. A program designed to write its output to the terminal, such as ls, can be told to write its output into a file:

```
ls >myfiles
```

or directly to a printer:

```
ls >/dev/lp
```

It makes no difference to ls, because disk files, printers, tape drives, and modems present the same interface to the program.

Because the UNIX designers chose to fit devices in the scheme of the UNIX file system, the names of devices look the same as those of any other file. In fact we find that a device such as a terminal or a printer must be allocated an inode in some filesystem. Because an inode must be cross-referenced to one or more directory entries to be used, this leads to the curious situation of finding devices listed in directories, or even in subdirectories of directories. For example, a path name for the primary system disk drive might be /dev/dsk/0s0; a printer might be referred to as /dev/lp.

Normally, all devices are listed in the /dev directory or in one of its subdirectories, but this is merely a convention. There would be nothing wrong in making a directory entry for the system printer in your own home directory, although this would be highly unusual. For example

```
/u/joe/devices/printers/line_printer_1
```

The catch is that a directory entry for a device can only be created by the superuser, and most superusers are conservative folks who follow standard UNIX conventions.

Unfortunately for the operating system, merely creating a directory entry for a printer does not make the printer work like a disk file. The kernel must detect that an attempt to write to /dev/lp is an attempt to write to a printer, and must compensate for that fact by interpreting the program's write requests in a manner appropriate to a printer device. To do that, the kernel must first know that the /dev/lp path name is a character device and not an ordinary disk file. This distinction is recorded in the inode for /dev/lp by showing the file type as a character-special file as opposed to a regular file.

The value of st_mode in the inode entry for a special file is S_IFCHR if it is a character-special file, or S_IFBLK if it is a block-special file. These values are distinct from S_IFREG, which indicates a regular file, and S_IFDIR, which indicates a directory. Thus, the first thing the kernel does when opening a file, beyond reading its inode, is to check the inode file type. If the file type indicates S_IFCHR or S_IFBLK, subsequent read and write requests will get the specialized handling they need.

The inodes for special files differ from other inodes in another important respect. To access a device, the kernel must know which device to access. The file name of the special file cannot be used for this purpose because it is a name for the device, and the kernel requires a unique address to identify the device. To put it another way, two different devices might have the same file name, or the same device might have two or more different file names. For example, /dev/printers/a and /dev/tapes/a both have the same file name, namely *a*, yet they refer not only to different devices, but to different kinds of devices. On the other hand, some programs might require a tape drive to have the file name /dev/mt0, but other programs might require the name /dev/mt/0m. The system programmer can solve this problem by executing the following command:

```
ln /dev/mt0 /dev/mt/0m
```

This creates a second file name to refer to the same device.

The ambiguity of file names is circumvented by reserving a field in the inode to contain a device identifier. The st_rdev field of the inode serves this purpose. The contents of the field are meaningless for most file types, but for character- and block-special files, the st_rdev field contains the device number, and uniquely identifies the physical device represented by the special file.

The value of st_rdev is made up of two parts: the major device number and the minor device number. The major device number identifies the device driver to be called when I/O to the device is needed. You can think of it as an identifier for the class of devices to which this device belongs, for example disk, tape, terminal, or printer; but no such formal list of device classes exists. It is generally true that only one kind of driver is present in the system for disks, only one kind of driver for terminals, and so on, but this is coincidence and not due to any restriction. The freedom to install more than one device driver for printers allows you to attach diverse kinds of printers.

The device driver may have been written by the same people who developed the operating system, but often a driver is written by the manufacturer of a device and is part of the package you get when you buy the device. If you are the system administrator, it will be your job to install the device driver into the UNIX kernel before installing the device on the system. (Instructions for installing a device driver are provided in your system documentation, and vary from one version of System V to another. Additional instructions may also be included in the vendor's package for the device.)

The minor device number is used by the device driver to select a particular device in the group of devices supported by the driver. The UNIX kernel does nothing with the minor device number. It merely passes the minor device number to the driver when requesting an I/O service from it.

You can discover the major and minor device numbers of particular devices by invoking the `ls` command to display the inode for one of the file names of the device. For example, the command

```
ls -l /dev/lp
```

produces the following on my system:

```
crw-rw----    2 lp        adm          7,   0 Mar 18  1986 /dev/lp
```

The first character of the line, as always, identifies the type of the file. In this case it is *c*, indicating that `/dev/lp` is a character-special file. There are two links to this inode. One link is this path name, `/dev/lp`. We cannot tell what the second link is from this listing. The owner of the device is listed as `lp`, and the group owner is `adm`. Both have read and write permission for the device, but other users can neither read nor write to this particular printer.

So far these fields are all familiar (although a file type of *c* might be new to you). The next two fields are the contents of `st_rdev` exploded into its constituent major and minor device numbers, and take the place of the file size that normally appears in this position of the output line. For `/dev/lp`, the major device number is 7 and the minor device number is 0. From this we could conclude that printers are in device class 7. Therefore, we would expect any other attached printers to have a major device number of 7 also.

A full listing of all attached printers bears this out. For example:

```
crw-rw----    2 lp        adm          7,   0 Mar 18  1986 /dev/lp
crw-rw----    2 lp        adm          7,   0 Mar 18  1986 /dev/lp0
crw-rw-rw-    1 root      sys          7,   1 Mar 18  1986 /dev/lp1
crw-rw-rw-    1 root      sys          7,   2 Oct 19  1986 /dev/lp2
```

Judging from the minor device numbers shown, we can also see that `/dev/lp0` is the other file name for the first printer attached to the system. Two other printers might also be present, one designated by minor device number 1, and the other designated by minor device number 2.

You must be wary of assuming that a device exists merely because a special file for the device exists. It is not unusual for shipped versions of System V to come complete with a special file already created for every device that the included drivers can support, because this saves the system administrator the burden of figuring out the proper major and minor device numbers to use.

In the discussion so far, I have touched on only the rudiments of special device handling. We now need to look more closely at how the system administrator manages special devices.

Defining Special Files

The steps in adding a device to the system configuration are roughly as follows:

1. Write or get a driver routine for the device.

2. Update the system configuration tables to describe the new device and device driver.

3. Regenerate the kernel to include the new device drivers.

4. Create at least one special file for each new device.

In this chapter, we are most concerned with the final steps involving special files.

A special file is created with the `mknod` command or the `mknod` system call. The format of the command is

```
/etc/mknod special type [ major minor ]
```

where

❏ *special* is the term used in most UNIX documentation to describe the path name of a special file. This operand is usually replaced with a full path name, such as `/dev/mt/0m`.

❏ *type* must specify one of the one-character codes: `c` to create a character-special file, `b` to create a block-special file, or `p` to create a named pipe.

❏ *major* must be specified for block-special and character-special files, and should *not* be specified for a named *pipe*. A numeric value (in decimal or octal notation) that specifies the major device number for the device is expected. The major device number identifies the driver routine used with this device. The correlation between the major device number and the device driver routine is established by tables in the `master` configuration file.

❏ *minor* specifies the minor device number for the block-special or character-special file; it should not be specified for a named pipe. The numeric value may be specified in decimal or octal notation (octal numbers start with a leading 0; decimal numbers do not). The proper value to be used depends on the specific device driver; consult the driver's documentation. Typically, though, the value is an integer, starting at 0, that sequentially numbers each of the devices to be controlled by this driver.

When a new class of devices is added to the system, the system configuration tables must be modified and the kernel regenerated to include the new device driver. A unique major device number is assigned at this time to identify the device driver and its corresponding class of supported devices.

But when the only change to the configuration is to add additional devices of a type already supported, rebuilding of the kernel may not be necessary. One of the system configuration files (called *dfile* in some versions of System V) specifies the number of devices supported for each device driver. As long as the number of attached devices of that type is not exceeded, you can define the new device merely by creating the appropriate special file.

Thus, the special file serves two useful functions in UNIX System V. It allows applications such as shell scripts and C programs to access devices in the same manner as disk files. In addition, in many cases it allows you to extend the system configuration without having to regenerate the kernel.

Permissions

The `mknod` command or system call always creates a special file with the default permissions 666 (`rw-rw-rw-`), except as overridden by the *umask* value. These permissions are not appropriate for all devices. The system administrator must decide what are the best permissions for a particular device, and set the desired permissions using the `chown` and `chmod` commands.

Block-special files usually represent disk devices. Some versions of System V may also consider other types of devices to be block devices, such as diskette drives and magnetic tape drives. The point is that a block-special file can be formatted as a filesystem, using the `mkfs` command, and can be mounted. When a filesystem is mounted, users can access files and directories in the filesystem. Reading a block-special file directly when it is already mounted as a filesystem ignores any copies of disk blocks that the kernel may be holding in memory buffers, and can give an appearance of a damaged or inconsistent filesystem even though nothing is wrong. Worse, writing to a block-special file while it is mounted can destroy the filesystem it contains.

For these reasons, it is customary to allow only root to have write access to block-special files. Read permission can safely be granted to other users, although they must recognize and accept the risk of accessing a block-special file when it is mounted as a filesystem. Some installations even withhold read permission for block-special files from other users, because a program that understands the physical organization of the filesystem can bypass the system permissions mechanism and read any file in the filesystem, which some installations may consider to be a security violation. The permissions mechanism cannot protect against such accesses because a block-special file looks like a single file to the operating system, and thus has only one set of access permissions.

Permissions can be freer for character-special devices. User terminals, for example, are often set up to allow anyone to write to the terminal. (Without this permission, the `write` command is unusable and the `mesg` command is meaningless.) A user who has logged on at a terminal must be able to both read and write to the terminal. The `getty` and `login` programs are designed to force the owner-ID and permissions of the terminal special file to the required values.

You should not, however, give everyone unrestricted write access to a printer because if two or more users attempt to write to the same printer at the same time, their output will be jumbled together. Printers are therefore usually owned by the `root` or `lp` users, and other users are not normally allowed write access.

It is not my intention to give a complete catalog of how to set up device ownership and permissions. The best settings for your system depend to some extent on how you intend to use the system. I have tried to give examples of the considerations that go into determining the ownership and permissions for a special file. No single answer is appropriate for all situations, and in real life most permission schemes are compromises that must be constantly adjusted and modified as needs change. The successful system administrator will not hesitate to experiment with different approaches, and will be sensitive to the changing needs of the user community that he or she is supposed to support.

Block Devices

I have mentioned block-special and character-special files without giving any precise definition of these terms. But these terms have specific meanings in the UNIX environment, as you will see.

A block device is any device that transfers data in fixed-size blocks, and can access any data block in roughly the same amount of time as any other. Disk and diskette drives are typical examples of block devices. Because of their high-performance design, these devices always read or write full blocks of data. Moreover, different kinds of disk drives often specify different block sizes. To provide an application program with greater flexibility and to isolate it from the need to be aware of the characteristics of a specific device, the operating system makes it appear as if an arbitrary number of bytes can be read or written at any location on the disk. But this capability is provided by the operating system I/O routines, not by the hardware.

Other kinds of devices, such as terminals, printers, and magnetic tape drives, generally do not define a fixed block size and cannot provide fast random access to arbitrary segments of the recorded data. They require an I/O interface quite different from block devices, and therefore UNIX treats block devices and character devices differently.

Because of the large capacity of disk drives and their comparatively high cost, it would be impractical to use an entire disk drive to hold a single file. The operating system provides a sophisticated file management system that allows many files to be stored on a single drive. This file management system requires that the disk drive be formatted to contain a filesystem. When a disk contains a valid filesystem, the filesystem can be mounted, after which it appears to the user as a hierarchy of directories containing files.

Diskette drives do not have the large capacity of disk drives, and the cost of the storage medium (the floppy disk) is much lower. For this reason, even though a diskette drive is a block device, users may sometimes choose not to format it as a filesystem but rather to use it in a manner similar to a magnetic tape containing one large file. This is convenient for bulk storage of files, such as for archival or backup purposes. To access the device in this manner, you just open the block-special file corresponding to the device.

The filesystem can be read and examined, and even written and modified through the block device interface, if this is allowed by the read-write permissions of the block-special file, and if the device contains a formatted filesystem. The mkfs program must have write access to a block-special file to initially create a filesystem on a disk drive. The fsck (filesystem checker) program also requires write access to block-special files because it must access parts of the filesystem that cannot be accessed as normal files, such as the inode table.

However, accessing a filesystem through the block device interface can be misleading or dangerous because of disk buffer caching. The UNIX kernel imposes an additional layer of software between the application program and the block device driver that is not present for character devices. This layer, the *disk buffer cache*, consists of processing routines for read and write requests, and a pool of disk buffers each the same size as a disk block. The number of disk buffers may be a system configuration parameter, or may be computed dynamically at boot time. The purpose of the disk buffer cache is to hold frequently referenced disk blocks in memory to reduce the total number of disk I/O operations.

The processing of both read and write requests begins with an attempt to locate the requested disk block in the buffer cache. If it is found in one of the buffers, the requested data is returned to the application program without the need to perform any disk I/O. But if the requested disk block is not present, the device driver is called to read it into memory. Because only a fixed number of buffers are available, it will frequently happen that a buffer which already contains a valid disk block must be reused to hold the new block. The kernel implements an algorithm for reusing buffers that is designed to keep frequently referenced blocks in memory.

Regardless of the algorithm used, the block that currently occupies the buffer must be written back to disk if it has been changed and no longer matches the copy on disk; only then can the new block be read into the buffer. Thus, a single read or write request by the application program might result in two disk accesses, one to write the modified contents of a buffer back out to disk, and another to read the new block into the buffer made available by the write.

The data recorded on the disk can be out of date with respect to the image viewed by the system because caching may cause recent changes to linger in the system's disk buffers until they are written back to disk. For this reason, most programs that process filesystems using the block-special file require that the filesystem be offline (not mounted) while the program is running. This ensures that the system is not caching any of the disk blocks, and that the image on disk is the current image of the filesystem. When the filesystem is processed while mounted, such as always occurs when running `fsck` against the root filesystem, inconsistencies and errors may be discovered which do not actually exist. The `sync` system call can be used to flush disk buffers out to disk, but offers no guarantee that the image on disk will remain current.

It is nearly impossible to write a truly portable program to access a filesystem through its block-special file. The format of the superblock and the inodes is highly system-dependent. Thus, if you write such a program, be prepared to port the program to each system on which you want to execute it.

Character Devices

The original UNIX definition of a character device was any device that transferred data a character at a time. This is how some simple types of devices such as ASCII terminals and low-speed printers behave. But as technology has evolved, devices have grown more sophisticated. Today, the term *character device* is a catchall for any device that does not fit the definition of a block device.

Typical kinds of character devices include terminals, magnetic tape drives, modems, and printers. Disk and diskette drives may also support a character device interface in addition to the required block device interface, for reasons I will discuss later.

A typical character-special file (character device) is unable to respond properly to lseek (and therefore to fseek as well). The current file pointer of a character device is, in general, undefined, and you can read or write only from the current position. This does not mean that the device does not support ways to affect its positioning. Terminals, for example, often respond to control-character sequences that move the cursor and therefore allow data to be placed at arbitrary positions on the display. Similarly, printers often respond to control characters that advance the device to the top of the next sheet of paper, or space down three blank lines. Nonetheless, the lseek function remains ineffective with these devices because these devices usually cannot be positioned to arbitrary byte offsets in the file. All control and positioning of the device must be performed in a device-dependent manner, and the behavior expected of lseek cannot be promised for most character devices. Hence, the device driver does not respond to lseek requests.

Magnetic tapes and disk drives, when their character-device (or "raw") interface is used, can write a continuous stream of characters in much the same manner as an ordinary file. This interface is often used for special purposes such as initializing a new disk drive with a *format* program. The manual page for the utility program normally specifies when the raw device should be used with the program instead of the usual block device.

The raw interface for a block device is represented by a different special file that usually has a path name similar but not identical to the path name of the block device, and that has a different major device number than the block device. The raw device must be represented by a character-special file, and the block device must be represented by a block-special file. On my system, for example, the block device for the primary disk drive is

```
brw-r--r--   1 root      sys      0,  0 May 17 19:25 /dev/dsk/0s0
```

and the raw device for the same drive is

```
crw-r--r--   2 root      sys      4,  0 Sep 14  1987 /dev/rdsk/0s0
```

The raw interface for block devices presents some special difficulties that can be difficult to overcome. For example, when the raw interface is used, no end-of-file marker is defined and the effective end of file is the end of the physical medium. This implies that a program that works correctly with standard disk files may work improperly if redirected, by a shell command or other means, to use a raw character device. This problem would show up later as reading past the end of the file and attempting to interpret garbage as if it were part of the file. Applications that are designed to work with raw devices such as tar and cpio write their own end-of-file markers to avoid this problem.

Another potential difficulty is that raw device drivers often require that I/O requests specify a fixed block size when reading or writing data. With most such drivers, the block size used is not important, as long as every read or write specifies the same size. This restriction can be difficult to meet when using the stdio package because when the file is closed, the close routine may attempt to write a short block, possibly running afoul of the raw device driver's restriction on block size. A violation of this restriction results in an I/O error indication.

You can encounter these problems even when redirecting the standard input or output of a program to a raw device using the shell redirection operators. There are three sure fixes for the problem: use a program designed to support raw devices such as tar or cpio, modify the program to read and write the correct block size (if you can find out what it is), or avoid the problem entirely by using the block device instead of the raw device.

These problems do not occur with true character devices such as terminals and printers, which are designed to transmit arbitrary character streams of data. The problem is limited to the character-special file interface for block devices, called the raw device interface. The reason why one might want to use the raw interface when the block device interface is more predictable is that the raw interface is usually faster. The operating system performs buffer caching only for block-special files.

When a very large file is read from or written to a medium such as magnetic tape, buffer caching by the operating system achieves no benefit because no block will be read more than once. Using the raw device interface avoids this excess system activity.

Another reason to use the raw device interface when processing very large stream files on magnetic media is that the raw interface may support very large block sizes, allowing very high data transfer rates to be achieved. When a device is accessed with the block device interface, all reads and writes must be passed through the system buffers, and are therefore limited to the file system block size (typically 1K or 2K bytes). When using the raw device, block sizes of 32K or larger may be allowed.

To summarize, remember that the character device interface is *always* used for some kinds of devices such as printers and terminals. The character device interface *may* be supported for some kinds of block devices to achieve performance gains in special applications that are not possible with the usual block device interface. File positioning is not defined for *any* file accessed as a character device, and the end of file usually has a device-specific meaning that may not be dependent on what is read from or written to the device. In fact, the end of file is not defined for printers, and has only a conventional meaning for terminals.

Different kinds of devices may define a device position, such as the current line on printed output or the cursor position on a terminal, but the device position may not be subject to program control or may require special device-dependent programming to be used. In general, the `lseek` and `fseek` standard UNIX calls have no effect on the current device position for character-special files. Therefore, not all programs that work properly with disk files will work properly also with character-special files.

The only way to know how a specific device will behave is to consult its operation and programming manuals. Fortunately, devices of similar type are often programmed in the same way. Printers usually work like terminals, and terminal interfaces are fairly well described by the *termio* conventions (*termio* is the name of a manual page entry). There are virtually no standards for magnetic tape support between versions of UNIX, however. In general, your best course for dealing with magnetic tape drives is to access them with special-purpose system utilities (for example, `tar` and `cpio`), thus offloading the handling details to the operating system implementers.

I realize that this list of warnings make the character device interface seem chaotic. But the situation is not quite that bad.

Programs fall into two broad categories: those that do not care about device characteristics, and those that are concerned with I/O to one particular class of devices. For device-independent programs, most of these warnings are irrelevant and the generic `stdio` function package will meet the program's needs.

Programs specializing in the control of a particular class of device also are unaffected by these warnings. The program simply assumes that the device provided by the user matches the required type, and lets the user worry about whether the program is appropriate to the device.

Pipes

Named pipes are similar to regular pipes, although more general in purpose and application. To make proper use of named pipes, you must first understand the programming and usage rules that apply to regular pipes.

Regular Pipes

A pipe is a kind of file, formally classed as a special file though quite different from character-special and block-special files. Pipes are normally created by the `pipe` system call. Unlike the `open` and `creat` system calls, both of which provide access to a regular file and return one file descriptor, the `pipe` system call always returns two file descriptors, the first opened for input and the second opened for output. By definition, data written to the output file descriptor is immediately made available for reading from the associated input file descriptor.

A pipe is more than just a conduit for information, though. It is also a queue mechanism, specifically a first-in first-out (FIFO) queue, which simply means that data read from the pipe is retrieved in the same byte order in which it was stored.

One of the tasks the system performs when it creates a pipe is to allocate a buffer in kernel memory to hold data that has been written to the pipe but not yet read. The buffer is managed as a wraparound queue such that the last byte of the buffer is followed by its first byte.

The system executes a `write` call by copying the user's data into the buffer associated with the pipe. Data is added at the logical end of the buffer, wrapping around from the last position of the buffer to the first if necessary. The end pointer is then advanced to point to the next position following the last byte copied. Similarly, a `read` call is executed by copying data from the system buffer into the user's buffer. Data is retrieved starting at the logical start of the buffer, wrapping around from the last position to the first if necessary, and proceeding until either the number of bytes requested have been copied or the start pointer becomes equal to the end pointer (signifying an empty buffer). The start pointer is then left pointing at the next byte in the buffer that has not been read.

Notice that this procedure implies that data can be retrieved from the buffer in different sized chunks than it was added. The system does not organize the buffer contents into lines, records, or blocks, even if it was written that way. Rather, the system treats the buffer contents as a continuous series of bytes. It is the user's responsibility to ensure that the buffered data is read in a meaningful manner. This is not difficult to achieve if, for example, only two processes are using the pipe and they both read and write records of the same length.

Both the read and write requests are considered completed as soon as the copying operation is finished. Therefore, as long as there is enough space in the buffer to complete a write, or enough data in the buffer to satisfy a read, no synchronization is enforced between the reading and writing processes. Data written to the buffer may remain in the buffer an indefinite period of time before it is retrieved. The pipe acts like a mail box, where data can be stored and held until retrieved.

Another implication of this procedure is that the system makes no guarantee that data written to the pipe will ever be delivered to another process. Before accepting data from a write request, the system requires that at least one process has the pipe open for input. But after data has been stored in the pipe, nothing prevents the processes that might read it from terminating and abandoning the unread data. For most applications of pipes, this is not a problem. But any application requiring assurance that all written data is delivered must provide that assurance by its own means, because the pipe mechanism does not.

The usual purpose in creating a pipe is to provide a path for information flow between two processes, such that information written into the pipe by one process is passed to the other process without the need to store the data in an intermediate file. The operating system provides a read-write interface to the pipe that is essentially the same as for any other file, making pipes very easy to use.

Unlike standard disk files, the lseek call cannot be used with a pipe. Data written to the pipe must be read in the same order, and skipping around is not permitted.

The following is an example of creating a pipe and using it to pass lines to the sort program. The example uses the fork and exec system calls because the purpose in using a pipe is to process the data without writing it to an intermediate file. This implies that the data generating program and the data processing program must be simultaneously active. Otherwise, the data would have to be passed between the programs in a file.

```
main()
{
        FILE    *names;    /* Input file of names */
        FILE    *sort;     /* Output file piped to sort */
        int     fd[2];     /* File descriptors for pipe */
        int     c;         /* Current input char */

        if ((names = fopen("names", "r")) == NULL)
            perror("names file"), exit(1);

        if (pipe(fd)) /* Able to create a pipe? */
            perror("pipe"), exit(2); /* No, create failed */

        if (fork() == 0) { /* Successful fork? */
            /*
             * The following code is executed by the child process
             */
            close(0);        /* Close std input file descriptor */
            dup(fd[0]);      /* Dup pipe input to stdin position */
            close(fd[0]);    /* Discard redundant file descriptor */
            close(fd[1]);    /* Don't use write side of pipe */
            execlp("sort", "sort", NULL);
            exit(255);       /* If reached, couldn't load 'sort' */
        }
```

```
close(fd[0]);    /* Don't use pipe input side */

if ((sort = fdopen(fd[1], "w")) == NULL)
      perror("sort"), exit(3);
      /* Unable to open pipe output */

while ((c = getc(names)) != EOF)
      putc(c, sort);  /* Copy data to sort program */

fclose(names);
fclose(sort);
return (0);               /* Finished, return to shell */
}
```

This program may be somewhat confusing at first sight. A short description of the fork and exec system calls is given in the "Reference" section, and more in-depth discussions appear in Chapter 13, "Kernel Internals," and Chapter 14, "Writing Multiprocessing Programs." The close and dup calls, which may seem unnecessary, are actually an essential part of creating an interprocess pipe.

When the call to fork is executed, the two file descriptors that were opened by pipe are automatically duplicated in the child process. This achieves our goal of attaching the pipe to both processes but leaves us with too many file descriptors.

The parent process (main) will only be writing to the pipe. It therefore needs the fd[1] file descriptor, which is open for output. But the program has no use for fd[0], which is open for input. (The program has no interest in reading back the data it writes.) Therefore, the program closes fd[0] as soon as the pipe has been passed to the child process through fork.

Similarly, the child process (the sort program) will only be reading from the pipe. Therefore, the write side of the pipe is useless and fd[1] is closed to avoid wasting a file descriptor.

Of the four file descriptors we had after the fork call, only two are now open. The child process, however, must reassign the read side of the pipe as the standard input file for the sort program. This is accomplished by first closing standard input (i.e., file descriptor 0). Then dup is called to make a copy of fd[0] in the lowest unused file descriptor slot, which will now be file descriptor 0. The pipe is then accessible by either file descriptor 0 or the file descriptor returned from pipe. Once again, this is one too many file descriptors. Only one of them is needed, so the child process closes fd[0].

After executing one dup and four close calls, the program has finally arranged to have the right set of file descriptors, one of them open for output in the parent process, and the other (standard input) open for input in the child process. The parent process then creates a stream file for the pipe (the fdopen call), and copies its data into the pipe. When the end of file is reached, it is only necessary to close the two remaining files and exit.

This program, while perhaps more complicated than we would like, still omits a lot of error checking that should always be performed in real production programs. For example, none of the `close` and `dup` calls are checked, and a possible error return from `fork` is ignored. In addition, the program does not make any provision for retrieving the completion status of the `sort` program, which should be done to avoid leaving zombie processes around to clutter up the system.

The example code could have been more easily written using the `popen` library function, as follows:

```
main()
{
        FILE    *names;             /* Input file of names */
        FILE    *sort;              /* Output file piped to sort */
        int     c;                  /* Current input char */
        if ((names = fopen("names", "r")) == NULL)
                perror("names file"), exit(1);

        if ((sort = popen("sort", "w")) == NULL)
                perror("popen"), exit(2); /* Couldn't open pipe */
        while ((c = getc(names)) != EOF)
                putc(c, sort);   /* Copy data to sort program */
        fclose(names);
        pclose(sort);
        return (0);                 /* Finished, return to shell */
}
```

This version of the program is much easier to write and understand than the first example, because the operating system interfaces have been hidden inside the `popen` and `pclose` library functions.

The first example discloses an important feature of pipes. From our experience writing UNIX shell scripts, we might suspect that pipes are mainly useful for redirecting the standard input and standard output files. But pipes are a generalized mechanism intended to support direct interprocess communication.

Named Pipes

A *named pipe* differs from a regular pipe in only one important respect: the manner in which it is created. As shown in the preceding section, regular pipes are created by the `pipe` system call and become linked between two processes as a side effect of the `fork` system call, which always duplicates all open file descriptors.

A named pipe is created by executing the /etc/mknod command or the mknod system call. (The /etc/mknod program is a simple wrapper providing a command interface to the mknod system call.) This action results not in the creation of a pipe, but in the creation of a directory entry representing the pipe. The directory entry has a unique file type of S_IFIFO to distinguish it from other kinds of files. A directory entry of this type always has a file size of 0 bytes, because no data is ever written to disk. When this directory entry is opened for input or output, however, a pipe is created with one end connected to the opening process. The other end of the pipe is inactive until some other process opens the same directory entry for the opposite type of I/O. As you might expect, the pipe mechanism is automatically dismantled when both ends of the pipe have been closed, although the directory entry representing the pipe remains in existence waiting for another process to open it.

Any number of processes can open the same named pipe for input or output simultaneously, because the system establishes no interlocks to prevent it. That is, a named pipe can at once be open for input by *n* processes, and open for output by *m* processes. The kernel assumes no responsibility for the validity of this situation. The permissions flags for the named pipe directory entry must be set to prevent it, or the applications using the pipe must be programmed to tolerate it.

The behavior of a pipe is influenced not only by the number of processes opening it for input and output, but also by the size of the system buffer and by the setting of the O_NDELAY flag in the file descriptor used to access the pipe. There is no requirement that all file descriptors for a pipe have the same O_NDELAY setting; instead, the flag setting for a file descriptor influences only those I/O operations directed to that file descriptor.

The rules governing the operation of pipes are set forth in the following list. The rules are best presented as a set of cases, where the behavior of a pipe for any given I/O request conforms to the rule with a matching set of conditions. The rules are presented in terms of writing to a pipe, but reading from a pipe behaves in a similar fashion.

1. *Write to a pipe; there is enough room in the buffer to hold the number of bytes requested.* In this case, the system guarantees a synchronous write: all the bytes to be written will be placed in consecutive locations in the buffer, and will not be interleaved with bytes written by other processes. Because there is enough room to hold the user data, it is copied into the buffer at once and the writing process resumes execution immediately. The O_NDELAY flag has no effect.

2. *Write to a pipe; the number of bytes to be written exceeds the current amount of space in the buffer, but not its total capacity.* As in the previous case, the system guarantees a synchronous write so that the data to be written will not be interleaved with bytes written by other requests. Because there is not enough room in the buffer to service the request immediately, however, execution of the request must be delayed until enough bytes are retrieved from the buffer to make room for this write.

   If the O_NDELAY flag is set, the system returns immediately with a return value of 0, which signifies that no data was written into the buffer. Otherwise, the requesting process waits until the write can be satisfied or until a signal becomes pending for the requesting process. If the return value is 0, or if a signal is caught and the signal-catching routine returns, the process attempting to write is expected to try its request again. But even if the process waits, the system does not guarantee that the next block of data to be stored in the buffer will be that of the current request, only that when the data is eventually stored, it will be stored as an uninterrupted series of bytes.

3. *Write to a pipe; the number of bytes to be written is greater than the total capacity of the buffer.* In this case, the system cannot perform the write operation in a single attempt, and therefore cannot guarantee that all the bytes to be written will be stored consecutively in the buffer. The number of bytes equal to the space remaining in the buffer are stored. If the O_NDELAY flag is set, write returns the number of bytes stored as the value of the function. Otherwise, the requesting process is suspended until more space becomes available. The operation is retried, storing consecutive portions of the data into the buffer as space becomes available, until all the requested data has been stored. The system then returns the total number of bytes written, which should be equal to the number requested. If other processes are competing to store data in the buffer, the segments stored by this request may be interleaved with data written by other processes.

Certain cautions are in order concerning signals and error handling when you use pipes. First, if all the processes reading a pipe close it while at least one process still has the pipe open for output, the next attempt to write to the pipe will result in a *broken pipe* error. (This descriptive term is meant to suggest that any data written to the pipe "leaks out," in the sense that it does not go where intended.) The error results in a signal (SIGPIPE) being sent to the writing process *before the write returns.* If the action for the SIGPIPE signal is SIG_DFL (the default action), the writing process is terminated immediately without any opportunity to issue an error message; the parent process may or may not issue an error message indicating death of a child due to a signal. If it does not, it will appear that the writing process has simply vanished, with no explanation of what happened.

On the other hand, if the signal action is SIG_IGN (ignore the signal) or a user signal-catching function, the writing process will survive the signal and write will return a value of -1 with *errno* set to EINTR, because the system still could not write any data to the pipe. A write operation described by case 1 or 2 in the preceding list may safely be retried without any confusion, because no data was stored in the buffer by the interrupted write.

However, in case 3, any number of bytes may have been written into the buffer—*and* retrieved and used by other processes—before the signal occurred. If the signal does not result in termination of the writing process and the write operation is retried, the data that was already read and used is stored into the pipe again. Because the writing process has no way to know how many bytes of the interrupted write were successfully stored (the return value from write was -1, not the number of bytes written), there is no practical way to determine where to restart the interrupted write. The only way to avoid this situation is to refrain from writing to the pipe blocks of data that may exceed the total size of the system buffer. Unfortunately, there is no guaranteed minimum size for the system buffer, and no easy way to determine the buffer size at run time. A rule of thumb that should always be safe to follow is to avoid writes for any length greater than BUFSIZ as defined in the stdio.h header file. Depending on the version of UNIX being used, this value can range from a low of 512 bytes to a high of 4096 bytes.

After reviewing these rules and warnings, you may feel that using pipes is fraught with peril and best avoided. Not so. There are a number of rules of procedure that you should follow when writing programs and administrating systems. If these rules are observed, you will experience very few, if any, difficulties.

A few of these rules follow. When developing your applications, review this list of rules until you know it by heart, then never break a rule unless you know precisely why it will be safe to do so in a particular situation.

1. Named pipes should always be protected with permissions that allow only applications that were programmed to use it to access the named pipe. Do not make it possible for malicious or curious users to throw garbage into the named pipe.

2. Whenever possible, use the `unlink` system call to delete a named pipe when there is no one to read it, so that programs designed to write to the pipe won't mysteriously "hang up."

3. If you invoke a pipeline from a shell, always check its exit code. Sometimes, the exit code is the only indication that the program aborted because of a broken pipe.

4. If you execute a program from within a program using `fork` and `exec`, always retrieve its exit status with `wait`, always test the exit status for termination due to a signal, and always document the termination by an informative message to `stderr`.

5. If you use the `popen` library function, always test for a negative return value and report it with the `perror` call, because it indicates a failure of the `fork` or `exec` calls in `popen`.

6. Always document a nonzero return value from `pclose`, because that might be the only indication that the program invoked by `popen` failed.

7. If more than one process may be writing to a named pipe, and you use the stream I/O functions to write the data, either issue an `fflush` call after each line of output or execute `setvbuf` to force physical writing to occur after each line. This is the only way to ensure that lines written by different processes do not become scrambled together.

8. Always try to use a record size of less than 512 bytes for data written to a pipe.

9. Use the `read` and `write` calls in preference to stream I/O when reading and writing pipes; you will have better control over when I/O occurs, and over the size of the data written.

10. Always check the return value from reads and writes to a pipe for a return value of -1, and always retry an operation that failed with an *errno* value of `EINTR`. If you do not, you may lose data without any explanation.

11. Programs performing I/O to a pipe should trap the SIGPIPE signal or set the signal action to `SIG_IGN`. An action of `SIG_DFL` can result in the "vanished program" syndrome.

Please remember that these rules sometimes are best ignored. For example, consider the following shell command:

```
sort foo ¦ pg
```

This command is intended to view a file in sorted sequence without modifying the file. If, after looking at the first screenful of information, you decide that you need to see no more, and tell pg to quit, the pipe will be broken. The quit command of pg is not communicated back to the sort program, which continues to try to write sorted lines into the pipe even though the pg command has gone away. This results in a broken pipe. Try it yourself. You will see that both programs quietly go away. The sort program vanishes with no error message because it does not set up a signal-catching routine to detect the broken pipe condition. Instead, it is terminated with no error report. In this situation and many like it, the fact that the sort program issues no error message in the case of a broken pipe is an advantage because it keeps the terminal from being cluttered with useless error messages.

The alternative is probably familiar to SCCS users, where the familiar command sequence:

```
get -p -s s.filename ¦ pg
```

does result in a broken-pipe error message if you quit the pg command before it completes. If this has ever happened to you, you know how annoying the "tidy" broken-pipe error message is.

Summary

The UNIX operating system handles devices in a manner unique among operating systems, and quite distinct from the usage of MS-DOS.

The use of a file to represent a device, called a *special* file, enables the system administrator to assign any name he wants to the device. In fact, because different directory entries can point to the same file, the same device can be known by more than one name.

The use of special files to represent devices often enables the system administrator to add new devices to the system configuration without having to rebuild the kernel. The address of the device is one of the characteristics of the special file. So as long as the kernel already contains support for the device to be added, creating a special file for the device is sufficient to define the device to the system.

There are three kinds of special files: block-special, character-special, and the named pipe.

Block-special files describe disk drives (or sections of disk drives called *partitions*), and other devices that can be accessed in a manner similar to disk drives. The block-special file naming a disk drive is actually a map of the entire drive, and provides access to the device outside the constraints of the file system; this capability is used by a number of system utilities such as /etc/mkfs, to create a new filesystem, and by /etc/format to initially format the disk. The block-special file is often protected so that only the superuser can write to it. The characteristics of a block-special file are well defined, and programs written to access them (such as the UNIX kernel itself) can work with any device model that may be attached to the system.

Character-special files describe any device that does not conform to the characteristics of a disk drive. Printers, terminals, modems, and mice are examples of character devices. Unlike block devices, character devices may differ radically in their operation and capabilities. There are special facilities for handling character devices such as the ioctl function and the *termio* interface. Unfortunately, programs written to support one type of character device are rarely usable with another type of character device. UNIX can provide some measure of device independence when the device is accessed purely as a stream of bytes, for example by redirecting one of the standard files to the device.

Named pipes are essentially the same as regular pipes, the only difference being that a directory entry exists for a named pipe, allowing unrelated processes to open the pipe for input or output. This chapter described the rules for performing I/O to pipes, both regular and named. Pipes can exhibit unpredictable behavior when incautiously programmed; by following the rules, you can avoid unpredictable behavior of your programs using pipes.

The next chapter, the last one dealing with the UNIX input/output system, discusses one important class of character devices: the terminal interface. The terminal interface also supports remote terminals that connect through communications lines, with or without a modem. UNIX provides special support for this class of devices, as you shall see.

12

Programming
Serial Devices

Regardless of the methods used to physically attach terminals, modems, printers, and other similar devices to the computer, UNIX provides a common application program interface to such devices. This interface is called the *serial communications interface,* or sometimes just the *serial interface.* We will examine how it works in this chapter.

What Is Serial Communication?

Serial communication is the protocol used to transfer data between the computer and a serial device. A serial device is two devices in one: a transmitter and a receiver. The transmitter takes bytes written by the program, converts them to a bit stream, and sends the resulting bits out one at a time on the transmit data line. The receiver reads each bit from the receive data line, assembles groups of bits into bytes, and returns the bytes received to the application program.

Some kinds of devices vary this procedure slightly. On a memory-mapped console screen, for example, serial data transfer does not occur; nonetheless, the device driver presents a serial interface to the application program to allow programs to use the device in the same manner as other terminals. A modem may send or receive groups of bits in a single packet rather than individually, but again, the device driver supports the serial communications interface to simplify application programming.

In addition to the receive and transmit lines, a serial communications port uses other signal lines for control. These signals, called *modem control signals,* are not needed for communicating with a locally connected terminal.

The serial interface is one of two common techniques for connecting a device to a computer; the other is the *parallel interface,* which uses multiple wires to send or receive an entire byte of data at a time. Generally, the parallel interface is used with high-speed devices, and the serial interface is used with low-speed devices.

With most versions of UNIX, the serial interface expects the device to understand the ASCII character set. In this chapter, we will assume that the ASCII character set is used. However, nothing in the definition of the serial interface forces this restriction.

Serial communication under UNIX is usually *asynchronous,* which means that each character is transmitted independently from the others. Start and stop bits mark the start and end of each character. Many devices also allow a parity bit to accompany each data byte so that transmission errors can be detected. For example, the letter *A* (0x41), when encoded with seven data bits and even parity, produces the serial bit stream shown in figure 12.1.

Fig. 12.1. Serial bit stream.

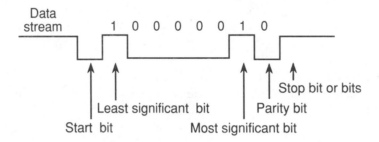

The hardware converts bytes to a serial bit stream, computes the parity bit, and automatically generates the start and stop bits. You have to specify the type of parity desired, the number of stop bits used by the attached device, and the speed at which the bits are transferred. This chapter will show you how to control these settings, as well as how to send and receive the individual characters.

Standard I/O and Serial Communications

UNIX performs all I/O by reading and writing a stream of bytes to a file descriptor. When writing to a disk file, the system buffers the bytes into blocks and calls the device driver to write filled blocks to the disk. In contrast, when the file descriptor refers to a serial port, read and write requests are passed directly to the device driver, which immediately transmits the bytes using the current settings of the serial port. To the programmer, there is no difference between writing to a disk file and writing to a serial communications port. It does not matter whether a compiled program or a command shell generates the output.

The UNIX login shell predefines three files when it is started. These are standard-in on file descriptor 0, standard-out on file descriptor 1, and standard-error on file descriptor 2. The shell normally connects these three file descriptors to the terminal. Thus, file descriptor 0 is available for reading characters you type on the keyboard, and file descriptors 1 and 2 are available for writing messages to the screen. There are two files for output so that if the standard-out file descriptor is redirected, standard-error is still available for writing error messages to the screen.

Accessing the Terminal

The /dev/tty pseudodevice name always refers to your terminal, whether you are logged into the UNIX system through a serial communications port, the system console, or a network protocol using serial communications emulation (rlogin and telnet are examples of network programs that emulate serial communications). You can always read or write to the terminal by opening /dev/tty or using the shell to redirect standard-out to /dev/tty. References to /dev/tty are equivalent to opening or redirecting to the path name of your terminal. By always referring to the current terminal as /dev/tty, you can avoid the need to determine which device is currently the login terminal. A special device driver internally maps this device name to the correct terminal for each process. This is the preferred way for you to access the terminal from your program or shell script when standard-in or standard-out are redirected to other files.

If you need to to determine the real device name of the current terminal, the tty command writes the full path name of the current terminal to standard output, or the string not a tty if standard input is not connected to a terminal.

Accessing Other Serial Communications Devices

It is often desirable to access serial communications devices other than the current terminal. Each communications device has its own directory entry. These entries have path names just like ordinary files, but a directory listing of these entries looks different from those of a normal file. Here is the long directory listing for the serial communications device /dev/ttya on my system:

```
crw-rw-rw- 1 uucp 12, 0 Jan 15 1990 /dev/ttya
```

The c as the first character of the permissions (crw-rw-rw-) indicates that this directory entry describes a character device.

The unusual part of the directory listing is the file size field. Although for ordinary and directory files it gives the number of bytes in the file, for device entries it shows the major and minor numbers of the device separated by a comma. The first number, the major device number, tells the UNIX kernel that this is a serial communications device, and identifies the driver to be called when handling an I/O request. The device driver uses the second number, the minor device number, to select the device from among the set of devices it controls. The minor device number may also be used by some drivers to associate I/O options with the read or write request.

Some device drivers use a range of minor device numbers to distinguish between the two different ways of using a serial port. The base number (and, of course, the device file name having the base minor device number), would be used for a local terminal. By combining a mask with the base number, the driver understands that the port uses full modem control signals.

This is not an unusual use of minor device numbers. Because the UNIX system does not include a table of device addresses and characteristics, device drivers cannot tell just from the device address whether a special device feature should be used. Therefore, device drivers are often written to check for certain option bits in the minor device number. This places the burden on the UNIX system administrator to set up device directory entries with minor device numbers that correspond to the requirements of the actual device.

As an example of this method, let us suppose that a terminal driver expects minor device numbers to be 8-bit numbers in the format

```
0r000xxx
```

The *xxx* bits specify the device number. Therefore, this driver would be capable of controlling up to eight terminals. The r bit might be used to indicate whether modem control signals should be used with the device. With this scheme, you could then define two character-special files for each terminal as follows:

File name	Minor device number	Meaning
/dev/tty2a	2	Local terminal, port 2
/dev/tty2A	66	Dial-up modem, port 2

In binary, the minor device number for device /dev/tty/2a is 00000010. Notice that the r bit is 0, indicating to the device driver that modem control signals should not be used with port 2. The minor device number for /dev/tty2A, however, is 01000010, which sets the r bit to 1. The driver would therefore use modem control signals when reading and writing to file name /dev/tty2A.

Which device name would you use for port 2? That would depend on the device that is actually attached at port 2. If it is a local terminal, you should use device name dev/tty2a to access port 2. If it is a modem, you should use device name dev/tty2A. By choosing the file name to be used to access the device, you tell the driver how to access it.

Please understand that not all device drivers recognize option bits in the minor device number. This technique is popular, however, and you are likely to encounter it at some point in your work with UNIX.

By convention, all device entries are in the /dev directory. Serial communications devices are usually labeled ttyXX. Some administrators prefer to place the files in the tty directory under /dev. Then the device name would be of the form /dev/tty/XX. You can execute the command

    ls /dev

to determine the naming convention used by your system. If the ls command prints a list of entries all starting with tty, your system uses the first, or ttyXX, method. In either case, the choice for the XX portion of the file name is up to the system administrator. It usually takes the form of one or two letters, a number, or a combination of a number and a letter, such as ttyaa, tty22, or tty2a.

Often, when the minor device number is used to indicate modem control options, there will be two or more similar names for the same device: a lowercase version of the name, which is the port without modem control, and an uppercase version of the name, which includes modem control. Examples of ports with two names are ttyaa or tty2a without modem control and ttyAA or tty2A with modem control.

The directory entry for a device does not have to be in the /dev directory, nor does it have to be named in the format ttyXX. Sometimes the file is given a mnemonic name, such as modem1 or Laser-printer. It is only convention that places the files in the /dev directory. The long directory entry, however, is always similar to the one shown at the beginning of this section, regardless of the name assigned by the systems administrator.

Input versus Output

A serial port has two lines, one for the receive and one for the transmit bit stream. However, there is only one device entry to access both lines. A read to the device automatically accesses the receive line, and a write to the device automatically accesses the transmit line. To both read and write the serial port, open it twice, once for reading and once for writing. In C it is possible to open it for both reading and writing at the same time. When you are using I/O redirection in the shell, redirect both standard input and standard output. Redirect standard error to standard output if access to the port is desired for both streams, for example:

```
command arg1 arg2 < /dev/tty/aa > /dev/tty/aa 2>&1
```

Controlling the Serial Port Configuration

Unlike a disk file, which can be read from or written to immediately after you open it, you must first configure a serial communications line by setting a number of options, including line speed, word length, parity, and number of stop bits. When you log in, the getty program reads the default options for the port from its startup file, /etc/gettydefs. This is why it is not necessary for you to change the port configuration each time you login. It is up to you to configure any serial port you use other than your login terminal.

These settings last only as long as the port is kept open by some process. When the last process closes the port, the settings revert back to the defaults.

The stty Command

UNIX provides the stty command to display the current settings of the communications port, and also to change those settings. Typed with no options, its output looks like this:

```
$ stty
speed 9600 baud; evenp hupcl clocal
intr = ^c; erase = ^h; kill = ^u; swtch = ^';
brkint -inpck icrnl -ixany onlcr tab3
echo echoe echok
```

With no options, the command shows only the settings that differ from the defaults for your login terminal. Adding the –a option instructs stty to print all the settings. On/off parameters are printed with no leading sign if set, and with a leading minus sign if cleared. All other parameters are printed with their current value.

Typing stty –a at the shell prompt produces output similar to the following:

```
$ stty -a
speed 9600 baud; intr = ^C; quit = ^\; erase = ^H; kill = ^U;
eof = ^D; eol = ^@; swtch = ^@
-parenb -parodd cs8 -cstopb hupcl cread clocal
-ignbrk brkint ignpar -parmrk -inpck -istrip -inlcr -igncr
      icrnl -iuclc
ixon -ixany -ixoff
isig icanon -xcase echo echoe echok -echonl -noflsh
opost -olcuc onlcr -ocrnl -onocr -onlret -ofill -ofdel
cr0 nl0 tab0 bs0 vt0 ff0
$
```

The following section lists the meaning of all the stty parameters:

speed   Bit rate of the communications line in bits per second. 50, 75, 110, 134, 150, 200, 300, 600, 1200, 1800, 2400, 4800, 9600, exta, and extb. With some versions of System V, 19200 and 38400 are also accepted as valid line speed designations for the stty command. exta is usually 19200 bits per second. However, some systems assign it the speed of the console terminal or some other value. Many systems take 19200 as an alternate name for *exta*. *extb* is usually 38400 bits per second. Again, some systems assign it a different speed. Many systems take 38400 as an alternative name for *extb*.

intr   Interrupt character. The keyboard key you press to generate an INTR signal. To specify a control character, enter the corresponding alphabetic key preceded by a caret (^).

quit   Quit character. The keyboard key you press to generate a QUIT signal. If prefixed with a caret (^), the specified character is taken to be the corresponding control character.

erase   Erase character. The key you use to cancel the previously typed character and remove it from the input stream. To specify a control character, enter the corresponding alphabetic key preceded by a caret (^).

kill   Kill character. The key you use to cancel the current input line. To specify a control character, enter the corresponding alphabetic key preceded by a caret ($^\wedge$).

eof   End of file character. A single character used to signal the end of file. To specify a control character, enter the corresponding alphabetic key preceded by a caret ($^\wedge$).

eol   Alternate end of line character. A single character used to end the current input line. The NL character is the default end-of-line character. To specify a control character, enter the corresponding alphabetic key preceded by a caret ($^\wedge$).

swtch   Switch character. The key used to generate a shell layer switch signal (suspend). To specify a control character, enter the corresponding alphabetic key preceded by a caret ($^\wedge$).

parenb   Enables (disables, if preceded with -) parity generation on output and parity checking on input. If -parenb is specified, the parodd parameter is ignored.

parodd   Generates odd parity on output and checks odd parity on input. The -parodd setting forces even parity generation and checking. This parameter is ignored if -parenb is set.

cs5, cs6, cs7, cs8
     Number of data bits per character not counting stop bits or the parity bit. Values are cs5, cs6, cs7, or cs8 according to whether the character size is five, six, seven, or eight bits, respectively.

cstopb   If set, two stop bits are generated for each output character, and two stop bits are expected for each received character. The -cstopb setting forces one stop bit per character.

hupcl   If set, forces the modem to drop the DTR (data terminal ready) line, thus forcing a hang up, after the last close on the port.

cread   Enables the receiver. If not set, no characters are received.

clocal   If set, ignores modem control signals. The -clocal setting forces the use of full modem control signals.

ignbrk   If set, the break signal (framing error with all data bits 0) is ignored.

brkint   If set, the break signal generates an INTERRUPT signal.

ignpar   If set, characters with parity or other framing errors are ignored.

parmrk	If set, a character received with a framing or parity error is read as the three-character sequence 0377, 0, *character-in-error*. If 0377 is read, it is converted to 0377, 0377 to avoid ambiguity.
inpck	If set, input parity checking is performed; otherwise, input parity errors are ignored. This allows for suppressing input parity checking while still generating output parity.
istrip	If set, mask all characters received so as to clear the eighth bit. Otherwise, all eight bits are used.
inlcr	Translate a received NL (newline) character to a CR (carriage return) character.
igncr	If set, ignore all CR (carriage return) characters.
icrnl	If set, translate a received CR (carriage return) character to NL (newline).
iuclc	If set, translate received uppercase characters to lowercase.
ixon	If set, start/stop output control is enabled. Receipt of an XOFF (DC3) character stops output. Receipt of an XON (DC1) character resumes output.
ixany	If set, any character received after an XOFF resumes output.
ixoff	If set, input start/stop control is enabled. The system generates XON and XOFF flow-control characters as needed to avoid overflow of the terminal input buffer.
isig	If set, each input character is checked for the INTR or QUIT characters, and the appropriate signal is generated.
icanon	If set, each input character is checked for the ERASE, KILL, EOF, EOL, and SWTCH characters. It also instructs the system to buffer all input into lines. If not set, input is unbuffered.
xcase	If set, precede each uppercase character for both input and output with a \ character. All characters not so preceded are lowercase.
echo	If set, echo each character typed.
echoe	If set, echo the erase character as "backspace space backspace."
echok	If set, the NL (newline) character is echoed when the KILL character is received.
echonl	If set, the NL (newline) character is echoed even if echo is not set.

`noflsh` If set, normal flushing of the queues is not performed when the INTR or QUIT characters are processed.

`opost` If set, enable output character post-processing; if clear, ignore all output post-processing flags.

`olcuc` If set, translate lowercase characters to uppercase on output.

`onlcr` If set, the NL (newline) character is output as CR NL (carriage return newline).

`onocr` If set, no CR (carriage return) character is output if the line is empty.

`onlret` If set, the NL (newline) character is assumed to do both CR (carriage return) and NL.

`ofill` Use the fill character for delays instead of just pausing the output.

`ofdel` If set, the DEL character is used as the fill character; otherwise the ASCII NUL character is used. This parameter is ineffective if `-ofill` is in effect.

`cr0, cr1, cr2, cr3`
Specifies the amount of delay to generate after sending a CR (carriage return) character, as follows:

`cr0`	none
`cr1`	varies by line length
`cr2`	0.10 seconds
`cr3`	0.15 seconds

`nl0, nl1` Specifies the amount of delay to generate after sending an NL (newline) character, as follows:

`nl0`	none
`nl1`	0.10 seconds

`tab0, tab1, tab2, tab3`
Specifies the amount of delay to generate after sending a tab character, as follows:

`tab0`	none
`tab1`	varies by line position
`tab2`	0.10 seconds
`tab3`	convert tabs to the appropriate number of spaces

`bs0, bs1` Specifies the amount of delay to generate after sending an NL (newline) character, as follows:

`bs0`	none
`bs1`	0.05 seconds

vt0, vt1 Specifies the amount of delay to generate after sending a VT (vertical tab) character, as follows:

     vt0   none
     vt1   enabled

ff0, ff1 Specifies the amount of delay to generate after sending an FF (form feed) character, as follows:

     ff0   none
     ff1   enabled

The stty command also takes keywords called *combination parameters*. These parameters change more than one of the simple parameters. You use them as a shorthand to change many parameters at once. Table 12.1 lists the combination parameters supported by the stty command, and shows the parameter values the combination parameter actually sets.

Table 12.1. *STTY Combination Parameter Definitions*

Combination	Definition	Evaluates to
evenp	Set even parity and 7 bits	parenb cs7 -parodd
parity	Same as evenp	parenb cs7 -parodd
oddp	Set odd parity and 7 bits	parenb cs7 parodd
-parity	Clear parity mode and set 8 bits	-parenb -parodd cs8
-evenp	Same as -parity	-parenb -parodd cs8
-oddp	Same as -parity	-parenb -parodd cs8
raw	Enable character-at-a-time input; Disable input characterprocessing	Many changes, including -icanon
-raw	Reenable line buffering and character processing. However, not the opposite of raw.	Many changes, including icanon

Table 12.1 continues

Table 12.1 *continued*

Combination	Definition	Evaluates to
cooked	Same as -raw	Many changes, including
nl	cr to nl translations	icanon
-nl	Reset cr to nl translation	-icrnl -onlcr
lcase	Convert uppercase to lowercase	icrnl onlcr -igncr -ocrnl -onlret
-lcase	Do not convert uppercase to lowercase	xcase iuclc olcuc -xcase -iuclc -olcuc
LCASE	Same as lcase	xcase iuclc olcuc
-LCASE	Same as -lcase	-xcase -iuclc -olcuc
tabs	Do not convert tabs to spaces	tab0
-tabs	Convert tabs to spaces	tab3
ek	Reset the erase and kill characters back to their defaults	erase # kill @
sane	Resets all modes to a reasonable default	Many changes

For example, you can enter the command:

```
stty evenp
```

instead of the equivalent command:

```
stty parenb cs7 -parodd
```

Both commands have the same effect. Note that an exact equivalence is not shown for raw, -raw, cooked, and sane. The effect of these combination parameters is not constrained by the System V Interface Definition, and varies from one version of System V to another.

Using stty from the Shell Interactively

The `stty` command operates on the serial port connected to standard input. When you type `stty` with no I/O redirection, you are changing the modes of your current terminal. When you redirect the standard input of the `stty` command, you change the modes of the serial port to which it was redirected.

Changes you make with the `stty` command remain in effect until changed by another `stty` command, changed by some other program, or all opens of the communications port are closed. When you log out, the system closes the communications port, and the parameters are reset.

Using stty from a Shell Script

When you run `stty` in a shell script, standard input may already be redirected. To ensure that `stty` changes the parameters of your terminal, redirect the standard input of the `stty` command from `/dev/tty`, as shown in the following example:

```
stty echo < /dev/tty
```

However, `stty` commands that you already redirect to affect other communications ports should not be changed.

Resetting the Serial Port Modes to a Known State

When the modes of your login terminal are mangled, as indicated when the terminal is not acting correctly, `stty` provides a combination parameter that restores the modes of your terminal to a default condition, called `sane`. The modes set by this parameter are not the same as the defaults that the port is reset to on the last close. Instead, the `sane` option forces a reasonable set of modes for normal communications. It does not, however, change the speed of the port.

Another way to quickly reset the modes of the serial port to a known state is to use the `-g` option of the `stty` command. This option writes a single line of numbers separated by colons that together indicate the complete current state of the terminal settings. The `stty` output in the prior examples, using the `-g` option, produces:

```
526:1805:dad:3b:3:1c:8:15:4:0:0:0
```

To use the output of the `-g` option, append the generated string to the `stty` command. This restores the port to the same state as when the `stty -g` command was issued. With these techniques, it is easy to make a shell alias or a shell script that contains the mode reset for your terminal. Here is a Bourne shell script to place such a command in your home directory:

```
echo "stty 'stty -g'" > $HOME/reset
chmod +x $HOME/reset
```

Anytime your terminal is in an unexpected state, just type

```
$HOME/reset
```

to restore your terminal parameters. It is sometimes worthwhile to place the two lines that save the state of the terminal into your login start-up script (.profile if you use the Bourne shell) so that the reset script is updated every time you log in.

Dead Terminals

Sometimes a terminal appears to be dead—typing characters produces no output, and typing a carriage return does not produce a prompt. This can be caused by the termination of any program that sets the -icanon or raw mode. These modes can disable echoing and also disable the conversion of the carriage return to a newline, so that pressing a carriage return appears to do nothing.

To recover from this mode, remember that it is not necessary for the characters you type to be echoed for UNIX to process the command. Just type:

```
^Jstty sane^J
```

The first control-J (shown as ^J) sends an end-of-line, and will probably result in some error message about how the system was unable to find a command based on the characters left in the input buffer; you can safely ignore such errors. The stty sane command restores the parameters, but you must end the command with another control-J instead of a carriage return because the mapping of carriage returns to newlines is suppressed while the terminal is in raw mode.

Alternately, you could use the $HOME/reset script you created in the preceding section. This would restore the modes exactly as they were saved.

In either case, note that you cannot use the erase character to correct your typing mistakes. If you make a mistake, just type a control-J to send a newline and start over.

Forcing a Communications Port to Hang Up

On serial connections that are connected to modems or network connections and are not in clocal mode (modem control signals are being used on the port), you can force the modem to hang up the phone line or force the network to simulate a hang-up by dropping the network connection. The DTR signal controls the hang-up. When you drop DTR it causes the connection to be terminated. To drop the DTR signal, set the line speed of the port to 0.

Programming a Serial Device

Although the stty command works well for interactive use and shell scripts, it is awkward to spawn a shell from a C program just to change the parameters of a serial port. Because the stty command is just an application program, UNIX provides ways for any C program to perform the same functions as stty.

Opening the Port

Before you can change any of the serial port parameters, you must first associate a file descriptor with the port, either by using shell I/O redirection on one of the preconnected descriptors (standard input, standard output, or standard error) or by opening the port using the standard open system call.

You open a serial port in the same way as you open any other file under UNIX. A separate file descriptor should be opened for input and for output, if both are desired. Although you are not required to open separate file descriptors for input and output, the stream I/O library does require you to use separate streams for input and output. Using separate file descriptors simplifies keeping track of the separate streams used by the stream I/O library. The fcntl.h header file contains definitions for each of the parameters used in the open(2) system call. Because the device entry must already exist, the creat(2) call is not supported with serial devices. The following code fragment shows how to open a terminal for input and output:

```
#include <stdio.h>
#include <fcntl.h>
#include <termio.h>

...
int input, output;

...
input = open("/dev/tty", O_RDONLY);
output = open("/dev/tty", O_WRONLY);
```

You perform all input, output and parameter changes using the file descriptors. You can change the parameters using the input or output file descriptor. The stty command uses its standard input file descriptor for parameter changes, but UNIX does not impose that restriction.

You can also use fopen(3) to open the serial port. If you use the stream I/O routines, however, you cannot use unbuffered input. Because fopen returns a FILE structure instead of a file descriptor, you make parameter changes by accessing the file descriptor in the FILE structure.

Serial Communications Port ioctl Calls

Because a write to the port causes output on its transmit line, and a read from the port waits for date to be received on the input line, parameter changes require a way of accessing the port without reading or writing characters. UNIX provides access to a device for non read/write functions through the `ioctl` system call. Serial ports use the `ioctl` system call for parameter changes, and for out-of-band signaling. An out-of-band signal is information transferred without sending or receiving a character. For serial communications, this includes flow control and the break signal.

The serial driver `ioctl` functions are symbolically enumerated in the `termio.h` header file. Three of the functions (`TCSBRK`, `TCXONC`, and `TCFLSH`) perform out-of-band signaling; the remainder perform parameter changes. All are described in table 12.2.

Table 12.2. Serial Communications Driver ioctl Functions

Name	Description
TCGETA	Retrieve the current parameters.
TCSETA	Immediately change the parameters.
TCSETAW	After the pending output has finished, change the parameters.
TCSETAF	After the pending output has finished, flush any typed ahead characters and then change the parameters.
TCSBRK	Wait for pending output, then optionally send a break character. A break is 0.25 seconds of 0 bits.
TCXONC	Start or stop output. Acts like flow control.
TCFLSH	Flush pending input, output, or both input and output.

The following is an example of using the `ioctl` system call with serial ports. This code fragment flushes the input and output queues and then sends a break signal:

```
/* Flush both the input and output queues */

ioctl(output, TCFLSH, 2);

/* Now send a break signal */

ioctl(output, TCSBRK, 1);
```

The termio Structure

Configuration parameters are reported in the `termio` structure defined in `termio.h`. The `termio` structure uses bit fields to hold the parameter information. The header file contains symbolic definitions of each of the mode bits, as well as the definition of the `typedef` for the `termio` structure. The `termio` structure contains four bit fields for the parameters, as well as a table of the character values. The bits in each bit field contain 1 if the option is set, or 0 if the option is cleared. The option names match the `stty` command parameter names. Some names, however, start with the letter of the mode word in which it is contained. See the `include` file for a complete listing of all the parameter names and command flags. The `termio` structure follows:

```
struct termio {
        unsigned short  c_iflag; /* input modes */
        unsigned short  c_oflag; /* output modes */
        unsigned short  c_cflag; /* control modes */
        unsigned short  c_lflag; /* line discipline modes */
        char            c_line;  /* line discipline */
        unsigned char   c_cc[NCC]; /* control chars */
};
```

The following code fragment shows how to obtain the current configuration parameters for the serial port associated with the `input` file descriptor, then set the echo bits for character, erase, and kill echoing. This fragment is how you would restore echoing if it was currently disabled.

```
{
        struct termio curparms, newparms;

        ioctl(input, TCGETA, &curparms);
        newparms = curparms;
        newparms.c_lflag |= (ECHO | ECHOE | ECHOK);
        ioctl(input, TCSETA, &newparms);
}
```

The sgtty Structure

An older method of reporting and changing the terminal parameters was used before the current `termio` method was adopted with the release of UNIX System III. It is based on the `stty(2)` and `gtty(2)` system calls. System V supports an emulation mode for these calls, and some older programs still use them, but they are obsolete. These system calls used the `sgtty` structure defined in `sgtty.h`.

The `sgtty` structure included a byte for input and output speeds, a byte for the erase character, a byte for the kill character, and a short integer for the flags. Note that with this structure you cannot change all the character parameters; you can change only the erase and kill characters. Also, the `sgtty` structure and system calls use a different set of flags. Because there are fewer flags (only sixteen possible values), fewer choices are possible. Therefore, there is not a one-to-one mapping of modes in sgtty and termio. Setting any of the flags in the sgtty structure is emulated by changing an appropriate set of flags in the termio structure. Resetting any of the flags in the sgtty structure will also cause a change in an appropriate set of flags in the termio structure. However, the set of flags changed in the termio structure when a sgtty parameter is set and the set of termio flags changed when a sgtty parameter is cleared may not be the same. Thus, you cannot reset the terminal back to the same state by setting and then clearing a flag in the sgtty structure.

The gtty(2) system call retrieves the current parameters. The stty(2) system call immediately changes the parameters. None of the delay options are supported. Any programs that still use the obsolete sgtty structure should be converted to the current termio structure.

Error Recovery

When you develop programs that change the parameters of the controlling terminal, it is important for you to consider error recovery. Your program should always return the parameters to their original state before exiting, even if the exit is due to an error.

One way to ensure this during development is to wrap your program invocation with a shell script that saves the terminal state, then restores it after the program exits. For example:

```
oldparms=`stty -g`
trap "stty $oldparms" 0 1 2 3 4 5 6 7 8 10 12 13 14 15
16
program-to-run$*
```

This script uses the stty command's -g option to save the current parameters, and the trap command of the shell to execute another stty command to set the parameters back to the original values on every trapable exit condition. Note that signal 9 (kill) and 11 (segmentation violation) are not recoverable and are omitted from the trap list. These signals are received by the shell, not the program being run. Thus, even if you send a kill-9 signal to the program, the shell still executes the restore, because the shell sees only the trap0 for the normal exit from the script.

After you have debugged the program, you must add the appropriate signal traps to the program to restore the terminal parameters to their original values. Your signal-catching routine should call a routine to restore the terminal parameters by using the TCGETA ioctl call. For more information on signals, see Chapter 14, "Signals and IPC."

Reading and Writing the Serial Port from a C Program

Now that you have opened the port and set the parameters, you can send and receive characters using the port. Using the file descriptors you have opened and the `read(2)` and `write(2)` system calls, you can read the receive data stream and write to the transmit data stream. The following is a simple example of how to copy characters from the input stream to the output stream:

```
{
        char    c;

        while (read(input, &c, 1) > 0)
                write(output, &c, 1);
}
```

This loop reads one character at a time from the input buffer, then writes that character to the output file. It ends when an end-of-file is detected on the input file, causing the read to return EOF (-1). This loop is very simple, but not very efficient. It causes two system calls for each character copied. System calls are an expensive resource and their use should be optimized. If the `icanon` option is set, the loop is executed only after an end of line is reached, because UNIX buffers the characters and makes them available to your program only after it receives a line termination character. Thus, the user would type an entire line, and then the loop would execute for each character in the line.

A more efficient method would be to take advantage of buffering by having your program read a line at a time. This modification would change the code fragment to:

```
{
        char    buf[BUFSIZ];
        int     len;

        while ((len = read(input, buf, BUFSIZ)) > 0)
                write(output, buf, len);
}
```

The new loop reads a single line, or at most `BUFSIZ` characters. `BUFSIZ` is a symbol defined in `stdio.h` that specifies a good value for buffer size. UNIX will read a single line, truncate the read, then return the line including the line termination character. This differs from disk reads, in which the read is truncated only at the end-of-file. Reading from a serial communications port always returns at most one line when in `icanon` mode. This loop only uses two system calls per line, a more efficient method.

Using Stream I/O

An even more efficient method is to use the stream I/O routines. These routines use the FILE structure and an automatically allocated buffer to reduce the number of system calls. UNIX also provides several useful subroutines to read and write lines of text when using streams. The stream I/O routines are fopen, fflush, fclose, fread, fwrite, fgets, fputs, fgetc, getc, getw, fputc, putc, putw, fprintf, and fscanf. When the stream is either standard input or standard output, you can use the additional functions gets, puts, getchar, putchar, printf, and scanf, which assume the standard input or standard output file.

The stream I/O routines ending in c read or write a single character to the stream. Those ending in w read or write a binary word to the stream. Those ending with s write a string or read a line. The printf routines make formatted conversions to build strings and output those strings. The scanf routines extract items from a line or string using a format description. Both the printf and scanf routines have many options. Refer to the "Reference" section for more information.

Because stream I/O is buffered, the fflush routine is provided to force the I/O to occur even if the buffer is not full. (The read and write routines perform their I/O immediately.) Rewriting the preceding code fragment to use stream I/O to copy our file to standard output yields the following code fragment:

```
#include <stdio.h>

main(argc, argv)
int     argc;
char    *argv[];
{
        char    buf[BUFSIZ];
        FILE    *in_file;

        if ((in_file = fopen(argv[1], "r")) == NULL) {
                fprintf(stderr,
                    "Unable to open the input file %s\n",
                    argv[1]);
                exit(1);
        }
        while (fgets(buf, BUFSIZ, in_file)) {
                puts(buf, stdout);
        }
        fclose(in_file);
}
```

This code fragment uses fgets and fputs to read and write the string for each line. Note that this fragment looks identical to the fragment that would be used to copy disk files. This is because to UNIX, there is no difference in reading or writing disk or device files even though the buffering of these items differs, so your program must be able to handle truncated reads. The stream I/O routines handle this difference automatically.

ICANON (Line-at-a-Time) Mode

So far, the code fragments have dealt with the port in icanon mode. In this mode, UNIX buffers the characters into lines, performs editing to erase characters that you backspaced over, deletes lines that you killed, and processes the end-of-file characters. This mode is very useful in that it does not differ from the same method you used to read disk files. The drawback is that your program does not see any input until the newline character is typed. Thus, your program waits when it performs the read until an entire line is entered.

Despite these disadvantages, icanon mode is the most efficient way to handle terminal input because it allows the characters to be read and written with the least number of system calls. You should use icanon mode unless your program needs to read single keystrokes immediately.

RAW Mode

Whereas icanon mode processes a full line with each read, -icanon, often called *raw* mode, reads characters one at a time. Each character typed is returned immediately and the read is terminated by the input of a character instead of a line. The -icanon mode is useful for programs that respond to single keystrokes, but also wasteful of CPU resources. For each character received, UNIX must switch the active context to the user's program to process the character, then switch the context back to receive the next character.

When in raw mode, no checking is made for the special characters that handle erase, kill, and end-of-file; your program must handle any line editing that is needed. Thus, all characters are valid for input. When a read is posted, your program blocks until a single character is typed. Then that character is returned to the program. Any additional characters are buffered and returned on subsequent reads.

Because it is wasteful to read characters one at a time, and keyboard input often occurs in bursts (such as function key strings), recent versions of UNIX provide a way to read more than one character at a time, and still return with less than a complete line. Two of the special character parameters are given a different meaning when in raw mode, namely the MIN and TIME parameters. By controlling the values of these two parameters, you can vary the amount read and the time when the program unblocks and is able to process the pending characters.

MIN is the minimum number or characters that must be read before a read system call will return the buffered characters to your program. The system may return more than MIN characters to you on a read call, but never less.

TIME is a time-out value in tenths of a second. Your program will not be delayed longer than this time when you issue a read to the terminal. If fewer than MIN characters have been read in TIME tenths of a second, the system will return the characters it has read despite the MIN limitation.

If either MIN or TIME is 0, the corresponding function is disabled, as follows:

❏ MIN = 0, TIME = 0. This case reads exactly the number of characters requested in the read call. There is no time-out value, so the program will block indefinitely until the read request is satisfied.

❏ MIN = 0, TIME > 0. This case reads for TIME tenths of a second, or until the requested number of characters in the read call have been received. If TIME tenths of a second occur before the characters are read, the read short terminates, even if no characters have been read. In this case, the return of zero characters read by the read call is not an error.

❏ MIN > 0, TIME = 0. Because TIME is 0, the timer is not used. The read waits until at least MIN characters, but less than the requested number of characters, are available. Those characters are returned, completing the read call. If the read requests less than MIN characters, the program still blocks until MIN characters are read, but only the requested number are returned to the program in that read request. The remainder wait in the input buffer for the next read request.

❏ MIN > 0, TIME > 0. TIME is now an intercharacter timer and is activated after the first character is received. The program blocks indefinitely until the first character is received. Then it waits until at least MIN characters are received, or TIME tenths of a second have occurred between the receipt of two characters. The read request returns the smaller of the requested number of characters or the number of characters read before the time-out expired. Any remaining characters stay in the input buffer for the next read. This case always returns at least one character because the timer is not activated until one character is read, and may take longer than TIME tenths of a second because the timer is restarted every time a character is received.

It is important to note that MIN is just a minimum number of characters to read. If due to scheduling constraints, more than MIN number of characters have been received before the read call is made, the characters are buffered by UNIX and returned to the program in the first read call. The maximum number of characters returned by a read call is controlled by the length argument of the read system call. For more information on the effects of MIN and TIME in raw mode, see the termio(7) section of the manual for your system.

Time-outs Using Alarms

By using the appropriate value of TIME and MIN while in raw mode, you can provide for a read time-out. Yet the efficient mode of TIME > 0 and MIN > 0 does not allow a time-out until at least one character has been received. Also, icanon does not allow a read time-out. UNIX does provide a method of handling these time-outs.

One of the software interrupt signals supported by UNIX is the alarm clock timer. You can set this timer to expire at some integral number of seconds. By setting a timer with the alarm system call and defining a user signal-handling function for the SIGALRM signal with the signal system call, the read can be halted after a time-out. You can use this method, for example, to allow a user sixty seconds to enter a password, and then abort the program if more than sixty seconds are used to enter the password. It is more efficient that polling the keyboard, because UNIX can assign the CPU elsewhere until the read completes or the alarm triggers.

When the alarm expires, it generates a SIGALRM software interrupt. This interrupt also interrupts any serial communications read in progress. The interrupted read returns 0 because no characters are returned. If the read does complete before the alarm expires, however, you must cancel the alarm. If you don't cancel the alarm, it will still be triggered when it expires.

The following code fragment will read a yes-or-no answer and time out in thirty seconds if no answer is received:

```
#include <stdio.h>
#include <signal.h>
#include <ctype.h>

static int alarm_received = 0;

void alarm_catcher()
{
    alarm_received = 1;
}

int yesno(prompt)
{
    char    ans[20];
    void    (*oldalarm)();
/*
 *    Set up our signal-catching routine, and save the
```

```
    *    old one to be restored later.
    */
        oldalarm = signal(SIGALRM, alarm_catcher);

    /*
    *    Output the prompt to standard-out and use fflush to
    *    force the output even though it does not end with
    *    newline.
    */
        printf("%s: (y/n) ? ", prompt);
        fflush(stdout);
    /*
    *    Clear the alarm flag, start the alarm, and start the read
    */
        alarm_received = 0;
        alarm(30);
        gets(ans);
    /*
    *    The read has returned, so clear the alarm and restore
    *    the prior alarm signal handler.
    */
        alarm(0);
        signal(SIGALRM, oldalarm);

        if (alarm_received) {
                return(-1);

        }

        return(tolower(*ans) == 'y');
}
```

This code fragment returns -1 for a time-out, 0 for any answer other than a word starting with *Y* or *y*, and 1 otherwise. It saves and restores the prior signal handler for the alarm signal, and initializes the alarm_received variable each time, so that the routine can be used more than once. Further information on signals is available in Chapter 14, "Signals and IPC."

Modems

Up to this point, only a side mention has been made of modems and the modem control signals. A directly connected terminal is always available to handle input and output, although flow control may delay the processing of characters. Modems, however, are not permanently connected. The session is connected only as long as the modem is talking to the user at the remote modem. When the user hangs up, the computer must close the connection. If this is not done, the next person to use the modem would be connected in the middle of the prior user's session. UNIX uses the modem control signals provided by the modem to determine that the user has hung up and to terminate the session.

Modem Control Signals

A modem indicates that it has accepted a call and is in communication with another modem by the use of modem control signals. These signals are also used to indicate that the system is ready to make a connection, and to force the modem to hang up on the connection. The standard three signals for a directly connected serial port are transmit, receive, and signal-ground. A modem adds the signals listed in the following:

DSR   Data Set Ready. This signal indicates that the modem is powered up and ready to make a connection. If this signal is not present, no communications will occur with the modem.

DTR   Data Terminal Ready. This signal indicates to the modem that the computer is ready to accept a connection. If this signal is on, and the modem is so configured, the modem is allowed to answer the phone when it rings. If not set, the modem hangs up on any current connection. By dropping this signal, you cause the modem to hang up.

CD   Carrier Detect. This signal indicates that the connection is complete. The modem has recognized and properly connected to another modem, and all the signals are stable. If the remote modem hangs up, this signal is dropped.

RTS   Request to Send. The computer raises this signal when it has data to send. The modem looks for this signal before receiving characters.

CTS   Clear to Send. The modem raises this signal when it is ready to process incoming characters. It is raised in response to RTS being raised by the computer. When a full duplex modem is used, RTS is held high by the computer and CTS is held high by the modem for the full duration of the connection.

RI   Ring Indicator. The modem raises this signal when it detects a ring on the telephone line. It follows the ringing signal. It is used if the computer wants to count the rings and raise DTR to answer the phone itself after the appropriate number of rings.

UNIX uses most of these signals. RI, however, is usually ignored, and the modem internally determines when to answer the phone.

The standard login process uses the `getty` program to open the port. This raises DTR. The modem already has DSR high if it is powered on, and sees the raising of DTR as permission to answer the phone. When a connection completes, the modem raises CD and the `getty` program's open completes.

This allows the getty program to print the banner and ask for the login name. The getty program then starts the login program, and the login program starts the user's shell. On logging out, the last close of the port causes DTR to drop. This signals the modem to drop the connection, which drops CD. The process is now ready to be repeated.

If CD drops due to the modem losing the connection (for example, by the user hanging up without logging out), UNIX sends a HANGUP signal to all processes that own the device. This allows the process to recover and close the port, forcing a local hang up.

Opening a Modem Port

If a standard open is given to a port configured for modem control, the open will wait for a connection to complete and the modem to raise CD. The open causes UNIX to raise DTR, and this instructs the modem to answer the phone. However, if the modem is being opened for an outbound call, in which it is necessary to talk to the modem before it raises CD to ask it to dial the call, it will be impossible to talk to the modem before the call is completed.

UNIX does provide for a way around this impasse. By setting the O_NDELAY flag in the open options, the open will complete without CD being raised. The following code fragment shows the proper use of the O_NDELAY flag.

```
#include <stdio.h>
#include <fcntl.h>

...
int modem;

...
modem = open("/dev/tty/aa", O_RDWR | O_NDELAY);
```

Locking a Port

Many UNIX utilities access the serial ports. For some devices, the device driver enforces exclusive access, which means that only one process can open the device. This is not true of serial devices. It is not even desired, because a controlling program that is waiting for the connection to complete might invoke a dialer program that opens the port with O_NDELAY.

There is a convention in UNIX for reserving access to a serial port. This convention creates a small file in a known directory before opening the file. If the file already exists, the port is in use. However, sometimes the program that reserved the port has died and did not remove its lock file. To accommodate this condition, the convention requires writing the process-ID of the process locking the serial port into the lock file. A check for the existence of this process would then indicate that the lock is still active. If the process is not found, the lock is considered stale. The lock file may be removed, and the locking attempt can be retried.

Currently, all serial port locks are placed in the /usr/spool/uucp directory, primarily because the uucp and cu programs are the principal users of serial ports. Serial port locks are called LCK..portname. If the port is /dev/tty/aa, the lock file would be LCK..ttyaa. The subdirectory marker between the directory name of the port directory (if any) and the port name is not used in the lock name. Thus, the same lock file names would be used for both /dev/ttyaa and /dev/tty/aa.

The following code fragment creates a lock, if possible, or returns with a return value of -1 to indicate that the port is already locked:

```
#include <stdio.h>
#include <fcntl.h>
#include <ctype.h>
/*
 * Create a lock file to advise that we are going to use this
 * port. If it already exists, return -1; else return 0.
 * port = the full name, including the /dev/ on the front.
 */
lock(port)
char *port;
{
        char lock_name[BUFSIZ], *c, lock_contents[10];
        int  lock_fd, lock_pid;
        /*
         * Form the lock name: skip over /dev/ first;
         * allow both /dev/tty/aa and /dev/ttyaa forms
         */
        port += 5;
        c = strchr(port, '/');
        if (c && *c != '\0') {
                *c++ = '\0';
                sprintf(lock_name, "/usr/spool/uucp/%s%s",
                        port, c);
        } else {
                sprintf(lock_name, "/usr/spool/uucp/%s", port);
        }
        /*
         * Now try and read the lock file, and if pid is
         * no longer active, remove the lock file
         */
        if ((lock_fd = open(lock_name, O_RDONLY)) != -1) {
                if (read(lock_fd, lock_contents, 10) > 0) {
                        lock_pid = atoi(lock_contents);
                        if (lock_pid) {
                                if (kill(lock_pid, 0)) {
                                        unlink(lock_name);
```

```
                            }
                        }
                    }
                    close(lock_fd);
            }
            /*
             * Now try to create it.
             */
            if ((lock_fd = open(lock_name, O_WRONLY | O_CREAT |
                O_EXCL, 0444))
                  != -1) {
                        sprintf(lock_contents, "%d", getpid());
                        write(lock_fd, lock_contents,
                              strlen(lock_contents));
                        close(lock_fd);
                        return(0);
            }
            /*
             * lock failed
             */
            return(-1);
    }
```

The locks created by this method are called *advisory locks* because it is up to the program to check to see whether the device is locked. UNIX does not enforce the lock, and any attempt to open and use the port will succeed. This will cause interference between the two programs that are attempting to use the port at the same time. If you use advisory locking, be sure that all programs that access the port also use the same advisory locking method.

Another type of locking is *mandatory locking.* Various standards activities are working on adding mandatory locking to UNIX, but at present it is best not to depend on it being available.

The Hangup Signal and Forcing the Modem to Hang Up

As mentioned, UNIX sends the SIGHUP signal to the program when it detects a hang up (loss of the CD signal) on the serial communications port. However, this signal is only sent when modem control signals are being honored. The port must not be in `clocal` mode, and if the system uses a different device name for modem control ports, the device must be one of the ports that has the modem control bits set.

After the SIGHUP signal is received, it is up to the program to close the port and thus force the dropping of DTR. If you want to wait for another call, your program will have to drop DTR without closing the port. Just set the line speed to 0. UNIX will hold DTR low as long as the speed is 0. Resetting the speed to the desired speed reasserts DTR.

Terminal Program

As a summary of all that was presented in this chapter, this section presents a program to access a modem on a modem-controlled serial communications port and communicate with a remote system. Note that UNIX already includes such a program, either as cu or tip.

The program accepts command-line parameters for the line and speed, locks the line, opens the line, sets the parameters for the port, and receives and transmits characters to the port and the user's keyboard and screen. It takes two processes to do this, because characters may be received for the screen while the keyboard read is in progress. The characters received on the communications line should not be delayed in being processed and displayed on the user's screen just because a read of the keyboard is pending and has the program blocked. The program must use a second process to allow both to run in parallel. This example uses the fork system call to split into two processes to handle the two reads in parallel.

To keep the application simple, it does not dial the modem, but sends all characters typed at the keyboard to the terminal. To dial a remote connection, you need only type the modem control command to dial the desired telephone number. Also, the program provides no command keystroke escapes except for the keystroke sequence to drop CD and cause the line to drop. The remote terminal program follows:

```
 1   #include <stdio.h>
 2   #include <fcntl.h>
 3   #include <signal.h>
 4   #include <termio.h>
 5   #include <ctype.h>
 6   #include <string.h>
 7   #include <sys/types.h>
 8   #include <sys/stat.h>
 9
10   char    portname[64];
11   int     speed;
12   int     receive_pid = 0;
13   int     modem, modem;
14   struct termio init_termio, cur_termio, modem_termio;
15   #define IN_LINE 0
16   #define AT_NEWLINE 1
17   #define AT_TILDE 2
18   /*
19    * This program support only these speeds:
```

```
20    */
21   struct speedtable {
22      int    speed;
23      int    parm;
24   } speeds[] = {
25      { 300, B300 },
26      { 1200, B1200 },
27      { 2400, B2400 },
28      { 4800, B4800 },
29      { 9600, B9600 },
30      { 19200, EXTA },
31      { 0, 0 } };
32
33   /*
34    * Create the lock file to advise that we are going to use
35    * this port. If it already exists, return -1; else return
36    * 0. port=the full name, including the /dev/ on the front.
37    */
38   lock(port)
39   char  *port;
40   {
41      char   lock_name[BUFSIZ], *c, lock_contents[10];
42      int    lock_fd, lock_pid;
43      /*
44       * Form the lock name: skip over /dev/ first;
45       * allow both /dev/tty/aa and /dev/ttyaa forms
46       */
47      port += 5;
48      c = strchr(port, '/');
49      if (c && *c != '\0') {
50         *c++ = '\0';
51         sprintf(lock_name, "/usr/spool/uucp/%s%s",
52            port, c);
53      } else {
54         sprintf(lock_name, "/usr/spool/uucp/%s",
55            port);
56      }
57      /*
58       * Now try and read the lock file, and if pid is
59       * no longer active, remove the lock file
60       */
61      if ((lock_fd = open(lock_name, O_RDONLY)) != -1) {
62         if (read(lock_fd, lock_contents, 10) > 0) {
63            lock_pid = atoi(lock_contents);
64            if (lock_pid) {
65               if (kill(lock_pid, 0)) {
66                  unlink(lock_name);
67               }
68            }
69         }
```

```
 70          close(lock_fd);
 71      }
 72      /*
 73       * Now try to create it.
 74       */
 75      if ((lock_fd = open(lock_name,
 76          O_WRONLY | O_CREAT | O_EXCL, 0444)) != -1) {
 77          sprintf(lock_contents, "%d", getpid());
 78          write(lock_fd, lock_contents,
 79              strlen(lock_contents));
 80          close(lock_fd);
 81          return(0);
 82      }
 83      /*
 84       * lock failed
 85       */
 86      return(-1);
 87  }
 88
 89  /*
 90   * Remove lock file for this port, we are done with it.
 91   */
 92  unlock(port)
 93  char  *port;
 94  {
 95      char  lock_name[BUFSIZ], *c;
 96      /*
 97       * Form the lock name. Skip over /dev/ first;
 98       * allow both /dev/tty/aa and /dev/ttyaa forms
 99       */
100      port += 5;
101      c = strchr(port, '/');
102      if (c && *c != '\0') {
103          *c++ = '\0';
104          sprintf(lock_name, "/usr/spool/uucp/%s%s", port, c);
105      } else {
106          sprintf(lock_name, "/usr/spool/uucp/%s", port);
107      }
108      /*
109       * Now unlink the lock file.
110       */
111      return(unlink(lock_name));
112  }
113
114  /*
115   * On any signal, restore the terminal parameters,
116   * cleanup, and exit
117   */
118  catch_sig()
119  {
```

```
120     if (receive_pid)
121         kill(receive_pid, SIGKILL);
122     ioctl(0, TCSETA, &init_termio);
123     unlock(portname);
124     printf("Exiting due to caught signal\n");
125     exit(0);
126  }
127
128
129
130  main(argc, argv)
131  int    argc;
132  char   *argv[];
133  {
134      char  c, buf[BUFSIZ], *bufptr;
135      int    len, state;
136      struct stat statbuf;
137      struct speedtable *speedsptr;
138
139      extern int  optind;
140      extern char *optarg;
141      /*
142       * The default values
143       */
144      strcpy(portname, "/dev/ttyaa");
145      speed = B9600;
146
147      if (ioctl(0, TCGETA, &init_termio)) {
148          printf("Unable to get current parameters\n");
149          exit(1);
150      }
151      /*
152       * Get the run-time arguments
153       */
154      while ((c = getopt(argc, argv, "l:s:")) != EOF) {
155          switch {
156          case 'l': /* line to use */
157              sprintf(portname, "/dev/%s", optarg);
158              if (stat(portname, &statbuf)) {
159                  printf("Unable to stat line %s\n", portname);
160                  exit(1);
161              }
162              if ((statbuf.st_mode & S_IFMT) != S_IFCHR) {
163                  printf("Line %s is not a character device\n",
                            portname);
164                  exit(1);
165              }
166
167              break;
168
169          case 's': /* speed of the line */
170              speed = atol(optarg);
```

```
171              for (speedsptr = speeds; speedsptr->speed;
                     speedsptr++) {

172                  if (speedsptr->speed == speed) {
173                      speed = speedsptr->parm;
174                      break;
175                  }
176              }
177              if (speedsptr->speed == 0) {
178                  printf("Invalid speed %d\n", speed);
179                  exit(1);
180              }
181              break;
182
183          default: /* an illegal argument */
184              printf("usage: modem [-l line] [-s speed]\n");
185              exit(1);
186          }
187      }
188      /*
189       * Set signal catch routine to restore and unlock
190       * on any error or interrupt
191       */
192      signal(SIGHUP, catch_sig);
193      signal(SIGINT, catch_sig);
194      signal(SIGQUIT, catch_sig);
195      signal(SIGILL, catch_sig);
196      signal(SIGTRAP, catch_sig);
197      signal(SIGBUS, catch_sig);
198      signal(SIGTERM, catch_sig);
199      /*
200       * Try and lock the line
201       */
202      if (lock(portname)) {
203          printf("Unable to lock %s\n", portname);
204          exit(1);
205      }
206      /*
207       * Now open the port, and set up the line options
208       */
209      if ((modem = open(portname, O_RDWR | O_NDELAY)) < 0) {
210          printf("Unable to open %s for read\n", portname);
211          unlock(portname);
212          exit(1);
213      }
214      /* Set the parameters for the line: basically 8 bits,
215       * no parity, no time-out on read, and return with
216       * at least one character.
217       */
218      modem_termio.c_iflag = IGNBRK | ISTRIP;
219      modem_termio.c_oflag = 0;
220      modem_termio.c_cflag = CS8 | CREAD | speed;
```

```
221      modem_termio.c_lflag = 0;
222      modem_termio.c_line = 0;
223      modem_termio.c_cc[VMIN] = 1;
224      modem_termio.c_cc[VTIME] = 0;
225
226      if (ioctl(modem, TCSETA, &modem_termio)) {
227          printf("Unable to configure %s\n", portname);
228          close(modem);
229          unlock(portname);
230          exit(1);
231      }
232      /*
233       * Now split into two processes, one to read the
234       * terminal, and one to read the modem line.
235       */
236      if (receive_pid = fork()) {
237          if (receive_pid == -1) {
238              printf("Unable to fork\n");
239              close(modem);
240              unlock(portname);
241              exit(1);
242          }
243          /* This is the parent side. This side will read
244           * to the terminal and write to the modem.
245           * Configure the terminal for -icanon mode.
246           */
247          cur_termio = init_termio;
248          cur_termio.c_iflag = IGNBRK | ISTRIP;
249          cur_termio.c_oflag = cur_termio.c_oflag & ~(OLCUC |
                 ONLCR | OCRNL | ONLRET);
250          cur_termio.c_lflag = 0;
251          cur_termio.c_cc[VMIN] = 1;
252          cur_termio.c_cc[VTIME] = 0;
253          if (ioctl(0, TCSETA, &cur_termio))
254              goto exit_cleanup;
255          state = AT_NEWLINE;
256          /* Now loop, reading the keyboard and
257           * sending to the modem
258           */
259          while ((len = read(0, buf, BUFSIZ - 1)) >= 0) {
260              buf[len] = '\0';
261              /*
262               * Check for exit characters
263               */
264              for (bufptr = buf; *bufptr; bufptr++) {
265                  if (*bufptr == '\r')
266                      state = AT_NEWLINE;
267                  else if (*bufptr == '~' && state == AT_NEWLINE)
268                      state = AT_TILDE;
269                  else if (*bufptr == '.' && state == AT_TILDE)
270                      goto exit_cleanup;
```

```
271                  else
272                      state = IN_LINE;
273              }
274          /*
275           * Write these characters
276           */
277          write(modem, buf, len);
278      }
279      /*
280       * Error condition received, go do cleanup
281       */
282      goto exit_cleanup;
283  } else {
284      /*
285       * This is the child. Loop reading the modem, and
286       * write the terminal. No checking needed here.
287       */
288      while ((len = read(modem, buf, BUFSIZ)) >= 0)
289          write(1, buf, len);
290      exit(0);
291  }
292  exit_cleanup:
293      /*
294       * First, kill the child process. Then close the
295       * modem, restore our modes, and release the lock.
296       */
297      kill(receive_pid, SIGKILL);
298      close(modem);
299      ioctl(0, TCSETA, &init_termio);
300      unlock(portname);
301      exit(0);
302  }
```

This remote terminal program uses the lock subroutine described previously in this chapter, as well as a simple addition, unlock, that removes the lock file. Both use the same code fragment to determine the name of the lock file.

To prevent errors leaving the terminal port in an inconvenient state, where carriage returns are not mapped to newlines and the characters are not echoed, the signal-catching routine at lines 114-126 restores the terminal parameters to those read at program start up. It also sends a forced termination signal to the cooperative receive process whose pid was saved in the receive_pid global variable.

The main routine saves the terminal state at line 147 so that the terminal parameters can be restored later. You should perform this save early in the program, before any changes have been made to the terminal state.

Lines 151-187 use the getopt routine to parse command-line options. This loop processes the -l and -s options. See the manual page for getopt for more details on its use and parameters. This loop also does some basic error checking on the supplied arguments. Note at lines 158-165 the check that the file name is a character-special device. The s t a t call returns the file type in st_mode. By masking the permissions and comparing the result against the character-special device entry, it is easy to perform a reasonableness check of the line name parameter. However, it is not as easy to determine whether the file is a serial character device or some other character device. If it is not a serial character-special device, a later i o c t l call fails, as the *TCxxxxxx* i o c t l commands are valid only for serial devices.

Lines 218-230 configure the serial port with appropriate parameters. It is not necessary to first obtain the existing parameters because the port was closed before this and was kept in a reset state by the system. The parameters shown set 8 bits, no parity, and 1 stop bit.

Line 236 uses the f o r k system call to split this process into two processes. The parent process becomes the side that reads the terminal keyboard and writes the modem line. The child process reads the modem and writes the terminal. The parent process, rather than the child process, reads from the terminal so that it can receive the exit signal when the user decides to terminate the program.

The state loop at lines 255-273 checks the characters read to detect the sequence, "return, tilde, dot." This is the sequence the user should enter to terminate the program. When this sequence is detected, the program does its exit cleanup.

The exit cleanup at lines 292-303 basically is identical to the exit cleanup of the signal processing code. In both cases, the parent process kills the child process, restores the terminal parameters to their default values, and exits. It is not strictly necessary to close the modem port before exiting because the program exit closes all open files.

Advanced Issues

Most of this chapter has dealt with sending characters to and receiving characters from a terminal. However, serial communications is also used for computer-to-computer communications. Terminals usually use 7-bit ASCII with or without parity, wherease computer-to-computer communications send and receive 8 bits using a binary protocol.

Eight-Bit Binary Input and Zero Bytes

Because UNIX is written in C, the operating system inherits the conventions of the C runtime library, including the convention that strings are terminated by null (zero) characters. As a result, it is not possible to read a string that contains embedded null characters because the first null would end the string. Binary communications, however, often need to send zero bytes. The only way to treat null characters as data is to read and write data streams in the unbuffered mode. You must perform 8-bit binary communications using -icanon mode. Using the appropriate MIN and TIME values also allows for efficient data transfer, and for lost character time-outs. This makes for ease and efficiency when programming a communications protocol.

Buffering

When you program a serial communications application, the level of buffering you use affects the appearance of output on the terminal screen. The C function library supports multiple levels of buffering.

The highest level is private buffering, in which your program accumulates characters into blocks using its own buffers. To cut down on the number of system calls, it is a good idea to use buffers, rather than multiple write calls, to build strings. When you keep the number of system calls down, the performance of the system and your program improves, and output to the terminal looks normal. Frequent system calls, on the other hand, result in output being displayed intermittently in short bursts of characters, because other processes are continually stealing time from your process on each system call.

The next level of buffering is stream I/O. You can control the size and type of buffering used by the stream I/O package with the setbuf and setvbuf function calls. By default, standard output and standard error use line buffering when connected to a terminal and full buffering otherwise. Line buffering flushes the internal stream I/O buffer whenever a newline character is written; full buffering only flushes the buffer when it is full. Either buffering method writes the contents of the internal buffer when an explicit flush is requested with fflush or when the file is closed. When you use full buffering, several lines are written to the terminal at once, ending with the first part of the last line, then the terminal appears to pause. Line buffering forces only whole lines to be written.

The lowest level of buffering occurs in the kernel. A system buffer holds the data while it is being written to the device. If the data will fit in one system buffer, all the characters will appear on the screen at once. For input, this buffering holds the characters the user types ahead. The length of the type-ahead buffer is limited, and any characters typed beyond the limit of the type-ahead buffer can cause the loss of the entire type-ahead buffer. However, this buffer is large enough to handle most situations. Usually, the buffer can hold between 128 and 256 characters.

Modem/Serial Port Speed Detection

The getty program can adjust to any one of several line speeds to match that of your terminal during the login process. The getty program first tries a default line speed defined by your system administrator. If the login message from getty appears garbled on your screen, you can force getty to try another line speed by sending a BREAK character. Multiple breaks may be needed to find the right speed. The gettydefs system file defines the speeds supported by each communications line. Normally, getty supports only a limited set of line speeds on any given communications line. However, it is possible to do speed detection, where the computer automatically determines the speed that the modem or terminal is using.

Automatic speed detection requires that the program enable the receipt of error information from the device driver, and use the error information to detect line speed mismatch. Detection of the speed can be performed on a character by character basis, almost in real time. When you use an application program, however, you may need to have the user type several recognition characters until the system responds.

Typically, a known recognition character is chosen, for example, several carriage returns. Configure the port for the most likely speed, and set it up to pass errors with flagging as to the error type (parmrk option). If the received character is the recognition character (the carriage return), the speed is the default and the speed detection is complete. If not, examine the portion of the recognition character that was correctly detected and try to guess the correct line speed.

If the modem speed is less than the terminal speed, the character will fill only part of the byte, and several bits will be dropped; all remaining bits will be the stop bit. If the modem speed is faster than the terminal speed, the character will be expanded, and the bits will appear to be repeated with the end of the byte being lost.

If the recognition character is a carriage return, for example, the expected value is 0x0d for no parity or odd parity, and 0x8d for even parity. If you see either of these values, the speed is correct. If the modem speed is 1200 and the terminal speed is 2400, however, the received byte is either 0xF3 or 0xF2 for odd parity or no parity, respectively. For even parity, it could be 0xF3, 0xF2, 0xFB, or 0xFA, because the modem could read either the 0 bit or the 1 bit, depending on the timing when two consecutive bits are received.

If the speed is 300, the received byte will be 0xF0 regardless of parity. Also, a second character might be received following that of 0x00. This is because the first 1 bit lasts four bit times, and the next 0 bit also lasts four bit times.

Because these two results differ, you can detect whether to go up or down in speed for the next guess. Just remember that the bits are received from least significant to most significant, and that bits are repeated if the terminal speed is too low, and dropped if the terminal speed is too high.

Streams Drivers and Serial Protocols

Recent UNIX systems support a feature called *streams,* not to be confused with the stream I/O library. The stream I/O library is a C subroutine library that buffers read and write calls; a streams driver permits some device driver functions to be performed by the user process. Through a well-defined interface, it allows the addition of user programs to process every I/O request to a streams device.

For example, if it is always necessary to do character set translation for a particular port, you could write a user program that performs the translation. Then the program would be pushed onto the protocol stack for the device, and all bytes read and written with that device would first pass through your program. However, the application program would not need to change; the conversion would be transparent to the application.

This is not only useful for character set conversion, but also used to implement many serial protocols, such as X.25 or SLIP. Some recent UNIX systems even make the standard `termio` serial driver just a streams module.

A discussion of streams drivers is beyond the scope of this chapter. Several books fully explain the programming of streams drivers, and the UNIX manual set devotes a complete volume to this topic.

Summary

There are two aspects to terminal handling: managing your own terminal, and programmed terminal I/O.

To manage your own terminal, you must understand and use the `stty` command and its options. Some options, such as `clocal`, line speed, word size, and parity settings will be set for you automatically when you log in; you will rarely need to modify these settings. Other options, such as `icrnl`, `xcase`, and `echoe` must be set according to the type of terminal you are using; the system cannot necessarily determine the proper setting for these options, and you may have to modify the settings to receive readable output. A third set of options, including `intr`, `kill`, `erase`, and `eod`, can be set according to your preferences; there is no "proper" setting for options in this category.

This chapter contains tables that explain the meaning and use of each of the stty options. Often, though, no amount of explanation will clarify the effect of an option. Try different settings on your terminal and observe the effect. Add an stty command to your profile to set the options that work best for you. Also, remember that if you log in at a different terminal, you may need to change some of the stty options you normally use.

Programming for serial devices (a terminal is one type of serial device) is much more difficult. When your program drives the device, there is no /bin/getty to automatically select the stty options; your program is responsible for setting all of them, including the line speed, word size, and parity options. From within a C program, the ioctl function performs the same services as the stty command. This chapter presents an example of using the ioctl function to set options.

If a serial device is locally attached, performing I/O to the device is simply a matter of issuing the appropriate read and write calls. This chapter discusses alternative methods for performing I/O to a terminal; the method you use is determined by analyzing the trade-off between the needs of your program and system performance considerations.

If a serial device is remotely attached through a modem, you will have to issue instructions to the modem to dial the remote terminal (or to wait for an incoming call and then answer it) before you can read and write to the device. This chapter does not contain instructions for controlling modems because there are many kinds of modems, some of which use different control procedures than others.

Having opened the device and set its stty options appropriately, you are free to send whatever data you like to the device. UNIX does not specify or constrain the device to operate in any particular way. To work with a specific kind of terminal or serial device, you must be familiar with the device and know how to program it. Some terminals, for example, recognize the character sequence ESC,H,ESC,J as a code to clear the screen; but not all terminals do. You send these control codes to the device just like any other data. Similarly, code sequences emitted by the device, such as a function key code, are read using the normal input functions. Because the control codes used by a device are peculiar to the device, this chapter does not discuss device control codes.

This chapter is the last that explicitly discusses the UNIX I/O system. The remaining chapters deal with other UNIX services, such as process management. However, advanced techniques for managing input/output depend on these other UNIX services. We will not finish discussing I/O techniques until the end of Chapter 15, "Writing Multiprocessing Programs."

Part IV

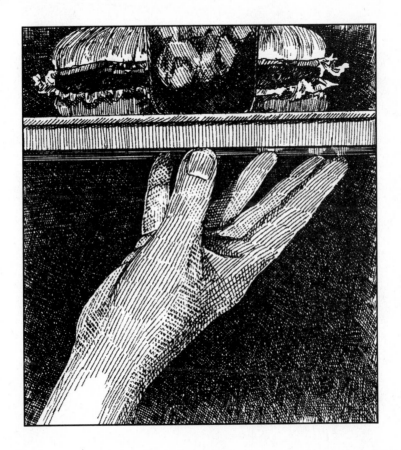

Operating System
Services

13

Kernel Internals

I n this chapter I will talk about the UNIX kernel. Although I might at times appear to be discussing UNIX's internals, every topic is really intended to permit you to use your UNIX system more effectively, whether you are a user, a system administrator, or a programmer.

The kernel provides a number of services whose descriptions do not fit well into other chapters, but these services are of central importance. One of these is process management. We will see what processes are, how they are created, how the system manages and controls them, and how to use processes effectively.

The UNIX kernel also manages system memory. There are several different kinds of system memory. The most important to programmers is the *process address space*, which is the memory available to a user program. We will examine the UNIX concept of memory management in as much detail as we can tolerate, while trying to emphasize portability as much as possible.

Process Internals

In any multiuser operating system, one of the most difficult concepts to describe and to understand is a *process*.

Basically, a process is simply one execution of a program. If I type the ls command at my terminal, the system creates a *process* to execute the ls *program*. If three different users simultaneously enter the ls command at their terminals, three processes are created even though the users all run the same program.

Similarly, if I enter a pipeline command, such as

```
pr report | lp
```

then three processes are involved: the active shell process that reads and interprets the pipeline command; a process created by that shell to execute the pr command; and another process also created by the shell to execute the lp command.

All three processes appear to execute at the same time. With most computers, however, this is not literally possible. A single computer can execute only one instruction at a time, so how does the system make it look as though three different programs are running?

Each of the three processes is interrupted many times during its execution, such as when requesting a system service, or when another user presses some key on his or her terminal. When a running process is interrupted, the kernel saves its *state*, which includes a notation regarding what instruction would have been executed next by the process, and also the contents of the machine registers at the time of the interrupt. Having saved this information, the kernel is free to go about other business. Later, when the kernel determines that the computer has nothing better to do, it will reload the saved information and let the computer resume execution of the interrupted process.

The appearance of the simultaneous execution of two or more processes, then, is due to two facts:

1. The computer runs very fast, so delays in the execution of any one process are generally not noticeable.

2. Most programs, during their execution, have to wait for certain external events to occur, such as for a group of bytes to be read from disk.

The concept of process, not being native to the machine itself, is created out of whole cloth by the operating system, and it really consists of the system's responsibility to return to an interrupted program. The system fulfills this responsibility by setting aside an area of memory to remember the existence of the process, and its state at the time of its last interruption.

Having taken the major step of suspending a program's in-flight execution, the kernel, once it has taken care of the cause of an interruption, is soon faced with a big decision. There might be more than one process currently waiting to regain control of the machine, and the kernel must decide which interrupted process gets that scarce resource. Making that decision is called *scheduling* a process, and it is a major function of the kernel.

Because UNIX is a multiuser operating system, it sometimes actually forces an interruption of a currently executing process to keep any one user from monopolizing the computer. When that happens, the kernel arranges to delay resumption of that process until some other user processes have had a chance to execute. The maximum amount of time the kernel is willing to allow a process to monopolize the system is called a *time slice*. The system uses time slicing to force sharing of the computer among competing processes, and successively steals the computer from one process to loan it to the next until all have had a chance to execute. When this occurs, we say that the kernel is implementing a *round robin* scheduling algorithm.

Time slicing of user process execution is the principal reason that UNIX is called a *time-sharing* system.

Process Identification

UNIX associates seven different identifiers with each process in the system, each identifier having its own significance and use. The following sections explain each of these identifiers.

The process identifier, more commonly called the *process-ID*, or *PID*, is a positive integer in the range of 1 to 30,000. (The actual upper limit of the process-ID can be larger or smaller on some systems.) The process-ID is assigned to a process when it is created with the fork system call, and is guaranteed to be unique at the time it is created.

The process-ID of the current process is returned by the getpid system call.

The process-ID of a process cannot be changed.

Eventually a process-ID value will be reassigned if the system is not rebooted before all 30,000 values have been used, but even for large systems with many users, a process-ID value will remain unique for a significant period of time.

The parent-process-ID is the process-ID of the process that created the current process. When a fork system call is executed, the process-ID of the child process is returned to the parent process as the return value of fork; the process-ID of the parent process becomes permanently associated with the child process as its parent-process-ID.

The parent-process-ID of the current process is returned by the getppid system call.

The parent-process-ID of a process cannot be changed.

Because each knows the other's process-ID, the parent and child processes can send signals to one another.

The real user-ID of a process is an unsigned integer value in the range of 0 to 60,000. (The maximum user-ID value can be larger or smaller on some systems.) The real user-ID of a process is inherited from its parent process, and is ultimately inherited from the login shell created by the /bin/login program; its value is taken from the third field of that line of the /etc/passwd system file that contains the login user name as its first field. This value is intended to identify the user on whose behalf the current process is executing, and is a primary component of the UNIX data security facility.

The real user-ID of the current process is returned by the getuid system call.

The real user-ID of the current process can be altered to a new value by the setuid system call, but only if the current process has the authority of the superuser.

The effective user-ID of the current process is an unsigned integer value similar in meaning, usage, and value range to the real user-ID. The effective user-ID of a process is set whenever a new program text is loaded by one of the exec system calls; its value is set to the value of the real user-ID, unless the file from which the program text was read contains the setuid flag among its permissions. In that case, the effective user-ID of the process is set to the owner-ID of the file.

An effective user-ID value of 0 grants superuser privileges to the process.

The effective user-ID of the current process is returned by the geteuid system call.

The effective user-ID of the current process can be changed by the setuid system call. If the currently executing program was loaded from a set-uid file, then the effective user-ID can be set to either the real user-ID of the process, or to the owner-ID of the file from which the program was loaded. If the currently executing program was *not* loaded from a set-uid file, then the effective user-ID can be set only to the real user-ID value of the current process. But if the current process is superuser, setuid will set both the real and effective user-ID of the current process to the value specified.

The set-uid flag and its implications and uses are discussed further in Chapter 9, "Ordinary Files."

The real group-ID of a process is an unsigned integer value in the range of 0 to 60,000. (The maximum group-ID value may be larger or smaller on some systems.) The real group-ID of a process is inherited from its parent process, and is ultimately inherited from the login shell created by the /bin/login program; its value is taken from the fourth field of the line of the /etc/passwd system file that contains the login user name as its first field. This value is intended to identify the user group of which the current user is a member, and on whose behalf the current process is executing. It is a primary component of the UNIX data security facility.

The real group-ID of the current process is returned by the getgid system call.

The real group-ID of the current process can be altered to a new value by the setgid system call, but only if the current process has the authority of the superuser.

The effective group-ID of the current process is an unsigned integer value similar in meaning, usage, and value range to the real group-ID. The effective group-ID of a process is set whenever a new program text is loaded by one of the exec system calls; its value is set to the value of the real group-ID, unless the file from which the program text was read contains the set-gid flag among its permissions. In that case the effective group-ID of the process is set to the group-ID of the file. An effective group-ID value of 0 has no special significance.

The effective group-ID of the current process is returned by the getegid system call.

The effective group-ID of the current process can be changed by the setgid system call. If the currently executing program was loaded from a set-gid file, then the effective group-ID can be set to either the real group-ID of the process, or to the group-ID of the file from which the program was loaded. If the currently executing program was *not* loaded from a set-gid file, then the effective group-ID can be set only to the real group-ID value of the current process. If the current process is superuser, however, setgid will set both the real and effective group-ID of the current process to the value specified.

The set-gid flag and its implications and uses are discussed further in Chapter 9, "Ordinary Files."

Process Groups

The process-group-ID identifies the *process group* of which the current process is a member. The process-group-ID is the process-ID of the group leader of the process group. The current process inherited its process-group-ID from its parent process when it was created. A new process-group-ID is created by getty when it invokes the login processor, and is inherited by the login shell created as the result of a successful login. Therefore, each login shell has a unique process-group-ID and is normally the group leader of that process-group; all processes invoked by the login shell, either directly or indirectly, automatically become members of that process-group by the method of inheritance.

The process-group-ID of the current process is returned by the getpgrp system call.

The process-group-ID can be changed by invoking the setpgrp system call, which results in setting the process-group-ID to the process-ID of the current process. The current process becomes the group leader of a new process group consisting of one process: itself.

When a process invokes setpgrp to become the group leader of a new process group, its association with the control terminal is broken; it no longer has a control terminal.

The first terminal to which a new process group leader performs I/O becomes associated with the group leader and the process group as the *control terminal*. Signals generated by the control terminal are issued to all members of the process group; these include the SIGHUP, SIGINT, and SIGQUIT signals (see Chapter 14, "Signals and IPC," for a discussion of signals).

It is often desirable, when you create a daemon process, to use setpgrp to break the association of the current process with a control terminal. This keeps you from receiving signals from the control terminal which are irrelevant to the daemon process.

All this business about process groups amounts to showing how UNIX uses a complicated mechanism to achieve a fairly simple objective; namely, to give a login user some measure of control over all the processes he or she creates, whether directly by entering commands, or indirectly as processes created by those commands. This also applies to the background processes one can start with the & shell operator. This control is little more than the ability to send an interrupt signal with the INTR key—usually Ctrl-C—but we do tend to find even this meager control useful and desirable. The process-group-ID is therefore the kernel's method of tracing the relationship between your terminal and any programs you cause to be executed.

Process Creation

With only two notable exceptions, discussed shortly, all processes in the system are created by the fork system call.

There is an elegant simplicity about the fork system call that I have never seen in any other operating system; in other respects, it has all the subtlety of a sledgehammer. More than any other aspect of UNIX, the ability of a machine to efficiently execute the fork operation determines how fast UNIX will run on that machine. This is because fork makes a complete copy of the current process's state and its entire address space, and sets this identical copy up so as to be scheduled by the kernel as a new process. On some types of hardware, this copying has to be performed as a literal copy and is very slow; on other machines, the copy can be done very quickly using the characteristics of a virtual-memory paging scheme, which we will not discuss here.

Regardless of how quickly it executes and the operations actually performed by the machine to accomplish it, fork achieves a complete cloning of a process so that, whereas one program was running before, now two are running.

This method of creating a new process is so conceptually simple that the fork system call requires no arguments; its calling syntax is merely the following:

```
int fork (void)
```

Fortunately, the function returns a value to the caller, otherwise the future course of events in the new process would be an identical mirror of the actions in the original process, a useless thing to do indeed. It is only by this return value that the two processes differ in any respect at all, but this difference is enough to allow the new process (called the *child* process) to follow a different execution path from the original process (called the *parent* process).

I must emphasize at this point just how completely fork duplicates the parent process. The next instruction to be executed by the new child process is the same instruction that the parent process will execute, namely the one following the fork call itself. The same program is in memory for both processes. The contents of all static data areas is identical. The same function is active, and the contents of its automatic variables are identical. The complete stack is identical between the two processes, so that the function to which the current function will return is identical in both processes. The same files are open in both processes and even on the same file-descriptor numbers. The contents of dynamic memory previously allocated by malloc is identical, and the process memory of the two processes even contains the same malloc control tables so that the two appear to have the same amount of unused memory available to malloc. The signal actions are the same for both processes, even if some of the signal actions are set to invoke a signal-catching function.

I cannot emphasize strongly enough that when you receive control back from the fork call, you are really programming now for two processes; and everything you do in your program from this point forward will be done by both processes *unless* you check the return value from fork. If the return value is 0, your program is currently executing the new child process; if it is nonzero and positive, your program is executing as the original process; and if it is negative, you are also the parent process because the fork failed and no child process was created.

A typical course of events after returning from the fork call is to test its return value. If the return value is found to be 0, you will often want to load and execute another program using one of the variety of exec system calls. This is in fact how one program calls another in UNIX; the caller forks, and the new child process then executes the exec system call to load another program into memory and begin its execution. Of course, this means that the (possibly laborious) copying of the parent process in order to create the child process will turn out to be a complete waste of time, to be thrown away and replaced with a new program in the space of a handful of instructions; but if you ever wondered how the system library function works, that's it in a nutshell.

It's only fair to point out, before leaving this subject, that the parent and child processes differ in a few respects besides in the return value from fork.

The two processes have different process-IDs, of necessity, because otherwise the process identifier would not serve to identify a unique process.

The two processes also have different parent process IDs; that is, the return value from getppid differs for the two processes. Once again, UNIX is really forced to this conclusion, because the two processes do in fact have different parents.

Fortunately, the child process does not inherit any file locks that might be owned by its parent; otherwise, the two now-independent processes could stomp all over each other's files, a possibility enhanced by the fact that they start out having the same files open.

The semadj values of the parent process, if any, are not inherited by the child process either. Otherwise, termination of the child process (whether benign or catastrophic) would cause the related IPC semaphores to be adjusted to back out operations that the child process had never performed.

Lest you become too enthusiastic about forking and invent an application that quickly forks into hundreds of processes, be aware that the system imposes a limit on the number of processes that can be created. There are actually two limitations.

First, the existence of a process in the system requires dedication of a slot in the kernel's process table, and that table is statically allocated. The number of entries is a configuration parameter, so it varies from system to system, but it is nonetheless a fixed upper limit on the total number of processes that can exist. If no free slot in the process table is available when fork is called, the function returns a value of -1 and sets *errno* to EAGAIN, indicating that the system is unable to satisfy the request right now and that your program should try again later when some of the currently active processes might have terminated.

Secondly, the system imposes an arbitrary numeric limit on the number of processes allowed for any given user-ID. Typical values for this limit are in the range of 25 to 30. An attempt to fork more than this number of processes results in the same EAGAIN error indication, even though a slot might be available in the system's process table. Do not retry the fork call in this second case unless there is a definite possibility that some of your active child processes might terminate, otherwise your program will be in an endless loop.

Process 0 and Process 1

When you boot the system, you start a series of events that result in loading the kernel into memory from a file in the root directory of the root filesystem. Once loaded, control is transferred to the initialization routine in the kernel, and this routine begins the task of setting up system tables and preparing the system for normal operation.

This initialization routine, being part of the kernel, executes in kernel mode. One of its steps is to issue the first fork system call in the new system, and then call exec to load the /bin/init program into memory and begin its execution as process 1, called the init process.

The kernel initialization routine then forks other kernel processes, which must normally be present but are generally invisible to the user, and then transforms itself into process 0, called swapper. It remains active in kernel mode throughout the life of the system, and performs memory swapping I/O for the kernel as needed. This task is relegated to a process, albeit a kernel-mode process, because swapping address spaces in and out of memory necessarily entails a lot of waiting for I/O to complete. Waiting for any length of time in the kernel would be very bad for system performance, but it is easily done in a process; swapper is therefore best run as a process.

When we left process 1 (init), it had just been loaded into memory and was starting its execution. This process now takes over the job of getting the system going, because at this point the kernel initialization routine has finished its work, transformed itself into swapper, and become idle waiting for some work to do; yet there are still no user processes in the system.

init takes the role of starting up processes to perform odd jobs for the system. The first odd job to be done is to get the getty program running for each of the terminals attached to the system, so that we can get some users logged on. Yet the init program has no idea what terminals are attached and what communications lines are available for use as dial-up connections, or even whether dial-up connections are wanted at this time.

init therefore reads a script file that tells it what to do. The script file is prepared by the system administrator, who bears the responsibility of installing the system in the first place, and making sure that it stays in good working order. Each line of this script file, /etc/inittab, specifies a process that init should start. See Chapter 3, "UNIX in Action," for a complete description of /etc/inittab and the system initialization procedure.

Memory Management

System memory falls into two main categories: *kernel memory* and *process address spaces*.

Kernel memory consists of all real memory and can also include a virtual address space for the use of kernel routines. User programs are not allowed direct access to kernel memory, although a rudimentary form of access is sometimes permitted through the /dev/mem and /dev/kmem pseudo-device special files.

The memory belonging to an active process that is accessible to a user program is called the *process address space*; it is virtual memory, meaning that it is in one sense imaginary but usable nonetheless. The term *virtual* means that only those parts of a program and its data which are currently needed actually reside in real memory; the rest of the program and data are left on disk until referenced.

The process address space begins at address location 0 and extends up to the maximum *break address* permitted for a process. The address space is divided into two subsections, one called the *text segment* and the other called the *data segment*. The text segment contains the program's instructions and constant data, and is protected against modification. The data segment contains the program's initialized data, statically allocated areas, and the program stack. The program can write only in the data segment. An attempt to modify a location in the text segment will result in a program error signal, usually SIGBUS.

The main divisions of the process address space are defined by the external labels

```
extern void etext();
extern edata;
extern end;
```

all of which are defined automatically by the C compiler. The contents of these variables are not significant; in fact, an attempt to reference them will likely cause a program error. Their significance lies in their address. `etext` defines the end of the program text segment, `edata` defines the end of the data segment, and `end` defines the end of the program as a whole. When a program begins execution, its break address is equal to `&end`, so that it indicates the first memory location beyond the end of the loaded program.

The text segment can neither be extended nor reduced in size. Its size is that which will contain the instructions and constant data of a program.

The size of the data segment can be changed with the `brk` and `sbrk` system calls, which change the current value of the break address. The system will allow the break address to be adjusted downward, but will complain if the new break address would truncate any part of the program stack. It is not considered an error to place the break address within the program data area, in effect deleting some of it from memory, as long as the validity of the stack is not affected. The break address can be adjusted upward, but the system will not allow its new value to overlap any currently attached shared-memory segment (see Chapter 14, "Signals and IPC"), or to exceed a system-defined upper limit.

The maximum allowable break address can be determined by invoking the `ulimit` function with the `cmd` argument value of *3*:

```
maxbrk = (void *) ulimit(3);
```

(Note the use of `void *` to denote a generic address, as called for by the ANSI standard. K&R compilers would require the use of `char *` to designate a generic address.) The return value of `ulimit` is normally a `long`, and therefore must be cast to a pointer before being interpreted as an address.

The *program stack* is allocated with an initial default size when a program begins execution. If the program later overflows the upper limit of the stack, the kernel automatically adjusts the break address upward and extends the stack, allowing it to grow as needed. If the maximum break address is exceeded, however, the stack is not extended and the program receives an error signal.

The *link editor* (the `ld` command) provides a complex, powerful language for assigning portions of a program to areas within the process address space. If you care to take the time to learn how to use it, you can arrange your text, data, and stack segments in memory any way you please, though care must be taken not to disturb assumptions made by the C compiler if any portion of the executable program is written in C. Assembler programmers, of course, have no such concerns.

You should generally avoid using the brk and sbrk functions because their behavior can vary from one implementation of System V to another. The malloc function package provides an interface which is portable across all implementations, and is easier to use.

Using brk

The brk system call is declared as follows:

```
int brk (void *endds);
```

The break address is set to the end-of-data-segment address specified by endds. If the call is successful, brk returns a value of 0, otherwise it returns -1.

The value of endds may be chosen to change the current break address either upward or downward. If your program attaches shared segments with shmat, you may want to explicitly specify their address, but whether you do so or allow the system to choose the address of a shared segment, brk will not permit you to set the addressable range of the data segment so as to include any shared segment. The two ranges must not overlap at any time. If you do not use shared segments, the only causes for brk to fail are an attempt to lower the break address into the range of the program stack, or an attempt to extend it beyond the maximum break address.

This operation is straightforward for versions of System V supporting a machine with a continuous range of addresses. Some machines, however, might require memory to be allocated in discontiguous address ranges. In such a case, it is an error to set the break address within an illegal address range. To avoid this, some operating systems may allocate memory to the process address space in *blocks*, allocating a new block for each brk request. In such cases, some of the address range between the old break address and the new may be invalid. (There is no easy way to find out where such holes might lie.)

Using sbrk

The sbrk system call is declared as follows:

```
void *sbrk (int size);
```

in which size is the number of bytes by which the usable space in the data segment should be increased, and the return value of the function designates the first address in the allocated range (*not* the new break address). If the call is unsuccessful, sbrk returns a value of (void *)(-1).

The value of size can be positive or negative to set the break address either upward or downward. If your program attaches shared segments with shmat, sbrk will not allow the break address to be extended into the range of any attached shared segment. The shared segment with the lowest address thus becomes the effective maximum break address for the process. If you do not use shared segments, the only cause for sbrk to fail is an attempt to lower the break address into the range of the program stack, in an attempt to extend it beyond the maximum break address.

Note that the current break address cannot be increased by more than the maximum positive value of an integer, nor decreased by more than the maximum negative value of an integer. This might result in the need to allocate a desired amount of storage using multiple sbrk requests; the system does not guarantee, however, that the storage allocated by successive sbrk calls is necessarily contiguous.

This problem does not occur on machines supporting a large continuous range of addresses, but some do not. Some machines might require that all memory be allocated in *blocks* which may or may not be of fixed size but probably cannot exceed some largest size. Implementing System V for these machines does not guarantee that all the address range between the previous break address and the new break address is valid. It *is* guaranteed, however, that size bytes of valid address space will have been allocated between the address returned by sbrk and the new break address.

Using malloc

As you can see from the previous discussions of brk and sbrk, the system calls for storage allocation can be difficult to use properly on some kinds of machines supported by System V. Worse, even if brk and sbrk work in the normal fashion, programs depending on this operation might not port successfully to other machine environments, even where the same release of System V is in use.

For this reason, two packages of functions that provide a reliable and portable interface for dynamic storage management have been provided in the standard C function libraries. The first of these two (which I will call the *standard* package) is provided in the standard C library, whereas the newer (*optimized*) function package is stored in the libmalloc.a archive.

To include the standard package with your C program, do nothing. To include the optimized package, include the -lmalloc operand on the cc command when compiling or linking your program.

Both packages include the basic functions malloc, calloc, free, and realloc. The optimized package also includes the mallopt and mallinfo functions.

The standard package provides a good all-around facility that serves most needs adequately. It suffers from a performance defect, however, that led eventually to the development of the optimized package. The older functions were not replaced, because the newer functions operate slightly differently, having side effects which could affect the validity of programs written to use the old functions. Also, the performance characteristics of the two packages differ markedly such that the standard functions are more suitable for programs which make only occasional use of dynamic storage allocation, whereas the optimized functions are more appropriate for programs that make heavy and continuous use of storage allocation.

The standard package organizes all available storage in its charge (the *heap*) in a linked list, and keeps both active and free blocks in the list. When `malloc` is called, it searches the list for a free block that is large enough to satisfy the request, and begins the search with the last block freed by the `free` function. `malloc` accepts the first block it finds that is equal to or larger than the requested size; that is, it uses the `first fit` algorithm.

Only when no block on the list is large enough does `malloc` extend the process break address by calling `sbrk`.

A program can take advantage of the `malloc` algorithm by arranging the sequence of `free` and `malloc` calls to *compact* the heap, meaning to remove holes between allocated areas. The sequence of calls can also be arranged to make the most efficient use of released storage. Note, however, that this behavior was not originally documented for `malloc` and `free`, so programs making use of this feature are depending on a specific implementation of the function package. Nevertheless, this behavior has been well known among the UNIX community for many years, so many older programs use it.

The other difference between the two packages lies in the internal operation of the `free` function itself. The older version of `free`, which is still used by default, does not modify the released storage area in any way; its contents remain intact until the block or some portion of it is selected to satisfy a subsequent `malloc` request. As a result, some programs rely on this behavior by first calling `free` and then accessing the contents of the area just released, confident that it is valid to do so as long as no `malloc` call is issued. The optimized package, on the other hand, normally destroys a portion of the block released by `free` immediately. This is such a handy feature, though, that the implementers of the optimized package provided an option that can be specified via the `mallopt` call to force the newer package to work the same way.

I should emphasize that programmers should avoid dependence on either operational characteristic whenever they are not themselves responsible for the packaging of their modules into programs. If someone else were to code the -lmalloc option on the cc command when compiling such dependent modules, bugs that are quite difficult to diagnose would appear in the resulting program.

The optimized package uses a radically different storage allocation strategy from the standard package. The major performance problem with the older implementation is that it can waste an incredible amount of CPU time searching the list because it has to examine every block, whether free or currently in use. When only a few blocks have been allocated and the list is short, the searching overhead is minor and has no noticeable effect on a program's overall run time. But when malloc is used frequently, and a large number of blocks tend to be outstanding at any given time, the time spent searching becomes prohibitive. If the execution time of an application program seems excessive to you and you're looking for ways to speed it up, I would recommend that you use the compiler profiling option and look for where the execution time is being spent. (Use the -p option of the cc command to recompile all the program modules, and run the prof command after executing your program to see the profile.) If malloc is the culprit, replacing it with the optimized package or a custom storage allocation routine of your own making could dramatically improve the program's run time.

You would not always use the optimized package because it is a more complex routine than the conventional malloc, and could therefore actually increase a program's run time when there are, on the average, only a few blocks in the free list. This is just like the old trade-off between sequential and binary searching; sequential searches are cheaper for short lists, binary searches are cheaper for long lists. Although the optimized malloc does not perform binary searches, the same principle applies.

If you choose to use the optimized package with your program, you must learn something about its operation. The run-time behavior of the optimized package is influenced by the settings of three parameters. You must specify values for these parameters to obtain any benefit from the new package. If no parameters are specified, the new package defaults to operating the same way as the old, but with a more complicated algorithm that might actually worsen performance rather than improve it.

The names for these parameters are defined in the malloc.h header file. Values for the parameters are specified by invoking mallopt with its cmd argument set to one of the parameter names, and its value argument set to the value to be assigned to the parameter.

M_MXFAST defines the largest request size that will be processed by suballocating a *holding block*; requests for a size larger than the M_MXFAST value will be handled in the same manner as the old malloc. The concept of a holding block is therefore at the core of the new algorithm. The idea is simple: To avoid searching long lists of available blocks that vary widely in size, allocate one large block that can contain a number of smaller blocks and then just chop off pieces to satisfy requests for these small sizes. To do this efficiently, the new malloc keeps a holding block available for each possible partition of M_MXFAST. This results in reserving a larger total amount of data space than would be used by the standard package, because at any given time only a portion of each holding block is likely to be in use. If sufficient memory is available, however, the improvement in the execution speed of malloc can be dramatic.

M_GRAIN defines the smallest unit of storage that will be allocated. Requests for areas smaller than M_GRAIN are satisfied by allocating an area M_GRAIN bytes long. Values of M_GRAIN that are too large for a program's pattern of memory allocation waste memory, because many blocks of size M_GRAIN would be only partially filled. On the other hand, small values of M_GRAIN result in a greater number of holding blocks used by the new malloc, because at least one holding block can be allocated for each multiple of the grain size that is smaller than M_MXFAST.

For example, if M_GRAIN is 4 and M_MXFAST is 512, a different holding block might exist for each of the request sizes 4, 8, 12, 16, ..., up to 512 bytes, a total of 128 different sizes. If a particular size is never actually requested, no holding block for that size will be allocated. Also, if a holding block is full or nearly full of areas currently in use, little or nothing is being wasted; I'm discussing *tendencies* that are true on the average.

M_NLBLKS specifies the number of suballocated areas a holding block is to contain. The size of a particular holding block is therefore equal to the particular multiple of the M_GRAIN size for which the block will be used, multiplied by the M_NLBLKS value. In the previous example, one of the possible multiples of M_GRAIN is 128 bytes, therefore an M_NLBLKS value of 100 would mean that a request for a storage area from 125 to 128 bytes long would be satisfied from a holding block of 12,800 bytes.

To summarize, the following rules of thumb should be applied when using the optimized malloc:

❏ If the program makes only a few allocation requests, or tends to have only a few blocks in use at a time, do *not* use the optimized package.

❏ Smaller values of M_NLBLKS are preferable to larger ones in order to keep to a minimum the total memory space needed to run the application, but values that are too small force the allocation of new holding blocks too often, defeating the effectiveness of the algorithm.

❏ Larger values of M_GRAIN are preferred over smaller ones to keep the number of holding blocks to a minimum and reduce the total memory requirement, but values that are too large result in wasting space for each request that is smaller than M_GRAIN.

❏ The M_MXFAST value should be large enough that *frequently* requested sizes are satisfied from holding blocks, and large, infrequently occurring requests bypass holding blocks and use the old space-efficient algorithm.

If you don't know what the pattern of requests is for your program, try several parameter values and print the contents of `struct mallinfo` at the end of each trial run. Call the function `mallinfo` to get a copy of the `struct`. Don't choose the combination of parameter values that yields the most efficient space utilization; the standard `malloc` package does that automatically. You're looking for an optimum combination of execution speed and memory usage, so use profiling together with `mallinfo` to find the cost in execution speed for a given combination of parameter values.

If the optimized `malloc` package seems complicated to understand and to use, you can write your own custom memory management routines. But you should only do so under the following conditions:

1. You know that the standard package is causing unacceptable performance of your programs and something *must* be done to improve the situation.

2. There are patterns in the way your program uses memory that neither the standard nor the optimized package can take advantage of, and that lead to a simple implementation for you.

I do not, by the term *memory management routine*, refer to the use of wrappers for the conventional function calls. Even when the standard or optimized function package serves your needs quite well, there are advantages to embedding the calls in functions of your own, which I call *wrappers*. I provide the following as an example of a wrapper for the `malloc` call:

```
void *getmem (size_t size)
{
    void *ptr;

    if ((ptr = malloc(size)) == NULL) {
        fprintf(stderr, "Out of memory.\n");
        exit(123);
    }
    memset(ptr, 0, size);
    return ptr;
}
```

This particular wrapper performs two valuable services for the rest of your program: it catches an error return from malloc and terminates after printing a standard error message, and it always initializes the allocated area to 0s. If you always call this function to allocate storage, you will avoid the temptation to skip error return checking for every malloc call, a standard error message will always be issued on error, and you will never experience bugs that arise from failing to initialize the allocated area.

Wrappers can be easily created for all the malloc functions. Their use will improve the overall reliability of your programs, and simplify your coding effort as well.

But when wrappers don't suffice and you must replace the call to malloc, you can write your own memory allocator.

It makes sense to write your own routine, for example, when your program tends to allocate many areas but rarely releases any at all. You need an allocator for *permanent* memory, and this is very easy to write. The following program is an example of one design for such an allocator. It is based on the concept of using malloc to allocate very large areas infrequently, and subdivide these areas into smaller pieces on request.

```
#if __STDC__    /* Defines for ANSI C compiler */
#include <stdlib.h>
typedef void *MEMPTR;
#else           /* Defines for K&R C compiler */
#include <stdio.h>
#include <malloc.h>
#include <memory.h>
typedef unsigned int size_t;
typedef char *MEMPTR;
extern void exit();
#endif


/* ALLOCATION PARAMETERS */

#define GRAIN   16  /* Smallest allocated block size */
#define NBLOCKS 100 /* Grains per "page" */
#define NULLPTR ((MEMPTR)0)    /* Null pointer */

/* STORAGE ALLOCATION CONTROL BLOCKS */

typedef union {
    long    aligned;
    char    bytes[GRAIN];
} MEMBLK;

static struct {
```

```
        MEMPTR   start;      /* Start of current large block */
        MEMPTR   next;       /* Next available byte in block */
        size_t   free;       /* Number of grains remaining   */
} page;

MEMPTR
getmem(size) size_t size;
{

        MEMPTR area;
        size_t nbytes;

        /* Compute the request size in "grains" */
        size = (size + sizeof(MEMBLK) - 1) / sizeof(MEMBLK) ;
        nbytes = size * GRAIN;

        /* If requesting 0 bytes, oblige him */
        if (size == 0)
            return NULLPTR;
        if (size > NBLOCKS) {
            /* Request is too large, use malloc */
            if ((area = malloc(nbytes) == NULLPTR) {
                fprintf(stderr, "Out of memory!\n");
                exit(123);
            }
            return area;
        }

        /* If not enough room in current page, get another */

        if (size > page.free) {
            page.start = malloc(NBLOCKS * GRAIN);
            if (page.start == NULLPTR) {
                fprintf(stderr, "Out of memory!\n");
                exit(123);
            }
            page.next = page.start;
            page.free = NBLOCKS;
        }

        /* Chop a piece off the end of the current page */

        area = page.next;
        page.next += nbytes;
        page.free -= nbytes;
        memset(area, 0, nbytes);
        return area;
}

main()
{
```

```
long area;
int ctr;

for (ctr = 0; ctr < 4; ctr++) {
    area = (long)getmem(60);
    printf("area = %#lx\n", area);
}

return 0;
}
```

The allocator shown in the example program uses malloc in two cases. If the number of bytes requested exceeds the size of a standard memory block, the allocation is performed using malloc; these large requests are presumably infrequent (otherwise, increase the NBLOCKS value) so program performance should not suffer. A call to malloc is also issued when the current memory block (called a page in the example) is not large enough to contain the size requested: malloc is used to acquire another working memory block.

The point of this approach is to reduce the number of calls to malloc by collecting small areas together into one larger area. Because fewer large areas will be allocated than if malloc had been used directly, the memory chain used by malloc will contain fewer elements and will be searched much faster.

Programs can also benefit from using the memory allocator in the preceding listing when areas allocated for some purposes must be released. Use getmem for allocating permanent areas, and use malloc (or a wrapper for malloc) for allocating temporary areas. The overall performance will still be improved by the proportion of permanent to temporary allocations.

The very same getmem can be used for collecting short-term requests together, and freeing the storage they occupy all at once. For this usage, you need to modify the program to keep better track of the large blocks allocated, so that they can be released when no longer needed. Each large block will need to be kept on a chain. The page.start variable is provided in the listing to serve as an anchor for such a list of large blocks, but is actually not used.

Combining these approaches, you might use one set of large blocks for long-term requests, and one or more additional sets for temporary memory allocation; in this scheme, only the temporary blocks would ever be released. This memory allocation strategy soon leads to the more formal concept of *memory pools*, in which each list of large blocks is anchored by its own page struct, and each pool (or cluster of large blocks) is used for a different purpose. With modest extensions to the code, an entire memory pool can be released in one operation if the blocks in the pool are kept on a list. Memory pools might differ in grain size or block size, depending on your requirements.

getmem could also have been written to use brk or sbrk rather than malloc for allocating the large blocks. The disadvantage to such a strategy is in maintaining program portability, but where performance is critical and an increased porting cost can be accepted, or where program portability is not a requirement, the system calls will execute much faster than any malloc-based implementation.

The point of all these strategies is to reduce the number of calls to malloc by performing most memory allocations with application program code, based on the assumption that custom programming can satisfy typical requests more easily, and with less complex code, than malloc can. The strategy will be defeated if the custom memory allocator becomes more complex than malloc itself; consider this a danger sign when designing your allocator, and either rethink your allocation strategy if its complexity becomes too great, or go ahead and use malloc. If your needs are that complex, you will probably not be able to improve on it.

The fork/exec Paradigm and How It Works

There are six different versions of the exec system call: execl, execle, execlp, execv, execve, and execvp. They differ in minor ways, but they all perform the same function of loading and running a new program.

The steps performed by the exec kernel routine are roughly as follows:

1. The argument strings are copied into a temporary buffer in kernel memory where they will be held during the exec procedure.

2. The environment strings, specified either to exec or the current environment by default, are also copied into kernel memory.

3. The address space of the invoking process is then completely discarded.

4. A new address space is constructed and attached to the process, consisting of a text segment and a data segment, each sized according to specifications contained in the executable file.

5. The program instructions and data are then copied from the executable file into the corresponding areas of the new address space.

6. Address constants in the loaded text and data are modified as necessary to account for any difference between the link address of the program and its actual load address.

7. The data segment is extended by the amount needed to contain the saved argument and environment strings.

8. The argument strings are copied into the new address space, building a list of pointers to each of the strings.

9. The environment strings are copied into the new address space and a pointer list built.

10. The process table entry for the calling process is set up with a next instruction pointer that points to the start address of the new program.

11. The exec routine exits to the kernel scheduler.

12. Eventually the process is selected to resume execution, and control returns from the exec call, but to a different program.

The result of the preceding steps is that the program calling exec is destroyed and replaced with a new program. When execution of the calling process continues, it begins at the start of the new program. Note that although the program issuing the call is destroyed, the same process is running both before and after the call. It has merely taken on a new program identity.

There can be no return from a successful exec call to the program that called it, because the original program has been replaced in memory and is not to be found there anymore. As we noted earlier, the kernel does in fact return to the calling process, but the process table entry describing the process has been modified so that the return transfers control to the beginning of the new program and not to the original calling program.

The exec strategy can be useful when an application is naturally constructed as a series of consecutive steps. Each program, when finished, needs merely to invoke the exec system call to load the next program and begin its execution. This is more efficient than executing each of the programs individually with a separate shell command, because the same process and the same process address space continues to exist from one program to the next; there is no need for the system to alternately build up a complete process and address space, then tear it down again. This strategy is especially useful when you can make good use of the fact that open files remain open across an exec call; each program can use the working files of the previous program simply by referencing the proper file-descriptor number.

But exec is more often used together with fork to call another program. When used this way, the calling program is not destroyed because the exec call is performed in another process (the child process created by fork). This is the principle on which the system and popen library functions are based. These two functions are adequate for most purposes and should be used instead of writing your own fork-exec service. There are times, however, when neither library function quite fits an application need, and then you must write your own.

For an example, assume that your program needs to call a user program dbsfilt, which may be an executable binary (probably written in C), or a shell script. The called program expects the file it is to process to be open on standard input, and it will write its output on standard output. The output file will be a temporary, and your program will process the temporary output of dbsfilt when it is finished. You decide to write a function to encapsulate this interface, called filter. Its calling format will be the following:

```
int filter (char *progname, FILE *in, FILE *out);
```

in which the return value will be the exit value of dbsfilt, in will be an open stream file to be read by dbsfilt, and out will be where a pointer to an open temporary stream file containing the output of dbsfilt will be stored.

The filter function is implemented as shown in the following example.

```
#include <stdio.h>
#include <string.h>
#include <errno.h>

#define STDIN   0           /* Standard-input file descriptor */
#define STDOUT  1           /* Standard-output file descriptor */
#define ERROR       (-1)    /* Error return from function */

extern void     perror();
extern void     exit();

filter (command, cmdin, cmdout)
char *command;
FILE *cmdin, *cmdout;
{
    int  pid, wpid;     /* Process-ID of child process */
    int   status;       /* Exit value from wait() */
    int   sig_num;      /* Signal that terminated the child */

    /*
     * Create the child process.
     */
    if ((pid = fork()) == 0) {
```

```
/*      Redirect standard-I/O files      */

close(STDIN);
if (dup(fileno(cmdin)) != STDIN)
      goto child_fails;
close(fileno(cmdin));

close(STDOUT);
if (dup(fileno(cmdout)) != STDOUT)
      goto child_fails; close(fileno(cmdout));

/*      Execute the 'command' program      */

execlp(command, command, NULL);
if (errno == ENOEXEC)
      /* Program not binary, try shell */
      execl("/bin/sh", "sh", "-c", command, NULL);

child_fails: /* If we get here, the exec didn't work */
      perror("filter"); /* Document the specific cause */
      exit(255);        /* Tell parent of failure */
   }
/* As parent process, wait for child to finish and
 * return his exit value.
 */

while ((wpid = wait(&status)) != pid)
    if (wpid == ERROR && errno != EINTR)
        return ERROR;

/* Process concluded, but why? */
if ((sig_num = status & 0177) != 0) {
    /*
     * Process terminated due to signal.
     * No shell to document failure, so we do it.
     */
    fprintf(stderr, "Terminated [%d]: sig %d",
        pid, sig_num);
    if (status & 0200)
        fputs(" - dumped", stderr);
    fputc('\n', stderr);
    return 255;
    }
/* Normal completion, return exit code to caller */
return ((status >> 8) & 0377);
}
```

   The function really has no preliminary work to do, so it begins with a call to
fork, creating a child process to run the user program. If the return value from
fork is 0, then the code is being executed by the child process; otherwise the
code skips around to handle the continuation of the parent (calling) process.

The code inside the i f statement has two objectives:

1. To redirect the standard-input and standard-output files of the child process to the appropriate files.

2. To invoke the filter program itself, which in our hypothetical example would be the dbsfilt program.

All the code included in the TRUE part of the first i f statement is executed only by the child process, yet it is still code contained in the calling program. This is in fact one of the key characteristics of the UNIX design: that it enables the calling program to initialize the environment of the called program.

The initialization consists of redirecting the two standard files. Redirection is actually accomplished by the dup system call, which duplicates an open file descriptor. By closing file descriptor 0 (standard input) before calling dup, it is virtually guaranteed that that file descriptor will be chosen by dup as the target of the copy. (If you do not remember how dup works, check Part V of the Reference section, "C Library Functions.") After the dup, there are actually two open file descriptors for the input file. This wastes one of the file descriptors of the child process, so the original file descriptor is closed.

The same actions are then repeated, reassigning the output file cmdout to be the standard-output file for the child process.

Note that no fclose is performed to discard the original stream files, nor is fdopen or freopen used to initialize standard input and standard output. This is because the next thing the child process will do is to call exec, and this will result in discarding the entire memory contents of the process including the FILE blocks; setting up new streams for standard input and standard output would therefore be a waste of effort, and the code does not bother with such useless tidying up.

The final step in this start-up routine for the child process is to attempt to invoke the target program itself. I use execlp to do that because execlp will search the directories named in the $PATH environment variable for the desired filename, whereas execl will not. If execlp succeeds in finding the named file, but it is not a loadable binary file, it sets the ENOEXEC error. Because that is the only error I anticipate, I let other errors fall through to be properly diagnosed, but in this one case I attempt to call the shell to run the user's program. For this second try, I use execl because the standard system shell is always provided in the /bin directory, eliminating the need to search the $PATH directory list.

If control returns from the execl call for the shell, this implies that execl was unable to load the shell; it does *not* mean that the shell could not find the user program, nor does it mean that the user program returned an error.

Remember, exec calls do not return if they are successful, therefore any return indicates that the exec call itself failed, and that the shell was never even entered.

In any case, a return from exec indicates that the user program cannot be called. The only thing to do is to describe the error and abandon the child process, using perror to print a descriptive error message, and exit to terminate the child process. It is *necessary* to print the error message here; the parent process cannot do it because the parent would require the *errno* value to print an appropriate message. Returning the value of *errno* here, however, could be confused by the parent process as a return value from command. In other words, there is no way except by using a special return value to indicate what happened to the parent process—the parent and child processes are using distinct copies of *errno*, and the parent process cannot examine the *errno* value in the child's process address space.

This completes the preamble for the child process: either exec fails and the code performs an exit to terminate the child, or else the exec succeeds and the process continues in the command program (or the shell).

If the return value from fork was *not* 0, the program is executing the continuation of the parent process. The task here is simple in purpose, although somewhat complicated in execution: to wait for the child process to complete its execution, capture its exit value, and return to the original calling routine.

The wait system call is used to wait for the termination of a child process. It is not intended to be used for any other purpose, and normally it returns only when one of the child processes terminates; if there are none, or if a child process has already terminated by the time wait is called, it returns immediately.

wait can return an error indication, EINTR and ECHILD being the most common. ECHILD is the *errno* value used by wait to complain when it is called but no child processes exist; EINTR is the *errno* value set when wait cannot finish waiting for a child process to terminate because it was interrupted by a signal. In the latter case, the correct action is to repeat the wait call until something other than EINTR happens. For any other error return, I pass the error back to the caller of filter. This is actually an ambiguous action to take, because the calling routine will assume that the child process was not executed and that the output file cmdout is empty; however, this might not be the case. But something unusual has certainly happened, the user program may or may not have executed, and I just don't have an exit value to be returned. It is safest to return a value of -1, indicating total failure of the filter.

If the wait call is successful, it returns the process-ID of the child that has terminated. The program continues to execute the wait operation until the returned process-ID matches the process created by the previous `fork`. The program calling `filter` might not create any other child processes, but the function will be safe to use in any program if it includes this check.

The termination status of the user program is now available in `status`. Unfortunately, the caller of `filter` is expecting the return value to be the user program exit value, and is presumably not prepared to handle anything more sophisticated. Yet the contents of `status` might indicate that the child process was terminated by a signal and never terminated of its own accord. In this case, no exit value from the user program is available. Worse yet, if the child process was terminated by a signal, it might have been aborted due to a programming error and not just by the user at the terminal pressing the Ctrl-C key to cancel the program. Normally the shell will report the cause of a signal termination so that a programming error can be identified as such and corrected; `filter`, on the other hand, might have called the user's filter program without going through the shell, in which case it's not available to print the report. The `filter` routine therefore has to take on that responsibility. This signal reporting action is necessary even when the program invoked by `exec` was the shell rather than the user program, because the standard shell traps signals only when it is invoked as an *interactive* shell, which is not the case here. The shell itself might therefore have been terminated by a signal, and hence it cannot be relied on to produce the signal report either.

Having successfully reported the cause of the signal termination, there is still the question of what to report to the caller of `filter`. A return value of 0 would clearly be inappropriate. A return value of -1 would probably cause the caller of `filter` to execute a `perror` call, but in this case there is nothing significant in *errno*; the last function called was `fprintf` to write the signal report message, and either it was successful or else its error condition is completely inappropriate to the situation. I therefore return a value of 255, which is similar to the return value that would have been received had an intermediate shell been called and had it been unable to process the shell script.

Finally, if nothing unusual occurred, the exit code is waiting in bits 8-15 of the `status` variable, so it is only necessary to convert it to a simple integer value and return it to the caller of `filter`.

This concludes our example of using the `fork-exec` interface. I would guess that it is more complicated than you expected. This is the main reason that the documentation warns you to use the `system` or `popen` library functions whenever possible. You might not always be able to heed that advice, however. I strongly advise you to carefully study the descriptions of all the pertinent system calls: `fork`, `exec`, and `wait`. Once mastered, you might be interested in developing some extensions to the `system` call. Some extensions that would be useful include the following:

1. Write a version of system that would close files that are open in the parent process before calling the child process. As long as the closes are performed *after* the fork call, only duplicate file descriptors are being closed, so the action has no effect on the parent process. On the other hand, closing all open file descriptors prevents child processes from terminating because they do not have enough file descriptors. This problem can arise because the default value of the close-on-exec file descriptor flag is 0, meaning do not close open files when exec is called. There are two ways to get around this: either use fcntl before calling fork to set the flag to 1 for all file descriptors greater than 2 (standard error), or call close after the fork.

2. Separate the system function into two functions, one performing the fork and exec calls, the other performing the wait system call. This version enables your calling routine to continue execution in parallel with the called program, and to wait for its completion at a later time. You would have to decide whether the second part would wait for any child process to terminate, or would return the status of the next child process to terminate. You might even want to provide a list of functions to be called, depending on which child terminates next. A good implementation is not as simple as just separating the sample program into two parts!

One final word before going on to the next subject. The previous sample listing demonstrates that there are many possible causes for a return value of -1 from the system and pclose library functions. You would be well advised not to ignore this return value in your programs, but rather to always use perror to report the cause of the failure.

Switching and Swapping

A process is interrupted many times throughout its life.

Sometimes these interruptions are caused by the process itself, such as when initiating an I/O operation. At other times an event entirely unrelated to the process's execution occurs while the process is running, causing a *trap* to be taken so that the kernel can handle the event. Regardless of the cause, interruption of the active process has certain consequences.

One of these consequences is that an interruption always causes a *context switch*. The purpose of a context switch is to leave the current process and begin the execution of a kernel routine, or to exit the kernel and resume process execution. Either of these actions causes a significant change in the *state* of the machine, and entails a significant cost in machine cycles.

Switching the machine from executing a user process to executing a kernel routine requires the following hardware actions:

❑ Preserving the current instruction address of the machine in the process table entry of the interrupted process.

❑ Storing all the machine registers in a space reserved for this purpose in the process table entry of the interrupted process.

❑ Disabling the memory mapping hardware that supports virtual storage image, thereby returning the machine to the real memory addressing required by the base kernel routines.

❑ Blocking further interrupts of the same type so that the kernel routines can execute uninterrupted.

❑ Placing a description of the interruption in some hardware register so that the kernel can identify its source and cause.

❑ Loading a new current instruction address from an *interrupt vector table* to find the correct kernel routine to be entered.

❑ Resuming normal instruction execution in the new machine state.

Some of these tasks are simplified and made more economical by advanced hardware design, whereas other machines might not even be capable of performing all these steps unassisted, leaving some to be performed by software. The efficiency and speed with which a particular computer performs these actions, as well as the precise manner in which they are performed, largely determines the number of users and the number of devices that can practically be supported by the system.

When these hardware actions are complete, the system has only begun to process the interrupt, for now the kernel interrupt routine begins execution and it might be a long way back to the interrupted process.

The amount of effort involved in processing the interrupt depends largely on the source and cause of the interrupt. Good software design strives to handle the most frequently occurring interruptions with a minimum of effort. If this is not possible, the operating system designer often chooses to defer the full processing of the interrupt, merely making a record of the event in the interrupt-handling routine, then turning control over to the kernel's scheduling routines to determine according to priorities what tasks should be done next.

The most frequently occurring interruptions in any UNIX operating system are usually the character device interrupts, by which a device such as a terminal presents an input character to the system, or requests the next character to be output from the system. These routines use real-memory buffers (clists) to allow most interrupts to be completely processed in only a few cycles. These buffers are loaded with the data to be written prior to starting an output operation, so that when the interrupts start, the data is ready at hand. When data is received from the device, it is stuffed into clists with no regard for whether any process has asked for it, or how much will be accepted; such higher-level matters are deferred to the interruptible kernel routines that will eventually process the data.

Another frequent class of interrupts is the *system call*, a call executed by a process similar to a function call. Unlike function calls that amount to little more than stack operations, a system call requires a context switch into kernel mode so that the appropriate kernel routine can be executed to process the request.

Interrupt routines conclude in one of two ways. Those interrupts that are executed very quickly and that do not change the dispatch status of any process often simply exit, allowing the hardware to return control to the interrupted program. Such interrupt routines reap the benefits of hardware-effected returns. They have to save little or none of the machine state beyond that automatically saved by the hardware.

This kind of fast exit cannot be used when the dispatch status of processes is changed, or could be changed, as a result of the interrupt processing. An example of such an interrupt is the humble timer interruption that occurs when a preset value loaded into the hardware timer expires. This interrupt should be simple to handle because it requires no transfer of data and the hardware itself is simple to control.

It's entirely possible, however, that the timer interruption signals the end of an interval currently being awaited by a sleeping process. If so, the system has to wake the process up by attaching it back into the list of active processes eligible for execution. The relative priorities of the processes in the active list must be reevaluated to determine where in the list the newly awakened process should be inserted. Finally, the system has to perform a context switch to change the current machine state from kernel mode into the virtual memory protected mode in which user processes execute.

This series of operations consists of two main steps, *scheduling* and *dispatching*.

When scheduling processes, the system reevaluates the relative priorities of each of the processes eligible for execution. The factors used to compute a process's effective priority include the process nice value specified by the process itself with the nice system call, the amount of virtual storage required to run the process, the amount of time elapsed since the process was last allowed to run, and a number of other weighted factors that count for or against the process. The scheduling algorithm tends to attach a higher priority to processes that do a lot of I/O to the terminal, while deferring processes that gobble CPU time without producing any immediate results.

Dispatching a process consists of restoring the machine state that was in effect when that process was last interrupted. Although dispatching is straightforward in most respects, consisting mainly of stuffing saved values back into machine control and data registers, one issue complicates things enormously, namely, reloading the active portions of the process's instruction and data space back into system memory.

Most machines do not have enough real memory to simultaneously hold all the programs and data areas of all the processes currently executing. The most obvious solution to this problem—executing only the number of processes that will fit in memory—is not a very acceptable solution to most users.

UNIX therefore frees the real memory occupied by a process when that process ceases execution; for example, by being first interrupted and then passed over when the kernel scheduling algorithm selects some other process to receive control. Because in general *some* portion of a program's instructions and data happen to be on disk when it is selected for execution, it tends to follow that something currently in memory will need to be written out before the newly selected process can begin execution. In fact, if this is not the case, or only rarely so, the system is being underutilized because it has been specifically designed to support a larger virtual address space than the machine's real address space.

Because of this effect, dispatching a process often involves writing to disk some portion of the memory currently in use, then reading in the portions of the selected process that will be called for when its execution resumes. This act of trading one set of memory contents for another is called *swapping*. It is a vitally important feature of the UNIX operating system, because it permits a large number of users to make effective use of even a modest-sized system.

The interruption-handling techniques, process-scheduling algorithms, and memory-swapping features of UNIX, although interesting in themselves, are of concern to both system administrators and application programmers.

System administrators are required to allocate the disk space to hold the swapped-out portions of active programs, to decide the number of buffers that will be available for character device operation, and in other ways specify system configuration parameters that will beneficially or adversely affect system performance. Some understanding of the underlying kernel design is essential to understand the effects of these decisions.

Application programmers (by which I mean anyone not writing kernel routines or device drivers) can write programs that allow for the operational characteristics of UNIX and thus achieve a satisfying level of performance, or they can use techniques that disregard these characteristics, and suffer the consequences. For the most part, you should form your judgments about efficient program design using an informed understanding of the way UNIX works.

Some conclusions, though, are so readily apparent and generally true that they are worth mentioning here.

One of these is the importance of using proper *buffering* for all program input and output, for example, by using the stdio package. When using low-level I/O system calls (read and write, primarily), each transfer of data necessarily requires the following: two context switches (one to get into the kernel routine, one to return to the program); at least one pass through the kernel scheduler; and (if luck is against you) a swap-out and swap-in of part or all of your process address space. The larger the buffers used, the less frequently the kernel needs to be called to physically transfer data between your program and the device. So, there is nothing "sissy" about using the stdio package at all; it makes good sense to do so whenever possible.

Another conclusion is that *any* system calls should be issued outside loops, or at least outside the innermost loops, whenever possible. This is because every system call entails the entire process scheduling, dispatching, and swapping overhead I just described, and this work, if needless, detracts from the performance of everything running in the system, not just your own process.

Character I/O is overhead-intensive, but is rarely something to be avoided, and the design of UNIX does everything possible to make character I/O reasonably efficient. You can help the system by allowing full buffering whenever possible for character device streams; avoid the use of setbuf or setvbuf to select line buffering or unbuffered I/O unless you really need it. Unbuffered character I/O, in which every character entered into the terminal has to be immediately passed to your program, is the worst choice for system performance, although sometimes it is the best possible choice for a clean, easy-to-use user interface. I do not advise against its use, only against unjustified use of this feature of UNIX.

Unfortunately, one of the worst offenders for doing unbuffered character I/O is the curses terminal interface. Although no one would argue against the usefulness and attractiveness of full-screen terminal operation for some applications, using curses for nearly everything would cut the apparent level of system performance to a mere fraction of what we're accustomed to.

Processing Priority: nice

The nice system call is issued by a user process to reduce its priority. The kernel scheduling routine uses the nice value as one of the factors in the formula for dispatching priority. Higher nice values result in a lower dispatching priority, deferring execution of the process in favor of other processes.

A program is typically written to reduce its priority with the nice system call when it is computation-intensive, meaning that it tends to use a lot of machine time to produce a small amount of output. The typical command invoked interactively by users at their terminals, on the other hand, performs only a minor amount of processing, produces its output very quickly, then ends. People learn to expect fast response from these commands, and become frustrated when they don't get it. If computation-intensive programs are allowed to steal much time from these other programs, the overall system response time will appear to suffer, even though the machine is working just as fast as ever. Changing the nice value of one of these "crunchers" is considered a courtesy to others; hence the name nice.

The net effect of increasing the nice value of a process is to cause it to execute in the gaps of system activity, when people are thinking about their next command entry or chatting with others instead of keying into their terminals. Because the computation-intensive program tends also to be a long-running program, the additional delay in receiving its results is often not important.

The nice command is provided to allow a user to increase the nice value of a program even when it does not do so itself. An enterprising system administrator might write a number of shell scripts for common chores such as compilations, nroff runs, and the like, combining the nohup and nice commands to run these programs in the background with an increased nice value. These alternate forms of longrunning commands (for example, make) can replace the standard command using a shell script similar to the following:

```
:
# @(#) make - a background version of the 'make' command
nohup nice /bin/make $* &
```

Summary

This chapter discussed the UNIX services for process and memory management.

Process management refers to the way in which UNIX executes programs. The distinction between *process* and *program* is important: A program is executable code, whereas a process is code in execution. Executable code is static and lifeless; it just lies there in a file someplace. It is not until a process begins to execute the program that the program has life and performs actions.

This chapter has explained how processes are identified, how they are created and destroyed, and how you can manipulate them. Central to the discussion are the fork and exec system calls; the chapter provides examples of using these calls. Creating processes with fork is easy. Properly handling the termination of a process with the wait system call can be difficult. When you try programming with processes, pay particular attention to the status information returned by wait, and do not ignore any returned status unless you know what you're doing.

This chapter has also discussed memory management. UNIX provides many different kinds of memory; the two main classes are *kernel* memory and *process* memory. Kernel memory is owned and managed by the UNIX kernel. Your application programs cannot directly access kernel memory in any way, so this chapter says little about kernel memory. Process memory is that memory which is unique to a process, and in most cases constitutes all the memory that your program can access.

Process memory can be allocated statically, in which case the memory is reserved as a part of your program and is actually allocated by the system's program loader when your program is brought into memory. Process memory can also be allocated dynamically, in response to requests from your program. The system calls for allocating memory are brk and sbrk. The UNIX standard C library also contains a function package called malloc that includes the malloc function among others.

You should always avoid using the brk and sbrk system calls; they behave differently in different versions of UNIX. The malloc function should form the basis of your dynamic memory allocation. Although malloc is flexible and portable, it is not always efficient. You can improve the performance of your programs in many cases by writing your own routines to allocate and release memory areas. This chapter contained an example of a user-written memory management routine.

You do not often have to worry about the relative priorities of your processes; UNIX contains built-in scheduling routines to balance the system's work load, and to assure each terminal user of an equal share of the machine's time. This chapter explains the concept of process priority, and shows how to use the `nice` command or system call to change it. You should consider using the `nice` command or system call when preparing a program for execution in the background, and when the program will place a heavy burden on the system.

Notably absent from the discussions in this chapter is the subject of signals. Signals, and interprocess communications services, are discussed in Chapter 14.

14

Signals and IPC

S ystem V provides three main tools for interprocess communication.

Signals provide a means for interrupting a process and causing a pre-defined action to be taken. The proper use of signals is important to many types of applications. This chapter explores signals in depth.

Named pipes (also called *FIFOs*) provide another means for passing information between processes. Named pipes are discussed in Chapter 11, "Special Files and Pipes."

Finally, System V includes a number of system calls that are lumped together under the general heading of *IPC* (*Interprocess Communication*). These facilities were introduced in Release 2, but have found wide acceptance and are now also supported in the current releases of XENIX. The major portion of this chapter concentrates on the IPC functions because they are more often poorly understood than signals. The IPC functions support a broad range of interesting applications and are a very important addition to the *System V Interface Definition*.

Signals

UNIX terminology about signals can be a little confusing, so here are a few definitions.

A *signal* is a request for an interruption. The act of originating a request for interruption is called *generating a signal*, or sometimes *raising a signal*. When a signal is generated, the party generating it designates in one fashion or another which process or processes should be interrupted; these are called the *signaled processes.*

A signal can be generated by the system or by a user program. A signal is only a request, because it can be ignored by the process that would receive the signal (in which case no interruption occurs), or it can be delayed if the system is otherwise occupied and cannot handle the signal at the time it is generated. It can even be discarded if an interruption is already pending at the signaled process for another signal of the same type.

If the signal is generated by the system, the type of signal implies the processes that are to receive the signal. If the signal is generated by a user program, the program must specify the process or processes to receive the signal.

If the system decides to interrupt the signaled process, we say that an interruption becomes *pending* for the process. The interruption can remain pending indefinitely while the system is working with other processes, although the delay is usually slight.

When the interruption is actually "taken," the system suspends the sequential flow of instructions being executed by the process, and makes a note of what instruction was to be executed next. It then diverts the program flow to an interruption-handling function designated by the user process to handle the signal. Alternatively, the user process can specify that no *signalhandling* function is provided and the system should take the default action. In almost all cases, the default action is to terminate the process as if the e x i t function had been called as the next instruction in the process.

From the preceding discussion, you can see that there are three main types of *signal action* that might be taken when an interruption occurs. First, the default signal action can be taken, which results in immediate termination of the signaled process. Second, the signal can be ignored, in which case the signal is discarded and no interruption occurs. Finally, a user-defined function can be executed to take whatever action the programmer wants. Because the system saves the address of the next instruction to be executed when the interruption occurs, the user signal-handling function can elect to return to that point in the process. This has the effect of returning to the interrupted code as if no interruption had occurred.

If a user-defined function is provided for a given signal type, and an interruption of that type occurs, we say that the process *traps* or *catches* the signal; hence, the user signal-handling function is often called a *trap* or a signal-catching function. I make no apologies for the variety of terms; it is a fact of life that all these different terms are used to describe the same thing.

With all this discussion, you might feel that you've missed any mention of what information is actually passed to the signaled process by the signal. Actually, there is none. (For a couple of signal types caused by hardware error, additional information describing the error might be presented to the signaled process along with the signal, but this is the exception rather than the rule.) The entire information content of the signal is contained in its occurrence.

The sole effect of the keyboard cancel key (usually Ctrl-C) is just to generate a signal. As with any signal, a process can elect to ignore the signal, to provide a signal-handling function (such as a clean-up routine, which would be appropriate in this case), or to simply allow the default action to be taken, which is to terminate the process. The only information contained in the Ctrl-C signal is the fact that it occurred, but this is sufficient to achieve the desired effect.

As a result, although signals are listed under the heading of interprocess communication facilities, they actually communicate very little. They are like a tap on the shoulder to get your attention. The signaled process, if properly programmed, can take a desired action in response to the signal, if the action does not require knowledge of who generated the signal or other application-related information. This is why signals can be used to perform a rudimentary form of interprocess communication.

Only two functions exist for managing this complex signaling process: `kill` and `signal`. Oddly, the function used by a program to generate a signal is called `kill`, probably because in the early days of UNIX, only one type of signal could be generated, and its effect was always to terminate the signaled process. A command called `kill` is also available; it takes the same arguments as the `kill` function and simply executes the `kill` function with the values provided on the command line.

The `kill` function has the following general format:

```
int kill (int pid, int sig);
```

in which `pid` specifies which process or processes should receive the signal and `sig` is one of the valid signal types.

The header file `signal.h` contains a definition of each of the signal types valid for your system. There are at least 15 signal types in any UNIX system. I briefly describe each of these signal types using the signal names defined in the header file. Your programs should always include the `signal.h` header file and refer to signals by name, because different numbers can be assigned in different implementations. The signal types are as follows:

SIGHUP: Hang up. This signal is generated when you log out, shut off your terminal, or hang up when using a dialed remote connection.

SIGINT: This is the signal generated by the terminal device driver for the interrupt key (usually Ctrl-C).

SIGQUIT: Generated by the terminal device driver for the quit key (set up by `stty quit x`).

SIGILL: Generated by the attempted execution of an illegal instruction.

SIGTRAP: Trace trap (not reset when caught). Generated by `trace` when a breakpoint has been reached.

SIGFPE: Floating point exception. A floating-point overflow or underflow occurred during the last executed machine instruction.

SIGKILL: Kill. This signal always results in the termination of the signaled process regardless of the signal action defined.

SIGBUS: Bus error. Can have a number of causes, including attempted use of an invalid address.

SIGSEGV: Segmentation violation. Usually generated as the result of using an invalid address to reference storage.

SIGSYS: Bad argument to system call. Generated by a system call when passed an invalid argument.

SIGPIPE: Generated by issuing a `write` to a pipe with no one to read it.

SIGALRM: Alarm clock. Generated when a time interval set up by `alarm` has expired.

SIGTERM: This is the signal generated by default by the `kill` command.

SIGUSR1: User-defined signal 1. This signal is reserved for use by user-written processes. It is never generated by the system.

SIGUSR2: User-defined signal 2. This signal is reserved for use by user-written processes. It is never generated by the system.

SIGCLD: Death of a child. Generated when a signal-catching function has been set up for the signal SIGCLD and a child process terminates. The signal is not generated when the signal action is set to either ignore or default.

Signal number 0 is reserved and is not normally generated. When specified as the value of the `sig` argument to `kill`, signal number 0 causes the normal execution of the `kill` function to be bypassed, and no real signal is generated. The `pid` argument is checked by the `kill` function, however, for being the process-ID of a currently active process, and so the call

```
kill(pid, 0)-
```

can be used to test whether the process identified by the value of `pid` is currently active.

The value of the `pid` argument determines the process or processes to receive the signal (presuming that the value of `sig` is not 0). Its simplest use is to specify the process-ID of some active process; the signal `sig` is then presented to that process. From the viewpoint of the program issuing `kill`, the effect of presenting signal `sig` to the specified process is unpredictable, because the action that occurs is the signal action defined by the receiving process for that signal. You cannot test what signal action is currently set up by another process, so use signals only in accordance with their conventional meanings.

The signals SIGINT and SIGTERM are traditionally used to attempt to terminate a process gracefully, whereas SIGKILL forces the immediate termination of a process and does not allow any cleanup by that process because, by definition, SIGKILL cannot be trapped. Signals SIGUSR1 and SIGUSR2 are reserved for situations in which two related processes, presumably parts of the same application, want to signal one another; the programs are free to apply their own interpretation to these signals.

The `pid` value can be used for more complicated purposes. You can issue a signal to all the processes in your *process group* by specifying a `pid` value of 0. (Think of a process group as all the active child processes of a login shell, with the shell itself playing the role of group leader.) This capability is often used with the `kill` command to terminate all of the still-running asynchronous processes that were created with the `&` shell operator.

You can send the signal `sig` to all the processes in an arbitrary process group by specifying for `pid` the negative value of the appropriate process group number.

A `pid` value of -1 also has a special effect: The signal `sig` is issued to all the processes having a real user-ID equal to the effective user-ID of the issuing process. This could be used to issue a signal to all processes owned by a particular user, regardless of the terminal with which a process was associated.

If the program issuing the `kill` system call has an effective user-ID of superuser, and the value of `pid` is -1, the signal is issued to all active processes (excluding only processes 0 and 1, the `swapper` and `init` processes created by the system boot). This facility is used by the system administration command `shutdown` to terminate active user processes.

Now that you know what signals are and have some idea of how to send signals to processes, let's look at how to specify signal actions and how to set up a signal-catching routine.

Generally, programmers write signal-catching functions for one of the following reasons:

❑ Prevents the program from being unexpectedly terminated while sensitive or must-complete processing is being performed.

❑ Performs clean-up actions such as removing temporary files before terminating.

❑ Allows use of the system's interval timer facility (see the alarm function) without being terminated when the alarm goes off.

❑ Writes specialized applications using the SIGUSRn signals in which certain server processes perform a desired action when receiving one of the user signals.

signal is the function invoked by a user process to specify the action to be performed for one signal type. Contrary to what you might expect from its name, the function does not generate signals. Rather, it specifies the manner in which the reception of a signal is to be handled.

The signal function has the following prototype declaration:

```
void (*signal(int sig, void action())))()
```

This is one of those horrid "complex declarations" mentioned in the C programming language manual. Let's see what it really says.

The traditionally recommended method for reading a complex declaration suggests that we read it inside out, starting with the name of the declared function. Following this advice, the first construct we pick out is as follows:

```
signal(int sig, void action())
```

A rather large chunk, but we have to follow the rule of parentheses before pointers. This piece says that signal is a function. That's clearly true; in fact, signal is a system call. It also indicates that the function takes two arguments, one of them an int and the other a function returning a void. But functions themselves cannot be passed, either as arguments or as return values. Actually, C always interprets a function name as a pointer to the function, so by convention, we read this as "pointer to function returning void." These are indeed the two arguments required by the signal function.

If we delete the part of the declaration we have already recognized, what remains is

```
void (*)()
```

This is simple enough to read directly. It says, "pointer to a function returning void." We already had "signal is a function," so, putting these two together, we have "signal is a function returning a pointer to a function returning void."

What this really means is that signal returns as its value the signal action that was in force prior to this invocation of signal.

Sometimes, even the authors of UNIX systems get confused about the signal function. Some earlier versions of the operating system provide an incorrect declaration in the signal.h header. You might at times see a declaration such as

```
int (*signal())()
```

in the older K&R style, which says that "signal is a function returning a pointer to a function returning int." But this is wrong. signal is defined to return the previous value of the signal action, and a signal action is of type "pointer to function returning void." Clearly this must also be the type of value returned by signal. Fortunately, the new ANSI standard for the C programming language corrects this error, and you are not likely to see it on newer systems.

Often you won't care what the previous signal action was; you're only trying to set it to something new. On the other hand, the fact that signal returns the previous signal action allows you to write very general routines that can temporarily change a signal action, and then restore the signal action to its previous value.

For the sig argument, you must specify the signal type for which this action applies. The same set of signal names that you used for the kill function should be used with signal. This is only natural, because for every signal you can generate with kill, you should be able to specify a signal action with signal.

For the action argument, you can code a pointer to the signal-catching function you want executed, should that signal be received by your program. Of course, the function must have been previously declared before you can write its name in the call to signal. The value of a function name is always, according to C conventions, interpreted as a pointer to the function. Therefore, to provide a value for the action argument, all you really have to do is write the name of your signal-catching function. Simple, isn't it?

I said earlier that there were three general types of signal actions: a default action, an ignore action, and an action you implement in a signal-catching function. We've seen how to name your signal-catching function to signal, but how do you specify the ignore or default actions?

The signal.h header file that I mentioned earlier defines two symbolic values for you over and above the names of the signals themselves. These are SIG_IGN—which is an acceptable value for the action argument, signifying that signal s i g is to be ignored—and SIG_DFL, which specifies that the action for s i g is to be the d e f a u l t action. These symbols are actually defined to be the numerical values 0 and 1, neither of which could validly be the address of a function. Therefore, the s i g n a l routine easily distinguishes these values from a pointer to a signal-catching function.

Let's take a look at a sample program that applies these concepts.

```
/*
NAME
      clock - Display the current time
DESCRIPTION

This program shows an example of using the alarm() and
signal() functions to implement a simple clock. An alarm
interruption is scheduled every 10 seconds. When the alarm
occurs, the signal-catching routine for SIGALRM is activated and
prints out the current time.

*/
#include <stdio.h>
#include <signal.h>
#include <sys/types.h>
#include <time.h>
#define INTERVAL 10      /* Seconds between time display */
/*
 * onintr - the signal-catching routine
 */
void onintr (int sig)
{
        struct tm *      local;
        time_t           now;
        /* Print out the current time */
        time(&now);
        local = localtime(&now);
        fprintf(stderr, "Time is %02d:%02d:%02d\n",
                local->tm_hour, local->tm_min, local->tm_sec);
        /* Start another time interval */
        signal(SIGALRM, onintr);
        alarm(INTERVAL);
}
/*
 * main - the program main driver
 */
void main (void)
{
        onintr(0);
        for (;;) pause();
}
```

This program implements a simple clock. Once started, it runs forever, printing the current time every ten seconds. It consists of two main parts, a signal-catching function `onintr` that is entered every time the SIGALRM signal is received, and a main driver `main` that starts everything.

Despite the brevity of this example, it brings out some interesting points. When the system calls a user signal-handling function, it passes one argument, the signal number. This is not generally useful information, and `onintr` pointedly ignores it. On the other hand, this single argument to your signal-handling function enables you to use the same function to handle several different signals and still perform slightly different processing for each type of signal handled.

After printing the current time, the `onintr` routine starts another time interval to keep the clock running. Without this, the program would print the current time only once and then go into a useless loop with nothing to do.

Before exiting, the `onintr` routine executes another call to `signal`, specifying itself as the signal-handling function for the SIGALRM signal. Why is this necessary? Whenever the system enters a signal-handling routine, it changes the signal action to the default (SIG_DFL) action, to avoid recursively entering the signal-handling routine. It is also a safeguard against a program-error signal-handling routine that itself contains a program error!

Unfortunately (or so it would seem), the system does not restore the original signal action when the function exits. In general, once one of your signal-handling functions is called, it is not called again. If you're not aware of this and fail to restore the desired signal action before leaving your handling function, it can lead to some confusing bugs.

Actually, this only *seems* unfortunate. If the system were to automatically restore the signal action, you would not be able to select the subsequent signal action within your routine; the system would always alter whatever action you set back to the original action. Once you're aware of this system behavior, you can take advantage of it.

The main function calls `onintr` itself. There is nothing that forbids other functions in your program from calling a signal-handling function. It is a function just like any other, unusual only in the manner in which it is sometimes called. `main` capitalizes on this fact because the system alarm clock has to be initialized, and the signal-handling function set up, before `main` can "go to sleep"; calling `onintr` is the simplest way to do that initialization.

`main` uses the system call `pause` to wait for the next alarm interruption, rather than using the more obvious

```
for (;;) ;
```

Although the latter spin loop would work, it would waste many CPU cycles simply jumping to itself. The call to `pause` suspends process execution until an interruption occurs, so it wastes no CPU time.

gsignal and ssignal

All releases of System V also include two functions, `gsignal` and `ssignal`, that together provide a *software signaling* facility. Although these functions appear to implement the same kind of mechanism as basic signaling, they differ in that `gsignal` and `ssignal` do not involve interprocess communication; all signaling using these functions occurs between linked modules of the same program and requires no operating system support.

Software signaling was implemented to solve a fundamental problem arising in the design of general-purpose library function packages, namely, what to do when error conditions are encountered. Although it is often feasible for a packaged function to simply return an error value, this approach can distort the function's interface. As an alternative, you would do better to allow users of the function package to define their own routines that can be called when an error occurs.

To support user error routines, the functions in the package must know the names of the user routines to be called in the event of error. Typical ways to accomplish this are to pass a pointer to the user's error routine with every function call, or to have the package set aside one or more reserved names for user error routines. Both these approaches are awkward.

The `gsignal` and `ssignal` functions provide a solution to the problem of user routine names. A function package can define up to 15 different classes of error or alert conditions by associating a signal number with each one of the classes.

The `gsignal` function supports 15 different signals, numbered 1 to 15. The meaning of a signal is defined by the application; the signal names defined in `signal.h` can be used, but the 15 software signals bear no relation to the 15 system-defined signals. The meaning of a software signal can be different from one application to the next, as long as no conflict in usage occurs between the parts of the application.

The `ssignal` function allows a user-written program to define an action for each of the signal numbers. Just as with the basic signaling facility, there are three possible signal actions: to allow a default action to be taken (SIG_DFL), to ignore the signal (SIG_IGN), or to designate a user routine to be invoked when the signal is raised. In turn, the function package can activate one of the user's signal actions by executing the `gsignal` function.

The internal mechanism used by gsignal and ssignal is simple but elegant. An internal table is maintained containing one slot for each of the signal types. The ssignal function stores the action value in the table slot corresponding to the signal number sig. A subsequent gsignal call inspects the value in the table slot, and if it is SIG_DFL or SIG_IGN, returns 0 or 1 to the caller of gsignal, respectively. It takes no other action. If the table value is a function address, gsignal sets the action for the signal to SIG_DFL and calls the user function passing it the signal number as the sole argument. When the user function returns, gsignal returns in turn to its caller, passing the return value from the user signal-handling function as its return value. The signal action is not restored to its original value; the user signal-handling function can do so by calling ssignal.

Interprocess Communication (IPC)

The Interprocess Communication tool set of System V has been an official component of the operating system since Release 2. Portions of it have been in existence much longer than that.

As with named pipes, portions of IPC were implemented internally by AT&T to support the development of high-performance transaction processing systems. These kinds of systems require the capability to store information in a central database while allowing access to the database from other (possibly unknown) processes. Signals do not provide a way to transport information between processes, and named pipes are often awkward to use. The IPC tools provide a means for communicating requests for data between consumer processes that will actually use the data, and a server process that controls the data resources, possibly a collection of files, terminals, or communications lines.

Although these tools are essential for constructing efficient database systems and transaction processing systems, they have other uses as well. This section examines not only the tools themselves, but practical ways to use them, some of which you might find useful in your own applications.

General Concepts

The IPC tools fall into three main categories of functionality:

❏ Message queueing

❏ Semaphores

❏ Shared memory

Message Queueing

Message queueing provides a tool similar to named pipes in that it is used to transport data called *messages* (which can be records of any description) from one process to another. Message queues are much easier to manage effectively and efficiently than named pipes, because the kernel does most of the work organizing and controlling the flow of data.

Message queues are accessed and manipulated using the `msgget`, `msgctl`, `msgsnd`, and `msgrcv` functions.

Semaphores

Semaphores provide a tool of great flexibility that can be used for managing any shared resource easily and effectively. (A shared resource does not have to be an IPC object to be synchronized with IPC semaphores.) The semaphores implemented by IPC can be used in a number of different ways. An IPC semaphore can be used to implement an "event control block" representing the occurrence of an event; any number of processes can wait for the event to be posted, at which time the waiters wake up and resume execution.

An IPC semaphore can also be used to represent an allocatable pool of resources consisting of an arbitrary number of units; consumer processes can remove and return units, automatically waiting when the number of units desired is not available. Semaphores can also implement a form of file locking with much greater flexibility than the file-segment locking implemented by `fcntl`.

Semaphores are accessed and manipulated using the `semget`, `semctl`, and `semop` functions.

Shared Memory

Semaphores were included in the IPC tool set primarily to provide a means for coordinating access to shared memory. Shared memory, the third class of IPC tools, overcomes the normal isolation between process address spaces and allows windows of memory to be shared among a number of processes. Shared memory can be used in a great many ways, but because it is not interlocked, difficulties can arise when independent processes attempt to modify an area in shared memory. Semaphores can be used to lock an arbitrary user-defined subset of shared memory so that it can be updated by a process while other processes, also wanting to access the shared memory, are blocked until the lock is released. Some amount of programming is needed to implement these locks; it is not automatic, and all processes wanting to use shared memory must test and set the appropriate semaphores if synchronization is to be maintained.

Shared memory is set up using the shmget, shmctl, shmat, and shmdt functions. Shared memory is accessed and manipulated using normal instructions.

Using a Key with an IPC Object

An IPC object, whether a message queue, a set of semaphores, or a segment of shared memory, has a name, called a *key*. This key is the name by which a specific object is identified. The key corresponding to an IPC object is assigned by the user program that creates the object; it must be known to all the programs in the application set that use it. Otherwise, there is no way to access it because IPC objects do not physically reside in process memory. On the other hand, different objects cannot have the same key, because the key is the only identifier for an object. You must be careful in selecting a key identifier because a conflict over keys between unrelated applications usually causes the malfunction of one or both programs.

At some point, you will want to know whether a key naming a message queue can be the same as a key naming a semaphore set or shared-memory segment. This is a question about name spaces, asking whether each of the three classes of IPC object has its own name space or whether all IPC objects have only one name space. The answer is that three name spaces exist, one for each class of IPC object. The same key value can be used in the msgget, semget, and shmget functions, yet a different object is created in each case. That is, a message queue with a key of 10 and a semaphore set with a key of 10 can both exist at the same time.

The ftok library function can be used to form keys that are both unique to an application set and yet readily determined by the application programs. The use of this function is recommended when applications using IPC are developed independently of one another, creating the risk that key identifiers will collide. The ftok function is discussed fully in the section, "Using ftok."

IDs and Permissions

Associated with each IPC object is a set of IDs and permissions. The permissions include read and write flags for owner, group, and other that are analogous to the permission flags for files. (Execute permissions are not relevant and are ignored.) Read and write permissions determine which functions a process can perform on an IPC object. IPC objects also have an owner user-ID and a group-ID that identifies the processes having owner or group privilege. Unlike files, which have only one owner-ID, IPC objects also have a creator user-ID. This allows ownership privileges to be assigned to another process, while the process that originally created the object retains the capability of removing it.

When an IPC object is first created, the creator user-ID and the owner user-ID are both set to the effective user-ID of the creating process, and the group-ID of the object is set to the effective group-ID of the creating process. The permission flags are set to the value of the nine low-order bits of the `flags` argument of the `msgget`, `semget`, or `shmget` function that was invoked to create it. These functions perform a service analogous to the `creat` function for creating files.

IPC objects, although created by individual processes, are global to the entire system. They are not deleted simply as a result of the termination of any process. An IPC object is removed from the system only when a process with the proper permissions executes the `msgctl`, `semctl`, or `shmctl` function with a command argument of `IPC_RMID`. The process must have an effective user-ID equal to superuser, the owner user-ID of the object, or the creator user-ID of the object; it is not sufficient to have write permission.

The `xxxctl` functions also provide a means to retrieve information describing an IPC object, similar to a `stat` call for a file. The IPC_STAT command argument causes a structure describing a message queue, semaphore set, or shared-memory segment to be stored at a user-specified location. The format of the stored structure differs for each of the three types of object. These structures, `msqid_ds` defined in `sys/msg.h`, `semid_ds` defined in `sys/sem.h`, and `shmid_ds` defined in `sys/shm.h`, are images of the information actually maintained by the kernel to describe an active message queue, semaphore set, or shared-memory segment. They are analogous to the inode describing a disk file.

Finally, the `xxxctl` functions provide a means to modify the user and group-IDs and the permission flags of an IPC object. This service is invoked by specifying an operation of IPC_SET for the function's command argument. The process must have an effective user-ID of superuser or be the same as the owner or creator user-ID of the IPC object. This service is analogous to the `chown` and `chmod` functions for files.

Using ftok

Before we discuss the use of `ftok` to create IPC object keys, you should understand that its use is not mandatory. If you are creating a set of applications that will use IPC services and these applications will run in an environment under your control, you can select whatever key values you want and code them as literals in your programs.

Because most System V implementations have IPC keys that are represented as 32-bit numbers, it is extremely unlikely that keys you pick at random will duplicate keys in other applications (such as purchased software).

On the other hand, vendors writing software for public use will prefer to use `ftok` to minimize the chance that users of their software will have problems. The challenge in selecting IPC keys for such software is to come up with values that no other programs could reasonably be using, but that programs in your own package can easily determine. As long as `ftok` is used by all IPC application programs, its methods come as close as possible to fulfilling these requirements.

The calling format for `ftok` is as follows:

```
key_t ftok (const char *path, int c);
```

in which `path` is the pathname of a file or directory and `c` is an integer value in the range 0 to 255.

Eight of the 32 bits in the generated key are set to the value of `c`. This is the part of the key that you specify; it can be any code you want. Typically, it is set to the same value for all IPC objects used by an application. You might then arrange for each of your application packages to use a different code. This would guarantee that, although key collisions might still occur between your software and someone else's, they could not occur between your own applications.

The other 24 bits of the key are set by `ftok` in a manner that depends on the path name you provide. Implementations of `ftok` typically construct the bits using the eight-bit minor device number of the filesystem containing `path`, and 16 bits of the inode number of the file. (The name `ftok` is modeled after the name of the function `atoi`, which converts ASCII to integer values and suggests that `ftok` converts filenames to keys.) A variation of this scheme might be used on systems where inode numbers can exceed 16 bits in size.

Regardless of the details of the implementation, the effect of this strategy is to base the uniqueness of the generated key value on the uniqueness of the path name. If your application uses certain files that are always present, you can choose one of these files to serve as the basis for manufacturing keys. Another possibility is to use the path name of one of the programs in the application itself, typically in some `bin` directory, as the key-generating path name. Having selected the file to serve as the `ftok` basis, every program in the application then calls `ftok` as part of its initialization code, specifying the chosen path name as the value of the `path` argument, to compute the key to be used in `msgget`, `semget`, or `shmget` calls.

I used `ftok` in a slightly different way in one of the applications I wrote. The programs needed to use IPC semaphores to lock certain files, preventing updates to these files while other programs were using them. Because these files were unique to the application, the semaphore keys were constructed by calling ftok with the pathname of the file to be locked. This generated a unique semaphore key for each file while also assuring uniqueness with respect to other applications, because no other application would reasonably be expected to refer to one of these files. Further, all programs using these locked files would generate the same semaphore keys for the files.

One danger with ftok: Because it uses the inode number of a file rather than the path name itself to construct the key, repeated removes and creates of the basis file result in a different inode being assigned by the system and consequently result in different keys being generated by ftok. The file used as the basis for ftok should therefore exist at all times. Some editors and utilities update files by making a copy, removing the original file, and then renaming the copy to the original file name. Because this technique continually changes the file's inode number, such a file would not work as a basis for ftok.

If ftok does not meet your needs, you are free to invent other means for generating IPC key values, because IPC kernel routines concern themselves with only the values of the keys.

Using Message Queues

I begin the discussion of using IPC message queues by looking at the associated functions: msgget, msgctl, msgsnd, and msgrcv.

msgget

The msgget function connects an application program to a message queue. The calling syntax is

```
int msgget (key_t key, int flags);
```

in which *key* is the IPC key identifier for the message queue and *flags* specifies the message queue's access permissions in its nine low-order bits. *flags* can also specify one or more of the following values:

IPC_PRIVATE: if set, a unique message queue is always created. The value of *key* is ignored. The message queue is defined by the system so that no possible key value could be used by another program to connect to this message queue, guaranteeing that its existence and use is restricted to the creating process. A queue created this way is a private queue because the only way another process could access this queue, either to add messages to it or to receive messages from it, is to first obtain the internal `msqid` identifying the queue from the process that created it.

IPC_CREAT: if set, indicates that the message queue should be created by the system if it does not already exist. Ordinarily, only one program in an application package "expects" to create the message queue while other programs connect with the queue to submit messages to its server. These programs have no desire to become queue servers, so they should not set the IPC_CREAT flag. If the IPC_CREAT flag is not set, and the message queue corresponding to `key` doesn't already exist, an error value is returned to the caller and `errno` is set to ENOENT.

IPC_EXCL: if set and if a message queue already exists with the specified key, causes an error value to be returned and `errno` to be set to EEXIST. If the message queue already exists, this flag is used with IPC_CREAT to force an error return. If IPC_EXCL is not set and the queue already exists, the IPC_CREAT flag is ignored and the `msqid` for the existing queue is returned. Typically, a program expecting to create and service a queue sets this flag with IPC_CREAT and interprets a return value of EEXIST as indicating that the program is already active as another process.

Multiple flags can be combined by ORing them together with the | operator (adding them together with + has the same effect).

The value returned by `msgget` is called the `msqid` or *message queue identifier*. Its value is used as the queue identifier on all the other message queue functions because its value is meaningful to the kernel, whereas the key is not. Any process having the `msqid` can perform message operations on the queue, even if the queue was originally created with the IPC_PRIVATE flag.

msgctl

The `msgctl` function has the following calling syntax:

```
int msgctl (int msqid, int command, struct msqid_ds *buf);
```

The action taken by `msgctl` is determined by the value of `command`, which must be one of the following values as defined in `sys/ipc.h`:

IPC_STAT: causes the contents of the message queue descriptor identified by `msqid` to be copied from kernel memory into the area in user memory pointed to by `buf`. The format of the `msqid_ds` structure is defined in the header file `sys/msg.h` and contains at least the following members:

```
struct msqid_ds {
      struct ipc_perm msg_perm;
      ushort    msg_qnum;
      ushort    msg_qbytes;
      ushort    msg_lspid;
      ushort    msg_lrpid;
      time_t    msg_stime;
      time_t    msg_rtime;
      time_t    msg_ctime;
}
```

in which `msg_perm;` describes the permissions associated with this message queue. This structure is described in the `sys/ipc.h` header file. Its members include the creatingprocess user-ID and group-ID, the owner user-ID and group-ID, and the permissions flags. A typical declaration is the following:

```
/* Common IPC Access Structure */
struct ipc_perm {
            ushort   uid;    /* owner's user id */
            ushort   gid;    /* owner's group id */
            ushort   cuid;   /* creator's user id */
            ushort   cgid;   /* creator's group id */
            ushort   mode;   /* access modes */
            ushort   seq;    /* slot sequence number */
            key_t     key;  /* key */
};
```

`msg_qnum`: a count of the number of messages on the queue.

`msg_qbytes`: the maximum number of data bytes in all messages allowed in the queue.

`msg_lspid`: process-ID of the last process that added a message to the queue with `msgsnd`.

`msg_lrpid`: process-ID of the last process that retrieved a message from the queue with `msgrcv`.

`msg_stime`: time-of-day as a system clock value when the last `msgsnd` operation was performed for this queue.

`msg_rtime`: time-of-day as a system clock value when the last `msgrcv` operation was performed for this queue.

`msg_ctime`: time-of-day as a system clock value when the last `msgctl` operation was used to change the permissions associated with this queue.

The `msg_qbytes` member is of particular interest. The kernel buffers all queued messages in kernel memory while they are waiting for delivery. Because only a limited amount of kernel memory is available, a restriction is placed on the total amount of data that can be actively stored in message queues. When this restriction is reached and an attempt is made to add another message with the msgsnd function, the process is suspended until some space has been freed by the execution of msgrcv. The maximum can be changed; downward, by any creator or owner of the queue, or upward as well if the requesting process has an effective user-ID of superuser. Application packages doing message queueing may want to include a command the superuser can execute to increase the amount of kernel memory allocated to the application's message queues, because this would improve application performance (albeit at the expense of performance for other processes).

IPC_SET: causes the values of certain members of the msqid_ds structure associated with the message queue msqid to be replaced with the corresponding values found in the structure in user memory pointed to by buf. The values that can be changed are msg_perm.uid (the owner user-ID of the queue), msg_perm.gid (the group-ID of the queue), msg_perm.mode (the permission bits), and msg_qbytes. Any process can adjust the value of msg_qbytes downward, but only the superuser can adjust the value upward. A nonzero value is returned and errno indicates EPERM if the requestor is not the superuser or the owner or the creator of the message queue.

IPC_RMID: deletes the message queue corresponding to msqid. The msqid_ds structure in kernel memory defining the message queue, as well as all messages in the queue at the time of the request, are destroyed. The kernel takes steps to ensure that the msqid value identifying the queue remains unused and therefore invalid for a long time, to ensure that attempts to reference the message queue by active processes do not result in an improper reference to some other message queue. Any processes waiting for a message to be added to or removed from the queue are wakened; the interrupted msgsnd or msgrcv is set to return an error value and errno indicates EIDRM.

In general, an application should include a utility command to remove message queues. Although removal may be performed as a part of normal application cleanup procedures, it does not occur when the system terminates the application abnormally. The IPC_RMID call can be packaged in a small program for cleaning up after such terminations. Similarly, the IPC_STAT call could be packaged in a small utility that would dump the contents of the msqid_ds structure, which would prove useful for both debugging and system administration.

msgsnd and msgrcv

The most important message queueing functions, of course, are msgsnd and msgrcv.

msgsnd adds a message to the queue. The arguments it requires in order to do this job are as follows:

msqid: the message-queue identifier returned by a previous call to msgget, (an int).

msgp: a pointer to your message buffer.

msgsz: an integer specifying the size of the data portion of the message buffer.

msgflg: an integer value comprised of flags defined in the sys/ipc.h and sys/msg.h header files.

The msgrcv function is very similar to msgsnd, adding one additional argument to the list:

msgtyp: the message type to be received from the queue or 0 if any message in the queue should be retrieved.

msgsnd and msgrcv are concerned with transporting blocks of data between processes. Data is always transported as a single block of bytes, which you may choose to think of as a *record,* but which IPC calls a *message.* IPC is totally uninterested in the way you structure the data in a message; it may consist of character strings, integers, structures, or anything else useful. To transport the message, IPC must perform two steps. First, the message is copied into an area of kernel memory where it is held until some process retrieves it; and second, the message is copied from the holding buffer in kernel memory into the buffer provided by the receiving process when the message is received.

To perform this transport, the kernel requires two pieces of information from you: the address where your message is stored so that it can be copied from there, and the message size. These values are specified by the msgp and msgsz arguments of both the msgsnd and msgrcv functions.

Your message buffer must have the following general format:

```
struct msg {
      long    type;
      char    data [n];
};
```

The type value must always be present and nonzero, but its interpretation is entirely at the discretion of your program. If you have no use for it, set it to some arbitrary constant value; the system won't care. However, the message type can be used to build some remarkable queueing systems; you'll see why in a moment. Also, note that although I've described the message data as a character array, the data portion of the message can contain any kind of data that you might like, except for pointers. The receiver of the message is normally a different process than the one that sent the message, so the message data is stored in a different address space than it occupied when it was sent. Pointers of any kind are meaningless to the message receiver, even pointers to areas within the data area of the message, because the message is not likely to be stored at the same address.

The message size is specified with the `msgsz` argument. Its value must be the size of `struct msg` excluding the `long type` member. For `msgsnd`, the system uses this value to know how much data to copy into its internal buffers while transmitting the message. For `msgrcv`, the size value is used to check that the receiving process has set aside a large enough area to hold the message; if it won't fit, the system does not store the message. Unfortunately, you have only two options for handling oversize messages: You can advise the system (by including the MSG_NOERROR value in the `msgflg` argument of `msgrcv`) that you will accept oversize messages, causing them to be truncated to fit in the area you have provided but without any error indicating that a truncation occurred; or you can indicate that you do not want to accept truncated messages, in which case, the system stores no portion of the oversize message at all, but gives you an error return value from `msgrcv` to indicate that you would have received such a message.

It would be ideal if the system could reject an oversize message when an attempt is made to place it in the queue, but that's not possible because at that time, the system has no idea what process will eventually retrieve the message, and therefore no way to know what buffer size will be available for storing it. Second-best would be to return an error indication to the process that originated the oversize message so that the message can be rebuilt and re-sent. That won't work either, because the time delay between sending and receiving the message is unspecified; the process that created the message may not even be present in the system by the time the attempt to store the message occurs.

Because of this situation, your program that receives messages from the queue must determine what to do with oversize messages. Ignoring them completely (by not specifying the MSG_NOERROR flag) could mean that the sending process goes to sleep forever waiting for you to take the expected action on the message. You have to decide what is the best course of action in the context of your applications. A general procedure you might use is always to store the process-ID of the process creating the message, and the actual length of the message, in the message data itself, and to receive messages with the MSG_NOERROR flag set so that you receive all messages sent to you. You can then check for truncation and use the process-ID in the message to send an error note to the sending process (perhaps using kill to send a user-defined signal, or using msgsnd to send an error message). If your application is very sophisticated, you may also need to include a message sequence number in the message data so that the receiving process can identify the failing message to its sender.

These schemes can get quite complex, however, and the best design avoids the problem entirely by using fixed message sizes or ensuring that no message that can properly be sent can exceed the size of your msgrcv buffers.

Your system has a maximum message size that it can support. The actual value of this limit is not specified as part of the System V Interface Definition, but in general, terms your message size must always be less than or equal to the value of the msg_qbytes member in the msqid_ds structure. To find the value for msg_qbytes, use the msgctl function's IPC_STAT command to retrieve the msqid_ds structure. As a general rule of thumb, avoid sizes larger than 5,120 bytes, although many systems implement a larger limit.

Absence of the IPC_NOWAIT flag causes your process to wait if the function is msgsnd and the system limits for message queue sizes would be exceeded by adding your message to the queue. Execution resumes when some messages have been removed from the queue and enough room is available for the new message. For msgrcv, waiting occurs when no message of the requested type is currently present in the message queue; execution resumes when a message of the requested type is added.

Both types of waits can be interrupted, for example, by a signal. If this happens, an error value (-1) is returned by msgsnd or msgrcv, and errno is set to EINTR. As usual, you should repeat the interrupted function call again; no loss of data occurs because the interruption nullifies the action that would be taken by the interrupted function call.

If one of the causes for waiting arises and the IPC_NOWAIT flag is set, a value of -1 is returned by either function and errno is set to EAGAIN to indicate that you should try your request again later. Retrying the request immediately probably only delays execution of the processes that would remove messages from the queue (or add messages for msgrcv to receive). If you elect not to wait when the queue is full, it is your program's responsibility to decide when to reattempt sending the message.

Message Types

I've delayed talking about the message type value while covering the basics of sending and receiving messages. I examine the uses of message type now, as well as the one argument of msgrcv that I haven't discussed yet, namely msgtyp.

For clarity, here's the full calling format for msgrcv:

```
int msgrcv (int msqid, struct msg *msgp, int msgsz,
    long msgtyp, int msgflg);
```

As you might guess, the value of msgtyp has something to do with the value of type in struct msg. The relationship is this: If the value of msgtyp is 0, msgrcv retrieves the next message of any type from the message queue. If the value of msgtyp is positive, the next message with the same type as msgtyp is retrieved, if one exists, or msgrcv waits until a message of that type is added to the queue. (Of course, waiting does not occur if msgflg contains the value IPC_NOWAIT; in this case, msgrcv returns -1 and errno indicates ENOMSG.)

With a negative value of msgtyp, you indicate a desire to retrieve a message currently in the queue and of the lowest type having a type less than or equal to that of msgtyp taken as an unsigned number. In other words, although a msgtyp value of 5 only retrieves a message of type 5, a msgtyp value of -5 retrieves a message of type 1, a message of type 2 if no messages of type 1 exist, or a message of type 3 if no messages of type 2 exist, and so on. The message retrieved is the first message queued of the selected type (it is, after all, a queueing system).

As I hinted before, your application decides the significance of the message type value. I can suggest some possible uses for message type, and you probably can think of more.

Some message queueing systems as implemented by other non-UNIX operating systems built in a scheme for prioritizing messages. System V does not encumber its message queueing mechanism with priority schemes, but you can build one using the message type. To do so, assign priorities to your messages, numbering the priorities from 1 to 10, for example, with a priority of 1 indicating the highest priority and 10 the lowest. The following retrieves the highest-priority message:

```
rc = msgrcv(qid, &msgbuf, msgsz, -9L, IPC_NOWAIT);
if (rc == ERROR && errno == ENOMSG)
    rc = msgrcv(qid, &msgbuf, msgsz, 0L, 0);
if (rc == ERROR)
    /* error handling */
```

This code first tries to receive a priority message from the queue. Failing that, it executes a receive operation for any message type, because of one of the following conditions:

❑ Either there are no messages in the queue at all, so the next message added, by definition, is the highest priority message in the queue.

❑ The queue contains only priority-10 (ordinary) messages, so a nonspecific receive operation retrieves the next one of those.

Another possible use of message types involves replying to messages. Many applications of message queueing involve sending requests for data to a central database server; the server must respond to the request with an error message or with a data record. There are a number of ways that could be used to send responses or data back to a message originator, but message queueing offers a rather unique capability—that of using the message queue as a bidirectional channel.

This scheme calls for using the message type as a channel number; that is, a value that indicates the intended recipient of the message. Although some extremely sophisticated schemes are possible, consider this simple one: Every database request addressed to the server process sets the message type to 1; every response message generated by the server is added to the queue with a message type equal to the process-ID of its intended recipient.

Message queues are not fundamentally directional in nature; they are more like a stew pot containing any number of messages, each marked with a message-type value. Any process with the required permissions may reach into the pot and draw out a message. In the previously described scheme, the message-type value simply is the process-ID of the process to which a message is addressed, except that the database server process always retrieves messages of type 1. This way, user processes do not have to know the process-ID of the server to the queue.

The general algorithm for making database requests is now clear:

❑ Queue a message to the server by setting its message type to 1.

❑ Issue a `msgrcv` call specifying a `msgtyp` value equal to one's own process-ID.

Any number of response messages can be sent from the server to the consumer process—including a complete copy of the database—by sending each record as a response. The consumer process must have some way to decide from each message when the last response has been read, but the procedure itself is quite straightforward.

Message queues place no restrictions, other than permissions, on which processes can remove a message from a queue. Normally, we think of a producer-consumer relationship in which every message is sent from one process to another, but IPC message queues are not so limited. If message types are suitably assigned, it's possible for one process to place a message in the queue that might be of interest to any number of other processes; the first process issuing a msgrcv operation for that message type gets the message. Such a design basically implements a *multiserver* system in which the first free server resource processes the message. Perhaps you find it even less intuitive that a process may remove a message from the queue that it added to the queue. If you think of this as canceling a message to which no process responded, its potential usefulness is apparent.

In server systems in which response messages are sent back to requesters, the possibility always exists that the process originating a message may be, for one reason or another, no longer around when the response enters the queue. If this message is allowed to remain there indefinitely, the queue eventually may become clogged with messages for which no receiver exists. A robust server system should periodically attempt to retrieve response messages it has sent out; those that have already been received and processed are no longer in the queue; those that have not been picked up by their intended recipients are retrieved and free the queue of trash. If a message pulled back this way has not been left on the queue long enough, it can be put back simply by executing another msgsnd operation.

As you can see, IPC message queues are a surprisingly versatile tool. It is well suited to solving multiuser problems that can be difficult to handle with other more traditional UNIX methods. A good example of this is in supporting multiuser access to a common collection of files to be updated. In the sample application that I will show you, you will use message queueing to implement a simple checkout system for a common collection of files.

UNIX makes it very easy to set up a collection of directories and files to which a group of users all have access. When group read-write permissions for the files is set, any user who has that group-ID, or who can execute the newgrp command to enter that group, can read and write the files in that group. The problem is that there are no interlocks to prevent the classic lost-update problem, where

1. User A edits a file x in the set, and the editor chosen reads the file into memory.

2. User B also edits the file x, and his editor also reads the file into memory; the image he reads is identical to that read by user A.

3. After making a number of changes, user A writes the file back successfully because his process group-ID matches the group-ID of the file and the file has group write permission set. At this point, the file contains the modifications written by user A.

4. User B, having made all of his changes, then writes the modified file back. This write succeeds because of group permissions. The

> file now contains the modifications made by user B but none made by user A.

Of course, more horrible scenarios are possible if the two users begin writing the file back only moments apart; the resulting file is a meaningless mixture of parts of the two copies edited by A and B. UNIX offers no built-in mechanism to guard against this sort of thing.

We now look at a tool that can provide the necessary synchronization controls.

Sample Application of Message Queuing

Before looking at the code, let's look at an overview of the tool's operation. To make the discussion easier, I call the tool fs, for file sharer.

The first thing is to ensure that only the tool can read and write the files to be shared. Otherwise, you will not have reliable assurance of their integrity. The tool therefore has a command for placing a file under fs control:

```
fs share dirname [user ...]
```

Anyone can execute this command to place a directory he owns under file-sharer control.

If no errors occur, fs changes the owner-ID of every file and directory in the named directory to its own user-ID and sets file permissions to 444 (read only) and directory permissions to 775 (read/write by owner [fs], read/write by group [the original owner of dirname], and read-only for everyone else). This action means that the original directory owner can still add and remove files in the directory (using group permissions), but only fs has control of the ownership and permissions of the files and directories in the shared directory.

The share command also allows the user to specify a number of user-IDs of users who will be allowed to modify the files in the shared directory. If none are specified, initially no one but the file's original owner is allowed to modify it. You can add more users to the share list by executing the share command again; because the shared directory is already set up, the only effect is to add user names to the share list.

You can drop users from the share list by executing the command,

```
fs drop filename [user ...]
```

If no user names are specified, the shared directory is returned to the exclusive ownership of the original owner. (Note: I don't include the code for this command in the sample because its implementation teaches little. This command is essentially the inverse of the fs share command.)

We need two more commands: One to be used by an allowed user to check out a shared file and one to check in an updated version of the file. The checkout function is performed by the command,

```
fs get filename
```

and the check-in function is performed by

```
fs put filename
```

When a file is checked out, we want to (a) remember to whom temporary ownership of the file has been given, (b) reserve the file so that no one else can check it out, and (c) provide a copy of the file with which the user can work. All this can be achieved by changing the owner-ID of the file to be checked out from f s to that of the user checking it out, and changing its permissions to 644, read/write by the (new) owner, and read-only by everyone else. This enables the new file owner to modify the file directly.

When checking the file back in, f s simply resets the file ownership to f s and the permissions to 444.

The program f s is written as a set of source modules to be linked together and a header file containing definitions global to the program.

```
/*
 * fs.h - common header file for modules of 'fs'
 */

/* Include all system headers here */

#include <stdio.h>        /* Needed for stream I/O */
#include <errno.h>        /* Needed for error checking */
#include <ftw.h>          /* Needed for directory set-up */
#include <pwd.h>          /* Convert names to uid's */
#include <signal.h>       /* Used to shutdown the daemon */
#include <string.h>       /* General usage */
#include <sys/types.h>    /* Required for stat.h */
#include <sys/ipc.h>      /* IPC common definitions */
#include <sys/msg.h>      /* IPC message queue defs */
#include <sys/stat.h>     /* For file attribute checking */

/* Symbolic values - NOT expected to change! */

#define OK      0         /* Successful return value */
#define ERROR   (-1)      /* Error return value */
#define TRUE    (1)       /* Logic 'true' value */
#define FALSE   (0)       /* Logic 'false' value */
#define NOSTR   ((char *)NULL) /* Null string pointer */
#ifdef GENERATE
# define GLOBAL
#else /* not in fs_main.c, define globals as externals... */
#  define GLOBAL extern
#endif
```

```
/* Program Parameters - adjust to suit environment */

#define FS_KEY (key_t) 0x66730000    /* 'fs' IPC key */
#define FS_DAEMON 1                  /* Daemon msgtyp */
#define F_ALLOW ".allow"             /* Permissions file */
#define F_ERRLOG "/tmp/fs_errlog"    /* Daemon error log */
#define MAXPATH 512                  /* Longest pathname */

/* External function declarations */

extern void     ipc_send(), ipc_recv(), ipc_reply();
extern void     perror();
extern void     exit();
extern ushort   getuid(), geteuid(), getgid(), getegid();
extern struct passwd *getpwnam(), *getpwuid();

/* Format of a record in .allow */

struct allow {
    ushort  uid;                /* User-id to be allowed */
    char    uname[L_cuserid]; /* Name of user */
};

/* Check-out request message */

struct request {
    long    type;                /* Message addressee */
    struct get {
        int     pid;     /* Process-id of requestor */
        int     uid;     /* User-id of requestor */
        char    path[1]; /* Path of file to 'get' */
    }       get;             /* Format for get message */
    char    path [MAXPATH];  /* Space for pathname */
};

/* Request response message */

struct reply {
    long    type;                /* Message addressee */
    ushort  status;              /* Status of request */
    ushort  reason;              /* Reason for failure */
};

/* IPC Message Sizes */

#define RCVSIZE (sizeof(struct request) - sizeof(long))
#define RPLSIZE (sizeof(struct reply) - sizeof(long))
        /* Global Variables */
GLOBAL int      qid;             /* Message queue identifier */
GLOBAL int      shutdown;        /* Request daemon shutdown */
GLOBAL int      usr_uid;         /* Real user's uid */
```

```
GLOBAL int      usr_gid;          /* User's group-id */
GLOBAL int      fs_uid;           /* uid of fs */
GLOBAL int      fs_gid;           /* group-ID of fs */
GLOBAL struct request    msg;     /* Checkout message */
GLOBAL struct reply      reply;   /* Status reply from daemon */
```

The header file, fs.h, is shown in the preceding listing. This header file performs the following services:

❏ Includes the header file sys/ipc.h because it's needed when any IPC facility is used, and sys/msg.h provides definitions needed for using IPC message queues. The header file sys/types.h must be included to use the IPC headers.

❏ Defines the key value for the IPC message queue as a constant. No particular file in this application is suitable for use with ftok, and only one key value is used, so a key value is selected that ordinarily does not conflict with any keys generated by ftok.

❏ Defines the msgtyp value (FS_DAEMON) for sending checkout requests to the fs daemon, which always receives messages of type 1.

❏ Defines the file name (F_ALLOW) where user-IDs specified on the fs share command are kept.

❏ Defines a file where the fs daemon can write error messages (F_ERRLOG). This file serves as a substitute for standard error, because the daemon should not be writing internal error messages to random user terminals.

❏ Defines the longest path name of a file to be checked out, because the file's path name has to be stored in the IPC message sent to the fs daemon.

❏ Declares some system functions not otherwise declared in headers, as well as the ipc_xxxx functions that actually issue the IPC message calls.

❏ Defines the format of a user record kept in the .allow file. Each record identifies one user who has been authorized by the fs share command to check files in and out of the file sharing directory.

❏ Defines a global static area which is used to construct messages to be sent to the fs daemon. Only one such area is needed for any given fs command.

❏ Defines a global static area into which daemon replies to requests are received.

❏ Defines symbolic values for the calculation of message lengths. These calculations are complicated by the fact that the message type must not be included in the message length passed to the `msgsnd` and `msgrcv` calls.

❏ Either allocates storage for, or declares as external variables, the global values used throughout the program. The setting of the GENERATE preprocessor symbol is used to control whether global values are allocated or set up as `externs`.

The format of checkout and status-reply messages is permanently defined by this header file; the remainder of the program source merely uses these formats.

The checkout message contains the following data members:

`get.pid`: Used to identify the process originating the checkout request. A reply indicating the success or failure of the request is sent by the daemon to the process identified here.

`get.uid`: Identifies the user making the checkout request. This user-ID is checked against the list of authorized users in the `.allow` file that was written by the `fs share` command. The daemon refuses to execute a checkout request unless this user-ID is found in the `.allow` file.

`get.path`: Defines the beginning of the area to contain the name of the file to be checked out. The path name field is defined in a peculiar fashion. It starts here, in `struct get`, and yet space for the full path name is reserved after the `struct get`. The reason for this is so that the size of a checkout request message can be calculated exclusive of the path name string; the length of the string has to be added to the basic `struct get` size to compute the actual size of the message.

The global variables `usr_uid` and `usr_gid` contain user and group IDs for the user executing the `fs` command, whereas `fs_uid` and `fs_gid` contain the user and group IDs associated with the `fs` facility itself. The `fs` command is a set-uid program so that the ownership of files can be assigned to the `fs` facility.

```
/* fs_main
        Main program driver. The first command arg is checked
        for being one of the strings "share", "get", or "put".
        If no valid operation is specified, write a usage message.
        */


#define GENERATE
#include "fs.h"
```

```
main(argc, argv)
int     argc;
char    *argv[];
{
        char *command;

        if (argc > 2) {/* Need at least two arguments */
                argv++;
                command = *argv++;      /* Save command name     */
                usr_uid = getuid();     /* Fetch real user-id     */
                usr_gid = getgid();     /* Fetch real group-id    */
                fs_uid = geteuid();     /* Fetch fs user-id       */
                fs_gid = getegid();     /* Fetch fs group-id      */
                if (strcmp(command,"share") == 0)
                        return fs_share(argv);
                if (strcmp(command, "get") == 0)
                        return fs_get(argv);
                if (strcmp(command, "put") == 0)
                        return fs_put(argv);
        }
        /* Print command usage */
        fprintf(stderr, "usage: fs share directory user ...\n");
        fprintf(stderr, "       fs get pathname\n");
        fprintf(stderr, "       fs put pathname\n");
        return (1);
        }
```

The preceding listing shows the main driver for the fs command. The main function is quite straightforward. It determines which program function has been requested by the first command argument (actually the second element of the argv array) and calls the appropriate routine to execute that function. If the command is improper, control falls all the way through to the end, where a brief description of the command format is printed on the user's terminal.

```
/* fs_share
        Handler for the command 'fs share dirname user ...'
        The dirname operand must be the pathname of a directory.
        All files in the directory will be made eligible for sharing
        by setting their ownership to the 'fs' user and permissions
        to 444 - these settings indicate "available for checkout".
*/

#include "fs.h"

fs_share(args)
char    *args[];
{
```

```
int     setperms();
FILE    *allowf;
char    *dirname;
struct stat dir;
struct allow udef;
struct passwd *pw;

/* Save a pointer to the user's directory "dirname" */
dirname = *args++;
if (stat(dirname,&dir)) {
        /* Can't stat the directory */
        perror(dirname);
        return(2);
}

/* Test if "dirname" is really a directory */
if ((dir.st_mode & S_IFMT) != S_IFDIR) {
        fprintf(stderr, "fs: %s: not a directory\n", dirname);
        return(3);
}

/*  If the directory's owner is not 'fs' it must be set
 *  up for fs operations
 */
if (dir.st_uid != fs_uid) {

        /* Set the effective user-ID to the user's, so
         * that we can modify its contents.
         */

        if (setuid(usr_uid)) {
                perror("fs setuid");
                return(3);
        }

        /* Use ftw to visit all the subdirectories and files */
        ftw(dirname, setperms, 5);
}
/* Fs owns the directory now, so restore the effective user-ID */
   */

if (setuid(fs_uid)) {
        perror("fs setuid");
        return(3);
}
if (chdir(dirname)) {
        perror(dirname);
        return(4);
}
}
```

```
        if ((allowf = fopen(F_ALLOW, "a")) == NULL) {
                /* Can't create or extend the .allow file */
                perror(F_ALLOW);
                return(4);
        }
        for (; *args; args++) {
                /* Look up the user name in /etc/passwd */
                if ((pw = getpwnam(*args)) == NULL) {
                        fprintf(stderr,
                            "%s: unknown user, ignored\n", *args);
                        continue;
                }
                /* Now have his uid, so write the allow record */
                udef.uid = pw->pw_uid;
                strcpy(udef.uname, pw->pw_name);
                fwrite( (char *)&udef, sizeof udef, 1, allowf);
        }
        fclose(allowf);
        return OK; /* Successful operation */
}
/******************************************************************/
/*      SETPERMS  Called by ftw during fs_share setup            */
/******************************************************************/
setperms(path,sbuf,flag)
char    *path;
struct stat *sbuf;
int     flag;
{
        if (!strncmp(path, "HOME=", 5))
                return OK; /* Ignore this ftw call */
        if (!strcmp(path, ".") || !strcmp(path, ".."))
                return OK; /* No change to these dirs */
        switch(flag) {

        case FTW_F: /* File found */
                /* File MUST be owned by current user, otherwise we
                 * won't be able to 'control' it
                 */

                if (sbuf->st_uid != usr_uid)
                        fprintf(stderr, "%s: wrong file owner\n", path);
                else if (chmod(path, 0444) || chown(path, fs_uid, usr_gid))
                        perror(path);
                else
                        printf("checked in: %s\n", path);
                break;
```

```
case FTW_D: /* Directory found */

        /* Subdirectories must also be set to fs ownership */

        if (sbuf->st_uid != usr_uid)
                fprintf(stderr, "%s: wrong file owner\n", path);
        else if (chmod(path, 0775) || chown(path, fs_uid, usr_gid))
                perror(path);
        else
                printf("sharing dir: %s\n", path);
        break;

case FTW_DNR: /* Unreadable directory */
case FTW_NS: /* Stat failed, don't know what it is */
        fprintf(stderr, "%s: not shareable\n", path);
        break;

}
return OK;

}
```

The preceding listing presents the processing for the fs share command. The fs_share routine sets up the directory named by the dirname command argument for use by the file-sharing system.

Of interest are the use of the ftw function (discussed in Chapter 10, "Directories") and the policies used for initializing directories contained within the target directory. At first it might seem that no changes would need to be made to the ownership and permissions of nested directories; only the files are switched between ownership by fs and ownership by a user who has checked out the file. The problem however lies in the placement of the .allow file; fs has to be able to find it even though only the path name of the file to be checked was specified by the user on the fs get command.

The solution, to be implemented by the checkout server daemon, is to look for the .allow file in the directory containing the specified file, and if the .allow file is not found there, to look in the parent directories. This process is stopped by accessing a parent directory of the target file and finding that its owner-ID is not fs. Use directory ownership, therefore, to learn to what nesting depth the share directory hierarchy extends.

Having set up the user's directory for sharing, we can now accept and process requests to borrow from that library.

```
/* fs_get
        Attempt to check out the file named on command line.
        Command format: fs get <filename>
```

```
        Check out is done by passing the request to the fs daemon.
        If the daemon is not already running, we start it here.
*/

#include "fs.h"

fs_get(args)
char    *args[];
{
        void    fs_daemon();

        /*      First, 'connect' to the fs message queue */

        if ((qid = msgget(FS_KEY, 0)) == ERROR) {
                fs_daemon(); /* Start the daemon. */
                if ((qid = msgget(FS_KEY,0)) == ERROR) {
                        fprintf(stderr, "fs: no daemon\n");
                        exit(2);
                }
        }

        /*    Send the check-out request message */

        msg.type = FS_DAEMON;          /* Address to fs-daemon */
        msg.get.pid = getpid();        /* Identify sender */
        msg.get.uid = usr_uid;         /* And requesting user */
        strncpy(msg.get.path, *args, MAXPATH);
        ipc_send();

        /* Process status reply */

        ipc_recv(getpid());
        errno = reply.reason;
        switch (reply.status) {
        case 1: /* Can't stat the target file */
                perror(*args);
                break;
        case 2: /* Not a regular file */
                fprintf(stderr, "%s: not a file\n", *args);
                break;
        case 3: /* Already checked out */
                fprintf(stderr, "already checked out (%d)\n", errno);
                break;
        case 4: /* Not on share list */
                fprintf(stderr, "permission denied.\n");
                break;
        case 5: /* chmod didn't work */
                perror("chmod");
                break;
```

```
            case 6: /* chown didn't work */
                    perror("chown");
                    break;
            }

            return reply.status;
    }
```

The fs_get function, shown in the preceding listing, services those requests. On inspecting its code, we discover that it contains nothing relating to management of the file to be checked out.

The program begins by connecting to the fs message queue. We intend to set up one process in the entire system whose task is to execute file checkout requests; this is the server for the checkout facility. By allowing only one process to check out a file, we ensure that nearly simultaneous requests to check out the same file don't result in both users getting it.

Consequently, fs_get processing consists solely of structuring the IPC message to be sent to the server process and in analyzing the status message it returns. To the user issuing the command, it appears as if fs_get actually processed the request and issued any error messages; actually, fs_get is acting as a slave of the fs server.

The program contains an interesting but cryptic function call to the fs_daemon routine. This call is not intended to process the checkout request; rather, the call is intended to install the server as a system daemon if the server is not already active. This policy has the effect that any execution of the fs command starts the daemon.

```
/* fs_daemon
        Runs as child of init process after fs get command exits
        Performs the checkout function for any user in the system.
*/

#include "fs.h"

/***************************************************************/
/*          Signal handling functions                          */
/***************************************************************/

void terminate()
{
        if (++shutdown > 1) {
                /*
                 * Not the first time we have been asked.
                 * Something must be stopping flushing of the
                 * message queue, so bail out immediately.
                 */
```

```
                msgctl(qid, IPC_RMID);
                exit(1);            /* Immediate shutdown */
        }

        /* Restore the signal trap */
        signal(SIGTERM, terminate);
}

/**********************************************************/
 /*      ALLOWED         Test whether a check-out is allowed
/**********************************************************/

static char *
allowed()
{
        FILE    *allowf = NULL;          /* Allow file */
        char    *sep;                    /* Separator character '/' */
        char    *filename = NOSTR;       /* Filename to check out */
        struct allow udef;               /* User definition record */
        struct stat sbuf;                /* Stat buffer */
        char    dirname [MAXPATH+1];     /* Share directory */

        /* Try to cd into the share directory */

        strcpy(dirname, msg.get.path);
        while ((sep = strrchr(dirname,'/')) != NULL) {
                *sep = '\0';
                if (*dirname == '\0')    /* Don't look above root! */
                        return NOSTR;
                if (stat(dirname,&sbuf)) /* Object doesn't exist! */
                        return NOSTR;
                if ((sbuf.st_mode & S_IFMT) != S_IFDIR)
                        continue;        /* Not a directory */
                if (sbuf.st_uid != fs_uid)
                        return NOSTR;    /* Not owned by fs */
                if (chdir(dirname))      /* Try to cd in there */
                        continue;        /* Unsuccessful, try higher */
                if (allowf = fopen(F_ALLOW,"r"))
                        break;           /* Found the allow file */
        }

        if (allowf == NULL)
                return NOSTR; /* Didn't find the .allow file */
```

```
        /* Search for user-id */

        while (fread((char *)&udef, sizeof udef, 1, allowf))
                if (udef.uid == msg.get.uid) {
                        /* Found the user listed */
                        filename = msg.get.path + strlen(dirname) + 1;
                        break;
                }
        fclose(allowf);

        return filename;
}

/*****************************************************************/
/*      FS_DAEMON         System daemon to service fs get requests */
/*****************************************************************/

/*
**      A global system daemon is used to perform file check-out
**      primarily because a delay between testing the file for
**      available status, and setting the file to checked-out status
**      could result in another user sneaking in and grabbing the file.
**      The use of a daemon serializes access to the file, and thus
**      prevents confusion about its status.
*/

void
fs_daemon()
{
        int     sig, pid;
        char    *filename;
        struct stat sfile;

        /*      step 1: create the message queue       */

        if ((qid = msgget(FS_KEY, IPC_CREAT | IPC_EXCL | 0600)) == ERROR)
                if (errno == EEXIST) /* Queue already exists */
                        return;
                else /* Error creating queue */ {
                        perror("create");
                        exit(1);
                }
        /*      step 2: create the daemon process      */

        if ((pid = fork()) == ERROR)
                perror("fork"), exit(1);
```

```
if (pid != 0) /* Parent process? */
        return ; /* Resume fs_get processing */
if (freopen(F_ERRLOG, "a", stderr) == NULL)
        exit(1); /* Can't get an error-log file */
if (setvbuf(stderr, _IOLBF, NULL, 512))
        exit(1); /* Can't allocate a buffer */


/*      step 3: set up signal traps            */

for (sig = 1; sig <= NSIG sig++)
        signal(sig, SIG_IGN);
signal(SIGTERM, terminate);

while (!shutdown) {
        /* step 4: wait for a message to be received */
        ipc_recv(FS_DAEMON);

        /* step 5: attempt to check the file out */

        if (stat(msg.get.path,&sfile))
           reply.status = 1,
               reply.reason = errno;

        else if ((sfile.st_mode & S_IFMT) != S_IFREG)
               reply.status = 2;

        else if (sfile.st_uid != fs_uid)
               reply.status = 3,
                   reply.reason = sfile.st_uid;

        else if ( (filename = allowed()) == NULL)
               reply.status = 4;

               /* Request ok - now check out the file */
        else if (chmod(filename, 0644))
               reply.status = 5,
                   reply.reason = errno;

        else if (chown(filename, msg.get.uid, fs_gid))
               reply.status = 6,
                   reply.reason = errno;

        else /* successful */
               reply.status = 0,
                   reply.reason = 0;

        /* step 6: send success-or-failure message back to requestor */
        ipc_reply(msg.get.pid);
}

/* Shutdown requested - close message queue and exit */
```

```
        msgctl(qid, IPC_RMID);   /* Remove the queue */
        exit(0);                 /* Terminate the daemon process */
}
```

Look at fs_daemon in the preceding listing and see how the daemon is actually created and how it executes checkout requests.

The first function encountered in the listing is terminate. This routine is a signal-catching function and is set up when the daemon is started. Its purpose is to respond to the SIGTERM signal, normally issued by the shutdown command when the system is turned off at the end of the day. The terminate routine increments a global variable called shutdown, which is tested by the daemon periodically. When the variable goes from 0 to 1, terminate returns quietly and allows daemon activity to continue. In fact, the daemon might be in the middle of altering the status of files, changing permissions and owner-IDs, when the shutdown signal is received. By merely setting a flag that the daemon can test, such processing can proceed to its normal stopping point and the daemon can then terminate itself.

If terminate is called twice, though, it's clear that something is delaying the daemon's termination, so rather than ignore the termination request forever, the signal-catching function finally takes matters into its own hands and forcibly terminates the message queue and the daemon process. Deleting the fs message queue is usually enough to halt the daemon's operation, but terminate exits at this point anyway; and because it is running as part of the daemon process, its exit results in exit and termination of the daemon process itself.

This function is followed in turn by allowed, a subroutine that is called by the daemon mainline to test whether the requesting user is marked in the .allow file as authorized to check out files. This routine has to get over a major hurdle before it can actually scan the .allow file for the presence of a record for this user: it must *find* the .allow file.

This is done by stripping off the last component of the path name of the file to be checked out, using a loop that progressively removes tails of the path name. This results in looking for .allow first in the directory containing the file to be checked out, and then searching upward in the directory hierarchy for the directory containing the .allow file. You can tell when you've gone too far, thanks to the initialization performed by fs_share, by finding a parent directory not owned by fs. At this point, you can assume that the file name on the original fs get command was simply a bad file name, and either no such file exists or the file is not located in a file-sharing directory.

Note that the .allow file is read and written with the fread and fwrite functions. This is done to keep the program simple (the authorization records themselves have a very simple format) and using these functions avoids the overhead involved in fscanf to identify fields of the record.

The mainline of the daemon really consists of two parts: a preliminary section of code that installs the daemon process, and the remainder that processes checkout requests from the message queue.

A daemon is simply a free-running process not associated with any specific user or terminal and that exists primarily to service requests from other processes. Daemons characteristically manage some system resource shared among all system users. The fs daemon is really no exception because the files of each file-sharing directory are a unique resource that has to be allocated among the system users who might compete for them.

The method by which daemon processes are created is really quite simple: If the parent process exits and a child process continues its execution, the system automatically switches the child's parent process-ID to 1, the process-ID of the init system task. If that child process then continues to run until forcibly terminated, it's called a daemon.

The procedure used to create the fs daemon is as follows:

1. Attempt to create the fs message queue. If it already exists, the fs daemon must already be running, so just return to the caller.

2. Use the fork system call to create a new process. The process becomes the parent process; it is the process that started out as the fs_get routine, and it continues in that role by simply returning to the caller to continue checkout processing.

3. The child process, which soon becomes the fs daemon, remains executing in the fs_daemon function and never leaves until terminated. Its first task is to try to receive a checkout request message from the newly created IPC message queue. It waits on the msgrcv function call until such a message is received, because the IPC_NOWAIT flag is not specified in the flags argument.

The process, which returned to the fs_get mainline, is now free to send a message to the fs daemon. It doesn't matter that, at the moment, the daemon is actually a child process of fs_get.

Eventually the fs_get function receives a reply message. It examines the status field of the reply; a nonzero value here indicates that the checkout request failed or was denied, so the reason code is used to construct an appropriate message to explain the failure to the user who issued the command.

At this point, the process that started out life as the fs get command now exits. This has no effect on its child process, which continues execution. At the precise moment that the fs get command completes, and the user gets a shell prompt for the next command, the now abandoned child process of the fs command is turned into a daemon, because it lives on.

The main loop of the daemon is a complex if statement sandwiched between two message-queue operations. At the top of the loop, it retrieves the next checkout request message in the queue. The if statement evaluates whether the request is to be allowed and goes on to perform the chmod and chown system calls that actually implement the checkout of the requested file. The loop ends by sending a reply message to the same process that sent the original request. The whole loop then cycles back to the top, consuming request messages and spewing out status replies as quickly as it can, with little regard for where the messages are coming from.

The message queue was created with access permissions of 0600 (specified in the call to msgget at the top of the function) to ensure that only the fs program itself could place messages in the queue, thus eliminating the need to deal with improperly formatted messages that might otherwise be sent by "alien" programs.

Note that the fs_daemon routine does not directly issue the msgsnd and msgrcv function calls. These have been placed in another source module so that all IPC calls are handled in one small set of routines. This is not strictly necessary, but it helps to ensure that once the programmer gets the set-up and coding for these calls right, they can be used without the need for further debugging.

The following listing shows the inner workings of the functions that actually execute the message operations.

```
/* fs_ipc.c
        Package of IPC message queueing interfaces.

        ipc_send:       sends a request message
        ipc_recv:       receives a message or reply
        ipc_reply:      sends a reply message
*/

#include "fs.h"

void ipc_send()
{
        int     msglen;

        msglen = sizeof(struct get) + strlen(msg.get.path);
```

```
            while ( msgsnd( qid, (struct msgbuf *)&msg, msglen, 0))
                    if (errno != EINTR) { /* Unexpected error */
                            perror("msgsnd");
                            exit(12);
                    }
}


void ipc_reply(pid)
{

        reply.type = pid;

        while ( msgsnd( qid, (struct msgbuf *)&reply, RPLSIZE,
            IPC_NOWAIT))
                    /* Check for retry-able error */
                    if (errno == EAGAIN) {
                            kill(pid,SIGTERM);
                            break;
                    }
                    else if (errno != EINTR) {
                            /* Unknown error, terminate */
                            perror("msgsnd");
                            exit(12);
                    }
}


void ipc_recv(msgtyp)
{
        struct msgbuf *buf;
        int     size;

        if (msgtyp == FS_DAEMON)
                    /* Expecting request message */
                    buf = (struct msgbuf *)&msg,
                        size = RCVSIZE;
        else /* Expecting status reply */
                    buf = (struct msgbuf *)&reply,
                        size = RPLSIZE;

        while ( msgrcv( qid, buf, size, (long)msgtyp, 0) == ERROR)
                    switch(errno) {
                    case EINTR: /* Interrupted */
                            break;
                    case E2BIG: /* Oversize message */
                            fprintf(stderr, "msgrcv: oversize message\n");
                            break;
                    default: /* Unexpected error */
                            perror("msgrcv");
                            exit(12);
                    }
}
```

None of these routines passes back a return code, because errors in message handling are dealt with immediately. Those that are recoverable are retried without any involvement of the calling program; those that are not understood are assumed to be programming errors, and result in the immediate termination of the calling process. This technique provides a clean interface to the mainline routines and ensures that error handling techniques need be coded only once.

For msgsnd, only one error is recoverable: the interruption of msgsnd. The msgsnd operation merely needs to be retried, so msgsnd is executed as a loop that iterates until something other than EINTR happens. Any other error is fatal, and results in documentation of the error in the log file and termination of the calling process.

The ipc_reply function also performs a msgsnd operation, but executes the call in quite a different manner. Its objective is to stuff a status reply message into the message queue to be retrieved by the user process that originated a checkout request. However, user processes place checkout requests into the queue as fast as the system allows. If the fs daemon were to do the same thing with replies, it could get stuck, unable to send a reply until it removes a request message from the queue because the queue is full, and unable to remove a request message until it sends the reply. The only way to avoid this deadlock situation is to use a nonwaiting technique for sending replies. This at least keeps the daemon active and removing request messages.

If a reply message cannot be sent, ipc_reply calls kill to send a termination signal to the process that will not receive a reply. If something isn't done, the user process waits forever for a reply that it never receives; the termination signal circumvents that error. The termination actually does no harm, because the request already has been completely processed by the daemon. If the request is successful, the checkout request already has been granted. If unsuccessful, users learn that the request failed as soon as they try to use the file that they tried to check out. In either case, the fs get command could be safely reissued by the user.

The implementation of the daemon leaves one problem unsolved in message-queue handling. There is no checking to ensure that reply messages put in the queue are ever taken out. The user might become frustrated waiting for his checkout request to get through a clogged message queue, and might cancel the fs get command.

In such a case, the reply message would remain in the queue until the system is rebooted, wasting kernel buffer space and exacerbating a problem with full or nearly full message queues. You can solve the problem by using any of several different approaches, one of the most obvious being to keep a list of the process-IDs to which replies have been sent, and to periodically attempt to retrieve those replies from the queue.

The programmer using IPC message queues must be prepared at all times to deal with the problem of nondelivery of messages, because IPC offers no guarantee that messages placed in the queue are delivered. Consider the situation that would result if the IPC message daemon were to terminate unexpectedly, leaving its message queue in place. When restarted, the fs_get routine would not create a new daemon process because the message queue already exists. Instead, the routine would place a checkout request message in the queue and then wait forever for the dead daemon to reply to the message, apparently hanging until someone terminates it. You should try to develop your own solutions to this problem.

The following listing shows an implementation of the fs_put function for returning a checked-out file to the control of fs, equivalent to returning a borrowed book.

```
/* fs_put
        Returns a previously checked-out file to fs control.
        Requires no services from the fs daemon, just sets the
        owner-ID of the file back to 'fs' and permissions to 444.
*/

#include "fs.h"

fs_put(args)
char     *args[];
{
        struct stat file;
        int      exit_code = 0;

        /*
         * Need to have user's uid to chmod/chown files checked out
         * to him, since the files now have his user-ID.
         */
        if (setuid(usr_uid))
                perror("setuid"), exit(1);

        /*
         * More than one file can be checked back in with one
         * fs put command... the check-in routine is iterated once
         * for each argument.
         */
        for (; *args; args++) { /* Read current file status */
                if (stat(*args, &file)) {
                        perror(*args);
                        exit_code++;
                        continue;
                }
```

```
        if (file.st_uid != usr_uid) {
                fprintf(stderr, "%s: not checked out.\n", *args);
                exit_code++;
                continue;
        }

        /* Return ownership to 'fs' */
        if (chmod(*args, 0444) || chown(*args, fs_uid, usr_gid)) {
                perror(*args);
                exit_code++;
                continue;
        }

        /* Return to fs was successful */
        fprintf(stderr, "%s: ok\n", *args);
}

return (exit_code);
}
```

This function uses a radically different approach than fs_get. Because the user issuing the fs put command is already the sole owner of the file to be checked in, fs_put does not use the services of the fs daemon at all, but changes the permission flags and file ownership back to those fs uses for an available file, thus returning the file to general availability.

The test in fs_put to ensure that the user is already the owner of the file is not strictly necessary, because the chmod and chown system calls would fail if the user were not the file owner. However, as implemented here, fs_put would blindly switch ownership of any file owned by the user to fs, probably an undesirable characteristic.

A better implementation would use some method to confirm that the file to be returned actually resides in a file-sharing directory and was originally checked out by fs. I leave this problem with you, the reader, because its solution is beyond my objective of demonstrating the use of IPC message queue processing.

Using Semaphores

Semaphores are the second main component of the System V Interprocess Communications tool set. In many respects the semaphore tool set is just like IPC message queues, so in this section, I concentrate on the ways in which semaphores differ from message queues. Before reading further, you should review the entries semget, semctl, and semop in the Reference section (Part V) of this book.

But what is a semaphore? The word itself comes from the Greek *sema*, meaning *flag* or *signal*, and *phore*, meaning *bearer of* or *producer of*. Interpretations like *producer of signal* give the wrong impression because a semaphore is a relatively passive object. It is a flag that can be set to one value or another, but that has no effect on your program unless you test it (examine its value in some way).

Consider a problem in which you need to synchronize access to a shared file. A single bit flag is sufficient to coordinate access to the file, if we let the 1 value of the flag represent the available state and the 0 value of the flag represent the locked state. If a program needs to modify the file, it must always follow this procedure to do so:

1. Inspect the value of the lock flag.

2. If its value is 0, go back to step 1.

3. Set the value of the lock flag to 0.

4. Modify the file as desired.

5. Set the value of the lock flag to 1.

6. Exit.

Unfortunately, this algorithm doesn't work if the lock flag is only a conventional variable. If two independent processes both attempt to use the same file, and their instructions are being executed closely enough together, you could see the following scenario occur:

1. Process x tests the lock flag and sees a value of 1.

2. Process y then tests the lock flag immediately after the test by process x and also sees a value of 1.

3. Process x sets the lock value to 0.

4. Process y sets the lock value to 0.

5. Both processes now modify the file at the same time, turning it into garbage as they read and write blocks of the file on top of one another.

The reason the lock flag failed to work is that another process was able to "sneak a peek" at its value in the time gap between the first process's testing and its setting of the flag's value. Semaphores don't allow this kind of peeking. Between the time its value is inspected and the time its value is changed, no other process can access the semaphore.

The lock flag just described is an example of a *binary* semaphore. The semaphores implemented by IPC are *counting* semaphores, because the value of the semaphore is represented by an integer rather than a single bit. It can have an arbitrary positive or 0 value. (An IPC semaphore is never allowed to become negative.)

IPC semaphores are manipulated with the `semop` function, which has an unusual user interface but yields a surprisingly high-powered tool:

```
int semop (int semid, struct sembuf *sops, int nsops);
```

The first argument, `semid`, is familiar from our study of message queues. It is simply the integer value returned by `semget` that identifies the semaphore set to the kernel.

The meaning of the second argument, `sops`, is not at all self-evident and requires some explanation. For its value, you must provide a pointer to an array of semaphore operations. The pointer declaration is used because the C compiler considers an array name to be the same as a pointer.

Each member of the array (or more properly, list) that you provide is itself a single semaphore operation: it makes one inspection, or one alteration, to the value of a semaphore. Each semaphore operation specifies three values: the number of the semaphore in the semaphore set on which it operates, the adjustment to the semaphore value that should be made, and the ever-present flags value.

You can provide as few as one element in the operation array (`nsops` specifies a value of 1), or as many as you like, but the semaphore operations cannot be scattered in memory. They must be organized into a continuous array so that the kernel can easily step through the array, executing each operation in turn. The kernel makes certain guarantees about the effect of doing several semaphore operations in a list, as opposed to executing each action with a separate `semop` call; these guarantees are rather complex, so I explain them as you go along.

Remember that when you defined the semaphore set with `semget`, you specified the number of semaphores in the set. This group of semaphores is treated as an array, so the first semaphore in the set is element number 0, the second is element number 1, and so on. When specifying a semaphore operation, therefore, you must indicate which of the semaphores is the target of the operation.

The adjustment value (called the `semadj` value) can be a positive, negative, or zero number. What happens when the adjustment is attempted depends on the sign of the adjustment value. The adjustment you specify might not actually occur or its occurrence could be delayed, in which case your process might have to wait for the adjustment to be made.

If you specify a zero value, the value of the semaphore is tested for equality to zero. If the semaphore value is not zero, your process waits until it becomes zero (unless the IPC_NOWAIT flag is specified in `flags`). That is, a test for zero blocks your process until the semaphore value is equal to zero. If this test is performed all by itself in a list consisting of only this one operation, the test is basically useless. When the `semop` call designating this operation completes, you know that the semaphore value became zero while the `semop` call was executing, but another process could "sneak in" right after `semop` returns to you (and before the next instruction in your program is executed), and change the semaphore value. In other words, nothing about the test for zero operation forces the semaphore value to remain zero. This operation is usually combined with other operations in a list.

If you specify a positive adjustment value, the current value of the semaphore is incremented by the specified number, that is

```
semval[semnum] += semadj;
```

This operation is nonblocking and always succeeds. It causes the current semaphore value to be increased by the amount specified, and has no other effect. If more semaphore operations are in the `sops` list, the kernel just goes on to the next one.

The most complicated case occurs when you specify a negative adjustment value. Technically, the current semaphore value is reduced by the specified amount, but if you request an adjustment that would cause the semaphore value to become negative, your process must wait. The kernel never allows a semaphore value to actually become negative, so your process waits until the semaphore is incremented sufficiently by other processes so that your negative adjustment can be applied and still result in a zero or positive semaphore value. Note that the kernel is not the slightest bit "concerned" with the likelihood of this ever happening. It is entirely your responsibility to design your application in such a fashion that your process doesn't wait forever on a negative adjustment.

The third value you must specify in a semaphore operation, `flags`, provides a couple of options that govern the effect of semaphore operations. The two values you might specify for flags, individually or together, are SEM_UNDO and IPC_NOWAIT.

The IPC_NOWAIT flag has the expected effect: If at any point during the execution of a list of semaphore operations, your process becomes blocked and normally would be forced to wait, and if the IPC_NOWAIT flag is specified in the flag's value for the operation that would have caused the wait, the kernel undoes all the operations that were performed on the semaphore by this list up to that point and returns from `semop` with a return value of -1 and `errno` set to EAGAIN.

This undoing of the operations preceding a return that is forced by IPC_NOWAIT also occurs if the IPC_NOWAIT flag is not specified and your process has to wait. The difference is, when you allow the wait to occur, the kernel retries the entire semaphore operations list when the semaphore value is next changed by some other process. This procedure of "try to execute the list, and if unsuccessful, undo all the operations, wait, and try the whole list over again" continues indefinitely until the kernel can get all the way through the list, executing every semaphore operation in turn, without becoming blocked by either a zero or negative adjustment. Only when the operation list can be executed completely, all the way through without waiting, does the semop call finally return to your process.

The reason for this peculiar behavior is subtle, and best explained by an illustration. Suppose that you have a parts inventory application that consists of

❏ A parts inventory file

❏ An inquiry program used by sales clerks to check for the availability of parts when taking phone orders

❏ An order program that removes inventory when an order is placed.

The two programs are designed so that they execute for a very short time. To check the availability of a part, the sales clerk enters the command

```
in 3671424
```

As a response, the program writes back

```
3671424 - 47 on hand
```

The order program, on the other hand, reads the complete order and then checks and decrements units on hand for all the items ordered at one time.

In this application, the problem to be solved with semaphores is to synchronize accesses to the file. We actually need two kinds of locks for the parts file: *exclusive-use*, in which the file is locked for the exclusive use of a single program, and a *shared-use* lock, set by the inquiry program to keep an order program from disturbing the database while it is being examined. The exclusive-use function is needed to keep a second order program from trying to update the file at the same time as the first order program.

This is a fairly common type of locking arrangement and is instructive for you to examine. You need the following semaphore operation lists:

```
struct sembuf
        lock_exclusive[] = {
                0, 0, 0,            /* Wait for sem#0 = 0 */
                1, 0, 0,            /* Wait for sem#1 = 0 */
                1, 1, SEM_UNDO,     /* Increment sem#1 */
        },
```

```
lock_shared[] = {
        1, 0, 0,            /* Wait for sem#1 = 0 */
        0, 1, SEM_UNDO,     /* Increment sem#0 */
},
unlock_excl[] = {
        1, -1, SEM_UNDO,    /* Decrement sem#1 */
},
unlock_shr[] = {
        0, -1, SEM_UNDO,    /* Decrement sem#0 */
};
```

Semaphore #0 is used to count the number of processes currently using the parts file for shared (read) access. Any number of processes can read the file at the same time, but no process can update the file while it is being read. Semaphore #1 counts the number of processes currently updating the parts file; no other processes can use the file for either read or update while a process is updating the file.

The semaphore operation list for acquiring an exclusive lock consists of three steps: Wait for the number of shared users to equal 0, wait for the number of exclusive users to equal 0, and increment the number of exclusive users. The list for acquiring a shared lock contains only two steps: Wait for the number of exclusive users to equal 0, and increment the number of shared users. The value of semaphore 0 can be large, but the value of semaphore 1 can never exceed 1.

Return to the kernel's rules for executing semaphore operations now. Suppose that the kernel used the more obvious approach of waiting at the point in the list where it becomes blocked and resumes from that point when the semaphore operation succeeds. The operations list for exclusive use wouldn't work! If the first step succeeds and the number of shared users is 0 and the program then becomes blocked waiting for semaphore 1 to become 0 (another process is currently updating the parts file), the kernel must go back and test that the number of shared users is 0 again. After all, any delay is possible between the time the update program releases its lock and your program resumes. In that time, an inquiry program could gain control and lock the file for shared use.

The problems that would occur after a wait if the kernel did not restart scanning the operations list at the top would be the same kinds of problems your own program would experience if you performed each of the semaphore operations with a separate semop call: You can never get past checking the first semaphore for 0, because it could become nonzero between that check and the next instruction in your program. (If this doesn't sound right to you, you might be forgetting that UNIX is a multiprocessing system. When more than one process executes at once, it appears to the system as a whole that sections of code from each active process are interleaved. Each active process only appears to execute continuously.)

There is a big difference between executing a series of semaphore operations in a list and executing each operation individually. When multiple operations are placed in a list, you are guaranteed that a condition tested or established by a previous operation continues to hold true throughout the remainder of the list. The operation list for gaining an exclusive-use lock is based on this guarantee, because it assumes that when the test for 0 for semaphore 1 is complete, semaphore 0 also still has a 0 value.

The operation lists in our sample parts inventory application specify the SEM_UNDO flag. The effect of this flag is to save our application from disaster if a program owning a shared or exclusive lock exits without releasing a held lock. The system maintains a record of the semaphore operations performed by a process when that process executes semaphore operations having the SEM_UNDO flag set. When the program exits for any reason, all the changes it has made to any semaphores are backed out as if it had never made any changes at all.

As you can imagine, this insurance is fairly expensive in terms of system overhead. You should use it sparingly and only where needed.

At this point, it is appropriate to look at some actual code using semaphores. The example application I choose is the `fs` program discussed earlier in this chapter. This program already has a problem dealing with an overloaded message queue: If too many processes attempt to send checkout messages at the same time, the queue can become full and the checkout daemon is then unable to send a reply message to the process for which it has completed a request.

We can use semaphores to solve this problem. Because the message queue has a limited capacity, modify the system so that no message can be placed in the queue unless there is also room for a reply. Insert the following code immediately following the creation of the message queue in the `fs_daemon` function:

```
static struct makeroom = { 0, 1, 0 };

/* Find out how big the queue is */
if (msgctl(qid, IPC_STAT, &stat) == ERROR)
        crash("msgctl(IPC_STAT)");
makeroom.sem_op = stat.msg_qbytes / MSGSIZE - 1;

/* Create the queue capacity semaphore */
if ((semid = semget(FS_KEY, 2, IPC_CREAT | IPC_EXCL | 0600))
    == ERROR) /* Unable to create the semaphore? */
        crash("semget");
    if (semop(semid, &makeroom, 1) == ERROR)
            crash("makeroom");
```

Because there are now so many reasons for failing to initialize the daemon properly, we need a new routine to abandon the attempt entirely. The `crash` routine provides that service in the following way:

```
void crash (const char *reason)
{
        perror(reason);            /* Explain failure */
        msgctl(qid, IPC_RMID);     /* Abandon the message queue */
        semctl(semid, IPC_RMID);   /* Kill semaphores if exist */
        exit(25);                  /* Crash the fs_get program */
}
```

This routine attempts to destroy the message queue and the semaphore set without worrying about failure to do so. Nothing can be done about these failures anyway.

At this point, we have a semaphore set in addition to the message queue. We've calculated how many checkout messages can fit in the queue (these are the large messages; replies are much smaller) and initialized the semaphore value to that number.

We now go to the `fs_ipc.c` module and adjust the `ipc_send` function as follows:

```
void ipc_send()
{
        int      msglen;
        static struct sembuf reserve = {
                0, -1, 0 };

msglen = sizeof(struct get) + strlen(msg.get.path);

semop(semid, &reserve, 1);

while ( msgsnd( qid, (struct msgbuf *)&msg, msglen, 0))
          if (errno != EINTR) { /* Unexpected error */
                perror("msgsnd");
                exit(12);
          }
}
```

Strictly speaking, we should check the `semop` call for errors, but as you will see, our application will make this unnecessary.

The semaphore operation performed by `ipc_send` attempts to decrement the value of semaphore 0. This semaphore is initialized with the number of messages that can safely be placed in the queue, but every time you want to add a message to the queue, you decrement that count first. Hence, if the count goes to 0, the next `semop` performed by `ipc_send` attempts to make the semaphore go negative, and `ipc_send` is forced to wait. It is therefore impossible (in theory) for the `msgsnd` operation to find the queue full, and it should never have to wait.

The real advantage to this, however, is calculating the queue limit so that there always is room for a reply message. Consequently, the likelihood is greatly reduced that ipc_reply will fail on its IPC_NOWAIT call and then will have to use kill to restart execution of the waiting fs_get process.

We have one more task to perform in the update to fs: we have code to decrement the semaphore value, but somewhere we need to put back the unit of queue space this reserves. The most obvious place to do this is in the fs_get function after having received the reply to a message. This would have the effect of allowing the same message queue slot that was used to send the checkout request in the first place to remain reserved for sending the reply—not a bad approach. On the other hand, this would leave two of the three semaphore operations to be located in the daemon, while one was located in the fs_get function, and this seems untidy.

A better approach is to place the increment operation in the ipc_recv function. Because receiving a message is the opposite of sending one and ipc_send decrements the semaphore, its opposite function should increment the semaphore. The revised ipc_send function would be coded as follows:

```
void ipc_recv(msgtyp)
{
        static struct sembuf release = {
                0, 1, 0 };
        struct msgbuf *buf;
        int     size, semnum;

        if (msgtyp == FS_DAEMON) /* Expecting request message */
                buf = (struct msgbuf *)&msg,
                release.sem_num = 0,
                size = RCVSIZE;
        } else { /* Expecting status reply */
                buf = (struct msgbuf *)&reply;
                release.sem_num = 1;
                size = RPLSIZE;
        }

        while (msgrcv( qid, buf, size, (long)msgtyp, 0) == ERROR)
                switch(errno) {
                case EINTR: /* Interrupted */
                        break;
                case E2BIG: /* Oversize message */
                        fprintf(stderr, "msgrcv: oversize message\n");
                        break;
                default: /* Unexpected error */
                        perror("msgrcv");
                        exit(12);
                }
```

```
        semop(semid, &release, 1);
}
```

This change causes the semaphore to be decremented once for each message sent, but you incremented twice: once when the daemon receives the checkout message and again when fs_get receives the status reply message. It appears that the number of message slots represented by the semaphore value would continually creep upward until queue flooding could once again be a potential problem.

Yet the symmetry of this arrangement suggests that it shouldn't be abandoned casually. Certainly, when the daemon receives a checkout message, queue space has been made available for another message. Why not let it be used? Maybe you need to arrange for another balancing decrement of the semaphore someplace to compensate for the two increments.

You might recall that the fs algorithm presented two problems, not one. The second problem is concerned with allowing unreceived status replies to remain in the queue, which is probably a problem whenever fs_get is cancelled by the user (or other causes!) before the status reply message is received. If you arrange for ipc_reply to decrement the semaphore value after sending the reply, it is forced to wait until the reply has been received before proceeding. This looks promising, because it allows a kind of "signal" to be sent back from fs_get to the daemon, indicating that the status reply message was properly received.

Modified for this capability, the ipc_reply function is written as follows:

```
void ipc_reply(pid)
{
        static struct sembuf received = {
                1, -1, 0 };

        reply.type = pid;

        while (msgsnd(qid, (struct msgbuf *)&reply, RPLSIZE,
            IPC_NOWAIT)) /* Check for retry-able error */
                if (errno == EAGAIN) {
                        kill(pid,SIGTERM);
                        break;
                }
                else if (errno != EINTR) {
                        /* Unknown error, terminate */
                        perror("msgsnd");
                        exit(12);
                }
        semop(semid, &received, 1); /* Wait for status received */

}
```

Note what happens if `fs_get` actually receives the reply message and increments the semaphore before the `ipc_reply` routine gets around to waiting for the reply acknowledgement. In the normal case, the sequence of events is as follows:

1. `ipc_reply` queues a status reply message.

2. `ipc_reply` attempts to decrement the semaphore value, but it is already 0, so the daemon is forced to wait.

3. `ipc_recv` receives the status reply message and increments the semaphore, making its value equal to 1.

4. The kernel notes that the semaphore value has changed and retries the `ipc_reply` operation list again. This time the semaphore value is 1, so the decrement succeeds and the daemon resumes normal execution.

The other possible scenario is the following:

1. `ipc_reply` queues a status reply message.

2. `ipc_recv` receives the status reply message and increments the semaphore, making its value equal to 1.

3. `ipc_reply` attempts to decrement the semaphore value and, because it has a value of 1, succeeds. The daemon resumes normal execution.

Because IPC semaphores are counting semaphores, the order in which they are incremented and decremented is largely immaterial. What counts is the balance of operations. This makes them well suited for event-waiting applications of the classical "post" and "wait" type, in which the `post` operation marks the occurrence of an event, and `wait` waits until the event occurs. If the event occurs before the wait, the semaphore has already counted it, and the decrement used to wait for the event succeeds at once.

You might have noticed that in the preceding modifications to the `ipc_recv` and `ipc_reply` functions, reply waiting used semaphore number 1, whereas semaphore 0 was used for checkout messages. I chose this approach in order to force absolute synchronization between sending a reply and signaling its successful receipt. If semaphore 0 were used for both types of messages, the receipt of a checkout message by the daemon could be taken as a successfully received reply. The books would still balance eventually, but at any given moment, it would be impossible to tell whether an imbalance was due to a checkout message pending in the queue or a reply message pending in the queue.

The approach as written means that the daemon always knows the process-ID of the process for which a reply is currently outstanding. If the `ipc_reply` routine were now to be extended to start an alarm clock before waiting for the reply to be received, waiting a reasonable period of time on the order of a minute before the alarm goes off, we could then take measures to assure that no reply message ever hangs in the queue due to a dead receiver process.

I present now the final version of `ipc_reply`, modified to catch unreceived status replies:

```
void timeout()
{
}

void ipc_reply(pid)
{
        static struct sembuf received = { 1, -1, 0 };

        reply.type = pid;

again:  /* Retry sending the reply */
        while ( msgsnd( qid, (struct msgbuf *)&reply, RPLSIZE,
            IPC_NOWAIT)) /* Check for retryable error */
                if (errno == EAGAIN) {
                        /* THE QUEUE IS FULL !! */
                        kill(pid,SIGTERM);
                        return; /* Don't wait for receipt of reply */
                }
                else if (errno != EINTR) {
                        /* Unknown error, terminate */
                        perror("msgsnd");
                        exit(12);
                }

        signal(SIGALRM, timeout);        /* Prepare to catch a timer */
        alarm(30);                       /* Goes off in 30 seconds */
        if (semop(semid, &received, 1) == ERROR && errno == EINTR
            /* Semaphore wait failed due to timeout */
        && msgrcv(qid, (struct msgbuf *)&reply, RPLSIZE,
            (long)pid, IPC_NOWAIT) != ERROR
            /* Successfully retrieved the reply message */
        && (kill(pid,0) != ERROR || errno != ESRCH))
                /* got reply back && target process is still there */
                goto again;

        /*
```

```
        Either the target process received the reply and posted sem1,
        or the status reply was successfully fished back and the
        target process was dead, or the reply was not in the queue,
        or the msgrcv failed for mysterious reasons.
        In any event, there is nothing more we can do, so just
        return to continue normal process operations.
        */
        alarm(0);            /* Cancel any outstanding timer interrupt */
}
```

Using Shared-memory Segments

Shared-memory segments are the third and final tool in the IPC tool set. With shared-memory segments, you can establish areas of memory that are simultaneously accessible to more than one process, overcoming the normal strict separation between process address spaces.

A shared-memory segment is like a window onto a segment of common memory provided by the kernel. Shared-memory segments are not restricted to any fixed standard size, although there is a largest size that any given implementation of System V and your particular installation can support. The term *segment* merely suggests that it is an area of storage which can be substituted for a subrange of the addresses in your process address space. The actual address at which a shared-memory segment is attached can be controlled with the shmat function (discussed more later). Segments can be attached at a different address in each address space (in this case, care must be taken with any pointers in the segment itself, because they point to a different location in each address space) or a segment can be attached at the same address in some or all of the processes sharing it, simplifying the use of pointers in the segment itself.

In some respects, shared-memory segments are more like semaphores than message queues, because a shared-memory segment continues to exist in the system even if the process that originally created it dies. Shared segments are not special to any one process, so a segment can continue to exist whether or not it is currently attached to any process. This means that a segment can be set up at any time and that processes can attach and detach the segment when necessary. If at any given moment, no process has attached the segment, it lies dormant somewhere under kernel control, invisible but waiting to be attached to the next process that requires it.

Normally, one thinks of shared segments as a way to establish a communication path or a scratch-pad work area between two or more simultaneously executing processes. This is not the only way to use them, however. Shared segments can also be used to provide a long-term working memory shared between successively executed processes. Thus, whereas the use of an IPC message queue tends to imply the use of one or more daemon processes to serve the message queue, no daemon processes need be used at all in some types of shared-memory applications. The sample program I show is an example of this type of use.

Shared-memory segments are created or identified using the `shmget` function, which is similar in operation to the `msgget` and `semget` functions previously discussed. As with message queues, shared-memory segments can be created with the IPC_PRIVATE flag so that no other process can use the segment unless the creating process first passes the segment identifier (`shmid`) to it. Publically sharable segments are identified by a key, which is defined in the same manner as for message queues and semaphores.

Also similar to the support for queues and semaphores is the `shmctl` function, which is used to examine the status of a segment (IPC_STAT command), to destroy the segment and remove all traces of it from the system (IPC_RMID command), or to modify the access privileges associated with the segment (IPC_SET command).

The most important functions, though, are the shared-memory operations, specifically the `shmat` and `shmdt` function calls.

To use the `shmat` (`attach`) function, you must first know the shared-memory identifier (`shmid`) for the segment. You get this by executing the `shmget` function, either to create a new segment or to locate an existing segment.

You must next decide where (at what address range) you want the segment to be attached. Typically (and in the best program designs), you won't care, and you can let the system determine a good address for you. With a call of the form

```
shmat(id, (char *)NULL, 0)
```

you indicate that you have no preference for the address of the segment, and the system chooses an address range that is currently invalid for your process.

However, if the segment contains pointers to locations within the segment, you probably wish to attach the segment at a constant address so that you can safely use those pointers. To do so, you must select some address range that does not conflict with the text, data, and stack areas of any of your programs, typically by being higher than any address used. You run two risks by attempting this, however, as follows:

1. An unusually large program might overlap the address range you have chosen for the segment, especially if future corrections or enhancements to the program increases its size.

2. There is an overall system limit on process size that is configurable by the system administrator, so you must know this limit in advance of building your application (or publish the minimum process size you require as an installation requirement for your application).

Having overcome these obstacles, you specify the attachment address with a call of the form

```
shmat(id, (char *)(0x7f2300), 0)
```

The kernel makes every attempt to attach the segment at that address, but if it cannot, it returns the error value

```
((char *)(-1))
```

and sets the value of errno to the following:

ENOMEM if the system-defined limit on process size would be exceeded;

EINVAL if the address you specified would overlap the data or stack segments of your program.

If you're seriously considering the attachment of segments at addresses you specify, you need to provide for the proper alignment of the segment so that data areas in the segment fall on the correct address boundaries as required by the machine. The SHM_RND flag value (meaning round), if specified as the third argument of shmat, causes the system to round automatically the address you specify to a system-defined standard boundary. The documentation for shmat refers to a value called SHMLBA; this is not a value you specify or that you need to know, but simply a symbolic name for the rounding factor the system uses when SHM_RND is specified. To use rounding, the shmat call must be in the form

```
shmat(id, (char *)(myaddr), SHM_RND)
```

in which, once again, myaddr is the address where you want the segment attached. After rounding, the resulting address is tested for validity, and the same errors may result (ENOMEM or EINVAL) as for a nonrounding call.

Supposing that you have managed to create or locate the desired segment with shmget, and to attach it with shmat, your troubles are not over. You might be able to read the memory (inspect the values of variables in the segment) but be unable to write (modify) the memory; this is the case when the access permissions set up by the creator of the shared-memory segment grant only read permission to your process.

If you have write access, you must be prepared to handle the case in which some other process has also attached the shared-memory segment with write access and might attempt to read or write areas of the segment at the same time as your process. Even if you are limited to read-only access, other processes with write access might disturb the contents of the segment while your process is attempting to read it, and you might find chains broken while they are being updated, or other apparent damage to the data simply because you are "sneaking in" while the other processes are midway through updates to the data.

If there is any chance that another process might modify the segment while your process is using it, you must synchronize these accesses. The easiest way to achieve this is to use one or more semaphores as locks on various areas of the shared-memory segment. To use locks in this fashion, you need to establish a convention between your programs about which semaphores represent locks on which areas of the segment, then always lock an area using the established semaphore before accessing it, and unlock the area after you are finished.

You might be unfamiliar with the use of semaphores as locks, so the following sample program uses locking semaphores to synchronize access to the contents of a segment. The sample program is not sophisticated, so one semaphore is sufficient to represent the locked or unlocked state of the entire segment; more sophisticated applications might use more than one semaphore so that processes that do not actually interfere with one another (because they access unrelated parts of the shared-memory segment) don't have to wait unnecessarily.

The sample application is a personal time-accounting facility. Its purpose is to assist in tracking the amount of time spent working on various projects. Although it could be used to track time whether the computer is part of the work or not, the package is oriented toward accounting for work time spent actually logged onto and using the system.

The application uses IPC facilities because most UNIX systems allow a user to be logged on at more than one terminal at a time. More traditional approaches are difficult to use because they do not as naturally allow for multiple process operations.

The strategy used by the application is straightforward. A shared-memory segment is created by the `shmcs` (create segment) program, essentially opening the facility for use. The shared-memory segment is used to contain the list of projects the user is currently working on and notes whether a particular project is currently active, the time when work started, and the amount of time accumulated on the project so far.

The shmset command can be used to start recording time against a particular project, using the format

```
shmset project-name on
```

and recording can be stopped by entering

```
shmset project-name off
```

When recording is stopped, the amount of time elapsed since the last on command is computed and added to a total maintained for that project. The program thus supports working on a project piecemeal and also allows recording time against more than one project at a time.

Besides the shmcs and shmset commands, the facility also includes two utilities. The shmstat command displays the current status of the shared-memory segment, as well as the time that has been logged against each project. The segment status is obtained by an IPC_STAT call to shmctl, so it shows working code that uses that service. The shmkill function dismantles the shared-memory segment when the user no longer has any use for it.

The package ought to include a program for storing the accumulated project times in a permanent file, but because the program would demonstrate no new concepts in shared-memory management, it has not been included.

Because the package includes more than one source module, a header file is defined to ensure commonality between components.

```
/*
 * shmcom - common definitions for shared-memory application
 */

#include <stdio.h>
#include <string.h>
#include <sys/types.h>
#include <sys/ipc.h>
#include <sys/sem.h>
#include <sys/shm.h>
#include <time.h>
#include <errno.h>

#define OK      (0)
#define ERROR   (-1)
#define L_KEY   0x74000000
#define CREATE  (IPC_CREAT | IPC_EXCL | 0600)
#define MAXPRJ  20
#define SHMATFAIL ((char *)ERROR)

typedef struct {
        ushort   nproj;              /* Number of active projects */
        time_t   start;              /* Time log was started */
        struct shmproj {
```

```
                char      name[16];        /* Account identifier */
                time_t    total;           /* Cumulative seconds */
                time_t    start;           /* Start time */
        }         proj [MAXPRJ];           /* Table of active projects */
} SHMSEG;

extern void     perror();
extern void     exit();
extern time_t   time();
extern char     *shmat();
extern unsigned short  getuid();

int     semid;          /* Semaphore id */
int     shmid;          /* Shared-memory id */

struct sembuf
        seize = { 0, -1, 0 }    /* Seize the segment */
        relse = { 0, 1, 0 };    /* Release the segment */
```

The contents of the `shmcom.h` file are shown in the preceding listing. This header includes all the other headers needed by the time-accounting package; this avoids having to repeat the lengthy list of includes in every program. Of special importance are the `sys/ipc.h` and `sys/shm.h` headers, both of which must be present to work with the shared-memory facility.

The label SHMATFAIL is declared in the header to simplify checking for an error return from the `shmat` system call. As with most system calls, `shmat` returns a value of -1 on error. Because, however, the function is declared to return a value of type `pointer to character`, the -1 must be cast to this type when comparing it to the function's return value, hence its peculiar definition.

The function also defines the semaphore operations needed to lock (`seize`) and unlock (`relse`) the shared segment; this saves the trouble of defining these operations by hand in every application program.

The shmcs Command

The `shmcs` program, shown in the next listing, must be executed to initialize the time-logging facility.

```
/*
 * shmcs.c - Shared-memory Create Segment
 */

/*
This program, an experiment with shared-memory segments,
creates a segment for sharing. When created, it terminates,
leaving the segment in the system but unattached to anything.
```

A semaphore set is also created to be used in synchronizing
update access to the segment.

This program could be extended into a personal time-logging facility,
since the shared segment is unique per user-ID, and registers start
and stop times for up to 20 activities. A program run at logout time
could record the information in a disk file and destroy the segment.

```
*/
#include "shmcom.h"
/*****************************************************************/
/*      CRASH              Abandon setup
/*****************************************************************/

static void crash(msg)
char *msg;
{
        fprintf(stderr, "shmcs: ");
        perror(msg);
        semctl(semid, IPC_RMID);
        semctl(shmid, IPC_RMID);
        exit(12);
}


/*****************************************************************/
/*      MAIN              Initializes the segment & semaphores
/*****************************************************************/

main()
{
        key_t     key;          /* object key to use */
        ushort    uid;          /* Real user-ID */
        SHMSEG   *base;         /* Ptr to active shm segment */

        uid = getuid();
        key = (key_t)(L_KEY | uid);
        if ((semid = semget(key, 1, CREATE)) == ERROR)
                crash("semcreate");
        if ((shmid = shmget(key, sizeof(*base), CREATE)) == ERROR)
                crash("shmcreate");

        /* Attach the segment and initialize it */

        base = (SHMSEG *) shmat(shmid, (char *)NULL, 0);
        if (base == (SHMSEG *)SHMATFAIL)
```

```
                crash("shmat");
        base->nproj = 0;
        time(&base->start);

        /* Release the facilities and exit */

        fprintf(stderr, "shmcs: no projects active\n");
        if (semop(semid, &relse, 1) == ERROR)
                crash("semop");
        if (shmdt((char *)base) == ERROR)
                crash("shmdt");
        return 0;

}
```

The program begins by calculating the IPC key value that will be used to identify the shared-memory segment. I intend to use a distinct segment for each user of the facility in the system, although only one such segment will exist for a given user no matter how many times he may be logged in. It therefore seems only logical to use the user-ID as part of the IPC key. To form the key, this routine sets the high-order bits to the application code 0x7400 (a purely arbitrary number), and the low-order bits to the user-ID.

This key is then used in a `shmget` call to attempt to create the shared-memory segment. The symbol CREATE is defined in the header file to set both the IPC_CREAT and IPC_EXCL flags; thus, if the segment is already known to the system, the create will fail. The user will need to execute the `shmcs` program only once; other login sessions can use the segment that is already set up.

The locking semaphore is also created at this time, because the segment cannot be used without it. Notice that the same IPC key is used for the semaphore as for the shared-memory segment; this is valid, and results in one semaphore per application user (and per shared segment) regardless of the number of times the user is logged in.

The semaphore is automatically initialized with a semaphore value of 0 when it is created. We will use the convention that a semaphore value of 0 corresponds to the locked state, and a value of 1 corresponds to an unlocked condition. Happily, this means that the semaphore already indicates that the segment is in use when we create it.

The program next attaches the newly created segment by calling `shmat`. Note that creating the segment with `shmget` does not automatically attach it, so we must do that in a separate step in order to initialize its contents. The code properly checks the return value from shmat for equality with the SHMATFAIL value. Note that, because the return value of shmat (a pointer to the first byte of the newly attached segment) has already been cast to the type pointer to SHMSEG, we must cast the SHMATFAIL value to that type also.

After initializing the segment to indicate that no project entries are currently defined, and saving the time at which the project record starts, the program finishes by detaching the segment and releasing the lock semaphore. The relse operation increments the semaphore to a value of 1, indicating that another process can now use the segment.

The shmset Command

shmset is the main program in the facility. Its purpose is to start or stop recording time against specific projects. The program shown allows project names to be up to 15 characters in length and does not verify the user-specified name against any list of valid projects. You can therefore specify any desired project name on the command line.

```
/*
shmset.c - Shared-memory segment operations

Command format is:

shmset project on
shmset project off

The project code is expected to be 1-15 characters. If the function
is 'on' and the project is not listed in the project table,
the project is added and the start time is noted, otherwise
a new timing interval is started.

If the function is 'off' and the project is not listed in the table,
an error message is given, otherwise the cumulative time is updated,
and the project is marked off.

*/

#include "shmcom.h"

main(argc, argv)
int     argc; char *argv[];
{
        key_t  key;
        ushort uid;
        int    n, hrs, min, sec;
        time_t now;
        struct shmproj *proj;
        SHMSEG *base;
```

```
/* Check the operands */
if (argc != 3 || (strcmp(argv[2],"on") && strcmp(argv[2],"off")))
{
        /* Invalid arguments, give usage */
        fprintf(stderr, "Usage: %s <project> on|off\n", *argv);
        exit(1);
}

/* Connect the user logging table */

uid = getuid();
key = (key_t)(L_KEY | uid);
if ((semid = semget(key,1,0)) == ERROR) {
        fprintf(stderr, "shmstat: can't attach semaphores\n");
        exit(errno);
}
if ((shmid = shmget(key,sizeof(*base),0)) == ERROR) {
        fprintf(stderr, "shmstat: can't attach segment\n");
        exit(errno);
}

/* Reserve the resource */
base = (SHMSEG *) shmat(shmid, (char *)NULL, 0);
if (base == (SHMSEG *)SHMATFAIL) {
        fprintf(stderr, "%s: no table, run shmcs\n", *argv);
        exit(errno);
}
if (semop(semid, &seize, 1)) {
        fprintf(stderr, "%s: seize failed\n", *argv);
        exit(errno);
}

/* Locate the project-id in the table */
n = base->nproj;
for (proj = base->proj; n--; proj++)
        if (strcmp(argv[1],proj->name) == 0)
                break;

/* set a project 'on' */
if (strcmp(argv[[2],"on") == 0) {
        if (n < 0) { /* New project code */
                base->nproj++;
                strcpy(proj->name, argv[1]);
                proj->total = 0;
                time(&proj->start);
                fprintf(stderr, "%s: started new\n", proj->name);
```

```
        } else if (proj->start)
                fprintf(stderr, "%s: already on\n", proj->name);
        else { /* Start new interval */
                time(&proj->start);
                fprintf(stderr, "%s: started\n", proj->name);
        }
}
/* set a project 'off' */
else if (strcmp(argv[[2],"off") == 0) {
        if (n < 0) /* No such project code */
                fprintf(stderr, "%s: invalid project code\n",
                        argv[1]);
        else {  /* Update the cumulative time */
                time(&now);
                proj->total += (now - proj->start);
                proj->start = 0;
                hrs = proj->total / 3600;
                min = proj->total % 3600;
                sec = min % 60;
                min /= 60;
                fprintf(stderr,
                    "%s off: time: %d hrs, %d min, %d sec\n",
                    proj->name, hrs, min, sec);
        }
}
/* Finished, release the resources */
if (semop(semid, &relse, 1))
        perror("semop-relse");
return OK;
}
```

This program must begin with the same steps as the shmcs program, first by calculating the IPC key value. The semaphore and shared segment are located next with the semget and shmget functions, but this time the calls use a flag of 0 rather than (IPC_CREAT ¦ IPC_EXCL), because the segment should already exist and you only want to connect to them. Next, the shared segment is attached. Finally, the semop call is used to lock the segment against modification by other processes while your process is working with it. If the semaphore is already in the locked state, locking it again results in an attempt to decrement a semaphore value of 0, forcing your process to wait until the other process releases the segment and the lock.

The program then updates the project table according to the command-line values and logs a message to document the action taken. Notice how much easier this is than updating a project file would be, and how simply the interlock against simultaneous update by other processes is arranged. This simplicity and ease is the hallmark of applications that are well suited to the use of IPC facilities, shared-memory segments in particular.

After updating the project table, the program then releases the lock on the segment, detaches the segment, and exits. The detach operation (shmdt) is not strictly necessary because it would be performed automatically when the program exits (a segment cannot be attached to a nonexistent process!), but I have coded the operation here to illustrate its use.

The semaphore operation is absolutely necessary, however. There is nothing about exiting the program to imply that the system should change the value of the semaphore, and in fact, no such automatic unlocking would occur on exit. Omission of the release operation would therefore leave the segment in the locked state with no process to unlock it, and the application would become inoperative. (We have left one way out of this, namely to execute the shmkill utility program to kill the entire subsystem. The user could then start over with shmcs.)

The shmstat Command

The shmstat command displays the status of the shared segment, as well as the on/off status of each project, and is useful for inquiring about the project time that has been recorded and for diagnosing problems with the application.

```
/*
shmstat.c - Shared-memory status

This utility displays the current shmid_ds values for the
current user.
*/

#include "shmcom.h"

main(argc, argv)
int     argc;
char    *argv[];
{
        key_t   key;
        ushort  uid;
        SHMSEG  *base;
        int     n;
        int     hrs, min, sec;
        time_t  now, total;
        struct shmproj *proj;
        struct shmid_ds stat;
```

```
uid = getuid();
key = (key_t)(L_KEY | uid);
if ((semid = semget(key,1,0)) == ERROR) {
        fprintf(stderr, "shmstat: can't attach semaphores\n");
        exit(errno);
}
if ((shmid = shmget(key,sizeof(*base),0)) == ERROR) {
        fprintf(stderr, "shmstat: can't attach segment\n");
        exit(errno);
}
if (shmctl(shmid,IPC_STAT, &stat)) {
        fprintf(stderr, "shmstat: shmctl failed\n");
        exit(errno);
}

printf("shared-memory segment status:\n");
printf("\tkey=%#lx, shmid=%d, seq=%d\n",
    stat.shm_perm.key, shmid, stat.shm_perm.seq);
printf("\tmode=%#o cuid=%d, cgid=%d, uid=%d, gid=%d\n",
    stat.shm_perm.mode,
    stat.shm_perm.cuid, stat.shm_perm.cgid,
    stat.shm_perm.uid, stat.shm_perm.gid);
printf("\tseg size=%u, nattch=%u, cnattch=%u\n",
    stat.shm_segsz, stat.shm_nattch, stat.shm_cnattch);
printf("\tcreator pid=%u, last shmop pid=%u\n",
    stat.shm_cpid, stat.shm_lpid);
printf("\tlast shmat  at %s", ctime(&stat.shm_atime));
printf("\tlast shmdt  at %s", ctime(&stat.shm_dtime));
printf("\tlast shmctl at %s", ctime(&stat.shm_ctime));

/* Reserve the resource */
base = (SHMSEG *) shmat(shmid, (char *)NULL, 0);
if (base == (SHMSEG *)SHMATFAIL) {
        fprintf(stderr, "%s: no table, run shmcs\n", *argv);
        exit(errno);
}
if (semop(semid, &seize, 1)) {
        fprintf(stderr, "%s: seize failed\n", *argv);
        exit(errno);
}

if (base->nproj) {
        time(&now);
        printf("\nproject status:\n");
        n = base->nproj;
        for (proj = base->proj; n--; proj++) {
                total = proj->total;
                if (proj->start)
                        total += (now - proj->start);
```

```
                    hrs = total / 3600;
                    min = total % 3600;
                    sec = min % 60;
                    min /= 60;
                    printf("\t%-15s  %3s  %2dh %2dm %2ds\n",
                        proj->name,
                        proj->start ? "on" : "off",
                        hrs, min, sec);
            }
    } else
            printf("\nno projects active.\n");

/* Release the resource */
if (semop(semid, &relse, 1))
        perror("semop-relse");

return OK;
}
```

The key operation in this program is the call to shmctl with the IPC_STAT argument. This causes the current values in the shmid_ds structure to be copied from kernel memory into the program's buffer.

The program also locks the shared segment while displaying the contents of the project table. This is not absolutely necessary. I do so here mainly to remind you that even read-only accesses can be disturbed by interference from other processes. The effects of simultaneous update could be seen by the user if a relationship normally exists between the data elements displayed: Incomplete update to some values by another process might cause the normal data relationships to appear to be violated in the output report. The locking performed here is more a matter of good practice than strict necessity.

The shmkill Command

The shmkill command executes the IPC_RMID function to destroy the shared segment. It can be executed whenever the facility is no longer required. In a complete application, this program would be called by a logout shell to record the accumulated times in a permanent file.

```
/*
shmkill.c - Shared-memory segment terminate

This utility destroys the shared-memory segment.
*/

#include "shmcom.h"

main()
{
```

```
key_t    key;
ushort   uid;
int      rc1, rc2;
SHMSEG   *base;

uid = getuid();
key = (key_t)(L_KEY | uid);
if ((semid = semget(key,1,0)) == ERROR) {
        fprintf(stderr, "shmkill: can't attach semaphores\n");
        exit(errno);
}
if ((shmid = shmget(key,sizeof(*base),0)) == ERROR) {
        fprintf(stderr, "shmkill: can't attach segment\n");
        exit(errno);
}

/* Destroy the segment */
if (rc1 = shmctl(shmid, IPC_RMID))
        perror("shmctl(IPC_RMID)");
if (rc2 = semctl(semid, 0, IPC_RMID))
        perror("semctl(IPC_RMID)");

return ((rc1 == OK && rc2 == OK) ? OK : 5);
}
```

The IPC tools are designed to support one another. Not coincidentally, you have had occasion to combine semaphores with both the message queueing application and the shared-memory segments. You might expect to find applications in which all three facilities can be combined in a single application. Often, problems solved with IPC tools are difficult, awkward, or even impossible to solve with other methods. You are therefore well advised to write some exercises of your own, or improve and extend those I have shown, until you feel comfortable working with the IPC functions. In the long run, I am sure you will find a knowledge of the IPC functions to be an important and useful addition to your UNIX programming skills.

Summary

Signals, involving asynchronous program events as they do, may be a new concept to you. The UNIX implementation of signals is fairly generalized, allowing your programs to use signals in many different ways. One of the most common and straightforward uses of signals is to perform cleanup actions and then to terminate your process. If you do not catch the signals, your program will be terminated anyway, so you might as well call exit, but before you do, you can close files, remove work files, and release system resources (such as IPC objects) before exiting.

Interprocess communications is a much more difficult subject to understand than signal handling, because it offers powerful, general purpose mechanisms for exchanging data between unrelated processes, and the way to use IPC calls depends largely on what you want to do. This chapter described the three kinds of IPC objects: message queues, semaphore sets, and shared-memory segments.

IPC message queues provide a mechanism for sending packets of data to another process. The size of a message should be fairly small, to avoid filling the system's message buffers. For this reason, message queues are not well suited to the exchange of large amounts of data, such as might occur in an implementation of a database server. Message queues are an appropriate way to transmit service requests to a server process, however, and this chapter discussed an example of such a server.

The IPC implementation of semaphores provides counting semaphores, which allow for the construction of several types of useful program objects including locks, resource allocation queues, and post/wait events. The operating system support for semaphores guarantees that an operation on a semaphore occurs all at once as seen by other processes, thus assuring that simultaneous access to a semaphore by two processes does not yield unpredictable results.

The third IPC facility, shared-memory segments, allows an area of memory to be established that is shared in common between two or more processes. The processes can then communicate with each other by exchanging data in the common area. A shared segment can be quite large, making it possible to efficiently pass very large amounts of data between the processes. Shared-memory segments are the preferred basis for implementation of database managers for UNIX. Because shared memory by itself provides no means for interlocking accesses to a common storage area, applications using shared memory often use IPC semaphores to coordinate memory updates.

All three IPC facilities associate a *key* with a message queue, semaphore set, or shared-memory segment. The key serves as an identifier, naming the object so that unrelated processes can reference it. The key is assigned by the process that creates an object. A process that wants to use an existing object must supply the key naming the object. Care must be taken when choosing a key value so that unrelated applications do not use the same key values. The ftok library function provides a means for assigning unique but guessable key values to IPC objects.

There are potential difficulties you must overcome when using any of the IPC objects. Message queues can become full, potentially causing an unending wait between processes sharing the message queue. Semaphores can be incremented or decremented by a process, indicating a reservation of some resource, and then terminate abnormally without releasing the resource, leaving the resource permanently unavailable. Only a limited number of shared memory segments can be created, and simultaneous accesses to a common area of a segment must be controlled with a separate facility, such as semaphores, to avoid destructive updates to data in memory.

There are solutions to all these problems, but first you must know that a problem exists before you can solve it. If you find some of the material in this chapter difficult to follow, try writing the sample application yourself, without looking at the solution given in the book. Carefully check your work against the specifications of the IPC functions in the "C Library Functions" reference section in this book, or the *UNIX Programmer's Reference Manual* for your system. Test your program carefully, and as you find problems, reread the pertinent text in this chapter. Gradually you should find the issues addressed becoming clearer in your mind. You have to actually use an IPC facility to fully understand how it works.

15

Writing Multiprocessing Programs

This chapter discusses some of the more exotic aspects of UNIX. Our subject is multiprocessing—performing a single logical task using more than one execution thread.

You're already familiar with the concept of a subroutine. The equivalent multiprocessing concept is that of a *coroutine* (as in co-routine). At its simplest, coroutines are routines which call each other; they share the work to be done in roughly equal proportions. A number of UNIX data structures support the development of coroutines, named pipes being a prime example.

The *daemon* is a special kind of coroutine. There is usually only one instance of a particular daemon process in the system, and its function typically involves the management of a global system resource. Familiar examples of daemon processes include the time-based scheduling facility called cron, and the printer spooler lp. There is nothing inherently difficult about implementing daemons.

This chapter rounds out the discussion of files, processes, and system administration topics that you have been wading through for the past six chapters. We will put to work in this chapter many of the concepts previously presented. If you have been skipping around in your reading, this is probably not a good time for you to read this chapter. Make sure you are comfortable with the material presented in Chapter 13, "Kernel Internals," before reading on.

Coroutines

A coroutine cannot exist by itself. Its very nature is to cooperate as an equal partner in some task or job. Execution tends to alternate between cooperating coroutines, with the flow of control proceeding first in one of the routines, then continuing in the other, then switching back to the first again. The proportion of execution time between the two routines is not important; rather, it is the sense of sharing the workload that distinguishes coroutines from the more familiar caller/callee relationship of subroutines.

A *pipeline* provides a good example of coroutines at work. Consider the simple command,

```
sort myfile | pg
```

Which of these would you say is the main program? Certainly sort is doing the more important work, because its actions determine what is displayed. On the other hand, the primary user interaction occurs with the pg command as you use it to scroll forward and back through the output of sort. Both commands share equal responsibility for the work performed. Surely we would be wrong to imply that either one is a subroutine of the other—both programs have a equal status, and either one could be executed without the other.

One important use of coroutines in application development is to overcome implicit waiting. An implicit wait, to put it simply, is a wait that you didn't ask for. There are a number of situations in which the C programmer might choose to wait for the completion of an action, or to continue execution now and check for completion later. Examples are writing a record to a pipe, adding a message to an IPC message queue, and invoking a child process. I/O requests, though, are *blocking* requests; they cause the program requesting the I/O to wait for its completion before control returns to the program. This waiting is built in to the read and write calls, and is therefore also an integral part of the stream I/O operations printf, getchar, fread, and others.

Implicit waiting is detrimental to the performance of an individual program, but advantageous to the system as a whole.

The operating system prefers implicit waiting because it simplifies the design of the kernel, and it encourages the user to write programs that are easily overlapped with the execution of other programs. This latter reason is particularly important to a time-sharing system, because if all programs tended to be runnable all the time, the switching from process to process that gives the appearance of multiple simultaneous program executions would be destroyed. The UNIX operating system therefore *biases* program design toward having all those little windows of idle time in user programs.

A prime example of the hurtfulness of implicit waiting arises in a typical chore: making backup copies of the system disks. Consider a program that first reads a record from the disk, then writes it to the output magnetic tape. The program must wait while the disk record is read in, and then wait again while the record is being written out. On the other hand, the machine is quite capable of sustaining simultaneous I/O to both the disk and the tape. If the backup program could *buffer* disk records in memory, in effect reading ahead so that at least one output buffer is always full, then a record would always be available to be written to the tape drive whenever it finishes with the previous write. The tape drive would tend to run at top speed, and the backup chore would finish sooner. Because system backups are often performed in single-user mode, this would mean either that users could get back on the system more quickly, or that the night operator could go home sooner.

So, how does one overcome the implicit waiting built in to the I/O system calls? By using coroutines. In our daily backup example, the utility program should execute as two processes: one reading records from disk, and the other writing records to tape. The tape output process could then proceed at full speed, even when the disk input process is waiting for an input record. The two processes would act as coroutines, each performing half the job.

Let's try to develop a backup program that uses coroutines to overlap disk reading and tape writing.

It takes only one f o r k system call to split a process into two processes, so the basic mechanism for creating coroutines is available. A problem we'll have to overcome, however, is finding some way to pass data between the two processes. You'll remember from the discussion of memory management in Chapter 13 that the address spaces of different processes are completely separate, so we have to find a way to allow the tape output process to retrieve data from the disk input process data buffers.

There are at least two methods to do this.

One way is to use a pipe to transport data between the input process and the output process. A disadvantage of pipes is that the system must first copy data *into* the pipe when a record is written to it, and then copy it back *out* when it is read. Both copying steps are wasteful, because the tape output routine could just as well write directly from the disk input buffer.

Another problem could arise if tape output blocks are very large. If the size of tape blocks approaches or exceeds the size of the system's pipe buffer, the disk input process will never be allowed the chance to get significantly ahead of the tape drive. Instead, it will race to fill the pipe, then wait while the tape output process drains the entire pipe, then race to fill the pipe again when it is suddenly drained.

This problem with "bursty" tape I/O can be remedied by setting the O_NDELAY flag in the file descriptor for the output side of the pipe which is read by the tape process. The disk process can then be programmed to store input data in its own buffers when the pipe buffer is full. Even if the entire pipe is drained by a single read from the tape output process, it can be quickly refilled from the private disk input buffers.

When tape output occurs in 512-byte or 1024-byte blocks (not unusual for many UNIX implementations), the interprocess pipe serves well as a speed-matching buffer. The disk input process can then read ahead of the tape drive, and the tape output process will always, or almost always, find data in the pipe ready to be written.

Ultimately, you the programmer have to decide whether to let the pipe perform all the buffering between the read and write processes, or to set O_NDELAY and use extra private buffers in the disk input process. If the program is intended for use on a single system or type of system, you can adapt the program to the particular disk and tape block sizes of that system. If the program is intended for wider distribution, however, the extra buffering should be included in the program design to guarantee good performance in any environment.

There is another way to pass data between the disk input and tape output processes: a shared-memory segment can be set up between the two. Both of the problems that can occur with interprocess pipes can be avoided when using shared-memory segments. Data need not be copied twice on the way from the input process to the output process, because the shared-memory segment is simultaneously accessible to both processes. Output blocks can be read directly into the shared-memory segment, and they can be written directly from it as well. The problem with burst tape I/O is also avoidable by using a large shared segment which can contain two or more tape buffers. Each buffer should be at least as large as a tape block.

The use of shared memory gives rise to different technical difficulties.

The main problem with the use of shared memory is synchronization. It would not do to have the tape output process writing from shared buffers which haven't been filled yet, or which are currently being filled by the disk input process. Neither must the disk input process disturb a buffer currently being written out by the tape process. We must arrange some method whereby the buffers in the shared segment are *locked* for the exclusive use of one or the other of the two processes. Fortunately, this is not difficult. We don't even have to resort to IPC semaphores.

Let us suppose that the program always keeps five I/O buffers in the shared-memory segment. A lock will also be associated with each buffer in the segment, consisting of two integers, or *lock words*. One of the lock words will be set to a nonzero value when the disk input process is using the corresponding buffer, and the other lock word will be nonzero when the tape output process is using it.

Either process can then *acquire* the buffer (to fill or to drain) by using the following algorithm:

```
get-buffer:
     set lock[me] = 1;
     while (lock[other] != 0) ;
     return &buffer;

free-buffer:
     set lock[me] = 0;
     return;
```

This semaphore scheme works without kernel supervision because:

❏ Each process sets only its own lock word, and tests only the other's lock word, so no possibility exists that both processes will try to update the same memory location at the same time

❏ The size of a lock word is equal to a machine unit of storage, so no possibility exists that a lock word can be seen by a process when it has been only partially updated.

The algorithm shown uses *busy waiting*, a simple loop that tests the lock word repeatedly until its value changes. This will probably be acceptable for a backup utility to do, because it is likely to be the only program running in the system at the time. But busy waiting will not be acceptable for all applications of coroutines.

To avoid busy waiting, try the following technique: When a lock is found to be owned by the other process, put the process that wants the lock to sleep by calling the `pause` function. When releasing a resource (in our example, a buffer), notify the coroutine by sending a signal to wake it up. The algorithm would be modified as follows:

```
null-trap:
     signal(SIGUSR1, null-trap);
     return;

get-buffer:
     signal(SIGUSR1,null-trap);
     set lock[me] = 1;
     while (lock[other] != 0) pause();
     return &buffer;

free-buffer:
     set lock[me] = 0;
     kill(other-pid, SIGUSR1);
     return;
```

Two notes about this changed algorithm. First, the `signal` call shown in `get-buffer` need not be executed every time `get-buffer` is called; it is sufficient to call `signal` once during program initialization. I show the call to `signal` here to remind you that it must be called somewhere. Second, the two processes have to arrange some way to tell each other their respective process-ID values. This could be done by storing the two PID values somewhere in the shared segment, along with the lock words and buffers. In the algorithm pseudo-code, I have written *otherpid* where the PID of the other process should be used.

Also, note that one of the processes should use the value *0* for *me* and *1* for *other*, whereas the values should be reversed for the other process.

I will now show you a sample implementation of the backup utility using a shared-memory segment as the data transport mechanism.

```
/* bu - a Tape Backup Utility using Coroutines */

#include <stdio.h>
#include <errno.h>
#include <fcntl.h>
#include <signal.h>
#include <memory.h>
#include <sys/types.h>
#include <sys/ipc.h>
#include <sys/shm.h>

#define STDIN   0               /* Standard input file
descriptor */
#define STDOUT  1               /* Standard output file
descriptor */
#define ERROR   (-1)            /* Error return value */
#define SHMATFAIL ((BPOOL *)ERROR)

#define RDR     0               /* ID of disk reader process */
#define WTR     1               /* ID of tape writer process */
#define NBUFS   10              /* Num of buffers per segment */

extern void    perror(), exit();
extern char*   shmat();
```

This listing shows a typical set of preliminary definitions. The number of header files needed is increased by the use of IPC facilities, but is large primarily because of the number of different types of system services being used.

The definitions for STDIN and STDOUT are present because the program will use low-level I/O and will need to refer to the file descriptor numbers for these files. The terms `stdin` and `stdout` refer to the stream files for standard input and standard output, and hence cannot be used as file descriptor numbers.

The definitions for RDR and WTR set up some internal identifiers for referring easily to the disk input reader and the tape output writer processes; they are present as a matter of convenience.

The definition for NBUFS is particularly important. It will be used to determine the number of block transfer buffers defined in the shared segment. A value that is too small will give poor performance, whereas too large a value will waste memory. The value for NBUFS given here worked well in my tests, but some other value might be optimal for you. A reasonable alternative design might accept the NBUFS value as a command-line parameter or look for it as an environment variable. I chose to use a `#define` declarative to keep the program simple.

Each buffer in the shared segment looks like this:

```
/* DECLARE A SHARED SEGMENT BUFFER */

typedef struct {
        int     owner;          /* ID of buffer owner */
        int     nbytes;         /* Number of bytes in buffer */
        char    data[BUFSIZ];   /*  The buffer itself */
} BUFFER;
```

Each buffer contains an identifier of the process currently using the buffer, the number of data characters actually in the buffer, and space for BUFSIZ characters. (The symbolic value BUFSIZ is defined in the `stdio.h` header file.)

The `owner` field will always contain a value of RDR or WTR. When its value is RDR, the buffer is currently owned by the disk input process, and is either empty or only partially filled with data. When the disk input process has filled the buffer, it will change the value of `owner` to WTR, allowing the tape output process to access the buffer. The disk input process will not regain control of the buffer until the output process has completely written its contents to the tape and changed the value of `owner` back to RDR.

This method of synchronizing access to the buffer is safe, because only the process that currently owns the buffer will attempt to change the value of the `owner` field.

The shared-memory segment is described by the following declaration:

```
typedef struct {
    int     pid[2];       /* Pid of me & other */
    BUFFER  iobuf[NBUFS];    /* Buffers with locks */
} BPOOL;
```

Notice that this `typedef` statement describes the sharedmemory segment but allocates no space for it. The space is allocated by the `shmget` system call because the segment will actually reside in kernel memory. Access to the segment is later acquired by the shmat call when the segment is installed at an address in the process address space.

Besides the buffers themselves, the only additional information I have chosen to keep in the shared-memory segment is the process-ID's for the RDR and WTR processes. By storing these PID values here, it is easier to write general routines for acquiring and releasing buffers. The array of PID values is intended to be indexed with the RDR and WTR values used as generic identifiers for the disk input and tape output processes.

```
BPOOL      *bpool;     /* Pointer to shared segment */
int   me;              /* My process flag (0 or 1) */
int   other;`          /* Process flag of 'other'*/
int   bufwaits;        /* Num of buffer waits */

void rinput();         /* Input reader process */
BUFFER *getbuf();      /* Allocate an I/O buffer */
int   relbuf();        /* Release an I/O buffer */
```

The example presents the few global variables needed by the program. The bpool variable will contain the address of the shared-memory segment. By setting this variable before calling fork to create the disk input process, it will be defined for both processes. This is because fork duplicates the active process address space when creating the new process.

The me, other, and bufwaits variables, although global, will contain values unique to each process. Because the two process address spaces are actually distinct, different values can be carried in these fields for each process even though they are declared only once in the program.

This completes the definitions and declarations for the program. The first procedural sections to be written will be the signal catching routine trap, which is used to prevent the input and output processes from being killed by a signal, and the main function.

```
/*
**      trap
**              Signal catcher. Ignores the signal, but wakes up
**              a pause() call anyway.
*/
void trap()
{
/* Restore the trap */ signal(SIGUSR1, trap);
}
```

The program will use a SIGUSR1 signal to wake up a process that is waiting for a buffer. The trap routine is needed to allow the use of signals for that purpose. Setting a signal action to trap is very similar to setting it to SIG_IGN, except that an ignored signal will not terminate a call to pause, whereas a signal handled by a user-written function will cause pause to return.

Now let's look at the program's `main` function.

```
/*
**    main
**         Initializes the program, then acts as the output
**         writer process.
*/
main(argc,argv)
int argc;
char *argv[];
{
    int   shmid,      /* ID of shared segment */
          nb,         /* Num of bytes returned by read */
          bnum = 0;   /* Current buffer index */
    BUFFER  *buf;     /* Ptr to current buffer */

    if (argc < 2) {
        fprintf(stderr, "usage: %s filenames\n", *argv);
        exit(1);
        }

    /* Initialize the shared-memory segment */
    shmid = shmget(IPC_PRIVATE, sizeof(BPOOL),
            (IPC_CREAT | 0600));
    if (shmid == ERROR)
        perror("shmget"), exit(1);
    if ((bpool = (BPOOL *)shmat(shmid, NULL, 0)) == SHMATFAIL)
        perror("shmat"), exit(1);

    /* Start the input reader process */

    signal(SIGUSR1, trap);
        /*
        ** If set up before the fork in rinput, the trap
        ** is automatically defined for both processes. */
    me = WTR;
    other = RDR;
    bpool->pid[me] = getpid();
    rinput(argv + 1);

    while ((buf = getbuf(bnum)) != NULL)
    {
        if ((nb = write(STDOUT, buf->data, BUFSIZ)) != BUFSIZ)
        {
            if (nb == ERROR && errno == EINTR)
                continue; /* Just try again */
            fprintf(stderr, "write error %d (nb=%d)\n",
                errno, nb);
            exit(3);
        }
```

```
        bnum = relbuf(buf);
    }
    close(STDOUT);

    /* Discard the shared-memory segment */

    shmctl(shmid, IPC_RMID);

    /* Retrieve the zombie rinput exit status */

    for (;;)
    {
        if (wait((int *)NULL) == ERROR)
        {
            if (errno == ECHILD)
                /* No more children, stop waiting */ break;
            if (errno != EINTR)
                /* Document unexpected error,
                but keep waiting! */
                perror("wait");
        }
    }
    fprintf(stderr, "WTR: bufwaits = %d\n", bufwaits);
    return 0;
}
```

Although there is a fair amount of code in this function, main has a straightforward design.

It begins by checking that the command line names at least one file to be copied (*argc* > 1). The program would be simpler to use if the list of files to be copied were read from standard input, giving it an external interface similar to the cpio command. If you're interested in developing this program further, you might modify it to read pathnames from standard input, or to use ftw so that it will automatically copy all the files in the named directories, as does tar. The approach shown here was chosen merely for its simplicity.

The most important initialization step is the creation of the shared-memory segment that will be shared between the program's input process and its output process. This step is performed by calling shmget and then shmat. (See Chapter 14 for a discussion of these calls.) Notice that a key of IPC_PRIVATE is used. This is acceptable (in fact desirable) because the segment will be used only by the main process and its child, and there is no need to define a key by which other processes can identify the segment.

Once initialization is complete, the rinput function is called to actually create the disk input process. It will call fork, causing program execution to split into two separate paths. One path, the child process, will continue execution in rinput, opening each of the filenames listed on the command line, reading each of the files and stuffing their contents into shared-memory buffers as fast as possible. The other path, the parent process, will return to the caller (main) and begin writing shared-memory buffers to standard output, which presumably has been redirected to the tape drive.

The remainder of the routine, the tape output process, consists of two parts. The first, a loop, successively acquires buffers in the shared memory segment and writes them out, going from one to the next until the end of the segment is reached, then starting over at the beginning. The input process is designed to fill buffers in the same order.

Terminating the loop is a bit tricky, because the tape output process (this routine) might have to write several buffers after the disk input process has already reached the end of the last input file and quit. The getbuf routine, which we will look at next, has been programmed to complain if the calling process attempts to acquire a buffer currently owned by the other process, but the other process is dead. Waiting for the buffer to become available in this case would be a mistake, because the other process, being dead, will never assign the buffer to the calling process. This condition can occur only if the input process has finished *and* the output process has drained all remaining buffers; it is therefore taken as the indication that tape output is finished and that the output loop should be abandoned.

The output process, which is eventually the only surviving process, concludes by retrieving the exit status of its child the disk input process, and finally exits.

Although the main and rinput functions perform the work of the program, the getbuf and relbuf routines are critical to successful use of the shared-memory segment as a data pathway between the two coroutines. Let's look at getbuf and relbuf next.

The getbuf and relbuf Routines

The getbuf and relbuf routines are designed to work very closely together. The getbuf routine is called whenever one of the processes needs a buffer to read into or write from. Rather than taking an active role in acquiring the buffer, it waits for the buffer in question to be assigned to the requesting process. The process making the request is always identified by the value of the global variable me, which is equal to RDR if called by rinput, or to WTR if called by main. If the value of the owner field for the buffer is equal to me, then getbuf returns its address to the caller. Otherwise it calls pause to wait for the buffer to become available. It is therefore expecting to receive some kind of signal when the buffer is assigned to the requesting task; this signal is issued by the relbuf function, which calls kill to send the SIGUSR1 signal whenever it changes the value of owner.

```
/*
**     getbuf
**          Reserve a buffer. Wait if it's in use.
*/
BUFFER *
getbuf(index)
{
     BUFFER  *buf;
     int  wcnt = 0;

     buf = bpool->iobuf + index;
     while (buf->owner != me)
     {
          if ( bpool->pid[other] == 0)
               /* The other process is dead: DONT WAIT! */
               return NULL;
          wcnt = 1;
          pause();
     }
     bufwaits += wcnt;
     return buf;
}
/*
**     relbuf
**          Release a buffer to the other process.
**          Sends a SIGUSR1 signal to 'other' in case he's
**          currently waiting for a buffer.
*/
int
relbuf(buf) BUFFER *buf;
{
     int  index, him;

     index = buf - bpool->iobuf;
     buf->owner = other;
     if (him = bpool->pid[other])
          kill(him, SIGUSR1);
     return (++index % NBUFS);
}
```

There is a catch to this basic scenario, for both `getbuf` and `relbuf`.

`getbuf` doesn't want to wait for the signal if the other process is dead, because such a signal will never arrive. It tests for this by examining the `pid` value in the shared segment for the other process. If this value is 0, `getbuf` assumes that the other process has given up the ghost, and returns a NULL pointer value instead of waiting for the buffer. This of course implies that when one of the two coroutine processes terminates, it must set its `pid` value in the shared segment to 0. But the output process executed by `main` will always be the last to terminate, so this responsibility is really being laid exclusively on the `rinput` routine.

On the other side of the coin, relbuf has to watch out for a 0 value in pid[other], because if it sends a signal using a 0 process-ID, kill will actually kill *all* of the active processes for the current user. This could result in the termination of other processes the user is running, for example, with the & shell operator. So, if pid[other] is 0, relbuf does nothing, assuming that there is no need to wake up a dead process.

The getbuf and relbuf routines also cooperate in another respect. Whereas getbuf requires a buffer *index* as its calling argument and returns a buffer *pointer*, the relbuf routine requires a buffer *pointer* as its argument and returns a buffer *index*. This is a little strange, but this has allowed me to embed the incrementation and wrapping of buffers in the buffer management routines. As a result, main and rinput themselves are totally unaware that the buffer pool in the shared segment is finite. relbuf automatically returns the buffer index of the next buffer in the pool, which is just the index needed by getbuf to acquire that buffer. This scheme works because both the input and output processes step from buffer to buffer sequentially.

The Disk Input Process

There is only one piece remaining to examine in the program: namely, the disk input process. The rinput routine which follows reads blocks of data from disk and stores the blocks in shared memory buffers.

```
/*
**    rinput
**        This is the disk input reader process. It reads data
**        into a buffer and when filled, moves on to the next
**        buffer. It waits only when there are are no empty
**        buffers.
*/
void
rinput(files) char *files[];
{
      char *filename;
      BUFFER  *buf;
      char *ioptr;
      int   bnum = 0;
      int   input, pid;
      int   nb, space;

      if ((pid = fork()) != 0) {
          /* In parent process ... */
          if (pid == ERROR)
              perror("fork"), exit(12);
          bpool->pid[RDR] = pid;
          return ;
          }
```

```
/* In disk input process ... */
me = RDR;
other = WTR;

buf = getbuf(bnum);
buf->nbytes = 0;
ioptr = buf->data;
space = BUFSIZ;

while (filename = *files++) {
    if ((input = open(filename,O_RDONLY)) < 0) {
        perror(filename);
        continue;
        }
    while ( nb = read(input, ioptr, space)) {
        if (nb == ERROR) {
            if (errno == EINTR)
                /* Just try again */
                continue;
            perror(filename);
            break;
            }
        ioptr += nb;
        buf->nbytes += nb;
        if ((space -= nb) == 0) {
            bnum = relbuf(buf);
            buf = getbuf(bnum);
            buf->nbytes = 0;
            ioptr = buf->data;
            space = BUFSIZ;
            memset(ioptr, 0, BUFSIZ);
            }
        }
    close(input);
    }
/* Finished */
bnum = relbuf(buf);
bpool->pid[me] = 0; /* Tell other I'm no longer working */
if (bpool->pid[other])
    kill(bpool->pid[other], SIGUSR1);
    /* In case he's waiting */
fprintf(stderr, "RDR: bufwaits = %d\n", bufwaits);
exit(0);
}
```

This function has two exits. The first, a return statement, occurs near the top of the program and is executed only by the parent process that originally called rinput. The second is the exit call at the end of the function; this is executed only by the child process that acts as the disk input coroutine. The disk input process is born and dies all in this one function.

`rinput` is passed the argument list originally given to `main` when the program began. `rinput` scans each argument in turn. It assumes that each argument is a filename. The file is opened and read. Each read stores data in the current shared-segment buffer. When a buffer is full, `rinput` calls `relbuf` to release the buffer, relinquishing it to the output process. `rinput` then acquires the next buffer, resets it to an empty condition, and begins filling it.

When the end of the last file is reached, `rinput` zeroes its `pid` value in the shared segment and exits. The tape output process must finish dumping out the buffers that still contain any data, and then the program is finished.

I have run this program on my system and it appears to work. I embedded a counting mechanism in `getbuf` to count the number of times the disk input process and the tape output process have to wait for an available buffer. Normally one would hope that the disk input process often has to wait, while the tape output process always finds a full buffer waiting and drives the output medium at its maximum speed. In practice, I found that this depends on the amount of disk fragmentation there is in the files to be dumped. Some models of tape drive are quite fast, especially when operated in streaming mode. On the other hand, a heavily fragmented disk file can require many seeks to read. I actually found some situations in which the disk input process never had to wait, while the tape output process waited frequently.

In either case, the program represents a significant improvement over the performance achieved by conventional implementations, because it always executes in the time needed to read the slowest medium.

Daemons

In UNIX terminology, a *daemon* is any process that runs as a child of `init`, has no associated control terminal, and does not die. A daemon exists to manage a global system resource, or to provide a service to all users. Common examples of daemons include:

❑ `lp`, which manages printers owned by the system on behalf of all users, scheduling user print jobs so that all users can share the printers in an orderly fashion

❑ `cron`, a component of the system that provides a mechanism for scheduling commands to be run at a specific date and time

❑ `getty`, a routine that watches a specific terminal or communications line for input, establishes the correct line speed and terminal settings for a login session, and initiates the login sequence.

Often, `getty` is not considered a daemon because, unlike most daemons, a particular `getty` is associated with a specific terminal. Nevertheless, the process that runs the `getty` is long-lived because, once a terminal is successfully connected, the process is transformed into the `login` routine by a call to `exec`, and then into the login shell by another call to `exec`. It is therefore the same process that eventually becomes associated with a user as his login shell.

I must emphasize that the purpose of a daemon is to perform a global service for the system. It is rarely connected in any permanent way with a specific user. An example of an application-oriented daemon would be the process that serves an IPC message queue. (See Chapter 13, "Kernel Internals.") In typical examples of IPC message queueing, the queue server provides some service that any number of user processes can request, such as accessing an application database. Although the database is related to a specific application, any number of users might choose to work with that application at any given time. By placing the database under the control of a daemon, it becomes a system resource that is potentially available to any user even though accesses to the database are serialized through a central server.

Another interesting application of daemons, not related to any specific application, is a *tape server*. This type of daemon is given ownership of all mountable devices in the system, such as tape drives and floppy disk drives. Any user may request that the daemon mount a specified volume on the device; the daemon in turn confirms that the request was issued by an authorized user, issues a message to the system operator to mount the named volume, automatically executes the `mount` command if necessary, and assigns ownership of the device to the requesting user. The daemon acts as a *scheduler*, allocating a scarce resource (devices, in this case) to users on demand.

Other examples of daemons include `tcp/ip` processes that provide a communications resource for users outside the system, responding to requests to send and receive mail, transfer files over communications lines, or execute programs and send the results back to the remote user. Daemons such as these do not provide services directly to any user of the system in which they run, and the global resource they manage is the system itself. They are, nevertheless, implemented as daemons because there is no specific logged-in user to perform the services; the daemons act as agents of the system. They must check for proper authority of the requester, and need superuser privileges to perform their services, just as if they were system call routines in the kernel.

As you can see, the range of applications for daemons is very broad and includes both system services and application-oriented operations. An understanding of methods for creating daemons and establishing their runtime environments is important for making full use of UNIX. As you will see, although daemon processes are fundamentally system objects and somewhat beyond the scope of most user programming objectives, they are easy to create and to program.

Creating Daemons with inittab

The objective in creating a daemon process is to arrange for the daemon to be a child of the `init` system process so that it can live forever, or at least as long as it wishes to live.

One way for a process to become a child of `init` is to be invoked by `init` itself with an appropriate command in the `/etc/inittab` script. This is the way the `getty` processes are created. There are a number of advantages to this approach:

❏ The daemon can be automatically initiated whenever a suitable system run mode is entered, such as the *multiuser* run mode

❏ `init` can be instructed to restart the daemon automatically if it should disappear for any reason

❏ This is the easiest way to get the daemon running with superuser privileges, a requirement for many applications of daemons (though by no means all).

To get a daemon running with this method, it is only necessary to add a line to the `/etc/inittab` script similar to the following:

```
dm:23:respawn:/usr/lib/prog < /dev/syscon > /dev/syscon 2>&1
```

The sample `inittab` line makes the following specifications:

1. This line of the inittab file is identified by the unique tag *dm*.

2. The daemon will be started when either system run mode *2* or *3* is entered, and killed when any other system run mode is entered.

3. If the daemon should exit for any reason, it will be started again immediately (*respawn*).

4. The program to be executed by the daemon is in the file `/usr/lib/prog`.

5. Any standard input requests from the daemon should be satisfied from the system console device `/dev/syscon`.

6. Standard output is written to the system console `/dev/syscon`.

7. Standard error output is to be written to the same location as standard output.

Notice that the sample `inittab` line shown previously explicitly names the files to be used for standard input, standard output, and standard error. This is required because `init` does not establish a default for these files. Any file not explicitly provided by a redirection is simply not open. Note that this differs from the environment established by `/bin/login`, which establishes the login terminal as the default location for the standard input, standard output, and standard error files. It also differs from the environment created by `cron`, which arranges to mail standard output and standard error lines to the user. `init` is a much more basic system service; for any process it might start, it has no idea what an appropriate destination for these files would be, so by default it assigns none.

A process initiated by `init` has only a skeletal environment in other ways as well. The real and effective user-ID of the process is 0, which gives the process superuser capabilities. The real and effective group-ID is also 0, although no special privileges are associated with that group. The current working directory is the root directory /, because that is the effective current directory of `init`. The environment consists of only the one variable, as follows:

```
PATH=/bin:/usr/bin:/etc
```

Note that some versions of the system might include only a subset of these search directories, or define them in a different search order. The other variables normally set up by login, including $LOGNAME, $HOME, and $MAIL, are not defined.

Just as you must assume responsibility for specifying the standard input, standard output, and standard error files to be used by the daemon, you must also use `chdir` to specify the desired working directory if it is not to be the root directory, and you must define any desired environment variables.

You might be getting the impression that a daemon must be a binary executable C program. This is not the case. The program executed by a daemon can be written in any desired programming language; it can even be written as a shell script.

`init` executes the command field of the line by the equivalent of issuing the command,

```
/bin/sh -c "exec $command"
```

so the `sh` shell is always invoked first. This results in the substitution of variable names and the redirection of files using normal shell facilities. Because of the presence of the `exec` shell command, the shell itself is usually replaced by the command program. If the program to be invoked is a shell script, however, `exec` will cause the shell to be reloaded in order to execute the script. The shell is then the primary program executed by the daemon, but its behavior is governed by the shell script, as you would expect.

Creating Daemons with fork

The other method to create a daemon is based on the fact that, whenever the parent of a process exits or is terminated, any surviving child processes are automatically attached to the init system process so that it is their new parent process. This action is taken by the kernel's process management routines because the death of a parent process does not require the death of its child processes. (If the parent is a process group leader, the SIGHUP signal is propagated to all its direct and indirect children, but the signal can be ignored. No SIGHUP signal is generated at all if the parent process is not a process group leader.) The operating system design requires that every process must have a parent process, hence the rather arbitrary rule of assigning init as the new parent.

It is possible to create a daemon process by accident, if a user process creates a number of child processes and is then terminated accidentally and no arrangement is made for killing the child processes. Such *orphan* processes (so called because their parent has died) are usually a problem because they were never designed to act as daemons, do not function properly or at all in this state, and end up just wasting space in the kernel's process table. But this is exactly the method you will want to use to create some kinds of daemons. The lp and cron daemons are initiated in just this manner. In a nutshell, the procedure is as follows:

1. A main program is started in a process simply by invoking the program as a command, or by calling it with the exec system call. The lp daemon is started by the /usr/lib/lpsched program, and the cron daemon is started by the /etc/cron program, both of which are normally invoked as commands in the system start-up procedures.

2. The main program calls fork to create a child process. This child process will eventually become the daemon.

3. The parent and child processes perform any initialization required to establish the run environment for the daemon.

4. The parent process then calls exit, turning the child process into an orphan that the kernel attaches to init as the foster parent.

5. The child process (now a daemon) usually issues the setpgrp system call at this point to divorce itself from the control terminal from which it was invoked, thus insulating it from any

subsequent SIGINT and SIGQUIT signals that might be generated by the user at that terminal.

The initial environment of a daemon created by this method is quite different from that of a daemon created by init. Because the daemon is created by fork, its environment is initially the same as that of the parent process. It has the same real and effective user-ID, the same real and effective group-ID, the same current working directory, and the same environment variable values. The method is suitable for creating a "private" daemon that is associated with some user and performs services on his behalf. The fs_get sample program shown in Chapter 14 is an example of a user daemon. Although it has the same capabilities as the user that *spawned* it, it still provides a global system service by allowing other users to access selected files belonging to that user. The fact that its user-ID is not root simply implies that fs_daemon is an application-oriented daemon rather than a system daemon.

If a daemon process must have superuser authority, it will have to be spawned by the superuser. This happens directly by executing the program as a command while logged in as root, or indirectly by being invoked from a crontab set up by the superuser, or by being called from a system initialization script such as /etc/rc2.

The following sample program demonstrates the procedure for creating a daemon process. It performs no useful function. It is merely a skeleton of the kind of code that might be written for creating a daemon via fork.

```
#include <stdio.h>
#include <signal.h>

#define ERROR (-1)

void trap() {}

main(int argc, char *argv[])
{
    int pid, sig;

    if ((pid = fork()) == 0) {
        /*
         * THIS IS THE CHILD PROCESS
         */
        /* Disconnect from the control terminal */
        setpgrp();
        /* Ignore all signals */
        for (sig = 0; sig < NSIG; sig++) signal(sig, trap);
        /* The main daemon routine just sleeps */
        for (;;)
            pause();
```

```
        exit(0); /* No way to get here */
        }

    if (pid == ERROR)
        perror("fork");
    else
        fprintf(stderr, "Daemon running (pid=%d)\n", pid);
    return (pid == ERROR);
}
```

This sample program differs from a more conventional coroutine or a program call by the fact that it never invokes the wait system call. After the fork that creates the child process, it simply exits, leaving the child process running. This is the precise action that transforms the child from a typical subprocess into a daemon.

The sample shown contains the programming for the daemon within it. This is undesirable if the main program is large, because it will continue to occupy system memory even though the daemon never uses its instructions or data. Inserting a call to exec as the first step of the child process would cause the main program's instructions and data to be discarded (for the child process only) and to be replaced with a program unique to the daemon. The effort of maintaining two programs, one to spawn the daemon, and one to execute the daemon's function, is not usually justified.

Communicating with a Daemon

Once a daemon process is created and running, some means must be established for communicating with it.

The getty process needs no special provision, because its command line specifies the terminal from which it is to solicit input. The program is inactive until data is received from the terminal, and when a connection is successfully established, getty immediately invokes /bin/login to continue the login process.

The lp and cron daemons, however, both require some interface by which users can issue requests to the daemon for service. Their solution to this problem is typical. The lp daemon creates a named pipe called FIFO in the /usr/spool/lp directory; cron creates a named pipe called FIFO in the /usr/lib/cron directory.

In both cases, the named pipe is created as part of the daemon initialization, and is destroyed by the daemon when it terminates. When a user process wishes to invoke the services of one of these daemons, the user must invoke a command intended for that purpose. The /usr/bin/crontab program is the command interface for requesting `cron` services, and `/usr/bin/lp` serves the same function for the `lp` daemon. Both of these programs are `set-uid`, and the corresponding named pipes have permissions that allow only the `root` user (in the case of `cron`) or the `lp` user (in the case of `lp`) to read or write the corresponding pipe. This prevents curious or fumble-fingered users from writing meaningless garbage into the pipe and possibly crashing the daemon.

When the `crontab` or `lp` commands have received a valid user request, they write a job record to their corresponding named pipe. This in turn is read by the `cron` or `lp` daemon in the same manner as reading a line from standard input. The job record describes the request, and might include such information as the user-ID, terminal, and process-ID of the user making the request. Sometimes the daemon writes a response indicating the disposition of the request to the user's terminal, as does the `lp` daemon, whereas some, such as the `cron` daemon, do not. The use of `set-uid` privilege and restricted permissions on the named pipe provides assurance that a valid user identification is always contained in the job records written to the pipe.

It is normal for the daemon initialization routine to create the named pipe that will be used for communication with the user, and for the daemon itself to remove the named pipe when it terminates. With both the `lp` and `cron` services, the user interface command must write a job record to the pipe, but if the daemon is not active, the write will remain outstanding until some process attempts to read it, which will probably never occur. Such a situation would leave the user command suspended waiting for completion of the write, and the user himself would lose otherwise productive time and peace of mind until he finally cancels the command. To avoid this situation, it is much better design to remove the pipe itself whenever the daemon is not active. This allows the command program to complain that the server is not active whenever the named pipe cannot be opened.

It is conceivable that a daemon might require a data file from the user in order to perform its function. This is certainly the case with the `lp` print spooling daemon, which is intended to print files generated by the user. Despite the attractiveness of the approach, files needed by the daemon should not be passed to it by writing them to the daemon's named pipe. If a server is in heavy demand, many processes might be trying to stuff job records into the pipe. Any attempt to write a file containing two or more lines to the pipe can result in job requests becoming interspersed with data files. This can be difficult, if not impossible, for the daemon process to sort out. Another technique is needed for passing files.

There are several means for passing a file to a daemon. The simplest case arises when the file already resides in one of the user's working directories. The interface command can then just pass the pathname of the file to the daemon in the job record. This is the approach used by lp when the file to be printed is named as an argument of the lp command.

Another technique is for the interface command (such as /usr/bin/crontab) to make use of its set-uid privilege to write the file in a directory known to the daemon process. (I will call such a directory the daemon's *work space*.) If this is practical, passing the name of the data file in the job record is once again possible, allowing the daemon to easily gain access to the file.

The problem that can arise with this latter approach is in attempting to ensure that files written simultaneously by several users have unique filenames. If there is no practical way to arrange this, only direct passing of the file will suffice.

To write a file from a user process to a daemon process, a second named pipe must be used. This second (or *data transfer*) pipe should be created by the interface command, but protected with suitable permissions so that only the interface command and the daemon can access it. The procedure required to use a data transfer pipe is as follows:

1. The interface command creates the data transfer pipe and stores its filename in the job record.

2. The interface command writes the job record to the daemon's job request pipe (usually called a *FIFO*).

3. The daemon reads the job record, extracts the name of the data transfer pipe, and opens it for input.

4. The interface command opens the data transfer pipe for output.

5. The interface command writes the data file through the data transfer pipe, probably using stream file I/O for efficiency, then closes the data transfer pipe.

6. The daemon reads the data file, storing it in its own work space.

7. The daemon closes the data file pipe when it receives end of file.

8. The interface command closes the data file pipe and destroys it with the unlink system call or the rm command.

9. The daemon continues to process the job request.

10. The interface command exits.

There are some control problems with the use of a named pipe for passing data. For example, if the daemon has opened the data transfer pipe for input but the interface command terminates before writing any data to it, the daemon will be suspended forever waiting for input. Similarly, if the interface command opens the data transfer pipe for output but the daemon fails at the attempt to open it for input, the interface command will be indefinitely suspended. These kinds of blocks can be broken by using the a l a r m system call to set a timer to interrupt the hanging read or write, and either of the two processes can arrange to send a signal with k i l l to ask the other side to cancel a request.

As a general conclusion, it should be clear that the safest method for passing data files to a daemon is to write them directly into a working directory owned by or accessible to the daemon. This will avoid the complexities of handling additional named pipes.

Summary

At the beginning of this chapter, I discussed coroutines and pointed to pipes as an example. Other examples of coroutines are plentiful, including the programs at opposite ends of a communications line, such as the two copies of uucico in a UUCP link, or a bbs program and your terminal emulation program. Daemons are also examples of coroutines, because a daemon does nothing useful until another program communicates with the daemon in some way. Coroutines, then, are simply two independently-executing routines in communication with each other. The method used to communicate, whether pipes, IPC message queues, or telephone lines, is of secondary importance.

There are a number of pitfalls the unwary programmer can fall into when developing coroutines. All of them involve improper use of the communications medium. Because the two routines execute independently, they may run at different speeds, or one of the routines may terminate while the other continues. To use coroutines successfully, you must provide for these possibilities.

Yet the advantages to using coroutines are compelling. Whether the application is as simple as a shell pipeline command, or as complex as X Windows or TCP/IP, the alternative implementation without coroutines is undesirable or even difficult to imagine. As your skills as a UNIX programmer develop, and the projects you tackle become more complex, you will sooner or later find yourself working with coroutines.

This chapter brings to a close our discussion of UNIX programming techniques. You are now ready to develop applications for UNIX systems. You also have gained the background needed to study some of the new and exciting things happening in UNIX, such as X Windows, network programming with TCP/IP, sockets, streams, and writing device drivers.

by Peter J. Holsberg

System V Release 4 Changes

I n 1975, Ken Thompson, the "father" of UNIX, took a sabbatical at the University of California at Berkeley. He and some graduate students in the Computer Science department put together a package of enhancements to the sixth edition (*circa* 1977) and released source code to anyone who had an AT&T UNIX source code license. Thus BSD (*Berkeley Software Distribution*) UNIX was born.

In 1979, UNIX System III, based on the seventh edition (*V7*) of "internal" UNIX, was AT&T's first commercial version of UNIX. In 1983, AT&T presented UNIX System V, Release 1, with a promise to maintain upward compatibility in future releases of UNIX. AT&T had become a software company!

In the early 1980s, Bill Joy, one of Thompson's graduate students, co-founded Sun Microsystems, which then developed SunOS, a variant of 4.2BSD. In the '80s, many other commercial organizations purchased source code licenses from AT&T and ported System V or BSD UNIX to their hardware, adding what they believed to be appropriate enhancements and needed changes. They created a large set of essentially incompatible, UNIX-like operating systems! Because the name *UNIX* belongs to AT&T, licensees made up their own names for their versions of this multiuser, multitasking operating system. Probably the most clever is the name made up by the Free Software Foundation. *GNU* is a recursive acronym that stands for *GNU's Not UNIX*. Table 16.1 shows some of the other variants and the companies that created them.

Table 16.1. *Variations on the UNIX Operating System*

UNIX Variations	Parent Company
AIX	IBM
A/UX	Apple Computer
CLIX	Fairchild
Concentrix	Alliant
CTIX	Convergent Technology
DG/UX	Data General
Distrix	Convergent Technology
DVIX	Northern Telecom
Dynix	Sequent
Eunice	The Wollongong Group
Genix	National Semiconductor
HP-UX	Hewlett-Packard
INIX	Compugraphic
IN/ix	Wang
IDRIS	Whitesmiths
Iris	Silicon Graphics
Mach	Carnegie-Mellon University
Minix	Andrew Tanenbaum
MPX	Philips
MS-UX	NEC
Mxelos	Perkin-Elmer
NDIX	Norsk Data
OSx	Pyramid
Primix	Pr1me
Scenix	Scientific Computer Systems
Sinix	Siemens
System V/AT	Microport
TOS	Nixdorf
UCOS	Honeywell-BULL
UniCOS	Cray
Uniq	Uniq Digital Technologys
UNOS	Charles River Data Systems
UTS	Amdahl
UTX/32	Gould
UTek	Tektronix
ULTRIX	DEC
XENIX	Microsoft
XINU	Doug Comer

When the dust had settled, there were three major "flavors" of UNIX and many, many variants of those flavors. The official AT&T UNIX was *System V*, at release level *3.2*, in 1989. The University of California at Berkeley had released its most recent offering, *4.3BSD*, in 1983. One of the first commercial ports of UNIX to microcomputers was done under the auspices of Microsoft and called *XENIX*; the current release is called *XENIX System V*. These versions of UNIX are similar but different. For example, if you have a binary (that is, executable) file that was created on a XENIX System V platform, it will run under UNIX System V Release 3.2 on a microcomputer that uses an Intel 80386 micro-processor. But it will not run under the System V Release 3.1 version or an earlier one. Furthermore, *no* BSD binary will run on any System V machine!

Clearly, object code incompatability was a problem that had held back the growth of UNIX into a mature commercial operating system. So, in 1988, AT&T, Microsoft, and Sun came to an agreement that the three heretofore diverging "Unices" would be merged into UNIX System V Release 4.0. In addition, System V Release 4.0 is a step forward from System V Release 3 in that it adheres to a number of industry standards that were developed outside of Bell Labs and AT&T.

An Overview of System V Release 4.0

First, we'll take a sweeping look at the new things that will be found in System V Release 4.0, and then we'll look in detail at some of the changes that affect programmers.

Basic System V Release 4.0 Operating System Services maintain XENIX system code compatibility (established in System V Release 3.2) for Intel 80386-based platforms. The System V Release 3 STREAMS facility gets en-hancements. The system call interface meets IEEE POSIX 1003.1 and ANSI X3J11C standards, and there is an X3J11C C compiler. BSD contributes the C shell, its fast file system, job control, symbolic links, and a number of commands and system calls. If you have ever had to configure a "portable" C program with lines upon lines beginning with "#ifdef...." to account for the differences among the flavors of UNIX, you have a treat in store for you! Finally, SunOS provides mapped files to System V Release 4.0.

System V Release 4.0 has enhanced networking capabilities. In addition to RFS (Remote File Sharing), TLI (Transport Level Interface), and UUCP, there is TCP/IP, `telnet`, `ftp`, and `smtp` from DARPA (Defense Advanced Projects

Research Agency); sockets compatibility and inted from BSD; and NFS (Network File System), RPC (Remote Procedure Call), and XDR (Extended Data Representation) from SunOS.

System V Release 4.0 includes System V Release 3.2 user interfaces: *curses*, *terminfo*, ETI (Extended Terminal Interface), FMLI (Form and Menu Language Interface), and FACE (Framed Access Command Environment). MIT provides the X Window System, and SunOS supplies *NeWS*. New for System V Release 4.0 is a set of OPEN LOOK tool kits.

One of the broadest changes in many commands was brought about by "internationalization," making commands adapt to multiple languages. System V Release 4.0 supports 8-bit and multibyte characters to accommodate European and Asian languages. Commands that display the date or information dealing with clock time, the so-called *time-of-day*, can achieve a display that takes into account the standards and practices of a country of choice. You can display error and other system messages in the local language, if you like, by implementing a message database and its manager.

Some Details of What's New in System V Release 4.0

UNIX System V Release 4.0 Commands and Shells

System V Release 3 users will find that some new commands have been added (many of these have been available as public domain source code from Usenet archives for years), and that some System V commands have been enhanced. Commands from BSD, SunOS, and XENIX have been added to the System V Release 3.2 command set, where possible. In addition, System V Release 4.0 includes four shells: Bourne, Korn, C, and the *job shell* (the *job shell* is just the Bourne shell with job control).

Commands

A problem that faced System V Release 4.0 designers was how to merge all the commands of System V Release 3, SunOS, BSD, and XENIX. The solution was to take those commands that could not be merged (that is, those that did not meet the System V Interface Definition SVID standard) and place them into a compatibility package. If users want to use these commands, they must place the compatibility bin directory (/usr/ucb for BSD and XENIX, /usr/5bin for SunOS) into their PATHs ahead of /usr/bin and /bin. "Compatibility" commands include the following:

adb	man	tset
addbib	newaliases	uptime
basename	notes	users
checkegn	nroff	vmstat
BSDs calendar	troff	vnews
dd	patch	whereis
diction	printenv	whoami
explain	ranlib	ypcat
hostid	ratfor	ypmatchg
hostname	readnews	yppasswd
install	readnotes	ypwhich
jove	sccs	biff
logger	spellout	fastboot
look	style	

Tables 16.2, 16.3, and 16.4 show the changes to common System V Release 3 commands, system calls, and functions. Terms that are not familiar to System V Release 3 users are explained later in the chapter.

Table 16.2. *New and Changed Commands*

Command	Changes
ar	Internationalized; recognizes *Extensible Linking Format* (ELF) files; the obsolete –l option has been removed
as	Produces ELF files
at	Internationalized; can read commands from a script file; can send mail after a job has been run
awk	Recognizes 8-bit characters; has new keywords: delete, do, func, return; can execute user-defined functions; has new built-in functions: atan2, cos, sin, rand, srand, gsub, sub, match, close system; has new predefined variables: FNR, SUBSEP, ARGC, ARGV, RSTART, RLENGTH; strings may contain *escape sequences;* the precedence of operators has been changed to match the precedence of C operators

Table 16.2 continues

Table 16.2 *continued*

Command	Changes
calendar	Internationalized
cat	Recognizes 8-bit characters
cb	Recognizes 8-bit characters
cc	Supports ANSI C semantics
chgrp	Can change the group of a symbolic link; can change group recursively on directories provided as arguments
chmod	Can change the mode of a symbolic link; can change owner recursively on directories provided as arguments
chown	Can change the owner of a symbolic link; can change owner recursively on directories provided as arguments
compress	From BSD UNIX, compresses files by the Lempel-Ziv method
cp	Has "safe" option; can preserve times and modes of copied files; can copy the subtree of a directory given as a "source" file
cpio	Internationalized; recognizes 8-bit and multibyte characters; can handle ASCII, ASCII with crc checking, and tar archives; can append a *cpio* archive to an existing disk file; supports symbolic links
cu	Recognizes 8-bit and multibyte characters
date	Internationalized; can adjust the system clock; can handle the date in UTC (Universal Coordinated Time, formerly known as Greenwich Mean Time [GMT])
dcopy	Supports *Virtual File System* (VFS); can return allocation in kilobytes, several new options
df	Supports the VFS architecture; can return allocation in kilobytes

Command	Changes
diff	Has about a dozen new options
echo	Supports both System V and SunOS versions, depending on the value of PATH
egrep	Recognizes multibyte characters; regular expressions have no fixed limits
ex	Provides a new option that aids in editing LISP programs
expr	Recognizes 8-bit and multibyte characters
file	Recognizes 8-bit and multibyte characters and symbolic links
find	Recognizes 8-bit and multibyte characters; can check for file type, inode number, ownership by a user who is not in /etc/passwd and/or /etc/group, and can prune the search tree; supports symbolic links
grep	Recognizes multibyte characters; regular expressions have no fixed limits
ld	Handles ELF files and the three modes of library binding (static, symbolic, and dynamic); -x, -m, -VF have been omitted
lint	Handles ANSI C types and function prototypes; has about 10 new options
ln	Can create symbolic links for files and directories
login	Reports time, date, and port of user's last login
lp	Internationalized
ls	Internationalized; recognizes 8-bit and multibyte characters, and symbolic links

Table 16.2 continues

Table 16.2 *continued*

Command	Changes
mail	Internationalized; can utilize *domain addressing*; the mailbox file has a new format
mailx	See mail
make	Recognizes multibyte characters
mv	Provides for a "safe" move; can move directories in a file tree within a physical file system
news	Internationalized
nohup	Now a shell built-in
od	Recognizes 8-bit and multibyte characters; has 7 new options
pg	Recognizes multibyte characters; internationalized; handles files with more than 32,767 lines; has better help screens and has correct exit codes on failure
pr	Internationalized; can fold long lines
ps	Can also use the /proc file system type; internationalized; recognizes 8-bit and multibyte characters
rmail	Recognizes symbolic links; accepts binary files; is independent of mail
sed	Recognizes multibyte characters; internationalized; no fixed limits on regular expressions
sh	Internationalized; recognizes multibyte characters; the built-in kill command can handle symbolic signal names; supports job control
size	Recognizes ELF files
sort	Internationalized; recognizes 8-bit and multibyte characters

Command	Changes
strip	Recognizes ELF files; removes all debugging information; -b, -l, -r options are obsolete
stty	Provides new options for POSIX compliance: control character, job control commands, control flags, window size; and for AT&T hardware flow control of ports
tar	Supports symbolic links
test	Supports symbolic links and is compatible with SunOS test
uucp	Can resume an interrupted file transfer where it left off
vi	Internationalized; recognizes 8-bit and multibyte characters; supports job control; can edit LISP programs
wall	Internationalized; can detect non-printable characters and print a reasonable facsimile
wc	Recognizes 8-bit and multibyte characters
who	Internationalized
write	See wall

Table 16.3. *New and Changed System Calls*

System Call	Changes
access	Recognizes symbolic links
chdir	Recognizes symbolic links
chmod	Recognizes symbolic links
chown	Recognizes symbolic links
creat	Recognizes symbolic links

Table 16.3 continues

Table 16.3 *continued*

System Call	Changes
exec	All support #! in a shell script to name explicitly the shell that interprets the script
fork	Enhanced so that a child process inherits the session ID as well as parental attributes
ioctl	Handles XENIX and BSD command convergence
mkdir	See chdir
mount	Recognizes symbolic links
open	Supports the O_PRIV oflag for devices; recognizes symbolic links
pipe	Now STREAMS-based; can be read from or written to from either end
read	Handles the POSIX non-block feature
signal	Recognizes six new signals: SIGCONT—a stopped process has been continued; SIGSTOP—the user has requested that a process be stopped (not ignorable); SIGTSTP—the user has requested that the foreground processes be stopped; SIGTTIN— a background process is attempting to read from the controlling terminal; SIGTTOU—a background process is attempting to write to a controlling terminal; and SIGCHLD—a child process has died
sigset	See signal
stat	Recognizes symbolic links
unlink	Recognizes symbolic links

Table 16.4. *New and Changed Functions*

Function	Changes
abort	Issues the SIGABRT signal instead of the SIGIOT signal; no longer closes files when SIGABRT signal is caught or ignored

Function	Changes
ctime	Can read the timezone description file if the value of TZ is the name of that file
curses	Has many enhancements
fprintf	Supports position-independent parameter substitution
fputs	Returns EOF on failure rather than 0
printf	See fprintf
puts	See fputs
sprintf	See fprintf
vfprintf	See fprintf
vprintf	See fprintf

There are about 600 user/administrator/programmer commands in System V Release 4.0, about 160 system calls, and about 1000 library subroutines!

Shells

System V Release 4.0 includes four shells: Bourne, Korn, C, and the *job shell*. The last three support job control signals as defined by POSIX P1003.1 and use the C shell job control user interface. Both the C shell and the Korn shell offer command-line editing and recall of previously executed commands. The Korn shell's programming language is upwardly compatible with older Bourne shell scripts and offers a number of enhanced programming features.

Job control has the following commands: ^Z suspends your current foreground job; bg puts it in the background; fg %x (in which x is the job ID number) brings a suspended or background job to the foreground; kill %x kills a background job; jobs lists your current jobs; and stop %x suspends a background job.

The C shell (*csh*) has several features not available with the older Bourne shell. The C shell has two startup files, .login and .cshrc (whereas the Bourne shell used only one, .profile). The .login file enables you to separate items that need to be executed only when you log in from others that are more general; for example, a list of aliases. The .cshrc file is executed every time you run a shell, for example, when you do a *shell escape* from a program; but .login is executed only when you log in. The C shell has a noclobber toggle that prevents you from overwriting an existing file on redirection. It also keeps a list of the last N commands you typed at the keyboard. You can see this list by typing

```
history
```

and you can reexecute a command using the ! operator.

For example, if you had edited a file with v i a few commands back, all you have to type to re-edit that file would be the following:

```
!vi
```

You use as many characters as you need to refer unambiguously to the command you want to recall. A special case is *!!*; this means *repeat the last command*.

C shell aliases are very handy. You can create an alias for a command like this:

```
alias ll "ls -al"
```

Then, typing l l is the same as typing l s -a l.

Like csh, the Korn shell (*ksh*) has two startup files. One of them is called .profile. The other can have whatever filename you like; you tell ksh its filename by setting the environment variable ENV to the pathname of the file. The latter file is analogous to csh's .cshrc. The ksh also has noclobber, command history and recall, aliases, and a very handy feature called *command-line editing*. Given a command line (either typed by hand or recalled from the history list), you can edit that line using either v i or the emacs editors (depending on the value of the environment variables EDITOR and VISUAL). A neat ksh trick is the command to return to the previous directory:

```
cd -
```

Of course, this is a toggle.

Login Services

One small but important change is that the Backspace key is automatically used for the erase function. There's no longer a need to execute the command

```
stty erase '^h'
```

to change the erase key from # to the Backspace key. This makes correcting errors during login much less frustrating.

When you log in, you will see a message telling you when you last logged in. This is intended to be a security measure: if the time reported doesn't match your recollection of when you last logged in, notify your system administrator. Someone might have gained illegal access to your account!

UNIX System V Release 4.0 File Operations

System V Release 4.0 has greatly enhanced file operations by including XENIX's file and record locking interface, SunOS's memory-mapped files, and features of the IEEE POSIX standard—renaming, truncation, synchronization, new error messages, and new modes. In addition, System V Release 4.0 has tunable parameters to set the maximum number of open files per process and for the system as a whole.

New system calls include `setrlimit`, `rename`, `truncate`, `ftruncate`, `lockf`, `fcntl`, `locking`, `fsync`, `mmap`, `munmap`, and `msync`.

Some old system calls get new flags. For example, `write` now allows `O_SYNC`, to ensure that the `write` call does not complete until the data is actually written (at a slight performance penalty).

Memory-mapped files provide the programmer with a method to access the contents of files without constantly using `read`, `lseek`, and `write` calls. The `mmap` call maps a file (or device) into the process address space and returns the base address of the mapped area. That address can then be manipulated just like any other address.

In System V Release 4.0, a filename can be almost any sequence of characters, although System V Release 4.0 considers that two files having the same characters in the first 14 positions are the same file.

UNIX System V Release 4.0 File Systems

System V Release 4.0 introduces the concept of a Virtual File System (VFS) to extend the old fixed static file system (the so-called *s5* file system) as implemented on System V Release 3 and earlier. VFS is the merger of the System V FSS (File Systems Switch) and the VFS mechanism from SunOS. This introduces the concept of the "virtual inode" or `vnode`, a kind of generalized inode that can deal with VFS file systems. VFS permits regular System V file systems to coexist with RFS, UFS (fast file system), `proc`, and NFS file systems, as well as permitting the addition of new types of file systems as they are defined and implemented. The VFS interface a programmer sees is independent of the actual file system being programmed.

The UFS file system is System V Release 4.0's version of the BSD "fast file system" (FFS). The FFS specifies a block size of 4096 bytes, but permits subdividing a block into *fragments* of either 512, 1024, or 2048 bytes each. Thus, FSS has the advantages of a large block size without its disadvantage.

The `proc` file system is a mechanism for accessing the address space of processes that are currently running. This permits programmers to apply file and/or device operations to a process, using an already well-defined interface. Under System V Release 4.0, the *s5* file system can have blocks of 512 bytes, 1KB or 2KB.

System V Release 4.0 introduces a new file system call, `statvfs`, to replace the obsolete System V Release 3 call, `statfs` (although `statfs` is retained for backward compatibility with existing System V Release 3 programs). Table 16.5 shows the file system description that `statvfs` returns.

Table 16.5. *File System Descriptions Returned by statvfs*

System Call	Description
f_bsize	Preferred block size
f_frsize	Fundamental block size
f_blocks	Total number of blocks of size f_frsize
f_bfree	Total number of free blocks
f_bavail	Number of blocks available to non-superuser processes
f_files	Number of inodes
f_ffree	Number of free inodes
f_favail	Number of inodes available to non-superuser processes
f_fsid	File system ID
f_basetype[FSTYPSZ]	Target file system type name, null-terminated
f_flag	Bit mask of flags
f_namemax	Maximum length of a file name
f_fstr[32]	File system-specific string
f_filler[7]	Reserved for future use

Symbolic links are a Berkeley enhancement. Essentially, a symbolic link is a file that contains the name of a target file. The target filename is an alias for some other filename. When the operating system operates on a symbolic link, it actually operates on the target file. Symbolic links can be established across file systems and can even be used to link directories, with almost no performance degradation. The files and directories can even be on other computers in the same network! Four new system calls support symbolic linking: `symlink`, `readlink`, `lstat`, and `lchown`.

System V Release 4.0 supports filesystem-independent routines for reading the contents of directory files. However, the physical organization of files and directories has been modified to facilitate sharing in a networked environment, to clearly separate differing subtrees, and to provide a rational means for installing new software.

Table 16.6 shows the directories contained in System V Release 4.0's root file system.

Table 16.6. *System V Release 4.0's Root File System*

Directory Name	Contents
stand	Standard programs and data for booting the system
sbin	Administrative and operations binaries
dev	Character and block special files
etc	Machine-specific configuration and system administration files
export	Default root of the exported file system tree
home	Default subtree for user directories
mnt	Default mount point for file systems
opt	Root of subtree for add-on applications
proc	Root of the process file system
tmp	System-generated temporary files
usr	Subtree containing static sharable files
var	Subtree for varying files
spool	Directories for spool files
spool/lp	Printer spool files
spool/uucp	Queued uucp jobs
spool/uucppublic	Files deposited by uucp

The /bin directory is symbolically linked to /usr/bin, and there are two copies of the shell: one in /sbin for boot-up, the other in /usr/bin.

Files that were previously in /usr and were modified have been moved to /var. The /usr file system now contains the directories shown in table 16.7.

Table 16.7. *Directories Contained in the /usr File System*

Directory	Contents
bin	The majority of the system utilities
sbin	System administration binaries
games	Pretty obvious!
include	C program header files

Table 16.7 continues

Table 16.7 *continued*

Directory	Contents
lib	C program libraries and architecture-dependent databases
share	Architecture-independent sharable files
share/man	On-line manual pages
share/lib	Architecture-independent databases for source code license holders
ucb	BSD (or XENIX) compatibility package binaries
ucbinclude	BSD compatibility header files
ucblib	BSD compatibility libraries

The /var file system contains files and directories whose contents change over the lifetime of the system. Table 16.8 shows the files contained in the /var file system.

Table 16.8. *Files in the /var File System*

File Name	Contents
adm	System accounting files
cron	Log file for the cron command
mail	User mail files
news	News bulletins from the system administrator
opt	Root of subtree for add-on applications
preserve	Backup files for vi and ex
saf	Service Access Facility accounting files
tmp	Temporary files
uucp	Log and status files for UUCP

Almost all the XENIX system calls from System V Release 3.2 are included in System V Release 4.0 so that applications portability (on 80386-based computers) is maintained. System calls and subroutines that have been omitted or moved to the compatibility group include the following:

conv	nextkey	tgetflag
brkctl	store	tgetnum
dbm	fxlist	tgetstr
dbminit	nbwaitsem	tgoto
delete	shutdn	tputs
fetch	termcap	xlist
firstkey	tgetent	

UNIX System V Release 4.0
Input/Output Facilities

The complete STREAMS facility from System V Release 3 has been carried over into System V Release 4.0 and enhanced there. For example, STREAMS now includes all tty devices to make tty polling more efficient, and pipes are also part of STREAMS. The POSIX termios terminal manipulation interface is supported along with the System V Release 3 termio structure and its corresponding ioctls. *Named STREAMS* allows a process to attach a STREAMS file descriptor to a pathname.

System V Release 4.0 includes network access calls such as listen and inetd so that users can log in to a machine from across a LAN.

A new feature, SAF (Service Access Facility), controls access to a system by providing a common point of administration for ports. A *port monitor* detects activity on a set of homogeneous ports—for example, a group of serial communications lines—and can be installed and used by ordinary users and their applications. For terminals, ttymon replaces getty (and uugetty) and provides the capability to poll STREAMS-based ttys. For networks, listen is carried over from System V Release 3.

UNIX System V Release 4.0
Interprocess Communications

To the System V Release 3.2 Interprocess Communications (IPC) suite (message queues, named pipes, pipes, semaphores, shared memory, and TLI), System V Release 4.0 adds XENIX semaphores and shared data, BSD sockets, and SunOS RPC. RPC, sockets, and TLI are used in a networked environment that connects computers that use different operating systems (including MS-DOS, VMS, etc.). If all of the computers in the network use UNIX System V Release 4.0, named pipes and named STREAMS can be added to the list of usable IPC mechanisms. And, for IPC in a single computer, you can add message queues, pipes, semaphores, and shared memory to those previously listed IPC facilities! These single-machine IPC mechanisms generally offer higher performance over traditional programming approaches, and the network-based mechanisms permit the distribution of processing to occur in a fairly transparent manner. Thus, a programmer need no longer distinguish between IPC and networking for many applications.

UNIX System V Release 4.0 Processes

UNIX continues as a multiuser, multitasking operating system with several enhancements under System V Release 4.0. For example, demand-paged virtual memory increases the efficiency of memory utilization and provides support for processes that require more memory than is physically available. Also, POSIX P1003.1 job control provides the user with the capability to stop and restart a group of processes under keyboard control.

POSIX defines the following *signals* incorporated in System V Release 4.0 as shown in table 16.9.

Table 16.9. *System V Release 4.0 Signals*

Signal	Definition
SIGHUP	Hangup
SIGINT	Interrupt
SIGQUIT	Quit
SIGILL	Illegal instruction
SIGTRAP	Trace trap
SIGIOT	IOT instruction
SIGEMT	EMT instruction
SIGFPE	Floating point exception
SIGKILL	Kill
SIGBUS	Bus error
SIGSEGV	Segmentation violation
SIGSYS	Bad argument in system call
SIGPIPE	Write on a pipe with nothing to read it
SIGALRM	Alarm clock
SIGTERM	Software termination
SIGUSR1	User-defined
SIGUSR2	User-defined
SIGCLD	Death of child process
SIGPWR	Power failure
SIGWINCH	Window change
SIGPOLL	Selectable event is pending
SIGSTOP	Stop
SIGTSTP	Interactive stop
SIGCONT	Continue if stopped
SIGTTIN	Background read attempted from controlling terminal
SIGTTOU	Background write attempted from controlling terminal

System V Release 4.0 supports real-time processing via a change to the kernel's process scheduler. It now recognizes two process types: *timesharing* and *real time*, a method of processing in which program execution can be guaranteed to occur in specific time intervals. A new system call, `priocntl`, can change a timesharing process (the default process type) to a real-time one, and monitor and modify its priority rating and the size of its "time slice." In addition, certain BSD system calls having to do with time have been added: `getitimer`, `setitimer`, `gettimeofday`, `settimeofday`, and `adjtime`. The first two manipulate an interval timer that sends alarm signals at predetermined intervals. The BSD "time-of-day" calls provide finer granularity time specifications (if the underlying hardware supports it) than the equivalent System V Release 3.2 calls. `adjtime` permits updating the system time-of-day clock over an extended period of time; it's used in environments that cannot tolerate a large instantaneous change in that clock.

UNIX System V Release 4.0 Internationalization

For the first time in its existence, UNIX attempts to provide the capability to read input and generate output in a way that's understandable to users, regardless of their national language and local conventions. This includes permitting multibyte characters (for European and Kanji character sets), thus removing the USA-based assumptions on language, date and time formats, collating sequences, and numeric formats. You can do this with the `setlocale` system call (with accompanying header file `locale.h`) as simply as

```
setlocale(LC_ALL, "French");
```

in which LC_ALL causes collation, character type, money format, and date and time formats to use the style prevalent in *la belle France.* Individual categories may be selected by replacing LC_ALL with one of LC_COLLATE, LC_CTYPE, LC_MONETARY, LC_NUMERIC, or LC_TIME.

UNIX System V Release 4.0 Application Development Environment

In General

The C compiler distributed with System V Release 4.0, the so-called *C Issue 5.0,* conforms with ANSI X3J11C and its library with POSIX 1003.1. New features include *dynamic linking, process file system utilization*, and *message management*. Also, the new compiler can be used to compile older "K&R plus extensions" programs without requiring rewrites, and is actually a superset of the ANSI C Standard. Further, the libraries are a superset of the POSIX standard which itself is a superset of the ANSI standard.

ANSI C is an improvement over the original "K&R C" in that it provides for better type checking through *function prototypes*, new type qualifiers, and a more well-defined preprocessor. Function prototypes permit the compiler to check for the number and types of arguments that are passed to functions, so that lint need not be invoked. Further, the compiler performs *silent coercion* on arguments that are compatible with but not the same as the type defined in the prototype.

The compiler has three compilation modes:

❏ Transitional mode, the default, uses K&R semantics and produces warnings where ANSI interpretation is different from K&R interpretation.

❏ ANSI mode (*-Xa* option) uses ANSI semantics and provides warnings where ANSI interpretation is different from K&R interpretation.

❏ ANSI conforming mode (*-Xc* option) uses ANSI semantics, provides warnings where ANSI interpretation is different from K&R interpretation, and produces error messages where usage differs from ANSI.

The C Issue 5.0 compiler creates ELF files (explained later in the section "Extensible Linking Format").

The following libraries are provided with C Issue 5.0:

libc: standard I/O service routines, string operation routines, memory allocation routines, directory access routines, and routines that provide access to /etc/passwd and /etc/group

libsys: all system calls have been moved here

libgen: general purpose routines

libcrypt: DES encryption and decryption routines

libm: math routines

libmsg: message formatting routines

libcurses: screen I/O and management routines

libform: forms manipulation routines

libmenu: menu creation, display and navigation routines

libpanel: the opaque window library

libX: X Windows System X11 protocol library

libXt: the X11 tool kit library

libNDE: the BSD NeWS development environment library

libnet: the network selection and listener services routines

libnsl: TLI interface routines

librpc: BSD's Remote Procedure Call routines

libxdr: BSD's External Data Representation library routines

To support internationalization, the libraries include a message management routine, fmtmsg. This permits programmers to provide error messages for their programs that are consistent and that attempt to aid naive users by providing information on the severity of the error and the possible remedial action to take. For example, a typical error message created with fmtmsg might appear as follows:

```
$ lp myfyle
lp: WARNING: Cannot access the file:
          myfyle.
  TO FIX: Make sure file names are valid.
lp: ERROR: No (or empty) input files.
$
```

Extensible Linking Format (ELF)

System V Release 4.0 has a new object file format called ELF (Extensible Linking Format). It is used for relocatable objects (that is, *.o files), executable files (that is, of the form of a.out), and for *dynamic libraries* (a facility imported from SunOS). More flexible than COFF (the old object file format), ELF is also more portable (most information is in machine-independent form) and more extensible. System V Release 4.0 can exec COFF executables, but ELF executables cannot be executed on pre-System V Release 4.0 systems (except under System V Release 3.2.2 on 80386-based computers).

The System V Release 4.0 debugger is an enhanced version of sdb. A new command, gcore, will generate a core file for a given process without killing the process, and another new command, truss, is used to trace system calls. All three of these use the new proc file system facility, a mechanism for accessing the virtual address space of a process in a way that permits access using read and write.

System V Release 3 introduced *static shared* libraries, designed to reduce the size of the resulting a.out and thus reduce the per-process use of system memory. Instead of copying output modules from the libraries into the `a.out` file, the compiler now includes a section in `a.out` that alerts the kernel to link the needed routines into the process's address space (at specific fixed addresses). This means that every process can share the same code for such ubiquitous (and large) routines as `printf` and `scanf`. Further, if the shared library is updated, no one needs to relink programs to get the new linkages.

The major disadvantage of static shared libraries is their static nature: they use special files; there are fixed paths to locate the library; the process addresses that use them are fixed. In System V Release 4.0, AT&T has implemented the SunOS *dynamic linked library* mechanism with two big advantages over static shared libraries:

❑ Code in a dynamic library contains no absolute references to the process's memory space, and does not require relocation.

❑ Function calls are implemented by means of a table of function addresses that initially contains only references to the dynamic linker. When a function is called for the first time, the linker determines the address of the actual function, patches the table, and turns control over to the function. If the function is called again by the process, the linker will not be involved. Also, if the function is never called, it is never linked.

The Network Applications Environment

In 1981, BSD released *sockets*, a generic interface designed to streamline UNIX-to-UNIX communications over networks. In 1985, SunOS introduced NFS and RPC to provide transparent file sharing over a network. In 1986, AT&T released STREAMS, TLI (Transport Layer Interface), and RFS (Remote File Sharing).

STREAMS is an environment for network programming and includes systems calls, kernel resources, and utilities. It provides services for full-duplex communications between a user process and a kernel driver that "connects" directly to communications hardware. STREAMS network programs can be reused in the implementation of different protocols and ported to new machines, becoming transparent to network applications.

TLI is an interface between the "session" and "transport" layers in the Open Systems Interconnection (OSI) model of networking. It provides a facility for building programs that are independent of the details of the provider at the transport level. TLI could run on top of any number of transport providers, particularly TCP/IP protocol on, say, Ethernet, AT&T's Universal Receiver Protocol (URP) on Starlan, or on a STREAMS module on an appropriate stream.

RFS is "distributed UNIX." That is, it provides the facility through which a collection of computers—all running System V UNIX—can be treated as a single machine. The user sees file systems that physically belong to "other" machines as just ordinary file systems mounted on his or her machine. With System V/386, RFS can operate over STREAMS and over Ethernet or any other network that supports TCP/IP or NetBIOS. This was accomplished by tying RFS in with TLI.

System V Release 4.0 incorporates all these and more. From System V Release 3 comes UUCP, RFS, STREAMS, TLI, and the network listener for connection management. From BSD comes the sockets interface, support for DARPA's TCP/IP Internet package, the r* commands (rlogin, rcp, etc.), and inetd for server management. SunOS provides NFS, RPC, and XDR. And System V Release 4.0 adds revisions to the mail architecture, the *network selection* facility, and *name-to-address translation* for transparent handling of the network addresses of servers.

In a distributed processing environment, applications are frequently structured in the *client-server* model. A *service* specifies the functions that are offered (for example, open, read), the parameters required by the functions, the results that the functions return, the sequence in which functions may be invoked, and the method of invocation. A *server* executes the code that implements a service, whereas a *client* calls on the server to provide the services that the application requires. Over a network, clients and servers run as separate processes (and may even be on different machines) that communicate with each other via an IPC mechanism.

Particularly in the RPC mechanism, the client sends a message to the server, a message that contains the name of the service and the parameters required. Servers respond by sending back a message containing the results. To implement this, System V Release 4.0 networking software manages the connections between clients and servers through name/address translation, making and breaking the connections, and starting and stopping the servers. Messages are managed through specifying the format and encoding the messages, and by enforcing waiting for a response to a request. Finally, the System V Release 4.0 networking software provides a standard format for data, so that problems associated with byte ordering and alignment, word size, and data encoding (for example, 1's complement or 2's complement) are prevented.

System V Release 4.0's TLI has the capability to let the programmer achieve protocol and media independence over the network by defining some guidelines for the programmer. Thus, any network that conforms to the TLI specification can be accessed by a program via TLI.

The System V Release 4.0 distributed processing programming environment provides layers of facilities, each of which provides a standard solution that will fit many applications. The lowest layer deals with IPC, and is implemented with TLI (pipes within a single computer; sockets where appropriate for existing applications). The next level, data representation, is handled with XDR, a standard solution for a network of heterogeneous computers. Next is the RPC layer, which manages message formats, contents, and sequencing. On top of that is the applications program itself.

The network protocols in System V Release 4.0 are the DARPA TCP/IP Internet suite; these protocols are implemented using STREAMS. However, the responsibility for providing device drivers for the hardware falls to the manufacturers of that hardware, including Ethernet, Starlan, token bus and token ring LANs, and X.25 WANs. Specific information can be found in RFCs 793, 768, 791, 792, 826, 903, and 904.

BSD/SunOS sockets are fully supported in System V Release 4.0 at the source code level only. That is, existing applications must be recompiled and linked with the System V Release 4.0 libraries for them to run under System V Release 4.0. Because sockets provide functionality that is similar to that of TLI, AT&T encourages programmers to develop new applications using TLI rather than sockets.

UNIX System V Release 4.0 Networking

Networking was introduced to UNIX in 1975 with *UUCP*, the UNIX-to-UNIX CoPy suite of programs intended to be used from "point to point," that is, between two UNIX systems that were most likely connected over telephone lines with modems. UUCP is still widely used today, and System V Release 4.0's UUCP, based on the HoneyDanBer implementation, supports local area networks over TLI. The uucp command has been enhanced so that interrupted file transfers will be resumed from where they were interrupted rather than restarted from the beginning, and file transfers may be classified by *job grades* (high, medium, or low) to establish the priority of a transfer.

The UUCP command cu can now recognize 8-bit and multibyte characters, and has been enhanced with several additional *tilde* commands, shown in table 16.10.

Table 16.10. *New Tilde Commands with the cu Command*

Command	Function
~%b	Send a break to the remote
~%d	Toggle debugging
~t	Print the termio values for your terminal
~l	Print the termio values for the communications line
~%ifc	Toggle XON/XOFF input flow control
~%ofc	Toggle XON/XOFF output flow control
~%old	Toggle pre-System V Release 4.0 cu syntax

In addition, cu can specify a local area network rather than a communications line or phone number.

The TCP/IP Internet facility in System V Release 4.0 includes the applications shown in table 16.11.

Table 16.11. *Applications Provided with TCP/IP*

Application	Function
telnet	Terminal emulation
ftp	File transfer
tftp	File transfer using the UDP protocol
finger	Information about users
nictable/whois	Information from the NIC table (DARPA user directory service)
mail/mailx	Now support SMTP-based mail services
rcp	Remote file copy
rlogin	Remote login
rsh	Remote shell execution, not to be confused with the System V Release 3 *restricted shell*
rwho	Information on logged-in users
ruptime	Information on status of network hosts
ping, netstat	Network debugging and information
rmt	Remote tape operations

System V Release 4.0 now includes *YP* (Yellow Pages), a distributed data lookup facility that supports NFS.

Distributed file systems provide transparent access to remote directories and file systems. Files that are accessed this way are not copied to the local machine, but can be used by a number of users simultaneously so that changes become instantly available to all users.

Files can be centralized, easing the problems of making backups. Distributed file systems extend access to peripheral devices connected to remote computers. Peripheral-sharing is a potential system cost reducer.

The two types of distributed file systems provided in System V Release 4.0 are RFS, for remote file sharing in a UNIX System V environment, and NFS (from the SunOS) for remote file sharing in an environment that contains different types of operating systems. In System V Release 4.0, both exist under VFS (Virtual File System), but they cannot interoperate because each uses different protocols. Each provides access to any directory tree in its file system, and the syntax of administrative commands has been modified to provide a uniform interface. For example, `share` replaces both the RFS `adv` and the NFS `exportfs`. Once mounted, remote directory trees can be used as if they were local directory trees.

RFS maintains compatibility with System V Release 3, including file and record locking. RFS supports regular files, directories, named pipes, and special files (that is, devices). A single directory tree can be mounted by two or more remote machines and over multiple networks.

NFS provides remote file sharing over operating systems as diverse as MS-DOS and VMS, and uses an open, industry-standard protocol. However, NFS does not support mandatory file and record locking, nor access to remote special files.

RFS and NFS will operate on the same machine and over the same network, so that a single directory tree can be mounted simultaneously under both.

System V Release 4.0 User Interfaces

The traditional System V user interface employs character-oriented terminals, whereas workstation-based UNIX systems employ bit-mapped graphics devices. With the growing power of personal computers based on Intel microprocessors and their memory-mapped graphics video systems, more emphasis is being placed in UNIX development on the *GUI* (Graphical User Interface). Where the character-based terminal interface depends largely on a keyboard, the GUI uses a *pointing device* (for example, a *mouse)* as the user input device. Further, a GUI provides the user with multiple windows—areas on the screen that represent different applications running simultaneously.

System V Release 4.0 addresses both kinds of interface. The character-based interface is supported by two tool kits: *FMLI* (Frame and Menu Language Interpreter) and *ETI* (Extended Terminal Interface). System V Release 4.0 provides an FMLI application—*FACE* (Framed Access Command Environment)—to illustrate its usefulness. FACE provides (on an 80386 platform) a function-key-operated, menu-driven interface to a subset of the system administration commands. Similar to the *User Agent* provided with the AT&T 3B1/7300 computer, FACE is more window-oriented than the menu-driven *Sysadm* system provided on AT&T 3B2 computers.

The GUI is handled by OPEN LOOKTM, and supported by two tool kits. OPEN LOOK X Toolkit is based on the MIT *X Windows System* and permits a programmer to build applications having the "look and feel" associated with OPEN LOOK. The OPEN LOOK NeWS Development Environment (NDE), based on the SunOS *NeWS* graphical platform, complements the X Toolkit.

As in earlier UNIX System V releases, the underlying platform for the character interface is `curses/terminfo`. On top of that comes ETI and/or FMLI.

FMLI has a command syntax similar to that of the Bourne shell, and has its "look and feel" embedded in its command language. The language consists of a set of *descriptors* that define the attributes of the form or menu you are developing. Some of these attributes are as follows:

❑ Single choice or multiple selection

❑ Default selection

❑ Screen placement

❑ Action to be taken by each selection

❑ Closing the menu

❑ Title

❑ Validation of entered data

❑ Definition of function keys

ETI is a C language library for building forms, windows (called *panels* in ETI parlance), and menus. Thus ETI provides sophisticated programmers with the tools to create entities of their choice. For example, programming in ETI permits you to use stylistic borders and decorations, manage the cursor position, move windows, customize the look and feel, etc. Further, an ETI-based interface executes faster than an FMLI one.

OPEN LOOK is not a program, but rather a specification and a style guide for designing a graphical user interface. It provides a consistent standard GUI for all developers using an System V Release 4.0 platform for their applications development, and employs the "desktop" metaphor wherein each window is analogous to a piece of paper on your desk. It supports mice (mouses?) with from one to three buttons.

OPEN LOOK applications have two major components, *menus* and *windows*. There are two kinds of menus, *popup* and *submenus*. Each may contain *buttons* (click the mouse on a button to make a selection), *pushpins* (click the mouse on a pushpin in a popup window and the window stays on the desktop until you "dismiss" it), and a *window mark (shine)*.

There are three types of windows: *base*, *popup*, and *closed*. Popups come in four "flavors": *command*, *property*, *help*, and *notice*. All windows can have *buttons*, *pushpins*, *window marks*, *scroll bars* (to allow the user to move back and forth in a file in a window), *control areas*, *choices*, *toggles*, *messages*, and *resize corners* (used to shrink or expand the window).

System V Release 4.0 supports a *client-server* model of graphics interface. The server manages keyboard and mouse input as well as output and windows. A client requests that the server perform one or more of the management services; the client can be on a different machine in the network but the server must be running locally. This permits applications (that is, *clients*) to be developed so that they are independent of the operating system or hardware platform. The implementation in System V Release 4.0 is a merger of X11 and NeWS.

When developing graphical applications, the programmer should be aware of the differences between the X11 tool kit and the NDE tool kit. NDE places user interface components in the window server yielding fast execution, whereas X11 puts them with the client, reducing the amount of memory needed (and probably the amount of CPU power) on the server. Extensions to X servers are compiled into the server, whereas those for NDE are interpreted PostScript code, usually considerably slower in execution than compiled code. X11 uses a fast *raster* image, whereas NDE provides a slower but device-independent *stencil-paint* image. X11 uses X protocol that is supported by the *X Consortium*; NDE uses PostScript.

System V Release 4.0 Application Binary Interface (ABI)

The System V Release 4.0 ABI is a set of interfaces designed to achieve binary portability of applications programs on a particular processor. Thus, binary (that is, executable) software can be portable across different vendors' computers that use the same processor architecture. The goal is to emulate the binary portability that exists in the PC/MS-DOS world where programs compiled on an IBM PC, for example, will run on a Zenith AT/286 without change; that is, *shrink-wrap compatibility*. The targeted processors include the Intel 80386 (and 80486), Motorola 68000 and 88000 families, and the Sun SPARC. Others will be developed and added to System V Release 4.x.

Sources

Notes distributed at the UNIX System V Release 4.0 Software Developer Conferences, 1988.

Migration Guides for UNIX SV, BSD, SunOS, and XENIX.

Rosen et al, *UNIX System V Release 4—An Introduction*, Osborne/McGraw-Hill, 1990.

AT&T UNIX System V Release 4 Programmer's Reference Manual, Prentice-Hall, 1990.

Private email exchanges with Tony Hansen of AT&T Bell Labs. Hansen is the "owner of the `mail` command."

Part V

Reference

C Library Functions

This part of the reference section is a concise summary of UNIX System V system calls and library functions for the C language programmer.

UNIX System V includes an extensive collection of function libraries. Describing in this section every known function call is neither possible nor particularly desirable, mainly because of the sheer wealth of material, but also because many functions are highly specialized and not of much interest to the general programmer. This chapter, therefore, concentrates on the standard library functions usually found in `libc.a` and the math library functions found in `libm.a`. These functions have been a part of UNIX for many years. They provide a sound basis for application development. The functions covered include everything mentioned in Chapters 2 and 3 of the *UNIX Programmer's Reference Manual*, and possibly a little bit more. Chapter 16, "UNIX System V Release 4 Changes," covers functions unique to System V Release 4.

Function interfaces are described using the ANSI C syntax, although most UNIX systems do not yet support the ANSI standard. This rarely will be a problem for the programmer who must use a Kernighan and Ritchie (K&R) compiler, because this compiler does not require full function prototypes. ANSI C compilers, on the other hand, include the necessary function prototypes in the standard header files. As a result, you should never need to type the function descriptions into your programs.

UNIX System V has been ported to many different hardware environments. While these versions of System V comply closely with the UNIX System V Interface Definition (SVID), differences in hardware inevitably force some deviation from the official release. You must consult the documentation provided with your system for precise information when using hardware-dependent functions.

A word about the notational conventions used in this section is in order.

Occasionally, you will find a keyword highlighted next to the function name. These keywords note special usage considerations for the function. The meanings of the keywords are explained in the following table:

Symbol	Means
errno	Sets *errno* global
S	System call
KE	Requires kernel extensions
R3	Requires System V Release 3
M	Math library function

Functions located in the C standard library automatically are linked with your program during compilation. Functions located in other libraries, such as the math library, are linked only if you tell the compiler to search the library. The `-lm` option in the following command forces the compiler to search the math library while building the executable program `myprog`:

```
cc myprog.c -lm -o myprog
```

Anytime you intend to use functions from a nonstandard library, you must include the appropriate `-l`*lib* option on the `cc` command.

This reference section uses several different typefaces. Explanatory text is written in standard type. Italics are used to refer to the arguments of a function in the body of a description, and to highlight technical terms special to UNIX. A typeface similar to computer output printing is used for code listings, and when referring to a function name such as `read` or `wait`, which could easily be mistaken for the English word when the name of a function or command is intended.

Warning

You should pay special attention to warnings displayed like this one. These notes are intended to warn you of ways programmers often misuse a function call. Bugs caused by misusing a function can be incredibly difficult to find even when using a powerful debugger. Don't rely on debugging tools; learn to use functions correctly!

a64l

```
long a64l (const char *string);
```

Converts a string of 0 to 6 characters in base-64 notation to a long integer. In order from 0 to 63, the base-64 digits are . (0), / (1), 0-9, A-Z, and a-z. If the string is longer than 6 characters, only the first 6 are used.

Returns: The long integer value equivalent to the base-64 string pointed to by *string*.

Related Functions: `l64a`

abort

```
int abort (void);
```

Attempts to close all open files. The current process is then terminated by generating a signal that causes process termination with a dump.

Warning

`abort` does not behave as intended if the process catches or ignores the generated signal (usually SIGIOT).

Returns: Does not return.

Related Functions: `_exit, exit, signal`

abs

```
int abs (int i);
```

Computes the absolute value of its argument.

Returns: abs(*i*).

> **Warning**
>
> The machine implementation may not be able to represent the absolute value of the maximum negative integer.

access *errno S*

```
int access (const char *path, int amode);
```

Generates a return value that indicates whether the current user is permitted to access the file named by *path* for the types of access indicated by *amode*. The value of *amode* must be 0 or a combination of the bit values as indicated in the following table:

Bit Mask	Meaning
04	Test for read access
02	Test for write access
01	Test for execute (search) access

If *amode* is 0, only the existence of the file is tested.

Returns: 0 if the access is permitted, -1 otherwise.

> **Warning**
>
> access is intended to be used by set-uid programs to determine whether the real user is permitted the access.

Related Functions: chmod, execl, stat, setuid

acos *errno M*

```
double acos (double x);
```

Headers: math.h

Computes the principal value of the trigonometric arccosine of the argument *x* in radians.

Returns: arccos(*x*).

alarm *S*

```
unsigned alarm (unsigned sec);
```

Schedules the alarm signal SIGALRM to occur *sec* real seconds from the time that the function is invoked. Any outstanding previously scheduled alarm signal is canceled. If the value of *sec* is 0, no new time interval is started and the only effect is to cancel any outstanding alarm.

Returns: The amount of time remaining in the previously scheduled interval, or 0 if none exists.

> **Warning**
>
> 1. If the SIGALRM signal is not caught or ignored, it causes the process to terminate abnormally.
>
> 2. Depending on the amount of other system activity, the signal may occur an indeterminate length of time later than actually requested

Related Functions: pause, signal

asctime

```
char *asctime (struct tm *time);
```

Headers: time.h

Converts the values contained in the `tm` structure pointed to by *time* to a character string suitable for display. The fields in the result string are of fixed length, and express the date and time in the following format:

```
Sun Dec 17 09:19:13 1989\n\0
```

Returns: A pointer to an internal static character array containing the result string.

Related Functions: `ctime, gmtime, localtime, time, time.h`

asin *errno M*

```
double asin (double x);
```

Headers: `math.h`

Computes the principal value of the trigonometric arcsine of the argument x in radians.

Returns: `arcsin(x)`.

assert

```
assert (expression)
```

Headers: `assert.h`

Calculates the truth value of *expression*. If the result is TRUE (nonzero), nothing happens. Otherwise, a diagnostic message is written to the standard-error file identifying the line of the source program where the assertion appears and echoing that the assertion failed.

`assert` is intended to be used as a debugging aid. By embedding `assert` statements in the program, this function generates appropriate error messages when an unexpected value or relationship between variables occurs.

`assert` is a macro. By specifying the `cc` option `-DNDEBUG`, you can suppress the generation of `assert` statements.

Returns: Nothing.

atan *errno M*

```
double atan (double x);
```

Headers: `math.h`

Computes the principal value of the trigonometric arctangent of the argument *x* in radians.

Returns: `arctan(x)`.

atan2 *errno M*

```
double atan2 (double x, double y);
```

Headers: `math.h`

Computes the trigonometric arctangent of the tangent *x/y*. The result lies in the range of negative to positive pi radians. `atan2` can be used to avoid the calculation of

```
tan(h) = x/y
```

before computing the arctangent of *h*.

Returns: `arctan(x/y)`.

atof *errno*

```
double atof (const char *string);
```

Converts *string* to a double-precision floating-point number. The string may contain leading whitespace, an optional sign character, one or more decimal digits optionally containing a decimal point, an optional exponent consisting of an "e" or "E", an optional sign character, and one or more decimal digits. The first character in *string* that does not match this pattern stops the conversion.

Returns: The value of *string* as a double-precision floating-point number.

> **Warning**
>
> If an overflow or underflow occurs, this atof returns [+/-]HUGE or 0, and sets *errno* to EDOMAIN.

Related Functions: atof, scanf, strtol

atoi

```
int atoi (const char *string);
```

Returns the integer value represented by the contents of *string*. The string may contain leading whitespace, an optional sign character, and one or more decimal digits. The first character in *string* that does not match this pattern stops the conversion.

atoi is equivalent to (int) strtol(*string*, (char**)0, 10).

Returns: The integer value of *string*. If the value of *string* is too large, it is truncated modulo 32768.

Related Functions: atoi, scanf, strtod, strtol

atol

```
long atol (const char *string);
```

Returns the long integer value represented by the contents of *string*. The string may contain leading whitespace, an optional sign character, and one or more decimal digits. The first character in *string* that does not match this pattern stops conversion.

atol is equivalent to strtol(*string*, (char**)0, 10).

Returns: The long integer value of *string*.

Related Functions: atoi, scanf, strtod, strtol

brk *errno S*

```
int brk (void *endds);
```

Dynamically changes the break address (the first address beyond the end of the data segment) to the value of *endds*, thereby allocating or deallocating memory. *endds* must not fall in the text or stack areas, and must not exceed a system defined maximum. The initial break address is equal to the value of the external static symbol *end*.

Returns: 0 if successful, -1 otherwise.

> **Warning**
>
> The space allocated by brk is not necessarily contiguous. In particular, if the break address is adjusted upward, part or all of the address range between the old break address and the new break address may be inaccessible. You should use the malloc and free functions instead of brk.

Related Functions: sbrk, *end*, malloc

bsearch

```
void *bsearch (const void *key, const void *table,
unsigned nel, unsigned width, int (*compar)());
```

Headers: search.h

Performs a binary search of the array pointed to by *table* for an entry matching *key*. The table is assumed to contain *nel* elements of *width* bytes each.

compar is a user function declared

```
int compar (const void *entry1, const void *entry2);
```

which returns a 0, positive, or negative integer value when the table entry pointed to by *entry1* is equal to, greater than, or less than the table entry pointed to by *entry2*.

Returns: A pointer to the entry in *table* having a key value equal to the value pointed to by *key*, or NULL if no such entry exists.

> **Warning**
>
> The array entries must be in sorted sequence by their key values.

Related Functions: `hsearch, lsearch, tsearch, strcmp`

calloc *errno*

```
void *calloc (unsigned nelem, size_t size);
```

Headers: `malloc.h`

Allocates an area of storage large enough to contain an array of *nelem* elements each *size* bytes long. The area is properly aligned for any use and is initialized to binary 0. A NULL pointer value is returned if an area of the requested size cannot be allocated.

`calloc` uses the `malloc` routine to allocate storage areas. `mallopt` thus has the expected influence on allocations performed by `calloc`.

> **Warning**
>
> Accesses to storage outside the boundaries of the allocated array have unpredictable results, and may cause the program to terminate abnormally.

Related Functions: `free, malloc, mallopt, realloc`

ceil *M*

```
double ceil (double x);
```

Headers: `math.h`

Truncates *x* to the nearest smaller integer value.

Returns: The smallest integer not less than x.

> **Warning**
>
> The value of `ceil(2.7)` is 3, while the value of `ceil(-2.7)` is -2.

chdir *errno S*

```
int chdir (const char *path);
```

Sets the current working directory to the given *path*. Path names that do not begin with / are taken to be relative to the current working directory, as specified by the path argument. The directory named by *path* must exist and must be accessible to the effective user.

Returns: 0 for success, -1 otherwise.

chmod *errno S*

```
int chmod (const char *path, int mode);
```

Sets the access permissions of the file named by *path* to the 12 low-order bits of *mode*. The effective user must be superuser or the owner of the file.

Symbolic values, defined in the header file `sys/stat.h`, should be used to specify the mode bits, as shown in the following table:

Flag Bit	Meaning
S_ISUID	Set-user-ID flag
S_ISGID	Set-group-ID flag
S_ISVTX	Save-text-image flag
S_IREAD	Allow read by the owner of the file
S_IWRITE	Allow write by the owner of the file
S_IEXEC	Allow execute (search) by the owner of the file
S_IRGRP	Allow read by group
S_IWGRP	Allow write by group

Flag Bit	*Meaning*
S_IXGRP	Allow execute by group
S_IROTH	Allow read by others
S_IWOTH	Allow write by others
S_IXOTH	Allow execute by others

The effective group-ID of the process must be equal to the group-ID of the file to set the set-group-ID flag. The effective user-ID must be superuser to set the save-text-image flag.

Returns: 0 if successful, -1 if the file access permissions could not be changed.

> **Warning**
>
> The set-user-ID, set-group-ID, and save-text-image flags have no effect when set for a shell script or data file.

Related Functions: `chown, exec, mknod`

chown *errno S*

```
int chown (const char *path, int owner, int group);
```

Sets the owner-ID and group-ID of the file named by *path* to the numeric values of *owner* and *group* respectively. The effective user-ID of the current process must be superuser or the current owner of the file.

The set-user-ID and set-group-ID bits of the file access permissions are reset to 0 unless the superuser invokes `chown`.

Returns: 0 for success, -1 otherwise.

Related Functions: `chmod`

chroot *errno S KE*

```
int chroot (const char *path);
```

Makes the directory named by *path* the effective root directory of the calling process. `chroot` causes all searches for files to begin with *path*. The directory named by *path* must exist.

Returns: 0 for success, -1 otherwise.

> **Warning**
>
> Only the superuser can execute `chroot`. Once executed, files outside the directory tree beginning at *path* cannot be accessed.

clearerr

```
void clearerr (FILE *stream);
```

Headers: `stdio.h`

Resets any error or end-of-file indication preserved in the FILE block pointed to by *stream*, enabling normal stream-file I/O operations to continue.

Note that once the stream-file I/O functions detect an error or end-of-file indication, the indication is preserved in the FILE block, and further I/O operations for the file are inhibited until the indication is reset.

> **Warning**
>
> `clearerr` is implemented as a macro.

Related Functions: `feof, ferror, fopen`

clock

```
long clock (void);
```

Accumulates the time elapsed since the previous call to `clock`. Accumulated time wraps after 2147 seconds (35+ minutes).

Returns: The number of microseconds elapsed since the previous call to `clock`.

> **Warning**
>
> The resolution of the clock may be greater than 1 microsecond.

close *errno S*

```
int close (int handle);
```

Closes the file corresponding to *handle*. All locks that may be held on the file (see `open`) are released. The file descriptor corresponding to *handle* is marked not-in-use and may be opened for another file.

Returns: 0 if successful, -1 otherwise.

> **Warning**
>
> You should use this function only for files opened with `open`, `creat`, `dup`, or `pipe`.

Related Functions: `creat`, `exec`, `fclose`, `open`, `pipe`

closedir *errno R3*

```
void closedir (DIR *dirp);
```

Headers: `sys/types.h dirent.h`

Closes the directory file pointed to by *dirp* and releases all `malloc` storage associated with the open directory.

> **Warning**
>
> The pointer value of *dirp* is no longer valid after `closedir` is called; any subsequent reference to the DIR structure pointed to by *dirp* will have an unpredictable effect.

Returns: Nothing.

Related Functions: `opendir`, `readdir`, `rewinddir`, `seekdir`, `telldir`

cos *errno M*

```
double cos (double x);
```

Headers: math.h

Computes the trigonometric cosine of the argument *x* in radians.

Returns: `cos(x)`.

cosh *errno M*

```
double cosh (double x);
```

Headers: `math.h`

Computes the hyperbolic cosine of *x*.

Returns: `cosh(x)`.

creat *errno S*

```
int creat (const char *path, int mode);
```

If the file named by *path* does not already exist, this function creates it with access permissions equal to the nine low-order bits of *mode* as modified by the process file-creation mask (see `chmod` and `umask`). If the file already exists, it is truncated to zero length and its access permissions remain unchanged. The file is then opened and made available for writing, even if the access permissions do not allow writing.

The effective user must be the superuser or have write permission for the file if the file already exists.

You cannot use the `creat` function to create a directory, pipe, or special file.

Returns: The handle of the open file, or -1 if unsuccessful.

Related Functions: `chmod`, `fopen`, `mknod`, `open`, `pipe`, `umask`

crypt

```
char *crypt (const char *key, const char salt[2]);
```

Encrypts the string *key* using the password encryption algorithm and a hash code specified as salt. *salt* points to a string of two characters, each of which is one of the values "a" through "z", "A" through "Z", "0" through "9", "." or "/". The string pointed to by *key* is encrypted in a manner influenced by the value of *salt*. The return value points to the encrypted password in a static buffer that is reused on each call.

Only the first eight characters of *key* are used in the encryption process.

Returns: A pointer to the encrypted result as a string in a static internal buffer.

ctermid

```
char *ctermid (char *buf);
```

Headers: `stdio.h`

Returns a path name by which the terminal associated with the calling process can be accessed.

If the value of *buf* is not the NULL pointer, the same path name is stored as a null-terminated string in the character array pointed to by *buf*. The character array must be at least `L_ctermid` bytes in length; `L_ctermid` is defined in the `stdio.h` header file.

Returns: The pointer value of *buf*, if *buf* is not the NULL pointer, or a pointer to an internal static character array containing the result string.

> **Warning**
>
> `ctermid` always returns the literal path name `/dev/tty`.

Related Functions: `ttyname`

ctime

```
char *ctime (long *clock);
```

Headers: `time.h`

Converts the time-of-day value pointed to by *clock* to a character string suitable for display. The clock value expresses the number of seconds elapsed since midnight January 1, 1970. The fields in the result string are of fixed length, and express the date and time in the following format:

```
Sun Dec 17 09:19:13 1989\n\0
```

Returns: A pointer to an internal static character array containing the result string.

Related Functions: `asctime, gmtime, localtime, time`

cuserid

```
char *cuserid (char *buf);
```

Headers: `stdio.h`

Attempts to return the login name of the current user. *buf* is either a NULL pointer, or a pointer to a user-supplied character array at least `L_cuserid` bytes long where the login name will be stored. (`L_cuserid` is defined in the `stdio.h` header file.)

If the calling process was created by `/bin/login` or is a child of such a process, the returned value is equivalent to that returned by `getlogin`, and corresponds to the login name of the user.

If the calling process was created by the `batch` or `at` commands, or was created by a crontab entry, or if for any other reason no appropriate entry is found in the `/etc/utmp` file, the returned value is equivalent to that returned by `getpwuid` for the real user-ID of the calling process.

Returns: The pointer value of *buf* containing the null-terminated user name if *buf* is not the NULL pointer, or otherwise a pointer to a static buffer within the `cuserid` routine. If no appropriate user name can be found, the NULL pointer value is returned, and the character array pointed to by *buf* (if *buf* is not the NULL pointer) is set to the null string.

Related Functions: `getlogin`, `getpwuid`, `getuid`, `logname`

---

drand48

```
double drand48 (void);
```

Computes a double-precision pseudo-random number in the range 0-1 using a congruential multiplicative generator. The random number generator should be seeded before the first call using one of the seed functions `srand48`, `seed48`, or `lcong48`.

Returns: A random number in the range D-1.

> **Warning**
>
> If the random number generator is seeded with the same value on each program execution, or if no seed is introduced, the same series of pseudo-random numbers are generated for every execution of the program.

Related Functions: `erand48`, `jrand48`, `lcong48`, `lrand48`, `mrand48`, `nrand48`, `rand`, `seed48`, `srand48`

---

dup *errno S*

```
int dup (int handle);
```

Copies the open file descriptor corresponding to *handle* into the first unused file descriptor slot, and returns the handle of the copy. Both file descriptors share the same file pointer; a read or write using either file descriptor changes the current position of the file for both file descriptors.

`dup` is primarily used to change the assignment of the standard input, standard output, and standard error files using a sequence similar to the following:

```
fd = open(path, O_WRONLY); /* Open a new output file */
close(1);                  /* Close current stdout file */
dup(fd);                   /* Copy new file descriptor to stdout */
close(fd);                 /* No longer needed */
```

Returns: The handle of the new file descriptor, or -1 if unsuccessful.

Warning

`dup` provides no way to specify which unused file descriptor should be used. When using `dup` to reassign a specific file descriptor, you must carefully ensure that all lower-numbered file descriptors are in use (open).

Related Functions: `close, exec, fcntl, open, pipe`

---

ecvt

```
char *ecvt (double num, int prec, int *exp, int *sign);
```

Converts the double-precision value of *num* to the equivalent base-10 representation as a string of *prec* decimal digits. Leading zeroes are not stored, and the last digit is rounded.

The radix point is assumed to be at the left of the first digit; the integer pointed to by *exp* is set to the number of bytes by which the assumed radix point should be shifted left (negative values) or right (positive values) to obtain the true value of the number. The integer pointed to by *sign* is set to 0 if *num* is 0 or positive, or to -1 if *num* is negative.

Returns: A pointer to the first character of the decimal digit string.

Related Functions: `fcvt, gcvt, printf`

edata

```
extern edata;
```

This external variable contains no data; rather its address (`&edata`) points to
the first memory location beyond the end of the initialized-data portion of the
data segment of the program. Systems not employing a segmented memory
model may define the address of `edata` identically with the address of `end`.

This variable is defined automatically by the C compilation system (`cc`
command).

Related Functions: `end, etext`

encrypt

```
void encrypt (char buffer[64]);
```

Encrypts the contents of *buffer* using the key last set by `crypt`. The buffer must
contain 64 characters, each of which is an ASCII 0 or 1. The characters, divided
into eight groups of eight, represent the binary code of an eight-byte string. The
character-sized bits in the buffer are encrypted in place using the `crypt`
algorithm.

Returns: Nothing.

Related Functions: `crypt`

end

```
extern end;
```

This external variable contains no data; rather its address (&end) points to the first memory location beyond the end of the program. In systems employing a segmented memory model, this location is equivalent to the location following the uninitialized portion of the data segment.

The program break address is set to coincide with the address of end when the program is loaded by the exec functions.

The C compilation system (cc command) automatically defines this variable.

Warning

Attempts to reference the end address may result in a segmentation violation or other abnormal termination condition.

Related Functions: edata, etext

endgrent

```
void endgrent (void);
```

Closes the internal file used by getgrent. The file descriptor and any storage allocated with malloc are released.

Use endgrent to recover resources acquired by the functions getgrent, getgrgid, and getgrnam when group file access is no longer needed.

Returns: Nothing.

Related Functions: getgrent, setgrent

endpwent

```
void endpwent (void);
```

Closes the internal file used by getspent. The file descriptor and any storage allocated with malloc are released.

Use endpwent to recover resources acquired by the functions getpwent, getpwuid, and getpwnam when you no longer need password file access.

Returns: Nothing.

Related Functions: getpwent, setpwent

endspent

```
void endspent (void);
```

Closes the internal file used by getspent. The file descriptor and any storage allocated with malloc are released.

endspent recovers resources allocated by getspent and getspnam.

Returns: Nothing.

Related Functions: getpwent, getspent, setpwent

endutent

```
void endutent (void);
```

Closes the internal file used by getutent. The file descriptor and any storage allocated with malloc are released.

Use endutent to recover resources acquired by the functions getutent, getutid, and getutline when utmp file access is no longer needed.

Returns: Nothing.

Related Functions: getutent, setpwent, utmp.h

environ

```
extern char *environ[];
```

A global variable automatically defined by the C compilation system. It points to an array of string pointers terminated with the NULL pointer; each element of the array points to one of the `name=value` strings in the environment.

You can reference the environment using the `environ` pointer even if the *envp* pointer is not declared as the third argument of the `main` function.

> **Warning**
>
> Alterations to the environment using the `putenv` function are reflected in the value of `environ` but do not affect the *envp* pointer.

Related Functions: `execle`, `getenv`, `putenv`

erand48

```
double erand48 (unsigned short lvalue[3]);
```

Generates a double-precision pseudo-random number in the range 0-1 using a consequential multiplicative algorithm.

The user-supplied array pointed to by *lvalue* is expected to contain a 48-bit value before invocation; on return, the array contains the *X*-value that is used to generate the next number in the random series. Before the first call to `erand48`, some value should be introduced into the array to "seed" the generator.

You can use `erand48` to generate multiple independent random number series by maintaining a separate *lvalue* array for each of the desired series.

Returns: A double-precision number in the range 0-1.

Related Functions: `drand48`, `jrand48`, `lcong48`, `lrand48`, `mrand48`, `nrand48`, `rand`, `seed48`, `srand48`

erf *M*

```
double erf (double x);
```

Headers: math.h

Computes the value of the error function for the argument *x*.

Returns: erf(*x*).

erfc *M*

```
double erfc (double x);
```

Headers: math.h

Computes the value of the complement of the error function for the argument *x*.

Use erfc to avoid loss of significance when erf(x) is a very small value.

Returns: 1.0 - erf(*x*).

errno

```
extern int errno;
```

Headers: errno.h

The errno external variable is set by all system calls and most library functions whenever an error occurs; the value of errno explains the type of error that occurred. You can use the value of the variable as an index into sys_errlist, an array of pointers to message strings. The errno.h header file defines symbolic values for most of the errors that can occur.

> **Warning**
>
> The value of `errno` is not meaningful unless an error was otherwise indicated by the function, usually by a return value of -1.

Related Functions: `sys_errlist, sys_nerr, perror`

etext

```
extern void etext();
```

This external variable is not a usable function; rather its address (`&etext`) points to the first memory location beyond the end of the code (also called *text*) segment of the program. Systems not employing a segmented memory model may define the address of `etext` identically with the address of `end`.

The C compilation system (`cc` command) automatically defines this variable.

> **Warning**
>
> Attempts to invoke the *etext* function may result in a segmentation violation or other abnormal termination condition.

Related Functions: `edata, end`

exec *errno S*

```
int execl (char *path, char *arg0, ... , (char *)0);
int execle (char *path, char *arg0, ... , (char *)0, char *envp[]);
int execlp (char *file, char *arg0, ... , (char *)0);
int execv (char *path, char *argv[]);
int execve (char *path, char *argv[], char *envp[]);
int execvp (char *file, char *argv[]);
```

Discards the current contents of the process address space and loads the executable file named by *path* into memory, then begins executing the loaded program at its entry point. Control cannot be returned to the program calling `exec`. No new process is created. Files that are open remain open, except those for which the close-on-exec flag has been set (see `fcntl`). Signal actions remain in effect, except those for which the action is *function address* (see `signal`), which are set to the default action.

If the access permissions of the executable file include the set-user-ID flag, the effective-user-ID of the process is set to the owner-ID of the file. If the access permissions of the executable file include the set-group-ID flag, the effective-group-ID of the process is set to the group-ID of the file.

The file named by *path* or *file* must exist, must have the appropriate execute permission, and must be a valid executable file. For `execlp` and `execvp`, the directories in the PATH environment are searched for the named *file*.

The arguments *arg0, ...* must be pointers to character strings. The list must be followed by a NULL pointer marking the end of the argument list. The argument strings are copied into the new address space and passed to the invoked program as a standard argument list.

argv must point to an array of pointers to character strings. The last element in the array must be a NULL pointer to mark its end. The strings are copied into the new address space, and become the argument list for the new program.

envp must be an array of pointers to character strings. The last pointer must be followed by a NULL pointer to mark the end of the pointer list. Each string must be an expression of the form *varname=value*.

If the `exec` function cannot be successfully completed, control returns to the calling program and `errno` indicates the reason for failure.

Returns: -1 if unsuccessful, otherwise does not return.

Warning

You must save argument and environment strings in a system buffer while the new process address space is being created. The total number of bytes available is limited, and may be as little as 5120 bytes. You should avoid long argument lists whenever possible.

Related Functions: `chmod`, `fcntl`, `signal`

exit *S*

```
void exit (int status);
```

Terminates the current process after performing cleanup actions, including the following:

❏ Closing all open files

❏ Detaching all attached shared-memory segments as if `shmdt` had been executed for each segment

❏ Adding the *semadj* value for each semaphore manipulated with the SEM_UNDO flag to the semaphore value

❏ Removing all outstanding file locks

The eight low-order bits of *status* are made available to the parent process as a return value.

If the parent process is not executing a `wait`, the calling process is transformed into a zombie process and remains in the process table until the parent process retrieves the termination status. The SIGCLD signal is posted to the parent process, unless the parent process has set the signal action to SIG_DFL or SIG_IGN.

Returns: Nothing.

Related Functions: `_exit, fcntl, lock, semop, shmat, wait`

exp *errno M*

```
double exp (double x);
```

Headers: `math.h`

Computes the value of *e* (the base of the natural logarithms, 2.718...) raised to the power of *x*.

Returns: e^x.

> **Warning**
>
> exp returns HUGE on overflow, or 0 on underflow, and sets *errno* to ERANGE.

fabs *M*

```
double fabs (double x);
```
Headers: math.h

Computes the absolute value of its argument.

Returns: abs(*x*).

fclose *errno*

```
int fclose (FILE *stream);
```
Headers: stdio.h

Closes the stream file pointed to by *stream*. The contents of the stream buffer, if any, are written to the external file or device. All dynamic storage allocated for the file, including the stream buffer and the FILE block, is released.

Returns: 0 if successful, -1 otherwise.

> **Warning**
>
> The object pointed to by *stream* no longer exists after fclose returns, hence any subsequent reference using this pointer would have an unpredictable effect.

Related Functions: close, exit, fflush, fopen, setbuf

fcntl *errno S*

```
int fcntl (int handle, int command, int arg);
```

Headers: fcntl.h

Manipulates an open file in the manner specified by *command*. The file corresponding to *handle* must be open.

For *command* specify one of the following:

F_DUPFD   Copy the file descriptor for *handle* to the file descriptor slot designated by *arg*, or the next higher unopen file descriptor. The handle of the new copy is returned as the value of the function.

F_GETFD   Return the value of the close-on-exec flag for the file descriptor *handle*. The return value will be 0 (not set) or 1 (set).

F_SETFD   Set the close-on-exec flag of the file descriptor *handle* to the value of *arg*. *arg* must have a value of 1 (set) or 0 (not set).

F_GETFL   Return the file status flags as the value of the function. The returned value will be one of the values O_RDONLY, O_WRONLY, or O_RDWR, possibly combined with one or more of the values O_NDELAY, O_APPEND, and O_SYNC.

F_SETF   Set the file status flags to the value of *arg*. Only the O_NDELAY, O_APPEND, and O_SYNC flags may be set.

F_GETLK   Change the flock structure pointed to by *arg* to describe the existing file lock that would prevent you from setting the lock described by the structure. If no conflict is found, the struct is not changed except that the lock type is set to F_UNLCK.

F_SETLK   Set the file segment lock described by the flock structure pointed to by *arg*, if possible. If the lock cannot be granted, a value of -1 is returned.

F_SETLKW   Same as F_SETLK, except that the process is set to wait until the lock can be granted.

The F_GETLK, F_SETLK, and F_SETLKW operations require *arg* to be a pointer to a struct flock that is declared in the fcntl.h header file. The struct contains at least the following members:

l_type   One of the values F_RDLCK, F_WRLCK, or F_UNLCK. A read lock (F_RDLCK) on a file segment prevents any other process from acquiring a write lock on any part of that segment, while a write lock (F_WRLCK) prevents any other lock on any part of that segment (exclusive use). The unlock type (F_UNLCK) releases an existing lock held by the caller.

l_start   The byte offset from the start of the file to the first byte of the file segment to be locked.

l_len   The number of bytes in the file segment. If 0, the segment extends to the end of the file, even if the length of the file later changes. If the value of l_start is also 0, the entire file is locked.

l_pid   Used only by F_GETLK to identify the process owning the conflicting file lock.

Returns: -1 if unsuccessful, otherwise as described in the preceding command definitions. The return value for F_SETFD, F_SETFL, F_GETLK, F_SETLK, and F_SETLKW is not defined.

Related Functions: close, exec, open

fcvt

```
char *fcvt (double num, int prec, int *exp, int *sign);
```

Converts the double-precision value of *num* to the equivalent base-10 representation as a string of decimal digits. The result string consists of the number of digits required for the integer portion of the number, followed immediately by *prec* fractional digits. Leading zeroes are not stored, and the last digit is rounded.

The radix point is assumed to be at the left of the first digit; the integer pointed to by *exp* is set to the number of bytes by which the assumed radix point should be shifted left (negative values) or right (positive values) to obtain the true value of the number. The integer pointed to by *sign* is set to 0 if *num* is 0 or positive, and to -1 if *num* is negative.

Returns: A pointer to the first character of the decimal digit string.

> **Warning**
>
> The result is stored in an internal static buffer, which is reused on each call.

Related Functions: `ecvt, gcvt, printf`

---

fdopen *errno*

```
FILE *fdopen (int handle, const char *type);
```

Headers: `stdio.h`

Creates and initializes a stream file environment, including a FILE block and a stream buffer, to support access of type *type* to the file corresponding to *handle*. The file descriptor *handle* must be open already, and must be compatible with the access type specified by *type*.

Returns: A pointer to the new FILE block, if successful, or a NULL pointer if unsuccessful.

Related Functions: `creat, dup, fopen, freopen, open, pipe`

---

feof

```
int feof (FILE *stream);
```

Headers: `stdio.h`

Checks the stream file *stream* for the presence of an end-of-file indication.

Note that once the stream-file I/O functions detect an end-of-file indication, the indication is preserved in the FILE block, and further I/O operations for the file are inhibited until the indication is reset.

Returns: The value EOF if an end-of-file condition previously was detected for the file *stream*; otherwise 0.

> **Warning**
>
> `feof` is implemented as a macro.

Related Functions: `clearerr, ferror, fopen`

ferror

```
int ferror (FILE *stream);
```

Headers: `stdio.h`

Checks the stream file stream for the presence of an error indication.

Note that once the stream-file I/O functions detect an error indication, the indication is preserved in the FILE block, and further I/O operations for the file are inhibited until the indication is reset by a call to `clearerr`.

Returns: A nonzero value if any previous error was detected for the file *stream*; otherwise 0.

> **Warning**
>
> `ferror` is implemented as a macro.

Related Functions: `clearerr, feof, fopen`

fflush *errno*

```
int fflush (FILE *stream);
```

Headers: `stdio.h`

Writes to the external file or device any output data currently buffered for the stream file pointed to by *stream*.

Returns: 0 if successful, -1 otherwise.

Related Functions: `fclose, setbuf`

fgetc

```
int fgetc (FILE *stream);
```

Headers: stdio.h

Reads the next character of the stream file *stream,* or a character inserted into the stream by a previous call to ungetc. The character value is expanded to an integer value before it is returned. The file pointer is advanced, or the character inserted by ungetc is deleted, as appropriate.

Returns: The value EOF at end-of-file or if an error occurs; otherwise fgetc returns the next character in the file.

> **Warning**
>
> It is machine-dependent whether sign extension occurs when the character value is expanded to an integer; this may cause the integer value of some characters to be negative.

Related Functions: fclose, feof, ferror, fgets, fopen, fputc, fread, fseek, getc, gets, putc, puts, read, scanf, ungetc

fgetgrent

```
struct group *fgetgrent (FILE *stream);
```

Headers: grp.h

Successive calls to fgetgrent retrieve each line of the stream file *stream* in turn. A line is parsed according to the format of the /etc/group system file, and the information is used to fill in an internal static struct of type group. A description of the group struct is given in the grp.h header file.

Returns: A pointer to an internal static group structure, or the NULL pointer if no more entries exist in the file.

> **Warning**
>
> The user is responsible for opening and closing the stream file pointed to by *stream*. The results are unpredictable if the format of the file *stream* does not match the format of the /etc/group system file.

Related Functions: endgrent, getgrent, getgrgid, getgrnam, getpwent, grp.h, setgrent

---

fgetpwent

```
struct passwd *fgetpwent (FILE *stream);
```

Headers: pwd.h

Successive calls to fgetpwent retrieve each line of the stream file *stream* in turn. A line is parsed according to the format of the /etc/passwd system file, and the information is used to fill in an internal static structure of type passwd. A description of the passwd structure is given in the pwd.h header file.

Returns: A pointer to an internal static passwd structure, or the NULL pointer if no more entries exist in the file.

> **Warning**
>
> The user is responsible for opening and closing the stream file pointed to by *stream*. The results are unpredictable if the format of the file *stream* does not match the format of the /etc/passwd system file.

Related Functions: endpwent, getpwent, getpwuid, getpwnam, getpwent, pwd.h, setpwent

---

fgets

```
char *fgets (char *buffer, int size, FILE *stream);
```
Headers: stdio.h

Reads characters from the stream file *stream* and stores them in the character array pointed to by *buffer* until a newline character is stored, *size* characters are stored, or end-of-file is reached. A null character is stored at the end of the input string.

Returns: A pointer to the stored string, that is, the value of *buffer*. If end-of-file occurs before any characters are stored, a NULL pointer value is returned.

Warning

If the input line is longer than *size* characters, each call to `fgets` returns a *size*-byte segment of the line until the last (possibly short) segment is read. This causes processing errors if the input stream file contains lines longer than the program expects.

The `gets` and `fgets` functions handle the newline character differently: `fgets` stores the newline at the end of the input string, but gets does not.

Related Functions: `ferror, fopen, fputs, fread, getc, gets, scanf`

---

fileno

```
int fileno (FILE *stream);
```

Headers: `stdio.h`

Returns the file descriptor on which the stream file pointed to by *stream* is currently open.

Returns: The file descriptor corresponding to the stream file *stream*.

Warning

`fileno` is implemented as a macro.

Related Functions: `fopen, open`

floor *M*

```
double floor (double x);
```

Headers: `math.h`

Returns: The largest integer not greater than *x*.

> **Warning**
>
> floor differs from the integer part of *x* for negative numbers; for example, floor(-2.7) is -3.

fmod *M*

```
double fmod (double x, double y);
```

Headers: `math.h`

Computes the modulus function for double-precision *x* and *y*.

Returns: $x \bmod y$, that is, the quantity *f* such that $x = iy + f$ for some integer *i*.

fopen *errno*

```
int fopen (const char *path, const char *type);
extern FILE *stdin, *stdout, *stderr;
```

Headers: `stdio.h`

Opens the file named by *path* for operations of type *type*. A FILE block and a stream buffer are allocated using `malloc`. The stream files `stdin`, `stdout`, and `stderr` are always open and may be used without an explicit `fopen` request.

Stream files buffer input and output to minimize the number of `read` and `write` calls to the kernel. The size of the buffer defaults to the value BUFSIZ defined in `stdio.h`, but can be overridden using `setbuf` and `setvbuf`.

The character string pointed to by *type* must specify one of the following values:

"r" Opens the file for reading. Sets the file pointer to the first byte of the file.

"w" Opens the file for writing. Creates the file if it does not exist; otherwise truncates it to zero length. Sets the file pointer to the first byte of the file.

"a" Opens the file for appending. Creates the file if it does not exist. Sets the file pointer to the end of the file.

"r+" Opens the file for updating. Returns an error indication if the file does not exist; otherwise, the file is opened for both reading and writing with the file pointer set to the first byte of the file. You cannot follow a read (write) operation with a write (read) unless an intervening fseek or rewind is performed, or the read operation detects end-of-file.

"w+" Opens the file for updating. Creates the file if it does not exist; otherwise the file is truncated to zero length. Either reading or writing can be performed, with the same restrictions noted for type r+. The file pointer is set to the first byte of the file.

"a+" Opens the file for updating. Creates the file if it does not exist; otherwise the file's length remains unchanged. The file pointer is set to the end of the file. Reading may be performed anywhere in the file using fseek or rewind, but all writes are forced to occur at the end of the file.

When a file is open for appending ("a" or "a+"), two or more processes may simultaneously write to the file without causing harm; the output will be interleaved, but will not overlap.

Returns: A pointer to the FILE block, if successful; otherwise the NULL pointer is returned and errno identifies the error.

Related Functions: clearerr, creat, fclose, fread, fseek, fwrite, rewind, setbuf, setvbuf, open

fork *errno S*

```
int fork (void)
```

Creates a new (child) process by making a copy of the current (parent) process. Both processes then continue execution of the same program.

The return value differs for the two processes: the parent receives the new process-ID of the child, while the child receives a return value of 0.

The file descriptors of the child process are initially a copy of the parent's; open file descriptors share a common file pointer. The child process inherits all signal actions in effect for the parent process. The child does not inherit the file locks or the semadj values of its parent. The parent and child processes form a process group sharing the same terminal; signals that are not process-specific are issued to all processes in the process group.

The parent process is notified of the termination of its child processes by the receipt of the signal SIGCLD ("death of a child"), or the parent process is notified of the termination of its child processes when the parent process requests such notification by calling the `wait` function.

Returns: -1 and fails if the system limit on the total number of processes is exceeded, otherwise 0 is returned to the child process, and the process-ID of the child is returned to the parent process.

Related Functions: `dup`, `exec`, `signal`, `wait`

fprintf *errno*

```
int fprintf (FILE *stream, const char *format, ...);
```

Headers: `stdio.h`

Differs from `printf` only in that `fprintf` writes the result string to the stream file *stream* instead of to standard output.

Returns: The number of characters written to *stream*, or a negative number if an error occurred.

> **Warning**
>
> The same cautions apply to fprintf as to printf.

Related Functions: printf, putc, puts, fscanf, sprintf, vfprintf

fputc

```
int fputc (int c, FILE *stream);
```

Headers: stdio.h

Writes the character *c* to the stream file *stream*. fputc differs from putc only in that fputc is a real function instead of a macro.

Returns: The value *c*.

> **Warning**
>
> fputc imposes more overhead than putc because of function entry and exit code; use putc whenever possible.

Related Functions: putc

fputs *errno*

```
int fputs (const char *string, FILE *stream);
```

Headers: stdio.h

Writes to the stream file *stream* the null-terminated string pointed to by *string*. Neither a newline character nor the ending null character are written.

fputs behaves as if the putc function were called to write each character of the string successively.

Returns: EOF if an error occurs, otherwise 0.

> **Warning**
>
> The `puts` and `fputs` functions use opposite conventions for writing a trailing newline character to the output.

Related Functions: `ferror, fgets, fopen, putc, puts`

fread *errno*

```
int fread (void *ptr, int size, int elems, FILE *stream);
```

Headers: `stdio.h`

Retrieves a number of data elements, each *size* bytes long, from the stream file *stream* and stores them in consecutive elements of the array pointed to by *ptr*. Reading stops when *elems* elements have been transferred, EOF is encountered, or an I/O error occurs. If the value of *elems* is 0 or negative, no elements are transferred.

One call can transfer 65,535 bytes at most.

Returns: The number of array elements actually stored.

Related Functions: `fopen, fwrite, getc, gets, putc, read, scanf`

free

```
void free (void *area);
```

Headers: `malloc.h`

Releases the storage block pointed to by *area*. The storage is made available for subsequent reallocation.

> **Warning**
>
> Undefined results occur if the value of *area* is not a pointer value previously returned by `malloc`, `calloc`, or `realloc`.

Returns: Nothing.

Related Functions: `calloc, malloc, realloc`

freopen *errno*

`FILE *freopen (const char *path, const char *type, FILE *stream);`

`Headers: stdio.h`

Closes the stream file associated with the FILE block pointed to by *stream*, then reopens the stream file on the file named by *path* for access type *type*. The reopen operation is identical to the operation performed by `fopen` for the specified *path* and *type*.

If the reopen operation fails, the FILE block pointed to by *stream* was closed, and in this case further reference to the pointer *stream* is invalid.

The `freopen` function is most useful for changing the file to which the standard FILE blocks `stdin`, `stdout`, and `stderr` are assigned.

Returns: The value of *stream* if the reopen is successful; otherwise the NULL pointer is returned and *errno* is set to indicate the error.

Related Functions: `fclose, fdopen, fopen`

frexp

`double frexp (double num, int *eptr);`

Returns: The mantissa of the base-2 logarithm of the double-precision number *num*. The characteristic is stored at the integer pointed to by *eptr*.

Related Functions: `ldexp`

fscanf *errno*

`int fscanf (FILE *stream, const char *format, ...);`

Headers: stdio.h

Differs from scanf only in that fscanf reads the stream file pointed to by *stream* instead of standard input.

Returns: The number of values converted and stored, or EOF if end-of-file was encountered before any values were stored.

Related Functions: fclose, ferror, fopen, fread, getc, scanf, sscanf

fseek

```
# include <unistd.h>
int fseek (FILE *stream, long offset, int origin);
```

Headers: stdio.h

Performs a logical seek for the stream file *stream* by setting an internal file pointer to a new byte offset within the file at which the next read or write request will begin transfer of data. Any end-of-file indication that may be preserved in the FILE block pointed to by *stream* is cleared.

The new byte offset is computed as the sum of the signed value of *offset* and a byte displacement implied by the value of *origin*. The following table shows the allowable values of *origin* as defined in unistd.h:

Origin	Implied Position in File
SEEK_SET	Beginning (offset=0)
SEEK_CUR	Current position
SEEK_END	End-of-file

Note that fseek(*stream*,0L,SEEK_SET) positions to the first byte of the file, fseek(*stream*,0L,SEEK_CUR) leaves the current file position unchanged, and fseek(*stream*,-1L,SEEK_END) positions to the last byte in the file.

You can use negative offsets, but only when the resulting file offset is not negative.

Returns: A nonzero value if the seek cannot be performed, or 0 if successful.

> **Warning**
>
> You cannot reposition some types of files, such as terminals, communication lines, and pipes. `fseek` is intended to be used with standard disk files; other uses may not be portable. `fseek` cancels the effect of any previous `ungetc`.

Related Functions: `ftell, fopen, lseek, rewind`

fstat *errno S*

```
int fstat (int handle, struct stat *buf);
```

Headers: `sys/types.h sys/stat.h`

Returns information about the open file associated with *handle* in the user-provided structure pointed to by *buf*. The format of the stat buffer is defined in the `stat.h` header file.

Returns: 0 if successful, -1 otherwise.

Related Functions: `access, stat, stat.h`

ftell

```
long ftell (FILE *stream);
```

Headers: `stdio.h`

Returns the current position of the stream file *stream* as a byte offset from the beginning of the file. The value returned by `ftell` can be used as the *offset* argument to `fseek` so that a read or write operation following the `fseek` reads from (or writes to) the same byte of the file as if the read (or write) were performed immediately after the `ftell`.

Returns: The current value of the file pointer for the file *stream*.

> **Warning**
>
> When *stream* is opened for a file type that does not support seek operations, the value returned by `ftell` is meaningless.

Related Functions: `fopen`, `fseek`

ftok

```
key_t ftok (const char *path, char id);
```

Headers: `sys/types.h` `sys/ipc.h`

Aids in forming unique keys for use by the `msgget`, `semget`, and `shmget` system calls.

path points to a null-terminated string giving the pathname of a file to which the caller has access. *id* is a single character that represents the caller's best effort to associate a unique identifier with the application.

Returns: A numeric value of type `key_t` that can be used with the `msgget`, `semget`, and `shmget` calls.

> **Warning**
>
> `ftok` forms the key by using the *inode* number associated with the given pathname; therefore, links to the same file yield the same key value even though they have a different pathname. There is no guarantee that the key value computed by `ftok` will not duplicate a key value used by an unrelated application.

Related Functions: `msgget`, `semget`, `shmget`

ftw

```
int ftw (const char *path, int (*fn)(), int depth);
```
Headers: `ftw.h`

Recursively descends the directory hierarchy beginning with the directory named by *path*, calling the user-supplied function *fn* for each file or directory encountered. When `ftw` finds a directory while reading a directory, the function opens a new file descriptor if the number of files it already opened is less than *depth*; otherwise `ftw` reuses one of the file descriptors already open.

The declaration of the user-supplied function *fn* is as follows:

```
int fn (char *filename, struct stat *statbuf, int flag);
```

where *filename* is a null-terminated string giving the name of the current file or directory, *statbuf* points to a structure containing the output from `stat` for the current file, and *flag* contains one of the following values:

FTW_F If the current object is a file

FTW_D if the current object is a directory

FTW_DNR if the current object is a directory that cannot be read

FTW_NS if stat could not be executed for the object. The contents of the structure pointed to by *statbuf* are meaningless in this case.

When traversal is complete or the user function returns a nonzero value, `ftw` closes all files that it opened, releases all storage obtained by calls to `malloc`, and returns.

Returns: The last value returned by the user function *fn*.

Warning

`ftw` can run out of free storage when traversing a very deep directory structure. `ftw` runs faster if the value of *depth* is at least as large as the deepest nesting level in the directory tree to be traversed.

Related Functions: `dir.h`, `opendir`, `stat`, `malloc`

---

fwrite *errno*

```
int fwrite (const void *ptr, int size, int elems, FILE *stream);
```

Headers: `stdio.h`

Writes successive elements of the array pointed to by *ptr*, each *size* bytes long, to the stream file *stream*. Writing stops when *elems* elements have been transferred or an I/O error occurs. If the value of *elems* is 0 or negative, no elements are transferred.

You can transfer 65,535 bytes at most in one call.

Returns: The number of array elements actually written.

Related Functions: `fopen, fread, printf, putc, write`

gamma *errno M*

```
double gamma (double x);
```

Headers: `math.h, values.h`

Computes the natural logarithm of the absolute value of the gamma function at *x*. The sign of the gamma function at *x* is stored in the global integer variable *signgam*. The actual gamma function can be computed as the product of *signgam* and exp(g), when g is not larger than LN_MAXDOUBLE as defined in the `values.h` header file.

Returns: The natural logarithm of the absolute value of the gamma function at *x*.

gcvt

```
char *gcvt (double num, int prec, char *buf);
```

Stores the base-10 representation of the double-precision value of *num*, rounded to *prec* digits of precision, in the character array pointed to by *buf*. The stored result contains a decimal point at the proper position, as well as a sign character if necessary.

An attempt is made to store the result in fixed-point notation; if the size of *buf*, as indicated by the value of *prec*, is insufficient, the result is stored in exponent notation.

Returns: The pointer value of *buf*.

Related Functions: `ecvt, fcvt, printf`

getc

```
int getc (FILE *stream);
```

Headers: stdio.h

Returns: The character at the byte offset indicated by the file pointer of the stream file *stream,* or a character inserted into the stream by a previous call to ungetc. Before it returns, the character value is expanded to an integer value. The file pointer is advanced, or the character inserted by ungetc is deleted, as appropriate.

The value EOF is returned at end-of-file or if an error occurs.

> **Warning**
>
> getc is implemented as a macro. Although getc is therefore faster than fgetc, unexpected side-effects can arise; for example, getc(*f++) causes multiple incrementations of the pointer f.

Related Functions: fclose, feof, ferror, fgetc, fgets, fopen, fputc, fread, fseek, gets, putc, puts, read, scanf, ungetc

getchar

```
int getchar (void);
```

Headers: stdio.h

Reads the next character from the stream file stdin. getchar is implemented as the following macro definition:

```
#define getchar() getc(stdin)
```

Returns: The character read, or EOF if stdin is at end-of-file.

Related Functions: fgetc, getc

getcwd *errno*

```
char *getcwd (char *buf, int size);
```

Stores the pathname of the current directory in the character array pointed to by *buf*; the length of the pathname stored will not exceed *size* bytes.

If the value of *buf* is the NULL pointer, a storage area *size* bytes long is allocated using `malloc` to hold the pathname string.

Returns: The NULL pointer if `malloc` cannot acquire storage, or if the size of the user-supplied character array indicated by *size* is less than the length of the pathname of the current directory. Otherwise a pointer to the pathname string is returned.

> **Warning**
>
> The pathname of the current directory is determined by reading the piped output of the `pwd` command. Not only does this entail significant overhead, but the `pwd` command cannot determine the pathname if the caller does not have search permission for all higher directories in the hierarchy.

getegid *S*

```
unsigned short getegid (void);
```

Returns the effective group-ID of the calling process.

Group-ID numbers are assigned in the `/etc/passwd` and `/etc/group` files. `exec` sets the effective group-ID when the calling program is loaded and executed.

Returns: The effective group-ID of the calling process.

Related Functions: `execl`, `getuid`, `getgid`

getenv

```
char *getenv (const char *name);
```

Searches the environment for a string of the format

```
name=value
```

where the string to the left of the = ("name") is equal to the string pointed to by *name*.

Returns: A pointer to the string following the = in the environment variable; but if no environment variable with a matching name is found, the NULL pointer is returned.

Related Functions: putenv

geteuid *S*

```
unsigned short geteuid (void);
```

Returns the effective user-ID of the calling process.

User-ID numbers are assigned in the /etc/passwd file. The exec system call set the effective user-ID when the calling program was loaded and executed.

Related Functions: execl, getuid, getgid, setuid

getgid *S*

```
unsigned short getgid (void);
```

Returns the real group-ID of the calling process. Group-ID numbers are assigned in the /etc/passwd and /etc/group files. You can change the real group-ID of the process using the setgid system call.

Related Functions: getuid, getegid, setgid

getgrent

```
struct group *getgrent (void);
```

Headers: grp.h

The first call to getgrent opens the group definition file /etc/group and stores the first line of the file in an internal group structure, the address of which is returned to the caller. Successive calls to getgrent retrieve each line of the /etc/group file in turn.

A description of the group struct is given in the grp.h header file.

Returns: A pointer to an internal static group structure, or the NULL pointer if no more entries exist in the file.

Related Functions: endgrent, fgetgrent, getgrgid, getgrnam, getpwent, grp.h, setgrent

getgrgid

```
struct group *getgrgid (int group_id);
```

Headers: grp.h

Searches the /etc/group file for a line having a matching group-ID. If found, getgrgid pauses the line into an internal group structure and returns a pointer to the structure. The grp.h header file contains a description of the group structure.

Returns: A pointer to an internal static group structure containing the record in the /etc/group file having a matching group-id, or the NULL pointer if the specified group-ID does not occur in the /etc/group system file.

> **Warning**
>
> The getgrgid function calls getgrent internally to scan the /etc/group file. If the endgrent function is not called, the group file remains open, reducing the number of file descriptors available for application use.

Related Functions: endgrent, fgetgrent, getgrent, getgrnam, grp.h, setgrent

getgrnam

```
struct group *getgrnam (const char *name);
```

Headers: grp.h

Searches the /etc/group file for a line having a matching *name*. If found, getgrnam pauses the line into an internal group structure and returns a pointer to the structure. The grp.h header file contains a description of the group structure.

Returns: A pointer to an internal static group structure containing the record in the /etc/group file having a matching *name*, or the NULL pointer if the specified group-ID does not occur in the /etc/group system file.

> **Warning**
>
> The getgrnam function calls getgrent internally to scan the /etc/group file. If the endgrent function is not called, the group file remains open, reducing the number of file descriptors available for application use.

Related Functions: endgrent, fgetgrent, getgrent, getgrnam, grp.h, setgrent

getlogin

```
char *getlogin (void);
```

Returns the login name of the current user.

Returns: A pointer to a null-terminated character string that is the login name of the current user, as found in the /etc/utmp system file. The NULL pointer is returned if the proper login name cannot be identified; if this is the case, the current process was probably initiated by the batch or at commands, or by the cron system facility.

> **Warning**
>
> The result string is stored in an internal static character array that is reused on each call.

Related Functions: `cuserid`, `getpwuid`, `getuid`, `logname`

getopt

```
int getopt (int argc, const char *argv[], const char *flags);
extern char *optarg;
extern int optind, opterr;
```

Parses option flags in the argument list *argv*, returning each keyletter found together with any value string that may be present. Each call to `getopt` returns the next option keyletter in the argument list.

Each letter in the null-terminated string pointed to by *flags* is considered to be a legal keyletter. If a keyletter is expected to have an accompanying value string, a colon (:) must follow that keyletter.

`getopt` is quite flexible in the formats that it accepts for keyletter options. Options not having an accompanying value string may occur as separate arguments, for example `-a` `-e` `-h`, or may be combined into one option argument, as in `-aeh`. When a value string is expected, the value string may immediately follow the keyletter that introduces it, or the value string may appear as the next argument; for example, both `-I/usr/lib` and `-I /usr/lib` are accepted as equivalent forms for the flag `I:`. The argument value `--` if found is always taken by `getopt` to mark the end of the option list; EOF is returned immediately and *optind* is adjusted to the index of the following argument.

Note that a keyletter with an accompanying value string must be the last keyletter in a combined group of flags; this is because all remaining characters in the argument string are assumed to be the value string for the keyletter.

optarg is set to point to the null-terminated value string accompanying the keyletter; if no value string is expected, *optarg* points to a zero-length string.

optind always indicates the index of the next unprocessed argument in the argument list. The value of this external variable can be used after `getopt` returns all option keyletters (and indicated EOF) to locate the remaining arguments.

opterr is a boolean flag that the user can set to indicate whether getopt should generate error messages for illegal keyletters found in the argument list. If the value of the external integer is 1, getopt generates error messages; if the value is 0, getopt does not write error messages. In either case, an ASCII value of ? is returned to the caller for an illegal option keyletter. The value of *opterr* is initialized to 1.

Returns: The next option keyletter found in the argument list as an integer ASCII code, or the integer code for the question mark character (?) if an illegal keyletter is found, or the value EOF if no more keyletters are found.

getpass

```
char *getpass (const char *prompt);
```

Writes the string pointed by *prompt* to the file /dev/tty, then reads input from the same device up to the next newline or end-of-file. All but the first eight characters of the typed input is discarded. The read is performed with echoing disabled so that the typed password cannot be seen.

Returns: A pointer to the typed input string, or NULL if an error occurs.

> **Warning**
>
> The input string is stored in an internal static array, which is reused on each call.

Related Functions: crypt

getpgrp *S*

```
int getpgrp (void);
```

Returns the ID of the process group of which the calling process is a member.

All processes sharing the same terminal are members of the same process group. One of the processes in the group is not the child of any other process in the group; this process is the group leader. The process group-ID is the same as the process-ID of the group leader.

Returns: The process group-ID of the caller.

Related Functions: `fork, getpid, getppid`

getpid *S*

```
int getpid (void);
```

Returns the process-ID of the current process. The process-ID is unique for each process, but numbers may be reused as long as no two active processes have the same process-ID.

Returns: The process-ID of the calling process.

Related Functions: `fork, getppid, getpgrp`

getppid *S*

```
int getppid (void);
```

Returns the process-ID of the parent process.

Related Functions: `fork, getpid, getppid`

getpwent

```
struct passwd *getpwent (void);
```

Headers: `pwd.h`

The first call to `getpwent` opens the password file `/etc/passwd` and stores the first line of the file in an internal structure, the address of which is returned to the caller. Successive calls to `getpwent` retrieves each line of the `/etc/passwd` file in turn.

The `pwd.h` header file provides a description of the `passwd` struct.

Returns: A pointer to an internal static `passwd` structure, or the NULL pointer if no more entries exist in the file.

Related Functions: `endpwent`, `fgetpwent`, `getpwuid`, `getpwnam`, `getpwent`, `pwd.h`, `setpwent`

getpwnam

```
struct passwd *getpwnam (const char *name);
```

Headers: `pwd.h`

Searches the `/etc/passwd` file for the next line matching *name*. If the line is found, `getpwnam` parses it and stores its fields into an internal `passwd` structure, and returns a pointer to the structure.

Returns: A pointer to an internal static `passwd` structure, or the NULL pointer if the specified login name does not occur in the `/etc/passwd` system file.

The `pwd.h` header file contains a description of the `passwd` structure.

> **Warning**
>
> The `getpwnam` function calls getpwent internally to scan the /etc/passwd file. If the `endpwent` function is not called, the file remains open, reducing the number of file descriptors available for application use.

Related Functions: `endpwent`, `fgetpwent`, `getpwent`, `getpwnam`, `pwd.h`, `setpwent`

getpwuid

```
struct passwd *getpwuid (int user_id);
```

Headers: `pwd.h`

Searches the `/etc/passwd` file for the next line matching *user_id*. If the line is found, `getpwuid` parses it and stores its fields into an internal `passwd` structure, and returns a pointer to the structure.

Returns: A pointer to an internal static `passwd` structure, or the NULL pointer if the specified user-ID does not occur in the `/etc/passwd` system file.

The `pwd.h` header file contains a description of the `passwd` structure.

> **Warning**
>
> The `getpwuid` function calls `getpwent` internally to scan the `/etc/passwd` file. If the `endpwent` function is not called, the file remains open, reducing the number of file descriptors available for application use.

Related Functions: `endpwent`, `fgetpwent`, `getpwent`, `getpwnam`, `pwd.h`, `setpwent`

gets

```
char *gets (char *buffer);
```

Headers: `stdio.h`

Reads characters from the standard-input file *stdin*, and stores them in the character array pointed to by *buffer*, until a newline character is read or end-of-file is reached. The newline character is not stored. A null character is stored at the end of the input string.

Returns: A pointer to the stored string, that is, the value of *buffer*. If end-of-file occurs before any characters are stored, a NULL pointer value is returned.

> **Warning**
>
> The `gets` function is dangerous because it attempts to store an indefinite number of characters in the array pointed to by *buffer*, possibly overrunning the end of the array. You should usually use `fgets` instead.

Related Functions: `ferror`, `fgets`, `fopen`, `fread`, `getc`, `puts`, `scanf`

getuid *S*

```
unsigned short getuid (void);
```

Returns the real user-ID of the calling process. User-ID numbers are assigned in the /etc/passwd file. You can change the real user-ID of the process by using the setuid system call.

Returns: The real user-ID of the calling process.

Related Functions: geteuid, getgid, setuid

getutent

```
struct utmp *getutent (void);
```

Headers: utmp.h

The first call opens the system file /etc/utmp (or, if utmpname has been called, a file in the same format as /etc/utmp) and stores the first record in the file in an internal structure, the address of which is returned to the caller. Successive calls to getutent retrieve each record of the file in turn.

The utmp.h header file provides a description of the utmp struct.

Returns: A pointer to an internal static utmp structure, or the NULL pointer at end-of-file.

Related Functions: endutent, getutent, getutid, getutline, pututline, setutent, utmp.h, utmpname

getutid

```
struct utmp *getutid (struct utmp *buf);
```

Headers: utmp.h

Searches for the next occurrence in the utmp file of a record where the *ut_type* value matches the value of *ut_type* in the struct pointed to by *buf*. If the value of *ut_type* in *buf* is INIT_PROCESS, LOGIN_PROCESS, USER_PROCESS or DEAD_PROCESS, the record must match both the *ut_type* and *ut_id* values in the struct pointed to by *buf*.

Returns: A pointer to an internal static struct containing the record that matches the search criteria, or the NULL pointer if a matching record is not found between the current file position and end-of-file.

> **Warning**
>
> The current contents of the internal static `utmp` struct are tested for a match before the next `utmp` record is read. Therefore, once a match is found, the user must clear the *ut_type* field (and *ut_id* field) in the struct before performing the next search.

Related Functions: `endutent,getutent,getutline,pututline,setutent,` `utmp.h, utmpname`

---

getutline

```
struct utmp *getutline (struct utmp *buf);
```

Headers: `utmp.h`

Searches for the next occurrence in the `utmp` file of a record where the *ut_line* value matches the value of *ut_line* in the struct pointed to by *buf*. Only records having a *ut_type* value of LOGIN_PROCESS or USER_PROCESS are examined.

Returns: A pointer to an internal static struct containing the record that matches the search criteria, or the NULL pointer if a matching record is not found between the current file position and end-of-file.

> **Warning**
>
> The current contents of the internal static `utmp` struct are tested for a match before the next `utmp` record is read. Therefore, once a match is found, the user must clear the *ut_line* field in the struct before performing the next search.

Related Functions: `endutent,getutent,getutline,pututline,setutent,` `utmp.h, utmpname`

---

getw

```
int getw (FILE *stream);
```

Headers: `stdio.h`

Returns: The next integer taken from the stream file *stream*. The number of bytes read is equal to the size of an integer, and the file pointer is advanced by a corresponding amount. No alignment of the file pointer is forced or assumed.

EOF is returned at end-of-file.

Warning

Because `getw` can return all legal values of an integer, you should check end-of-file with the `feof` function. The manner in which integers are stored in memory, and therefore on external media, differs among implementations of UNIX.

Related Functions: `feof, fopen, fread, fseek, getc, scanf`

gmtime

```
struct tm *gmtime (long *clock);
```

Headers: `time.h`

Converts the time-of-day value pointed to by *clock* to a *tm* structure (see Appendix C, "Important Header Files"). The values returned correspond to the GMT timezone.

Returns: A pointer to a static area in the format of a *tm* structure contained within the `gmtime` routine.

Related Functions: `asctime, ctime, localtime, time, time.h`

gsignal

```
int gsignal (int sig);
```

Headers: `signal.h`

Causes the action associated with signal *sig* to be executed. Actions are associated with signals by the `ssignal` function.

Returns:

0 if the action for signal *sig* is SIG_DFL

1 if the action for signal *sig* is SIG_IGN

n if the action for signal *sig* is a function. *n* is the value returned by the signal-catching function.

> **Warning**
>
> You should use signal numbers 1-15 only. The standard C function library can use other signal numbers.

Related Functions: ssignal

hcreate

```
int hcreate (int n);
```

Creates a new hash search table with sufficient space to hold *n* entries. The table is initially empty.

You must invoke hcreate before you can use hsearch. You can use only one hash table at a time.

Returns: 0 if insufficient space is available to create the table; otherwise a nonzero value.

Related Functions: hdestroy, hsearch

hdestroy

```
void hdestroy (void);
```

Deletes an existing hash table, releasing all storage dedicated to the table. You can create a new table with hcreate after executing hdestroy.

Related Functions: hcreate, hsearch

hsearch

```
void *hsearch (ENTRY item, int action);
```

Headers: `search.h`

Searches the hash table previously created by `hcreate` for an entry containing a specified key value. The *item.key* pointer specifies the key value to find. The value of *action* specifies the action to take if the key value is *not* found in the hash table: a value of ENTER causes *item* to be added to the hash table, while a value of FIND suppresses the insertion of *item*.

Returns: A pointer to the struct of type ENTRY in the hash table having a key value matching that of *item*, or a pointer to the new table entry if the key value of *item* is not found in the table and the value of *action* is ENTER, or a NULL pointer if the key value of *item* is not found in the table and the value of *action* is FIND.

Related Functions: `hcreate, hdestroy, search.h`

hypot *errno M*

```
double hypot (double x, double y);
```

Headers: `math.h`

Computes the hypotenuse of a triangle with legs x and y.

Returns: $sqrt(x*x + y*y)$ computed in a manner to avoid spurious overflow or underflow.

ioctl *errno S*

```
int ioctl (int handle, int request, ...);
```

Performs device-specific functions for character-special devices. Refer to section 7 of the *UNIX System V Programmer's Reference Manual* for specific information.

Returns: -1 if an error occurs; otherwise the value returned depends on the request.

> **Warning**
>
> The valid request types and their meaning vary among implementations of UNIX System V. In general, programs using `ioctl` are not portable across implementations, releases, or versions of UNIX.

Related Functions: `fcntl`

isalnum

```
int isalnum (int character);
```

Headers: `ctype.h`

Tests whether the value of *character* corresponds to the ASCII code for an uppercase letter, a lowercase letter, or a decimal digit (0-9).

Returns: A nonzero value if true, otherwise 0.

> **Warning**
>
> A meaningless result value is returned if the value of *character* is outside the range of valid ASCII codes (0127).

Related Functions: `isalpha, isascii, iscntrl, isdigit, isgraph, islower, isprint, ispunct, isspace, isupper, isxdigit`

isalpha

```
int isalpha (int character);
```

Headers: `ctype.h`

Tests whether the value of *character* corresponds to the ASCII code for an upper- or lowercase letter (a-z or A-Z).

Returns: A nonzero value if true, otherwise 0.

> **Warning**
>
> `isalpha` returns a meaningless result value if the value of *character* is outside the range of valid ASCII codes (0127).

Related Functions: `isalnum`, `isascii`, `iscntrl`, `isdigit`, `isgraph`, `islower`, `isprint`, `ispunct`, `isspace`, `isupper`, `isxdigit`

isascii

```
int isascii (int character);
```

Headers: `ctype.h`

Tests whether the value of *character* corresponds to a valid ASCII code. The function is defined for all possible values of *character*.

Returns: A nonzero value if true, otherwise 0.

Related Functions: `isalnum`, `isalpha`, `iscntrl`, `isdigit`, `isgraph`, `islower`, `isprint`, `ispunct`, `isspace`, `isupper`, `isxdigit`

isatty

```
int isatty (int handle);
```

Tests whether the device corresponding to the open file descriptor *handle* is a terminal device.

Returns: 1 if true, 0 otherwise.

Related Functions: `ctermid`, `ttyname`

iscntrl

```
int iscntrl (int character);
```

Headers: ctype.h

Tests whether the value of *character* corresponds to the ASCII code for a control character (less than 040 or equal to 0177).

Returns: A nonzero value if true, otherwise 0.

> **Warning**
>
> iscntrl returns a meaningless result value if the value of *character* is outside the range of valid ASCII codes (0127).

Related Functions: isalnum, isalpha, isascii, isdigit, isgraph, islower, isprint, ispunct, isspace, isupper, isxdigit

isdigit

```
int isdigit (int character);
```

Headers: ctype.h

Tests whether the value of *character* corresponds to the ASCII code for a decimal digit (0-9).

Returns: A nonzero value if true, otherwise 0.

> **Warning**
>
> isdigit returns a meaningless result value if the value of *character* is outside the range of valid ASCII codes (0127).

Related Functions: isalnum, isalpha, isascii, iscntrl, isgraph, islower, isprint, ispunct, isspace, isupper, isxdigit

isgraph

```
int isgraph (int character);
```

Headers: `ctype.h`

Tests whether the value of *character* corresponds to the ASCII code for a printable graphic. The space character is not considered a printable graphic.

Returns: A nonzero value if true, otherwise 0.

> **Warning**
>
> `isgraph` returns a meaningless result value if the value of *character* is outside the range of valid ASCII codes (0127).

Related Functions: `isalnum, isalpha, isascii, iscntrl, isdigit, islower, isprint, ispunct, isspace, isupper, isxdigit`

islower

```
int islower (int character);
```

Headers: `ctype.h`

Tests whether the value of *character* corresponds to the ASCII code for a lowercase letter (a-z).

Returns: A nonzero value if true, otherwise 0.

> **Warning**
>
> `islower` returns a meaningless result value if the value of *character* is outside the range of valid ASCII codes (0127).

Related Functions: `isalnum, isalpha, isascii, iscntrl, isdigit, isgraph, isprint, ispunct, isspace, isupper, isxdigit`

isprint

```
int isprint (int character);
```

Headers: ctype.h

Tests whether the value of *character* corresponds to the ASCII code for a printable graphic.

Returns: A nonzero value if true, otherwise 0.

> **Warning**
>
> isprint returns a meaningless result value if the value of *character* is outside the range of valid ASCII codes (0127).

Related Functions: isalnum, isalpha, isascii, iscntrl, isdigit, isgraph, islower, ispunct, isspace, isupper, isxdigit

ispunct

```
int ispunct (int character);
```

Headers: ctype.h

Tests whether the value of *character* corresponds to the ASCII code for a punctuation character; equivalent to

```
(!iscntrl(character) && !isalnum(character)).
```

Returns: A nonzero value if true, otherwise 0.

> **Warning**
>
> ispunct returns a meaningless result value if the value of *character* is outside the range of valid ASCII codes (0127).

Related Functions: isalnum, isalpha, isascii, iscntrl, isdigit, isgraph, islower, isprint, isspace, isupper, isxdigit

isspace

```
int isspace (int character);
```

Headers: `ctype.h`

Tests whether the value of *character* corresponds to the ASCII code for a space, tab, newline, carriage return, vertical tab, or form feed.

Returns: A nonzero value if true, otherwise 0.

> **Warning**
>
> `isspace` returns a meaningless result value if the value of *character* is outside the range of valid ASCII codes (0127).

Related Functions: `isalnum, isalpha, isascii, iscntrl, isdigit, isgraph, islower, isprint, ispunct, isupper, isxdigit`

isupper

```
int isupper (int character);
```

Headers: `ctype.h`

Tests whether the value of *character* corresponds to the ASCII code for an uppercase letter (A-Z).

Returns: A nonzero value if true, otherwise 0.

> **Warning**
>
> `isupper` returns a meaningless result value if the value of *character* is outside the range of valid ASCII codes (0127).

Related Functions: `isalnum, isalpha, isascii, iscntrl, isdigit, isgraph, islower, isprint, ispunct, isspace, isxdigit`

isxdigit

```
int isxdigit (int character);
```

Headers: ctype.h

Tests whether the value of *character* corresponds to the ASCII code for a hexadecimal digit (0-9, a-f, or A-F).

Returns: A nonzero value if true, otherwise 0.

> **Warning**
>
> isxdigit returns a meaningless result value if the value of *character* is outside the range of valid ASCII codes (0127).

Related Functions: isalnum, isalpha, isascii, iscntrl, isdigit, isgraph, islower, isprint, ispunct, isspace, isupper

j0 *errno M*

```
double j0 (double x);
```

Headers: math.h

Computes the value of the Bessel function of the first kind, of order 0, corresponding to the argument *x*. The function is defined for positive values of *x* less than some "large" value; other values cause a *matherr* condition to be recognized.

Returns: The computed value.

j1 *errno M*

```
double j1 (double x);
```

Headers: math.h

Computes the value of the Bessel function of the first kind, of order 1, corresponding to the argument x. The function is defined for positive values of x less than some "large" value; other values cause a *matherr* condition to be recognized.

Returns: The computed value.

jn *errno M*

```
double jn (double x);
```

Headers: math.h

Computes the value of the Bessel function of the first kind, of order n, corresponding to the argument x. The function is defined for positive values of x less than some "large" value; other values cause a *matherr* condition to be recognized.

Returns: The computed value.

jrand48

```
long jrand48 (unsigned short lvalue[3]);
```

Generates a pseudo-random number uniformly distributed over the range -2,147,483,648 to 2,147,483,647.

The user-supplied array pointed to by *lvalue* is expected to contain a 48-bit value before invocation; on return, it contains the X-value that is used to generate the next number in the random series. You should introduce some value into the array before the first call to jrand48 to "seed" the generator.

You can generate multiple independent random number series using jrand48 by maintaining a separate *lvalue* array for each of the desired series.

Returns: The computed random number.

Related Functions: drand48, erand48, lcong48, lrand48, mrand48, nrand48, rand, seed48, srand48

kill *errno S*

```
int kill (int pid, int sig);
```

Headers: signal.h

Sends the signal *sig* to the process or group of processes implied by the value of *pid*.

sig must be one of the signals defined for the signal function, or 0. If 0, no signal is actually sent but all other error checking is performed; this fact may be used to validate the process-ID *pid*.

The process-ID can be one of the following:

-*n* Sends the signal to all processes having a process-group-ID equal to the positive value of *n*.

-1 Sends the signal to all processes having a real user-ID equal to the effective user-ID of the calling process, but if the effective user is the superuser, the signal is sent to all processes.

0 Sends the signal to all processes having the same process-group-ID as the calling process.

n Sends the signal to the process with process-ID equal to *n*.

Returns: 0 if successful, -1 otherwise.

> **Warning**
>
> The effect of kill is determined by the value of *action* for the signal being sent, as defined by each process signaled.

Related Functions: getpid, setpgrp, signal

l64a

```
char *l64a (long arg);
```

Converts the long integer *arg* to a base-64 representation of 0 to 6 ASCII characters. The string is formed in a static internal buffer that is reused for each call. The string representation of the long integer is suitable for interchange between machine environments with incompatible representations of long integers.

Returns: A pointer to the static buffer containing the result string.

Related Functions: `a64l`, `ltol3`

lcong48

```
void lcong48 (unsigned short initializers[7]);
```

Performs a seeding operation for the random-number-generating functions `drand48`, `lrand48`, and `mrand48`.

The first three elements *initializers*[0] through *initializers*[2] replace the 48-bit *X*-value of the generator, the next three elements *initializers*[3] through *initializers*[5] replace the 48-bit multiplier, and *initializers*[6] replaces the 16-bit addend.

Returns: Nothing.

> **Warning**
>
> A subsequent call to `seed48` or `srand48` resets the multiplier and addend values of the linear-congruential algorithm to their default values.

Related Functions: `drand48`, `erand48`, `jrand48`, `lrand48`, `mrand48`, `nrand48`, `rand`, `seed48`, `srand48`

ldexp *errno*

```
double ldexp (double mantissa, int exp);
```

Computes the base-2 antilogarithm of *exp.mantissa* by multiplying *mantissa* by 2 raised to the *exp*th power.

Returns: The computated result; however, if overflow or underflow would occur, the value HUGE or 0 is returned respectively, and *errno* indicates ERANGE.

Related Functions: `frexp`

lfind

```
void *lfind (const void *key, const void *table, unsigned nel,
unsigned width, int (*compar)());
```

Headers: search.h

Returns a pointer to the entry in an unordered array having a key value matching the search key.

key points to the value identifying the entry to be found in the table.

table points to the first element in the table.

nel the number of entries in the table.

width is the length of an entry in bytes.

compar is a user function with an assumed declaration of

```
int compar (const void *entry1, const void *entry2);
```

The user function pointed to by *compar* must return a 0, positive, or negative integer value when the table entry pointed to by *entry1* is equal to, greater than, or less than the table entry pointed to by *entry2*.

Returns: A pointer to the entry in the table having a key value equal to the value pointed to by the *key* argument, or a NULL pointer if no such entry is found.

Related Functions: lsearch

link *errno S*

```
int link (const char *path1, const char *path2);
```

path1 must name an existing file, and the file *path2* must not exist. link creates a directory entry for *path2* that ensures that the same file is referenced by both pathnames. The directory entry for *path2* must be made in the same file system as the file pointed to by *path1*; that is, a link may not cross file systems.

Returns: 0 if successful, -1 otherwise.

> **Warning**
>
> Although link sets *errno* to indicate the cause of an error, it is not possible to attribute the error definitely to either *path1* or *path2* in all cases.

Related Functions: `unlink`

localtime

```
struct tm *localtime (long *clock);
```

Headers: `time.h`

Converts the time-of-day value pointed to by *clock* to a *tm* structure (defined in `time.h`). The values returned correspond to the local timezone.

Returns: A pointer to a static area in the format of a *tm* structure contained within the `localtime` routine.

Related Functions: `asctime, ctime, gmtime, time, time.h`

lockf *errno*

```
int lockf (int handle, int function, long size);
```

Headers: `unistd.h`

Provides an interface to the file-locking capabilities of the `fcntl` system call. *handle* must identify an open file descriptor. A segment of the file beginning at the current file position and extending forward or backward *size* bytes is locked, unlocked, or tested for conflicting locks according to the value of *function*. A *size* of 0 is taken to mean the end of the file.

Both F_LOCK and F_TLOCK lock the specified file segment if no conflicting locks exist. Otherwise, F_LOCK causes the process to sleep until the entire segment is available, while F_TLOCK returns a value of -1 with *errno* set to EACCES. Overlapping and adjacent locks set by the same process are merged into a single locked segment. Nonexistent parts of the file may be locked.

F_ULOCK unlocks all locked segments of the file included in the range specified by *size*. A segment may be partially unlocked.

F_TEST returns a value of 0 if no portion of the range overlaps a file segment locked by another process; otherwise F_TEST returns a value of -1 and sets *errno* to EACCES.

Returns: 0, if F_TEST finds no conflicting lock, or if F_LOCK, F_TLOCK, or F_ULOCK was successful. Otherwise, `lockf` returns -1 and *errno* identifies the error.

> **Warning**
>
> Some versions of the UNIX system can store the *errno* value EACCES as EAGAIN. Record and file locking is not generally compatible with stream files.

Related Functions: `fcntl, lseek, open`

log *errno M*

```
double log (double x);
```

Headers: `math.h`

Returns: The natural logarithm of *x* for positive *x*.

> **Warning**
>
> log returns -HUGE and sets *errno* to EDOM when *x* is nonpositive.

log10 *errno M*

```
double log10 (double x);
```

Headers: `math.h`

Returns: The base-10 logarithm of *x* for positive *x*.

logname

```
char *logname (void);
```

Returns the value of the $LOGNAME environment variable.

Returns: A pointer to a string giving the login name of the current user.

Related Functions: cuserid, getpwuid

longjmp

```
void longjmp (jmp_buf env, int code);
```

Headers: setjmp.h

Returns the user to the function corresponding to *env* rather than the calling function. The function to which return is effected is that which last used setjmp to set the value of *env*. To the function receiving control, the return value *code* appears to be the return value from setjmp; if the value of *code* is 0, it is forced to 1 so that a longjmp return can be distinguished from a normal setjmp return.

Related Functions: setjmp

lrand48

```
long lrand48 (void);
```

Generates a pseudo-random number uniformly distributed over the range 0 to 2,147,483,647.

You should seed the random number generator before the first call by using one of the seed functions `srand48`, `seed48`, or `lcong48`.

Returns: The generated random number.

> **Warning**
>
> If you seed the random number generator with the same value on each program execution, or if you don't introduce a seed, the same series of pseudo-random numbers are generated for each execution of the program.

Related Functions: `drand48`, `erand48`, `jrand48`, `lcong48`, `mrand48`, `nrand48`, `rand`, `seed48`, `srand48`

lsearch

```
void *lsearch (const void *key, const void *table, unsigned nel,
unsigned width, int (*compar)());
```

Headers: `search.h`

Returns a pointer to the entry in an unordered array having a key value matching the search key.

key points to a value in the same format as an array element, the key portion of which is the key to be found in the table.

table points to the first element in the table.

nel is the number of entries in the table.

width is the length of an entry in bytes.

compar is a user function with an assumed declaration of

```
int compar (const void *entry1, const void *entry2);
```

The user function pointed to by *compar* must return a 0, positive, or negative integer value when the table entry pointed to by *entry1* is equal to, greater than, or less than the table entry pointed to by *entry2*.

Returns: A pointer to the entry in the table having a key value equal to the value pointed to by the *key* argument. If no matching entry is found in the table, a new entry for the specified key value is added to the end of the table, and a pointer to the new entry is returned.

Related Functions: lfind

lseek *errno S*

```
long lseek (int handle, long offset, int whence);
```

Sets the file pointer of the file corresponding to *handle* to a new offset within the file.

The new file position is the sum of the value of *offset* and a value implied by *whence*, as follows:

0 The start of the file

1 The current file position

2 The end of the file

The next read or write of the file begins at the new position. If the file pointer is set beyond the end of the file, a subsequent read returns end-of-file, while a write increases the length of the file accordingly. Using lseek and write may introduce "holes" into a file by skipping some areas of the file while writing into others.

Returns: The new value of the file pointer if successful, or -1 if an error occurs.

> **Warning**
>
> You cannot reposition some files, such as a terminal file, or a pipe. In these cases, the current file pointer is undefined, the value returned by lseek is meaningless, and lseek has no effect.

Related Functions: creat, fseek, open

mallinfo

```
struct mallinfo mallinfo (void);
```

Headers: `malloc.h`

Returns a structure describing the current `mallopt` settings and storage allocation statistics.

The *mallinfo* structure contains these members:

arena	Total number of bytes available for allocation by malloc
ordblks	Number of ordinary blocks allocated
smblks	Number of small blocks allocated
hblkhd	Number of bytes used by holding-block headers
hblks	Number of holding blocks
usmblks	Number of bytes allocated in small blocks
fsmblks	Number of bytes in free small blocks
uordblks	Number of bytes allocated in ordinary blocks
fordblks	Number of bytes in free ordinary blocks
keepcost	Space penalty if M_KEEP option is in force

Returns: A pointer to an internal static buffer.

Related Functions: `malloc, mallopt`

malloc *errno*

```
void *malloc (size_t size);
```

Headers: `malloc.h`

Allocates an area of storage at least *size* bytes long, properly aligned for any data type. `malloc` returns the NULL pointer if an area of the requested size cannot be allocated.

Two versions of `malloc` are available, one from the standard library, and one from the `malloc` library. You get the latter when you supply the `-lmalloc` option on the `cc` command. The standard version optimizes the use of memory at the expense of execution speed, and the `-lmalloc` version optimizes execution speed but uses more memory.

Returns: A pointer to the allocated storage area, or NULL if the area could not be allocated.

> **Warning**
>
> Accesses to storage outside the range of allocated addresses have an undefined result, and may cause abnormal termination of the program. The storage area returned by `malloc` contains unpredictable values.

Related Functions: `calloc, free, mallopt, memset, realloc`

mallopt

```
int mallopt (int cmd, int value);
```

Headers: `malloc.h`

Modifies the algorithm used by `malloc`. You cannot call this function after the first "small block" is allocated.

For *cmd* specify one of the following values defined in the `malloc.h` header file:

M_MXFAST sets the *maxfast* value to *value*.

M_NLBLKS sets the *numlbks* value to *value*.

M_GRAIN sets the value of *grain* to *value*. A small value for *grain* causes a greater number of holding blocks to be retained. The default value of *grain* is a value that enables `malloc`, `calloc`, and `realloc` to properly align allocated storage for any data type. The specified *value* is rounded to a multiple of the default value.

M_KEEP, if set, causes data in a storage block released by *free* to be retained until reallocated.

Returns: A nonzero value if either *cmd* or *value* is invalid, or if storage is already allocated, thus inhibiting further changes to the allocation variables; otherwise 0.

Related Functions: `calloc, free, mallinfo, malloc, realloc`

memccpy

```
char *memccpy (void *s1, const void *s2, int c, int n);
```

Headers: `memory.h`

Copies characters from the array pointed to by *s2* to the array pointed to by *s1*. Copying stops when a character with the value of *c* is copied, or *n* characters are copied.

Returns: A pointer to the character in *s1* following *c*, or the NULL pointer if the function copies *n* characters without finding *c*.

> **Warning**
>
> The result is not defined if either *s1* or *s2* is the NULL pointer.

Related Functions: `memchr, memcmp, memcpy, memset, strcpy, strncpy`

memchr

```
char *memchr (const char *s, int c, int n);
```

Headers: `memory.h`

Searches the memory area pointed to by *s*, *n* bytes long, for the first occurrence of *c*.

Returns: A pointer to the first occurrence of the character *c* in the *n*-element character array pointed to by *s*, or a NULL pointer if the character *c* is not found.

> **Warning**
>
> The result is not defined if *s* is the NULL pointer.

Related Functions: `memccpy, memcmp, memcpy, memset, strchr`

memcmp

```
int memcmp (const void *s1, const void *s2, int n);
```

Headers: `memory.h`

Compares the *n* byte areas *s1* and *s2*. The return value indicates the result of the comparison.

Returns: A positive, negative, or 0 value as the *n*-element character array pointed to by *s1* that is greater than, less than, or equal to the character array pointed to by *s2*. `memcmp` treats the arrays as strings, except that it compares exactly *n* characters and treats any null characters it finds as data characters.

> **Warning**
>
> The result is not defined if either *s1* or *s2* is the NULL pointer.

Related Functions: `memccpy, memchr, memcpy, memset, strcmp, strncmp`

memcpy

```
char *memcpy (void *s1, const void *s2, int n);
```

Headers: `memory.h`

Copies *n* characters from the array pointed to by *s2* to the array pointed to by *s1*.

Returns: A pointer to the result character array, that is, *s1*.

> **Warning**
>
> The result is not defined if either *s1* or *s2* is the NULL pointer.

Related Functions: `memccpy, memchr, memcmp, memset, strcpy, strncpy`

memset

```
char *memset (void *s, int c, int n);
```

Headers: memory.h

Copies *n* occurrences of the character *c* to the array pointed to by *s*.

Returns: *s*.

Warning

The result is not defined if *s* is the NULL pointer.

Related Functions: memccpy, memchr, memcmp, memcpy

mkdir *errno S R3*

```
int mkdir (const char *path, int mode);
```

Creates a new directory with a path name equal to the nullterminated string pointed to by *path*. The access permissions of the new directory are set to the 12 low-order bits of *mode* as modified by the process file creation mask (see umask). The owner-ID and group-ID of the new directory are set to the effective user-ID and effective group-ID of the calling process, respectively.

The request fails if a file with the same path name already exists, or if the caller does not have write permission in the parent directory of the new directory.

Returns: 0 if successful, -1 otherwise.

Warning

The mkdir system call is not a direct substitute for the mkdir command, because the command creates the new directory with owner-ID and group-ID corresponding to the real user-ID and real group-ID of the calling process, respectively.

Related Functions: chmod, creat, mknod, rmdir, umask

mknod *errno S*

```
int mknod (const char *path, int mode, int dev);
```

Creates a new directory, special file, or named pipe with the name path. If the file to be created is not a named pipe, the effective user-ID must be the superuser.

The type of file to be created is determined by the value of *mode*. The header file sys/stat.h defines the following possible values for *mode*:

S_IFIFO = Named pipe

S_IFCHR = Character special

S_IFDIR = Directory

S_IFBLK = Block special

S_IFREG = Regular file

The access permissions of the file are set according to the 12 low-order bits of *mode* and have the same meanings described for the chmod function. mknod sets the owner of the file to the effective user-ID of the calling process, and sets the group-ID of the file to the effective group-ID of the calling process.

If *mode* indicates a block-special or character-special device, *dev* is an installation-dependent device designation; otherwise *dev* is ignored.

Returns: 0 if successful, -1 otherwise.

Warning

The mkdir function is available to the general user for creating a directory. Also, although you can use the mknod function to create a directory, the directory will be malformed and cause system processing errors unless you properly initialize it with links for the . and .. files.

Related Functions: chmod, creat, mkdir, umask

mktemp

```
char *mktemp (char *template);
```

Generates a unique filename for temporary files.

The last six characters of the string pointed to by *template* should be X X X X X X. The six Xs are replaced by an arbitrarily chosen letter and the five-digit current process-ID.

Returns: The value of *template*.

> **Warning**
>
> The letter that replaces the six Xs is drawn from a list internal to mktemp to ensure that no two filenames generated by mktemp are the same. If it generates a great many filenames, mktemp can run out of letters. The mktemp naming procedure does not sufficiently guarantee that the generated filename differs from other filenames that may already exist in the directory; the procedure only guarantees that filenames generated by an individual program employing the UNIX mktemp function are unique.

Related Functions: tmpfile, tmpnam

modf

```
double modf (double dn, double *iptr);
```

Extracts the integer and fractional parts of a floating-point number.

Returns: The fractional part of the double-precision number *dn*. The integer part is stored at the location pointed to by *iptr*.

monitor

```
void monitor (void (*lowpc)(), void (*highpc)(), WORD
*buffer, int bufsize, int nfunc);
```

Headers: `mon.h`

Activates the profiling facility using the `profil` system call; this function is somewhat easier to use than `profil` itself. Note that use of the `profil` or `monitor` calls is not required to perform execution monitoring; the `-p` option of the `cc` command provides a default level of monitoring. However, you can use the `profil` or `monitor` calls to acquire more detailed counts than are provided by default.

lowpc is a pointer to the lowest-address function to be profiled, and *highpc* is a pointer to the highest-address function to be profiled. During the execution of your program, the UNIX kernel, assisted by supporting functions linked from the C library, records all storage references between these two limits by incrementing the corresponding WORD in the user-provided *buffer*, an array of *bufsize* elements of type WORD. The value of *lowpc* cannot be zero. A maximum of *nfunc* function calls are recorded.

The `monitor` function converts the *bufsize* argument into the appropriate scaling factor for the *profil* call.

The following profiles the entire program:

```
extern void etext();
...
monitor ( (void (*)())2, etext, buf, bufsize, nfunc );
```

To stop execution monitoring and cause counts to be written to the `mon.out` file, use

```
monitor( (void (*)())0, (void (*)())0, (WORD *)0, 0, 0);
```

Returns: Nothing.

Related Functions: `etext`, `profil`

---

mount *errno S*

```
int mount (const char *special, const char *dir, int rofs);
```

Causes the file system contained on the block-special file pointed to by *special* to be mounted at the directory named by *dir*. You cannot access files and subdirectories originally contained in *dir* after completing the mount.

If the low-order bit of *rofs* is 1, the block-special file is mounted as a read-only file system; all write accesses to the file system will be inhibited.

The effective user-ID of the calling process must be superuser.

Returns: 0 if successful, -1 otherwise.

Related Functions: umount

mrand48

```
long mrand48 (void);
```

Returns a pseudo-random number uniformly distributed over the range -2,147,483,647 to 2,147,483,648.

You should seed the random number generator before the first call using one of the seed functions srand48, seed48, or lcong48.

> **Warning**
>
> If you seed the random number generator with the same value on each program execution, or if you don't introduce a seed, the same series of pseudo-random numbers is generated for every execution of the program.

Related Functions: drand48, erand48, jrand48, lcong48, lrand48, nrand48, rand, seed48, srand48

msgctl *errno S KE*

```
int msgctl (int msqid, int cmd, struct msqid_ds *buf);
```

Headers: sys/types.h sys/ipc.h sys/msg.h

Provides three different operations for managing message queues, identified by the value of *cmd* as follows:

IPC_RMID causes the system to delete the message queue corresponding to the message queue identifier *msqid*, and to destroy all undelivered messages. This operation can be performed only by the superuser or by the process that created the message queue.

IPC_STAT causes the current status of the message queue identified by *msqid* to be stored at the location pointed to by *buf*.

IPC_SET sets the value of selected attributes of the message queue identified by *msqid* to the contents of the corresponding members of the structure pointed to by *buf*. The following variables can be set: *msg_perm.uid*, *msg_perm.gid*, *msg_perm.mode*, and *msg_qbytes*. Both the superuser and the general user can reduce the value of *msg_qbytes* (the maximum number of data bytes that can be simultaneously held undelivered in the message queue), but only the superuser can increase the value.

The `msqid_ds` structure contains the following principal members:

msg_perm describes the permission settings for the message queue, and is itself a structure consisting of the following members:

> `uid`, the owner-ID of the message queue
>
> `gid`, the group-ID of the message queue
>
> `cuid`, the user-ID of the process that created the message queue
>
> `cgid`, the group-ID of the process that created the message queue
>
> `mode`, of which the low-order nine bits specify read and write permissions for the owner, group, and other users, in the same format as for file permissions

msg_qnum: holds the number of messages currently queued.

msg_qbytes: holds the maximum number of data bytes that can be stored in the queue. This value is initialized to the system maximum when the message queue is created; the value can be increased by the superuser, or be reduced by the superuser or the owner of the message queue.

msg_lspid: holds the process-ID of the last process that used `msgsnd` to add a message to the queue.

msg_lrpid: holds the process-ID of the last process that used `msgrcv` to retrieve a message from the queue.

msg_stime: holds the time of last `msgsnd` operation.

msg_rtime: holds the time of last `msgrcv` operation.

msg-ctime: holds the time the message queue was last created or last modified by the IPC_SET command of `msgctl`.

Returns: 0 if successful, -1 otherwise.

Related Functions: `msgget, msgrcv, msgsnd`

msgget *errno S KE*

```
int msgget (key_t key, int msgflg);
```

Headers: `sys/types.h sys/ipc.h sys/msg.h`

Returns a message queue identifier and may create a new message queue. The *key* argument specifies an arbitrary numeric value identifying the public server queue of an application, or it specifies the symbolic value IPC_PRIVATE defined in the `sys/ipc.h` header file; if IPC_PRIVATE is specified, `msgget` always creates a new message queue that cannot be discovered by any possible value of *key*, and hence cannot be discovered by any other process.

For *msgflg* specify the following symbolic values:

IPC_CREAT to request that the function create the message queue corresponding to *key* if the message does not already exist. If IPC_CREAT is not specified and the message queue does not exist, no queue is created, a value of -1 is returned, and *errno* is set to ENOENT.

IPC_EXCL to indicate that the message queue corresponding to *key* should not already exist; `msgget` returns a value of -1 and sets *errno* to EEXIST if the message queue already exists. This flag commonly is used together with IPC_CREAT when only one server process for a public application queue should exist; attempting to execute the server process again returns an error.

0400 to indicate that the owner of the queue may read messages from the queue.

0200 to indicate that the owner of the queue may write messages to the queue.

0060 to indicate that processes with the same effective group-ID as the creator of the queue may read (0040) and write (0020) to the queue.

0006 to indicate that other processes may read (0004) and write (0002) to the queue.

A process must call the `msgget` function to create or attach a message queue before the process can perform any other message queue operations for that queue. Normally, one process, a public server, creates the queue using an arbitrary *key* value unique to the application, while other processes wanting to send messages to the server use `msgget` and the same key value for the application to identify the message queue.

The IPC_PRIVATE facility enables a process to create a queue for receiving messages only from authorized processes; the process using IPC_PRIVATE must provide the message queue identifier to the authorized processes, perhaps by including the message queue identifier of the private queue in a message to the public server.

Note that the message-queueing operations provide one way of building interprocess communications facilities; the semaphore and shared-memory operations provide another.

Returns: An integer message queue identifier that must be used in the `msgsnd`, `msgrcv`, and `msgctl` operations; use the *key* value to identify the queue only for the `msgget` operation. If no message queue corresponding to *key* exists and IPC_CREAT is not specified, or if such a queue exists but IPC_EXCL is also specified, then a value of -1 is returned and *errno* is set to identify the error.

Warning

The user must ensure that the key value does not duplicate a key value used by another application. Using the `ftok` library function is one strategy for minimizing this possibility.

Related Functions: `msgctl`, `msgrcv`, `msgsnd`, `semctl`, `semget`, `semop`, `shmat`, `shmctl`, `shmdt`, `shmget`

---

msgrcv *errno S KE*

```
int msgrcv (int msqid, void *buf, int size, int msgtyp,
int msgflg);
```

Headers: `sys/types.h sys/ipc.h sys/msg.h`

Retrieves a message from the message queue identified by *msqid*. The message queue identifier *msqid* must be the return value from a previous successful `msgget` operation.

The received message is stored in the buffer pointed to by *buf*, in the following general format:

```
struct msgbuf {
        long    type;
        char    msg[1];
};
```

The length of the character array msg must be at least equal to *size*, which specifies the maximum number of bytes that this operation can receive. If the message to be received is longer than *size*, msgrcv returns a value of -1 and sets *errno* to E2BIG, and no message is stored; but if *msgflg* includes the MSG_NOERROR flag, the message is truncated to a length of *size* and stored, with no indication of the truncation error.

The value of *msgtyp* indicates the following:

❏ If equal to 0, the value indicates that the next message in the queue is received

❏ If greater than 0, the value indicates that the next message with a type equal to *msgtyp* is received;

❏ If less than 0, the value indicates that the next message with a type less than or equal to the absolute value of *msgtyp* is received.

The application can use the type field of the message, and the *msgtyp* argument, to support prioritized message queueing where the message type corresponds to the message priority. Alternatively, the type can be used to establish *channels* of communication, where the server accepts general messages of type 1, and then assigns a communicator to another channel for continued conversations. Of course, simple FIFO queueing is established when the application only uses a message type of 1.

The *msgflg* value can include the IPC_NOWAIT flag to select the action to be taken when no message is available: if IPC_NOWAIT is set, msgrcv returns a value of -1 immediately and sets *errno* to ENOMSG; if IPC_NOWAIT is not set, the process is suspended until a message of the requested type is made available.

Returns: A count of the number of bytes stored in the msg portion of the message buffer, if successful; otherwise -1 is returned and *errno* indicates the cause of the error. The following are notable error indications:

E2BIG if the message exceeds *size* bytes in length and the message therefore cannot be stored

ERMID if an attempt is made to receive from a message queue that was deleted (see msgctl)

ENOMSG if IPC_NOWAIT is specified and no message is available

EACCESS if an attempt is made to retrieve a message from a message queue where the requesting process does not have the proper permission

Related Functions: msgctl, msgget, msgsnd

msgsnd *errno S KE*

```
int msgsnd (int msqid, void *buf, int size, int msgflg);
```

Headers: `sys/types.h sys/ipc.h sys/msg.h`

Posts the message contained in *buf* to the message queue identified by *msqid*. The message queue identifier *msqid* must be the return value from a previous successful `msgget` operation.

The *buf* argument must point to a structure of the following general format:

```
struct msgbuf {
        long    type;
        char    msg[1];
};
```

where `type` is a value greater than 0 with a meaning determined by the message receiver (see `msgrcv`), and `msg` is a string of bytes of length *size* containing the message. The installation defines an upper limit on the length of `msg`.

The *msgflg* value determines the action to take if the target message queue already reached an implementation-defined capacity limit. If the value IPC_NOWAIT is specified, -1 is returned and *errno* is set to EAGAIN; otherwise the process is suspended until sufficient messages are removed from the queue to enable the queueing of the requested message.

Returns: 0 if successful; otherwise -1 is returned and *errno* is set to indicate the error.

> **Warning**
>
> If IPC_NOWAIT is not specified and the process waits, and a signal is subsequently presented to the process, a return value of -1 is returned and *errno* is set to EINTR to indicate that the msgsnd operation was not performed; retry the operation.

Related Functions: `msgctl, msgget, msgrcv`

nice *errno S KE*

```
int nice (int incr);
```

Increases or decreases the scheduling priority of the calling process by the value of *incr*, to a maximum value of 39 or a minimum value of 0. Smaller values of the scheduling priority increase the share of the CPU allocated to the calling process, while larger values reduce the share consumed by the process.

The effective user-ID must be superuser if *incr* is negative or greater than 40.

Returns: 20 less than the new *nice* value of the process, or -1 if unsuccessful.

nrand48

```
long nrand48 (unsigned short lvalue[3]);
```

Returns a pseudo-random number uniformly distributed over the range 0 to 2,147,483,647.

The user-supplied array pointed to by *lvalue* is expected to contain a 48-bit value before invocation; on return, the array contains the *X*-value that will be used to generate the next number in the random series. You should introduce some value into the array before the first call to nrand48 to "seed" the generator.

You can generate multiple independent random number series using nrand48 by maintaining a separate *lvalue* array for each of the desired series.

Related Functions: drand48, erand48, jrand48, lcong48, lrand48, mrand48, rand, seed48, srand48

open *errno S*

```
int open (const char *path, int oflags, int mode);
```
Headers: fcntl.h

Initializes an unused file descriptor to enable reading and writing of the file named by *path*. The file pointer is set to the beginning of the file, and the the close-on-exec flag is set to 0.

The specific actions taken by open are determined by flags set in *oflags*. Symbolic names for these flags are defined in fcntl.h, and include the following:

O_RDONLY opens the file for read access.

O_WRONLY opens the file for write access.

O_RDWR opens the file for both read and write access.

O_APPEND causes the file pointer to be reset to the end of the file before each write request.

O_CREAT causes open to create the file if it does not already exist. The *mode* argument must specify the 12 low-order bits of the access permissions (see chmod).

O_EXCL, when specified in combination with the O_CREAT flag, causes the open request to fail if the file to be opened already exists.

O_NDELAY affects the way in which open satisfies read and write requests. See the descriptions for read and write.

O_SYNC causes a return from write to be delayed until the data is actually written to the external medium.

O_TRUNC causes open to truncate an existing file to a length of 0 bytes.

You can specify only one of the O_RDONLY, O_WRONLY, and O_RDWR values in *oflags*. You can combine the flag values by adding together the desired flags.

Returns: The file descriptor of the file if successful, or -1 otherwise.

Warning

The system imposes an upper limit on the number of files, usually 20, that any one process can have open at the same time.

Related Functions: close, chmod, creat, lseek, read, umask, write

opendir *errno R3*

```
DIR *opendir (const char *path);
```

Headers: `sys/types.h dirent.h`

Opens the directory named by *path* for reading, and sets the current location in the directory to the first entry. The file named by *path* must be a directory and must exist, and must be accessible for reading.

Once opened, active directory entries can be read using the `readdir` function, and the current location can be controlled using the `seekdir`, `telldir`, and `rewinddir` functions.

Use the `closedir` function to close the directory.

Returns: A pointer to a DIR structure allocated using the `malloc` function, or the NULL pointer if the open is unsuccessful.

Related Functions: `closedir, readdir, rewinddir, seekdir, telldir`

pause *errno S*

```
int pause (void);
```

Suspends execution of the calling process. The process resumes execution only when a signal is received. The result of receiving a signal is determined by the action currently set by the process for that signal (see `signal`).

Returns: -1 and sets *errno* to EINTR.

Related Functions: `alarm, kill, signal, wait`

pclose

```
int pclose (FILE *stream);
```

Headers: `stdio.h`

Closes the stream file pointed to by *stream*, which is assumed to be one side of a pipe opened by `popen`, after waiting for the associated process to terminate.

Returns: The exit status of the command invoked by `popen`, as returned by `wait`. The exit status indicates the success (0) or failure (nonzero) of the command.

Related Functions: `fclose`, `popen`, `wait`

perror

```
void perror (const char *msg);
```

Writes the error message corresponding to the current value of *errno* to the standard-error file. The message text is preceded by the null-terminated string pointed to by *msg*, which you may use to explain the context in which the error occurred.

Related Functions: `errno`, `sys_errlist`, `sys_nerr`

pipe *errno S*

```
int pipe (int handle[2]);
```

Creates an I/O channel called a "pipe," consisting of two file descriptors, one opened for reading and one opened for writing. The read file descriptor is stored in `handle[0]`, and the write file descriptor is stored in `handle[1]`.

Data written to the pipe is accumulated in an internal system buffer up to 5120 bytes long; when the system buffer is full, any further attempt to write data into the pipe suspends the writing process.

`pipe` satisfies read requests up to the length specified or the amount of data in the buffer, whichever is less. If the buffer is empty, the `pipe` function suspends the reading process until data is written to the pipe.

Either file descriptor may be closed first. If, however, the read file descriptor is closed, and then data is written to the file descriptor open for writing, the SIGPIPE signal is posted to the writing process. This condition is called a "broken pipe," and indicates that no process is available to read the data being written to the pipe.

Note that no actual file is ever created, and no data is ever written to or read from an external medium.

Returns: 0 if successful, -1 otherwise.

Warning

You cannot use `lseek` to set the file pointer of a pipe forward or back; data must be read from the pipe in the same sequence that it is written.

Related Functions: `close, read, write`

plock *errno S KE*

```
int plock (int op);
```

Headers: `sys/lock.h`

Locks the text segment, data segment, or both segments of the calling process in real memory, depending on the value of *op*, as follows:

> PROCLOCK locks both the text and data segments in memory
>
> TXTLOCK locks the text segment in memory
>
> DATLOCK locks the data segment in memory
>
> UNLOCK removes any held locks.

A segment which is locked cannot be swapped out or written to the external paging device, thus improving performance of the calling process in some situations. It is an error to set a lock which is already held, or to unlock when no segments are locked.

Only a process with an effective user-ID of superuser may invoke the `plock` function.

Returns: 0 if successful, -1 otherwise.

popen *errno*

```
FILE *popen (const char *command, const char *type);
```

Headers: `stdio.h`

Passes the string *command* to the standard Bourne shell (/bin/sh) for execution.

If *type* points to the string r, the standard output of the command is opened for reading; reading the FILE pointer returned by popen reads the output of the command. If *type* points to the string w, the standard input of the command is opened for writing; writing to the FILE pointer returned by popen passes input to the command.

Returns: A pointer to an opened FILE block, or NULL if the command text could not be executed because either fork or exec failed.

The FILE pointer returned by popen must be closed using pclose, which waits for the command to complete execution and retrieve its exit status.

> **Warning**
>
> The exit status of the invoked command is not known until pclose is called. Output produced by the command may be incomplete or non-existent, or input passed to the command may be incompletely processed or ignored, but these conditions cannot be recognized until the exit status of the command is retrieved from pclose and examined.

Related Functions: fopen, pclose, pipe

pow *errno M*

```
double pow (double x, double y);
```

Headers: math.h

Computes x^y.

Returns: x raised to the power of y.

> **Warning**
>
> If the result would overflow or underflow, pow returns +-HUGE or 0 respectively and sets *errno* to ERANGE. The function sets *errno* to EDOM if x is 0 and y is negative, or if x is negative and y is not an integer.

printf *errno*

```
int printf (const char *format, ...);
```

Headers: stdio.h

Formats values taken from the argument list according to specifications contained in the string *format* and writes the result to the standard output file.

The format string consists of message characters and format specifiers. Message characters (any character other than %) are output without further processing.

A format specifier is a substring of the general form %*[flag][width][.prec]type*. As each format specifier is encountered, successive arguments of printf are fetched and converted. Excess arguments are ignored.

flag is one of the characters -, +, 0, #, or blank, when - causes a result to be left-justified in a field of *width* characters, + and blank both force the result to contain a sign, 0 causes a numeric result to be padded on the left with zeros, and # causes a special effect described below.

width is an optional string of digits or an asterisk (*) denoting the size of the output field. The result is right-justified in the field unless the - flag is present or the width is too short. An * causes the width to be taken from the argument list; the corresponding argument must be of type int.

prec is an optional string of digits denoting the number of fractional digits to appear in a floating-point result, or the number of digits in an integer result. The default value is 6 for floating-point conversions. You can also specify *prec* as *.

The *type* character, and its significance, is as follows:

%   Prints one % for each %% in the format string.

c   Prints the ASCII character corresponding to the integer argument.

d   Converts the integer argument to a decimal digit string prefixed with a sign if the argument is negative.

e or E   Converts the floating-point argument to exponential notation (+9.999e+99). The # flag forces an integral result to contain a decimal point.

f   Converts the floating-point argument to a fixed-point number (-ddd.ddd) with *prec* fractional digits. If you specify *prec* as 0, printf drops both the decimal point and the fractional digits from the result. The # flag forces the result to contain a decimal point.

g or G   Converts the floating-point argument to either the f or e (E) format, depending on the value of the argument. The # flag forces the result to contain a decimal point, and trailing 0s to be retained.

o   Converts the integer argument to an unsigned octal digit string and prefixes the result string with a 0 if the # flag is present.

s   Interprets the corresponding argument as a pointer to a character string. The *prec* value, if present, specifies a maximum number of characters to be printed. The string is right-aligned in a field of *width* characters.

u   Interprets the integer argument as an unsigned number and converts the argument to a decimal digit string.

x or X   Converts the integer argument to an unsigned hexadecimal digit string, extends the argument with 0s or truncates it on the left to a length of *prec*, and prefixes the argument with 0x or 0X if the # flag is present.

For conversion types d u o x X, an h or l can precede the conversion character. The h signifies a halfsize argument (short int), whereas an l signifies a long argument.

For conversion types e E f g G, an h prefix signifies an argument of type float, while l signifies a double argument. The default is double.

Returns: The number of characters written to standard output, or -1 if an error occurred.

Warning

If the number of arguments following *format* is less than the number of format specifiers, printf fetches garbage argument values from the stack. The user is responsible for ensuring agreement between the description of the arguments implied by the format specifiers, and the actual type of arguments supplied.

Related Functions: ecvt, fprintf, putc, puts, scanf, sprintf, vprintf

profil *S KE*

```
void profil (short *buf, int bufsiz, void (*offset)(), int scale);
```

Initiates a profiling facility for the caller's process. At periodic intervals, `profil` inspects the current program address to determine whether a reference is to be counted, and if so which word of *buf* is to be incremented.

buf is a pointer to an array of integers. `profil` increments an integer when the current program address is found to correspond to the relative position of the integer within the array, in such a way that the array is always sufficient to count references to the entire program segment.

bufsiz is the size of the array *buf* in bytes. If you specify 0, profiling is active but nothing is counted.

offset specifies an address in the text segment below which no reference counting occurs. The address of *offset* is set to correspond to the first word of *buf*.

For *scale* specify an unsigned fixed-point fraction representing the number of words in the buffer to which one word in the text segment corresponds. The value $0 \times ffff$ defines a scale of 1.0, and the value $0 \times 7fff$ defines a scale of 0.8 (hexadecimal), or 1/2 (that is, one word in the text segment corresponds to one half the range represented by one buffer element). Similarly, $0 \times 0fff$ maps 16 text segment words to one buffer word ($0 \times 0fff + 1 = 0.1000$ hex, or 1/16th).

You turn off profiling by specifying a scale of 0 or 1.

Returns: Nothing.

Related Functions: `monitor`

ptrace *errno S KE*

```
int ptrace (int request, int pid, void *addr, int data);
```

Enables a parent process to monitor the execution of a child process.

The value of *request* determines the action performed by `ptrace`, as follows:

0 Issued by the child task to initiate tracing

1,2 Returns the word at *addr* in the text (1) or data (2) segment of the child process

3 Returns the word at *addr* in the child's USER area of the system address space

4,5 Writes the value of the *data* argument into the text (4) or data (5) segment of the child process at the location specified by *addr*

6 Writes the value of *data* into the child's USER area of the system address space. The locations that can be written are restricted.

7 Resumes execution of the child process. If the value of *data* is 0, all signals, including the one that caused the child process to stop, are canceled. If the value of *data* is a valid signal number, `ptrace` posts that signal to the child task and cancels all other signals. The *addr* argument must have a value of 1.

8 Causes the child task to terminate as if it executed the `exit` system call.

9 Equivalent to 7, except that only one instruction is executed. You can use this value to single-step the child process.

putc

```
int putc (int c, FILE *stream);
```

Headers: `stdio.h`

Writes the character *c* to the stream file *stream*, at the byte offset indicated by the file pointer associated with *stream*. The file pointer is advanced by one byte.

`putc` immediately writes the character to the output file, unless the buffering mode for the output file *stream* is *line* or *full*. Full buffering delays writes to the output file until the stream buffer is full; line buffering also flushes the stream buffer when a newline character is written.

Returns: The value *c*, or EOF if an error occurs.

> **Warning**
>
> `putc` is implemented as a macro. Although `putc` is therefore faster than `fputc`, unexpected side-effects can arise; for example, `putc(*f++)` causes multiple incrementations of the pointer *f*.

Related Functions: `fclose, ferror, fopen, fputc, fseek, getc, putchar, puts, setbuf`

putchar

```
int putchar (int c);
```

Headers: `stdio.h`

Differs from `putc` only in that the character *c* is written to the standard output stream by default.

Returns: The value *c*.

Related Functions: `getchar, putc`

putenv

```
int putenv (const char *string);
```

Adds to the program environment the null-terminated string pointed to by *string*.

The string is assumed to be in the format *name=value*, where *name* is a variable name and *value* is the string value of the variable. No whitespace should occur between *name* and the = delimiter.

If *name* already occurs in the program environment, the existing environment string from the environment pointer table is dropped and replaced with the value of *string*.

Returns: 0 if successful. A nonzero value indicates that space to expand the environment pointer table could not be acquired with `malloc`; in this case, the string has not been added to the environment.

> **Warning**
>
> Modification of the character array pointed to by *string* alters the environment, because the pointer value of *string* is simply added to the environment pointer table.

> **Warning**
>
> Certain naming restrictions may apply if the environment variable is to be referenced by shell programs. For example, the Bourne shell (/bin/sh) requires a variable name to start with an initial letter, and to contain only letters and digits (the underscore is considered a letter).

Related Functions: environ, execle, getenv

putpwent *errno*

```
int putpwent (struct passwd *p, FILE *stream);
```

Headers: pwd.h stdio.h

Writes the password structure pointed to by *p* to the stream file *stream* as a text line in the format of the /etc/passwd file.

Returns: A nonzero value if an error occurs, otherwise 0.

Related Functions: fopen, getpwent, pwd.h

puts *errno*

```
int puts (const char *string);
```

Headers: stdio.h

Writes the null-terminated string pointed to by *string* to the standard output file, followed by a newline character. The ending null character is not written.

puts behaves as if each character of the string were successively written by the putchar function.

Returns: EOF if an error occurs, otherwise 0.

> **Warning**
>
> The puts and fputs functions use opposite conventions for writing a trailing newline character to the output; puts appends a newline, fputs does not.

Related Functions: ferror, fopen, fputs, gets, putchar

pututline

```
void pututline (struct utmp *buf);
```

Headers: utmp.h

Writes the contents of the utmp structure pointed to by *buf* into the proper position within the /etc/utmp file. (If you call the utmpname function, the file specified by the call to utmpname is used instead.)

Returns: Nothing.

Related Functions: endutent, getutent, getutid, getutline, setutent, utmp.h, utmpname

putw

```
int putw (int w, FILE *stream);
```

Headers: stdio.h

Writes the bytes comprising the integer *w* to the stream file *stream*, at the byte offset indicated by the file pointer associated with *stream*. The file pointer advances by the size of an integer. No alignment of the file pointer occurs, despite any alignment requirements that may normally be imposed by the machine or compiler implementation.

`putw` immediately writes the bytes to the output file, unless the buffering mode for the output file *stream* is *line* or *full*; in either case, writing to the output file is deferred unless the buffer does not contain enough space to hold the data.

Returns: 0 if successful, otherwise a nonzero value.

> **Warning**
>
> The ordering of the bytes written to the output file is determined by the machine and compiler implementation; use `printf` when you need portability.

Related Functions: `fclose`, `ferror`, `fopen`, `fseek`, `fwrite`, `getw`, `printf`, `putc`, `setbuf`

qsort

```
void qsort (const void *table, unsigned nel, unsigned width,
int (*compar)());
```

Sorts the elements of the array pointed to by *table* using the QuickSort algorithm. The user comparison function *compar* determines the resulting order of the elements in the array.

nel is the number of entries in the table.

width is the length of an element of the array in bytes.

compar is a user function with an assumed declaration of

```
int compar (const void *entry1, const void *entry2);
```

The user function pointed to by *compar* must return a 0, positive, or negative integer value when the table entry pointed to by *entry1* is equal to, greater than, or less than the table entry pointed to by *entry2*.

Returns: Nothing.

Related Functions: `bsearch`, `lsearch`, `strcmp`

rand

```
int rand (void);
```

Generates a random number.

Returns: A random number in the range 0 to 32,767. The generated series is completely determined by the seed value previously introduced by srand.

> **Warning**
>
> The generator used by rand is not particularly good. You should use one of the 48-bit generators for serious work.

Related Functions: drand48, srand

read *errno S*

```
int read (int handle, void *buffer, unsigned len);
```

Reads data from the file or device associated with *handle* and stores the data in consecutive positions of *buffer* until the number of bytes specified by *len* have been stored, the end of the file is reached, or, for terminals and communications lines, the available buffered data has been read.

For block-special devices and files stored on such devices, reading begins at the byte offset in the file given by the file pointer. Character-special files cannot be positioned and the file pointer is undefined; such files are read beginning with the next position defined by the device.

The O_NDELAY flag affects the completion of the read request when the input file is a pipe, terminal, or communications line and no data is available. If O_NDELAY is set, the read is terminated immediately and a value of 0 is returned; otherwise read suspends the calling process until data is available or, for a pipe, the pipe is closed.

Returns: 0 if no data is stored (usually signifies end-of-file, but see the description of the O_NDELAY flag in the preceding paragraph), -1 if an error occurred, or the number of bytes actually stored in *buffer*.

> **Warning**
>
> `read` can be interrupted, in which case the return value is -1 and *errno* specifies EINTR. You should retry the read request until read returns completes without interruption.

Related Functions: `creat, fcntl, ioctl, open, pipe`

readdir *errno R3*

```
struct dirent *readdir (DIR *dirp);
```

Headers: `sys/types.h dirent.h`

Reads the entry at the current location from the directory file corresponding to *dirp*, the value of which must have been obtained from a previous call to `opendir`. The current location in the directory advances to the entry following that returned by `readdir`.

If the directory entry at the current location is not an active entry, `readdir` skips successive entries until it finds an active entry or encounters the end of the directory. You can make a directory entry inactive by using the `unlink` or `rmdir` system calls, but in UNIX System V the entry is not removed, only marked as inactive. `readdir` does not return inactive directory entries.

The current location in the directory is set by `opendir` to the first entry in the directory, by `seekdir` to a specified directory entry, and by `readdir` to the directory entry following the last active entry read.

Returns: A pointer to a `struct dirent` containing the directory entry, or a NULL pointer if the end of the directory is found or if the current directory location is invalid because of a previous `seekdir`. The `dirent.h` header file describes the `dirent` structure.

Related Functions: `closedir, opendir, rewinddir, seekdir, telldir`

realloc *errno*

```
void *realloc (void *area, size_t size);
```

Headers: `malloc.h`

Extends (or reduces) the size of the storage area pointed to by *area* to a length of *size* bytes. If the area cannot be extended, the original area is released by a call to `free`, a new storage block of the requested size is allocated, and the contents of the original area are copied to the new area.

Returns: A pointer to an area of storage at least *size* bytes long, properly aligned for any data type. `realloc` returns the NULL pointer if an area of the requested size cannot be allocated.

> **Warning**
>
> If the requested storage cannot be allocated, the previous area already has been released and can no longer be accessed.
>
> Accesses to storage outside the range of allocated addresses will have an undefined result, and may cause the program to terminate abnormally.
>
> Undefined results occur if the value of *area* is not a pointer value previously returned by `malloc`, `calloc`, or `realloc`.

Related Functions: `calloc, free, malloc`

rewind

```
void rewind (FILE *stream);
```

Headers: `stdio.h`

Resets the current position of the stream file *stream* in such a way that the next byte read or written is the first byte in the file. Any end-of-file indication that may be preserved in the FILE block pointed to by *stream* is cleared.

`rewind` is equivalent to `fseek(stream,0L,0)`.

Returns: Nothing.

Related Functions: `fseek, ftell`

rewinddir *R3*

```
void rewinddir (DIR *dirp);
```

Headers: `sys/types.h dirent.h`

Sets the current location of the directory file associated with *dirp* to point to the first entry of the directory.

> **Warning**
>
> `rewinddir` is implemented as a macro.

Related Functions: `closedir, opendir, readdir, seekdir, telldir`

rmdir *errno S R3*

```
int rmdir (const char *path);
```

Removes the directory named by *path* if the directory is empty, if it is not a mount point, if it is not the current directory of any process, and if the calling process has write permission in the parent directory. The directory is considered empty when it contains only the . and .. entries.

Returns: 0 if successful, -1 otherwise.

Related Functions: `mkdir, unlink`

sbrk *errno S*

```
void *sbrk (int incr);
```

Increases or decreases the amount of usable space in the data segment by *incr* bytes. If the break address (the first address following the end of the data segment) would be reduced into the stack or the text segment, or increased beyond a system-defined maximum, an error is recognized and the break address is not changed.

Note that *incr* is a signed quantity. Negative values decrease the break address and the effective size of the data segment, and positive values increase the break address.

Returns: The new break address if successful; otherwise a value of (char *) (-1) is returned and *errno* is set accordingly.

Warning

Memory may be allocated and deallocated discontiguously on some hardware and software implementations. The break address may be increased or reduced by more than *incr* bytes if portions of the data segment address range are undefined. You should use the `malloc` and `free` functions instead of `sbrk`, because they allow for implementation-dependent considerations.

Related Functions: `brk`, `end`, `malloc`

---

scanf *errno*

```
int scanf (const char *format, ...);
```

Headers: `stdio.h`

Reads string data from the standard input file and converts the strings found into the equivalent internal representation. Reading continues until an input character fails to match the corresponding format specification, the end of the format string is reached, or EOF is found.

The character string pointed to by *format* controls the data conversion as follows. Characters other than % must be matched by characters from the input stream. A whitespace character in the format string causes any number of whitespace characters in the input stream to be skipped. A % appearing in the format string begins a format specifier, which causes data conversion to occur and a converted result to be stored at a user-defined location.

Each format specifier causes the next argument of `scanf` to be fetched and used as a pointer to store the conversion result. The format specifier implies the type of the pointer. The number of arguments following the format must be at least as large as the number of format specifiers in the format string, with one exception noted below.

The syntax of the format specifier is

`%[*][width]type`

If the optional * character is present, data conversion occurs normally but the result is not stored, and the corresponding pointer argument to `scanf` must be omitted. A specifier of this kind causes input data to be skipped, while confirming that it matches an expected format.

If the optional *width* value is present, at most that number of characters is taken from the input string and converted. You can use the *width* value to limit the amount of data stored (for types c, s, and [), or to break apart fields that are adjacent in the input stream. Excess input characters that otherwise would be processed by the format specifier are left on the input stream to be processed by the next format specifier.

The *type* value specifies the kind of conversion to be performed. *type* consists of an optional size modifier and a type character. The size modifiers are l and h, where l denotes a long or double result value, and h denotes a short or float result value. The following descriptions note the default size of the result for each conversion type.

A *type* character can be one of the following:

%   Matches the current input character against the %. No pointer argument should be provided for this specifier.

d,u   Specifies a string of decimal digits, optionally beginning with a minus sign. `scanf` converts the sign and digits to an integer value, and stores the result in a signed or unsigned integer.

o   Specifies a string of octal digits. `scanf` converts the digits to an integer value, and stores the result in a signed or unsigned integer.

x   Specifies a string of hexadecimal digits. The letters [a-f] and [A-F] are taken to mean the digit values 10-15. `scanf` converts the digits to an integer value, and stores the result in a signed or unsigned integer.

e,f,g

Specifies that the input string is an external floating-point number. The string may be prefixed with a sign character, and may be suffixed with an exponent (an e or E, optionally followed by a sign character, followed by one or more decimal digits). The number itself may contain one decimal point. The string is converted and stored in the `float` item pointed to by the next `scanf` argument.

s   Specifies a character string. The string is ended by the first
     whitespace character following the start of the string. The
     corresponding argument must point to a character array large
     enough to contain the string and an ending null (\0) character.

c   Stores the next input character (or *width* input characters) in the
     character array pointed to by the corresponding scanf
     argument. Whitespace characters are not skipped, but are stored
     if encountered. No null character is appended.

The opening bracket ([)

     Begins a character-set specification; the specifier must end with a
     matching]. The characters between the brackets specify a
     character set. Input is read and stored up to the first character
     not appearing in the set, and a trailing null character is
     appended. You can indicate a range of characters with the
     expression x-y. If the bracketed expression begins with the caret
     (^), the character set is the set of all ASCII characters not
     appearing in the bracketed expression. To include a] in the
     character set, place it immediately after the opening [or [^. No
     skipping of whitespace occurs either before or after processing.
     The corresponding argument of scanf must be a pointer to a
     character array.

Returns: The number of result values converted and stored, or EOF if the end
of the input stream is reached before any values are stored. Note that
successfully matching the pattern characters in the format string does not affect
the count returned.

Related Functions: getc, printf, strtod, strtol

seed48

```
unsigned short *seed48 (unsigned short seed[3]);
```

Sets the 48-bit value contained in the three elements of the array *seed* into the
X-value used internally by the drand48, lrand48, and mrand48 functions for
generating pseudo-random numbers. A given 48-bit value always causes the
same series of numbers to be returned by subsequent calls to the generator
function.

Returns: A pointer to the three-element array internal to seed48 containing
the 48-bit X-value last used for generating a random number. You can save this
value and use it later as a seed value to restart an interrupted program.

Related Functions: `drand48, erand48, jrand48, lcong48, lrand48, mrand48, nrand48, rand, srand48`

---

seekdir *R3*

```
void seekdir (DIR *dirp, long loc);
```

Headers: `sys/types.h dirent.h`

Sets the current location of the directory file associated with *dirp* to the value of *loc*. The value provided for *loc* should have been previously obtained from `telldir`. `seekdir` does not test the validity of the specified location.

Related Functions: `closedir, opendir, readdir, rewinddir, telldir`

---

semctl *errno S KE*

```
int semctl (int semid, int semnum, int cmd,
    union semun {
        int val;
        struct semid_ds *buf;
        unsigned short *array;
    } arg );
```

Headers: `sys/types.h sys/ipc.h sys/sem.h`

Performs the semaphore control operation specified by the value of *cmd* on the set of semaphores identified by *semid*. *semid* must be a value previously returned by a `semget` call.

The value of *cmd* must be one of the following:

GETVAL returns the value of semaphore *semnum*.

SETVAL sets the value of semaphore *semnum* to *arg.val* and clear the *semadj* value in all processes (see `semop`).

GETPID returns the process-ID of the last process that read or altered semaphore *semnum*.

GETNCNT returns the number of processes waiting for semaphore *semnum* to be incremented.

GETZCNT returns the number of processes waiting for semaphore *semnum* to become 0.

GETALL copies the current value of all semaphores in the set into the array pointed to by *arg.array*.

SETALL sets the value of each semaphore in the set to the value of *semval* in the corresponding entry of the array pointed to by *arg.array*. The *semadj* values of all processes are cleared.

IPC_STAT stores the current contents of the `semid_ds` structure associated with the semaphore set *semid* into the structure pointed to by *arg.buf*. The `sem.h` header file describes the `semid_ds` structure.

IPC_SET sets the values of selected members of the semid_ds structure associated with the semaphore set *semid* to the corresponding values of the structure pointed to by *arg.buf*. You can set only the values of the `sem_perm.uid`, `sem_perm.gid`, and `sem_perm.mode` members.

IPC_RMID removes the set of semaphores from the system. All processes currently suspended waiting for a semaphore event are awoken; subsequent calls to `semop` return the ERMID error.

Most commands require that the requestor have read access to the semaphore set, but write access is required for the SETVAL and SETALL commands, and the requestor must be the superuser or the owner of the set for the IPC_SET and IPC_RMID commands.

Returns: A value of 0 for all commands except GETVAL, GETPID, GETNCNT, and GETZCNT. If an error occurs, all commands return a value of -1 and *errno* is set appropriately.

Related Functions: `semget, semop`

semget *errno S KE*

```
int semget (key_t key, int count, int semflg);
```

Headers: `sys/types.h sys/ipc.h sys/msg.h`

Creates or acquires access to a set of semaphores for an application. The semaphores are used to manage resource allocation, or to schedule access to common facilities such as shared memory segments. The *key* argument specifies an arbitrary numeric value identifying the set of semaphores for an application, or it specifies the symbolic value IPC_PRIVATE defined in the `sys/ipc.h` header file. If you specify IPC_PRIVATE, `semget` always creates a new set of semaphores but the semaphores are known initially only to the creating process.

For *count* specify the number of semaphores in the set. Each semaphore is characterized by two values: its index in the set of semaphores (called *sem_num*), and its value (a signed integer value called *semval*). Also associated with each semaphore is the set of processes that may be waiting on the semaphore.

For *semflg* specify the following symbolic values:

IPC_CREAT to request that `semget` create the set of semaphores corresponding to *key* if the set does not already exist. If you do not specify the value and the set does not exist, no semaphores are created, a value of -1 is returned, and *errno* is set to ENOENT.

IPC_EXCL to indicate that the semaphore set corresponding to *key* should not already exist; if the set already exists, a value of -1 is returned and *errno* is set to EEXIST. This flag is commonly used together with IPC_CREAT when only one set of semaphores should exist in the system; an attempt to create another set returns an error.

0400 to indicate that the owner of the semaphores may read them.

0200 to indicate that the owner of the semaphores may alter them.

0060 to indicate that processes with the same effective group-ID as the creator of the semaphores may read or alter them.

0006 to indicate that other processes may read or alter the semaphores.

A process must call the `semget` function before any other operations can be performed on the set of semaphores. Normally one process creates the semaphores using an arbitrary *key* value unique to the application, and other processes use `semget` and the same key value to access the semaphores.

Returns: An integer semaphore identifier that must be used in the `semop` and `semctl` operations; the *key* value is used to identify the semaphores only for the `semget` operation. If unsuccessful, a value of -1 is returned and *errno* indicates the cause.

Warning

The user must ensure that the key value does not duplicate a key value used by another application.

Related Functions: `msgctl, msgget, msgrcv, msgsnd, semctl, semop, shmat, shmctl, shmdt, shmget`

semop *errno S KE*

```
int semop (int semid, struct sembuf **sops, int nops);
```

Headers: sys/types.h sys/ipc.h sys/sem.h

Executes the list of semaphore operations pointed to by *sops* on selected semaphores in the set identified by *semid*. *nops* is the the number of semaphore operations in the list.

sops is a pointer to an array of pointers to semaphore operations, where each operation is a structure of type sembuf consisting of the following elements as defined in the sem.h header file:

sem_num: is an integer from 0 to 1 less than the number of semaphores in the set, specified by the *count* argument of semget. The corresponding semaphore in the set is the one on which the operation is performed.

sem_flg: contains flags modifying the effect of the operation. The IPC_NOWAIT flag, if present, prevents suspension of the process when the operation causes the requestor to wait, and causes semop to return to the caller with a return value of -1 and *errno* set to EAGAIN. The SEM_UNDO flag is optional; if present, it causes this operation to update the *semadj* value associated with the process so that exit can undo the effects of semaphore operations. The UNDO capability provides a measure of protection against permanent reservation of resources acquired with semaphores when the reserving process is unexpectedly terminated.

sem_op: is a signed integer specifying the operation to be performed. The action taken depends on the sign of *sem_op*, as follows:

<0   If the result of adding *sem_op* to *semval* would be non-negative, <0 adds the value of *sem_op* to *semval* (thus reducing the value of the semaphore) and processing continues with the next operation in the list. If the sum would be negative, this sign sets the process to wait until the sum would be nonnegative, unless *sem_flg* includes the IPC_NOWAIT flag.

>0   The value of *sem_op* is added to *semval*, and any processes waiting for incrementation of the semaphore are awakened. Processing continues with the next operation in the list.

=0   If the value of *semval* is already 0, processing continues with the next operation in the list. Otherwise, =0 suspends the process until other processes cause the value of the semaphore to become 0. If the *sem_flg* includes the IPC_NOWAIT flag, this sign does not suspend the process, but `semop` returns immediately with a value of -1 and *errno* set to EAGAIN.

If all operations in the list cannot be executed successfully, then no operations are executed; actions taken by operations before the failure are negated before control returns. The net result is that semaphore operations appear immediate to other processes.

You can use a semaphore as an event, where the semaphore value represents the number of times the event occurred; posting corresponds to incrementing the value of the semaphore, and waiting corresponds to decrementing the value of the semaphore. You also can use a semaphore as a resource allocation facility: if the value of the semaphore represents the number of units of a resource that are currently available, `semop` can allocate resources by attempting to decrement the value of the semaphore by the number of units desired, while incrementing the semaphore returns the specified number of units to the allocation pool.

Returns: The semaphore value resulting from the last operation in the list, or -1 if an error occurred.

Related Functions: `semctl, semget`

setbuf

```
int setbuf (FILE *stream, char *buf);
```

Headers: `stdio.h`

Substitutes the character array pointed to by *buf* for the automatically acquired buffer associated with the stream file *stream*. The size of the new buffer must be equal to the value of BUFSIZ defined in the `stdio.h` header file.

If *buf* is the NULL pointer, the stream is unbuffered.

Returns: 0 if successful, otherwise a nonzero value.

> **Warning**
>
> You must call `setbuf` before the first read or write to *stream*.

Related Functions: `fopen, setvbuf`

setgid *errno S*

```
int setgid (int gid);
```

Sets the group-ID according to the value of *gid*, and the user who invokes the function:

If invoked by the superuser, setgid sets both the real and effective group-ID of the calling process to the value of *gid*.

If invoked by the general user, setgid sets the effective group-ID of the calling process to the value of *gid*. The real group-ID remains unchanged. The request fails unless *gid* is either the real group-ID of the calling process, or the saved group-ID found by exec.

The setgid function provides a means for system control programs such as /bin/login to initialize the group-ID of a process, and for programs having the set-group-ID flag set to switch the effective group-ID between the group-ID of the program file and the real group-ID.

Returns: 0 if successful, -1 otherwise.

Related Functions: chmod, exec, getegid, getgid, setuid

setgrent

```
void setgrent (void);
```

Repositions the internal file used by getgrent to its beginning; the next call to getgrent returns the first group definition in the /etc/group system file.

Use setgrent when repeated searches of the /etc/group file are required.

Related Functions: endgrent, getgrent

setjmp

```
int setjmp (jmp_buf env);
```

Headers: setjmp.h

Applications typically consist of many functions that call each other to perform the application task. When the application is built in this manner, error handling can be awkward when the error is detected in a deeply nested call. You can use `setjmp` to return control to a function other than the calling function.

The stack in effect for the function calling `setjmp` is saved in the variable *env* of type *jmp_buf*. (The `setjmp.h` header file defines the typename *jmp_buf*.) As long as the function that called `setjmp` does not itself return, you can use `longjmp` to restore the stack to the state saved by `setjmp`. The lower-level function using `longjmp`, therefore, appears to return from `setjmp`, and does not return to the function which called it.

Returns: 0, but when `longjmp` is used, the return value appears to be non-zero; the actual return value is obtained from an argument of `longjmp`. Normally, the application establishes a convention for the significance of nonzero return values set via `longjmp`.

Warning

The function executing `setjmp` must remain active for the contents of *env* to be usable; therefore, you should issue `setjmp` in one of the high-level functions of the program.

Related Functions: `longjmp`

---

setpgrp *S*

```
int setpgrp (void);
```

Sets the process group-ID to the same value as the process-ID of the calling process.

Returns: The new process group-ID.

Related Functions: `getpgrp, signal`

setpwent

```
void setpwent (void);
```

Repositions the internal file used by getpwent to its beginning; the next call to getpwent returns the first user definition in the /etc/passwd system file.

Use setgrent when repeated searches of the /etc/passwd file are required.

Related Functions: endpwent, getpwent, setspent

setspent

```
void setspent (void);
```

Repositions the internal file used by getspent to its beginning; the next call to getspent returns the first user definition in the /etc/shadow system file.

Use setspent when repeated searches of the /etc/shadow file are required.

Related Functions: endpwent, endspent, getpwent, setpwent

setuid *errno S*

```
int setuid (int uid);
```

Sets the user-ID according to the value of *uid*, and the user who invokes the function:

If invoked by the superuser, setuid sets both the real and effective user-ID of the calling process to the value of *uid*.

If invoked by the general user, setuid sets the effective user-ID of the calling process to the value of *uid*. The real user-ID remains unchanged. The request fails unless *uid* is either the real user-ID of the calling process, or the saved user-ID found by exec.

The `setuid` function provides a means for system control programs such as `/bin/login` to initialize the user-ID of a process, and for set-uid programs (programs having the set-user-ID flag set in the file access permissions) to switch the effective user-ID between the owner-ID of the program file and the real user-ID.

Returns: 0 if successful, -1 otherwise.

Related Functions: `chmod, exec, geteuid, getuid, setgid, setpgrp`

setutent

```
void setutent (void);
```

Repositions the internal file used by `getutent` to its beginning. The next call to `getutent` returns the first record in the file, or the next call to `getutid` or `getutline` searches the file from its beginning for the desired record.

Use `setutent` when repeated searches of the `utmp` file are required.

Related Functions: `endutent, getutent, getutid, getutline, pututline, utmp.h, utmpname`

setvbuf

```
int setvbuf (FILE *stream, char *buf, int type, int size);
```

Headers: `stdio.h`

Replaces the automatically acquired buffer associated with the stream file *stream* with the user-provided buffer *buf*. The value of *size* specifies the size of the new buffer in bytes.

type specifies the type of buffering to be performed for *stream*, and must be one of the following values defined in the header file `stdio.h`:

_IOFBF Full buffering.   If reading, the buffer is filled only when it is empty; if writing, the buffer is flushed only when a character is written and the buffer contains no space for the character.

_IOLBF Line buffering.   The buffer is filled or flushed when a complete line is processed.

_IONBF No buffering.   Reading and writing occur to the external file immediately. The values of *buf* and *size* are ignored in this case.

The optimum size for a stream buffer is defined in the stdio.h header file as BUFSIZ, although you can use any other value.

Returns: A nonzero value if an error occurs, otherwise 0.

Related Functions: `fopen`, `setbuf`

shmat *errno S KE*

```
void *shmat (int shmid, void *shmaddr, int shmflg);
```

Headers: `sys/types.h sys/ipc.h sys/shm.h`

Attaches the shared-memory segment identified by *shmid* to the address space of the calling process.

The address at which the segment is attached is determined by the value of *shmaddr* and the presence or absence of the SHM_RND flag in the value of the *shmflg* argument, as follows:

If *shmaddr* is equal to the NULL pointer, the system chooses the address at which the segment is attached; the address chosen is an address range that is the appropriate size, that is not currently in use, and that is not likely to conflict with normal growth of the stack and the break address (see `malloc`).

If *shmaddr* is not NULL and you specify SHM_RND, the segment is attached at an address which is the value of *shmaddr* rounded to align the segment at the next lower system-defined boundary.

If *shmaddr* is not NULL and you do not specify SHM_RND, the segment is attached at the address specified by *shmaddr*.

If *shmaddr* is not NULL and the address (after any rounding) would cause any part of the segment to overlap an existing valid area of memory, the attach fails and EINVAL is indicated in *errno*.

Besides the SHM_RND flag, the *shmflg* value may also include the

SHM_RDONLY flag, which causes the segment to be attached for read accesses, but prevents write accesses. If you do not specify SHM_RDONLY, any address in the range of the segment can be accessed for both read and write.

Returns: The actual address at which the segment is attached, or -1 if the segment could not be attached.

> **Warning**
>
> shmat attaches only the number of bytes specified by the *size* argument of the shmget function, although the segment may have been created with a larger size.

Related Functions: shmctl, shmdt, shmget

shmctl *errno S KE*

```
int shmctl (int shmid, int cmd, struct shmid_ds *buf);
```

Headers: sys/types.h sys/ipc.h sys/shm.h

Perform three different actions depending on the value of *cmd*, as follows:

IPC_RMID removes the definition of the shared-memory segment identified by *shmid* from the system. Subsequent attempts to attach the segment indicate an error with *errno* set to ERMID. Processes that have already attached the segment may continue to access it; physical memory committed to the segment is not released until all processes have detached the segment.

IPC_STAT returns information describing the current status of the shared-memory segment identified by *shmid* in the area pointed to by *buf*. The shm.h header file defines the contents of the shmid_ds structure.

IPC_SET sets the values of selected parameters of the shared-memory segment to the values of the corresponding members of the shmid_ds structure pointed to by *buf*. Only the values shm_perm.uid, shm_perm.gid, and the nine low-order bits of shm_perm.mode can be set. The caller must be the superuser or the owner of the segment.

Returns: 0 if successful, -1 otherwise.

Related Functions: shmat, shmdt, shmget

shmdt *errno S KE*

```
int shmdt (void *shmaddr);
```

Headers: `sys/types.h sys/ipc.h sys/shm.h`

Detaches the shared-memory segment, located in the current address space at the address of *shmaddr*, from the current address space.

Returns: 0 if successful, otherwise -1.

Related Functions: `shmctl, shmat, shmget`

shmget *errno S KE*

```
int shmget (key_t key, int size, int shmflg);
```

Headers: `sys/types.h sys/ipc.h sys/shm.h`

Returns a shared-memory identifier and may create a new shared-memory segment. The *key* argument specifies an arbitrary numeric value established by application convention that identifies a public shared-memory segment, or it specifies the symbolic value IPC_PRIVATE defined in the `sys/ipc.h` header file; if you specify IPC_PRIVATE, `shmget` always creates a new shared-memory segment that does not correspond to any possible value of *key*.

For *size* specify the size in bytes of the shared-memory segment. The specified size must fall between system-defined minimum and maximum limits.

For *shmflg* specify the following symbolic values:

IPC_CREAT to request that the shared-memory segment corresponding to *key* be created if it does not already exist. If you do not specify IPC_CREAT and the shared-memory segment does not exist, no segment is created, a value of -1 is returned, and *errno* is set to ENOENT.

IPC_EXCL to indicate that the shared-memory segment corresponding to *key* should not already exist; a value of -1 is returned and *errno* is set to EEXIST if the shared-memory segment already exists. This flag is commonly used to prevent the creation of multiple instances of a shared-memory segment.

0400 to indicate that the owner of the segment may attach the segment for read access.

0600 to indicate that the owner of the segment may attach the segment for read/write access.

0060 to indicate that processes with the same effective group-ID as the creator of the segment may access the segment.

0006 to indicate that other processes may access the segment.

A process must call the shmget function before the process can perform any other shared-memory operations for that segment. Normally one process creates the segment using an arbitrary *key* value unique to the application, and other processes wanting to access the segment use shmget and the same key value to acquire access.

The IPC_PRIVATE facility enables a process to create a segment accessible only to authorized processes; the process using IPC_PRIVATE must provide the shared-memory identifier to the authorized processes.

Note that the semaphore and shared-memory operations provide one way of building interprocess communications facilities; the message-queueing operations provide another.

Returns: An integer shared-memory identifier (*shmid*) that must be used in the shmat, shmdt, and shmctl operations; use the *key* value to identify the segment only for the shmget operation. If no shared-memory segment corresponding to *key* exists and you do not specify IPC_CREAT, or if such a segment exists but you also specify IPC_EXCL, then a value of -1 is returned and *errno* is set to identify the error.

> **Warning**
>
> You must ensure that the key value does not duplicate a key value used by another application.

Related Functions: msgctl, msgget, msgrcv, msgsnd, semctl, semget, semop, shmat, shmctl, shmdt

signal *errno S*

```
void (*signal (int sig, void (*func)()))()
```

Headers: `signal.h`

Defines the action that is to occur when the signal *sig* is posted to the calling process.

The `signal.h` header defines the valid signal names, and include at least the signals listed in the following table:

Name	No.	Meaning
SIGHUP	1	Hangup
SIGINT	2	Interrupt
SIGQUIT	3	Quit
SIGILL	4*	Illegal instruction (not reset)
SIGTRAP	5*	Trace interrupt (not reset)
SIGIOT	6*	IOT instruction
SIGEMT	7*	EMT instruction
SIGFPE	8*	Floating-point exception
SIGKILL	9	Kill (cannot be reset or ignored)
SIGBUS	10*	Bus error
SIGSEGV	11*	Segmentation violation
SISSYS	12*	Invalid argument to system call
SIGPIPE	13	Broken pipe
SIGALRM	14	Process alarm clock
SIGTERM	15	Software termination signal
SIGUSR1	16	User defined
SIGUSR2	17	User defined
SIGCLD	18	Death of a child process
SIGPWR	19	Power failure

* Causes a core file to be written to the current directory.

The value of *func* may be one of the following:

SIG_DFL terminates the process as if exit were called.

SIG_IGN ignores the signal; SIGKILL cannot be ignored.

The function address invokes the function pointed to by *func* as if called at the point of interruption, after setting the signal action to SIG_DFL. The declaration of the function is `void func(int` *sig*`)`. If the function returns, the process resumes execution from the point of interruption. The original signal action is not restored.

The action value for all signals is normally SIG_DFL until set to some other value, but note that the current setting of signal actions is inherited by child processes.

Returns: The previous action value for *sig*, if successful, or -1 otherwise.

Warning

If a signal condition is raised during one of the system calls `read`, `write`, `open` or `ioctl` (except for disk accesses), `pause`, or `wait`, the system call may return a value of -1 and set *errno* to EINTR. You can safely repeat the interrupted system call without losing data or improperly processing data.

Related Functions: `execl, fork, kill, pause, wait`

---

sin *errno M*

```
double sin (double x);
```

Headers: `math.h`

Computes the size of the argument.

Returns: The trigonometric sine of the argument *x* in radians.

---

sinh *errno M*

```
double sinh (double x);
```

Headers: `math.h`

Computes the hyperbolic size of the argument.

Returns: The hyperbolic sine of *x*.

sleep

```
unsigned sleep (unsigned sec);
```

Suspends program execution for a real-time interval of *sec* seconds. The amount of time slept may be less than *sec* if a signal is received before the specified time elapses, or greater if other system activity delays alarm-clock interruptions. Although sleep uses the process alarm clock, sleep saves and restores any value which may have been set.

Returns: The number of seconds remaining to be slept which could not be slept because of an interruption signal.

> **Warning**
>
> If a signal-catching routine is set up for the SIGALRM signal, the routine is entered as a result of sleep execution even if the program does not otherwise set an alarm interval.

Related Functions: alarm, pause, signal

sprintf *errno*

```
int sprintf (char *buf, const char *format, ...);
```

Headers: stdio.h

Differs from printf in that this function stores the result string in the character array pointed to by *buf* rather than writing to an output file. A null character (\0) is placed at the end of the result string.

Returns: The number of characters stored in *buf*, exclusive of the trailing null character.

> **Warning**
>
> `sprintf` overruns the end of the character array pointed to by *buf* if the array is too short to contain the result string. The warnings described for `printf` also apply to `sprintf`.

Related Functions: `ecvt, fprintf, printf`

sqrt *errno M*

```
double sqrt (double x);
```

Headers: `math.h`

Computes the square root of its argument.

Returns: The square-root of *x*.

> **Warning**
>
> `sqrt` returns 0 and sets *errno* to EDOM if *x* is negative.

srand

```
void srand (unsigned int seed);
```

Seeds the random number generator used by `rand`. If `srand` is not called, `rand` uses a default initial seed of 1.

Returns: Nothing.

Related Functions: `rand`

srand48

```
void srand48 (long seed);
```

Initializes to the value of *seed* the 32 high-order bits of the *X*-value used internally by the `drand48`, `lrand48`, and `mrand48` pseudo-random number generators. The 16 low-order bits are set to an arbitrary constant value.

A given value of *seed* always causes `srand` to subsequently generate the same series of pseudo-random numbers.

Related Functions: `drand48`, `erand48`, `jrand48`, `lcong48`, `lrand48`, `mrand48`, `nrand48`, `rand`, `seed48`

sscanf *errno*

```
int sscanf (const char *string, const char *format, ...);
```
Headers: `stdio.h`

Differs from the `scanf` function only in that `sscanf` scans the null-terminated string pointed to by *string* instead of standard input. `sscanf` does not alter *string*.

Returns: The number of values converted and stored, which can be 0 if no values were stored before the end of *string* was reached.

Related Functions: `fclose`, `ferror`, `fopen`, `fread`, `getc`, `scanf`, `sscanf`

ssignal

```
int (*ssignal (int sig, int (*action)())());
```
Headers: `signal.h`

Establishes *action* as the action to be taken for the software signal *sig*.

For *sig* specify a number in the range 1-15. The significance of a signal number is determined by user convention.

For *action* specify one of the following values:

SIG_DFL to take the default action for *sig*

SIG_IGN to ignore the signal

name to cause `ssignal` to invoke the named function when signal *sig* is generated. The declaration for the user function must be

```
int name (int sig);
```

where the only argument to the function is the signal number that caused it to be invoked. The function return value is the value returned by `gsignal`.

Signals generated by `gsignal` are handled only by `ssignal` actions.

Returns: The action that was previously in effect for signal *sig*.

Related Functions: `gsignal`, `signal`

stat *errno S*

```
int stat (const char *path, struct stat *buf);
```

Headers: `sys/types.h sys/stat.h`

Returns information about the file *path* in the structure pointed to by *buf*. The format of the stat buffer is defined in the `stat.h` header file.

The calling process must have search permission for all directories in the path; read permission for the file itself is not required.

Returns: 0 if successful, -1 otherwise.

Related Functions: `access`, `fstat`, `stat.h`

stime *errno S*

```
int stime (long *clock);
```

Sets the system time-of-day clock to the value pointed to by *clock*. The clock value is a number of seconds measured from midnight GMT, January 1, 1970. The time-of-day clock is always maintained in Greenwich Mean Time (GMT).

The effective user-ID of the calling process must be superuser.

Returns: 0 if successful, -1 otherwise.

Related Functions: `asctime, ctime, gmtime, localtime, time`

strcat

```
char *strcat (const char *s1, const char *s2);
```

Headers: `string.h`

Copies the string pointed to by *s2* to the end of the string pointed to by *s1*, forming a single unbroken string that is the concatenation of the two original strings. The character array pointed to by *s1* must be large enough to contain both strings plus a trailing null character.

Returns: The pointer *s1*.

Warning

The result is not defined if either argument is the NULL pointer.

Related Functions: `strchr, strcmp, strcpy, strcspn, strlen, strncat, strncmp, strncpy, strpbrk, strrchr, strspn, strtok`

strchr

```
char *strchr (const char *s, int c);
```

Headers: `string.h`

Searches string *s* for the first occurrence of the character *c*. The string pointed to by *s* must be terminated by a null (\0).

Returns: A pointer to the first occurrence of the character *c* in the string *s*, or a NULL pointer if the character *c* does not occur in *s*. The null character (\0) will always be found.

> **Warning**
>
> The result is not defined if *s* is the NULL pointer.

Related Functions: `strcat, strcmp, strcpy, strcspn, strlen, strncat, strncmp, strncpy, strpbrk, strrchr, strspn, strtok`

strcmp

```
int strcmp (const char *s1, const char *s2);
```

Headers: `string.h`

Compares the string *s1* to the string *s2*.

Returns: A negative, 0, or positive value when the string *s1* is less than, equal to, or greater than the string *s2*.

> **Warning**
>
> The result is not defined if either argument is the NULL pointer.

Related Functions: `strcat, strchr, strcpy, strcspn, strlen, strncat, strncmp, strncpy, strpbrk, strrchr, strspn, strtok`

strcpy

```
char *strcpy (const char *s1, const char *s2);
```

Headers: `string.h`

Copies the null-terminated string pointed to by *s2* to the character array pointed to by *s1*. It is the user's responsibility to ensure that the character array *s1* is large enough to contain the string to be copied plus a trailing null character.

Returns: The pointer *s1*.

> **Warning**
>
> The result is not defined if either argument is the NULL pointer.

Related Functions: strcat, strchr, strcmp, strcspn, strlen, strncat, strncmp, strncpy, strpbrk, strrchr, strspn, strtok

strcspn

```
int strcspn (const char *s1, const char *s2);
```

Headers: string.h

Returns: The length of the initial substring of *s1* that consists only of characters not in the string *s2*.

> **Warning**
>
> The result is not defined if either argument is the NULL pointer.

Related Functions: strcat, strchr, strcmp, strcpy, strlen, strncat, strncmp, strncpy, strpbrk, strrchr, strspn, strtok

strdup *R3*

```
char *strdup (const char *s);
```

Headers: string.h

Allocates an area of storage equal in size to the length of string *s*, including the trailing null character (\0), and copies *s* to the allocated storage area.

Returns: A pointer to the allocated storage area containing a copy of *s*, or NULL if the area could not be allocated. You should release the copy using free when it is no longer required.

> **Warning**
>
> The result is not defined if *s* is the NULL pointer.

Related Functions: `free, malloc strcpy, strncpy`

strlen

```
int strlen (const char *s);
```

Headers: `string.h`

Finds the length of the string pointed to by *s*.

Returns: The length of the string *s* excluding the trailing null character.

> **Warning**
>
> The result is not defined if *s* is the NULL pointer.

Related Functions: `strcat, strchr, strcmp, strcpy, strcspn, strncat, strncmp, strncpy, strpbrk, strrchr, strspn, strtok`

strncat

```
char *strncat (const char *s1, const char *s2, int n);
```

Headers: `string.h`

Copies the string pointed to by *s2*, up to a maximum length of *n* characters, to the end of the string pointed to by *s1*. The result forms a single unbroken string. The character array pointed to by *s1* must be large enough to contain the result string plus a trailing null character.

Returns: The pointer *s1*.

> **Warning**
>
> The result is not defined if either argument is the NULL pointer.

Related Functions: `strcat`, `strchr`, `strcmp`, `strcpy`, `strcspn`, `strlen`, `strncmp`, `strncpy`, `strpbrk`, `strrchr`, `strspn`, `strtok`

---

strncmp

```
int strncmp (const char *s1, const char *s2, int n);
```

Headers: `string.h`

Compares the *n*-byte character array pointed to by *s1*. The array at *s1* must be *n* characters long. If the string *s2* contains a null character (\0), the null character stops the comparison.

Returns: A negative, 0, or positive value if the array of *n* characters pointed to by *s1* compares less than, equal to, or greater than the first *n* characters of *s2*.

> **Warning**
>
> The result is not defined if either argument is the NULL pointer, or if either of the character arrays *s1* or *s2* is less than *n* bytes long.

Related Functions: `strcat`, `strchr`, `strcpy`, `strcspn`, `strlen`, `strncat`, `strncmp`, `strncpy`, `strpbrk`, `strrchr`, `strspn`, `strtok`

---

strncpy

```
char *strncpy (char *s1, const char *s2, int n);
```

Headers: `string.h`

Copies the string *s2* to the array *s1*. The result is truncated or padded with nulls to a length of *n* characters. No trailing null is stored unless the string *s2* is less than *n* characters long.

Returns: The pointer *s1*.

> **Warning**
>
> The result is not defined if either argument is the NULL pointer.

Related Functions: strcat, strchr, strcmp, strcpy, strcspn, strlen, strncat, strncmp, strpbrk, strrchr, strspn, strtok

---

strpbrk

char *strpbrk (const char *s1, const char s2);

Headers: string.h

Searches the null-terminated string *s1* for the first occurrence of any character in the null-terminated string pointed to by *s2*. The strpbrk function is useful for identifying an initial substring of *s1* delimited by one of several possible delimiters, specified in the string *s2*.

Returns: A pointer to the first occurrence of a character in the string *s1* that matches any of the characters in the string *s2*, or a NULL pointer if none of the characters in *s2* occurs in the string *s1*.

> **Warning**
>
> The result is not defined if either argument is the NULL pointer.

Related Functions: strcat, strchr, strcmp, strcpy, strcspn, strlen, strncat, strncmp, strncpy, strrchr, strspn, strtok

---

strrchr

char *strrchr (const char *s, int c);

Headers: string.h

Searches the null-terminated string *s* for the last occurrence of character *c* in *s*.

Returns: A pointer to the last occurrence of the character *c* in the string *s*, or a NULL pointer if the character *c* does not occur in *s*. The null character (\0) will always be found.

> **Warning**
>
> The result is not defined if *s* is the NULL pointer.

Related Functions: strcat, strchr, strcmp, strcpy, strcspn, strlen, strncat, strncmp, strncpy, strpbrk, strspn, strtok

strspn

```
int strspn (const char *s1, const char *s2);
```

Headers: string.h

Determines the number of leading characters of *s1* that occur in the string *s2*. The first character in *s1* that does not occur in *s2* stops the search. Both strings must be null terminated.

Returns: The length of the initial substring of *s1* that consists only of characters from the string *s2*.

> **Warning**
>
> The result is not defined if either argument is the NULL pointer.

Related Functions: strcat, strchr, strcmp, strcpy, strcspn, strlen, strncat, strncmp, strncpy, strpbrk, strrchr, strtok

strtod *errno*

```
double strtod (const char *string, char **ptr);
```

Converts the number string *string* to a internal floating-point number. The string may contain leading whitespace, an optional sign character, one or more decimal digits optionally containing a decimal point, and an optional exponent consisting of an e or E, an optional sign character, and one or more decimal digits. The first character in *string* that does not match this pattern stops the conversion, and a pointer to this character is stored in the location pointed to by *ptr* (unless the value of *ptr* is the NULL pointer).

Returns: The double-precision floating-point number represented by *string*.

> **Warning**
>
> If an overflow or underflow would occur, `strtod` returns HUGE or 0 is returned and *errno* is set to EDOMAIN.

Related Functions: `atof, scanf, strtol`

strtok

```
char *strtok (char *text, const char *delims);
```

Headers: `string.h`

Extracts the next token from the string *text*, in which tokens are separated by characters from the string *delims*.

If *text* is the NULL pointer, the search begins immediately following the last token returned by `strtok`; otherwise the search begins at the character pointed to by *text*.

All initial occurrences of any character in *delims* are skipped. The search then continues for a character occurring in *delims*; the first delimiter found is replaced with the null character, and `strtok` returns.

If the string pointed to by *text* contains none of the characters in *delims*, or *delims* is a string of length 0, the entire string is identified as a single token; any subsequent call of `strtok` with a NULL value for *text* returns NULL.

Returns: A pointer to the first character of the token, or a NULL pointer if no token is found.

Related Functions: `strcat, strchr, strcmp, strcpy, strcspn, strlen, strncat, strncmp, strncpy, strpbrk, strrchr, strspn`

strtol

```
long strtol (const char *string, char **ptr, int radix);
```

Converts the numeric string *string* to an internal long-integer number. The string may contain leading whitespace, an optional sign character, and one or more decimal digits. The first character in *string* that does not match this pattern stops the conversion, and a pointer to this character is stored in the location pointed to by *ptr* (unless the value of *ptr* is the NULL pointer).

The value of *radix* specifies the number base in which the number in *string* is expressed, and may be any value from 2-36 or 0. If the value of *radix* is 0, the string determines its own radix: numbers beginning with a leading 0 are assumed to be octal, numbers beginning with 0x or 0X are assumed to be hexadecimal, and numbers beginning with a nonzero digit are assumed to be decimal.

Returns: The long integer value represented by the contents of *string*.

Related Functions: atoi, atol, scanf, strtod

swab

```
void swab (const char *from, char *to, int nbytes);
```

Copies *nbytes* characters from the array pointed to by *from* to the array pointed to by *to*. The first and second bytes of each pair of bytes copied are exchanged. Use swab to assist in the conversion of data files exchanged between machine environments maintaining opposite byte-ordering conventions for numeric data.

sync *S*

```
void sync (void);
```

Schedules the writing of data to disk. A call to sync causes all data contained in system buffers for which no valid copy exists on disk to be scheduled for writing. The system may indefinitely delay the actual writing of data to disk after a successful `write` system call. `sync` forces the scheduling of all such delayed writes.

Physical writing of buffers may occur an indefinite time after the call to `sync`, because `sync` only schedules buffer flushing, but does not wait for its completion.

Returns: Nothing.

Related Functions: `open`

sys_errlist

```
extern char *sys_errlist [];
```

Headers: `errno.h`

Contains the error message text for each possible value of *errno*. `sys_errlist` is an array of pointers to null-terminated strings; when indexed by the value of *errno*, a pointer to the message text corresponding to *errno* is obtained.

You can use the `perror` function to retrieve the appropriate message text and write the text to the standard-error file.

Related Functions: `errno, sys_nerr, perror`

sys_nerr

```
extern int sys_nerr;
```

Headers: `errno.h`

The value of *sys_nerr* is the largest value of *errno* for which a corresponding message text pointer can be found in the *sys_errlist* table.

Related Functions: `errno, sys_errlist, perror`

system *errno*

```
int system (const char *command);
```

Passes the string contents of the array pointed to by *command* to a new copy of the shell for execution as a command. The shell invoked by *system* is always /bin/sh to enhance portability of programs; the -c option of the shell is used to limit shell execution solely to the command passed.

Returns: A negative value if the shell could not be invoked because the fork or exec system calls failed; otherwise the return value is the value returned by the shell.

Related Functions: execl, fork, popen

tan *errno M*

```
double tan (double x);
```

Headers: math.h

Computes the tangent of *x*, which must be given in radians.

Returns: The trigonometric tangent of the argument *x* in radians.

tanh *errno M*

```
double tanh (double x);
```

Headers: math.h

Returns: The hyperbolic tangent of *x*.

tdelete

```
void *tdelete (void *key, void **root, int (*compar)());
```

Headers: search.h

Removes that item in the binary tree pointed to by *root* which matches the item pointed to by *key*. The user function *compar* describes the ordering relation between items, and thus is used to identify the item in the tree matching *key* (see tsearch).

tdelete removes the matching item by altering pointers to items so that no item in the tree is linked to the item to be deleted. The user program may release the memory occupied by the deleted item, because that item is no longer a part of the tree.

Returns: A pointer to the parent item of the deleted item, or the NULL pointer if no match was found.

Related Functions: tfind, tsearch, twalk

telldir *R3*

```
long telldir (DIR *dirp);
```

Headers: sys/types.h dirent.h

Returns: The current location of the directory file pointed to by *dirp*.

Warning

The returned value is intended to be used as an argument to a subsequent seekdir call. Any other use, including altering the value, is at least non-portable and may cause unexpected results if you subsequently pass the altered value to seekdir.

Related Functions: closedir, opendir, readdir, rewinddir, seekdir

tempnam

```
char *tempnam (const char *dir, const char *prefix);
```

Headers: stdio.h

Generates a pathname for a temporary file.

If *dir* is not the NULL pointer, `tempnam` uses the pathname pointed to by *dir* as the directory. Otherwise, `tmpdir` uses the value of the TMPDIR environment variable if the variable is defined, or the directory defined by `P_tmpdir` in the `stdio.h` header file if that directory is writable by the caller, or the `/tmp` directory as a last resort.

The filename portion is generated in a way that results in unique filenames for all programs using the `tmpnam`, `tempnam`, or `mktemp` function. If *prefix* is not the NULL pointer, the filename begins with the string of up to five characters pointed to by *prefix*.

`tempnam` generates the pathname in an area allocated using `malloc`. The user program is responsible for creating and opening the temporary file, and for closing and removing the file after use.

Returns: A pointer to a null-terminated string containing the generated pathname, or NULL if `malloc` failed.

Warning

Temporary filenames generated by other means can be duplicated, although this is unlikely.

Related Functions: `creat`, `fopen`, `mktemp`, `tmpnam`, `unlink`

---

tfind

```
void *tfind (void *key, void **root, int (*compar)());
```

Headers: `search.h`

Searches a binary tree for an item matching the item pointed to by *key*. *root* must point to a pointer that in turn points to the root node of the tree; if the value of *root* is the NULL pointer, the tree is considered empty.

The user comparison function *compar* is declared as follows:

```
int compar (void *item1, void *item2);
```

compar must compare the identifying portions of the objects pointed to by *item1* and *item2*, and return an integer value that describes the ordering relation between *item1* and *item2*, as follows:

Negative if *item1* precedes *item2* in the desired ordering

0 if *item1* and *item2* occupy the same place in the desired ordering

Positive if *item1* follows *item2* in the desired ordering

`tfind` is similar to `tsearch` except that `tfind` does not insert an item into the tree if it is not found.

Returns: A pointer to the tree node matching the item pointed to by *key*, or the NULL pointer if no match is found. A node contains a pointer to the actual item.

Related Functions: `tdelete`, `tsearch`, `twalk`

time *errno S*

```
long time (long *buf);
```

Returns the current value of the system time-of-day clock as the value of the function. If *buf* is not the null pointer, `time` also stores the current system clock value at the location pointed to by *buf*.

Returns: The current time as the number of seconds elapsed since midnight Greenwich Mean Time (GMT), January 1, 1970.

Related Functions: `stime`

times *errno S*

```
int times (struct tms *buf);
```

Headers: `sys/types.h sys/times.h`

Returns, in the structure pointed to by *buf*, the amount of CPU time in seconds used by the calling process and all its child processes for which it issued a `wait` system call.

The `times.h` header file describes the format of `struct tms`.

Returns: 0 if successful, -1 otherwise.

tmpfile

```
FILE *tmpfile (void);
```

Headers: stdio.h

Creates a temporary file in the temp directory defined as P_tmpdir in the stdio.h header file. The file is opened for both reading and writing (w +); tmpfile automatically deletes the file when the calling process terminates.

Returns: A pointer to the open FILE block or, if the file could not be opened, a NULL pointer.

Related Functions: mktemp, tmpnam, tmpname

tmpnam

```
char *tmpnam (char *buf);
```

Headers: stdio.h

Generates a pathname for a temporary file, consisting of the directory name defined by P_tmpdir in the stdio.h header file, and a filename guaranteed to be unique for all programs using tmpnam, tempnam, or mktemp. The pathname is stored in the user buffer of at least L_tmpnam bytes pointed to by *buf* or, if *buf* is the NULL pointer, in an internal static area.

The user program is responsible for creating and opening the file, and for deleting the file after use.

Returns: A pointer to the generated pathname.

> **Warning**
>
> The generated filename can duplicate the name of another file in the P_tmpdir directory if other means are used to generate filenames, but the names are chosen in a way that is highly likely to be unique in any case.

Related Functions: creat, fopen, mktemp, tempnam, tmpfile, unlink

toascii

```
int toascii (int ch);
```

Converts the value of *ch* to a valid ASCII character code.

Returns: The converted result.

tolower

```
int tolower (int ch);
```

Converts an uppercase letter to the corresponding lowercase letter.

Returns: The ASCII code of a lowercase letter if the value of *ch* is the ASCII representation of the corresponding uppercase letter (65-90); otherwise the value of *ch* is returned.

Related Functions: `_tolower, toupper`

toupper

```
int toupper (int ch);
```

Converts a lowercase letter to the corresponding uppercase letter.

Returns: the ASCII code of an uppercase letter if the value of *ch* is the ASCII representation of the corresponding lowercase letter (97-122); otherwise the value of *ch* is returned.

Related Functions: `_toupper, tolower`

tsearch

```
void *tsearch (void *key, void **root, int (*compar)());
```

Headers: `search.h`

Searches a binary tree for the item pointed to by *key*, inserts the item if it is not present, and returns a pointer to the node containing the item. The object pointed to by *key* may contain any data; `tsearch` itself does not examine the contents of an item.

compar points to a user function

```
int compar (void *item1, void *item2);
```

that compares two items and returns a negative, 0, or positive value when *item1* is less than, equal to, or greater than *item2*. The comparison may be performed on any portion of the items, and may consider values of any data type.

root must point to a variable containing a pointer to the root node of the binary tree. If the value of **root* is the NULL pointer, the tree is considered empty. You can change the value of **root* by using `tsearch` and `tdelete`.

Returns: A pointer to the tree node matching *key*; the node contains a pointer to the item. The NULL pointer is returned if space for an insertion could not be `malloc`'d.

Warning

`tsearch` does not copy inserted items; the tree contains only pointers to items. The user must therefore preserve an item presented by the *key* pointer until the item is explicitly deleted by `tdelete`.

Related Functions: `bsearch, hsearch, lsearch, tdelete, tfind, twalk`

---

ttyname

```
char *ttyname (int handle);
```

Returns: A pointer to a null-terminated string in an internal static area, where the string gives the pathname of the terminal device on which the file descriptor *handle* is open, or the NULL pointer if the device corresponding to *handle* is not a terminal.

Related Functions: `ctermid, isatty`

ttyslot

```
int ttyslot (void);
```

Returns: The index to the entry in the /etc/utmp file corresponding to the current user.

Warning

ttyslot identifies the entry by searching for a terminal entry corresponding to the device on which standard input, standard output, or standard error (handles 0, 1, or 2) is currently open. A return value of 0 indicates that an error occurred.

Related Functions: getutent, ttyname

twalk

```
void twalk (void *item, void (*action)());
```

Headers: stdio.h

Traverses a binary tree as built by tsearch, or any subtree of a tree.

The *item* pointer must point to a node of the tree, either the root node or any node below the root. If the node is not the root, then twalk traverses only the node and its subordinate nodes.

The user function pointed to by *action* is called for each node as it is visited. The function declaration is

```
void action (void **item, VISIT order, int depth);
```

where

❏ *item* is a pointer to a node of the tree, which in turn points to the item contained in that node.

❏ *order* is one of the enumeration values

```
typedef enum { preorder, postorder, endorder, leaf } VISIT;
```

and indicates for which visit of the node the user routine has been called. The user routine visits each node three times. The *preorder* visit occurs before the user routine visits any of the child nodes; the *postorder* visit occurs after the user routine visits the left child and before the user routine visits the right; and the *endorder* visit occurs after the user routine visits both children.

❑ *depth* indicates the relative depth of the node with respect to the starting node.

The `twalk` function returns when the node pointed to by *item* and all its child nodes have been visited.

Returns: Nothing.

Related Functions: `tdelete, tfind, tsearch`

tzset

```
void tzset (void);

extern long  timezone;
extern char *tzname[2];
extern int   daylight;
```

Headers: `time.h`

Updates the variables *timezone, tzname,* and *daylight.* `tzset` is called by `asctime.`

timezone specifies the number of seconds to be added to Greenwich Mean Time (GMT) to obtain the local time. Positive values indicate time zones west of the prime meridian, and negative values indicate eastern time zones.

tzname points to an array of two pointers to strings. The first element gives the name of the local standard time zone, while the second gives the name of the local daylight saving time zone.

daylight contains 1 when a daylight saving time conversion should be applied to obtain the local time, and contains 0 otherwise.

The contents of these variables are derived from the TZ environment string, in the format

SSS[-]hhDDD

where *SSS* is the name of the local standard time zone, [-] denotes an optional minus sign, *bb* specifies the number of hours to be added to Greenwich Mean Time, and *DDD* is the name of the local daylight saving time zone.

Related Functions: `asctime`

---

uadmin *errno S*

```
int uadmin (int cmd, int func, int mdep);
```

Headers: `sys/uadmin.h`

Performs system administrative functions, according to the value of *cmd* and *func*, as follows:

A_SHUTDOWN halts the system. The value of *func* specifies the mode of system continuation, and may be one of the values AD_HALT, AD_BOOT, or AD_IBOOT to request that the CPU be shut off, automatically rebooted, or interactively rebooted respectively.

A_REBOOT bypasses the normal system shutdown and reboots immediately according to the value of *func*.

A_REMOUNT remounts the root file system.

The effective user-ID must be superuser.

Returns: 0 if successful, or -1 otherwise. For some functions of `uadmin`, control is not returned.

---

ulimit *errno S*

```
long ulimit (int cmd, long newlimit);
```

Returns one of the process limits as specified by *cmd* or sets the value of *newlimit*. The possible values of *cmd* are as follows:

1 Gets the file size limit. This value returns the maximum number of 512-byte blocks that the calling process can write to any one file.

2 Sets the file size limit. The limit may be adjusted upward only if the effective user-ID is the superuser.

3 Gets the maximum possible break address (see brk).

Returns: The requested value, or -1 if an error occurred.

umask *S*

```
int umask (int mask);
```

Sets the process file creation mask to the value of *mask*. The process file creation mask is exclusive-or'd with the nine low-order bits of the *mode* argument of the system call that creates a new file. Bits in the mask value that are set to 1 cause the corresponding access permission bit of the new file to be set to 0.

The value of the process file creation mask is inherited by all child processes.

Returns: The previous value of the file creation mask.

Related Functions: chmod, creat, mknod, open

umount *errno S*

```
int umount (const char *special);
```

Unmounts the file system contained on the block-special device identified by the pathname *special*; files that were contained on the file system no longer will be accessible, but the directory on which the file system was mounted become accessible.

A process must invoke the umount system call with an effective user-ID of superuser.

Returns: 0 if successful, -1 otherwise.

Related Functions: mount

uname *errno S*

```
int uname (struct utsname *buf);
```

Headers: sys/utsname.h

Stores the current operating system identification in the structure pointed to by *buf*.

Members of the structure are null-terminated character strings. Information returned includes the following:

sysname   The name of the current UNIX system

nodename   The name by which this system is known in a UUCP communications network

release   The release of the currently active operating system

version   The version of the currently active operating system

machine   The type of CPU being used

In general there are no standards for the format of the information returned.

Returns: 0.

ungetc

```
int ungetc (int c, FILE *stream);
```

Headers: `stdio.h`

Pushes a character back onto the input stream file *stream*. The next call to `getc` (or any input function in the standard-I/O package) returns the character *c* before reading of the input stream resumes.

Returns: The value of *c*, or EOF if the push could not be performed.

> **Warning**
>
> Pushing cannot be performed if the file *stream* is unbuffered, if no input has as yet been read, or if an `ungetc` was already performed without an intervening `getc`. `fseek` destroys the effect of `ungetc`.

Related Functions: `fseek, getc, setbuf`

unlink *errno S*

```
int unlink (const char *path);
```

Removes the directory entry for *path* if the calling process has write access to the directory containing the entry or has an effective user-ID of superuser, and the entry is not the last link for an executable file that is currently being executed or the mount point for a currently mounted file system.

If the removed directory entry is the last link to the file, the file also is removed. File removal occurs immediately if the file is not open by any process, or as one of the actions taken by the `close` system call when the last process having the file open closes it.

The effective user-ID must be superuser to remove a directory entry for a directory.

Returns: 0 if successful, -1 otherwise.

Related Functions: `link, mknod`

ustat *errno S*

```
int ustat (int dev, struct ustat *buf);
```

Headers: `sys/types.h ustat.h`

Returns statistics for the file system mounted on the device *dev* in an area provided by the user and pointed to by *buf*. The `ustat.h` header file includes a full description of struct `ustat`.

The structure contains at least the following members:

f_tfree   Number of free blocks remaining

f_tinode   Number of free inodes remaining

f_fname   Name of the file system

f_fpack   Name of the volume containing the file system

Returns: 0 if successful, -1 otherwise.

Related Functions: `mount, stat`

utime *errno S*

```
int utime (const char *path, struct {time_t actime,
mtime;} *times);
```

Headers: `sys/types.h`

Sets the access and modification times of the file named by *path* to the current time if *times* is a null pointer. The calling process must be the owner of the file or have write permission.

If *times* is not NULL, `utime` sets the access and modification times to the values of *actime* and *mtime* contained in the structure pointed to by *times*. The times are expressed as the number of seconds elapsed since midnight Greenwich Mean Time (GMT), January 1, 1970. The calling process must have an effective user-ID equal to the owner-ID of the file, or it must be the superuser.

Returns: 0 if successful, -1 otherwise.

Related Functions: `stat`, `time`

utmpname

```
void utmpname (const char *filename);
```

Headers: `utmp.h`

Closes the current `utmp` file and sets the name of the file to the pathname string pointed to by *filename*. The next call to `getutent`, `getutid`, or `getutline` opens the file.

Returns: Nothing.

Related Functions: `endutent`, `getutent`, `getutid`, `getutline`, `pututline`, `setutent`, `utmp.h`

va_arg

```
type va_arg (va_list list, type);
```

Headers: `varargs.h`

Retrieves the next argument from a variable-length argument list defined by the pointer variable *list*. The argument is presumed to be of type *type*; the argument pointer *list* is incremented by the size of a *type* variable so that the next argument can be accessed.

The `va_start` macro must be executed before the invocation of `va_arg`.

Returns: The value of the next argument.

Warning

`va_arg` passes function arguments on the stack, meaning that they are stored one after the other in a contiguous area of storage. The `va_arg` macro works by maintaining a pointer to the current argument in the stack; each call increments the pointer by the size of the argument value returned. If the size in bytes implied by *type* does not match the actual size of an argument, the pointer is set incorrectly for the next use of `va_arg`. The caller must therefore ensure that the type supplied in the `va_arg` call agrees with the actual type of the arguments.

Related Functions: `va_end, va_start`

---

va_end

```
void va_end (va_list list);
```

Headers: `varargs.h`

Use the `va_end` macro together with the `va_start` macro to access the unknown arguments of a function; the macro serves as the ending bracket to `va_start`. Code the `va_end` macro at the end of the range of instructions where use of the `va_arg` macro is intended.

Warning

The range of a `va_start-va_end` bracket may not extend beyond the end of the code block containing the `va_start`. (A "code block" is a group of instructions enclosed between { and } brackets.)

Related Functions: `va_arg, va_start`

va_start

```
va_start (va_list list, arg);
```

Headers: `varargs.h`

Use the `va_start` macro to access the undeclared arguments of a function, usually represented by `...` in the argument list. The pointer variable *list* is initialized to point to the argument named *arg*. Repeated calls to the `va_arg` macro retrieve arguments following *arg*.

Non-ANSI compilers implement a different format for `va_start`, namely

```
va_start (list);
```

where *list* is the name of a variable of type `va_list`. The variable is initialized to refer to the argument represented by the placeholder name `va_alist` in the function declaration; `va_alist` must be declared to be of type `va_dcl` with no ending semicolon. The following is an example:

```
int vprintf (format, va_alist)
char *format;
va_dcl
{
      va_list args;
      char *strptr;

      va_start(args);
      strptr = va_arg(args, char *);
      va_end(args);
}
```

> **Warning**
>
> The program is responsible for properly determining the type of an undeclared argument.

Related Functions: `va_arg, va_end`

vfprintf *errno*

```
int vfprintf (FILE *stream, const char *format,
va_list args);
```

Headers: stdio.h varargs.h

Performs the same function as fprintf except that vfprintf supplies the list of arguments as a *varargs* pointer. This form of fprintf is useful typically when you pass a list of arguments to a user-written function which in turn are to be processed as the arguments of fprintf; use vfprintf in this case.

Returns: The number of characters written to the stream file *stream*, or a negative number if an error occurred.

Related Functions: fprintf, printf, sprintf, va_start, vprintf

vprintf *errno*

```
int vprintf (const char *format, va_list args);
```

Headers: stdio.h varargs.h

Performs the same function as printf except that vprintf supplies the list of arguments as a *varargs* pointer. This form of printf is useful typically when you pass a list of arguments to a user-written function which are in turn to be processed as the arguments of printf; use vprintf in this case.

Returns: The number of characters written to standard output, or a negative number if an error occurred.

Related Functions: fprintf, printf, sprintf, va_start, vfprintf

wait *errno S*

```
int wait (int *status);
```

Provides a means for a parent process to wait for the completion of its child processes. The effect of a wait call is as follows:

If the calling process has no children (including zombie processes), an error is recognized, a value of -1 is returned, and *errno* is set to ECHILD. Otherwise, the calling process is suspended until one of the child processes terminates, or a signal is received. If a signal is received and caught, `wait` returns a value of -1 and *errno* indicates EINTR. This return value does not indicate the termination of a child process, and you should repeat the `wait` call.

When a child process terminates, status information is stored in the low-order 16 bits of the integer pointed to by *status*, and `wait` returns the process-ID of the terminated child process. The value stored in the status location indicates one of the following:

❑ The child process terminated normally. The low-order eight bits of the status are 0, and the high-order bits contain the exit value of the child process.

❑ The child process was terminated by a signal. The low-order seven bits of the status indicate the nonzero signal number that caused the termination, and the 0200 bit is set to 1 if a core file was written. The high-order bits of the status are zero.

❑ The child process stopped because of a trace condition. The high-order bits identify the trace condition, and the low-order bits are set to 0177.

Note that the low-order eight bits of the status location are always zero when the child process terminated by a call to `exit`, and never zero otherwise.

Returns: The process-ID of a child process that has terminated, or -1 if an error occurred. A return value of zero cannot occur.

Warning

If the signal SIGCLD (death of a child) is set to a signal-catching function, the wait system call will always indicate the EINTR error because it can never return normally.

There is no way to selectively wait for the termination of a specific child process; wait will return for the next child process that terminates.

Related Functions: `exit, fork, pause, signal`

write *errno S*

```
int write (int handle, void *buf, unsigned len);
```

Bytes of the character array pointed to by *buf* are taken consecutively in a left-to-right order and written to the device or file associated with *handle* until *len* bytes have been written, a capacity limit is reached, or an error occurs.

For block-special devices and files, writing begins at the next byte in the file or at the offset specified by lseek, except that if the file descriptor specifies the O_APPEND flag, the file pointer is set to the current end of file before writing begins.

For character-special devices and pipes, lseek has no effect, and bytes written to the device are stored in a manner defined by the device.

If the file size limit (see ulimit) is reached when writing to a disk file, or the output device becomes full, or when writing to a pipe, the system buffer becomes full, only the number of bytes for which there is space are written, and the return value specifies the number of bytes written. The next write will either suspend the process (writing to a pipe) or indicate an error.

Returns: The number of bytes actually written, or -1 if an error occurred.

Related Functions: creat, fcntl, lseek, open, pipe, ulimit

y0 *errno M*

```
double y0 (double x);
```

Headers: math.h

Returns: The value of the Bessel function of the second kind, of order 0, corresponding to the argument *x*. The function is defined for positive values of *x*; other values cause a *matherr* condition to be recognized.

y1 *errno M*

```
double y1 (double x);
```

Headers: math.h

Returns: The value of the Bessel function of the second kind, of order 1, corresponding to the argument x. The function is defined for positive values of x; other values cause a *matherr* condition to be recognized.

yn *errno M*

```
double yn (double x);
```

Headers: math.h

Returns: The value of the Bessel function of the second kind, of order n, corresponding to the argument x. The function is defined for positive values of x; other values cause a *matherr* condition to be recognized.

The UNIX Shell

The UNIX shell is both a command interpreter and programming language. Two versions of the shell are supplied with UNIX System V: the Bourne shell developed by Steven Bourne, and the newer Korn shell developed by David F. Korn, both of AT&T Bell Laboratories. The Korn shell, named *ksh*, has all the features of the Bourne shell (*sh*), some of the best features of the C shell (the UCB 4.X version of the shell developed by Bill Joy at the University of California at Berkeley), and many new features of its own.

This quick reference guide describes the features of the Bourne and Korn shells. The Korn shell supports all Bourne shell features. In most cases, there are no differences between the Bourne shell syntax and Korn shell syntax for a command. Any differences, as well as commands that apply only to the Korn shell, are indicated specifically with the notation **KSH only**.

Shell programming relies to a great extent on the numerous commands provided with UNIX. Knowing these commands and their use is invaluable when you develop shell programs. This reference section discusses some of the more common UNIX commands; however, you should have the *AT&T UNIX User's Reference Manual* available while you develop shell programs.

The "Shell Basics" section explains the fundamentals of the Bourne and Korn shells. Topics include how to enter simple, sequential, and group commands; the use of the shell metacharacters; input and output redirection; pipelines; and the shell environment. You can use this section to quickly locate the syntax of any shell convention.

"Shell Files and Processes" explains how the UNIX file system and process control mechanism can help you make the best use of the shell.

"Built-In Commands" explains commands built into the shell program.

"Shell Parameters and Variables" contains information for using shell parameters and variables, including any predefined variables and their default values. Also included are notations for constructing and using conditional parameter substitution.

"Programming Constructs" provides information about using the shell's built-in programming constructs `for`, `while`, `until`, `if`, `case`, `select`, `time`, and `functions`.

"Shell Programs" tells how to create, execute, and debug shell programs and also how to use the dot (.) command. This section also includes examples of useful shell programs and programming hints.

Finally, the section "Related UNIX Commands" contains brief descriptions of UNIX commands that are helpful when writing shell programs.

Throughout this reference guide, a number in parentheses, such as (1), indicates a UNIX command. A description of the command is in the corresponding section of the reference manuals in table 1.

Table 1. *UNIX Manual Structure*

Subject	*Section(s) Where Covered*
User Commands	1
System Calls	2
Library Functions	3
File Formats	4
Miscellaneous	7
Administrative Commands	1M, 7, and 8

Shell Basics

Commands

Simple Commands

A simple command is a sequence of words separated by blanks (spaces or tabs). The first word is usually the name of a UNIX command or a built-in shell command. Additional words are either the name of files to be processed or arguments that modify the command's behavior.

In the UNIX environment a command always returns a numeric value, called an *exit status*, to the shell when it exits. By convention, an exit status of 0 implies that the command executed without errors, and a nonzero exit status means that it encountered unusual conditions or terminated abnormally. When evaluating an if statement, the shell treats an exit status of zero as the true condition, and takes a nonzero exit status to mean false.

When a command terminates abnormally, it returns octal 200+*status*, where *status* is the value of the signal that caused the abnormal termination. For example, if you press the Del key to interrupt a command, the command exit status will be 130 (200 octal = 128 decimal + 02, the value of the interrupt signal). See signal(2) for a complete list of signals and their values.

A *pipeline* consists of one or more simple commands separated by the pipe symbol (¦). The output of each command is sent to the input of the next command in the pipeline. Each command is executed as a separate process. After the last command in the pipeline exits, the shell resumes reading input from the keyboard. The exit status of a pipeline is the exit status of the last command in the pipeline.

Sequential Commands

A sequential command list consists of one or more simple commands (or pipelines) separated by a semicolon (;), ampersand (&), double ampersand (&&), or double pipe symbol (¦¦). In a command list, these separators are evaluated from left to right with the following precedence:

❏ && and ¦¦

❏ ; and &

> **KSH only**
>
> ❏ A ¦& symbol may be used as a command terminator and has equal precedence with ; and & (see "Co-Processes").

A semicolon causes sequential execution of the list of commands. The shell waits for each command in the list to complete before executing the next command. The output of each command is sent to the standard output. You can use newlines in place of semicolons to delimit commands.

Commands separated by an ampersand (&) are executed asynchronously. The shell starts each command without waiting for the preceding command to complete execution.

The *and* operator (&&) causes the command following it to be executed only if the preceding command returns a 0 exit status. In the following example, the message "You have mail" is echoed only if the `mail -s` command returns a 0 exit status:

```
mail -s && echo You have mail
```

The *or* operator (¦¦) causes the command that follows it to be executed only if the preceding command returns a nonzero exit status. In the next example, the message "No mail" is echoed if the `mail -s` command returns a nonzero:

```
mail -s ¦¦ echo No mail
```

> **KSH only**
>
> The ¦& symbol used to separate commands in the Korn shell causes asynchronous execution of the preceding command or pipeline with a two-way pipe established to the parent shell. The standard I/O of the spawned command can be written to and read from by the parent shell by using the -p option to the read and print built-in commands. Only one asynchronous command can be active at any time.)

Group Commands

You can group a sequential list of commands together by enclosing the commands in parentheses. Standard input can be redirected into the group, and the standard output of the entire group can be redirected.

For example, in the following command

```
$ ls;who;date > status
```

only the output of the `date` command is sent to the file `status`. However, if the entire list is enclosed in parentheses

```
$ (ls;who;date) > status
```

the output of all three commands is sent to the file `status`.

To run the entire group asynchronously in the background, you use the following:

```
$ (ls;who;date) > status&
```

Command Substitution

The output of a command can be used as the input to another command or for variable assignment with command substitution.

Whenever the shell encounters a command enclosed in grave accents (` `` `), that command is executed first and its output becomes the input to another command or variable assignment. For example:

```
$ here=`pwd`
```

first executes the `pwd` command and then assigns its output to the variable `here`. Similarly,

```
$ pg `cat list`
```

displays all of the files named in the file `list`.

Command substitution is very useful for setting positional parameters with the set command. In the example

```
$ set `date`
$ echo $1
Wed
$ echo $2
Dec
$ echo $*
Wed Dec 27 09:21:29 EST 1989
```

the `set` command sets the positional parameters `$1` through `$6` to the successive words printed by the date command. Thus, `$1` contains the day (Wed), `$2` the month (Dec), and so on. The command

```
echo $*
```

prints all the positional parameters.

A backquoted command is always executed in a subshell. Interpretation of shell variables and wild cards is not performed before the command is read, except that backslashes used to escape other characters are removed. Backslashes (\) may be used to escape a grave accent (`) or backslash that is to be passed to another command within the command substitution. For example,

```
$ echo `basename \`pwd\``
```

would print the current directory's basename.

If a backslash is used to escape a newline character, both the backslash and newline are removed. Backslashes used to escape a dollar sign (\$) are removed also. This has no effect because no interpretation is done on the command before it is read. Backslashes used to escape the meaning of other special characters (other than \, `, ", newline, and $) are left intact when the command is read.

> ***KSH only***
>
> The notation $(cmd) can be used in place of `cmd`.

Comments -

The # is used to specify that all text following it up to a newline is a comment (to be ignored by the shell). Comments are useful within a shell program to document how the program works.

Blank Interpretation

After parameter and command substitution, the shell separates arguments according to the value of the internal field-separator variable IFS. By default, IFS is set to the space, tab, and newline characters. Explicit null arguments ("" and ") are retained; implicit null arguments (those resulting from parameters that have no value) are removed.

You can change the value of IFS to modify the way the shell separates its arguments. For example, setting IFS to a colon (:) allows the following command:

```
$ IFS=:
$ ls:-l
```

This method can be used to make the shell parse lines separated by characters other than spaces. In the following example:

```
$ grep bill /etc/passwd
bill:fXAdztStiQVIU:100:21:Book Author:/usr/bill:/bin/sh
$ IFS=:
$ set `grep bill /etc/passwd`
$ echo $1
bill
$ echo $5
Book Author
```

the shell separates the line from the /etc/passwd file into seven parameters determined by the current value of IFS (:). The command substitution used with the set command sets each of these seven fields into the positional parameters $1 through $7 (the shell uses the value of IFS to separate fields). Therefore, each field can then be addressed by its positional parameter value.

Notice that spacing for the description field ($5) remained intact. By applying this method, you can use the shell as a simple database management system.

You should never set the value of IFS to that of one of the special shell characters (*, >, ;, and so on).

Quoting

In many instances, you must prevent the shell from interpreting the meaning of special characters such as *, ?, [], spaces, tabs, and so on. For example, you may need to pass a special character through the shell to another program such as grep(1). To accomplish this, there are three ways of quoting to prevent the shell from interpreting special characters.

Single Quotation Marks

Anything enclosed in single quotation marks is passed through the shell intact; that is, the shell does not interpret a string enclosed in single quotation marks. In the following example:

```
$ echo '$TERM'
$TERM
```

the shell will not interpret the $ as starting a shell variable.

Double Quotation Marks

Double quotation marks prevent the shell from interpreting everything except the dollar sign ($), backslash (\), and grave accent (`) symbols. You use double quotation marks also when you include spaces or tabs in a string. The shell interprets all other special characters.

In the following example, the double quotation marks prevent the shell from interpreting the spaces, thus providing only one argument to the second echo command:

```
$ name="Tom Jones" # Keep the space intact.
$ echo $name       # Two arguments to echo
Tom Jones
$ echo "$name"     # One argument to echo
Tom Jones
```

Backslash

The \ not only prevents the shell from interpreting the character immediately following it, but also prevents interpretation of spaces, tabs, and the newline character. The following example shows how the \ is used:

```
$ echo *
chapt01 chapt02 chapt03
$ echo \*
*
```

File-name Generation

Certain characters, often called wild cards or shell metacharacters, have special meaning to the shell.

Before a command is executed, the shell scans the command line for the special file-name generation characters described in table 2.

Table 2. *Shell Wild Cards*

Character	Meaning
*	Match anything, including null string
?	Match any single character
[xyz]	Match the character x, y, or z
[a-z]	Match any character in the range a through z
[!a-z]	Match any character except the lowercase letters

If one of these characters is present, it is regarded as a special pattern-matching character; the shell attempts to generate a list of file names that match the meaning of the special character. If the shell finds no file names that match the pattern, the special character is left intact.

To specify a range of characters, use – to separate the characters enclosed in brackets. For example, [a-z] matches any single character in the range a through z. If the first character following the opening bracket is an exclamation mark, as in [!, any character not enclosed in the brackets is matched.

Tilde Substitution

> ### KSH only
>
> The Korn shell checks each word of an alias substitution to see whether it begins with a tilde (~). If it does, the shell checks whether the string up to the next / matches one of the tilde sequences in table 3.

Table 3. *Tilde Sequences*

Character	Meaning
~	Replace tilde with value of HOME.
~+	Replace string (up to /) with value of PWD.
~-	Replace string (up to /) with value of OLDPWD.
~*login*	Replace tilde with the home directory of the user named by *login*. If no such user exists, no replacement occurs.

A tilde followed by anything else is left unchanged.

If, in the value of a variable assignment, a tilde follows the equal sign, the Korn shell attempts tilde expansion using the preceding rules.

Invocation

When a user logs in, login(1) starts a shell process. A - is prefixed to the name of the login shell (-sh), which causes the shell to read commands from the files /etc/profile and $HOME/.profile, if they exist.

If you set the ENV variable, the Korn shell uses its value as the environment file name and reads this file whenever you invoke a new Korn shell process, either directly or as a subshell. Thus, functions, parameters, and other shell constructs set within this file are available to all Korn shell subshells.

Following invocation, the shell reads commands as described in table 4. The first argument is assumed to be the name of a file containing commands; the remaining arguments are passed as positional parameters to that command file, unless the -c or -s options are specified.

For descriptions of the remaining options and arguments, see the set built-in command.

Table 4. Shell Options

Option	Meaning
– c *string*	If the – c option is present, *string* is taken to be a shell command, and is executed.
– s	If the – s option is present or if no arguments remain, he shell reads commands from standard input. Any remaining arguments specify the positional parameters. Shell output (except as described under "Built-In Commands") is written to file descriptor 2.
– i	If the – i option is present or if shell input and output are attached to a terminal, the shell is interactive. In this case, the SIGTERM signal is ignored (so that the command kill 0 does not kill an interactive shell) and the INTERRUPT signal is caught and ignored (so that wait is interruptible). In all cases, the shell ignores the QUIT signal. (See the section "Signals" for further discussion of SIGTERM, INTERRUPT, and QUIT.)
– r	If the – r option is present, the shell is a restricted shell.

Arithmetic Operations

KSH only

The let command provides integer arithmetic operations using long arithmetic. You can represent a named variable internally by using the typeset – i command, as in the following example:

```
# Declare num as a integer variable
typeset -i num
```

A base between 2 and 36 may be specified with the typeset command to represent the radix of the number, for example

```
# Declare binary as a base 2 integer
typeset -i2 binary
```

You can provide arithmetic functions on declared integer variables by using the let command, as in the following example:

```
$ typeset -i num1 num2 ans
$ num1=5
$ num2=8
$ let ans="$num1 + $num2"
$ print $ans
13
```

Many of the arithmetic operators for the let command (*, <, >, and so on) require quoting to prevent the shell from interpreting them.

The notation ((. . .)) can be used in place of the let command. For example, the following is equivalent to the previous example:

```
$ ((ans = $num1 * $num2))
$ print $ans
40
```

Prompting

The shell variable PS1 (default value $) is used as the primary prompt string and is printed before the shell reads each command. If the shell expects additional input to complete a command, it prompts with the secondary prompt sign PS2 (default >).

Signals

A subshell inherits the signal values from its parent except that the INTERRUPT and QUIT signals for a command are ignored if the command is executed in the background (followed by an &). For more information and a list of signals used by the shell, see the trap command.

Execution

The shell executes commands as follows:

1. First, file-name generation, quoting, command substitution, variable substitution, and I/O redirection are resolved.

2. Built-in commands are then executed within the current shell.

3. The command name is then compared to names of the defined functions. If a match is found, the function is executed in current shell process with positional parameters ($1, $2, and so on) set as arguments to the function.

4. If a command is neither a built-in command nor a function, a new process is created and the shell attempts to execute the command via the system call exec(2).

The shell uses the value of the PATH environment to search for commands. The default value of PATH specifies a shell search order starting with the current directory, then the /bin directory, and then the /usr/bin directory. The current directory is specified by a null path name or a dot (.) and can appear immediately after the = sign, between two colon delimiters, or at the end of the list. The following examples show how to set the current directory in the PATH parameter:

```
# Search current directory first
PATH=:/bin:/usr/bin
# Search current directory second
PATH=/bin::/usr/bin
# Search current directory last
PATH=/bin:/usr/bin:
# Do not search current directory
PATH=/bin:/usr/bin
```

For security reasons, system directories such as /bin and /usr/bin should always be searched first, before local directories or the current directory.

If a command begins with /, denoting an absolute pathname, the search path is not used. Commands containing / anywhere in the command name cannot be executed with the restricted shell (/bin/rsh).

If the shell finds a file in the search path with a name that matches the command name and that has execute permission, but is not an a.out file (one that contains directly executable code), it is assumed to be a file containing shell commands. A subshell is spawned to read and execute the commands within the file.

The shell remembers the search path of each command it executes to help avoid unnecessary exec system calls. However, the location of a command found in a relative directory must be redetermined whenever the current directory is changed. The shell forgets all remembered locations whenever the hash -r command (see "Built-In Commands") is executed or when the PATH environment is changed.

Shell Exit Status

The shell normally returns the exit status of the last command executed or the value specified by the exit built-in command. If the shell detects an error, it returns a nonzero exit status. If the shell detects an error while executing a shell script, execution terminates immediately and a nonzero exit status is returned. The exit status is available in the special shell variable $?.

Background Processing

The shell can run a command in the background rather than interactively. When a command runs in the background, the shell immediately returns a prompt to the user. The user can continue interactive use of the shell or start additional background commands.

To start a background command, append an ampersand (&) to the command line as follows:

```
$ sort large_file > file.out&
1222
```

A command started in the background becomes detached from the user's terminal. The standard input is redirected from /dev/null instead of the user's terminal. Because the INTERRUPT and QUIT signals are disabled, you cannot use the Break and Del keys to terminate the job. However, the HANGUP signal still will be sent to any background jobs when the login shell terminates.

The shell still redirects standard output and standard error to the user's terminal when it executes background jobs. The standard output and standard error should be redirected to a file, if necessary, so that output from the background job does not interfere with output from interactive jobs (see "I/O Redirection").

When a background job is started, its process-ID (pid) is printed before the shell issues another prompt. You can use the ps command to determine the process-ID of any background jobs.

Use the kill command to terminate a background job:

```
$ kill -2 1222
```

In this example, -2 is the signal to be sent (see "Signals") and 1222 is the background job's process-ID.

To make a background command immune to the hangup signal, use the nohup ("no hangup") command. nohup often is used when a user wants to start a job and then log off. The following example shows how to start a job with nohup:

```
$ nohup sort database> db.out&
1245
```

You can use the wait command to wait on a background process and obtain its exit status. An optional argument (the process-ID of the job to be waited for) may be supplied on the `wait` command; however, if the process-ID does not exist, all background jobs are waited for and the exit status is set to 0.

To wait for a job with a process-ID of 1245, for example, enter the following command:

```
$ wait 1245
```

If you enter a `wait` command, the Break and Del keys send INTERRUPT and QUIT signals to the `wait` command instead of to the process being waited for.

A limit is set on the number of processes (commands) that each user can start. If this limit is exceeded, the error message

```
cannot fork, too many processes
```

is printed.

Job Control Mechanism

KSH only

An interactive shell associates a job with each command if the following option is turned on:

```
set -o monitor
```

The `jobs` command prints a list of currently running jobs. When you start a job in the background with `&`, the shell prints a line similar to the following:

```
$ sort largedata > sort.out&
[1] 1923
```

In the preceding line, `[1]` indicates that this is job number 1, and `1923` is its process-ID.

To refer to a job, use the character `%`. Follow it with an integer (`%1`, for example, to refer to job number 1) or with a string indicating the first part of a command name (`%so` to refer to the last job started, the name of which begins with "so").

The notations `%+` and `%-` refer to the current and preceding jobs, respectively. A `%%` refers to the current job.

When a process state changes, the shell is notified immediately. Prior to a prompt, the shell notifies the user when a job becomes blocked and cannot continue. Thus, the shell does not interrupt the user's work.

When a user tries to exit a shell in which background jobs are active (running or stopped), the following message is displayed:

```
You have running(stopped) jobs
```

If, after using the jobs command to see what the jobs are, the user immediately tries to exit, the shell does not repeat the warning and kills all background jobs. Use the `nohup(1)` command to prevent jobs from being terminated when exiting the shell.

When using a version of UNIX that supports job control, certain features of the shell provide more precise control of jobs. Pressing Ctrl-Z (^ Z) sends a STOP signal to the current job. The shell stops the job, prints `Stopped`, and prints another prompt. You can put the job into the background by using the `bg` built-in command; a background job, either running or stopped, can be brought into the foreground with the `fg` built-in command. A ^ Z takes effect immediately. Pending output and unread input are discarded.

Background jobs stop if they attempt to read input from the terminal, but normally they can send output to the terminal. To prevent background jobs from writing output, issue the command

```
stty tostop
```

With this option set, the shell stops background jobs when they try to produce output as they do when they try to read input.

Co-Processes

KSH only

You can start two processes that communicate with each other. The concept is simple: one shell program starts another (using the `|&` operator) and then, using the print `-p` and read `-p` commands, the two processes can exchange information between each other.

The process that is started, called a co-process, must do the following:

❑ Send all output to the standard output

❑ Place a newline character at the end of each message

❑ Flush its standard output at the end of each message

The following two programs illustrate the use of co-processes. The first program, the co-process, returns the sum of two numbers passed to it:

```
# Program: sum - add two numbers
while true
do
     read a b
     let ans="$a + $b"
     print  $ans
done
```

The second program, the main process, starts sum and then prompts the user for two numbers. It passes the two numbers to sum, receives the answer, and prints the answer on the terminal.

```
# Program: query
sum |& # Start-up sum
while true
do
     #    Ask for the first number
     print "Enter num1"
     read num1
     #    Ask for the second number
     print "Enter num2"
     read num2
     #    Pass the numbers to sum
     print -p $num1 $num2
     #    Get the answer
     read -p ans
     #    Print it on the terminal
     print "Sum of $num1 + $num2 = $ans"
done
```

The co-process (sum) continues to run until the main process (query) dies.

Using co-processes, you can develop transaction-oriented shell programs for database applications.

With versions of ksh newer than 06/03/86, you can start multiple co-processes. Each co-process (after the first) must be assigned a unique file descriptor for its input and output. To assign standard output for a co-process, use the notation exec3>&p; to reassign the standard input, use exec3<&p.

Within a co-process, output must be redirected to the file descriptor associated with the co-process. For example,

```
print $ans >&3
```

sends output of the `print` command to file descriptor number 3.

The main process would use the command

```
print -pu4 num1
```

to send output to the co-process associated with file descriptor number 4, and

```
read -pu4
```

to receive input from co-process number 4.

The following programs illustrate the use of more than one coprocess. They start two co-processes, `add` and `subtract`:

```
# Program: add
while true
do
read a b
let ans="$a + $b"
print  $ans
done

while true
do
read a b
let ans="$a - $b"
print -r $ans >&4
done
```

The following main program `query` associates file descriptor 4 with `add`, and file descriptor 5 with `subtract`. The program uses a `select` statement to determine which co-process to write to and read from.

```
# Program: query (2 co-processes)
PS3="Choose function: "
# Start up add co-process
add |&
# Move to file desc. 4
exec 4>&p
# Start-up subtract co-process
subtract |&
# Move to file desc. 5
exec 5>&p
while true
do
# Get 1st number
print "Enter num1"
```

```
read num1
# Get 2nd number
print "Enter num2"
read num2
# Select function to perform
select F in add subtract quit
do
      case $REPLY in
        1) # Write to add
            print -ru4 $num1 $num2
            # Read from add
            read -ru4 ans
            break ;;
        2) # Write to subtract
            print -ru5 $num1 $num2
            # Read from subtract
            read -ru5 ans
            break ;;
        3)
            exit ;;
      esac
done
# Print the answer
print "Answer = $ans"
done
```

Reentering Commands

KSH only

When the Korn shell executes a command, it appends the text of the command, by default, to a file named $HOME/.history. You can set the variable HISTFILE to change the name of this history file. The variable HISTSIZE is used to set the number of commands for which ksh will maintain a history; it defaults to a value of 128.

You can use the fc -l command to list all or part of the HISTFILE. To list only part of the file, specify the first and last commands that you want listed, as in the following example:

```
# List the last 16 commands
$ fc -l
# List commands 2 through 12
$ fc -l 2 12
```

```
# Display the last 5 commands
$ fc -l -5
```

The r (repeat) command, an alias of fc -e, is used to reexecute a previous command from the HISTFILE file. By default, with no arguments, r reexecutes the last command. You can specify a command by a positive or negative number, or by a partial string containing the first few letters of the command you want to reexecute, as in the following example:

```
# Repeat the last command
$ r
ls -l
# Repeat command number 8
$ r 8
who
# Repeat the 4th command back
$ r -4
ps
# Repeat the last command starting
# with an "l"
$ r l
ls -l
```

Command-line Editing

KSH only

The Korn shell supports command-line editing using either the emacs or vi editor. emacs is provided in two versions, emacs and gmacs. The only difference between the two versions is when you press Ctrl-t: emacs transposes the current character with the next character, and gmacs transposes the two previous characters.

To use the command-line editing features, you must set one of the following ksh options: emacs, gmacs, or vi. An example of such a setting is

```
set -o vi
```

If the value of either the VISUAL or EDITOR variables ends in emacs, gmacs, or vi, the corresponding ksh option is set automatically to that editor.

You use the value of the variable FCEDIT to select which editor to use with the `fc` command. If you do not set FCEDIT, `ed` is used as the default editor.

The `fc` command (*fix* command) is used to invoke the command-line-editing feature. Enter `fc` alone to invoke the editor (FCEDIT) on the last command stored in the HISTFILE. Enter `fc` with a number to invoke the editor on that number command from the HISTFILE. If the first and last options are specified to the `fc` command, the editor is invoked for that list of commands:

```
# Edit commands 5 thru 10
$ fc 5 10
```

In the preceding example, the first command is the fifth command and the last command is command 10. If a string is given, `fc` invokes the editor on the last command that starts with the string, as in the following example:

```
# Edit a command starting with w
$ fc w
```

On exiting the editor, the edited command(s) are printed and reexecuted.

If the name of the editor to the `fc -e` command is -, as in the following example, editing is skipped:

```
# Repeat the last command
$ fc -e -
```

The first command is reexecuted directly.

This form of the command also accepts substitutions such as `old=new`. Because `fc -e -` is aliased as `r`, the following command substitutes `usr` for `bin` in the last `ls` command.

```
$ r bin=usr ls
```

To invoke the command-line editing feature, enter the appropriate fetch previous command sequence: press Esc-k for `vi` or Ctrl-P in `emacs` or `gmacs`. You can enter other fetch commands to recall specific command lines (see the appropriate editing mode summaries later in this section).

A command that has been fetched is displayed in a single-line window COLUMNS wide. If you don't set the variable COLUMNS, the window is 80 columns wide. If a line is longer than the value of COLUMNS minus 2, a mark at the end of the line indicates that additional text follows. As the cursor moves and reaches the window's boundaries, the window is centered on the cursor. The marks >, <, and * indicate that the line extends to the right, left, or both sides of the window, respectively.

You can use the editing commands shown for emacs and vi modes in the following sections within the window, depending on the editor selected by the -o option of set. A RETURN or LINE FEED indicates the end of the editing mode; then the modified command line is executed.

emacs Editing Mode

KSH only

To set emacs editing mode, enter

```
set -o emacs
```

or

```
set -o gmacs
```

The only difference between the emacs and gmacs modes is the way Ctrl-t is handled (see table 5).

To edit a command line, first recall it by using a fetch command (Ctrl-p) and then move the cursor to the point needing correction. Insert or delete characters or words as necessary.

All editing commands consist either of control characters or escape sequences. Control characters are notated by Ctrl- followed by a character. For example, Ctrl-x is the notation for pressing the Ctrl key and the x key at the same time. Do not press the Shift key (although control sequences are indicated with capital letters).

Del indicates that you press the delete key.

Escape sequences are shown as Esc- followed by a character. For example, you enter Esc-d by pressing the Esc key, releasing it, and then pressing the d key. Esc-x indicates that you should press Esc and then x.

The Korn shell implements the emacs commands described in table 5.

Table 5. *emacs Commands in ksh*

Command	Meaning
Ctrl-f	Move cursor forward one character
Esc-f	Move cursor forward one word
Ctrl-b	Move cursor back one character
Esc-b	Move cursor back one word
Ctrl-a	Move cursor to start of line
Ctrl-e	Move cursor to end of line
Ctrl-]x	Move cursor to character x on current line
Ctrl-xCtrl-x	Transpose the cursor and the mark
Ctrl-h	Delete preceding character
Ctrl-d	Delete current character
Esc-d	Delete current word
Esc-Ctrl-h	Delete preceding word
Esc-h	Delete preceding word
Esc-Del	Delete preceding word. If the interrupt character is Del, this command will not work.
Ctrl-t	In emacs mode, transpose current character with next character. In gmacs mode, transpose two preceding characters.
Ctrl-c	Capitalize current character
Esc-c	Capitalize current word
Ctrl-k	Delete from cursor to end of line. If given a parameter of 0, delete from start of line to cursor.
Ctrl-w	Delete from cursor to mark
Esc-p	Push region from cursor to mark on the stack
Ctrl-g	Kill entire current line. If two kill characters are entered in succession, all subsequent kill characters cause a line feed. (This is useful when using hardcopy terminals.)
Ctrl-y	Restore last item removed from line
Ctrl-l	Cause a line feed and print current line
Ctrl-@	Set mark
Esc-{Tab}	Set mark

Command	Meaning
Ctrl-j	Execute current line
Ctrl-m	Execute current line
Ctrl-d	Terminate shell if current line is null
Ctrl-p	Fetch previous command. Whenever Ctrl-p is pressed, retrieve preceding command from HISTFILE.
Esc-<	Fetch least recent history line
Esc->	Fetch most recent history line
Ctrl-n	Fetch next command. Whenever Ctrl-n is pressed, retrieve next command in HISTFILE.
Ctrl-r*string*	Reverse search history for a previous command line containing *string*. If a parameter of 0 is given, search is forward. *string* is terminated by a Return or newline character.
Ctrl-o	Execute current line and fetch next line relative to current line from the HISTFILE
Esc-*num*	Define numeric parameter. The *num* is taken as a parameter to the next command. Commands that accept a parameter are Ctrl-f, Ctrl-b, Ctrld, Ctrl-k, Ctrl-r, Ctrl-p, Ctrl-n, and Del.
Esc-letter	Search alias list for the name _letter. If an alias of this name is defined, its value is inserted on the line. The letter must not be one of the preceding escape sequences.
Esc-_	Insert last parameter of preceding command on the line
Esc-.	Insert last parameter of preceding command on the line
Esc-*	Attempt file-name generation on current word
Ctrl-u	Multiply parameter of next command by 4
\-Tab	Escape special meaning of next character. Edit characters and erase, kill, and interrupt characters may be entered in a command line or in a search string if preceded by a \.
Ctrl-v	Display version of shell

vi Editing Mode

KSH only

To set vi editing mode, enter the following command:

```
set -o vi
```

You can also set the viraw option to specify character-at-a-time input. This mode is often set for terminals operating at 1200 baud or less and those that do not support two alternate end-of-line delimiters.

To edit a command line, fetch it into the edit window with the Esc-k command. Move the cursor to the appropriate place in the editing window, and insert and delete text as necessary. Press Return to execute the edited command.

Tables 6-10 summarize the vi editor commands built into ksh. Most escape sequences accept an optional repeat count prior to the command.

Table 6. vi Input Commands

Command	Meaning
Ctrl-h	Delete preceding character
Ctrl-w	Delete preceding word
Ctrl-d	Terminate shell
Ctrl-v	Escape character immediately following Ctrl-v
\	Escape next erase or kill character

Table 7. vi Cursor Commands

Command	Meaning
[count]l	Move cursor forward one character
[count]w	Move cursor forward one word
[count]W	Move cursor to beginning of next word that follows a blank
[count]e	Move cursor to end of word
[count]E	Move cursor to end of current word

Command	Meaning
[*count*]h	Move cursor back one character
[*count*]b	Move cursor back one word
[*count*]B	Move cursor to preceding blank separated word
[*count*]f*x*	Find next character *x* in current line
[*count*]F*x*	Find previous character *x* in current line
[*count*]t*x*	Move cursor to next character *x*
[*count*]T*x*	Move cursor to preceding character *x*
;	Repeat last single-character find command (f, F, t, or T)
,	Reverse last single-character find command
0	Move cursor to start of line
^	Move cursor to first nonblank character in line
$	Move cursor to end of line

Table 8. *vi Search Commands*

Command	Meaning
[*count*]k	Fetch previous command. Whenever k is entered, retrieve previous command from HISTFILE
[*count*]-	Equivalent to k
[*count*]j	Fetch next command. Whenever j is entered, next command from HISTFILE is retrieved.
[*count*]+	Equivalent to j
[*count*]G	Fetch command number count
/regexp	earch backward through history for a previous command containing the regular expression *regexp*. If *regexp* is null, the preceding search pattern is used. *regexp* is terminated by a Return or newline character.
?regexp	Same as / (except that search is forward)
n	Search for next match of last pattern to / or ? commands
N	Search for next match of last pattern to / or ?, but in reverse direction

Table 9. *vi Text Modification Commands*

Command	Meaning
a	Enter input mode and enter text after the current character
A	Append text to end of line. Same as $a.
[*count*]cdir	
c[*count*]dir	Delete current character through character dir, where dir is a cursor-movement command; then enter input mode. If dir is c, the entire line is deleted and input mode is entered.
C	Delete current character through end of line and enter input mode (same as c$)
S	Equivalent to cc
D	Delete current character through end of line
d[*count*]dir	
[*count*]ddir	Delete current character to which character dir moves the cursor. Same as d$. If dir is d, entire line is deleted.
i	Enter input mode and insert text before current character
I	Insert text before beginning of line. Equivalent to two-character sequence ^i.
[*count*]p	Place preceding text modification before cursor
[*count*]p	Place preceding text modification after cursor
R	Enter input mode and overlay characters on screen with characters you type
rc	Replace current character with c
[*count*]x	Delete current character
[*count*]X	Delete preceding character
[*count*].	Repeat preceding text-modification command
~	Toggle (or change) the case of current character and advance cursor
[*count*]_	Append the count word of preceding command and enter the input mode. The last word is used if *count* is omitted.
*	Append an * to the current word and attempt file name generation. If no match is found, the bell is rung; otherwise the word is replaced by matching pattern and the input mode is entered.

Table 10. *vi Miscellaneous Commands*

Command	Meaning
u	Undo last text-modifying command
U	Undo all text-modifying commands performed on the line
[*count*]v	Return the command `fc -e ${VISUAL:-${EDITOR:-vi}}` *count* in the input buffer. If *count* is omitted, current line is used.
Ctrl-l	Line feed and print current line. Has effect only in control mode.
Ctrl-j	Execute current line, regardless of mode
Ctrl-m	Execute current line, regardless of mode
#	Equivalent to I#-Return. Useful for causing current line to be inserted in history without being executed.

I/O Redirection

On UNIX, all input/output is performed through files. When a shell command is executed, three files described in table 11 are opened automatically and associated with the command.

Table 11. *Standard I/O Files*

File Descriptor	Name	Description
0	stdin	Keyboard
1	stdout	Terminal
2	stderr	Terminal

Commands normally accept input from `stdin`, which by default is assigned to the terminal keyboard. Command output is written to `stdout`, normally the terminal display screen. Error messages are written to `stderr`, which is also assigned by default to the terminal display screen.

You can redirect input and output by using special shell operators. The command line is scanned for these special characters; if any are found, the shell sets up redirection before the command is executed. When input or output is redirected, no file-name expansion occurs (in other words, use of the special characters `*`, `?`, and `[ ]` is not allowed).

If a command is followed by &, the default standard input for that command is the empty file /dev/null. Otherwise, the environment for execution of a command contains the invoking shell's file descriptors as modified by input/output specifications.

The syntax described in table 12 is used to specify redirection; unless otherwise noted, spacing is not critical.

Table 12. Shell Redirection Operators

Notation	Meaning
<*file*	Use file as standard input (file descriptor 0)
>*file*	Use file as standard output (file descriptor 1). If file does not exist, it is created; otherwise, it is truncated to 0 length.
>>*file*	Use file as standard output. If file exists, output is appended to it (by first seeking the end-of-file); otherwise, file is created.
<<[-]*word*	Shell input is read up to a line that is the same as *word*, or to an end-of-file. The resulting set of lines (called a *document*) becomes the standard input. If any character of *word* is enclosed in quotation marks, no interpretation is placed on the text of the document; otherwise, parameter substitution occurs, escaped newlines are ignored, and a \ must be used to quote the characters \, $, and _. If - is prefixed to *word* (leading spaces are not allowed), all leading tabs are stripped from *word* (but not until after parameter and command substitution) and from all shell input as it is read and before each line is compared with *word*. Shell input is read up to the first line that literally matches the resulting word, or to an end-of-file.
<&*digit*	Standard input is duplicated from file descriptor number *digit* (see dup(2)). The alternate form >&*digit* duplicates standard output. Do not place spaces between the < and &; doing so causes the shell to interpret the syntax as a background command.
<&-	Standard input is closed. Similarly, >&- closes standard output. Do not place spaces between the < and &.

If `<&`*digit* or `<&-` is preceded by a digit, the file descriptor created is that specified by the digit (instead of the default 0 or 1). For example, `2>&1` creates file descriptor 2, which is a duplicate of (that is, refers to the same file as) file descriptor 1.

The order in which redirections are specified is significant because the shell performs redirections in the order written. For example:

```
sort large_data > outfile 2>&1
```

first sets file descriptor 1 to write to the file `outfile`, and then dups file descriptor 1 to file descriptor 2, causing standard error to also be written to the file `outfile`. If the order of redirections are reversed, standard error is written to the terminal (assuming file descriptor 1 was) and standard output is written to the file `outfile`.

If a command consists of several simple commands, redirection is evaluated for the entire command before it is evaluated for each simple command. The shell evaluates redirection in the following order:

1. For the entire command list

2. For each pipeline within the list

3. For each command within each pipeline

4. For each list within each command

The following examples illustrate these evaluation rules:

```
# Output from just the date command
# is redirected to status:
$ who ; ls ; date > status
# Output from the entire list (group)
# is redirected to status:
$ (who ; ls ; date) > status
# Output from the entire list (group)
# is redirected to the sort command:
$ (grep FL database ; grep MA database) | sort
```

Redirection of output is not allowed in the restricted shell.

Environment

Whenever a user invokes a shell (including the login shell), it establishes a list of name-value pairs (called the current environment). The shell passes these name-value pairs to an executed program in the same way it passes a normal argument list. If the user or a program modifies the value of any of these variables or creates new name-value pairs, these modifications become part of the current environment. The `unset` command can remove a parameter from the current environment.

An environment variable must be made global (with the `export` command) before it can be accessed by subshells or commands invoked by the current shell. Any variables modified by a subshell remain unchanged in the parent shell, whether or not they have been exported in the subshell; in other words, exported parameters are only available to subsequently called shells.

The environment passed to a subshell or command consists of any unmodified name-value pairs that have been exported minus those removed by the `unset` command.

To set environment values for the login shell, place them in a file named `.profile`. The shell reads this file during login and initializes the login environment from name-value pairs found in this file. Changes made to this file do not take effect until you log in again (at which time your profile is automatically executed), or until you use the dot (.) command to force reexecution of your profile, as follows:

```
. .profile
```

To modify the environment for a simple command, prefix it with one or more value assignments, as in the following example:

```
$ DIR=/tmp echo $DIR
/tmp
```

The shell `-k` option causes all keyword arguments to be placed in the current environment, regardless of their position in the command line. Notice the results of the following two commands:

```
$ export name
$ echo name=tom $name
name=tom
$ set -k
$ echo name=tom $name
tom
```

The first `echo` command is interpreted as an echo of the string `name=tom` and the variable `$name`. Because `$name` is not set, only the string `name=tom` was echoed.

After the `set` command, the shell placed the assignment `name=tom` into the current environment even though it occurred in the middle of the `echo` command, thus printing `tom`.

Restricted Shell

`rsh` is an alternate form of the Bourne shell that restricts the capabilities of the user as follows:

- ❏ Changing directories is not allowed.
- ❏ The value of the PATH variable cannot be changed.
- ❏ Commands or paths containing a / cannot be executed or used.
- ❏ Output redirection (> and >>) is not allowed.

If the `rsh` shell is used as the login shell, then these restrictions are suspended until after the user's `.profile` has been processed.

You can invoke a restricted shell in any of the following ways:

1. Specify `/bin/rsh` as the login shell in the `/etc/passwd` file. The environment variable SHELL is set to `rsh`.

2. Use `/bin/rsh` or `rsh` to invoke a command.

3. Invoke the shell with the `-r` option.

Because `rsh` invokes `sh` to execute shell scripts, it is possible to give users the full power of the standard shell while limiting the commands they can execute. This allows the system administrator to set up a directory of shell scripts intended to be used in the `rsh` environment.

Normally, use of the restricted shell assumes that the user is placed in a separate subdirectory (normally not his login directory) and does not have both write and execute permissions in the same directory. By setting the PATH variable, working directory, and permissions, the creator of the user's `.profile` file has full control over which actions the user can perform.

Shell Security Features

UNIX System V Release 3 and later versions provide an enhanced Bourne shell that contains some additional security features. To determine whether you have the enhanced version of the shell, enter the following command:

```
$ what /bin/sh
```

If you are running the enhanced shell, you receive the message `/usr/adm/sh.sec.sl`.

The enhanced shell resets the effective user- or group-ID when one or more of the following is true:

❏ The real and effective user-ID are not equal

❏ The real and effective group-ID are not equal

❏ The effective user-ID or group-ID is less than 100 (excluding group-ID 1)

These enhancements help prevent executing set-uid commands that may give a user unauthorized root privileges.

KSH only

The following additional security features are implemented in ksh:

❏ The Korn shell resets the value of the IFS variable to the default value when you invoke a shell script. The value can only be set for the `read` built-in command and after parameter and command substitution. In other words, IFS cannot be changed for an interactive shell (for example, the login shell).

❏ Whenever the real and effective user-ID of a shell program are different, ksh switches into a protected mode. In this mode, the PATH variable is reset to a default value and the `.profile` and ENV files are not processed. Instead, the Korn shell reads and executes the file `/etc/suid_profile`. This gives an administrator control over the environment to set the PATH variable or to log setuid shell invocations. Security of the system is compromised if either the `/etc` directory or the `/etc/suid_profile` file is writable by all.

❏ The setuid root program `/etc/suid_exec` authenticates all requests to `exec` any shell scripts that cannot be opened for reading and that have their suid and/or setgid bits set. The program authenticates the request and `execs` a shell with the correct bits set to carry out the task. This shell is invoked with the requested file already open for reading. For security reasons, this program is given the full pathname `/etc/suid_exec` in `/bin/ksh`.

Shell Notes

1. Special shell metacharacters used within I/O redirection constructs are not interpreted. For example,

    ```
    ls -l > l*
    ```

    creates a file named `l*`.

2. Variables set in a pipeline have no effect on the parent shell because commands in a pipeline are run as separate processes.

3. If the current directory or its parent directory (the one above it) is removed, pwd may not give the correct responses. Use cd with a full path name to correct this problem.

4. In a pipeline with three or more stages, not all processes are children of the invoking shell and therefore cannot be waited for.

5. If, for the wait *n* command, *n* is not an active process-ID, all the shell's currently active background processes are waited for and the exit status is 0.

Shell Files and Processes

The UNIX file and process implementation method is what makes the shell so powerful. Because the shell can take advantage of both the UNIX file system and process control mechanism, an understanding of how these work will help you make the best use of the shell.

File System

The file system uses a hierarchical structure of files and directories to organize information. The file system starts at the root directory (/). Underneath the root directory are additional subdirectories. Each directory and subdirectory may contain files and directories. There is no limitation on the depth of a directory structure.

File Naming Conventions

On UNIX System V, a filename can consist of 14 characters. UNIX does not impose any file naming conventions; upper- and lowercase characters in a filename are distinct. Ordinarily, a filename should not contain any spaces, tabs, newlines, or characters that have special meaning to the shell (/, *, ;, and so on); files with such names can be very difficult to manipulate.

Filenames that begin with a . (dot) are not printed when the contents of a directory are listed with the ls command unless specifically requested by the -a option to ls.

A pathname is the name a command uses to locate a file or directory. An absolute pathname always begins with a / (slash) and contains all the components that tell where the file or directory is located. A relative pathname does not begin with / and in this case the command searches for the file or directory in relation to the current directory.

The filenames . (dot) and .. (dot-dot) are used to refer to the current directory and parent directory, respectively. The parent directory is the directory immediately above the current directory. The parent directory of the root (/) directory is the root directory itself.

File Permissions

Access to each file and directory is controlled at three levels: the owner of the file, the members of a group that the file belongs to, or all other users on the system. These three accesses are referred to as user, group, and other.

When a file or directory is created, it is assigned the effective user-ID and effective group-ID of the person creating it. File access permissions can be assigned as follows:

❏ Read access for the user, group, and/or others

❏ Write access for the user, group, and/or others

❏ Execute permission for user, group, and/or others

❏ Set user-ID (suid) and/or set group-ID (sgid) permissions. If these permissions are set on an executable file, then when the program is executed, the effective user-ID and/or effective group-ID of the process being executed is set to the same as the user-ID and/or group-ID of the file that contains the program. (Note: suid and sgid permissions have no effect when executing shell scripts under the Bourne shell. The Korn shell has special security features built into it to control suid/sgid programs. See "Shell Security Features" in the "Shell Basics" section.)

❏ Set sticky bit. When this bit is set, an executable program is not removed from the swap device (if possible) when the program terminates. This makes the invocation of the program faster.

A directory may have the following permissions:

❏ Read permission for the user, group, and/or others. Read permission on a directory allows a user to list the contents of the directory.

❏ Write permission for the user, group, and/or others. Write permission on a directory allows a user to update the directory contents, which means that any user who has write permission for that directory can create, move, and remove files and directories.

❏ Search permission for user, group, and/or others. With search permission set, the user can change directories into the directory.

❏ On some releases of UNIX, the sticky bit may be set on a directory. With this bit set, only the owner of the directory or the owner of a file in that directory may remove files in it.

The user controls the access permissions of a file or directory through the `chmod` command (see "Related UNIX Commands"). Each user can also establish a file-creation mask that disables specified permissions when a new file is created. The file-creation mask is a three-digit octal number set with the `umask` command. This number tells a process which permissions to "take away" when a new file is created. For example, a file-creation mask of 027 removes write permission for the group and read/write/execute permissions for others. The initial file/directory access permissions are assigned as follows:

❏ For directories, the initial mode is `drwxrwxrwx` minus the `umask` value.

❏ For new files created by commands other than `cp`, the initial mode is `-rwxrwxrwx` minus the user's `umask` value.

❏ For new files created by the `cp` command, the permissions are the same as those of the source file. The `umask` value does not have any effect when you create files using the `cp` command.

File Descriptors

When the shell is first started it opens three files, described in table 13, and associates each file with a number called a *file descriptor*.

Table 13. *Standard I/O Files*

File Descriptor	Name	Device
0	Standard Input	Keyboard
1	Standard Output	CRT
2	Standard Error	CRT

File descriptor 0, the standard input, is initially opened for reading from the keyboard. File descriptor 1, the standard output, is initially opened for writing to the terminal CRT. File descriptor 2, the standard error, is initially opened for reading and writing. Error messages from most programs are written on the standard error to prevent their output from being mixed in with the normal output from a command.

When you invoke a program, it inherits these three file descriptors. Thus, each program reads from the standard input, writes to the standard output, and prints error messages on the standard error. If a program opens additional files, then they are assigned new file descriptors in sequence. By default, there is a limit of 20 open files per process on UNIX.

Special Files

UNIX accesses hardware devices through special files. These special files simply provide an interface between the operating system and a physical device such as a terminal or printer. These special files are normally kept in the /dev directory.

Each terminal connected to UNIX is associated with a special file. To determine the name of the special device associated with your terminal, you can use the tty command. Through I/O redirection, the shell can read from and write to special files, if the file access permission is set correctly.

The special file /dev/null is a 0-length special file that is often referred to as the "bit bucket." Unwanted output can be redirected to this file.

Processes

The UNIX system uses processes as a means of executing programs. Each command a user enters causes a process to be created. A process is a program in execution. In addition to the actual program itself, a process has associated with it information about the user and system environments. Each process has a unique process-ID associated with it that the operating system uses to distinguish it from other processes.

A process that creates another process is called a parent process. Any processes a parent creates are called child processes. A child process knows its parent through the parent process-ID.

A process also has associated with it a process-group ID. A process-group consists of all processes with the same process-group ID. Each login shell can only have one process-group ID associated with it at a time. This is called the foreground process. If a user's process is not in the user's process-group ID that is associated with the user's login shell, then that process is a background process.

Also associated with each process are the real and effective user-ID, and the real and effective group-ID. The real user-ID and real group-ID are set by the login process and are inherited by all processes that the user creates. The effective user-ID is normally the same as the real user-ID but may be changed by programs that run as set user-ID (that is, su). Likewise, the real and effective group-IDs are normally the same but the effective group-ID can be changed by programs that run as set group-ID (for example, mail). The effective user-ID and effective group-IDs of a process are used to determine what permissions a process has for file/directory access (read, write, execute/search).

A process is created by either a fork or exec system call (a system call is a request a program makes to the operating system for system services).

fork System Call

A parent process creates a child process by means of the fork system call (see figure 1).

Fig. 1. *Process creation.*

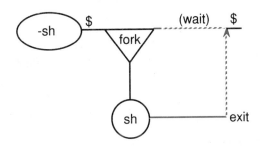

A fork creates a copy of the original process that is identical to the parent process with the exception of its process-ID. The child process is given its own unique process-ID. The parent process may suspend its execution (wait) until the child process completes. Normally, the shell runs commands by creating child processes and then waiting for the child to complete before issuing another shell prompt to the user. The child process inherits the following environmental information from the parent:

- ❏ Parent process-ID
- ❏ Process-group ID
- ❏ Open files
- ❏ Working directory
- ❏ File-creation mask (umask)
- ❏ Real and effective user-IDs
- ❏ Real and effective group-IDs
- ❏ File creation size limits
- ❏ Maximum memory limitations
- ❏ Signal setting actions
- ❏ Exported variables

Thus, a child process is initially identical to its parent. As the child process runs, it may modify its environment information. The parent process environment information is not affected by any changes the child process makes. For example, if the child process changes the value of a variable, the original value of the variable is still in effect when the child exits.

When a process completes, control returns to its parent. Any resources the process allocated return to the operating system for use by future processes. A child process also returns a number to its parent that indicates whether any errors occurred. This number is called the *return value* or *exit code*.

Normally, a return code of 0 indicates a success and a nonzero indicates an error.

exec System Call

An exec system call loads a new program into the memory space of the current process. Unlike fork, exec does not create a new process.

Figure 2 shows the effect of the exec system call.

The -sh was the login process and its parent was /etc/init. After the exec ls command was entered, the -sh process was overlaid with the ls process. Notice that the ls process inherits the process-ID (PID 895) of the -sh process. On completion of the ls command, control returned to the parent, /etc/init, which causes a login: prompt to be issued through /etc/getty.

Fig. 2. exec system call.

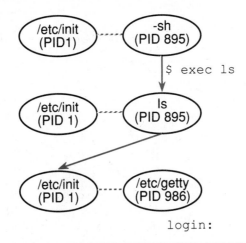

The Login Process

The events that occur during login illustrate how the fork and exec system calls work. The /etc/init process (PID 1) starts during system startup and continues to run until the system is shut down. /etc/init is a system process and is not attached to a terminal. Processes of this nature are often called daemons.

/etc/init continually examines the /etc/inittab file for work to be done. This file contains lines that tell /etc/init what commands it should execute for various system run levels and system events. Some lines in this file contain commands that print the login: prompt on each active terminal line. These lines are in the form of:

```
11:234:respawn:/etc/getty tty11 9600
```

This entry tells /etc/init to execute an /etc/getty command for tty11 at 9600 baud. The respawn indicates that each time the /etc/getty process dies it will be restarted by /etc/init. Figure 3 shows the events that occur when a user logs in.

First, /etc/init forks a /etc/getty process as indicated by the entry in /etc/inittab. The /etc/getty process prints the login: message on the terminal. When a user enters his login name at the login: prompt, /etc/getty execs /bin/login with the user's login name as an argument. /bin/login prompts the user for his password. After the user enters his password,

/bin/login validates the login name and password, and if both are correct, /bin/login execs /bin/sh, which prints the $ shell prompt after it reads the system /etc/profile and the user's $HOME/profile files.

Fig. 3. *Login process.*

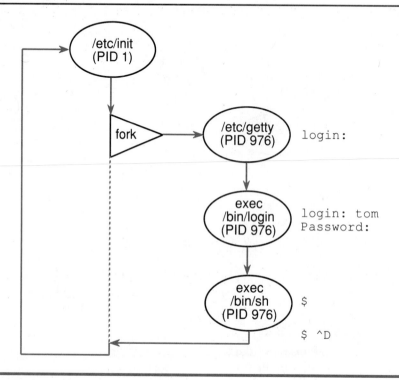

The shell continues to run until the user logs out (with Ctrl-D or exit). When the shell terminates, it returns to its parent process. The parent process for the shell is /etc/init. Because the shell was invoked through a series of fork and exec system calls, it inherited the parent process-ID (PPID 1) and process-ID (PID 976) of the processes that invoked it.

Simple Command Execution

A simple command consists of any single UNIX or shell command and its arguments. When you enter a simple command, the shell forks another shell and then an exec system call is made to execute the command. The parent shell waits until the child process is completed and then resumes control and issues another shell prompt. Figure 4 shows how an ls command is executed.

Fig. 4. *Simple command execution.*

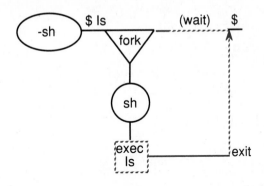

Sequential Command Execution

A sequential command consists of two or more UNIX or shell commands separated by semicolons (;), as in ls;date. When you enter a sequential command, the shell forks a subshell and then calls exec to execute the first command. When the first command completes, the shell forks another shell and then calls exec to execute the second command. This sequence continues until all commands in the sequential command line are executed, as shown in figure 5.

Fig. 5. *Sequential command execution.*

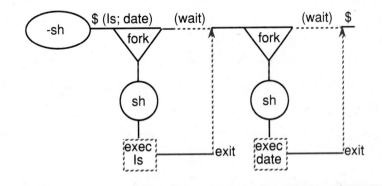

Notice that, on completion of each command in the sequential command line, control returns to the parent shell. Therefore, any environmental changes made by any command in the sequential command line will not affect subsequent commands. The return value to the parent shell is the return value of the last command in the sequential command line.

Group Command Execution

A group command consists of a sequential command enclosed in parentheses. Use group commands when the output of all commands in the sequential command line are to be redirected to a file or sent to the input of another command through a pipe.

When a group command is entered, the shell forks a subshell to execute the commands in the group (see fig. 6).

Fig. 6. *Group command execution.*

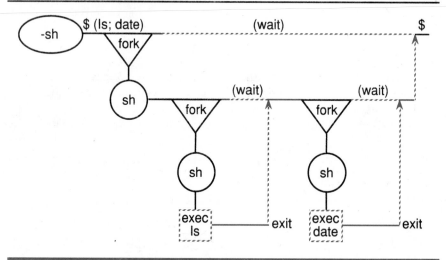

This subshell then forks another shell that calls exec to execute the first command. On completion of the first command, another shell is forked that execs the second command. This sequence continues until all the commands in the grouped sequential command line are executed. The return value from the group command is that of the last command in the group.

Pipe Command Execution

On recognizing the pipe (¦) special character in a command line, the shell starts up each process in the command line and establishes communications between them through a pipe special file. The last command in the pipe is started first, then the next to the last command, and so forth until all processes are created (see fig. 7).

Fig. 7. Pipe.

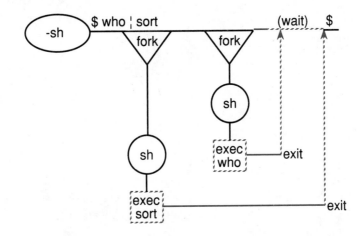

Each process in the pipeline reads from its standard input and writes to its standard output. The standard input and standard output from each adjacent command is connected by a pipe special file. When a process attempts to read from a pipe it does one of the following:

❏ Reads the data if another process has written to the pipe

❏ Suspends processing until another process writes data on the pipe

❏ Returns with an end-of-file indicator if no other process has the pipe open for writing

A process also can communicate with another process by signals. When a child process exits, it also communicates with its parent by the exit status.

Background Command Execution

You can invoke background command execution by following a UNIX or shell command with an ampersand (&). When you enter a background command, the shell forks a subshell that execs the command (see fig. 8).

***Fig. 8.** Background command execution.*

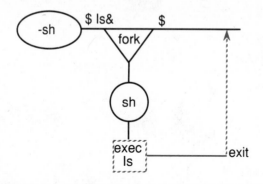

Control immediately returns to the parent shell, which issues another shell prompt ($). The shell can then execute additional UNIX or shell commands in either the foreground or background.

You can also enter background jobs sequentially or as a group. The following examples show various ways of entering background commands:

Example 1: Asynchronous Command Execution

The following shows how the ls and date commands can be executed asynchronously in the background.

```
$ ls & date &
```

Example 2: Group Background Command Execution

The following example shows how the ls and date commands can be executed in the background as a group.

```
$ (ls; date)&
```

Example 3: Asynchronous Group Command Execution

This example shows how two group commands can be executed asynchronously.

```
$ (ls; date) & (who; ps)&
```

Example 4: Sequential Background Execution

In this example, only the date command is executed in the background after completion of the ls command:

```
$ ls; date&
```

In each of these examples, output from the commands is printed on the terminal.

Process Notes

Shell programs are executed through `fork` and `exec`, which create additional processes. Any commands invoked within the shell program are also executed with `fork` and `exec`. Therefore, when writing shell programs that invoke other shell programs, you must be careful that the maximum number of user and/or system processes are not exceeded. This is especially important when writing shell programs that may be used by more than one user at a time. Although the program by itself may not exceed the allowable number of user processes, multiple copies of it may exceed the maximum allowable number of system processes.

Where possible, use functions within shell programs. They do not create additional processes for execution.

Be considerate of other users when invoking background processes. The more processes simultaneously executing on a UNIX system, the slower the system as a whole runs. If possible, schedule large jobs to run in the background at night when processor load is lower (see the `at(1)` and `nohup` commands).

Built-In Commands

These built-in commands are part of the shell. I/O redirection of these commands is allowed, with standard output being the default output file.

If a built-in command executes correctly, it returns an exit code of 0. The following conditions cause a nonzero exit code for the built-in command:

❏ Invalid options

❏ Incorrect number of arguments

❏ An incorrect argument

❏ Invalid I/O redirection

❏ Invalid variable assignment

KSH only

❏ Invalid alias name

❏ An attempt to expand a parameter that has not been set while the nounset option is in effect

: [*arg* ...]

Description: The : is a null operator and has no effect. The *args* to : are expanded.

Return Value: A 0 exit code is returned from :.

.*file* [*file* ...]

Description: The current shell reads and interprets commands in the file specified after the . (dot) built-in command. A subshell is not invoked. Use the search path specified by the PATH variable to find the directory containing the file to be read in by the . command.

Return Value: A 0 exit code is returned if the file was found and read.

alias [-tx] [*name*[=*value*] ...]

KSH only

Description: An alias enables you to rename commands within the shell. If an alias is defined, the command for that alias is substituted when you use the alias.

Table 14 describes the options to the alias built-in command.

Table 14. alias Command Options

Option	Meaning
-t	This option sets and displays tracked aliases. A tracked alias has the full path name for the command. If the PATH variable is changed, the alias becomes undefined but remains tracked. Tracked aliases execute faster because the shell does not have to search for the command.

Option	Meaning
-x	This option to the `alias` command causes the alias to remain in effect for shell programs that are invoked directly by their name and do not invoke a separate ksh process. Exported aliases do not migrate across separate invocations of the ksh; they must be put into the ksh environment file specified by the ENV variable (see "Invocation").

The `alias` command with no arguments lists the current aliases in effect. The current aliases are displayed, one per line, in the form *name=command*. If the -x or -t options also are specified, only exported or tracked aliases, respectively, are displayed.

If the command

```
$ alias whou
```

is given, the value of whou is displayed if it is set. Otherwise, the error message whou alias not found is printed. If you specify the -x or -t options with the name of a preset alias, the alias command sets those attributes (export and tracked) for the named alias. An alias is defined as follows:

```
$ alias whou="who -u"
```

Notice that you use double quotation marks to prevent the shell from interpreting the spaces to the command who -u.

The first character of an alias name may be any printable character; all other characters must be valid identifiers (a-z, A-Z, or 0-9). However, using a built-in shell metacharacter as the first character of an alias name may cause conflict with the shell's interpretation of the alias.

The command can be any valid shell program or UNIX command and may include built-in shell metacharacters. However, the first word of each command of replaced text is not be tested for additional aliases.

If an alias ends in a blank (space or tab), the word following the alias also is checked for alias substitution.

In the following example:

```
$ alias dir="ls "
$ alias opts="-CF"
$ dir opts
Src/        unit01.n    unit03.n
status*     unit02.n    unit04.n
```

dir is aliased as an ls command and followed by a space; opts is aliased as -CF; thus, the command

```
dir opts
```

is interpreted as if

```
ls -CF
```

was entered.

An alias is expanded when the shell first reads a shell program, not when the program is executed. To take effect, an alias must be defined before it is used within the shell program.

Quoting of alias values is important. Using double quotation marks expands any metacharacters to be performed when the alias is defined. Metacharacters to be expanded when the alias is used should be enclosed in single quotation marks.

The following exported aliases are compiled into the shell but can be unset or redefined:

```
echo='print -'
false='let 0'
functions='typeset -f'
history='fc -l'
integer='typeset -i'
nohup='nohup '
pwd='print - $PWD'
r='fc -e -'
true=':'
type='whence -v'
hash='alias -t'
```

Return Value: alias returns a 0 exit code if all names are valid aliases and valid attributes are specified. Otherwise, a nonzero exit code (the value of the number of names that are not aliases) is returned.

bg [*%job*]

> **KSH only**
>
> **Description:** On systems that support built-in job control, the `bg` command puts the current job in the background. If you specify *%job*, the shell puts that job in the background.

break [*n*]

Description: Use `break` to exit from a `for`, `while`, or `until` loop. You can specify an argument *n* to indicate the number of levels to break.

cd [*dir*]

Description: By default, `cd` changes the current directory to the directory specified by the HOME variable. Otherwise, *dir* becomes the current working directory.

You can use the shell variable CDPATH to set a search path for the directory containing *dir*. CDPATH contains a list of directories to search, separated by colons (`:`). The default path is the current directory, in which case `cd` attempts to change to *dir*. You can specify the current directory by a null path name that can appear immediately after the equal sign or between the colon delimiters anywhere in the path list. For example, to set the current directory as the first directory of the search path list, use the following:

```
CDPATH=:$HOME:$HOME/bin:/usr/games
```

Each directory in the search path is searched for *dir*, unless *dir* begins with a slash. */dir* is an absolute path name; the search path specified by CDPATH is not used.

You cannot use the `cd` command with the restricted shell rsh.

cd *old new*

> **KSH only**
>
> **Description:** In the ksh, the form
>
> ```
> cd old new
> ```
>
> substitutes the string new for the string old in the current directory name PWD and then attempts to change to that directory.
>
> **Return Value:** c d returns a 0 exit code if the command can change to the *dir* specified. Otherwise, the command returns a nonzero exit code.

continue [*n*]

Description: cont i nue causes a program to immediately return to the top of a for, while, or unt i l loop. If an argument *n* is specified, cont i nue resumes at loop number *n*.

echo [*args*]

Description: echo prints its *args* separated by blanks and a newline on the standard output. echo uses the C-language-type escape conventions listed in table 15 to represent built-in characters.

Beware of conflicts in the shell's use of the backslash (\). You should quote the backslash (with single or double quotation marks) or precede it with a backslash to prevent the shell from interpreting it.

n is a one-, two-, or three-digit octal code for an ASCII character. The first digit must always be 0.

echo is often used within shell programs to produce prompts or diagnostic messages.

Return Value: echo returns a 0 exit code if successful; otherwise, it returns a nonzero exit code.

Table 15. *Shell Backslash Characters*

Convention	Meaning
\b	Backspace
\c	Do not print a newline at end of echo command
\f	Form feed
\n	Output a newline
\r	Carriage return (without newline)
\t	Tab
\v	Vertical tab
\\	Backslash
\nnn	Octal-coded character

eval [*command-line ...*]

Description: eval reads and executes a normal command line. Use eval when "hidden" variable substitutions may cause conflicts. eval has the same effect as forcing the shell to scan the command line twice before executing the command. In the following example:

```
$ DIR='$HOME'
$ echo $DIR
$HOME
$ eval echo $DIR
/usr/billh
$
```

the variable DIR was set to $HOME because $HOME was enclosed in single quotation marks (which prevented interpretation of the variable lead-in character $). The eval executed the echo command after its arguments was expanded by the shell.

Return Value: eval returns the exit code of the command that it executes.

exec [*command-line ...*]

Description: The exec command executes the command line directly, without creating a new process. In effect, the current shell is replaced with the command specified on the command line. This command then returns to the parent of the process that was running before the exec. Unless the exec'd program is a shell, the command may return to init (the initialization process), thus logging out the user, as in the following example:

```
$ exec ls
chapt00.n
chapt01.n
chapt02.n
AT&T System V Unix
Login:
```

You can use exec also to rename or create new file descriptors. To change standard input from the keyboard to a file, use the exec command in the following form:

```
$ exec < file
```

All commands that normally read from standard input now read from file.

To change output redirection from the terminal to a file, use the following form:

```
$ exec > file
```

All output from a command now will go into file instead of being displayed on the terminal.

To reassign input/output back to the keyboard/terminal, use the exec command with the virtual file /dev/tty:

```
# Reassign standard input
$ exec < /dev/tty
# Reassign standard output
$ exec > /dev/tty
```

To open new file descriptors, use the exec command as follows:

```
# Open file descriptor 4 for input
$ exec <&4
# Open file descriptor 5 for output
$ exec >&5
```

Return Value: Because exec overlays the current process, no exit codes are returned.

exit [*n*]

Description: exit causes the shell to terminate with the exit status of *n* (*n* can be a positive integer between 0 and 255). If you omit *n*, the exit status is that of the last command executed.

export [*name ...*]

Description: If no arguments are supplied to the `export` command, it prints a list of all variables currently exported in the current shell. If you provide one or more arguments, the shell assumes that they are the names of variables to be exported. They are marked for automatic export to the environment of subsequently executed commands.

Note that you cannot export function names. If you use `export` within a function, a new local variable is not created.

> **KSH only**
>
> `export` is the same as `typeset -x`.

Return Value: export always returns a 0 exit status.

fc [-e *editor*] [-nlr] [*first*] [*last*]

> **KSH only**
>
> **Description:** The `fix` command (`fc`) provides access to the history file and is used with the command-line editor. Table 16 describes the `fc` options.
>
> *Table 16. fix Command Options*
>
> | Option | Meaning |
> | --- | --- |
> | -e *editor* | Edit and execute preceding command using editor. If you do not specify *editor*, `fc` uses the value of the FCEDIT environment variable as the editor. The default editor is `/bin/ed`. |
> | -n | Suppress command numbering when listing commands |
> | -l | List last HISTSIZE number of commands (default 16) |
> | -r | Reverse order of commands |

> When editing of commands is complete, ksh displays, reads, and executes them.

The values *first* and *last* let you specify the range of commands on which f c operates.

The HISTSIZE variable sets the size of the command list to be maintained (default 16).

You can specify *first* and *last* as positive numbers that indicate the command(s) to be fixed, negative numbers that are subtracted from the current command number, or a string that is used to match the most recent invocation of that command. If you do not specify *last*, its value is set to that of *first*.

If *first* and *last* are not specified, *first* is set to 16 if the – l option is specified; if – l is not specified, *first* is set to 1. *last* is then set to 1 (that is, the preceding command).

Return Value: f c returns the value of the last command reexecuted or, if you specify the – l option, a 0. Otherwise, a nonzero exit status is returned for invalid arguments or syntax errors.

fc -e - [*old=new*] [*command*]

> ***KSH only***
>
> **Description:** This command enables you to reexecute a previously executed command. The command is displayed before it is executed.
>
> The preset alias r can be used in place of f c -e -, with or without *old=new* and *command*.
>
> If you specify *old=new*, the string *new* replaces *old* when the command is executed.
>
> *command* specifies which command is to be reexecuted. The value of HISTSIZE limits the number of commands that can be reexecuted. You can specify *command* as any of the following:

❑ Nothing. Simply enter `r` or `fc -e -`. The preceding command will be reexecuted.

❑ A string or partial string. For example, `r ca` would reexecute the last command that started with the string `ca`.

❑ A positive number that indicates which command in the HISTSIZE list to reexecute.

❑ A negative number that is subtracted from the current command number; for example, `r -2` would reexecute the second to the last command previously executed.

Return Value: `fc` returns the value of the last executed command.

fg [*%job*]

KSH only

Description: This command brings *%job* into the foreground on systems that support built-in job control mechanisms. If you do not specify *%job*, `fg` brings the current job into the foreground.

getopts *optstring name* [*arg*]

KSH only

Description: `getopts` checks the positional parameters or the optional string *arg* for legal options.

A + or – begins the *arg* value. An *arg* not beginning with either of these characters delimits the end of the option list. The string – – also can delimit the end of the option list.

optstring contains the options that are to be processed by `getopts`. If an option is followed by a semicolon, then that option is expected to have an argument with it. The argument may or may not be separated from the option by spaces or tabs.

Each time you invoke `getopts`, it sets the value of the shell variable *name* to the next option letter. For example, + is prefixed to name if the *arg* is preceded by a +.

The index to the next *arg* is contained in the variable OPTIND. OPTIND is initially set to a 1 when a shell program is invoked. `getopts` places the option argument in the OPTARG variable, as required.

An *optstring* preceded by : changes how `getopts` reacts when it encounters an option not contained in *optstring*. If *optstring* does not contain a :, `getopts` displays an error message and sets *name* to ?. Otherwise, the option letter is put in OPTARG and sets name to ? for an unknown option, or sets name to : for a missing option argument. Otherwise, OPTARG is set to the option letter and, for an unknown option, *name* is set to ?; for a missing option argument, *name* is set to :.

Return Value: `getopts` returns true until it encounters the end of an option list.

hash [*-r*] [*commands*]

Description: The shell remembers each executed command's location in the search path. `hash` causes the shell to print a list of each command's search path, with the number of times the command was invoked (hits) and a measure of work required to locate a command in the search path (cost). In situations in which the stored location of a command must be recalculated, the hits information is followed by an asterisk (*). Cost is incremented when the calculation is completed.

If a command is supplied to `hash`, hits is reset to 0. The `-r` option causes the shell to forget all remembered locations.

Note that built-in shell commands and functions are not remembered and thus are not shown as part of the `hash` table.

> **KSH only**
>
> hash is a predefined alias of alias -t.

Return Value: hash always returns a 0 exit code.

jobs [*-l*]

> **KSH only**
>
> **Description:** The jobs command lists the active jobs. With the -l option specified, jobs also prints the process-IDs.

kill [-l] [*-sig*] *process* ...

Description: kill sends *sig* to the specified process, which can be either a process-ID or a job number.

You can specify *sig* as a signal number of the name of a signal listed by kill -l. Without *-sig*, kill -l sends a TERM (terminate) signal.

let *arg* ...

> **KSH only**
>
> **Description:** let evaluates arithmetic arguments as separate expressions. Because each *arg* is evaluated separately, it is important to quote expressions that contain spaces or tabs. Likewise, because many of the operators used within let statements (see following list) also have special meaning to ksh, they must be quoted. If only a single expression is to be evaluated, you can use the form *((expr))* in place of let. When you

use *((expr))*, you do not need to quote spaces, tabs, and other special characters; they are processed as if they were enclosed in double quotation marks.

All calculations are done as long integers and are not checked for overflow conditions. The operators in table 17, which are listed in decreasing order of precedence, are used.

Table 17. ksh Arithmetic Operators

Operator	Meaning
-	Unary minus. Changes sign of value given.
!	Logical negation
* / %	Multiplication, division, and remainder operators, respectively
+ -	Addition and subtraction
<= >= < >	Less than or equal to, greater than or equal to, less than, greater than
== !=	Equal to, not equal to
=	Assignment

Parameters to the let command must be predefined and have a value. Up to nine levels of recursion (grouping) are allowed.

Return Value: let returns 0 if the value of the last expression evaluated is nonzero. Otherwise, a nonzero exit code is returned.

newgrp [*group ...*]

Description: The newgrp command changes the user's group identification. With no arguments, the group is changed back to the group specified in the user's /etc/passwd file entry.

If you specify the - argument, newgrp changes the environment to what would be expected if the user actually logged in again as a member of the new group.

Before newgrp can change a user's group identifications, the user must be listed in the /etc/group file as member of the new group.

The id(1) command can be used to determine the group in which the user currently is working.

Return Value: newgrp always returns an exit code of 0 because it is run, in effect, as a command in the form exec newgrp group.

print [-Rnprsu[*n*]] [*arg ...*]

KSH only

Description: print replaces the echo command in the Korn shell. echo is aliased to print -. All echo conventions apply to the print command unless you specify the -R or -r options.

Table 18 describes the options used with the print command.

Table 18. ksh print Command Options

Option	Meaning
-	Process anything following the - as an argument, even if it begins with a -
-R	Do not use the echo conventions and process anything that follows (other than an -n) as an argument, even if it begins with -
-n	Do not add a trailing newline to the output
-p	Redirect all arguments to the print command to a co-process started with ¦&
-r	Do not use the echo conventions
-s	Redirect arguments into history file
-u	Redirect output to file descriptor n. Without n, file descriptor 1 is used; otherwise, file descriptor must be 1, 2, or a file descriptor previously opened with the exec command. -u option redirects standard output of print but does not cause the file to be opened and closed or the file descriptor to be duplicated each time.

pwd

Description: `pwd` prints the current working directory.

> **KSH only**
>
> The Korn shell defines the `pwd` command as `print - $PWD`.

read [-prsu[*n*]] [*name?prompt*] [*var1 var2 ...*]

Description: `read` reads one line from standard input and assigns the first word to *var1*, the second word to *var2*, and so on. If more words than *var*s are entered, all leftover words are assigned to the last variable.

If you enter no *var*s, `read` simply reads and ignores the input.

> **KSH only**
>
> The default *var* is the variable REPLY. If the option *name?prompt* is used and this is an interactive shell, the value of prompt will be displayed on the standard error.
>
> The options in table 19 can only be specified to the `read` command in the Korn shell.
>
> **Table 19. ksh read Command Options**
>
> | Option | Meaning |
> |--------|---------|
> | -p | Read input line from a co-process. The ksh disconnects from the co-process when an end-of-file or error condition occurs. |
> | -r | Do not append a newline on input text |
> | -s | Save input line as a command in history file |
> | -u | Read from file descriptor *n*. The default is file descriptor 0 (standard input). If file descriptor is other than 0 or 2, you must open the file with `exec` command before it is read from using -u. |

Return Value: `read` returns a 0 exit code unless it encounters an end-of-file, in which case it returns a nonzero exit code.

readonly [*name ...*]

Description: With no arguments, `readonly` prints a list of variables marked by the shell as read-only.

If you specify *vars*, the shell marks the variables as read-only. A read-only variable cannot be set or changed.

> **KSH only**
>
> `readonly` is the same as `typeset -r`.

Return Value: `readonly` always returns a 0 exit status.

return [*n*]

Description: `return` is used only within functions; it causes a function to exit with a value of *n*. If you do not specify *n*, the return status is that of the last command executed.

set [-- aefhkntuvx [*args*]]

> **KSH only**
>
> ```
> set [ -aefhkmnostuvx ] [ -o
> option ... ] [ arg ... ]
> ```

Description: There are two ways of invoking the set command. Certain *args* are valid for each way of invoking the command.

The set command is used to do the following:

1. Print a list of current variables and their values

2. Set arguments to the current shell

3. Set positional parameters for the current shell

With no arguments set, set prints a list of all variables and their values in effect in the current shell. Any defined functions are printed also.

The set command accepts the arguments listed in table 20.

Table 20. ksh set Command Arguments

Argument	Meaning
-a	Mark variables that are modified or created for export
-e	Exit immediately if a command exits with a nonzero exit status

KSH only	
-e	Execute the ERR trap and exit immediately if a command exits with a nonzero exit status. The -e option is not enabled while the profile files are being read.

-f	Disable file-name generation
-h	Locate and remember functions as they are defined (normally, functions are located and remembered when executed)
-k	Place in the environment for the command all keyword arguments, not just those that precede command name

KSH only	
-m	Run background jobs in a separate process group; on completion, print a message indicating the exit status

-n	Read commands but do not execute them

KSH only	
-p	Specifies privileged or protected mode. See following description of set for additional information.
-s	Sort positional parameters (the default in the Korn shell)

-t	Exit after reading and executing one command
-u	Treat unset variables as an error when substituting
-v	Print shell input lines as they are read
-x	Print commands and their arguments as they are executed
-	Turn off -x and -v options and stop examining arguments
--	Do not change any options (useful in setting $1 to -)

Using + rather than - causes these options to be turned off. The following command prints the current arguments that are set:

```
$ set $-
```

Other arguments to set are considered to be positional parameters and are assigned, in order, to $1, $2, and so on, in the current shell. These parameters can then be accessed by their individual position address or with $* and $a (see "Positional Parameters").

KSH only

The -o argument to the set command enables additional options to be displayed, set, or unset. With no options, set -o lists all the options listed in table 21 and their current status. You can specify one of the options listed in the table along with the -o option.

Table 21. ksh set -o Options

Option	Meaning
allexport	Same as -a
bgnice	Causes ksh to run all background jobs at a lower priority
errexit	Same as -e
emacs	Turns on emacs command-line editor mode
gmacs	Turns on gmacs command-line editor mode
ignoreeof	Ignores end-of-file. The shell no longer exits when a Ctrl-D (^D) is received; exit must be used to explicitly exit the shell.

Table 21. continues

Table 21. *continued*

Option	Meaning
keyword	Same as `-k`
markdirs	Appends / to all directory names resulting from file-name generation
monitor	ame as `-m`
noclobber	Prevents the > redirection operator from overwriting existing files. The notation >¦ must be used to overwrite an existing file.
noexec	Same as `-n`
noglob	Same as `-f`
nolog	Prevents function definitions from being stored in the history file
nounset	Same as `-u`
privileged	On versions of ksh released since 06/03/86, this option, when set, restores the effective user-ID and effective group-ID to their values when ksh is invoked. If this option is turned off, the effective user-ID is set to the real user-ID and the effective group-ID. The `privileged` option is set whenever the effective user-ID is not equal to the real user-ID or the effective group-ID is not equal o the real group-ID. When `privileged` is set, processing of `$HOME/.profile` is disabled and the file `/etc/suid_profile` is used instead of the file specified by the ENV variable value.
protected	In the 06/03/86 version of the Korn shell, the `protected` option is automatically turned on whenever the real and effective user-ID's are not equal and/or whenever the real and effective group-ID's are not equal. When this option is set, processing of `$HOME/.profile` is disabled, the PATH variable is reset to the default value, and the file `/etc/suid_profile` is used instead of the file specified in the ENV variable.
trackall	Same as `-h`
verbose	Same as `-v`
vi	Sets `vi` command-line editing mode
viraw	Processes each character as it is typed in `vi` command-line editing mode
xtrace	Same as `-x`

test [*expression*]

Description: `test` evaluates *expression* and returns an exit code indicating whether the expression was true (0) or false (nonzero). A nonzero exit code is set also if the test command has no arguments.

You can use the `test` command in one of the following forms:

`test` *expression*

`[` *expression* `]`

> **KSH only**
>
> `[[` *expression* `]]`

The *expression* consists of the primitives described in table 22.

Table 22. *test Expressions*

Primitive	Meaning
`-r` *file*	True if *file* exists and is readable
`-w` *file*	True if *file* exists and is writable
`-x` *file*	True if *file* exists and is executable
`-f` *file*	True if *file* exists and is not a directory
`-d` *file*	True if *file* exists and is a directory
`-c` *file*	True if *file* exists and is a character-special file
`-b` *file*	True if *file* exists and is a block-special file
`-p` *file*	True if *file* exists and is a named pipe (FIFO)
`-u` *file*	True if *file* exists and its set-user-ID bit is set
`-g` *file*	True if *file* exists and its set-group-ID bit is set
`-k` *file*	True if *file* exists and its sticky bit is set
`-s` *file*	True if *file* exists and its size is greater than 0
`-t` `[`*fildes*`]`	True if open file whose file descriptor number is *fildes* (1 by default) is associated with a terminal device
`-z` *s1*	True if length of string *s1* is 0
`-n` *s1*	True if length of string *s1* is nonzero
s1 `=` *s2*	True if strings *s1* and *s2* are equal
s1 `!=` *s2*	True if strings *s1* and *s2* are not equal
s1	True if *s1* is not the null string

Table 22. continues

Table 22. continued

Primitive	Meaning
n1 -eq *n2*	True if the integers *n1* and *n2* are algebraically equal. Any of the comparisons -ne, -gt, -ge, -lt, or -le may be used in place of -eq.

KSH only

-L *file*	True if *file* is a symbolic link
file1 -nt *file2*	True if *file1* is newer than *file2*
file1 -ct *file2*	True if *file1* is older than *file2*
file1	True if *file1* is linked tm

You can combine these primatives with the operators listed in table 23.

Table 23. test Operators

Operator	Meaning
!	Unary negation operator
-a	Binary *and* operator
-o	Binary *or* operator
(*expr*)	Parenthesis used for grouping

The -a (*and*) operator has higher precedence than -o (*or*). Note that all the operators and options are separate arguments to test. Note also that parentheses are meaningful to the shell and must be escaped.

If you own a file but its owner permission bit is not set, the test of that file (-r, -w, or -x) returns a nonzero even though the file may have the group and/or other bits set for that test (-r, -w, or -x permission). The correct exit status is returned if you are superuser.

The = and != operators have a higher precedence than (and cannot be used with) the -r through -n operators. The = and != must always have arguments.

If more than one argument follows the -r through -n operators, only the first argument is examined; the others are ignored unless the second argument is either -a or -o.

Return Value: test returns a 0 exit status if the evaluation is successful; otherwise the command returns a nonzero exit status.

times

Description: `times` prints the accumulated user and system times for processes run from the shell.

trap [*command*] [*signal*] ...

Description: `trap` sets up a *command* to be executed when the shell receives a *signal*. With no arguments, `trap` prints the `traps` currently in effect. If no *command* is specified, all `traps` for *signal* are reset. If *command* is null (`:`, `' '`, or `" "`), this shell and all commands it invokes ignore the signal. If *signal* is 0, `trap` executes *command* when it exits the shell.

The shell executes `trap` commands in order of signal number. If a signal that is ignored on entry to the current shell is trapped, the command is not executed.

The signals described in table 24 often are used with the `trap` command (see `signal`(2) in the *UNIX Programmer's Reference Manual*).

Table 24. Shell trap Signals

Signal	Meaning
0	Special signal for the shell. Executes command when shell exits.
1	Hangup. Sent when loss of DTR is detected.
2	Interrupt. Sent when the user presses Break key.
3	Quit. Sent when the user presses Del key.
15	Software termination. Set when a program exits.

KSH only

You can specify *sig* as a signal number or name. (Use `kill -l` to obtain a list of signal names.) Additionally, the pseudosignals ERR and EXIT are defined for `trap`.

The ERR signal executes the commands whenever a command has a nonzero exit code. The EXIT signal operates the same as signal 0.

type [*command*]

Description: `type` indicates how the shell interprets each command. `type` prints whether the command is a function, shell program, shell built-in, or standard UNIX command.

typeset -f[*tux*] [name]

KSH only

Description: This form of the `typeset` command (with the `-f` option) is used to display function names and values and to set and `unset` function attributes.

Table 25 describes the options used with `-f`.

Table 25. typeset Command -f Options

Option	Meaning
`-t`	Turns on `xtrace` option for function (see `set` command)
`-x`	Exports function definition so that it remains in effect across shell programs that are not a separate invocation of the ksh
`-u`	Specifies that the function name refers to an as yet undefined function. (Note: this option is available only in ksh versions released since 06/03/86.)

To display function names and their definitions, use the `typeset` command with the `-f` option. To display only function names, use the `+f` option.

Because function names are stored in the history file, `typeset` does not display function names if the history file does not exist or the `nolog` option was in effect when the function was read (see `set`).

Use `typeset` as follows:

- ❑ To display a single function, use the `typeset` *name* command with no options.

- ❑ To display all functions with a given attribute, specify the option with no function names.

- ❑ To display all functions, use `typeset -f`.

Return Value: `typeset -f` returns a 0 exit status if all names are defined functions or the `-u` option is specified. Otherwise, the command returns a nonzero exit status.

---

typeset [-FLRZefilprtux[*n*]
[*name*[=*value*]] ...]

KSH only

Description: Use the `typeset` command to do the following:

- ❑ Set and unset various attributes for variables and parameters

- ❑ Set and unset the value of variables and parameters

- ❑ Display variables and parameters and their attributes and values

With no options, the `typeset` command displays all variables and parameters in effect, as well as their type (export, read-only, and so on). Given a name, `typeset` displays the attribute for that variable or parameter.

If you use the + option, only the names of current variables and parameters are printed. If you specify a – option, the names and values of all current variables and parameters are printed.

Use the options described in table 26 to set (by typing a – before the option) or unset (by typing a + before the option) various attributes for variables and parameters:

Table 26. typeset Command Options

Option	Meaning
-u	Make variable uppercase
-l	Make variable lowercase
-i	Mark variable as an integer. An optional *n* can be specified to indicate the base. The following code, for example, sets the variable binary to 5, using base 2 notation:

```
$ typeset -i2 binary=5
$ print $binary
2#101
```

Option	Meaning
	When the variable value is printed, the base is printed first, followed by a #; then the value is printed in the base notation.
-L	Left justify the variable value. You can specify an optional *n* to indicate the field width.
-LZ	Left justify the variable; strip leading 0s. You can specify an optional *n* to indicate the field width.
-R	Right justify the variable value. You can specify an optional *n* to indicate the field width.
-RZ	Right justify the variable. You can specify an optional *n* to indicate the field width and fill it with leading 0s.
-Z	Fill the field with leading 0s. (This option is equivalent to -RZ. You can specify an optional *n* to indicate the field width.)
-r	Mark variable or parameter as read-only
-x	Mark variable as exported
-H	Map a UNIX system path name to a host operating system path name specification. (This option has no effect on UNIX systems)
-t	User-defined tag

If typeset is used within a function, a local variable of the name specified is created. When the function exits, the variable's value and attributes (if any) are restored.

Return Value: typeset returns a 0 exit status if no errors are encountered; otherwise, the command returns a nonzero exit status.

ulimit [-cdfmpt] [*n*]

Description: u l i m i t imposes a file size limit of *n* blocks for files written by the shell and any processes it executes. Files of any size can be read.

Without *n* specified, u l i m i t prints the current limit. Any user can lower his or her limit, but only the superuser can raise a limit.

unalias *name* ...

> **KSH only**
>
> **Description:** The u n a l i a s command removes aliases.
>
> **Return Value:** u n a l i a s returns a 0 exit code if all *name*(s) are valid aliases. Otherwise, the command returns a nonzero exit code.

umask [*mask*]

Description: u m a s k sets the file permission mask. If you do not specify *mask*, u m a s k prints the current mask.

u m a s k specifies which bits to take away when a file or directory is created. *mask* is an octal number in the range 000 to 777. This *mask* is the same as that used with the c h m o d command (see c h m o d(1) in the *UNIX User's Reference Manual*). *mask* specifies what permissions the system should remove when a file or directory is created.

Table 27 describes the useful values of u m a s k.

Table 27. *umask Command Values*

umask Value	File Permission	Directory Permission
000	-rw-rw-rw-	drwxrwxrwx
002	-rw-rw-r--	drwxrwxr-x
007	-rw-rw----	drwxrwx---
022	-rw-r--r--	drwxr-x---
027	-rw-r-----	drwxr-x---
077	-rw-------	drwx------

unset [-f] *name*   ...

Description: unset removes the variable or function name from the current shell. The -f option specifies unsetting of a function.

The variables PATH, PS1, PS2, MAILCHECK, and IFS cannot be unset.

Return Value: unset always returns a 0 exit status.

wait [*n*]

Description: wait waits for a specified process *n* to complete and then reports its termination status. If *n* is not specified, all currently active child processes are waited for until they exit and the return status is a 0.

Return Value: If *n* is specified, the return code is that of the process waited for. This is an effective way to obtain the return status of background processes.

whence [-v] *name ...*

Shell Parameters and Variables

Shell parameters are used to store values for the current shell or subshells to use later. A parameter may be one of the following types:

❏ A positional parameter

❏ A special parameter

❏ Named parameters (variables)

Positional parameters have a number as their name. Special parameters have one of the following characters as part of their name: * @ # ? - $!. A named parameter uses an identifier as part of its name and is often referred to as a variable.

A parameter value is available only to the current shell unless it is exported (see export under "Built-In Commands"), in which case its value can be accessed by subshells that the current shell creates.

The character $ references the value of a parameter. For example, $LOGNAME is read as "the value of LOGNAME."

There are no data types in the Bourne shell; all values are stored as character strings. The shell determines the data type when the parameter is used. For arithmetic functions in the Bourne shell, the expr(1) command must be used. The AT&T *UNIX User's Reference Manual* explains expr.

> **KSH only**
>
> You can declare parameters as integers by using the `typeset -i` command. The ksh also provides a built-in command, `let`, for performing arithmetic operations.

Positional Parameters

Positional parameters are values passed when a shell or subshell is invoked. You set positional parameters as arguments to a shell script or by using the `set` built-in command, and the parameters names are numbers such as 1, 2, and so on. The name of the current command (shell script) is referenced as `$0`. Any additional parameters passed to the shell script are referenced as `$1`, `$2`, and so on. Only nine positional parameters can be directly referenced as `$1` through `$9` in the Bourne shell. The special parameters `$@` and `$*` contain all the positional parameters starting with `$1`. The shell interprets `$@` to mean "`$1` `$2` `$3` `$4` ..." and `$*` to mean "`$1`" "`$2`" "`$3`", and so on (see "Quoting" in the "Shell Basics" section).

> **KSH only**
>
> Positional parameters greater than `$9` can be referenced with the notation `${n`. Thus, `${13}` refers to positional parameter 13.
>
> The ksh also supports one-dimensional arrays in the range of 0 through 511. You can subscript a parameter by using `[ ]`. The value of an array element is accessed with the notation `${var[n]}`. Referencing a parameter (without a subscript) that is part of an array is the same as referencing the first parameter of the array (*parameter[0]*).
>
> You do not need to declare parameter arrays before using them. Any reference to a parameter array with a valid subscript is acceptable and the array element is created when it is first assigned.

Special Parameters

Special parameters are set automatically whenever a shell is invoked. These parameters, described in table 28, have special meaning to the shell and cannot be modified directly.

Table 28. Special Parameters

Variable	Meaning
$@	Positional parameters as "$1 $2 $3 $4 ..."
$*	Positional parameters as "$1" "$2" "$3" "$4", etc.
$#	The number of positional parameters passed to the shell
$-	The flags passed to the shell on invocation, or set by the set command (see set under "Special Commands")
$?	The exit code of the last synchronously executed command
$$	The process number of the current shell
$!	The process number of the last background command invoked by the current shell

KSH only

$_ This special parameter holds:

❏ The last argument of the previous command

❏ The name of the matching MAIL file when checking for mail

❏ The value of the pathname of each program ksh invokes; this value is then passed in the environment. This argument is not set for commands that are asynchronous.

Named Parameters

A named parameter is called a shell variable and it must start with a letter or underscore and can be followed by zero or more alphanumeric or underscore characters. To set a variable, enter the name of the variable, followed immediately by an = sign, followed immediately by the value:

```
firstname=John
```

If the value of a variable contains blanks (spaces or tabs) then the value must be quoted:

```
myname="John Smith"
```

The value of a variable may be accessed by preceding the variable with a $:

```
$ echo $firstname
John
```

If the value contains blanks, then you should quote the variable to prevent the shell from interpreting the blanks:

```
$ echo "$myname"
John Smith
```

Braces must be used for variable names that are followed by a letter, digit, or underscore that is not part of the variable name itself:

```
$ filename=chapt
$ echo $filename0

$ echo ${filename}0
chapt0
```

Variables Set by the Shell

KSH only

The shell automatically sets the variables described in table 29.

Table 29. *Variables Set by the Shell*

Variable	Meaning
ERRNO	On versions of ksh newer than the 06/03/86 version, this variable contains the integer value of the most recently failed system call. ERRNO is primarily used for debugging shell scripts. ERRNO is set only for errors that occur in the current process environment. Setting ERRNO to 0 clears its value.
LINENO	Versions of ksh newer than the 06/03/86 version set LINENO to the current line number of a script or function before each command is executed. LINENO is often used as the value for the debug prompt PS4.
OLDPWD	This variable holds the previous working directory set by cd
OPTARG	Versions of ksh newer than the 06/03/86 version set OPTARG to the value of the argument of an option to getopts. See getopts for additional information on OPTARG.l

OPTIND	In versions of ksh newer than the 06/03/86 version, `getopts` sets OPTIND to the index of the argument to be processed. OPTIND is initially set to 1 whenever ksh, a shell script, or a function is invoked. Subsequently assigning OPTIND a value of 1 will reinitialize `getopts` to process another argument list.
PPID	Process number of the shell's parent.
PWD	Current working directory set by `cd` command.
RANDOM	Each time this parameter is referenced, a random integer is generated. You can initialize the sequence of random numbers by assigning a numeric value to RANDOM.
REPLY	This variable contains the value entered on the terminal when no arguments are supplied to the select or read built-in commands.
SECONDS	This variable contains an integer value that indicates the number of seconds that have elasped since ksh was invoked. If SECONDS is assigned a value, then the variable contains that value plus the number of seconds that have elasped since the assignment.

Variables Used by the Shell

The shell uses the variables described in table 30. These variables are often set by the system administrator in the `/etc/profile` file or by each user in his or her own `.profile` file. If values are not assigned to these variables, the shell does one of the following:

❑ Assigns an explict default value that can be printed

❑ Assigns an implicit default value that cannot be printed

❑ Does not assign a value; in this case, use of the null variable value may yield undesired results

Table 30. *Variables Used by the Shell*

Variable	Description
CDPATH	Search path for the `cd` command. The CDPATH takes precedence over the current directory when searching for a subdirectory. Thus, you should include the current directory in CDPATH by using the dot (`.`) notation. Example: `CDPATH=.:$HOME:/usr/project`

KSH only

Variable	Description
COLUMNS	If this variable is set, the value is used to define the width of the edit window for the shell edit modes and for printing select lists.
EDITOR	If the value of this variable ends in `emacs`, `gmacs`, or `vi` and the VISUAL variable is not set, then the corresponding option (see the discussion of set in the "Built-In Commands" section) is turned on.
ENV	If this parameter is set, then parameter substitution is performed on the value to generate the pathname of the script that will be executed when the shell is invoked. (See "Invocation" in the "Shell Basics" section.) This file is typically used for alias and function definitions.
FCEDIT	Default editor name for the `fc` command.
FPATH	In versions of ksh newer than the 06/03/86 version, this variable may be set to contain a colon (`:`) separated list of directories that ksh searches for a function definition file. The format of FPATH is the same as the PATH variable. FPATH is used with the `autoload` alias (`alias autoload= typeset-fu`).
HISTFILE	If this parameter is set when the shell is invoked, then the value is the pathname of the file that will store the command history.
HISTSIZE	If this parameter is set when the shell is invoked, then the number of previously entered commands that the shell can access will be greater than or equal to this number. The default is 128.

Variable	Description
HOME	Default argument (home directory) for the cd command. This variable is set by login(1).
IFS	Internal field separators, normally space, tab, and newline.

KSH only	
	(In versions of ksh newer than the 06/03/86 release, you cannot export IFS for security reasons.)
LINES	This variable contains the number of lines on a terminal and is used by ksh to print select lists (see the select built-in command). select lists are printed vertically until about two-thirds of the value of LINES lines are filled. The default value of LINES is 24.

MAIL	If this variable is set to the name of a mail file and the MAILPATH parameter is not set, the shell informs the user that mail has arrived in the specified file. This variable is set by login(1).
MAILCHECK	This parameter specifies how often (in seconds) the shell checks for the arrival of mail in the files specified by MAILPATH or MAIL parameters. The default is 600 seconds (10 minutes). If this parameter is set to 0, the shell checks before each prompt.
MAILPATH	A colon (:) separated list of file names. If this parameter is set, the shell informs the user that mail has arrived in any of the specified files. Each file name can be followed by a % and a message to be printed when the modification time changes. The default message is "you have mail."

KSH only	
MAILPATH	This variable contains a colon (:) separated list of pathnames of mail files to be checked for the arrival of new mail. Each pathname can be followed by a ? and a message to be displayed when new mail arrives. The default message is "You have mail in [mailfile]."

Table 30 continues

Table 30 *continued*

Variable	Description
PATH	Search path for commands. Users cannot change PATH if executing under rsh.
PS1	Primary prompt string, by default "$ "
PS2	Secondary prompt string, by default "> "

KSH only

PS3	Selection prompt string used within a select loop, by default ´ ´# ?
PS4	Debug prompt string. The value of PS4 is expanded and printed on the standard error output whenever the shell is ready to display a command during execution trace mode. The LINENO variable can be used as the PS4 prompt to display the line number of the script or function that corresponds to the line displayed by ksh. Example: `PS4='$LINENO '`

SHACCT	If this parameter is set to the name of a file writable by the user, the shell writes accounting records in the file for each shell procedure executed. Accounting routines such as `acctcom`(1) and `acctcms`(1M) can analyze the data collected.
SHELL	When the shell is invoked, it scans the environment for this variable. If it is found and there is an "r" in the value (such as in rsh or rksh), the shell becomes a restricted shell.
TERM	This variable contains the type of terminal you currently are using. Although not used directly by the shell, this variable is used by many programs for screen control.

KSH only

TMOUT	If this variable is set to a value greater than 0, the shell terminates when a command is not entered within the prescribed number of seconds. (Note that the shell can be compiled with a maximum bound for this value that cannot be exceeded.)

Variable	Description
VISUAL	If the value of this parameter ends in `emacs`, `gmacs`, or `vi`, then the corresponding option is turned on (see the discussion of set in the section "Built-In Commands").

Parameter Expansion

The shell provides a mechanism for conditionally evaluating parameters and performing substitution according to the parameter being set, not set, null, or non-null.

A parameter can be set or not set. If the shell has the parameter name in its internal list, then the parameter is considered to be set. The following shows how to set a parameter:

```
tmpdir=
```

This places the `tmpdir` parameter in the parameter list but it will not have a value.

A parameter can be null or have a value (non-null). In the previous example, `tmpdir` is null.

You can use the conventions described in table 31 to perform conditional substitution on parameters, depending on whether they are set, not set, null, or non-null:

Table 31. *Conventions Used for Parameter Substitution*

Convention	Description
${var}	Substitute the value of *var* if it is non-null. The braces are used when a *var* is followed by a letter, digit, or underscore that could be misinterpreted as part of the *var* name. If *var* is a digit then it is a positional parameter. If var is `*` or `@` then all positional parameters, starting with `$1`, are substituted and separated by spaces.

Table 31. continues

Table 31 *continued*

Convention	Description

	If a parameter is subscripted (part of an array) then the braces must be used:

```
$ user[5]="Tom Jones"
$ print "${user[5]}"
Tom Jones
```

If an array *var* with a subscript of * or @ is used, then the value of all elements of the array, separated by spaces, are substituted.

Convention	Description
${*var*:-*word*}	If *var* is set and non-null, use its value. Otherwise, substitute *word*. Note the keyword here is "substitute." If *var* is not set or is null, then *word* is used; there is no effect on *var*.
${*var*:=*word*}	If *var* is not set or is null, set it to *word*; the value of *var* is then substituted. After conditional substitution with this notation, *var* is set to *word*. Note: You can't assign positional parameters this way.
${*var*:?*word*}	If *var* is set and is non-null, substitute its value; otherwise, print *word* and exit from the shell. If *word* is omitted, the message `parameter null or not set` is printed.
${*var*:+*word*}	If *var* is set and is non-null, substitute *word*; otherwise substitute nothing.

KSH only

${#*var*}	Substitute the length of the value of *var* if *var* is not *. Otherwise, the number of positional *var*s is substituted.
${#*identifier*[*]}	Substitute the number of elements in the array identifier.

Convention	Description
$\{var\#pattern\}$	If the shell *pattern* matches the beginning of the value of *var*, then the value of this substitution is the value of the *var* with the matched *pattern* deleted; otherwise the value of this *var* is substituted. In the first form the smallest matching pattern is deleted and in the latter form the largest matching pattern is deleted.
$\{var\%pattern\}$	If the shell *pattern* matches the end of the value of *var*, then the value of *var* with the matched pattern is deleted; otherwise the value of *var* is substituted. In the first form the smallest matching pattern is deleted and in the latter form the largest matching pattern is deleted.

In the preceding structures, the shell does not evaluate *word* unless it is to be used as the substituted string. If the colon (:) is omitted from the preceding expressions, then the shell checks only whether *var* is set.

The following examples illustrate how you can set the parameter TERM using two different conditional constructs:

```
TERM=${TERM:-dumb}
${TERM:=dumb}
```

Programming Constructs

for

Usage:

```
for variable in words
do
   command-list
done

for variable
do
  command-list
done
```

Description: The `for` built-in command executes *command-list* once for each `$IFS`-delimited word in *words*, setting the value of *variable* to the next word in *words* on each iteration. If no words are given, `for` executes *command-list* once for each positional parameter set on the command line (`$*`).

Example: This first example runs spell on all files that match the pattern `unit??.n`; it redirects output to filenames consisting of the matched filenames suffixed with `_sp`.

```
$ ls unit??.n
unit01.n          unit02.n          unit04.n          unit12.n
$ for i in unit??.n
> do
> spell $i > ${i}_sp
> done
$ ls unit??*
unit01.n          unit02.n          unit04.n          unit12.n
unit01.n_sp       unit02.n_sp       unit04.n_sp       unit12.n_sp
```

To collect all output in a single file, you can use the following form of `for`. Notice where output redirection takes place:

```
for i in unit??.n
do
     echo "$i:"
     spell $i
     echo "\n"
done > spell.out
```

Return Value: `for` returns the exit code of the last command.

while

Usage:

```
while command
do
        command-list
done
```

Description: The `while` construct executes *command-list* repeatedly until the exit status of *command* is nonzero. If the first execution of *command* returns a nonzero value, *command-list* is never executed.

Examples: This first example monitors a user until she logs off, then prints a message to that effect:

```
while who ¦ grep linda > /dev/null
do
        sleep 10
done
echo "Linda just logged off" >/etc/watch_linda
```

The next example processes all the arguments to a shell script using $# (the number of positional parameters).

```
while [ $# -ne 0 ]
do
        spell $1 > $1.out
        shift
done
```

Return Value: while returns the exit status for the last iteration of *command-list* unless no commands were executed, in which case the while command returns 0.

until

Usage:

```
until command
do
                command-list
done
```

Description: The until construct executes *command* and, if its exit status is nonzero (*false*), executes *command-list*. Execution continues until *command* exits with a 0 (true).

Example: The following script watches for a user logging on to the system:

```
until who ¦ grep merlin > /dev/null
do
        sleep 10
done
echo "Merlin just logged on"
```

Return Value: until returns the exit status of the last iteration of *command-list* unless no commands were executed, in which case the until command returns 0.

if

Usage:

```
if command
then
                command-list
fi

if command
then
                command-list
else
                command-list
fi

if command
then
                command-list
elif command
then
                command-list
fi
```

Description: The command on the if line is executed; if it returns a 0 (true) exit status, the command list following the then is executed. The keyword fi terminates the if statement.

If the if command returns a nonzero exit status, the else command list is executed.

The shell executes the elif command if and only if *command* returns a nonzero exit status. The then command list associated with elif is executed if the exit status is zero.

Examples: The following example illustrates how you can use the if statement to evaluate a command's output:

```
if who | grep tom > /dev/null
then
     echo "Tom is logged on"
fi
```

The next example uses if with the else statement to print the type of file:

```
if [ -f status ]
then
     echo "status is a regular file"
else
     echo "status is not a regular file"
fi
```

You can use the elif construct To provide additional information:

```
if [ -f status ]
then
        echo "status is a regular file"
elif [ -d status ]
then
        echo "status is a directory"
fi
```

Return Value: The if statement returns a 0 exit status if no else or then clauses are executed; otherwise, the status of the last executed command list is returned.

case

Usage:

```
case word in
        pattern1)
          command-list
                ;;
        pattern2)
          command-list
                ;;
esac
```

Description: The case construct executes the command list associated with the first pattern that matches *word*. Each pattern clause must be terminated by a double semicolon (;;). Patterns are the same as those used for file-name generation.

Example: The following example shows how you can limit users to executing only certain commands:

```
echo "Enter command: \c"
read cmd
case $cmd
in
        ls)
                /bin/ls ;;
        who)
                /bin/who ;;
        date)
                /bin/date ;;
        *)
                echo "Invalid command" ;;
esac
```

Notice the use of the asterisk (*) to match everything else (normally called the *default* case).

Return Value: The case construct returns the exit status of the last command executed.

(command list)

Usage:

(command1; command2; ...)
(command1& command2& ...)

Description: This construct is called *command grouping*. The command list is executed in a subshell. The output of the group is sent to standard output and can be piped to another command or redirected into a file.

If the commands are separated by semicolons, each command is executed in sequence. If the commands are separated by ampersands, each command is executed in the background.

Example: The following example executes all three commands as a group, sending output to a file named status:

```
(date;ls;who) > status
```

Return Value: The exit status of the last command in the list is returned.

{ command list }

Usage:

{ command1; command2; ...; }
{ command1& command2& ...& ;}

Description: The command list is executed in the current shell. The output of the group is sent to standard output. Any environmental changes made by the commands in the list are effected in the current shell.

A space must follow the left brace ({); a semicolon (;) must follow the last command.

Example: In the following example, the current shell executes all three commands, sending output to a file named status:

```
{ date;who;ls; } > status
```

Return Value: The exit status of the last command in the list is returned.

functions

Usage:

```
name()
{
        commands
}
function
{
        commands
}
```

Description: `functions` defines the function *name*. You must follow the function identifier by left and right parentheses.

> **KSH only**
>
> The Korn shell uses the keyword `function` to define a function of *name*.

Functions are read into the current shell process and stored internally. To call a function, simply enter it as the name of a command (note that function names should never be the same as those of existing UNIX commands or built-in shell commands). The shell executes the commands within braces when the function is called.

A function has access to the variables set for the current shell.

> **KSH only**
>
> The `typeset` special command used within a function defines a variable as local to the function. The variable's scope is local to the current function and any functions it calls. The calling process does not have access to the variable, because the variable is unset when the function exits.
>
> You can use the `typeset -f` command to list functions and their text, and the `unset -f` command to undefine functions.

Example: This example shows how you can redefine the `ls` command to list the files in columns:

```
ls()
{
        /bin/ls -C
}
```

Notice the use of the full path name when naming functions with the same name as an existing command. (This scheme does not work for redefining built-in shell commands.)

Return Value: The `functions` construct returns the exit status of the last command in a function unless you set an explicit return value with the `return` built-in special command (see "Built-In Commands").

select

KSH only

Usage:

```
select variable in words
do
                commands
done

select variable
do
                commands
done
```

Description: The `select` command prints the words on the standard error output, each preceded by a number. If words are omitted, as in the second example of usage, the positional parameters are used.

Then the PS3 prompt is printed and a line is read from the standard input. If the line matches the number of one of the listed *words*, the value of *variable* is set to the *word* matching the corresponding number selected. If the line is empty, the selection list is printed again. If the line does not match one of the selection numbers, *variable* is set to null.

`select` saves the line read from the standard input in the REPLY variable. The *commands* are executed for each selection until a BREAK or end-of-file is encountered.

Example: The following example illustrates a simple menu using the
`select` command:

```
PS3="Enter item: "
select choice in ls date who quit
do
        case $REPLY in
            1)
                ls ;;
            2)
                date ;;
            3)
                who ;;
4¦Q¦q)
                exit ;;
            *)
                print "Invalid Choice" ;;
        esac
done
```

time

Usage:

```
time command
```

Description: *command* is executed and the amount of real, user, and system
time it took to execute is printed. time is useful for checking the efficiency of
shell programs. For example:

```
$ time status

real    0m1.61s
user    0m0.16s
sys     0m1.31s
```

Shell Scripts

A shell script is simply a file that contains built-in shell commands, functions,
and UNIX commands. Shell scripts frequently are used when a sequence of
commands must be executed more than once.

Creating and Executing Shell Scripts

To create a shell script, use your favorite editor to enter the commands you want to execute into a file.

To execute a shell script, you can do either of the following:

❏ Change the mode of the file so that it is executable, and then enter its name on a command line as you would enter other UNIX commands

❏ Invoke it, using the `sh` command with options, as in the following examples:

```
$ sh myprog
```

or

```
$ sh -x myprog
```

Both of these methods of execution create a subshell to execute the commands within the file.

The name of a shell script should not be the same as that of an existing UNIX command, built-in shell command, or function. Remember that the shell first executes built-in commands, then functions, then UNIX commands or shell scripts. A common mistake is to name a shell script `test`, only to discover that the shell script does not execute because `test` is a built-in shell command, which is executed before the shell script. The same is true for all other built-in shell commands.

Giving a shell script the same name as an existing UNIX command has the following undesirable effects:

❏ The shell script is executed instead of the UNIX command (if the PATH variable is set to search local directories first)

❏ The UNIX command is executed instead of the shell script (if the PATH is set to search system directories first)

Debugging Shell Scripts

If the shell encounters a syntax error while executing a shell script, it terminates execution and returns a nonzero exit status. Several methods can be used to try to find the error.

First, you should closely examine the shell script to determine whether the program is syntactically correct (all quotes in balance, correct spelling of commands, and so on).

Next, you can use the `-x` option of the `sh` or `ksh` command as follows

```
$ sh -x myprog
```

to print the commands and their arguments as they are executed. The `-x` option can be turned on also by placing the command

```
set -x
```

anywhere in the shell script file itself. This option lets you watch the execution of the shell script to see where it is failing.

Another method of debugging is to place `echo` commands in the file to print out information as the shell script is executed. `echo` commands can be used to print the value of variables or, if `echo` precedes a command, to print how the command would be interpreted by the shell:

```
echo "rm chapt??.n"
rm chapt01.n chapt02.n chapt03.n
```

For a "divide and conquer" method of debugging, use the `exit` command. By having the program exit at various places, you can test specific portions of the program to determine exactly where the problem lies.

The Dot Command

When a shell script is invoked either by its name or by running the shell with the name of a program as its argument (as in `sh prog1`), a separate subprocess is created to execute commands within the program. Changes made to the environment from within the program, such as changing directories, creating new variables, or changing the values of variables, do not remain when the program exits.

The dot (`.`) command causes the current process to execute the program directly, in its environment. Arguments can be passed to a program invoked with the `.` command.

The dot command is commonly used, for example, when changes are made to a user's `.profile` file. Instead of logging out and then logging back in to have the changes take effect, you need only enter the following command

```
$ . .profile
```

to force the login shell to read and execute the commands within the `.profile` file.

Used from within shell scripts, the . command is very useful for reading files that contain variable assignments and function declarations. Instead of entering variable assignments and functions into each shell program, use the . command to read the file that contains them.

Shell Script Examples

Processing Command-line Arguments

A shell script commonly is used to process command-line arguments and generate a new command line before invoking a UNIX command. The following examples illustrate various methods of processing command-line arguments.

```
# Checking number of command-line arguments
if [ $# -ne 5 ] # Arguments not equal to 5
then
      echo "Usage: $0 args"
fi

# Using a for loop to process arguments
for arg # Default word list
do
      echo $arg
done

for arg in $* # Wordlist is all arguments
do
      echo $arg
done

# Using a while loop to process arguments
while [ $# -ne 0 ] # Check number of arguments
do
    echo $1 # Process first argument
    shift   # Shift $2 to $1, etc.
done

while [ "$1" ] # Check $1 not the null string
do
    echo $1 # Process $1
    shift   # Shift $2 to $1, etc.
done
```

```
# This example allows the user to specify a command line
# argument. If no argument is supplied, the program prompts
# for one.
if [ $# -eq 0 ]
then
     echo "File Name: \c"; read fname
else
     fname=$1
fi
```

Data Management

You can use the shell as a data-management tool with ASCII files that have a record-field structure. A good example of this type of file is /etc/passwd. Each line represents a record for a user on the system; within each line, a colon separates the fields.

The following script shows how to use the shell to read each line and separate the fields:

```
IFS=: # Set the input field separator to :
exec < /etc/passwd # Redirect stdin from /etc/passwd
while read line # Read a line from stdin (/etc/passwd)
do
     set -- $line # Set positional parameters
     echo "Login: $1"
     if [ ! "$2" ]
     then
     echo "Passwd: None"
else
        echo "Passwd: Set"
     fi
done
```

This sample script uses exec to redefine the source of input. Then the while loop continues to read a line from /etc/passwd until end-of-file is reached. Each time a line is read, the set command and the value of IFS (:) are used to break the input line into its component fields.

Programming Hints

The following hints can help make your programs run faster and more efficiently:

1. Use built-in shell commands wherever possible. Unlike UNIX commands, they do not cause creation of subprocesses.

2. Take advantage of a command's capabilities. For example, because sort can open files,

```
sort file
```

is much more efficient than

```
cat file | sort
```

3. Use input and output redirection. For example:

```
$ lp < file
```

is better than

```
$ cat file | lp
```

4. Use `exec` to invoke commands that do not need to return to the calling shell; or, to return to the parent, use `exec` in both the parent and child processes.

5. Think about the number of bytes to be processed.

```
$ grep pattern file | sort
```

requires the `sort` command to process fewer bytes than

```
$ sort file | grep pattern
```

6. Use functions within your shell scripts. They execute much faster than subshells.

7. Use the dot (`.`) command to invoke subshells that modify variables. If you use the dot command, you won't have to pass information back and forth between the two programs.

8. Use command substitution instead of the pipeline mechanism. For example, use

```
$ sort `cat file`
```

instead of

```
$ cat file | sort
```

because more overhead is needed for creating the pipe mechanism than for using command substitution.

9. Redirect the output of commands within a loop once, at the end of the loop, instead of after each command. For example, use the following:

```
for i in 01 02 03 04 05
```

```
do
   sort unit$i
done > tmp
```

instead of

```
for i in 01 02 03 04 05
do
        sort unit$i >> tmp
done
```

The output of loops can also be piped to a command:

```
for i in 01 02 03 04
do
        sort unit${i}
done|lp
```

instead of

```
for i in 01 02 03 04
do
        sort unit${i} | lp
done
```

10. Use pipes instead of creating temporary files, wherever possible:

```
cat unit?? | tr [a-z] [A-Z]
```

instead of

```
cat unit?? > tmp
tr [a-z] [A-Z] < tmp
```

11. Become familiar with all the UNIX commands so that you can choose the most efficient one to do the job. For example, find is more efficient than ls in some cases:

```
$ find . -type d -print
```

is faster than:

```
# Find directories
$ ls -lR | grep "^d"
```

Similarly, sometimes awk is better to use for searching and processing information in a file than grep or sed.

12. Plan file-naming and directory structures before you begin a project. Using shell wild cards is more efficient than using shell programs that build lists of file and directory names.

13. The shell uses the PATH variable to locate commands. To improve performance, set up your search path (in the PATH variable) or organize your directory structure so that the shell doesn't have to make extensive searches.

14. Use the `cd` command in shell scripts to change to a directory before processing files or executing commands. The shell can locate files and commands more quickly if they are in the local directory. In the following shell script:

```
for i in /usr/john/documents/book1/*
do
   format $i
done
```

each name in the list contains `/usr/john/documents/book1`. Parsing takes longer and you could overflow a shell buffer.

A better method, using `cd`, follows:

```
cd /usr/john/documents/book1
for i in *
do
   format $i
done
```

15. Keep files and directories small, when possible. File access is much faster for small (<10K) files; directory searches are much faster for small directories (<286 entries).

16. Have your programs clean up temporary files on exit.

Related UNIX Commands

The following commands are not part of the shell but are extremely helpful when you write shell programs. (For a complete description of these commands, see the *AT&T UNIX User's Reference Manual*.)

basename *pathname* [*suffix*]

Description: `basename` strips the final filename from *pathname*, removes any trailing portion that matches *suffix*, and prints the result to standard output. The `basename` command is most often used in command substitution expressions. For example, the following command, if called from within a shell script, prints only the filename of the script, regardless of whether it was invoked with a full or partial pathname:

```
echo `basename $0`
```

The following example strips off the trailing .c suffix from C program source code files:

```
for i in *.c
do
  basename $i .c
done
```

Return Value: basename always returns 0.

cat [*filename ...*]

Description: The cat command writes all its input files as one file to standard output. If no filenames are given on the command line, or – is one of the arguments, cat reads the standard input.

Use caution when redirecting standard output to a file. The shell executes I/O redirections before invoking commands. therefore, the command

```
$ cat unit01.n unit02.n > unit01.n
```

yields only a copy of the file unit02.n because the file unit01.n was truncated to a length of 0 by the redirection before cat begins. The command

```
$ cat unit01.n unit02.n > unit01.new
```

would produce the desired results.

Return Value: cat returns a 0 exit status if the command can successfully copy all input files. Otherwise, a nonzero exit status is returned.

chmod *mode path*

Description: The chmod command changes the file access permissions of *path* as directed by the *mode* operand. Only the owner of file or directory, or the superuser, can change permissions.

mode may be specified as an octal value or as a symbolic expression. To specify *mode* in octal notation, add together one or more of the values listed in table 32.

Table 32. *Octal File Permissions*

Permission	Octal Value
Read by owner	400
Write by owner	200
Execute by owner	100
Read by group	040
Write by group	020
Execute by group	010
Read by others	004
Write by others	002
Execute by others	001

For example, to change the file permissions so that only the owner and group can read and write it, enter the following command:

```
$ chmod 664 file
```

The symbolic form of *mode* enables you to combine symbolic operators in the format *who op permission*. Table 33 lists these operators.

Table 33. *chmod Symbolic Operators*

who		operator		permission	
user	u	add	+	read	r
group	g	takeaway	-	write	w
other	o	absolute	=	execute	x
				suid/sgid	s

The following example shows how to remove write and execute permissions for group and other:

```
$ chmod og-wx file
```

Using the symbolic method, you can also specify more than one operation by separating each with a comma:

```
$ chmod u+w,g-wx,o-rwx file
```

Notice that there are no spaces between the symbols in this example.

Return Value: If it can change the mode, `chmod` returns a 0 exit status. If the user is not the owner of the file and is not the superuser, `chmod` fails and returns a nonzero exit status.

cp *filenames target*

Description: `cp` copies the files specified to *target*. *target* can be a directory, an existing file, or a new file. You can specify multiple filenames only when *target* is a directory.

If *target* is a directory, then all files are copied into that directory with the same filenames. If *target* is an existing file, then the input file is copied to it and the mode, owner, group, and links remain intact. If *target* is a new file, then the input file is copied to it and the mode, owner, and group of the new file remain the same as the old file.

Return Value: If the copy is successful, `cp` returns a 0 exit status. Otherwise, a nonzero exit status is returned.

date [+*format*]

Description: The `date` command prints the current date and time on the standard output in the form

```
Sat May 19 12:38:57 EDT 1990
```

`date` uses the value of the TZ variable to convert system clock time to local time (UNIX stores the time as Greenwich Mean Time).

You can specify an optional format string, preceded by a % sign, to print the date in a format more useful for your shell program. The format string is constructed from the one-character codes described in table 34.

Using the `date` command with one of these format strings is very useful within shell programs. For example, to set a variable equal to the current date as MM/DD/YY, use the following:

```
today=`date +%D`
```

Return Value: If the conversion is successful, `date` returns a 0 exit status. A nonzero exit status is returned if the conversion fails or an invalid format specification character is entered.

Table 34. *date Command Format String Character Codes*

Code	Meaning
n	Insert a newline character
t	Insert a tab character
m	Print the month of year (01 to 12)
d	Print the day of month (01 to 31)
y	Print the last 2 digits of year (00 to 99)
D	Print the date in MM/DD/YY format
H	Print the hour (00 to 23)
M	Print the minute (00 to 59)
S	Print the second (00 to 59)
T	Print the time in HH:MM:SS format
j	Print the day of the year (001 to 366)
w	Print the day of the week (Sunday = 0)
a	Print the abbreviated weekday (Sun to Sat)
h	Print the abbreviated month (Jan to Dec)
r	Print the time in AM/PM notation

dirname *pathname*

Description: dirname prints the initial part of *pathname*. For example, to find out the file system a user is on, use the following:

```
$ echo $HOME
/usr/tom
$ filesys=`dirname $HOME`
$ echo $filesys
/usr
```

Return Value: dirname always returns a 0 exit status.

env [-] [*name=value*] [*command*]

Description: The env command obtains the current environment, modifies it according to its arguments, and then executes a command with the modified environment. The – flag causes the inherited environment to be completely ignored so that the command is executed with only the environment specified by *name=value* pairs.

Like the set command, env prints the current environment if no arguments are specified.

env is a stand-alone UNIX command and is not part of the shell. env is useful for modifying the current shell environment before executing a command.

Return Value: env returns a 0 exit status if its arguments and commands are successful; otherwise, the exit status is that of the command.

expr *expression*

Description: expr is an expression evaluator used for evaluating strings and performing mathematical functions. expr is used in the Bourne shell for performing arithmetic operations, and is used in either shell when the test command does not provide the particular operation needed.

For example, to increment the value of a variable, use the following:

```
# Increment i by 1
i=`expr $i + 1`
```

Return Value: expr returns a 0 exit status if the evaluation is successful; otherwise, a nonzero exit status is returned.

false

Description: false always returns a nonzero (255) exit status. You can use it to control an until loop as follows:

```
until false
do
  ...
done
```

Return Value: false always returns a nonzero exit status.

find *directory expr*

Description: find locates files and directories that match the values specified in *expr*. The first argument to find must be a starting directory. The expressions described in table 35 can be used to construct the *expr* for files and directories to locate.

Table 35. *find Command Expressions*

Expression	Meaning
-print	Always true. Prints the current pathname.
-name *filename*	Specifies the name of a file/directory to find. Returns true if the file is found.
-perm *mode*	True if mode exactly matches the mode of a file/directory. If *mode* is prefixed by -, more flag bits are compared.
-type *t*	True if the file type is *t*. *t* can be d for a directory or f for a file.
-size [+/-]*n*	True if the size of the file is *n* blocks long. If *n* is followed by a *c*, then the comparision is made for that many characters.
-mtime [+/-]*n*	True if the file was modified exactly *n* days ago.
-atime [+/-]*n*	True if the file was accessed exactly *n* days ago.
-ctime [+/-]*n*	True if the file mode was changed exactly *n* days ago.
-exec *command*	*command* is executed on the found files. True if the command returns an exit status of 0. The end of the command must be punctuated with a semicolon (but note that the semicolon is a shell metacharacter, and normally must be escaped: \;).

A + in front of a number indicates greater than, and - means less than.

By default, juxtaposed expressions are assumed to stand in an *and* relation to one another; use the operators described in table 36 to alter the binding between expressions.

Table 36. *find Command Operators*

Operator	Meaning
!	Unary negation operator
-a	Logical *and*
-o	Logical *or*

The following are examples of uses for the `find` command:

```
# Find all files in the current directory
# which are readable by others
$ find . -type f -perm -002 -print

# Change the mode on all files
# so they are not writable by
# group and others
$ find . -type f -exec chmod og-w {} ;
```

Return Value: `find` returns a 0 exit status if the expression evaluates true. Otherwise, a nonzero exit status is returned.

grep [*opts*] *pattern* [*file(s)*]

Description: The `grep` command searches each of the file(s) specified for *pattern* and, without any options, prints each matching line on the standard output. If more than one filename is given on the command line, then the name of the file also is printed preceding each matching line.

`grep` uses patterns in the form of regular expressions. Table 37 describes a number of useful options to `grep`.

Table 37. *grep Command Options*

Option	Meaning
- i	Ignore upper/lowercase distinction when making comparisons
- l	Only display the name of the file (once) for each file with a matching pattern
- c	Print a count of matching lines

The following examples can be useful with shell scripts:

```
# Find all files that contain the string "UNIX"
$ grep UNIX *
# Build a list of filenames that contain "FL"
flist=`grep FL *`
# Count the number of records in a file
# which contain the string "Manager"
grep -c Manager employees
```

If the *pattern* consists of more than one word or contains special characters that are meaningful to the shell, then the pattern must be enclosed in quotes (" or `).

Be careful of the following:

```
# Find a greater-than (>) symbol in
# a file
$ grep > employees
```

In this example, the terminal appears to hang until the Del or Break key is pressed. You then find that the file employees is truncated to 0 length. This is because the shell took the > symbol as the redirection operator, opened the file employees for output, and stripped both the > and employees strings from the command line. Therefore, the grep command found no filenames on the command line and attempted to read from standard input. The correct command syntax is as follows:

```
$ grep ">" employees
```

Return Value: The grep command returns a nonzero exit status if the pattern is found. A exit status of 1 is returned if no patterns were found in the file(s). grep returns an exit status of 2 for syntax errors.

id

Description: The id command prints the real user-ID and group-ID numbers and names. id prints a line on standard output that looks like this:

```
uid=100(bill) gid=1(other)
```

If the effective and real user- or group-IDs are different, then id prints both:

```
uid=100(bill) gid=1(other) euid=102(tom) egid=3(sys)
```

Return Value: The id command always returns a 0 exit status.

kill [*-sig*] PID

Description: The `kill` command terminates a process. Without *sig*, `kill` sends signal 15 (TERMINATE) to the process specified by *PID*. Signal 15 normally kills processes that do not catch or ignore signals.

If a number is specified for *sig*, then that signal is sent to the process. The command

```
kill -9 PID
```

terminates any process.

Only the owner of a process or the superuser can kill a process.

Return Value: The `kill` command returns a 0 exit status if it can terminate the process; otherwise, a nonzero exit status is returned.

ln *file(s) target*

Description: The `ln` command links *file(s)* to *target*. If *target* names a directory, then the new links are created in that directory with the same name as the original file. If *target* names a file, then the original file is linked to the new file name. The new file must not exist before the `ln` command is invoked.

The `ln` command is useful for creating multiple references to a single file, especially when the original file is large. However, the permissions on linked files should be set so that the files are only readable by a group and others, to prevent multiple updates from being made at the same time.

You cannot link files across file systems.

Return Value: If the link is successful, `ln` returns a 0 exit status. Otherwise, a nonzero exit status is returned.

lp [*file(s)*]

Description: The `lp` command directs the named files to the print spooler. An optional `-d` *dest* operand may be specified to route the print job to a printer other than the system default printer.

lp uses the shell variable LPDEST (if set) to determine the default printer destination for the user.

Return Value: lp returns 0 if the files were successfully queued for printing, and returns a nonzero value for various errors such as invalid destination.

ls [*opts*] [*file/directory*]

Description: The ls command lists files and directories. Without any options or without a filename specified, ls lists all of the files in the current directory. If you specify the name of a file, only that file is listed. If a directory name is given, then the files in the specified directory are listed.

There are a bewildering variety of options for the ls command. Table 38 describes some of the more commonly used options.

Table 38. *ls Command Options*

Option	Meaning
-l	Produce a long listing showing file access permissions, link count, owner, group, size, the date that the file was last modified, and the name of the file
-a	List all files and directories, even those beginning with dot (.)
-t	List the files in sorted order according to the time they were last modified, with the most recent file being listed first
-r	List the files in reverse order
-C	List the files in columns
-F	Display a trailing / after directory names, * after executable files, and @ after symbolic links.

Return Value: ls returns a 0 exit status if it is successful. Otherwise, a nonzero exit status is returned and a diagnostic message is printed.

mkdir *directory*

Description: mkdir creates a new directory named *directory*. The mode of the new directory is set to 777 as modified by the file-creation mask.

The `mkdir` command requires that the parent directory have write permission set for the user making the new directory.

Return Value: If the new directory was created successfully, `mkdir` returns a 0 exit status. Otherwise, a nonzero exit status is returned and `mkdir` displays an error message.

mv *file(s) target*

Description: The `mv` command moves or renames the specifed files to target. The file and target cannot be the same.

If the target is a directory, then the named *file(s)* are moved to the directory with their same names. If the target is an existing file, `mv` first determines whether the file can be overwritten. If so, then the file is moved to the target file name. If the target file cannot be written to, then `mv` prints the target file permission mode and asks for a response. `mv` then reads from the standard input for a line beginning with `y` and moves the file if permissible. Otherwise, `mv` exits with a nonzero exit status.

`mv` requires write permission for the directory that the file is to be moved into. `mv` does not require write permission on the file.

You can specify the `-f` option to suppress the prompting for the move on existing files that do not have write permission.

Return Value: If the move is successful, `mv` returns a 0 exit status. Otherwise, a nonzero exit status is returned.

nohup *command*

Description: `nohup` runs *command* with HANGUP and QUIT signals ignored. If output is not redirected, then both standard output and standard error are sent to a file named `nohup.out`.

`nohup` is useful to start commands in the background and then log off. For example, a large sort job may be started at the end of the day.

Return Value: If the *command* can be executed, `nohup` returns a 0 exit status. Otherwise, a nonzero exit status is returned.

pg *opts file(s)*

Description: The pg command displays the named files on the terminal a screenful at a time. After each screenful of information, pg pauses and displays a colon (:) prompt. Table 39 describes the commands you can enter at the prompt.

Table 39. *pg Commands*

Command	Meaning
Space	Display the next screenful of information
-	Display the previous screenful of information
h	Display help information
q	Quit

In addition to the preceding commands, pg accepts regular expressions as search patterns and skips to the appropriate position in the file that matches the regular expression.

Return Value: If pg can open and paginate the file(s), it returns a 0 exit status. A nonzero exit status is returned for non-existent files, invalid arguments, or syntax errors.

rm [*opts*] *file(s)*

Description: The rm command removes specified files. Removal of a file requires write permission for the directory the file is in but does not require write or read permission for the file itself.

If the file does not have write permissions for the user attempting to remove it, then the rm command displays the file's permissions and prompts for input from the terminal. Responding with y causes the file to be removed if the user can write in the file's directory. Entering anything other than y will not remove the file.

Table 40 describes the options you can use with the rm command.

Table 40. *rm Command Options*

Option	Meaning
-f	Forcibly remove the file if possible. This option suppresses the prompting for removal of files that do not have write permission and suppresses error messages for non-existent files.
-r	Recursively remove files and directories. rm first removes all files in a directory and then removes the directory itself.
-i	Interactively remove files, asking whether you want to delete each file. A y response causes the file to be deleted. Any other response retains the file.

Return Value: rm returns a 0 exit status if it successfully removed the file or you specified the -f option. A nonzero exit status is returned if the user does not have permission to remove the file.

rmdir *directory*

Description: The rmdir command removes the directories specified as arguments to it. The directory must be empty.

If rmdir fails and an ls of the directory does not show any file names, try

```
ls -la
```

to print files that have a dot (.) as the first character of their file name. Remove those files and then remove the directory.

Return Value: If the directory was removed, rmdir returns a 0 exit status. Otherwise, a nonzero exit status is returned and rmdir displays an error message.

sleep *num*

Description: The sleep command suspends execution of the shell for *num* seconds. To sleep for one minute, enter

```
sleep 60
```

Used within shell scripts, sleep gives the user time to read error or warning messages.

Return Value: sleep always returns 0.

sort [*opts*] [*file(s)*]

Description: The sort command sorts the lines in the file specified on the command line. If no files are specified, sort reads from standard input.

By default, sort sorts the lines in a file in ascending order. Table 41 describes options you can specify to modify the sort output.

Table 41. sort Command Options

Option	Meaning
-n	Sort by numeric order
-o *outfile*	Put the output in *outfile* instead of sending it to the standard output
-t*c*	Use *c* as the field separator character instead of the default tabs and spaces.
+*n*	Sort on field number *n*. The sort command numbers fields starting with 0.
-r	Sort in reverse order

The following examples illustrate the use of the sort command:

```
# Sort the employee file
$ sort employees

# Sort the employee file in reverse order
$ sort -r employees

# Sort the /etc/passwd file by user id
$ sort -t: +2 -n /etc/passwd
```

Return Value: sort returns a 0 exit status if the sort was successful. A nonzero exit status is returned and a diagnostic message is printed if sort fails.

tail [[±]*num*] [-f] [*file(s)*]

Description: The tail command prints the last part of a file. By default, the last ten lines of the specified file are printed. If a +number argument is specified, tail starts that many lines from the beginning of the file. If a -number is specified, then tail begins printing at that many lines from the end of the file.

If the -f option is specified, tail does not exit when it detects an end-of-file, but continues to read the file as it is growing. This option is useful for monitoring the output of commands redirected to a file that is being extended by a background program.

The following examples show various uses for the tail command:

```
# Display the last 5 files that were modified
$ ls -ltr | tail -5

# Watch the output of a background sort command
$ sort employees -o employee.out&
$ tail -f employee.out
```

tee [-a] *file(s)*

Description: The tee command reads from standard output and writes to both the standard output and the file(s) specified on the command line. The -a option causes tee to append to the file(s).

The following is a example of how to use tee to create three files with the output of the who command:

```
$ who | tee who1 who2 who3
```

tr [-c] [-d] [-s] [*string1* [*string2*]]

Description: The tr command translates the characters in *string1* to those in *string2*. *string1* and *string2* may contain single characters, a group of characters enclosed in brackets, or a range of characters in the form *a-z* also enclosed in brackets. Nonprintable characters may be specified by their octal notation (for example, carriage return is '\012'). You should enclose *string1* and *string2* in quotes to prevent them from being interpreted by the shell.

Table 42 describes the options you can specify to the tr command.

Table 42. *tr Command Options*

Option	Meaning
-c	Complements the set of characters in *string1* with respect to the character set. In other words, the -c option specifies all characters not in *string1*.
-s	Squeezes multiple occurrences of characters in *string2*.
-d	Deletes input characters specified in *string1*.

The following example capitalizes all characters in the file employees:

```
$ tr "[a-z]" "[A-Z]" < employees
```

true

Description: The true command always returns a 0 exit status; it is used to create a endless while loop:

```
while true
do
      echo "More?"
      read ans
      if [ "$ans" = "n" ]
      then
          break
      fi
done
```

Note the use of the break statement to exit the loop.

Return Value: The true command always returns a 0 exit status.

uniq [-c] [-d] [-u] [*infile* [*outfile*]]

Description: The uniq command eliminates any adjacent lines in a file that are duplicated. The input file should be in sorted order.

Table 43 describes the options you can specify to the uniq command.

Table 43. *uniq Command Options*

Option	Meaning
-c	Prints a count of the number of times each line occurs in the file. The -c option suppresses the -d and -u options.
-d	Displays only duplicated lines
-u	Displays only lines that are not duplicated

uniq is useful for determining the number of times a specific line occurs in a file. For example, the following script tells how many times each word is used:

```
# First, put each word on a line by itself
tr -cs "[a-zA-Z]" "[ 12*]" < $1 > $1.tmpa
# Now sort the file
sort < $1.tmpa > $1.tmpb
# Then, perform a unique word count
uniq -c $1.tmpb
# And clean up the temporary files
rm -f $1.tmp?
```

wc [-w] [l] [c] [*file(s)*]

Description: The wc command counts the number of lines, words, and characters in a file. If a file name is not specified on the command line, wc reads from standard input. Otherwise, wc prints the counts for each file and then prints the total of lines, words, and characters for all specified files.

The -l option causes only the number of lines to be printed, the -w option prints only the number of words, and the -c option prints only the number of characters.

The following shows how `wc` can be used to determine the number of files in a directory:

```
$ ls | wc -l
```

Return Value: `wc` always returns 0.

who [am i]

Description: The `who` command displays a list of users currently logged on to the UNIX system along with their terminal ID and the time they logged in.

The command `who am i` prints only the information for the user logged on to the terminal from which the command was invoked. This form of the command is useful within shell scripts to determine whether the user running the script is authorized to do so:

```
set -- `who am i`
case $1 in
tom | mary | joe)
    # Authorized user
    ;;
*)
    # Unauthorized user
    echo "Sorry"
    exit
    ;;
esac
```

Regular Expressions

M any of the most useful UNIX commands are involved one way or another with searching files of text for strings that match a pattern. There are many other commands and programs that allow you to use string pattern matching to enhance the usefulness of the program. To make the most of your UNIX system, therefore, you must be able to write pattern matching expressions that will do what you want.

Definitions

All these programs use the same basic notation for describing a string pattern. This system of notation is called *regular expression*. Although not all commands support the full regular-expression notation, the meaning of an expression is the same in all commands that support it.

A regular expression (often called an *RE* in UNIX manuals) is itself a string of characters, some of which have special meaning (called *operators*) and others which simply stand for themselves (called *literal* characters). For example, the character * is an operator because it has a special meaning in a regular expression. The characters a through z are literals because they just represent themselves.

A regular expression can be simple or compound. A simple regular expression describes one character. A compound regular expression describes a sequence of characters and is written by running together a series of simple or compound regular expressions.

Operators

Table A.1 describes all the one-character regular expressions and operators in the full system of notation.

Table A.1. *Regular Expression Operators*

Operator	Meaning
.	Match any single character.
[*abc*]	Match *a*, *b*, or *c*.
[*a-z*]	Match range, matches any lower-case letter.
[^*e*]	Match any characters not in the set *e*, for example [^a-z] matches any character except a lowercase letter.
[]...]	Matches a right-bracket character in addition to any other characters or ranges specified.
^	Matches the beginning of a line of text.
$	Matches the end of a line of text.
a ¦ b	Matches either the expression *a* or the expression *b*.
( )	Groups a compound expression into a single expression or reference by operators such as * or ?.
*	Matches 0 or more occurrences of the immediately preceding single-character expression.
+	Matches one or more occurrences of the immediately preceding single-character expression.
?	Matches 0 or one occurrences of the immediately preceding single-character expression.
\(\)	The characters from the pattern space that are matched by the regular expression between these brackets are *noted*. They can be referenced later in the expression by the terms \1 (to reference the characters matched by the first \(\) term), \2 (second \(\) term), and so on.

Supported Regular Expressions

Table A.2 shows which regular-expression operators are supported by the various UNIX commands. All programs support the basic set of operators consisting of `.`, `[]`, `*`, `^`, and `$`. Additional support is shown in the table.

Table A.2. *Regular Expressions Supported by Various Commands*

Command	\(\)	|	+	?	0
awk	N	Y	Y	Y	Y
ed	Y	N	N	N	N
egrep	N	Y	Y	Y	Y
expr	Y	N	N	N	N
grep	Y	N	N	N	N
sed	Y	N	N	N	N
ex,vi	N	N	N	N	N

Examples

```
sed 's/\([a-z]\)\1/--/'
```

All occurrences of a doubled lowercase letter are changed to the string `--`. For example, the preceding sentence is changed to

```
A-- o--u--ences of a doubled lowercase le--er are
changed
      to the string --.
```

```
egrep '(^|[^a-zA-Z])(and¦or)([^a-zA-Z]¦$)' sample
```

This command prints every line of the file `sample` that contains the word `and` or `or`, but ignores letter sequences of the form `...and` (such as `command`) or `..or..` (such as `for`).

```
grep '^\.D[SE]' myfile
```

Presuming that `myfile` contains `nroff` text, this command displays all .DS and .DE macros in the file, allowing visual verification that they are present in matched pairs.

```
egrep 'this¦that¦those'
```

Every line in the standard input file that contains one or more of the words `this`, `that`, or `those` is printed.

B

Error Codes

The variable *errno* is fundamentally important to C programming in the UNIX environment. Every system call, and most of the standard library functions, return a value of -1 (or NULL) to indicate that an error was encountered during execution of the call. The error may be due to passing improper arguments to the function, external conditions (such as interruption of the function by a signal), or a great many other possible causes. Whenever a library function returns a value of -1, the function also will have set the *errno* variable to indicate the actual cause of the error.

Using errno

Your code can examine the value of *errno* to determine what kind of error occurred and what to do about it. In most cases, errors detected in system calls or library functions do not cause your program to terminate. You must check for the error and determine whether it is fatal. Then you should determine whether a recovery action should be taken, a warning message written, or the error ignored.

To examine the value of `errno`, you must include the `errno.h` header file in your source file using the instruction:

```
#include <errno.h>
```

which will not only declare the *errno* for the various error codes placed in *errno*, but also will declare the variable *errno* itself.

The exact list of errors that can occur varies from one UNIX system to another, and from one release or port of System V to another. The contents of errno.h defines the error codes that are common to all System V implementations, as well as those that are unique to your version. Consult the header file and your system's documentation to identify the complete list.

Many programs do not need to include the errno.h header file, and do not need to check *errno* for specific values, because it is often sufficient to just display the appropriate error message and terminate when an error occurs. A list of standard error messages is linked with your program in the form of an array of string pointers, such that the value of *errno*, when used as an index to this array, returns a pointer to the proper message text for the error. If you want to access the message text directly, include the following declarations in your program:

```
extern char *sys_errlist[];/* Array of system error messages */
extern int sys_nerr;       /* Highest legal array index */
```

When these values have been declared, you can include code such as the following in your program:

```
if ((input = fopen(filename, "r")) == NULL) {
    if (errno > sys_nerr)
        fprintf(stderr, "%s: Unknown error %d\n", filename,
errno);
    else
        fprintf(stderr, "%s: %s\n", filename, sys_errlist[errno]);
    exit(2); /* Abandon processing */
}
```

However, there is an easier way to print the message text corresponding to an errno value. Use the perror function.

The code sample above can be more easily written as follows:

```
if ((input = fopen(filename, "r")) == NULL) {
    perror(filename);  /* "filename: message" written to stderr */
    exit(4);           /* Abandon processing */
}
```

One final word of caution about using errno: system calls and library functions do not set the value of errno unless an error occurs. If no error occurs in function processing, the value of errno after the function call is *unpredictable*. You must always receive an error return from the function as a precondition to testing the value of errno. The following code is *wrong*:

```
pid = fork();          /* Create a child process */
if (errno == EAGAIN) { /* Not enough system resources */
    perror("fork");    /* Write error message */
        exit(31);      /* And exit. */
}
```

and the following code is *right*:

```
pid = fork();          /* Create a child process */
if (pid == -1) {       /* Error return from fork? */
    perror("fork");    /* Write error message */
    exit(31);          /* And exit. */
}
```

errno Values

The remainder of this appendix defines the error codes that can occur in all implementations of System V and the message text printed for each error. The codes have become relatively standard and are safe to use in programs intended to be portable.

You are cautioned against checking the value of errno for specific numeric values. Such code is *not* portable and will cause problems when you try to compile your program on another version of UNIX.

EPERM   *Not superuser.*

This error is returned when a system service that can only be performed by the superuser has been requested (i.e., a process having an effective user-ID value of 0). Functions returning this error include stime, nice when attempting to reduce the process scheduling priority, and unlink when attempting to remove a directory. This error can also be returned by kill when attempting to send a signal to a process not in the caller's process group.

ENOENT   *No such file or directory.*

Returned by open, creat, or unlink when one of the components of the specified pathname does not exist, by link when one of the components of the from pathname does not exist, and by the IPC functions msgget, semget, and shmget when the specified key does not exist and the IPC_CREATE flag is not specified in the call.

ESRCH *No such process.*

Returned by `kill` when no process exists with the specified process-ID.

EINTR *Interrupted system call.*

Returned by various system calls when a signal becomes pending for the process while the system is working. Any action taken by the system call is nullified, and control returns to the process after any user-defined signal-catching routine completes. The system call that returned this error should be retried. Note that this error cannot be caused by a signal for which the action is SIG_DFL (which causes the signaled process to be terminated) or SIG_IGN (which causes the signal to be ignored and, therefore, cannot interrupt the process or any system routine working on behalf of the process).

EIO *I/O error.*

This error can occur only as a result of a `read` or `write` call (or a library function such as `fprintf` that internally executes a `read` or `write` call) to a character-special file, and indicates that the device driver was unable to complete the I/O request because of a condition at the device. The condition need not be transient or directly hardware-related; for example, an attempt to write varying-size records to a tape drive may return this error. Additional information describing the I/O error is not made available to the user process, but may be recorded by the system error daemon, or be logged at the system console.

ENXIO *No such device or address.*

This error indicates that the system could not access the device defined by the major and minor device numbers of a special file. It is usually the result of an improperly created special file.

E2BIG *arg list too long.*

This error, returned by the `exec` system calls, indicates that the total length of all the argument strings to be passed to the called program is greater than can be held in the system buffer set aside for the purpose. The only circumvention is to attempt to pass fewer or shorter arguments to the called program. This error can also be returned by library functions that indirectly invoke the `exec` system calls, such as `system` and `popen`.

ENOEXEC   *exec format error.*

Returned by the `exec` system calls when the filename or pathname specified points to a file that is not in loadable binary format. Technically, it indicates that the file does not begin with a *magic number* recognized by the loader. This error is often the result of an attempt to execute a shell script with the `exec` calls. Scripts can only be executed indirectly by calling the appropriate shell program and passing the filename of the script as an argument to the shell.

EBADF   *Bad file number.*

Returned by the `read`, `write`, `close`, `lseek`, `fcntl`, or `ioctl` system calls when the file descriptor specified is not open. You must open the file first with the `open`, `creat`, or `pipe` system call.

ECHILD   *No children.*

Returned by the `wait` system call to indicate that there are no child processes for which to wait. Not normally a fatal error, this condition is returned to indicate to the calling program that no exit status was returned by the call.

EAGAIN   *No more processes.*

The EAGAIN error indicates that a service request could not be satisfied because of a temporary shortage of system resources. The request should be tried again later (not *immediately*) when some processes have terminated and relinquished their resources. Typical causes are calling `fork` when the system process table is full, or attempting to lock a file segment that is already locked by another process. This error is also returned by the `semop` function when attempting to decrement a semaphore, the attempt must be delayed, and IPC_NOWAIT is specified; by `semget`, `msgget`, and `shmget`, when the system limit on the total number of resources of that type has already been reached; and by `msgsnd` when the system limit on the number of queued messages has already been reached.

ENOMEM   *Not enough core.*

Returned by brk and sbrk when an attempt is made to adjust the process break address upward beyond the maximum allowed process size. Because the malloc, calloc, and realloc library functions internally call brk and sbrk, this error may be returned by one of those functions as well.

EACCES   *Permission denied.*

A service was requested that requires permissions the calling process does not have. Normally returned by open or creat when trying to read a read-protected file, to write a write-protected file, or to create a new file in a directory where the calling process does not have write permission. This error may also be returned by the msgctl, msgsnd, msgrcv, semctl, semop, shmctl, shmat, and shmds system calls when the calling process does not have permission to access or modify the specified message queue, semaphore, or shared-memory segment.

EFAULT   *Bad address.*

This error can be returned by any system call that is passed a pointer to an area in user process memory, when the pointer does not designate an address that is legal for the type of operation. In general, a memory area must be accessible by the user in the manner implied by the system call (fetch or modify) before the system routine will agree to operate on the memory area in that manner.

ENOTBLK   *Block device required.*

This is a catchall error returnable by file system management calls, such as mount, that require a block-special file as an argument, when the argument does not specify a block-special file. It is *not* returned as a response to an lseek call issued to an inappropriate device.

EBUSY   *Mount device busy.*

Returned by the mount system call when the named block-special file is already mounted, or another filesystem is already mounted at the directory specified as the mount point. Returned by the umount system call when the filesystem to be unmounted is in use and cannot be un-mounted (for example, when one or more files in the filesystem is currently open, or when one or more users has his current directory set to a directory in the filesystem).

EEXIST   *File exists.*

Returned by the `link` system call when the pathname specified by the *to* argument already exists.

EXDEV   *Cross-device link.*

Returned by the `link` system call when the pathname specified by the `to` argument would be created in a filesystem differing from the filesystem in which the directory entry for the `from` pathname exists. All directory entries for a given data file must be created in the same filesystem as the data file itself. This error cannot occur when creating symbolic links using the `symlink` system call.

ENODEV   *No such device.*

Returned by `read`, `write`, or `ioctl` when the device driver exists but has no entry point for the requested operation (for example, when attempting to read from a write-only device such as a printer). Unlike ENXIO, ENODEV is usually caused by user error.

ENOTDIR   *Not a directory.*

Returned by system calls (for example, `mount` or `chdir`) when an argument required to be the pathname of a directory does not point to a directory.

EISDIR   *Is a directory.*

Returned by `open` or `creat` when an existing file would be opened for output, and the file is a directory.

EINVAL   *Invalid argument.*

Returned by numerous functions to indicate that one of the arguments to the function does not have an acceptable value, and is often returned when the value of a coded argument is not one of the recognized codes. This error is caused by incorrect programming, or by using an improper value supplied to the program in a system call.

ENFILE   *File table overflow.*

Returned by open, creat, or pipe when there is no space in the system file table to make an entry for a new open file. This condition is not caused by user error; it is a result of the system being temporarily overloaded by the active set of processes. The open, creat, or pipe system call may succeed if tried again later.

EMFILE   *Too many open files.*

The installation-defined maximum number of files per user process has been exceeded when this error is returned by open, creat, or pipe. Unlike ENFILE, which can be retried, the only ways to circumvent an EMFILE error are to reduce the number of files the program attempts to open at one time, or to rebuild the kernel to support a larger maximum number of files per user process.

ENOTTY   *Not a typewriter.*

Returned by system calls, such as isatty and ioctl, that require the argument file descriptor to designate a terminal.

ETXTBSY   *Text file busy.*

Returned by unlink as a result of trying to remove an executable file while the file is being executed by some active process. UNIX will not remove a file while it is being executed.

EFBIG   *File too large.*

The file size set by ulimit would have been exceeded by a write system call. Only the number of bytes allowed by the file size limit were written.

ENOSPC   *No space left on device.*

This error occurs when no more space is available on the output device to write the full number of bytes requested. This error, when set by fcntl, indicates that there was no space available in the kernel tables to store a file lock description.

ESPIPE   *Illegal seek.*

Set by the lseek system call when the argument file descriptor designates a pipe or a FIFO (named pipe).

EROFS   *Read only file system.*

The EROFS error can be set by `chmod`, `chown`, `link`, `unlink`, or an I/O system call that attempts to modify a directory or file in a read-only file system

EMLINK   *Too many links.*

A maximum of 1000 links to a file are permitted. Note that the link created by `open` or `creat`, as well as links created by the `link` system call, counts toward this limit.

EPIPE   *Broken pipe.*

This error is set when any write to a pipe or FIFO is executed without the pipe open for input. Because the default action for the SIGPIPE signal is to terminate the process, the EPIPE error can be returned only when the signal (SIGPIPE) generated by this condition is caught or ignored by the process.

EDOM   *Math arg out of domain of func.*

Returned by various functions in the *math* (`-lm`) package to indicate that no valid result can be computed for the argument or arguments supplied.

ERANGE   *Math result not representable.*

This error is indicated when the result of a math function would be smaller than the smallest representable floating-point number, or larger than the largest representable floating-point number. The actual result returned will be `-HUGE` or `+HUGE` respectively as defined in the `math.h` header file. Note that this error cannot be caused by integer arithmetic.

ENOMSG   *No message of desired type.*

The `ENOMSG` message is displayed by the `perror` function when the actual value of `errno` is larger than `sys_nerr`, meaning that no message text exists for the error. The actual value of `errno` should never be ENOMSG.

EIDRM   *Identifier removed.*

If a process is blocked waiting for one of the IPC operations `msgsnd`, `msgrcv`, `semop`, `shmat`, or `shmds` to complete, *and* the message queue, semaphore, or shared-memory segment which is the target of the operation is removed by another process, the system awakens the suspended process and sets the EIDRM error as the reason for abandoning the operation. The program should abandon all attempts to access the resource because it no longer exists.

EDEADLK   *Deadlock condition.*

The f c n t l system call may return the EDEADLK error when an F_SETLKW operation could result in permanent blockage of the process. This condition can only arise when the process requesting a file-segment lock with F_SETLKW already holds one or more other file locks for which other processes are waiting. A program using file or record locking must employ algorithms which avoid deadlock situations. As a general rule, a process that already owns a resource for which other processes may be waiting should not request other resources. If it does, it should be prepared to tolerate the unavailability of additional resources.

C

Important Header Files

For the C programmer, the UNIX system is characterized more by the collection of header files and standard library functions than by the system's command set. This is as it should be. The UNIX user interface can be customized, as the success of graphical user interfaces such as OSF/Motif and Open Look testifies, but the C programming tools are fundamental to UNIX. The header files of a system contain declarations that are unique to that system, yet the symbols defined have become fairly standard. The header files have, therefore, become more than just a convenience; they are a cornerstone of portable UNIX programming in C.

This appendix presents the information you need to use the C library functions and UNIX system calls effectively. For example, to use the stat and fstat system calls, you need to know the contents of the structure they return; the entry for sys/stat.h contains that information. To use signals, you have to know the name and meaning of each signal code; that information is provided in the entry for signal.h.

This appendix provides a useful sample of the contents of each header file. However, because one of the purposes of header files is to allow for variations between machine types, system implementations, and compiler differences, the code should only be taken as illustrative. The actual values of constants and the data types of structure members are subject to change from one system to another. An actual structure declaration may contain more members than this book describes. As long as your programs make no assumptions about the values of constants and the data types or relative offsets of members within structures, these differences should not affect the validity of your source code.

The header files defined here are based on those provided with AT&T System V UNIX Release 3.2. Release 4 and the ANSI C standard introduce some additional new header files, while slightly earlier releases of System V omit some header files. This should not be too great a concern to you because the designers of System V attempted to preserve compatibility between the various releases of the system. Most programs do not and should not depend on the slight differences between each release of System V. If you base your programming on the information contained in this book, you should be able to compile and run your program on all releases of System V, and on many other UNIX implementations as well.

assert.h

Usage:

```
#include <assert.h>
```

Defines the `assert()` macro function.

ctype.h

Usage: `#include <ctype.h>`

Defines the following macros: `isalpha`, `isupper`, `islower`, `isdigit`, `isxdigit`, `isalnum`, `isspace`, `ispunct`, `isprint`, `isgraph`, `iscntrl`, `isascii`, `_toupper`, `_tolower`, `toascii`.

dirent.h

Usage:

```
#include <sys/types.h>
#include <dirent.h>
```

Defines elements of the portable directory access package.

Contents:

```
#include <sys/dir.h>            /* To define struct dirent */
```

```
typedef struct {
        int     dd_fd;      /* file descriptor */
        int     dd_loc;     /* offset in block */
        int     dd_size;    /* amount of valid data */
        char    *dd_buf;    /* -> directory block */
} DIR;                      /* stream data from opendir() */

extern DIR              *opendir  (char *path);
extern struct dirent    *readdir  (DIR *dirp);
extern off_t            telldir   (DIR *dirp);
extern void             seekdir   (DIR *dirp, off_t loc);
extern void             rewinddir (DIR *dirp);
extern int              closedir  (DIR *dirp);
```

errno.h

Usage:

```
#include <errno.h>
```

Provides access to the *errno* external variable.

Contents:

```
extern int errno;

#define EPERM   1    /* Not superuser              */
#define ENOENT  2    /* No such file or directory  */
#define ESRCH   3    /* No such process            */
#define EINTR   4    /* interrupted system call    */
#define EIO     5    /* I/O error                  */
#define ENXIO   6    /* No such device or address  */
#define E2BIG   7    /* Arg list too long          */
#define ENOEXEC 8    /* Exec format error          */
#define EBADF   9    /* Bad file number            */
#define ECHILD  10   /* No children                */
#define EAGAIN  11   /* No more processes          */
#define ENOMEM  12   /* Not enough core            */
#define EACCES  13   /* Permission denied          */
#define EFAULT  14   /* Bad address                */
#define ENOTBLK 15   /* Block device required      */
#define EBUSY   16   /* Mount device busy          */
#define EEXIST  17   /* File exists                */
#define EXDEV   18   /* Cross-device link          */
#define ENODEV  19   /* No such device             */
#define ENOTDIR 20   /* Not a directory            */
#define EISDIR  21   /* Is a directory             */
#define EINVAL  22   /* Invalid argument           */
#define ENFILE  23   /* File table overflow        */
#define EMFILE  24   /* Too many open files        */
```

```
#define ENOTTY   25   /* Not a typewriter           */
#define ETXTBSY  26   /* Text file busy             */
#define EFBIG    27   /* File too large             */
#define ENOSPC   28   /* No space left on device    */
#define ESPIPE   29   /* Illegal seek               */
#define EROFS    30   /* Read only file system      */
#define EMLINK   31   /* Too many links             */
#define EPIPE    32   /* Broken pipe                */
#define EDOM     33   /* Arg out of domain of func  */
#define ERANGE   34   /* Result not representable    */
#define ENOMSG   35   /* No message of desired type */
#define EIDRM    36   /* Identifier removed         */
#define EDEADLK  45   /* Deadlock condition.        */
```

fcntl.h

Usage:

```
#include <fcntl.h>
```

Defines symbolic constants for use in the open() and fcntl() system calls,
the fcntl_arg union used as the type of the third fcntl argument, and struct
flock for describing a lock request.

Contents:

```
/* Flag values accessible to open() and fcntl() */
/*  (The first three can only be set by open) */

#define O_RDONLY 0       /* Read-only file descriptor */
#define O_WRONLY 1       /* Write-only file descriptor */
#define O_RDWR   2       /* Both read and write to file */
#define O_NDELAY 04      /* Do not wait on I/O to pipe */
#define O_APPEND 010     /* Append to file */
#define O_SYNC   020     /* Force output to occur on write */

/* Flag values accessible only to open */

#define O_CREAT 00400     /* Create file if it does not exist */
#define O_TRUNC 01000     /* Truncate existing file to zero length */
#define O_EXCL  02000     /* Fail if file already exists */

/* fcntl() requests */

#define F_DUPFD  0   /* Duplicate fildes */
#define F_GETFD  1   /* Get fildes flags */
#define F_SETFD  2   /* Set fildes flags */
#define F_GETFL  3   /* Get file flags */
#define F_SETFL  4   /* Set file flags */
#define F_GETLK  5   /* Get file lock */
```

```
#define F_SETLK    6    /* Set file lock */
#define F_SETLKW   7    /* Set file lock and wait */

/* file segment locking request - passed to system by user */

struct flock {
    short       l_type;          /* Type of request, see below */
    short       l_whence;        /* Origin for l_start, see unistd.h */
    long        l_start;         /* Starting offset of file segment */
    long        l_len;           /* Length of file segment */
    int         l_pid;           /* Set by system for F_GETLK request */ };

/* file segment locking types */

#define F_RDLCK 01    /* Read lock */
#define F_WRLCK 02    /* Write lock */
#define F_UNLCK 03    /* Remove lock */

/* Union for the third argument of fcntl */

union fcntl_arg {
        struct flock    *sfparg;
        int             iarg;
};
```

ftw.h

Usage:

```
#include <ftw.h>
```

Defines the constants FTW_F, FTW_D, FTW_DNR, and FTW_NS.

grp.h

Usage:

```
#include <grp.h>
```

Defines struct group and the /etc/group file access functions.

Contents:

```
struct group {
    char        *gr_name;        /* Name of group */
    char        *gr_passwd;      /* Password for newgrp(1) command */
    int         gr_gid;          /* Group-ID */
    char        **gr_mem;        /* Login names of members of group */
};
```

```
extern struct group *     getgrent (void);
extern struct group *     getgrgid (int group_id);
extern struct group *     getgrnam (char *name);
extern void               setgrent (void);
extern void               endgrent (void);
extern struct group *     fgetgrent(FILE *);
```

limits.h

Usage:

```
#include <limits.h>
```

New with System V Release 3.2 and required by the ANSI C standard, the limits.h header defines values that are dependent on the machine, operating system environment, or system configuration. The following symbolic values should be used in preference to hard-coded constants whenever possible.

Contents:

CHAR_BIT	Number of bits in a char variable.
WORD_BIT	Number of bits in an int variable.
CHAR_MAX	Maximum value of a char variable.
CHAR_MIN	Minimum value of a char variable.
SHRT_MAX	Maximum value of a short variable.
SHRT_MIN	Minimum value of a short variable.
INT_MAX	Maximum value of an int variable.
INT_MIN	Minimum value of an int variable.
USI_MAX	Maximum value of an unsigned integer variable.
LONG_MAX	Maximum value of a long.
LONG_MIN	Minimum value of a long.
FLT_DIG	Number of digits of precision of a float.
DBL_DIG	Number of digits of precision of a double.
FLT_MIN	Minimum representable value of a float.
FLT_MAX	Maximum representable value of a float.
DBL_MIN	Minimum representable value of a double.

DBL_MAX	Maximum representable value of a `double`.
HUGE_VAL	Error value returned by math library on overflow.
LINK_MAX	Maximum number of links to a single file.
OPEN_MAX	Maximum number of files a process can have open at one time.
NAME_MAX	Maximum number of characters in a file name.
PATH_MAX	Maximum number of characters in a path name.
STD_BLK	Number of bytes in a physical I/O block.
PIPE_MAX	Maximum number of bytes to write to a pipe.
PIPE_BUF	Maximum number of bytes in atomic write to pipe.
ARG_MAX	Maximum length of argument strings supported by the `exec` system calls.
CLK_TCK	Number of clock ticks per second.
SYS_NMLN	Length of the strings returned by the `uname` system call.
PID_MAX	Largest process ID that can occur.
UID_MAX	Largest user or group ID that can be represented.
PASS_MAX	Maximum number of characters in a password.
FCHR_MAX	Maximum filesize in bytes.
CHILD_MAX	Maximum number of processes allowed per user-ID.

malloc.h

Usage:

```
#include <malloc.h>
```

Required when using the `malloc`, `calloc`, `realloc`, `mallopt` and `mallinfo` functions.

Contents:

Defines the constants M_MXFAST, M_NLBLKS, M_GRAIN, and M_KEEP. Defines the structure filled in by `mallinfo` as follows:

```
struct mallinfo {
    int arena;      /* total space in arena */
    int ordblks;    /* number of ordinary blocks */
    int smblks;     /* number of small blocks */
    int hblks;      /* number of holding blocks */
    int hblkhd;     /* space in holding block headers */
    int usmblks;    /* space in small blocks in use */
    int fsmblks;    /* space in free small blocks */
    int uordblks;   /* space in ordinary blocks in use */
    int fordblks;   /* space in free ordinary blocks */
    int keepcost;   /* cost of enabling keep option */
};

extern void *   malloc  (size_t size);
extern void *   calloc  (size_t nelems, size_t elemsize);
extern void *   realloc (void *block, size_t size);
extern void     free    (void *block);
extern int      mallopt (int cmd, int value);
extern struct mallinfo mallinfo(int max);
```

math.h

Usage:

```
#include <math.h>
```

Required when using any of the math library functions.

Contents:

```
extern int errno, signgam;

extern double atof(), frexp(), ldexp(), modf();
extern double j0(), j1(), jn(), y0(), y1(), yn();
extern double erf(), erfc();
extern double exp(), log(), log10(), pow(), sqrt();
extern double floor(), ceil(), fmod(), fabs();
extern double gamma();
extern double hypot();
extern int matherr();
extern double sinh(), cosh(), tanh();
extern double sin(), cos(), tan(), asin(), acos(), atan(), atan2();

#define M_E         2.7182818284590452354
#define M_LOG2E     1.4426950408889634074
#define M_LOG10E    0.43429448190325182765
#define M_LN2       0.69314718055994530942
#define M_LN10      2.30258509299404568402
#define M_PI        3.14159265358979323846
#define M_PI_2      1.57079632679489661923
#define M_PI_4      0.78539816339744830962
```

```
#define M_1_PI      0.31830988618379067154
#define M_2_PI      0.63661977236758134308
#define M_2_SQRTPI  1.12837916709551257390
#define M_SQRT2     1.41421356237309504880
#define M_SQRT1_2   0.70710678118654752440
#define MAXFLOAT      /* A machine dependent value */
#define HUGE      MAXFLOAT

#define _ABS(x) ((x) < 0 ? -(x) : (x))
#define _REDUCE(TYPE, X, XN, C1, C2)    { \
        double x1 = (double)(TYPE)X, x2 = X - x1; \
        X = x1 - (XN) * (C1); X += x2; X -= (XN) * (C2); }
#define _POLY1(x, c)    ((e)[0] * (x) + (e)[1])
#define _POLY2(x, c)    (_POLY1((x), (e)) * (x) + (e)[2])
#define _POLY3(x, c)    (_POLY2((x), (e)) * (x) + (e)[3])
#define _POLY4(x, c)    (_POLY3((x), (e)) * (x) + (e)[4])
#define _POLY5(x, c)    (_POLY4((x), (e)) * (x) + (e)[5])
#define _POLY6(x, c)    (_POLY5((x), (e)) * (x) + (e)[6])
#define _POLY7(x, c)    (_POLY6((x), (e)) * (x) + (e)[7])
#define _POLY8(x, c)    (_POLY7((x), (e)) * (x) + (e)[8])
#define _POLY9(x, c)    (_POLY8((x), (e)) * (x) + (e)[9])

struct exception {
    int type;
    char *name;
    double arg1;
    double arg2;
    double retval;
};

#define DOMAIN      1
#define SING        2
#define OVERFLOW    3
#define UNDERFLOW   4
#define TLOSS       5
#define PLOSS       6
```

memory.h

Usage:

```
#include <memory.h>
```

Provides convenience declarations for the byte-handling functions.

Contents:

```
extern void     *memccpy (void *s1, const void *s2, int c, size_t n);
extern void     *memchr  (const void *s, int c, size_t n);
extern void     *memcpy  (void *s1, const void *s2, size_t n);
extern void     *memset  (void *s, int c, size_t n);
extern int       memcmp  (const void *s1, const void *s2, size_t n);
```

pwd.h

Usage:

```
#include <pwd.h>
```

Required when using the /etc/passwd file access functions getpwent, getpwuid, getpwnam, fgetpwent, setpwent, and endpwent.

Contents:

```
/* The passwd struct breaks out a line of the /etc/passwd file.
 * Note that unspecified or omitted fields are zero-length strings.
 */
struct passwd {
        char    *pw_name;       /* User login name */
        char    *pw_passwd;     /* Encrypted password */
        int     pw_uid;         /* User id */
        int     pw_gid;         /* Group id */
        char    *pw_age;        /* Password aging or not used */
        char    *pw_comment;    /* Not used */
        char    *pw_gecos;      /* Fifth field of passwd line */
        char    *pw_dir;        /* Home directory pathname */
        char    *pw_shell;      /* Login shell pathname */
};

extern struct passwd *  getpwent (void);
extern struct passwd *  getpwuid (int user_id);
extern struct passwd *  getpwnam (char *name);
extern void             setpwent (void);
extern void             endpwent (void);
extern struct passwd *  fgetpwent(FILE *);
extern int              putpwent (struct passwd *, FILE *);
```

setjmp.h

Usage:

```
#include <setjmp.h>
```

Must be included when using the longjmp() or setjmp() library functions.

Contents:

```
#define _JBLEN   ? /* Machine-dependent value */
typedef int     jmp_buf[_JBLEN];

extern int      setjmp (jmp_buf env);
extern void     longjmp (jmp_buf env, int code);
```

shadow.h

Usage:

```
#include <sys/types.h>
#include <shadow.h>
```

In System V Release 3.2 and later, password information is not returned in the `passwd` structure. Instead, `pw_passwd` points to the string "x", and the password can be obtained only by use of one of the shadow password functions `getspent`, `fgetspent`, or `getspnam`. These functions return a `spwd` structure, which is described in the `shadow.h` header file.

Contents:

```
#define PASSWD      "/etc/passwd"
#define SHADOW      "/etc/shadow"
#define OPASSWD     "/etc/opasswd"
#define OSHADOW     "/etc/oshadow"
#define PASSTEMP    "/etc/ptmp"
#define SHADTEMP    "/etc/stmp"

#define DAY         (24L * 60 * 60)
#define DAY_NOW     (time_t)time((time_t *)0) / DAY

struct spwd {
    char      *sp_namp;       /* User login name */
    char      *sp_pwdp;       /* Encrypted password */
    time_t    sp_lstchg;      /* Date of last password change */
    time_t    sp_min;         /* Minimum age of password */
    time_t    sp_max;         /* Maximum age of password */
};
```

signal.h

Usage:

```
#include <signal.h>
```

Must be included when using the `signal` system call.

Contents:

```
extern void (*signal(int sig, void (*handler)()))();

#define SIGHUP  1   /* Hangup */
#define SIGINT  2   /* Interrupt key */
#define SIGQUIT 3   /* Quit key */
```

```
#define SIGILL  4    /* Illegal instruction (not reset) */
#define SIGTRAP 5    /* Trace trap (not reset) */
#define SIGIOT  6    /* System error */
#define SIGEMT  7    /* System error */
#define SIGFPE  8    /* Floating point exception */
#define SIGKILL 9    /* Kill (cannot be caught or ignored) */
#define SIGBUS  10   /* Bus error */
#define SIGSEGV 11   /* Segmentation violation */
#define SIGSYS  12   /* Bad argument to system call */
#define SIGPIPE 13   /* Broken pipe error */
#define SIGALRM 14   /* Alarm clock expired */
#define SIGTERM 15   /* Termination signal from kill */
#define SIGUSR1 16   /* Reserved for user signal 1 */
#define SIGUSR2 17   /* Reserved for user signal 2 */
#define SIGCLD  18   /* Death of a child */
#define SIGPWR  19   /* Power-fail restart */

#define NSIG    20   /* Number of signals */

#define SIG_DFL (void (*)())0
#define SIG_IGN (void (*)())1
```

stdio.h

Usage:

```
#include <stdio.h>
```

Required when using the standard I/O function package, and whenever the machine-dependent values EOF or NULL are used. As a general rule, this header file should be included in all C programs.

Contents:

The contents of the stdio.h header file are highly machine-dependent. The following is intended only to be taken as an example.

```
/* @(#) stdio.h 1.1
 * standard-I/O interface definitions
 */
#ifndef NULL
#define NULL    ((void *)0)
#endif

#ifndef EOF
#define EOF     (-1)
#endif

#define _NFILE  20      /* Max number of open files per process */
#define BUFSIZ  1024    /* Default buffer size for stdio files */
#define _SBFSIZ 8       /* suggested buffer size for unbuffered files */
```

```
typedef struct {
#if || vax || u3b || u3b5
        int       _cnt;
        unsigned char    *_ptr;
#else
        unsigned char    *_ptr;
        int       _cnt;
#endif
        unsigned char    *_base;
        char      _flag;
        char      _file;
} FILE;

/* Values for _flag */

#define _IOFBF      0000    /* Fully buffered file */
#define _IOREAD     0001    /* Input file */
#define _IOWRT      0002    /* Output file */
#define _IONBF      0004    /* Unbuffered file */
#define _IOMYBUF    0010    /* Buffer was allocated by stdio */
#define _IOEOF      0020    /* End of file indicator */
#define _IOERR      0040    /* I/O error indicator */
#define _IOLBF      0100    /* Line-buffered file */
#define _IORW       0200    /* Both read and write */

#define stdin       (&_iob[0])
#define stdout      (&_iob[1])
#define stderr      (&_iob[2])

/* Define macros for performance */
#define getc(iob)       ...
#define putc(c, iob)    ...
#define getchar()       getc(stdin)
#define putchar(e)      putc((e), stdout)
#define clearerr(iob)   ...
#define feof(iob)       ((iob)->_flag & _IOEOF)
#define ferror(iob)     ((iob)->_flag & _IOERR)
#define fileno(iob)     (iob)->_file

extern FILE    _iob[_NFILE];
extern FILE    *fopen(), *fdopen(), *freopen(), *popen(), *tmpfile();
extern long    ftell();
extern void    rewind(), setbuf();
extern char    *ctermid(), *cuserid(), *fgets(), *gets();
extern char    *tempnam(), *tmpnam();

#define L_ctermid       9
#define L_cuserid       9
#define P_tmpdir        "/usr/tmp/"
#define L_tmpnam        (sizeof(P_tmpdir) + 15)
```

---

string.h

Usage:

```
#include <string.h>
```

Declares functions in the string-handling package.

Contents:

```
/* @(#) string.h 1.1
 * Interface to the string-handling package
 */

char *    strcat   (char *s1, const char *s2);
char *    strchr   (const char *s, int c);
int       strcmp   (const char *s1, const char *s2);
char *    strcpy   (char *s1, const char *s2);
size_t    strcspn  (const char *s1, const char *s2);
char *    strdup   (const char *s);
size_t    strlen   (const char *s);
char *    strncat  (char *s1, const char *s2, size_t n);
int       strncmp  (const char *s1, const char *s2, size_t n);
char *    strncpy  (char *s1, const char *s2, size_t n);
char *    strpbrk  (const char *s1, const char *s2);
char *    strrchr  (const char *s, int c);
size_t    strspn   (const char *s1, const char *s2);
char *    strtok   (char *s1, const char *s2);
```

---

sys/dir.h

Usage:

```
#include <sys/types.h>
#include <sys/dir.h>
```

The `sys/dir.h` header file is not required to be present. If present, it describes the format of a directory entry on disk. Note that the `dirent.h` header and function package should be used for reading directories whenever possible.

Contents: Traditionally, the directory entry contains only two members, `d_ino`, giving the inode number that describes the file, and `d_name`, giving the filename of the directory entry. Modern filesystem implementations may include additional members in the directory entry, may support variable-length filenames, or may deviate from traditional formats in other ways.

```
#define DIRSIZ  14       /* Maximum length of a filename */
```

```
struct direct {
        ino_t   d_ino;
        char    d_name[DIRSIZ];
};
```

sys/ipc.h

Usage:

```
#include <sys/types.h>
#include <sys/ipc.h>
```

Defines manifest constants, data structures, and functions used by the various IPC function calls. This header must be included when using any IPC function.

Contents:

```
/* format of the operation permissions structure */
struct ipc_perm {
        ushort   uid;        /* Owner's user id */
        ushort   gid;        /* Owner's group id */
        ushort   cuid;       /* Creator's user id */
        ushort   cgid;       /* Creator's group id */
        ushort   mode;       /* Access permissions */
};

#define IPC_CREAT  0001000    /* Ok to create new entry */
#define IPC_EXCL   0002000    /* Fail if key exists */
#define IPC_NOWAIT 0004000    /* Fail if request must wait */

#define IPC_PRIVATE ((key_t)0)  /* Private key */

/* Control Commands. */
#define IPC_RMID      0       /* Remove identifier */
#define IPC_SET       1       /* Set options */
#define IPC_STAT      2       /* Get options */
```

sys/msg.h

Usage:

```
#include <sys/types.h>
#include <sys/ipc.h>
#include <sys/msg.h>
```

Gives definitions required for IPC message-queue operations.

Contents: At least the following macros and structures must be defined by the sys/msg.h header. The indicated values are illustrative.

```
/* Message operation flags */
#define MSG_NOERROR 010000      /* no error if big message */

/* Message-queue identification structure */
struct msqid_ds {
        struct ipc_perm msg_perm; /* operation permission struct */
        ushort   msg_qnum;          /* Num of messages on queue */
        ushort   msg_qbytes;        /* Max num of bytes on queue */
        ushort   msg_lspid;         /* Pid of last msgsnd */
        ushort   msg_lrpid;         /* Pid of last msgrcv */
        time_t   msg_stime;         /* Last msgsnd clock time */
        time_t   msg_rtime;         /* Last msgrcv clock time */
        time_t   msg_ctime;         /* Last change clock time */
};

/* User message buffer */
struct msgbuf {
        long     mtype;             /* message type */
        char     mtext[1];          /* message text */
};
```

sys/sem.h

Usage:

```
#include <sys/types.h>
#include sys/ipc.h>
#include <sys/sem.h>
```

Gives definitions required for IPC semaphore operations.

Contents: At least the following macros and structures must be defined by the sys/sem.h header. The indicated values are illustrative.

```
/* Semaphore operation flags */
#define SEM_UNDO 010000 /* adjust semval on exit */

/* semctl commands */
#define GETNCNT 3
#define GETZCNT 4
#define GETPID  5
#define GETVAL  6
#define SETVAL  7
#define GETALL  8
#define SETALL  9

/* semaphore identification structure */
struct semid_ds {
        struct ipc_perm sem_perm; /* operation permission struct */
        ushort   sem_nsems;         /* Num of semaphores in set */
        time_t   sem_otime;         /* Last semop clock time */
```

```
        time_t  sem_ctime;        /* Last change clock time */
};

/* semop operation structure */
struct sembuf {
        ushort  sem_num;          /* semaphore number */
        short   sem_op;           /* operation */
        short   sem_flg;          /* flags */
};
```

sys/shm.h

Usage:

```
#include <sys/types.h>
#include sys/ipc.h>
#include <sys/shm.h>
```

Gives definitions required for IPC shared-memory operations.

Contents: At least the following macros and structures must be defined by the
sys/shm.h header. The indicated values are illustrative.

```
/* Message operation flags */
#define SHM_RDONLY 010000     /* attach read-only */
#define SHM_RND    020000     /* round attach address to SHMLBA */

/* Shared-memory identification structure */
struct shmid_ds {
        struct ipc_perm shm_perm; /* operation permissions */
        uint    shm_segsz;        /* segment size */
        ushort  shm_cpid;         /* pid of creator */
        ushort  shm_lpid;         /* pid of last shmop */
        ushort  shm_nattch;       /* current # attached */
        time_t  shm_atime;        /* last shmat time */
        time_t  shm_dtime;        /* last shmdt time */
        time_t  shm_ctime;        /* last change time */
};
```

sys/stat.h

Usage:

```
#include <sys/types.h>
#include <sys/stat.h>
```

Declares the stat structure returned by the stat() and fstat() functions.

Contents:

```
struct stat {
        dev_t    st_dev;          /* Filesystem containing this inode */
        ino_t    st_ino;          /* Inode number */
        ushort   st_mode;         /* file type and permissions */
        short    st_nlink;        /* number of links */
        ushort   st_uid;          /* owner ID */
        ushort   st_gid;          /* group ID */
        dev_t    st_rdev;         /* major & minor device numbers */
        off_t    st_size;         /* Size of file in bytes */
        time_t   st_atime;        /* Clock time of last access */
        time_t   st_mtime;        /* Clock time of last modify */
        time_t   st_ctime;        /* Clock time of last inode change */
};

#define S_IFMT    0170000         /* File mode, one of */
#define S_IFDIR   0040000         /* is directory */
#define S_IFCHR   0020000         /* is character-special */
#define S_IFBLK   0060000         /* is block-special */
#define S_IFREG   0100000         /* is regular */
#define S_IFIFO   0010000         /* is fifo (named pipe) */
#define S_ISUID   04000           /* set user id on execution */
#define S_ISGID   02000           /* set group id on execution */
#define S_ISVTX   01000           /* save swapped text even after use */
#define S_IREAD   00400           /* read permission for owner */
#define S_IWRITE  00200           /* write permission for owner */
#define S_IEXEC   00100           /* execute permission for owner */
```

sys/types.h

Usage:

```
#include <sys/types.h>
```

Gives typedef names for data types special to the system. This header file must be included in front of any other header containing system-dependent data.

Contents: The following is only a suggestion. Your system may define additional data types, or may define the types differently.

```
/* BSD style typenames */
typedef unsigned char    u_char;
typedef unsigned short   u_short;
typedef unsigned int     u_int;
typedef unsigned long    u_long;

/* System V style typenames */
typedef unsigned short   ushort;
typedef unsigned int     uint;
typedef unsigned char    unchar;
```

```
/* Common data types */
typedef u_int    size_t;        /* Size of a memory area in bytes */
typedef long     time_t;        /* Clock value */
typedef long     fpos_t;        /* File pointer */
typedef u_short  uid_t;         /* User id */
typedef u_short  gid_t;         /* Group id */
typedef long     key_t;         /* IPC key */

/* Miscellaneous data types */
typedef long     daddr_t;       /* Disk address */
typedef char *   caddr_t;       /* String address */
typedef u_long   ino_t;         /* inode number */
typedef long     dev_t;         /* Filesystem identifier */
typedef long     off_t;
typedef long     paddr_t;
typedef short    cnt_t;
```

termio.h

Usage:

```
#include <termio.h>
```

Defines the `ioctl` serial terminal interface.

Contents:

```
#define NCC      8   /* Number of elements in c_cc */

/* c_cc control characters */
#define VINTR    0   /* keyboard INTERRUPT character */
#define VQUIT    1   /* keyboard QUIT key */
#define VERASE   2   /* keyboard ERASE key (discard last char) */
#define VKILL    3   /* keyboard KILL key (discard last line) */
#define VEOF     4   /* keyboard EOF key */
#define VEOL     5   /* line delimiter (ASCII LF) */
#define VEOL2    6   /* additional line delimiter (ASCII NUL) */
#define VMIN     4   /* min chars to satisfy read */
#define VTIME    5   /* max time to wait for input */
#define VSWTCH   7   /* switch between shell layers */

/* default control chars */
#define CINTR    0177   /* DEL */
#define CQUIT    034    /* FS, Ctrl-| */
#define CERASE   '#'
#define CKILL    '@'
#define CEOF     04     /* Ctrl-D */
#define CSTART   021    /* Ctrl-Q */
#define CSTOP    023    /* Ctrl-S */
#define CSWTCH   032    /* Ctrl-Z */
#define CNSWTCH  0
#define CESC     '\\'
```

```
#define CNUL      0
#define CDEL      0377

/* c_iflag - input mode flags */
#define IGNBRK    0000001    /* Ignore BREAK */
#define BRKINT    0000002    /* Signal INTR on break */
#define IGNPAR    0000004    /* Ignore parity errors */
#define PARMRK    0000010    /* Mark parity errors */
#define INPCK     0000020    /* Enable input parity check */
#define ISTRIP    0000040    /* Strip eighth bit */
#define INLCR     0000100    /* Map NL to CR on input */
#define IGNCR     0000200    /* Ignore CR on input */
#define ICRNL     0000400    /* Map CR to NL on input */
#define IUCLC     0001000    /* Map upper to lower case */
#define IXON      0002000    /* Enable start/stop control */
#define IXANY     0004000    /* Restart output on any char */
#define IXOFF     0010000    /* Disable start/stop control */

/* c_oflag - output mode flags */
#define OPOST     0000001    /* Enable other flags          */
#define OLCUC     0000002    /* Map lower-case to upper      */
#define ONLCR     0000004    /* Map NL to CR-NL on output     */
#define OCRNL     0000010    /* Map CR to NL on output        */
#define ONOCR     0000020    /* Suppress CR at column 0       */
#define ONLRET    0000040    /* NL performs CR function       */
#define OFILL     0000100    /* Use fill chars for delay      */
#define OFDEL     0000200    /* Fill is DEL, else NULL        */
#define NLDLY     0000400    /* Delay after newlines:         */
#define NL0       0          /*    "    no delay selected     */
#define NL1       0000400    /*    "    about 0.10 secs        */
#define CRDLY     0003000    /* Delay after carriage returns  */
#define CR0       0          /*    "    no delay selected     */
#define CR1       0001000    /*    "    depends on column      */
#define CR2       0002000    /*    "    about 0.10 secs        */
#define CR3       0003000    /*    "    about 0.15 secs        */
#define TABDLY    0014000    /* Delay after horizontal tabs:  */
#define TAB0      0          /*    "    no delay selected     */
#define TAB1      0004000    /*    "    depends on column      */
#define TAB2      0010000    /*    "    about 0.10 secs        */
#define TAB3      0014000    /*    "    expand tabs to spaces  */
#define BSDLY     0020000    /* Delay after backspace:        */
#define BS0       0          /*    "    no delay selected     */
#define BS1       0020000    /*    "    about 0.05 secs        */
#define VTDLY     0040000    /* Delay after vertical tab:     */
#define VT0       0          /*    "    no delay selected     */
#define VT1       0040000    /*    "    about 2 secs           */
#define FFDLY     0100000    /* Delay after form feed:        */
#define FF0       0          /*    "    no delay selected     */
#define FF1       0100000    /*    "    about 2 secs           */

/* control modes */
#define CBAUD     0000017    /* Baud rate:         */
#define B0        0          /* Hang up            */
```

```
#define B50     0000001     /* 50 bps            */
#define B75     0000002     /* 75 bps            */
#define B110    0000003     /* 110 bps           */
#define B134    0000004     /* 134.5 bps         */
#define B150    0000005     /* 150 bps           */
#define B200    0000006     /* 200 bps           */
#define B300    0000007     /* 300 bps           */
#define B600    0000010     /* 600 bps           */
#define B1200   0000011     /* 1200 bps          */
#define B1800   0000012     /* 1800 bps          */
#define B2400   0000013     /* 2400 bps          */
#define B4800   0000014     /* 4800 bps          */
#define B9600   0000015     /* 9600 bps          */
#define EXTA    0000016     /* 19,200 bps        */
#define EXTB    0000017     /* External B        */
#define CSIZE   0000060     /* Character size:   */
#define CS5     0           /* 5 bits            */
#define CS6     0000020     /* 6 bits            */
#define CS7     0000040     /* 7 bits            */
#define CS8     0000060     /* 8 bits            */
#define CSTOPB  0000100     /* Two stop bits, else one */
#define CREAD   0000200     /* enable receiver   */
#define PARENB  0000400     /* Parity enable     */
#define PARODD  0001000     /* Odd parity, else even */
#define HUPCL   0002000     /* Hang up on last close */
#define CLOCAL  0004000     /* Local, else modem control */
#define LOBLK   0010000     /* Block layer output    */

/* c_lflag - line discipline 0 mode flags */
#define ISIG    0000001     /* Enable signals */
#define ICANON  0000002     /* Canonical input (erase and kill) */
#define XCASE   0000004     /* Canonical upper/lower presentation */
#define ECHO    0000010     /* Enable echo */
#define ECHOE   0000020     /* Echo erase as BS-SP-BS */
#define ECHOK   0000040     /* Echo NL after kill char */
#define ECHONL  0000100     /* Echo NL */
#define NOFLSH  0000200     /* Disable flush after INTR or QUIT */

#define SSPEED  13          /* default speed: 9600 baud */

/*
 * Ioctl control packet (ioctl arg 3)
 */
struct termio {
        unsigned short  c_iflag;            /* Input modes */
        unsigned short  c_oflag;            /* Output modes */
        unsigned short  c_cflag;            /* Control modes */
        unsigned short  c_lflag;            /* Line discipline modes */
        char    c_line;                     /* Line discipline */
        unsigned char   c_cc[NCC];          /* Control chars */
};
```

```
/*
 * Ioctl commands (ioctl arg 2)
 */
#define TIOC    ('T'<<8)
#define TCGETA  (TIOC|1)
#define TCSETA  (TIOC|2)
#define TCSETAW (TIOC|3)
#define TCSETAF (TIOC|4)
```

time.h

Usage:

```
#include <sys/types.h>
#include <time.h>
```

Declares date and time handling functions. Declares the `tm` structure.

Contents:

```
struct tm {
        int     tm_sec;   /* Seconds (0-59)          */
        int     tm_min;   /* Minutes (0-59)          */
        int     tm_hour;  /* Hours (0-23)            */
        int     tm_mday;  /* Day of month (1-31)     */
        int     tm_mon;   /* Month (0-11)            */
        int     tm_year;  /* Year - 1900             */
        int     tm_wday;  /* Day of week (Sunday = 0) */
        int     tm_yday;  /* Day of year (0-365)     */
        int     tm_isdst; /* Daylight saving time    */
};

struct tm *gmtime(time_t *clock);
struct tm *localtime(time_t *clock);
char    *asctime(strúct tm *tm);
char    *ctime(time_t *clock);
void    tzset(void);
time_t  timezone;
int     daylight;
char    *tzname[];
```

unistd.h

Usage:

```
#include <unistd.h>
```

Provides definitions for various manifest constants.

Contents:

```
/* access() mode (arg 2) */
#define R_OK    4    /* Test for read permission */
#define W_OK    2    /* Test for write permission */
#define X_OK    1    /* Test for execute permission */
#define F_OK    0    /* Test for existence of file */

/* lockf() function (arg 2) */
#define F_ULOCK 0    /* Unlock a previously locked segment */
#define F_LOCK  1    /* Lock a segment for exclusive use */
#define F_TLOCK 2    /* Test and lock a segment for exclusive use */
#define F_TEST  3    /* Test a segment for other process locks */

/* lseek origin (arg 3) */
#define SEEK_SET 0   /* Relative to begin of file */
#define SEEK_CUR 1   /* Relative to current position */
#define SEEK_END 2   /* Relative to end of file */
```

ustat.h

Usage:

```
#include <sys/types.h>
#include <ustat.h>
```

Declares the structure returned by ustat.

Contents:

```
struct   ustat {
         daddr_t   f_tfree;      /* total free blocks */
         ino_t     f_tinode;     /* total free inodes */
         char      f_fname[6];   /* filsystem name */
         char      f_fpack[6];   /* volume name */
};
```

utmp.h

Usage:

```
#include <sys/types.h>
#include <utmp.h>
```

Declares the utmp structure and the file access functions.

Contents:

```
#define UTMP_FILE    "/etc/utmp"
#define WTMP_FILE    "/etc/wtmp"
#define ut_name ut_user
```

```
struct utmp {
        char ut_user[8];                /* User login name */
        char ut_id[4];                  /* /etc/lines id(usually line #) */
        char ut_line[12];               /* device name (console, lnxx) */
        short ut_pid;                   /* process id */
        short ut_type;                  /* type of entry */
        struct exit_status {
            short e_termination;        /* Process termination status */
            short e_exit;               /* Process exit status */
        } ut_exit;                      /* The exit status of a process
                                         * marked as DEAD_PROCESS.
                                         */
        time_t ut_time;                 /* time entry was made */
};

/* Definitions for ut_type */

#define EMPTY               0
#define RUN_LVL             1
#define BOOT_TIME           2
#define OLD_TIME            3
#define NEW_TIME            4
#define INIT_PROCESS        5           /* Process spawned by "init" */
#define LOGIN_PROCESS       6           /* A "getty" process waiting for login */
#define USER_PROCESS        7           /* A user process */
#define DEAD_PROCESS        8
#define ACCOUNTING          9

/* Largest legal value of ut_type */
#define UTMAXTYPE           ACCOUNTING

/*      Special strings used in the ut_line field when      */
/*      accounting for something other than a process.      */

#define RUNLVL_MSG      "run-level %c"
#define BOOT_MSG        "system boot"
#define OTIME_MSG       "old time"
#define NTIME_MSG       "new time"
```

values.h

Usage:

```
#include <values.h>
```

Defines machine-dependent values. Although superceded in principle by the limits.h header file, the values.h header is provided with most versions of the system to maintain compatibility with earlier versions. The limits.h header values should be used when writing new programs.

Contents:

```c
/* These values work with any binary representation of integers
 * where the high-order bit contains the sign. */

/* a number used normally for size of a shift */
#define BITSPERBYTE    8
#define BITS(type)     (BITSPERBYTE * (int)sizeof(type))

/* Integer values with only the most-significant bit set on */
#define HIBITS         ((short)(1 << BITS(short) - 1))
#define HIBITI         (1 << BITS(int) - 1)
#define HIBITL         (1L << BITS(long) - 1)

/* Largest short, regular and long int */
#define MAXSHORT       ((short)~HIBITS)
#define MAXINT         (~HIBITI)
#define MAXLONG        (~HIBITL)

/* Floating-point values */
#define MAXDOUBLE      1.79769313486231410e+308
#define MAXFLOAT       ((float)3.40282346638528860e+38)
#define MINDOUBLE      4.94065645841246544e-324
#define MINFLOAT       ((float)1.40129846432481707e-45)
#define _IEEE          1
#define _DEXPLEN       11
#define _HIDDENBIT     1
#define DMINEXP        (-(DMAXEXP + DSIGNIF - _HIDDENBIT - 3))
#define FMINEXP        (-(FMAXEXP + FSIGNIF - _HIDDENBIT - 3))
#define _LENBASE       1
#define _EXPBASE       (1 << _LENBASE)
#define _FEXPLEN       8
#define DSIGNIF        (BITS(double) - _DEXPLEN + _HIDDENBIT - 1)
#define FSIGNIF        (BITS(float)  - _FEXPLEN + _HIDDENBIT - 1)
#define DMAXPOWTWO     ((double)(1L << BITS(long) - 2) * \
                           (1L << DSIGNIF - BITS(long) + 1))
#define FMAXPOWTWO     ((float)(1L << FSIGNIF - 1))
#define DMAXEXP        ((1 << _DEXPLEN - 1) - 1 + _IEEE)
#define FMAXEXP        ((1 << _FEXPLEN - 1) - 1 + _IEEE)
#define LN_MAXDOUBLE   (M_LN2 * DMAXEXP)
#define LN_MINDOUBLE   (M_LN2 * (DMINEXP - 1))
#define H_PREC         (DSIGNIF % 2 ? (1L << DSIGNIF/2) * M_SQRT2 \
                           : 1L << DSIGNIF/2)
#define X_EPS          (1.0/H_PREC)
#define X_PLOSS        ((double)(long)(M_PI * H_PREC))
#define X_TLOSS        (M_PI * DMAXPOWTWO)
#define M_LN2          0.69314718055994530942
#define M_PI           3.14159265358979323846
#define M_SQRT2        1.41421356237309504880
/* The following are defined for compatibility */
#define MAXBEXP        DMAXEXP
#define MINBEXP        DMINEXP
#define MAXPOWTWO      DMAXPOWTWO
```

varargs.h

Usage:

```
#include <varargs.h>
```

Defines the `va_start`, `va_end`, and `va_list` macros. Because the definition of these macros varies significantly between system and compiler implementations, no generally applicable example implementation can be shown.

Glossary of Terms

S VID: System V Interface Definition, a document published by AT&T Corporation that describes in detail the common features of a version, release, or implementation of UNIX that complies with the System V definition.

application: When using System V interprocess communications (IPC) facilities, a group of programs intending to share the use of common message queues, semaphores, or memory segments. The programs comprising the application are expected to form "keys" identifying the shared resources in such a manner that no duplication occurs with key values used by any other application.

block-special: A special file corresponding to a block-oriented I/O device, usually a disk or tape volume. A block-special file refers to the entire device; reading and writing to such a filename ignores any organization of the device medium into directories and files.

break address: The address immediately following the highest valid address in the data segment of a process address space. Adjustment of the break address upwards or downwards increases or decreases the size of the process address space dynamically. The break address cannot be adjusted downward into the text or stack areas, or upward beyond a system-specified limit.

character-special: A special file corresponding to a character-oriented I/O device such as a terminal, printer, or communications line. The character-special filename refers to the device, which may or may not include a recording medium as such. Reading and writing occurs as a serial stream of bytes which are fetched and stored in a manner defined by the device. The `ioctl` function may provide some control over the device, depending on the device drivers used; the use of `ioctl` is dependent not only on the version of UNIX System V being used, but also on the device driver being addressed.

effective group-ID: The group identifier usually used for checking access permissions. The effective group-ID is equal to the real group-ID, except when a program is invoked with one of the `exec` system calls and the program permissions include the *set-group-ID* flag; the effective group-ID is then set equal to the group-ID of the program file.

effective user-ID: The user identifier usually used for checking access permissions. The effective user-ID is equal to the real user-ID, except when a program is invoked with one of the `exec` system calls and the program permissions include the *set-uid* flag; the effective user-ID is then set equal to the owner-ID of the program file.

file system: The logical organization of information recorded on a *block-special* device. A file system is created by the `mkfs` utility program, which writes a "superblock" at the beginning of the volume, followed by an inode table. The remainder of the volume is treated as free disk blocks which are organized into a chain. A file system is made accessible by the `mount` function call, and taken offline by the `umount` function call.

group-ID: Strictly, a numerical identifier in the range 0 to 30,000 denoting the affiliation of a user or a file with a named group of users. The group-ID of a file identifies the group of users that may have access to the file according to the group permissions. A *real group-ID* and an *effective group-ID* are also associated with each process in the system; these identifiers are used for checking access rights of the process to files it may reference.

group leader: The process in a process group whose parent process is not in the same process group. Every process which invokes the `setpgrp` function becomes a group leader, and all child processes of the group leader (and their children) become member processes of the process group.

inode: One entry in an inode table. Every *file system* contains an inode table as well as free and used disk blocks. The inode is known by its index in the table, which is an integer ranging from 2 to the number of table entries. Each inode is either free or in use. An in-use inode describes a file in the file system, or a device (see *special file*). The information contained in the inode consists of the values returned by the *stat* system call, as well as pointers to disk blocks which have been allocated to the file.

kernel: That portion of the UNIX System V operating system which is permanently resident in real memory; also called "supervisor" or "nucleus" in other operating systems. The kernel controls all elements of the computing system, and provides basic services to other programs. Kernel service routines are known as *system calls*.

link: A directory entry. A directory entry provides a name for a file, and a pointer to the inode that describes the location, size, permissions, and other attributes of a file. A file may be described by more than one directory entry; such a file is said to have "multiple links." Newcomers to UNIX often believe that one of the directory entries represents the real file, while the others are "aliases." This is not true. A file continues to exist as long as at least one directory entry also exists with the inode number corresponding to the file. A file is physically removed only when the last directory entry for the file is removed. See also *inode*.

nice value: A value set by the n i c e system call and used by the process scheduler to determine the execution priority of a process. The nice value is so-called because it is usually set to a positive integer by programs requiring large amounts of CPU time but where the duration of its execution is unimportant; by reducing its execution priority, the impact of its execution on the performance of other active programs is diminished.

owner-ID: The *user-ID* associated with a file when it is created, or set by the c h o w n system call. The owner of the file has certain access rights to the file which are shared by no one else, including the right to change the permissions associated with the file.

pipe: A type of file in which no external recording medium or device exists, but which passes all data written to the file via a system buffer to the process which issues a read to the same pipe. A pipe consists of two file descriptors and a system buffer; one of the file descriptors is open for reading, and the other is open for writing. Data flow in a pipe is always unidirectional. A pipe is most often used as an intermediate file for passing data between concurrently executing processes, and is usually created by a special utility program called a "shell," but pipes may be created and used by any program. See the p i p e and p o p e n function descriptions.

process: A task. The term refers to the system resources created by the kernel to maintain an independent execution thread, including a virtual process address space, a process state, process ID, process group ID, parent process ID, real and effective user ID, real and effective group ID, file creation mask, file descriptors, signal actions and other control variables. A process is created by the fork system call and is destroyed by the _exit system call. The program to be executed by the process is defined by the exec system calls. When multiple processes are concurrently executing, the operating system switches the CPU between competing processes using a scheduling algorithm that calculates the priority of each process; the relative priority can be influenced by the user by adjusting the *nice* value. A process which is not a member of a login process group is called a "daemon." A process which has terminated and can no longer execute, but which has not yet been removed from the system's process table, is called a "zombie."

process-ID: A small number assigned by the system to uniquely identify a process. Process identifiers are not reused until the system is rebooted, thus allowing a process-ID to refer to one specific process throughout an operational period of the system. The process-ID numbers 0 and 1 are special, in that they refer to the swap task and the init task by definition.

process group: A set of processes having a common parent called a "group leader." By convention, every login process is a group leader (/bin/login invokes the setpgrp function), and all subshells and executed commands are processes in the user's process group.

real group-ID: The group-ID of the actual user, as taken from the /etc/passwd file, ignoring any substitution that may be performed by an exec system call. The real group-ID is often used when the group affiliation of the user is important rather than his permissions.

real user-ID: The user-ID of the actual user, as taken from the /etc/passwd file, ignoring any substitution that may be performed by an exec system call. The real user-ID is often used when the identity of the user is important rather than his permissions.

signal: An interruption directed to a process or a group of processes. A signal may be automatically generated by the system as a result of a hardware or software event, or it may be generated under program control using the kill system call. A process to which the signal is directed may elect to be terminated by the receipt of the signal (the default), to ignore the signal, or to have a user function called to handle the signal. Signals are the most rudimentary kind of interprocess communication.

special file: A directory entry representing a peripheral device rather than a disk file. UNIX System V uses filenames to refer to peripheral devices to minimize the need for device-dependent considerations in utility programs. Directory entries for special files are usually collected in the /dev directory. A directory entry for a special file can be created by the mknod system call, and can be removed by the `unlink` system call. See also *block-special* and *character-special*.

superuser: The system maintenance and administration user, usually identified in the `/etc/passwd` file by the login name of "root." Authorization and permission mechanisms of the operating system are bypassed when the current user is the superuser, although error checks are still performed. UNIX recognizes any process having an effective user-ID of 0 as the superuser.

system call: A function implemented in the kernel. System calls are invoked just like any other function, but the code retrieved from the function library is only an interface that passes the function arguments to the kernel routine. The use of system calls in portable programs is discouraged because the implementation of system calls is less uniform between versions of UNIX than the implementation of other library functions.

user-ID: An unsigned number in the range 0 to 30,000 established by the `/etc/passwd` system file as a unique identifier for an authorized system user. The user-ID of 0 is reserved to always identify the superuser of the system. See also *real user-ID* and *effective user-ID*.

zombie: A process which has terminated and can no longer be executed, but which cannot yet be removed from the system's process table. See *process*.

Index

E

F

T